Essential Readings in World Politics

The Norton Series in World Politics
Jack Snyder, General Editor

Essential Readings in World Politics

EDITED BY

KAREN MINGST AND JACK SNYDER

W · W · NORTON & COMPANY   NEW YORK · LONDON

The text of this book is composed in Minion with the display set in Optima
Composition by PennSet, Inc.
Manufacturing by Maple-Vail

Library of Congress Cataloging-in-Publication Data
Essential readings in world politics / edited by Karen Mingst and Jack Snyder.
    p.   cm.—(The Norton series in world politics)
Includes bibliographical references.
    ISBN 0-393-97697-1 (pbk.)
    1. International relations.   2. World politics.   I. Mingst, Karen A., 1947–   II. Snyder, Jack L.
    III. Series.

JZ1305 .E85 2001
327—dc21
                                                                00-050111

W. W. Norton & Company, Inc., 500 Fifth Avenue, New York, N.Y. 10110
www.wwnorton.com
W. W. Norton & Company Ltd., Castle House, 75/76 Wells Street, London W1T 3QT
3 4 5 6 7 8 9 0

CONTENTS

PREFACE   ix

CHAPTER 3 ⌒ NEW FRONTIERS IN INTERNATIONAL POLITICAL THEORY

CHAPTER 4 ⌒ THE INTERNATIONAL SYSTEM

CHAPTER 5 ⌒ THE STATE

CHAPTER **6** ✑ THE INDIVIDUAL

CHAPTER **7** ✑ WAR AND STRIFE

CHAPTER **8** ✑ INTERNATIONAL POLITICAL ECONOMY

CHAPTER **9** ✑ QUEST FOR GLOBAL GOVERNANCE

CHAPTER **10** ❧ NATIONALISM

CHAPTER **11** ❧ THE DEMOCRATIC PEACE DEBATE

CHAPTER **12** ❧ GLOBALIZATION AND GLOBALIZING ISSUES

PREFACE

This reader is a collaborative effort of the two co-editors and Rob Whiteside of W. W. Norton. In a flurry of E-mails during the summer of 2000, the co-editors suggested articles for inclusion, rejected or accepted them, traced their sources, and defended choices to skeptical colleagues. It became apparent during the process that the co-editors, while both international relations scholars, read very different literatures. This book represents a product of that collaborative process and is all the better for the differences.

The articles have been selected to meet several criteria. First, the collection is designed to augment and amplify the core text of the series, *Essentials of International Relations*, written by Karen Mingst. Chapters 1 through 9 of this reader follow closely the organization and themes of that textbook. Other themes that cut across the text and are addressed in other books in the Norton Series in World Politics are also included, especially in chapter 3 and chapters 10 through 12. Second, the selections are purposefully eclectic. Key theoretical articles are paired with contemporary pieces found in the popular literature. Articles have been chosen to reflect diverse theoretical and national (non-American) viewpoints. Finally, the articles are meant to be readable and engaging to undergraduates. Thus, the co-editors struggled to maintain the integrity of the challenging pieces, while making them accessible to undergraduates at a variety of colleges and universities.

Special thanks go to the numerous individuals who provided reviews of earlier drafts and offered suggestions and reflections based on their teaching experience. Our product benefited from these evaluations, although had we included all the suggestions we received, the book would have been thousands of pages long! Rob Whiteside guided the process, reacting to our suggestions, mediating our differences, and sharpening our rationales and editing. To him, we owe a special thanks. While fully acknowledging that no set of readings will ever satisfy all the teaching objectives of our diverse colleagues in the field of international relations, we hope their students will find our selections stimulating and of enduring relevance.

Essential Readings in World Politics

1 ❧ APPROACHES AND HISTORY

Core ideas about international relations, introduced here in chapter 1 and elabo-
rated in chapter 3 of Karen Mingst's book Essentials of International Relations,
have emerged from historic events. The Peloponnesian War, as recorded by Thucy-
dides, produced the Melian Dialogue, a classic statement of the realist/idealist
dilemma. In this dialogue, the leaders of Melos ponder the fate of the island, decid-
ing whether to fight their antagonists, the Athenians, or to rely on the gods and the
enemy of Athens, the Lacedaemonians, for their safety.

The post–World War I peace process led to a clear statement of the liberal per-
spective. U.S. president Woodrow Wilson's "Fourteen Points," which he delineated
in an address to the U.S. Congress in January 1918, summarizes some of the key
points emerging from liberal theory. Wilson blamed power politics, secret diplo-
macy, and autocratic rulers for the devastating world war. He suggested that with
the spread of democracy and the creation of a "league of nations," aggression
would be stopped.

The Cold War, one of the most important series of events in contemporary
times, also provided the historical setting for the development of the realist and lib-
eral perspectives. In 1947, George F. Kennan, then director of the State Depart-
ment's policy planning staff, penned his famous "X" article, published in Foreign
Affairs. *In it, he assessed Soviet conduct and provided the intellectual justification*
for Cold War containment policy. Using realist logic, he suggested that to prevent
Soviet expansion, counterforce would have to be applied. Finally, in "The Long
Peace," John Lewis Gaddis, a diplomatic historian, describes the Cold War as a pe-
riod of prolonged peace. This article argues why, in the face of overwhelming odds,
the United States and the Soviet Union refrained from direct confrontation.

These writings provide an important foundation for the realist and liberal
theoretical debates, one of the major organizing themes in Mingst's Essentials of
International Relations *and a theme that is examined in greater depth both in*
this book and in other books of the Norton Series in World Politics.

SURESHT BALD

[Thucydides's] Melian Dialogue

It was the sixteenth year of the Peloponnesian War, but for the last six years the two great feuding empires headed by Athens and Sparta (Lacedaemon) had avoided open hostile action against each other. Ten years into the war they had signed a treaty of peace and friendship; however, this treaty did not dissipate the distrust that existed between them. Each feared the other's hegemonic designs on the Peloponnese and sought to increase its power to thwart the other's ambitions. Without openly attacking the other, each used persuasion, coercion, and subversion to strengthen itself and weaken its rival. This struggle for hegemony by Athens and Sparta was felt most acutely by small, hitherto "independent" states who were now being forced to take sides in the bipolar Greek world of the fifth century B.C. One such state was Melos.

Despite being one of the few island colonies of Sparta, Melos had remained neutral in the struggle between Sparta and Athens. Its neutrality, however, was unacceptable to the Athenians, who, accompanied by overwhelming military and naval power, arrived in Melos to pressure it into submission. After strategically positioning their powerful fleet, the Athenian generals sent envoys to Melos to negotiate the island's surrender.

The commissioners of Melos agreed to meet the envoys in private. They were afraid the Athenians, known for their rhetorical skills, might sway the people if allowed a public forum. The envoys came with an offer that if the Melians submitted and became part of the Athenian empire, their people and their possessions would not be harmed.

From Thucydides, *Complete Writings: The Peloponnesian War*, trans. Richard Crawley (New York: Modern Library, 1951), adapted by Suresht Bald, Willamette University, as excerpted in Karen Mingst, *Essentials of International Relations* (New York: Norton, 1999), chap. 3.

The Melians argued that by the law of nations they had the right to remain neutral, and no nation had the right to attack without provocation. Having been a free state for seven hundred years they were not ready to give up that freedom. Thucydides captures the exchange between the Melian commissioners and the Athenian envoys:

MELIANS: . . . All we can reasonably expect from this negotiation is war, if we prove to have right on our side and refuse to submit, and in the contrary case, slavery.

ATHENIANS: . . . We shall not trouble you with specious pretenses—either of how we have a right to our empire because we overthrew the Mede, or are now attacking you because of the wrong that you have done us—and make a long speech that would not be believed; and in return we hope that you, instead of thinking to influence us by saying that you did not join the Lacedaemonians, although their colonists, or that you have done us no wrong, will aim at what is feasible, . . . since you know as well as we do that right, as the world goes, is only in question between equals in power, while the strong do what they can and the weak suffer what they want. (331)

The Melians pointed out that it was in the interest of all states to respect the laws of nations: "you should not destroy what is our common protection, the privilege of being allowed in danger to invoke what is fair and right. . . ." (331) They reminded the Athenians that a day might come when the Athenians themselves would need such protection.

But the Athenians were not persuaded. To them, Melos' submission was in the interest of their empire, and Melos.

MELIANS: And how pray, could it turn out as good for us to serve as for you to rule?

ATHENIANS: Because you would have the advantage of submitting before suffering the worst, and we should gain by not destroying you.

MELIANS: So you would not consent to our being neutral, friends instead of enemies, but allies of neither side.

ATHENIANS: No; for your hostility cannot so much hurt us as your friendship will be an argument to our subjects of our weakness, and your enmity of our power. (332)

When the Melians asked if that was their "idea of equity," the Athenians responded,

As far as right goes . . . one has as much of it as the other, and if any maintain their independence it is because they are strong, and that if we do not molest them it is because we are afraid. . . . (332)

By subjugating the Melians the Athenians hoped not only to extend their empire but also to improve their image and thus their security. To allow the weaker Melians to remain free, according to the Athenians, would reflect negatively on Athenian power.

Aware of their weak position the Melians hoped that the justice of their cause would gain them the support of the gods, "and what we want in power will be made up by the alliance with the Lacedaemonians, who are bound, if only for very shame, to come to the aid of their kindred."

ATHENIANS: . . . Of the gods we believe, and of men we know, that by a necessary law of their nature they rule wherever they can. And it is not as if we were the first to make this law, or to act upon it when made: we found it existing before us, and will leave it to exist for ever after us; all we do is to make use of it, knowing that you and everybody else having the same power as we have, would do the same as we do. Thus, as far as the gods are concerned we have no fear and no reason to fear that we shall be at a disadvantage. But . . . your notion about the Lacedaemonians, which leads you to believe that shame will make them help you, here we bless your simplicity but do not envy your folly. The Lacedaemonians . . . are conspicuous in considering what is agreeable honourable, and what is expedient just. . . . Your strongest arguments depend upon hope and the future, and your actual resources are too scanty as compared to those arrayed against you, for you to come out victorious. You will therefore show great blindness of judgment, unless, after allowing us to retire you can find some counsel more prudent than this. (334–36)

The envoys then left the conference, giving the Melians the opportunity to deliberate on the Athenian offer and decide the best course for them to follow.

The Melians decided to stand by the position they had taken at the conference with the Athenian envoys. They refused to submit, placing their faith in the gods and the Lacedaemonians. Though they asked the Athenians to accept their neutrality and leave Melos, the Athenians started preparations for war.

In the war that ensued the Melians were soundly defeated. The Athenians showed no mercy, killing all the adult males and selling the women and children as slaves. Subsequently, they sent out five hundred colonists to settle in Melos, which became an Athenian colony.

*　　*　　*

WOODROW WILSON

The Fourteen Points

. . . It will be our wish and purpose that the processes of peace, when they are begun, shall be absolutely open and that they shall involve and permit henceforth no secret understandings of any kind. The day of conquest and aggrandizement is gone by; so is also the day of secret covenants entered into in the interest of particular governments and likely at some unlooked-for moment to upset the peace of the world. It is this happy fact, now clear to the view of every public man whose thoughts do not still linger in an age that is dead and gone, which makes it possible for every nation whose purposes are consistent with justice and the peace of the world to avow now or at any other time the objects it has in view.

We entered this war because violations of right had occurred which touched us to the quick and made the life of our own people impossible unless they were corrected and the world secured once and for all against their recurrence. What we demand in this war, therefore, is nothing peculiar to ourselves. It is that the world be made fit and safe to live in; and particularly that it be made safe for every peace-loving nation which, like our own, wishes to live its own life, determine its own institutions, be assured of justice and fair dealing by the other people of the world as against force and selfish aggression. All the peoples of the world are in effect partners in this interest, and for our own part we see very clearly that unless justice be done to others it will not be done to us. The program of the world's peace, therefore, is our program; and that program, the only possible program, as we see it, is this:

    I. Open covenants of peace, openly arrived at, after which there shall be no private

From Woodrow Wilson's address to the U.S. Congress, 8 January, 1918.

international understandings of any kind but diplomacy shall proceed always frankly and in the public view.

    II. Absolute freedom of navigation upon the seas, outside territorial waters, alike in peace and in war, except as the seas may be closed in whole or in part by international action for the enforcement of international covenants.

    III. The removal, so far as possible, of all economic barriers and the establishment of an equality of trade conditions among all the nations consenting to the peace and associating themselves for its maintenance.

    IV. Adequate guarantees given and taken that national armaments will be reduced to the lowest point consistent with domestic safety.

    V. A free, open-minded, and absolutely impartial adjustment of all colonial claims, based upon a strict observance of the principle that in determining all such questions of sovereignty the interests of the populations concerned must have equal weight with the equitable claims of the government whose title is to be determined.

    VI. The evacuation of all Russian territory and such a settlement of all questions affecting Russia as will secure the best and freest cooperation of the other nations of the world in obtaining for her an unhampered and unembarrassed opportunity for the independent determination of her own political development and national policy and assure her of a sincere welcome into the society of free nations under institutions of her own choosing; and, more than a welcome, assistance also of every kind that she may need and may herself desire. The treatment accorded Russia by her sister nations in the months to come will be the acid test of their good will, of their comprehension of her needs as distinguished from their own interests, and of their intelligent and unselfish sympathy.

VII. Belgium, the whole world will agree, must be evacuated and restored, without any attempt to limit the sovereignty which she enjoys in common with all other free nations. No other single act will serve as this will serve to restore confidence among the nations in the laws which they have themselves set and determined for the government of their relations with one another. Without this healing act the whole structure and validity of international law is forever impaired.

VIII. All French territory should be freed and the invaded portions restored, and the wrong done to France by Prussia in 1871 in the matter of Alsace-Lorraine, which has unsettled the peace of the world for nearly fifty years, should be righted, in order that peace may once more be made secure in the interest of all.

IX. A readjustment of the frontiers of Italy should be effected along clearly recognizable lines of nationality.

X. The peoples of Austria-Hungary, whose place among the nations we wish to see safeguarded and assured, should be accorded the freest opportunity of autonomous development.

XI. Rumania, Serbia, and Montenegro should be evacuated; occupied territories restored; Serbia accorded free and secure access to the sea; and the relations of the several Balkan states to one another determined by friendly counsel along historically established lines of allegiance and nationality; and international guarantees of the political and economic in-

dependence and territorial integrity of the several Balkan states should be entered into.

XII. The Turkish portions of the present Ottoman Empire should be assured a secure sovereignty, but the other nationalities which are now under Turkish rule should be assured an undoubted security of life and an absolutely unmolested opportunity of autonomous development, and the Dardanelles should be permanently opened as a free passage to the ships and commerce of all nations under international guarantes.

XIII. An independent Polish state should be erected which should include the territories inhabited by indisputably Polish populations, which should be assured a free and secure access to the sea, and whose political and economic independence and territorial integrity should be guaranteed by international covenant.

XIV. A general association of nations must be formed under specific covenants for the purpose of affording mutual guarantees of political independence and territorial integrity to great and small states alike.

In regard to these essential rectifications of wrong and assertions of right we feel ourselves to be intimate partners of all the governments and peoples associated together against the imperialists. We cannot be separated in interest or divided in purpose. We stand together until the end.

For such arrangements and covenants we are willing to fight and to continue to fight until they are achieved; but only because we wish the right to prevail and desire a just and stable peace such as can be secured only by removing the chief provocations to war, which this program does remove. We have no jealousy of German greatness, and there is nothing in this program that impairs it. We grudge her no achievement or distinction of learning or of pacific enterprise such as have made her record very bright and very enviable. We do not wish to injure her or to block in any way her legitimate influence or power. We do not wish to fight her either with arms or with hostile arrangements of trade if she is willing to associate herself with us and the other peace-loving nations of the world in covenants of justice and law and fair dealing. We wish her only to accept a place of equality among the peoples of the world—the new world in which we now live—instead of a place of mastery.

Neither do we presume to suggest to her any alteration or modification of her institutions. But it is necessary, we must frankly say, and necessary as a preliminary to any intelligent dealings with her on our part, that we should know whom her spokesmen speak for when they speak to us, whether for the Reichstag majority or for the military party and the men whose creed is imperial domination.

We have spoken now, surely, in terms too concrete to admit of any further doubt or question. An evident principle runs through the whole program I have outlined. It is the principle of justice to all peoples and nationalities, and their right to live on equal terms of liberty and safety with one another, whether they be strong or weak. Unless this principle be made its foundation no part of the structure of international justice can stand. The people of the United States could act upon no other principle; and to the vindication of this principle they are ready to devote their lives, their honor, and everything that they possess. The moral climax of this the culminating and final war for human liberty has come, and they are ready to put their own strength, their own highest purpose, their own integrity and devotion to the test.

GEORGE F. KENNAN ("X")

The Sources of Soviet Conduct

I

The political personality of Soviet power as we know it today is the product of ideology and circumstances: ideology inherited by the present Soviet leaders from the movement in which they had their political origin, and circumstances of the power which they now have exercised for nearly three decades in Russia. There can be few tasks of psychological analysis more difficult than to try to trace the interaction of these two forces and the relative role of each in the determination of official Soviet conduct. Yet the attempt must be made if that conduct is to be understood and effectively countered.

It is difficult to summarize the set of ideological concepts with which the Soviet leaders came

into power. Marxian ideology, in its Russian-Communist projection, has always been in process of subtle evolution. The materials on which it bases itself are extensive and complex. But the outstanding features of Communist thought as it existed in 1916 may perhaps be summarized as follows: (*a*) that the central factor in the life of man, the fact which determines the character of public life and the "physiognomy of society," is the system by which material goods are produced and exchanged; (*b*) that the capitalist system of production is a nefarious one which inevitably leads to the exploitation of the working class by the capital-owning class and is incapable of developing adequately the economic resources of society or of distributing fairly the material goods produced by human labor; (*c*) that capitalism contains the seeds of its own destruction and must, in view of the inability of the capital-owning class to adjust itself

From *Foreign Affairs* 25, no. 4 (July 1947): 566–82.

to economic change, result eventually and inescapably in a revolutionary transfer of power to the working class; and (*d*) that imperialism, the final phase of capitalism, leads directly to war and revolution.

*   *   *

Now it must be noted that through all the years of preparation for revolution, the attention of these men, as indeed of Marx himself, had been centered less on the future form which Socialism[1] would take than on the necessary overthrow of rival power which, in their view, had to precede the introduction of Socialism. Their views, therefore, on the positive program to be put into effect, once power was attained, were for the most part nebulous, visionary and impractical. Beyond the nationalization of industry and the expropriation of large private capital holdings there was no agreed program. The treatment of the peasantry, which according to the Marxist formulation was not of the proletariat, had always been a vague spot in the pattern of Communist thought; and it remained an object of controversy and vacillation for the first ten years of Communist power.

The circumstances of the immediate post-Revolution period—the existence in Russia of civil war and foreign intervention, together with the obvious fact that the Communists represented only a tiny minority of the Russian people—made the establishment of dictatorial power a necessity. The experiment with "war Communism" and the abrupt attempt to eliminate private production and trade had unfortunate economic consequences and caused further bitterness against the new revolutionary regime. While the temporary relaxation of the effort to communize Russia, represented by the New Economic Policy, alleviated some of this economic distress and thereby served its purpose, it also made it evident that the "capitalistic sector of society" was still prepared to profit at once from any relaxation of governmental pressure, and would, if permitted to continue to exist, always constitute a powerful opposing element to the Soviet regime and a serious rival for influence in the country. Somewhat the same situation prevailed

with respect to the individual peasant who, in his own small way, was also a private producer.

Lenin, had he lived, might have proved a great enough man to reconcile these conflicting forces to the ultimate benefit of Russian society, though this is questionable. But be that as it may, Stalin, and those whom he led in the struggle for succession to Lenin's position of leadership, were not the men to tolerate rival political forces in the sphere of power which they coveted. Their sense of insecurity was too great. Their particular brand of fanaticism, unmodified by any of the Anglo-Saxon traditions of compromise, was too fierce and too jealous to envisage any permanent sharing of power. From the Russian-Asiatic world out of which they had emerged they carried with them a skepticism as to the possibilities of permanent and peaceful coexistence of rival forces. Easily persuaded of their own doctrinaire "rightness," they insisted on the submission or destruction of all competing power. Outside of the Communist Party, Russian society was to have no rigidity. There were to be no forms of collective human activity or association which would not be dominated by the Party. No other force in Russian society was to be permitted to achieve vitality or integrity. Only the Party was to have structure. All else was to be an amorphous mass.

And within the Party the same principle was to apply. The mass of Party members might go through the motions of election, deliberation, decision and action; but in these motions they were to be animated not by their own individual wills but by the awesome breath of the Party leadership and the overbrooding presence of "the world."

Let it be stressed again that subjectively these men probably did not seek absolutism for its own sake. They doubtless believed—and found it easy to believe—that they alone knew what was good for society and that they would accomplish that good once their power was secure and unchallengeable. But in seeking that security of their own rule they were prepared to recognize no restrictions, either of God or man, on the character of their methods. And until such time as that security might be achieved, they placed far down on their scale of operational priorities the comforts and happiness of the peoples entrusted to their care.

Now the outstanding circumstance concerning the Soviet regime is that down to the present day this process of political consolidation has never been completed and the men in the Kremlin have continued to be predominantly absorbed with the struggle to secure and make absolute the power which they seized in November 1917. They have endeavored to secure it primarily against forces at home, within Soviet society itself. But they have also endeavored to secure it against the outside world. For ideology, as we have seen, taught them that the outside world was hostile and that it was their duty eventually to overthrow the political forces beyond their borders. The powerful hands of Russian history and tradition reached up to sustain them in this feeling. Finally, their own aggressive intransigence with respect to the outside world began to find its own reaction; and they were soon forced, to use another Gibbonesque phrase [from Edward Gibbon, *The Decline and Fall of the Roman Empire*], "to chastise the contumacy" which they themselves had provoked. It is an undeniable privilege of every man to prove himself right in the thesis that the world is his enemy; for if he reiterates it frequently enough and makes it the background of his conduct he is bound eventually to be right.

Now it lies in the nature of the mental world of the Soviet leaders, as well as in the character of their ideology, that no opposition to them can be officially recognized as having any merit or justification whatsoever. Such opposition can flow, in theory, only from the hostile and incorrigible forces of dying capitalism. As long as remnants of capitalism were officially recognized as existing in Russia, it was possible to place on them, as an internal element, part of the blame for the maintenance of a dictatorial form of society. But as these remnants were liquidated, little by little, this justification fell away; and when it was indicated officially that they had been finally destroyed, it disappeared altogether. And this fact created one of the most basic of the compulsions which came to act upon the Soviet regime: since capitalism no longer existed in Russia and since it could not be admitted that there could be serious or widespread opposition to the Kremlin springing spontaneously from the liberated masses under its authority, it became necessary to justify the retention of the dictatorship by stressing the menace of capitalism abroad.

*   *   *

Now the maintenance of this pattern of Soviet power, namely, the pursuit of unlimited authority domestically, accompanied by the cultivation of the semi-myth of implacable foreign hostility, has gone far to shape the actual machinery of Soviet power as we know it today. Internal organs of administration which did not serve this purpose withered on the vine. Organs which did serve this purpose became vastly swollen. The security of Soviet power came to rest on the iron discipline of the Party, on the severity and ubiquity of the secret police, and on the uncompromising economic monopolism of the state. The "organs of suppression," in which the Soviet leaders had sought security from rival forces, became in large measure the masters of those whom they were designed to serve. Today the major part of the structure of Soviet power is committed to the perfection of the dictatorship and to the maintenance of the concept of Russia as in a state of siege, with the enemy lowering beyond the walls. And the millions of human beings who form that part of the structure of power must defend at all costs this concept of Russia's position, for without it they are themselves superfluous.

As things stand today, the rulers can no longer dream of parting with these organs of suppression. The quest for absolute power, pursued now for nearly three decades with a ruthlessness unparalleled (in scope at least) in modern times, has again produced internally, as it did externally, its own reaction. The excesses of the police apparatus have fanned the potential opposition to the regime into something far greater and more dangerous than it could have been before those excesses began.

But least of all can the rulers dispense with the fiction by which the maintenance of dictatorial power has been defended. For this fiction has been canonized in Soviet philosophy by the excesses already committed in its name; and it is now anchored in the Soviet structure of thought by bonds far greater than those of mere ideology.

II

So much for the historical background. What does it spell in terms of the political personality of Soviet power as we know it today?

Of the original ideology, nothing has been officially junked. Belief is maintained in the basic badness of capitalism, in the inevitability of its destruction, in the obligation of the proletariat to assist in that destruction and to take power into its own hands. But stress has come to be laid primarily on those concepts which relate most specifically to the Soviet regime itself: to its position as the sole truly Socialist regime in a dark and misguided world, and to the relationships of power within it.

The first of these concepts is that of the innate antagonism between capitalism and Socialism. We have seen how deeply that concept has become imbedded in foundations of Soviet power. It has profound implications for Russia's conduct as a member of international society. It means that there can never be on Moscow's side any sincere assumption of a community of aims between the Soviet Union and powers which are regarded as capitalism. It must invariably be assumed in Moscow that the aims of the capitalist world are antagonistic to the Soviet regime and, therefore, to the interests of the peoples it controls. If the Soviet Government occasionally sets its signature to documents which would indicate the contrary, this is to be regarded as a tactical maneuver permissible in dealing with the enemy (who is without honor) and should be taken in the spirit of *caveat emptor* [let the buyer beware]. Basically, the antagonism remains. It is postulated. And from it flow many of the phenomena which we find disturbing in the Kremlin's conduct of foreign policy: the secretiveness, the lack of frankness, the duplicity, the war suspiciousness, and the basic unfriendliness of purpose. These phenomena are there to stay, for the

foreseeable future. There can be variations of degree and of emphasis. When there is something the Russians want from us, one or the other of these features of their policy may be thrust temporarily into the background; and when that happens there will always be Americans who will leap forward with gleeful announcements that "the Russians have changed," and some who will even try to take credit for having brought about such "changes." But we should not be misled by tactical maneuvers. These characteristics of Soviet policy, like the postulate from which they flow, are basic to the internal nature of Soviet power, and will be with us, whether in the foreground or the background, until the internal nature of Soviet power is changed.

This means that we are going to continue for a long time to find the Russians difficult to deal with. It does not mean that they should be considered as embarked upon a do-or-die program to overthrow our society by a given date. The theory of the inevitability of the eventual fall of capitalism has the fortunate connotation that there is no hurry about it. * * *

*   *   *

* * * [T]he Kremlin is under no ideological compulsion to accomplish its purposes in a hurry. Like the Church, it is dealing in ideological concepts which are of long-term validity, and it can afford to be patient. It has no right to risk the existing achievements of the revolution for the sake of vain baubles of the future. The very teachings of Lenin himself require great caution and flexibility in the pursuit of Communist purposes. Again, these precepts are fortified by the lessons of Russian history: of centuries of obscure battles between nomadic forces over the stretches of a vast unfortified plain. Here caution, circumspection, flexibility and deception are the valuable qualities; and their value finds natural appreciation in the Russian or the oriental mind. Thus the Kremlin has no compunction about retreating in the face of superior force. And being under the compulsion of no timetable, it does not get panicky under the necessity for such retreat. Its political action is a fluid stream which

moves constantly, wherever it is permitted to move, toward a given goal. Its main concern is to make sure that it has filled every nook and cranny available to it in the basin of world power. But if it finds unassailable barriers in its path, it accepts these philosophically and accommodates itself to them. The main thing is that there should always be pressure, increasing constant pressure, toward the desired goal. There is no trace of any feeling in Soviet psychology that that goal must be reached at any given time.

These considerations make Soviet diplomacy at once easier and more difficult to deal with than the diplomacy of individual aggressive leaders like Napoleon and Hitler. On the one hand it is more sensitive to contrary force, more ready to yield on individual sectors of the diplomatic front when that force is felt to be too strong, and thus more rational in the logic and rhetoric of power. On the other hand it cannot be easily defeated or discouraged by a single victory on the part of its opponents. And the patient persistence by which it is animated means that it can be effectively countered not by sporadic acts which represent the momentary whims of democratic opinion but only by intelligent long-range policies on the part of Russia's adversaries—policies no less steady in their purpose, and no less variegated and resourceful in their application, than those of the Soviet Union itself.

In these circumstances it is clear that the main element of any United States policy toward the Soviet Union must be that of a long-term, patient but firm and vigilant containment of Russian expansive tendencies. It is important to note, however, that such a policy has nothing to do with outward histrionics: with threats or blustering or superfluous gestures of outward "toughness." While the Kremlin is basically flexible in its reaction to political realities, it is by no means unamenable to considerations of prestige. Like almost any other government, it can be placed by tactless and threatening gestures in a position where it cannot afford to yield even though this might be dictated by its sense of realism. The Russian leaders are keen judges of human psychology, and as such they are highly conscious that loss of temper and of self-control is never a source of strength in political affairs. They are quick to exploit such evidences of weakness. For these reasons, it is a *sine qua non* of successful dealing with Russia that the foreign government in question should remain at all times cool and collected and that its demands on Russian policy should be put forward in such a manner as to leave the way open for a compliance not too detrimental to Russian prestige.

III

In the light of the above, it will be clearly seen that the Soviet pressure against the free institutions of the Western world is something that can be contained by the adroit and vigilant application of counter-force at a series of constantly shifting geographical and political points, corresponding to the shifts and maneuvers of Soviet policy, but which cannot be charmed or talked out of existence. * * *

*   *   *

IV

*   *   *

But in actuality the possibilities for American policy are by no means limited to holding the line and hoping for the best. It is entirely possible for the United States to influence by its actions the internal developments, both within Russia and throughout the international Communist movement, by which Russian policy is largely determined. This is not only a question of the modest measure of informational activity which this government can conduct in the Soviet Union and elsewhere, although that, too, is important. It is rather a question of the degree to which the United States can create among the peoples of the world generally the impression of a country which knows what it wants, which is coping successfully with the problems of its internal life and with the responsibilities of a World Power, and which has a spiritual vitality capable of holding its own among the major ideological currents of the time. To the extent that such an impression can be created and maintained, the aims of Russian Communism must appear sterile and quixotic, the hopes and enthusiasm of Moscow's supporters must wane, and added strain must be imposed on the Kremlin's foreign policies. For the palsied decrepitude of the capitalist world is the keystone of Communist philosophy. Even the failure of the United States to experience the early economic depression which the ravens of the Red Square have been predicting with such complacent confidence since hostilities ceased would have deep and important repercussions throughout the Communist world.

By the same token, exhibitions of indecision, disunity and internal disintegration within this country have an exhilarating effect on the whole Communist movement. * * *

* * * [T]he United States has it in its power to increase enormously the strains under which Soviet policy must operate, to force upon the Kremlin a far greater degree of moderation and circumspection than it has had to observe in recent years, and in this way to promote tendencies which must eventually find their outlet in either the break-up or the gradual mellowing of Soviet power. For no mystical, Messianic movement—and particularly not that of the Kremlin—can face frustration indefinitely without eventually adjusting itself in one way or another to the logic of that state of affairs.

*   *   *

NOTES

1. Here and elsewhere in this paper "Socialism" refers to Marxist or Leninist Communism. * * *

JOHN LEWIS GADDIS

The Long Peace: Elements of Stability in the Postwar International System

Systems Theory and International Stability

Anyone attempting to understand why there has been no third world war confronts a problem not unlike that of Sherlock Holmes and the dog that did not bark in the night: how does one account for something that did not happen? How does one explain why the great conflict between the United States and the Soviet Union, which by all past standards of historical experience should have devel-

From *International Security* 10, no. 4 (spring 1986): 92–142.

oped by now, has not in fact done so? The question involves certain methodological difficulties, to be sure: it is always easier to account for what did happen than what did not. But there is also a curious bias among students of international relations that reinforces this tendency: "for every thousand pages published on the causes of wars," Geoffrey Blainey has commented, "there is less than one page directly on the causes of peace."[1] Even the discipline of "peace studies" suffers from this disproportion: it has given far more attention to the question of what we must do to avoid the apocalypse than it has to the equally interesting question of why, given all the opportunities, it has not happened so far.

It might be easier to deal with this question if the work that has been done on the causes of war had produced something approximating a consensus on why wars develop: we could then apply that analysis to the post-1945 period and see what it is that has been different about it. But, in fact, these studies are not much help. Historians, political scientists, economists, sociologists, statisticians, even meteorologists, have wrestled for years with the question of what causes wars, and yet the most recent review of that literature concludes that "our understanding of war remains at an elementary level. No widely accepted theory of the causes of war exists and little agreement has emerged on the methodology through which these causes might be discovered."[2]

Nor has the comparative work that has been done on international systems shed much more light on the matter. The difficulty here is that our actual experience is limited to the operations of a single system—the balance of power system—operating either within the "multipolar" configuration that characterized international politics until World War II, or the "bipolar" configuration that has characterized them since. Alternative systems remain abstract conceptualizations in the minds of theorists, and are of little use in advancing our knowledge of how wars in the real world do or do not occur.[3]

But "systems theory" itself is something else again: here one can find a useful point of departure for thinking about the nature of international relations since 1945. An "international system" exists, political scientists tell us, when two conditions are met: first, interconnections exist between units within the system, so that changes in some parts of it produce changes in other parts as well; and, second, the collective behavior of the system as a whole differs from the expectations and priorities of the individual units that make it up.[4] Certainly demonstrating the "interconnectedness" of post-World War II international relations is not difficult: one of its most prominent characteristics has been the tendency of major powers to assume that little if anything can happen in the world without in some way enhancing or detracting from their own immediate interests.[5] Nor has the collective behavior of nations corresponded to their individual expectations: the very fact that the interim arrangements of 1945 have remained largely intact for four decades would have astonished—and quite possibly appalled—the statesmen who cobbled them together in the hectic months that followed the surrender of Germany and Japan.[6]

A particularly valuable feature of systems theory is that it provides criteria for differentiating between stable and unstable political configurations: these can help to account for the fact that some international systems outlast others. Karl Deutsch and J. David Singer have defined "stability" as "the probability that the system retains all of its essential characteristics: that no single nation becomes dominant; that most of its members continue to survive; and that large-scale war does not occur." It is characteristic of such a system, Deutsch and Singer add, that it has the capacity for self-regulation: the ability to counteract stimuli that would otherwise threaten its survival, much as the automatic pilot on an airplane or the governor on a steam engine would do. * * *

Does the post-World War II international system fit these criteria for "stability"? Certainly its most basic characteristic—bipolarity—remains intact, in that the gap between the world's two greatest military powers and their nearest rivals is not substantially different from what it was forty years ago.[7] At the same time, neither the Soviet Union nor the United States nor anyone else has been able wholly to dominate that system; the nations most active within it in 1945 are for the most part still active today. And of course the most convincing argument for "stability" is that, so far at least, World War III has not occurred. On the surface, then, the concept of a "stable" international system makes sense as a way of understanding the experience through which we have lived these past forty years.

But what have been the self-regulating mechanisms? How has an environment been created in which they are able to function? In what way do those mechanisms—and the environment in which they function—resemble or differ from the configuration of other international systems, both stable and unstable, in modern history? What circumstances exist that might impair their operation, transforming self-regulation into self-aggravation? These are questions that have not received the attention they deserve from students of the history and politics of the postwar era. * * *

* * *

The Structural Elements of Stability

BIPOLARITY

Any such investigation should begin by distinguishing the structure of the international system in question from the behavior of the nations that make it up.[8] The reason for this is simple: behavior alone will not ensure stability if the structural prerequisites for it are absent, but structure can under certain circumstances impose stability even when its behavioral prerequisites are unpromising.[9] * * *

* * *

Now, bipolarity may seem to many today—as it did forty years ago—an awkward and dangerous way to organize world politics.[10] Simple geometric logic would suggest that a system resting upon three or more points of support would be more stable than one resting upon two. But politics is not geometry: the passage of time and the accumulation of experience has made clear certain structural elements of stability in the bipolar system of international relations that were not present in the multipolar systems that preceded it:

(1) The postwar bipolar system realistically reflected the facts of where military power resided at the end of World War II[11]—and where it still does today, for that matter. In this sense, it differed markedly from the settlement of 1919, which made so little effort to accommodate the interests of Germany and Soviet Russia. It is true that in other categories of power—notably the economic—states have since arisen capable of challenging or even surpassing the Soviet Union and the United States in the production of certain specific commodities. But as the *political* position of nations like West Germany, Brazil, Japan, South Korea, Taiwan, and Hong Kong suggests, the ability to make video recorders, motorcycles, even automobiles and steel efficiently has yet to translate into anything approaching the capacity of Washington or Moscow to shape events in the world as a whole.

(2) The post-1945 bipolar structure was a simple one that did not require sophisticated leadership to maintain it. The great multipolar systems of the 19th century collapsed in large part because of their intricacy: they required a Metternich or a Bismarck to hold them together, and when statesmen of that calibre were no longer available, they tended to come apart.[12] Neither the Soviet nor the American political systems have been geared to identifying statesmen of comparable prowess and entrusting them with responsibility; demonstrated skill in the conduct of foreign policy has hardly been a major prerequisite for leadership in either country. And yet, a bipolar structure of international relations—because of the inescapably high stakes involved for its two major actors—tends, regardless of the personalities involved, to induce in them a sense of caution and restraint, and to discourage irresponsibility. * * *

(3) Because of its relatively simple structure, alliances in this bipolar system have tended to be more stable than they had been in the 19th century and in the 1919–1939 period. It is striking to consider that the North Atlantic Treaty Organization has now equaled in longevity the most durable of the pre-World War I alliances, that between Germany and Austria-Hungary; it has lasted almost twice as long as the Franco-Russian alliance, and certainly

much longer than any of the tenuous alignments of the interwar period. Its principal rival, the Warsaw Treaty Organization, has been in existence for almost as long. The reason for this is simple: alliances, in the end, are the product of insecurity;[13] so long as the Soviet Union and the United States each remain for the other and for their respective clients the major source of insecurity in the world, neither superpower encounters very much difficulty in maintaining its alliances. In a multipolar system, sources of insecurity can vary in much more complicated ways; hence it is not surprising to find alliances shifting to accommodate these variations.[14]

(4) At the same time, though, and probably because of the overall stability of the basic alliance systems, defections from both the American and Soviet coalitions—China, Cuba, Vietnam, Iran, and Nicaragua, in the case of the Americans; Yugoslavia, Albania, Egypt, Somalia, and China again in the case of the Russians—have been tolerated without the major disruptions that might have attended such changes in a more delicately balanced multipolar system. The fact that a state the size of China was able to reverse its alignment twice during the Cold War without any more dramatic effect upon the position of the superpowers says something about the stability bipolarity brings; compare this record with the impact, prior to 1914, of such apparently minor episodes as Austria's annexation of Bosnia and Herzegovina, or the question of who was to control Morocco. It is a curious consequence of bipolarity that although alliances are more durable than in a multipolar system, defections are at the same time more tolerable.[15]

In short, without anyone's having designed it, and without any attempt whatever to consider the requirements of justice, the nations of the postwar era lucked into a system of international relations that, because it has been based upon realities of power, has served the cause of order—if not justice—better than one might have expected.

INDEPENDENCE, NOT INTERDEPENDENCE

But if the structure of bipolarity in itself encouraged stability, so too did certain inherent characteristics of the bilateral Soviet-American relationship. * * *

＊　　　＊　　　＊

It has long been an assumption of classical liberalism that the more extensive the contacts that take place between nations, the greater are the chances for peace. Economic interdependence, it has been argued, makes war unlikely because nations who have come to rely upon one another for vital commodities cannot afford it. Cultural exchange, it has been suggested, causes peoples to become more sensitive to each others' concerns, and hence reduces the likelihood of misunderstandings. "People to people" contacts, it has been assumed, make it possible for nations to "know" one another better; the danger of war between them is, as a result, correspondingly reduced.[16]

＊　　　＊　　　＊

The Russian-American relationship, to a remarkable degree for two nations so extensively involved with the rest of the world, has been one of mutual *in*dependence. The simple fact that the two countries occupy opposite sides of the earth has had something to do with this: geographical remoteness from one another has provided little opportunity for the emergence of irredentist grievances comparable in importance to historic disputes over, say, Alsace-Lorraine, or the Polish Corridor, or the West Bank, the Gaza Strip, and Jerusalem. In the few areas where Soviet and American forces—or their proxies—have come into direct contact, they have erected artificial barriers like the Korean demilitarized zone, or the Berlin Wall, perhaps in unconscious recognition of an American poet's rather chilly precept that "good fences make good neighbors."

Nor have the two nations been economically dependent upon one another in any critical way. Certainly the United States requires nothing in the form of imports from the Soviet Union that it cannot obtain elsewhere. The situation is different for the Russians, to be sure, but even though the Soviet Union imports large quantities of food from the United States—and would like to import advanced technology as well—it is far from being wholly dependent upon these items, as the failure of recent attempts to change Soviet behavior by denying them has shown. The relative invulnerability of Russians and Americans to one another in the economic sphere may be frustrating to their respective policymakers, but it is probably fortunate, from the standpoint of international stability, that the two most powerful nations in the world are also its two most self-sufficient.[17]

*   *   *

It may well be, then, that the extent to which the Soviet Union and the United States have been independent of one another rather than interdependent—the fact that there have been so few points of economic leverage available to each, the fact that two such dissimilar people have had so few opportunities for interaction—has in itself constituted a structural support for stability in relations between the two countries, whatever their respective governments have actually done.

*   *   *

The Behavioral Elements of Stability

NUCLEAR WEAPONS

Stability in international systems is only partly a function of structure, though; it depends as well upon the conscious behavior of the nations that make them up. Even if the World War II settlement had corresponded to the distribution of power in the world, even if the Russian-American relationship had been one of minimal interdependence, even if domestic constraints had not created difficulties, stability in the postwar era still might

not have resulted if there had been, among either of the dominant powers in the system, the same willingness to risk war that has existed at other times in the past.

Students of the causes of war have pointed out that war is rarely something that develops from the workings of impersonal social or economic forces, or from the direct effects of arms races, or even by accident. It requires deliberate decisions on the part of national leaders; more than that, it requires calculations that the gains to be derived from war will outweigh the possible costs. * * *

For whatever reason, it has to be acknowledged that the statesmen of the post-1945 superpowers have, compared to their predecessors, been exceedingly cautious in risking war with one another.[18] In order to see this point, one need only run down the list of crises in Soviet-American relations since the end of World War II: Iran, 1946; Greece, 1947; Berlin and Czechoslovakia, 1948; Korea, 1950; the East Berlin riots, 1953; the Hungarian uprising, 1956; Berlin again, 1958–59; the U-2 incident, 1960; Berlin again, 1961; the Cuban missile crisis, 1962; Czechoslovakia again, 1968; the Yom Kippur war, 1973; Afghanistan, 1979; Poland, 1981; the Korean airliner incident, 1983—one need only run down this list to see how many occasions there have been in relations between Washington and Moscow that in almost any other age, and among almost any other antagonists, would sooner or later have produced war.

That they have not cannot be chalked up to the invariably pacific temperament of the nations involved: the United States participated in eight international wars involving a thousand or more battlefield deaths between 1815 and 1980; Russia participated in nineteen.[19] Nor can this restraint be attributed to any unusual qualities of leadership on either side: the vision and competency of postwar Soviet and American statesmen does not appear to have differed greatly from that of their predecessors. Nor does weariness growing out of participation in two world wars fully explain this unwillingness to resort to arms in their dealings with one another: during the postwar era both nations have employed force against third parties—in the case of the United States in Korea and Vietnam; in the case of the Soviet Union in Afghanistan—for protracted periods of time, and at great cost.

It seems inescapable that what has really made the difference in inducing this unaccustomed caution has been the workings of the nuclear deterrent.[20] Consider, for a moment, what the effect of this mechanism would be on a statesman from either superpower who might be contemplating war. In the past, the horrors and the costs of wars could be forgotten with the passage of time. Generations like the one of 1914 had little sense of what the Napoleonic Wars—or even the American Civil War—had revealed about the brutality, expense, and duration of military conflict. But the existence of nuclear weapons—and, more to the point, the fact that we have direct evidence of what they can do when used against human beings[21]—has given this generation a painfully vivid awareness of the realities of war that no previous generation has had. It is difficult, given this awareness, to produce the optimism that historical experience tells us prepares the way for war; pessimism, it appears, is a permanent accompaniment to our thinking about war, and that, as Blainey reminds us, is a cause of peace.

That same pessimism has provided the superpowers with powerful inducements to control crises resulting from the risk-taking of third parties. It is worth recalling that World War I grew out of the unsuccessful management of a situation neither created nor desired by any of the major actors in the international system. There were simply no mechanisms to put a lid on escalation: to force each nation to balance the short-term temptation to exploit opportunities against the long-term danger that things might get out of hand.[22] The nuclear deterrent provides that mechanism today, and as a result the United States and the Soviet Union have successfully managed a whole series of crises—most notably in the Middle East—that grew out of the actions of neither but that could have involved them both.

None of this is to say, of course, that war cannot occur: if the study of history reveals anything at all it is that one ought to expect, sooner or later, the unexpected. Nor is it to say that the nuclear de-

terrent could not function equally well with half, or a fourth, or even an eighth of the nuclear weapons now in the arsenals of the superpowers. Nor is it intended to deprecate the importance of refraining from steps that might destabilize the existing stalemate, whether through the search for technological breakthroughs that might provide a decisive edge over the other side, or through so mechanical a duplication of what the other side has that one fails to take into account one's own probably quite different security requirements, or through strategies that rely upon the first use of nuclear weapons in the interest of achieving economy, forgetting the far more fundamental systemic interest in maintaining the tradition, dating back four decades now, of never actually employing these weapons for military purposes.

I am suggesting, though, that the development of nuclear weapons has had, on balance, a stabilizing effect on the postwar international system. They have served to discourage the process of escalation that has, in other eras, too casually led to war. They have had a sobering effect upon a whole range of statesmen of varying degrees of responsibility and capability. They have forced national leaders, every day, to confront the reality of what war is really like, indeed to confront the prospect of their own mortality, and that, for those who seek ways to avoid war, is no bad thing.

THE RECONNAISSANCE REVOLUTION

But although nuclear deterrence is the most important behavioral mechanism that has sustained the post-World War II international system, it is by no means the only one. Indeed, the very technology that has made it possible to deliver nuclear weapons anywhere on the face of the earth has functioned also to lower greatly the danger of surprise attack, thereby supplementing the self-regulating features of deterrence with the assurance that comes from knowing a great deal more than in the past about adversary capabilities. I refer here to what might be called the "reconnaissance revolution," a development that may well rival in importance the "nuclear revolution" that preceded it, but one that rarely gets the attention it deserves.

The point was made earlier that nations tend to start wars on the basis of calculated assessments that they have the power to prevail. But it was suggested as well that they have often been wrong about this: they either have failed to anticipate the nature and the costs of war itself, or they have misjudged the intentions and the capabilities of the adversary they have chosen to confront.[23] * * *

* * * But both sides are able—and indeed have been able for at least two decades—to evaluate each other's *capabilities* to a degree that is totally unprecedented in the history of relations between great powers.

What has made this possible, of course, has been the development of the reconnaissance satellite, a device that if rumors are correct allows the reading of automobile license plates or newspaper headlines from a hundred or more miles out in space, together with the equally important custom that has evolved between the superpowers of allowing these objects to pass unhindered over their territories.[24] The effect has been to give each side a far more accurate view of the other's military capabilities—and, to some degree, economic capabilities as well—than could have been provided by an entire phalanx of the best spies in the long history of espionage. The resulting intelligence does not rule out altogether the possibility of surprise attack, but it does render it far less likely, at least as far as the superpowers are concerned. * * *

* * *

IDEOLOGICAL MODERATION

* * *

The relationship between the Soviet Union and the United States has not been free from ideological rivalries: it could be argued, in fact, that these are among the most ideological nations on the face of the earth.[25] Certainly their respective ideologies could hardly have been more antithetical, given the self-proclaimed intention of one to overthrow the other.[26] And yet, since their emergence as su-

perpowers, both nations have demonstrated an impressive capacity to subordinate antagonistic ideological interests to a common goal of preserving international order. The reasons for this are worth examining.

If there were ever a moment at which the priorities of order overcame those of ideology, it would appear to be the point at which Soviet leaders decided that war would no longer advance the cause of revolution. That clearly had not been Lenin's position: international conflict, for him, was good or evil according to whether it accelerated or retarded the demise of capitalism.[27] Stalin's attitude on this issue was more ambivalent: he encouraged talk of an "inevitable conflict" between the "two camps" of communism and capitalism in the years immediately following World War II, but he also appears shortly before his death to have anticipated the concept of "peaceful coexistence."[28] It was left to Georgii Malenkov to admit publicly, shortly after Stalin's death, that a nuclear war would mean "the destruction of world civilization"; Nikita Khrushchev subsequently refined this idea (which he had initially condemned) into the proposition that the interests of world revolution, as well as those of the Soviet state, would be better served by working within the existing international order than by trying to overthrow it.[29]

* * *

The effect was to transform a state which, if ideology alone had governed, should have sought a complete restructuring of the existing international system, into one for whom that system now seemed to have definite benefits, within which it now sought to function, and for whom the goal of overthrowing capitalism had been postponed to some vague and indefinite point in the future.[30] Without this moderation of ideological objectives, it is difficult to see how the stability that has characterized great power relations since the end of World War II could have been possible.

* * *

* * * American officials at no point during the history of the Cold War seriously contemplated, as a

deliberate political objective, the elimination of the Soviet Union as a major force in world affairs. By the mid-1950s, it is true, war plans had been devised that, if executed, would have quite indiscriminately annihilated not only the Soviet Union but several of its communist and non-communist neighbors as well.[31] What is significant about those plans, though, is that they reflected the organizational convenience of the military services charged with implementing them, not any conscious policy decisions at the top. Both Eisenhower and Kennedy were appalled on learning of them; both considered them ecologically as well as strategically impossible; and during the Kennedy administration steps were initiated to devise strategies that would leave open the possibility of a surviving political entity in Russia even in the extremity of nuclear war.[32]

All of this would appear to confirm, then, the proposition that systemic interests tend to take precedence over ideological interests.[33] Both the Soviet ideological aversion to capitalism and the American ideological aversion to totalitarianism could have produced policies—and indeed had produced policies in the past—aimed at the complete overthrow of their respective adversaries. That such ideological impulses could be muted to the extent they have been during the past four decades testifies to the stake both Washington and Moscow have developed in preserving the existing international system: the moderation of ideologies must be considered, then, along with nuclear deterrence and reconnaissance, as a major self-regulating mechanism of postwar politics.

"RULES" OF THE SUPERPOWER "GAME"

The question still arises, though: how can order emerge from a system that functions without any superior authority? Even self-regulating mechanisms like automatic pilots or engine governors cannot operate without someone to set them in motion; the prevention of anarchy, it has generally been assumed, requires hierarchy, both at the level of interpersonal and international relations. * * *

*   *   *

These "rules" are, of course, implicit rather than explicit: they grow out of a mixture of custom, precedent, and mutual interest that takes shape quite apart from the realm of public rhetoric, diplomacy, or international law. They require the passage of time to become effective; they depend, for that effectiveness, upon the extent to which successive generations of national leadership on each side find them useful. They certainly do not reflect any agreed-upon standard of international morality: indeed they often violate principles of "justice" adhered to by one side or the other. But these "rules" have played an important role in maintaining the international system that has been in place these past four decades: without them the correlation one would normally anticipate between hostility and instability would have become more exact than it has in fact been since 1945.

*   *   *

(1) *Respect Spheres of Influence.* Neither Russians nor Americans officially admit to having such "spheres," but in fact much of the history of the Cold War can be written in terms of the efforts both have made to consolidate and extend them. * * * But what is important from the standpoint of superpower "rules" is the fact that, although neither side has ever publicly endorsed the other's right to a sphere of influence, neither has ever directly challenged it either.[34]

*   *   *

(2) *Avoid Direct Military Confrontation.* It is remarkable, in retrospect, that at no point during the long history of the Cold War have Soviet and American military forces engaged each other directly in sustained hostilities. The superpowers have fought three major limited wars since 1945, but in no case with each other: the possibility of direct Soviet-American military involvement was greatest—although it never happened—during the Korean War; it was

much more remote in Vietnam and has remained so in Afghanistan as well. In those few situations where Soviet and American military units have confronted one another directly—the 1948 Berlin blockade, the construction of the Berlin Wall in 1961, and the Cuban missile crisis the following year—great care was taken on both sides to avoid incidents that might have triggered hostilities.[35]

*　　*　　*

(3) *Use Nuclear Weapons Only as an Ultimate Resort.* One of the most significant—though least often commented upon—of the superpower "rules" has been the tradition that has evolved, since 1945, of maintaining a sharp distinction between conventional and nuclear weapons, and of reserving the military use of the latter only for the extremity of total war. *　*　*

*　　*　　*

It was precisely this sense that nuclear weapons were qualitatively different from other weapons[36] that most effectively deterred their employment by the United States during the first decade of the Cold War, a period in which the tradition of "non-use" had not yet taken hold, within which ample opportunities for their use existed, and during which the possibility of Soviet retaliation could not have been great. The idea of a discrete "threshold" between nuclear and conventional weapons, therefore, may owe more to the moral—and public relations—sensibilities of Washington officials than to any actual fear of escalation. By the time a credible Soviet retaliatory capability was in place, at the end of the 1950s, the "threshold" concept was equally firmly fixed: one simply did not cross it short of all-out war.[37] *　*　*

(4) *Prefer predictable anomaly over unpredictable rationality.* One of the most curious features of the Cold War has been the extent to which the superpowers—and their respective clients, who have had little choice in the matter—have tolerated a whole series of awkward, artificial, and, on the surface at least, unstable regional arrangements: the division of Germany is, of course, the most obvious example; others would include the Berlin Wall, the position of West Berlin itself within East Germany, the arbitrary and ritualized partition of the Korean peninsula, the existence of an avowed Soviet satellite some ninety miles off the coast of Florida, and, not least, the continued functioning of an important American naval base within it. There is to all of these arrangements an appearance of wildly illogical improvisation: none of them could conceivably have resulted, it seems, from any rational and premeditated design.

And yet, at another level, they have had a kind of logic after all: the fact that these jerry-built but rigidly maintained arrangements have lasted for so long suggests an unwillingness on the part of the superpowers to trade familiarity for unpredictability. *　*　*

(5) *Do not seek to undermine the other side's leadership.* The death of Stalin, in March 1953, set off a flurry of proposals within the United States government for exploiting the vulnerability that was thought certain to result: *　*　* And yet, by the following month President Eisenhower was encouraging precisely that successor regime to join in a major new effort to control the arms race and reduce the danger of war.[38] The dilemma here was one that was to recur throughout the Cold War: if what one wanted was stability at the international level, did it make sense to try to destabilize the other side's leadership at the national level?

The answer, it appears, has been no. There have been repeated leadership crises in both the United States and the Soviet

Union since Stalin's death: one thinks especially of the decline and ultimate deposition of Khrushchev following the Cuban missile crisis, of the Johnson administration's all-consuming fixation with Vietnam, of the collapse of Nixon's authority as a result of Watergate, and of the recent paralysis in the Kremlin brought about by the illness and death of three Soviet leaders within less than three years. And yet, in none of these instances can one discern a concerted effort by the unaffected side to exploit the other's vulnerability; indeed there appears to have existed in several of these situations a sense of frustration, even regret, over the difficulties its rival was undergoing.[39] From the standpoint of game theory, a "rule" that acknowledges legitimacy of leadership on both sides is hardly surprising: there have to be players in order for the game to proceed. But when compared to other historical—and indeed other current—situations in which that reciprocal tolerance has not existed,[40] its importance as a stabilizing mechanism becomes clear.

*   *   *

The Cold War, with all of its rivalries, anxieties, and unquestionable dangers, has produced the longest period of stability in relations among the great powers that the world has known in this century; it now compares favorably as well with some of the longest periods of great power stability in all of modern history. We may argue among ourselves as to whether or not we can legitimately call this "peace": it is not, I daresay, what most of us have in mind when we use that term. But I am not at all certain that the contemporaries of Metternich or Bismarck would have regarded their eras as "peaceful" either, even though historians looking back on those eras today clearly do.

Who is to say, therefore, how the historians of the year 2086—if there are any left by then—will look back on us? Is it not at least plausible that they will see our era, not as "the Cold War" at all, but rather, like those ages of Metternich and Bismarck,

as a rare and fondly remembered "Long Peace"? Wishful thinking? Speculation through a rose-tinted word processor? Perhaps. But would it not behoove us to give at least as much attention to the question of how this might happen—to the elements in the contemporary international system that might make it happen—as we do to the fear that it may not?

NOTES

1. Geoffrey Blainey, *The Causes of War* (London: Macmillan, 1973), p. 3.
2. Jack S. Levy, *War in the Modern Great Power System, 1495–1975* (Lexington: University Press of Kentucky, 1983), p. 1. Other standard works on this subject, in addition to Blainey, cited above, include: Lewis F. Richardson, *Arms and Insecurity: A Mathematical Study of the Causes and Origins of War* (Pittsburgh: Quadrangle, 1960); Quincy Wright, *A Study of War*, 2nd ed. (Chicago: University of Chicago Press, 1965); Kenneth N. Waltz, *Man, the State and War: A Theoretical Analysis* (New York: Columbia University Press, 1959); Kenneth Boulding, *Conflict and Defense: A General Theory* (New York: Harper and Row, 1962); Raymond Aron, *Peace and War: A Theory of International Relations*, trans. Richard Howard and Annette Baker Fox (New York: Doubleday, 1966); Robert Gilpin, *War and Change in World Politics* (New York: Cambridge University Press, 1981); Melvin Small and J. David Singer, *Resort to Arms: International and Civil Wars, 1816–1980* (Beverly Hills, Calif.: Sage Publications, 1982); and Michael Howard, *The Causes of Wars*, 2nd ed. (Cambridge, Mass.: Harvard University Press, 1984). A valuable overview of conflicting explanations is Keith L. Nelson and Spencer C. Olin, Jr., *Why War? Ideology, Theory, and History* (Berkeley: University of California Press, 1979).
3. The classic example of such abstract conceptualization is Morton A. Kaplan, *System and Process in International Politics* (New York:

John Wiley, 1957). For the argument that 1945 marks the transition from a "multipolar" to a "bipolar" international system, see Glenn H. Snyder and Paul Diesing, *Conflict Among Nations: Bargaining, Decision Making, and System Structure in International Crises* (Princeton, N.J.: Princeton University Press, 1977), pp. 419–420; and Kenneth Waltz, *Theory of International Politics* (Reading, Mass.: Addison-Wesley, 1979), pp. 161–163. One can, of course, question whether the postwar international system constitutes true "bipolarity." Peter H. Beckman, for example, provides an elaborate set of indices demonstrating the asymmetrical nature of American and Soviet power after 1945 in his *World Politics in the Twentieth Century* (Englewood Cliffs, N.J.: Prentice Hall, 1984), pp. 207–209, 235–237, 282–285. But such retrospective judgments neglect the perceptions of policymakers *at the time*, who clearly saw their world as bipolar and frequently commented on the phenomenon. See, for example, David S. McLellan, *Dean Acheson: The State Department Years* (New York: Dodd, Mead, 1976), p. 116; and, for Soviet "two camp" theory, William Taubman, *Stalin's America Policy: From Entente to Detente to Cold War* (New York: Norton, 1982), pp. 176–178.

4. I have followed here the definition of Robert Jervis, "Systems Theories and Diplomatic History," in Paul Gordon Lauren, ed., *Diplomacy: New Approaches in History, Theory, and Policy* (New York: Free Press, 1979), p. 212. For a more rigorous discussion of the requirements of systems theory, and a critique of some of its major practitioners, see Waltz, *Theory of International Politics*, pp. 38–78. Akira Iriye is one of the few historians who have sought to apply systems theory to the study of international relations. See his *After Imperialism: The Search for a New Order in the Far East, 1921–1931* (Cambridge: Harvard University Press, 1965); and *The Cold War in Asia: A Historical Introduction* (Englewood Cliffs, N.J.: Prentice Hall, 1974).

5. See, on this point, Robert Jervis, *Perception and Misperception in International Politics* (Princeton, N.J.: Princeton University Press, 1976), pp. 58–62. Jervis points out that "almost by definition, a great power is more tightly connected to larger numbers of other states than is a small power. . . . Growing conflict or growing cooperation between Argentina and Chile would not affect Pakistan, but it would affect America and American policy toward those states. . . ." Jervis, "Systems Theories and Diplomatic History," p. 215.

6. "A future war with the Soviet Union," retiring career diplomat Joseph C. Grew commented in May 1945, "is as certain as anything in this world." Memorandum of May 19, 1945, quoted in Joseph C. Grew, *Turbulent Era: A Diplomatic Record of Forty Years, 1904–1945* (Boston: Houghton Mifflin, 1952), Vol. 2, p. 1446. For other early expressions of pessimism about the stability of the postwar international system, see Water Lippmann, *The Cold War: A Study in U.S. Foreign Policy* (New York: Harper Brothers, 1947), pp. 26–28, 37–39, 60–62. "There is, after all, something to be explained—about perceptions as well as events—when so much that has been written has dismissed the new state system as no system at all but an unstable transition to something else." A.W. DePorte, *Europe Between the Super-Powers: The Enduring Balance* (New Haven: Yale University Press, 1979), p. 167.

7. See, on this point, Waltz, *Theory of International Politics*, pp. 180–181; also DePorte, *Europe Between the Super-Powers*, p. 167.

8. Waltz, *Theory of International Politics*, pp. 73–78; Gilpin, *War and Change in World Politics*, pp. 85–88.

9. ". . . [S]tructure designates a set of constraining conditions. . . . [It] acts as a selector, but it cannot be seen, examined, and observed at work. . . . Because structures select by rewarding some behaviors and punishing others, outcomes cannot be inferred from intentions and behaviors." Waltz, *Theory of International Politics*, pp. 73–74.

10. Among those who have emphasized the instability of bipolar systems are Morgenthau, *Politics Among Nations* [*The Struggle for Power and Peace* (New York: Alfred A. Knopf, 1949)], pp. 350–354; and Wright, *A Study of War*, pp. 763–764. See also Blainey, *The Causes of War*, pp. 110–111.

11. "... [W]hat *was* dominant in their consciousness," Michael Howard has written of the immediate post-World War II generation of statesmen, "was the impotence, almost one might say the irrelevance, of ethical aspirations in international politics in the absence of that factor to which so little attention had been devoted by their more eminent predecessors, to which indeed so many of them had been instinctively hostile—military power." Howard, *The Causes of War*, p. 55.

12. Henry Kissinger has written two classic accounts dealing with the importance of individual leadership in sustaining international systems. See his *A World Restored* (New York: Grosset and Dunlap, 1957), on Metternich; and, on Bismarck, "The White Revolutionary: Reflections on Bismarck," *Daedalus*, Vol. 97 (Summer 1968), pp. 888–924. For a somewhat different perspective on Bismarck's role, see George F. Kennan, *The Decline of Bismarck's European Order: Franco-Russian Relations, 1875–1890* (Princeton, N.J.: Princeton University Press, 1979), especially pp. 421–422.

13. See, on this point, Roger V. Dingman, "Theories of, and Approaches to, Alliance Politics," in Lauren, ed., *Diplomacy*, pp. 247–247.

14. My argument here follows that of Snyder and Diesing, *Conflict Among Nations*, pp. 429–445.

15. Waltz, *Theory of International Politics*, pp. 167–169.

16. The argument is succinctly summarized in Nelson and Olin, *Why War?*, pp. 35–43. Geoffrey Blainey labels the idea "Manchesterism" and satirizes it wickedly: "If those gifted early prophets of the Manchester creed could have seen Chamberlain—during the Czech crisis of September 1938—board the aircraft that was to fly him to Bavaria to meet Hitler at short notice they would have hailed aviation as the latest messenger of peace. If they had known that he met Hitler without even his own German interpreter they would perhaps have wondered whether the conversation was in Esperanto or Volapuk. It seemed that every postage stamp, bilingual dictionary, railway timetable and trade fair, every peace congress, Olympic race, tourist brochure and international telegram that had ever existed, was gloriously justified when Mr Chamberlain said from the window of number 10 Downing Street on 30 September 1938: 'I believe it is peace for our time.' In retrospect the outbreak of war a year later seems to mark the failure and the end of the policy of appeasement, but the policy survived. The first British air raids over Germany dropped leaflets." *The Causes of War*, p. 28.

17. Soviet exports and imports as a percentage of gross national product ranged between 4 and 7 percent between 1955 and 1975; for the United States the comparable figures were 7–14 percent. This compares with figures of 33–52 percent for Great Britain, France, Germany, and Italy in the four years immediately preceding World War I, and figures of 19–41 percent for the same nations plus Japan for the period 1949–1976. Waltz, *Theory of International Politics*, pp. 141, 212.

18. See Michael Howard's observations on the absence of a "bellicist" mentality among the great powers in the postwar era, in his *The Causes of War*, pp. 271–273.

19. Small and Singer, *Resort to Arms*, pp. 167, 169.

20. For a persuasive elaboration of this argument, with an intriguing comparison of the post-1945 "nuclear" system to the post-1815 "Vienna" system, see Michael Mandelbaum, *The Nuclear Revolution: International Politics Before and After Hiroshima* (New York: Cambridge University Press, 1981), pp. 58–77; also Morgan, *Deterrence* [*A Conceptual Analysis* (Beverly Hills: Sage, 1977)], p. 208; Craig and George, *Force and Statecraft* [*Diplomatic Prob-*

lems of Our Time (New York: Oxford University Press, 1983)], pp. 117–120; Howard, *The Causes of War*, pp. 22, 278–279. It is interesting to speculate as to whether Soviet-American bipolarity would have developed if nuclear weapons had never been invented. My own view—obviously unverifiable—is that it would have, because bipolarity resulted from the way in which World War II had been fought; the condition was already evident at the time of Hiroshima and Nagasaki. Whether bipolarity would have lasted as long as it has in the absence of nuclear weapons is another matter entirely, though: it seems at least plausible that these weapons have perpetuated bipolarity beyond what one might have expected its normal lifetime to be by minimizing superpower risk-taking while at the same time maintaining an apparently insurmountable power gradient between the superpowers and any potential military rivals.

21. See, on this point, Mandelbaum, *The Nuclear Revolution*, p. 109; also the discussion of the "crystal ball effect" in Albert Carnesale et al., *Living With Nuclear Weapons* (New York: Bantam, 1983), p. 44.

22. For a brief review of the literature on crisis management, together with an illustrative comparison of the July 1914 crisis with the Cuban missile crisis, see Ole R. Holsti, "Theories of Crisis Decision Making," in Lauren, ed., *Diplomacy*, pp. 99–136; also Craig and George, *Force and Statecraft*, pp. 205–219.

23. Gilpin, *War and Change in World Politics*, pp. 202–203. Geoffrey Blainey, citing an idea first proposed by the sociologist Georg Simmel, has suggested that, in the past, war was the only means by which nations could gain an exact knowledge of each others' capabilities. Blainey, *The Causes of War*, p. 118.

24. A useful up-to-date assessment of the technology is David Hafemeister, Joseph J. Romm, and Kosta Tsipis, "The Verification of Compliance with Arms-Control Agreements," *Scientific American*, March 1985, pp. 38–45. For the historical evolution of reconnaissance satel-

lites, see Gerald M. Steinberg, *Satellite Reconnaissance: The Role of Informal Bargaining* (New York: Praeger, 1983), pp. 19–70; Paul B. Stares, *The Militarization of Space: U.S. Policy, 1945–1984* (Ithaca, N.Y.: Cornell University Press, 1985), pp. 30–33, 47–57, 62–71; also Walter A. McDougall, *The Heavens and the Earth: A Political History of the Space Age* (New York: Basic Books, 1985), pp. 177–226.

25. See, on this point, Halle, *The Cold War as History* [New York: Harper and Row, 1967], pp. 157–160.

26. Adam B. Ulam, *Expansion and Coexistence: The History of Soviet Foreign Policy, 1917–73*, 2nd ed. (New York: Praeger, 1974), pp. 130–131.

27. See, on this point, E.H. Carr, *The Bolshevik Revolution, 1917–1923* (New York: Macmillan, 1951–1953), Vol. 3, pp. 549–566; and Marshall D. Shulman, *Stalin's Foreign Policy Reappraised* (New York: Atheneum, 1969), p. 82. It is fashionable now, among Soviet scholars, to minimize the ideological component of Moscow's foreign policy; indeed Lenin himself is now seen as the original architect of "peaceful coexistence," a leader for whom the idea of exporting revolution can hardly have been more alien. See, for example, G.A. Trofimenko, "Uroki mirnogo sosushestvovaniia," *Voprosy istorii*, Number 11 (November 1983), pp. 6–7. It seems not out of place to wonder how the great revolutionary would have received such perfunctory dismissals of the Comintern and all that it implied; certainly most Western students have treated more seriously than this the revolutionary implications of the Bolshevik Revolution.

28. For Stalin's mixed record on this issue, see Shulman, *Stalin's Foreign Policy Reappraised*, *passim*; also Taubman, *Stalin's American Policy* [*From Entente to Detente to Cold War* (New York: Norton, 1982)], pp. 128–227; and Adam B. Ulam, *Stalin: The Man and His Era* (New York: Viking, 1973), especially pp. 641–643, 654. It is possible, of course, that Stalin followed both policies intentionally as a means

both of intimidating and inducing complacency in the West.

29. Herbert Dinerstein, *War and the Soviet Union:
Nuclear Weapons and the Revolution in Soviet
Military and Political Thinking* (New York:
Praeger, 1959), pp. 65–90; William Zimmer-
man, *Soviet Perspectives on International Re-
lations, 1956–1967* (Princeton: Princeton
University Press, 1969), pp. 251–252.

30. ". . . [P]layers' goals may undergo very little
change, but postponing their attainment to the
indefinite future fundamentally transforms the
meaning of . . . myth by revising its implications for social action. Exactly because myths
are dramatic stories, changing their time-
frame affects their character profoundly.
Those who see only the permanence of pro-
fessed goals, but who neglect structural
changes—the incorporation of common experiences into the myths of both sides, shifts in
the image of the opponent ('there are reasonable people also in the other camp'), and
modifications in the myths' periodization—
overlook the great effects that may result
from such contextual changes." Friedrich V.
Kratochwil, *International Order and Foreign
Policy: A Theoretical Sketch of Post-War International Politics* (Boulder: Westview Press,
1978), p. 117.

31. David Alan Rosenberg, " 'A Smoking, Radiat-
ing Ruin at the End of Two Hours': Documents on American Plans for Nuclear War
with the Soviet Union, 1954–55," *International
Security*, Vol. 6, No. 3 (Winter 1981/82),
pp. 3–38, and "The Origins of Overkill:
Nuclear Weapons and American Strategy,
1945–1960," *International Security*, Vol. 7, No.
3 (Spring 1983), pp. 3–71. For more general
accounts, see Fred Kaplan, *The Wizards of Armageddon* (New York: Simon and Schuster,
1983), especially pp. 263–270; and Gregg
Herken, *Counsels of War* (New York: Alfred A.
Knopf, 1985), pp. 137–140.

32. Rosenberg, "The Origins of Overkill," pp. 8,
69–71; Kaplan, *Wizards of Armageddon*,
pp. 268–285; Herken, *Counsels of War*,

pp. 140–165; and Stephen E. Ambrose, *Eisenhower: The President* (New York: Simon and
Schuster, 1984), pp. 494, 523, 564.

33. See, on this point, John Spanier, *Games Nations Play: Analyzing International Politics*, 5th
ed. (New York: Holt, Rinehart and Winston,
1984), p. 91.

34. "In general terms, acquiescence in spheres of
influence has taken the form of A disclaiming
what B does and in fact disapproving of what
B does, but at the same time acquiescing by
virtue of effectively doing nothing to oppose
B." Keal, *Unspoken Rules and Superpower
Dominance* [New York: St. Martin's, 1983],
p. 115.

35. Coral Bell, *The Conventions of Crisis: A Study
in Diplomatic Management* (New York: Oxford
University Press, 1971); Phil Williams, *Crisis
Management: Confrontation and Diplomacy in
the Nuclear Age* (New York: Wiley, 1976).
They have also managed successfully to con-
trol incidents at sea: see Sean M. Lynn-Jones,
"A Quiet Success for Arms Control: Prevent-
ing Incidents at Sea," *International Security*,
Vol. 9, No. 3 (Spring 1985), pp. 154–184.

36. With the exception of chemical weapons, for
which there appears to be an even deeper aversion than to the use of nuclear weapons. See,
on this point, Mandelbaum, *The Nuclear Revolution*, especially pp. 29–40. For the distinction
between nuclear and conventional weapons,
see Thomas C. Schelling, *Arms and Influence*
(New Haven: Yale University Press, 1966), pp.
132–134.

37. It is interesting to note that John F. Kennedy
began his administration with what appeared
to be a pledge never to initiate the use of nuclear weapons against the Soviet Union; after
protests from NATO allies, though, this was
modified into a promise not to initiate hostilities only. See Michael Mandelbaum, *The Nuclear Question: The United States and Nuclear
Weapons, 1946–1976* (Cambridge: Cambridge
University Press, 1979), p. 75.

38. Eisenhower speech to the American Society of
Newspaper Editors, April 16, 1953, *Eisenhower*

Public Papers: 1953 (Washington: U.S. Government Printing Office, 1960), pp. 179–188. For the origins of this speech, see Emmet John Hughes, *The Ordeal of Power: A Political Memoir of the Eisenhower Years* (New York: Atheneum, 1963), pp. 100–112.

39. See, for example, Lyndon B. Johnson, *The Vantage Point: Perspectives of the Presidency, 1963–1969* (New York: Holt, Rinehart and Winston, 1971), pp. 468–469; also Henry Kissinger, *Years of Upheaval* (Boston: Little, Brown, 1982), pp. 287–288.

40. I have in mind here the long history of dynastic struggles in Europe up through the wars of the French Revolution; also, and much more recently, the way in which a refusal to acknowledge leadership legitimacy has perpetuated the Iran-Iraq war.

2 ∽ CONTENDING PERSPECTIVES

Over the past century or more, the most prominent theoretical perspectives for understanding the basic nature of international politics have been realism, liberalism, and radicalism. These viewpoints have vied for influence both in public debates and in academic arguments. For that reason, Karen Mingst's Essentials of International Relations *is organized around the dialogue among these contending perspectives. In this chapter, the essays by Morgenthau, Doyle, and Gunder Frank flesh out each of these classic debates, respectively, while that by Tickner exemplifies the new directions in today's theory.*

The first essay in this chapter, by Stephen Walt, provides a brief overview of these prominent theories of international politics and sets them in the context of the new issues and approaches that are being debated in the field. The three following readings constitute some of the most concise and important statements of each of the three theoretical traditions. Hans Morgenthau, the leading figure in the field of international relations in the period after World War II, presents a realist view of power politics. His influential book Politics Among Nations *(1948), excerpted below, played a central role in preparing Americans intellectually to exercise global power in the Cold War period and to reconcile power politics with the idealistic ethics that had previously dominated American discussions about foreign relations.*

Michael Doyle advances the liberal theory of the democratic peace. His 1986 article in the American Political Science Review *pointed out that no two democracies had ever fought a war against each other. This sparked a huge and still ongoing debate among academics and public commentators about why this was the case and whether this meant that the United States and other democracies should place efforts to promote the further spread of democracy at the head of their foreign policy agendas.*

Andre Gunder Frank, a political economist who has written extensively on Latin America, draws on Marxist ideas in discussing the dependency of the developing countries in the global capitalist system. His 1966 essay reprinted below argues that the more economic contact a late developing country had with the wealthier and more powerful advanced capitalist states, the more likely it was to become impoverished and dependent. Though this diagnosis would have fewer adherents today, the problem of how late developing countries can accommodate to the challenges of economic globalization remains a pressing one.

Finally, the excerpt from Gender and International Relations *by J. Ann Tickner illustrates new currents in the study of international politics that fundamentally challenge the realist, liberal, and radical perspectives. Arguing from a feminist perspective, Tickner suggests that much of the warlike behavior realists attribute to the situation of international anarchy is better understood as a consequence of the way male identity has been constructed.*

Books in the Norton Series in World Politics by John Mearsheimer and by John Oneal and Bruce Russett offer the most up-to-date statements of the realist and liberal perspectives, respectively. The book in the series by Stephen Krasner provides a contemporary statement on international economic relations that addresses the insights of all three perspectives.

STEPHEN M. WALT

International Relations: One World, Many Theories

Why should policymakers and practitioners care about the scholarly study of international affairs? Those who conduct foreign policy often dismiss academic theorists (frequently, one must admit, with good reason), but there is an inescapable link between the abstract world of theory and the real world of policy. We need theories to make sense of the blizzard of information that bombards us daily. Even policymakers who are contemptuous of "theory" must rely on their own (often unstated) ideas about how the world works in order to decide what to do. It is hard to make good policy if one's basic organizing principles are flawed, just as it is hard to construct

From *Foreign Policy*, no. 110 (spring 1998): 29–44.

good theories without knowing a lot about the real world. Everyone uses theories—whether he or she knows it or not—and disagreements about policy usually rest on more fundamental disagreements about the basic forces that shape international outcomes.

Take, for example, the current debate on how to respond to China. From one perspective, China's ascent is the latest example of the tendency for rising powers to alter the global balance of power in potentially dangerous ways, especially as their growing influence makes them more ambitious. From another perspective, the key to China's future conduct is whether its behavior will be modified by its integration into world markets and by the (inevitable?) spread of democratic principles. From yet another viewpoint, relations between China and the rest of the world will be shaped by issues of culture and identity: Will China see itself (and be seen by others) as a normal member of the world community or a singular society that deserves special treatment?

In the same way, the debate over NATO expansion looks different depending on which theory one employs. From a "realist" perspective, NATO expansion is an effort to extend Western influence—well beyond the traditional sphere of U.S. vital interests—during a period of Russian weakness and is likely to provoke a harsh response from Moscow. From a liberal perspective, however, expansion will reinforce the nascent democracies of Central Europe and extend NATO's conflict-management mechanisms to a potentially turbulent region. A third view might stress the value of incorporating the Czech Republic, Hungary, and Poland within the Western security community, whose members share a common identity that has made war largely unthinkable.

No single approach can capture all the complexity of contemporary world politics. Therefore, we are better off with a diverse array of competing ideas rather than a single theoretical orthodoxy. Competition between theories helps reveal their strengths and weaknesses and spurs subsequent refinements, while revealing flaws in conventional wisdom. Although we should take care to emphasize inventiveness over invective, we should welcome and encourage the heterogeneity of contemporary scholarship.

Where Are We Coming From?

The study of international affairs is best understood as a protracted competition between the realist, liberal, and radical traditions. Realism emphasizes the enduring propensity for conflict between states; liberalism identifies several ways to mitigate these conflictive tendencies; and the radical tradition describes how the entire system of state relations might be transformed. The boundaries between these traditions are somewhat fuzzy and a number of important works do not fit neatly

into any of them, but debates within and among them have largely defined the discipline.

REALISM

Realism was the dominant theoretical tradition throughout the Cold War. It depicts international affairs as a struggle for power among self-interested states and is generally pessimistic about the prospects for eliminating conflict and war. Realism dominated in the Cold War years because it provided simple but powerful explanations for war, alliances, imperialism, obstacles to cooperation, and other international phenomena, and because its emphasis on competition was consistent with the central features of the American-Soviet rivalry.

Realism is not a single theory, of course, and realist thought evolved considerably throughout the Cold War. "Classical" realists such as Hans Morgenthau and Reinhold Niebuhr believed that states, like human beings, had an innate desire to dominate others, which led them to fight wars. Morgenthau also stressed the virtues of the classical, multipolar, balance-of-power system and saw the bipolar rivalry between the United States and the Soviet Union as especially dangerous.

By contrast, the "neorealist" theory advanced by Kenneth Waltz ignored human nature and focused on the effects of the international system. For Waltz, the international system consisted of a number of great powers, each seeking to survive. Because the system is anarchic (i.e., there is no central authority to protect states from one another), each state has to survive on its own. Waltz argued that this condition would lead weaker states to balance against, rather than bandwagon with, more powerful rivals. And contrary to Morgenthau, he claimed that bipolarity was more stable than multipolarity.

An important refinement to realism was the addition of offense-defense theory, as laid out by Robert Jervis, George Quester, and Stephen Van Evera. These scholars argued that war was more likely when states could conquer each other easily. When defense was easier than offense, however, security was more plentiful, incentives to expand declined, and cooperation could blossom. And if defense had the advantage, and states could distinguish between offensive and defensive weapons, then states could acquire the means to defend themselves without threatening others, thereby dampening the effects of anarchy.

For these "defensive" realists, states merely sought to survive and great powers could guarantee their security by forming balancing alliances and choosing defensive military postures (such as retaliatory nuclear forces). Not surprisingly, Waltz and most other neorealists believed that the United States was extremely secure for most of the Cold War. Their principle fear was that it might squander its favorable position by adopting an overly aggressive foreign policy. Thus, by the end of the Cold War, realism had moved away from Morgenthau's dark brooding about human nature and taken on a slightly more optimistic tone.

LIBERALISM

The principal challenge to realism came from a broad family of liberal theories. One strand of liberal thought argued that economic interdependence would discourage states from using force against each other because warfare would threaten each side's prosperity. A second strand, often associated with President Woodrow Wilson, saw the spread of democracy as the key to world peace, based on the claim that democratic states were inherently more peaceful than authoritarian states. A third, more recent theory argued that international institutions such as the International Energy Agency and the International Monetary Fund could help overcome selfish state behavior, mainly by encouraging states to forego immediate gains for the greater benefits of enduring cooperation.

Although some liberals flirted with the idea that new transnational actors, especially the multinational corporation, were gradually encroaching on the power of states, liberalism generally saw states as the central players in international affairs. All liberal theories implied that cooperation was more pervasive than even the defensive version of realism allowed, but each view offered a different recipe for promoting it.

RADICAL APPROACHES

Until the 1980s, marxism was the main alternative to the mainstream realist and liberal traditions. Where realism and liberalism took the state system for granted, marxism offered both a different explanation for international conflict and a blueprint for fundamentally transforming the existing international order.

Orthodox marxist theory saw capitalism as the central cause of international conflict. Capitalist states battled each other as a consequence of their incessant struggle for profits and battled socialist states because they saw in them the seeds of their own destruction. Neomarxist "dependency" theory, by contrast, focused on relations between advanced capitalist powers and less developed states and argued that the former—aided by an unholy alliance with the ruling classes of the developing world—had grown rich by exploiting the latter. The solution was to overthrow these parasitic élites and install a revolutionary government committed to autonomous development.

Both of these theories were largely discredited before the Cold War even ended. The extensive history of economic and military cooperation among the advanced industrial powers showed that capitalism did not inevitably lead to conflict. The bitter schisms that divided the communist world showed that socialism did not always promote harmony. Dependency theory suffered similar empirical setbacks as it became increasingly clear that, first, active participation in the world economy was a better route to prosperity than autonomous socialist development; and, second, many developing countries proved themselves quite capable of bargaining successfully with multinational corporations and other capitalist institutions.

As marxism succumbed to its various failings, its mantle was assumed by a group of theorists who borrowed heavily from the wave of postmodern writings in literary criticism and social theory. This "deconstructionist" approach was openly skeptical of the effort to devise general or universal theories such as realism or liberalism. Indeed, its proponents emphasized the importance of language and discourse in shaping social outcomes. However, because these scholars focused initially on criticizing the mainstream paradigms but did not offer positive alternatives to them, they remained a self-consciously dissident minority for most of the 1980s.

DOMESTIC POLITICS

Not all Cold War scholarship on international affairs fit neatly into the realist, liberal, or marxist paradigms. In particular, a number of important works focused on the characteristics of states, governmental organizations, or individual leaders. The democratic strand of liberal theory fits under this heading, as do the efforts of scholars such as Graham Allison and John Steinbruner to use organization theory and bureaucratic politics to explain foreign policy behavior, and those of Jervis, Irving Janis, and others, which applied social and cognitive psychology. For the most part, these efforts did not seek to provide a general theory of international behavior but to identify other factors that might lead states to behave contrary to the predictions of the realist or liberal approaches. Thus, much of this literature should be regarded as a complement to the three main paradigms rather than as a rival approach for analysis of the international system as a whole.

New Wrinkles in Old Paradigms

Scholarship on international affairs has diversified significantly since the end of the Cold War. Non-American voices are more prominent, a wider range of methods and theories are seen as legitimate, and new issues such as ethnic conflict, the environment, and the future of the state have been placed on the agenda of scholars everywhere.

Yet the sense of déjà vu is equally striking. In-stead of resolving the struggle between competing theoretical traditions, the end of the Cold War has merely launched a new series of debates. Ironically, even as many societies embrace similar ideals of democracy, free markets, and human rights, the scholars who study these developments are more divided than ever.

REALISM REDUX

Although the end of the Cold War led a few writers to declare that realism was destined for the academic scrapheap, rumors of its demise have been largely exaggerated.

A recent contribution of realist theory is its attention to the problem of relative and absolute gains. Responding to the institutionalists' claim that international institutions would enable states to forego short-term advantages for the sake of greater long-term gains, realists such as Joseph Grieco and Stephen Krasner point out that anarchy forces states to worry about both the absolute gains from cooperation and the way that gains are distributed among participants. The logic is straightforward: If one state reaps larger gains than its partners, it will gradually become stronger, and its partners will eventually become more vulnerable.

Realists have also been quick to explore a variety of new issues. Barry Posen offers a realist explanation for ethnic conflict, noting that the breakup of multiethnic states could place rival ethnic groups in an anarchic setting, thereby triggering intense fears and tempting each group to use force to improve its relative position. This problem would be particularly severe when each group's territory contained enclaves inhabited by their ethnic rivals—as in the former Yugoslavia—because each side would be tempted to "cleanse" (preemptively) these alien minorities and expand to incorporate any others from their ethnic group that lay outside their borders. Realists have also cautioned that NATO, absent a clear enemy, would likely face increasing strains and that expanding its presence eastward would jeopardize relations with Russia. Finally, scholars such as Michael Mastanduno have argued that U.S. foreign policy is generally consistent with realist principles, insofar as its actions are still designed to preserve U.S. predominance and to shape a postwar order that advances American interests.

The most interesting conceptual development within the realist paradigm has been the emerging split between the "defensive" and "offensive" strands of thought. Defensive realists such as Waltz, Van Evera, and Jack Snyder assumed that states had little intrinsic interest in military conquest and argued that the costs of expansion generally outweighed the benefits. Accordingly, they maintained that great power wars occurred largely because domestic groups fostered exaggerated perceptions of threat and an excessive faith in the efficacy of military force.

This view is now being challenged along several fronts. First, as Randall Schweller notes, the neorealist assumption that states merely seek to survive "stacked the deck" in favor of the status quo because it precluded the threat of predatory revisionist states—nations such as Adolf Hitler's Germany or Napoleon Bonaparte's France that "value what they covet far more than what they possess" and are willing to risk annihilation to achieve their aims. Second, Peter Liberman, in his book *Does Conquest Pay?*, uses a number of historical cases—such as the Nazi occupation of Western Europe and Soviet hegemony over Eastern Europe—to show that the benefits of conquest often exceed the costs, thereby casting doubt on the claim that military expansion is no longer cost-effective. Third, offensive realists such as Eric Labs, John Mearsheimer, and Fareed Zakaria argue that anarchy encourages all states to try to maximize their relative strength simply because no state can ever be sure when a truly revisionist power might emerge.

These differences help explain why realists disagree over issues such as the future of Europe. For defensive realists such as Van Evera, war is rarely profitable and usually results from militarism, hypernationalism, or some other distorting domestic factor. Because Van Evera believes such forces are largely absent in post–Cold War Europe, he concludes that the region is "primed for peace." By contrast, Mearsheimer and other offensive realists believe that anarchy forces great powers to compete irrespective of their internal characteristics and that security competition will return to Europe as soon as the U.S. pacifier is withdrawn.

NEW LIFE FOR LIBERALISM

The defeat of communism sparked a round of self-congratulation in the West, best exemplified by Francis Fukuyama's infamous claim that humankind had now reached the "end of history." History has paid little attention to this boast, but the triumph of the West did give a notable boost to all three strands of liberal thought.

By far the most interesting and important development has been the lively debate on the "democratic peace." Although the most recent phase of this debate had begun even before the Soviet Union collapsed, it became more influential as the number of democracies began to increase and as evidence of this relationship began to accumulate.

Democratic peace theory is a refinement of the earlier claim that democracies were inherently more peaceful than autocratic states. It rests on the belief that although democracies seem to fight wars as often as other states, they rarely, if ever, fight one another. Scholars such as Michael Doyle, James Lee Ray, and Bruce Russett have offered a number of explanations for this tendency, the most popular being that democracies embrace norms of compromise that bar the use of force against groups espousing similar principles. It is hard to think of a more influential, recent academic debate, insofar as the belief that "democracies don't fight each other" has been an important justification for the Clinton administration's efforts to enlarge the sphere of democratic rule.

*   *   *

Liberal institutionalists likewise have continued to adapt their own theories. On the one hand, the core claims of institutionalist theory have become more modest over time. Institutions are now said

Competing Paradigms

	Realism	*Liberalism*	*Constructivism*
Main Theoretical Proposition	Self-interested states compete constantly for power or security	Concern for power overridden by economic/political considerations (desire for prosperity, commitment to liberal values)	State behavior shaped by élite beliefs, collective norms, and social identities
Main Units of Analysis	States	States	Individuals (especially élites)
Main Instruments	Economic and especially military power	Varies (international institutions, economic exchange, promotion of democracy)	Ideas and discourse
Modern Theorists	Hans Morgenthau, Kenneth Waltz	Michael Doyle, Robert Keohane	Alexander Wendt, John Ruggie
Representative Modern Works	Waltz, *Theory of International Politics*	Keohane, *After Hegemony*	Wendt, "Anarchy Is What States Make of It" (*International Organization*, 1992)
	Mearsheimer, "Back to the Future: Instability in Europe after the Cold War" (*International Security*, 1990)	Fukuyama, "The End of History?" (*National Interest*, 1989)	Koslowski & Kratochwil, "Understanding Changes in International Politics" (*International Organization*, 1994)
Post–Cold War Prediction	Resurgence of overt great power competition	Increased cooperation as liberal values, free markets, and international institutions spread	Agnostic because it cannot predict the content of ideas
Main Limitation	Does not account for international change	Tends to ignore the role of power	Better at describing the past than anticipating the future

to facilitate cooperation when it is in each state's interest to do so, but it is widely agreed that they cannot force states to behave in ways that are contrary to the states' own selfish interests. On the other hand, institutionalists such as John Duffield and Robert McCalla have extended the theory into new substantive areas, most notably the study of NATO. For these scholars, NATO's highly institutionalized character helps explain why it has been able to survive and adapt, despite the disappearance of its main adversary.

The economic strand of liberal theory is still influential as well. In particular, a number of scholars have recently suggested that the "globalization" of world markets, the rise of transnational networks and nongovernmental organizations, and the rapid spread of global communications technology are undermining the power of states and shifting attention away from military security toward economics and social welfare. The details are novel but the basic logic is familiar: As societies around the globe become enmeshed in a web of economic and social connections, the costs of disrupting these ties will effectively preclude unilateral state actions, especially the use of force.

This perspective implies that war will remain a remote possibility among the advanced industrial democracies. It also suggests that bringing China and Russia into the relentless embrace of world capitalism is the best way to promote both prosperity and peace, particularly if this process creates a strong middle class in these states and reinforces pressures to democratize. Get these societies hooked on prosperity and competition will be confined to the economic realm.

This view has been challenged by scholars who argue that the actual scope of "globalization" is modest and that these various transactions still take place in environments that are shaped and regulated by states. Nonetheless, the belief that economic forces are superseding traditional great power politics enjoys widespread acceptance among scholars, pundits, and policymakers, and the role of the state is likely to be an important topic for future academic inquiry.

CONSTRUCTIVIST THEORIES

Whereas realism and liberalism tend to focus on material factors such as power or trade, constructivist approaches emphasize the impact of ideas. Instead of taking the state for granted and assuming that it simply seeks to survive, constructivists regard the interests and identities of states as a highly malleable product of specific historical processes. They pay close attention to the prevailing discourse(s) in society because discourse reflects and shapes beliefs and interests, and establishes accepted norms of behavior. Consequently, constructivism is especially attentive to the sources of change, and this approach has largely replaced marxism as the preeminent radical perspective on international affairs.

The end of the Cold War played an important role in legitimating constructivist theories because realism and liberalism both failed to anticipate this event and had some trouble explaining it. Constructivists had an explanation: Specifically, former president Mikhail Gorbachev revolutionized Soviet foreign policy because he embraced new ideas such as "common security."

Moreover, given that we live in an era where old norms are being challenged, once clear boundaries are dissolving, and issues of identity are becoming more salient, it is hardly surprising that scholars have been drawn to approaches that place these issues front and center. From a constructivist perspective, in fact, the central issue in the post–Cold War world is how different groups conceive their identities and interests. Although power is not irrelevant, constructivism emphasizes how ideas and identities are created, how they evolve, and how they shape the way states understand and respond to their situation. Therefore, it matters whether Europeans define themselves primarily in national or continental terms; whether Germany and Japan redefine their pasts in ways that encourage their adopting more active international roles; and whether the United States embraces or rejects its identity as "global policeman."

Constructivist theories are quite diverse and do not offer a unified set of predictions on any of these issues. At a purely conceptual level, Alexander Wendt has argued that the realist conception of anarchy does not adequately explain why conflict occurs between states. The real issue is how anarchy is understood—in Wendt's words, "Anarchy is what states make of it." Another strand of constructivist theory has focused on the future of the territorial state, suggesting that transnational communication and shared civic values are undermining traditional national loyalties and creating radically new forms of political association. Other constructivists focus on the role of norms, arguing that international law and other normative principles have eroded earlier notions of sovereignty and altered the legitimate purposes for which state power may be employed. The common theme in each of these strands is the capacity of discourse to shape how political actors define themselves and their interests, and thus modify their behavior.

DOMESTIC POLITICS RECONSIDERED

As in the Cold War, scholars continue to explore the impact of domestic politics on the behavior of states. Domestic politics are obviously central to the debate on the democratic peace, and scholars such as Snyder, Jeffrey Frieden, and Helen Milner have examined how domestic interest groups can distort the formation of state preferences and lead to suboptimal international behavior. George Downs, David Rocke, and others have also explored how domestic institutions can help states deal with the perennial problem of uncertainty, while students of psychology have applied prospect theory and other new tools to explain why decision makers fail to act in a rational fashion.

The past decade has also witnessed an explosion of interest in the concept of culture, a development that overlaps with the constructivist emphasis on the importance of ideas and norms. * * * This trend is partly a reflection of the broader interest in cultural issues in the academic world (and within the public debate as well) and partly a response to the upsurge in ethnic, nationalist, and cultural conflicts since the demise of the Soviet Union.

Tomorrow's Conceptual Toolbox

While these debates reflect the diversity of contemporary scholarship on international affairs, there are also obvious signs of convergence. Most realists recognize that nationalism, militarism, ethnicity, and other domestic factors are important; liberals acknowledge that power is central to international behavior; and some constructivists admit that ideas will have greater impact when backed by powerful states and reinforced by enduring material forces. The boundaries of each paradigm are somewhat permeable, and there is ample opportunity for intellectual arbitrage.

*   *   *

In short, each of these competing perspectives captures important aspects of world politics. Our understanding would be impoverished were our thinking confined to only one of them. The "compleat diplomat" of the future should remain cognizant of realism's emphasis on the inescapable role of power, keep liberalism's awareness of domestic forces in mind, and occasionally reflect on constructivism's vision of change.

HANS MORGENTHAU

A Realist Theory of International Politics

This book purports to present a theory of international politics. The test by which such a theory must be judged is not *a priori* and abstract but empirical and pragmatic. The theory, in other words, must be judged not by some preconceived abstract principle or concept unrelated to

From Hans Morganthau, *Politics Among Nations: The Struggle for Power and Peace* (1948; reprint, New York: Knopf, 1960), chaps. 1, 3. Some of the author's notes have been omitted.

reality, but by its purpose: to bring order and meaning to a mass of phenomena which without it would remain disconnected and unintelligible. It must meet a dual test, an empirical and a logical one: Do the facts as they actually are lend themselves to the interpretation the theory has put upon them, and do the conclusions at which the theory arrives follow with logical necessity from its premises? In short, is the theory consistent with the facts and within itself?

The issue this theory raises concerns the nature

of all politics. The history of modern political thought is the story of a contest between two schools that differ fundamentally in their conceptions of the nature of man, society, and politics. One believes that a rational and moral political order, derived from universally valid abstract principles, can be achieved here and now. It assumes the essential goodness and infinite malleability of human nature, and blames the failure of the social order to measure up to the rational standards on lack of knowledge and understanding, obsolescent social institutions, or the depravity of certain isolated individuals or groups. It trusts in education, reform, and the sporadic use of force to remedy these defects.

The other school believes that the world, imperfect as it is from the rational point of view, is the result of forces inherent in human nature. To improve the world one must work with those forces, not against them. This being inherently a world of opposing interests and of conflict among them, moral principles can never be fully realized, but must at best be approximated through the ever temporary balancing of interests and the ever precarious settlement of conflicts. This school, then, sees in a system of checks and balances a universal principle for all pluralist societies. It appeals to historic precedent rather than to abstract principles, and aims at the realization of the lesser evil rather than of the absolute good.

*   *   *

* * * Principles of Political Realism

Political realism believes that politics, like society in general, is governed by objective laws that have their roots in human nature. In order to improve society it is first necessary to understand the laws by which society lives. The operation of these laws being impervious to our preferences, men will challenge them only at the risk of failure.

Realism, believing as it does in the objectivity of the laws of politics, must also believe in the possibility of developing a rational theory that reflects, however imperfectly and one-sidedly, these objective laws. It believes also, then, in the possibility of distinguishing in politics between truth and opinion—between what is true objectively and rationally, supported by evidence and illuminated by reason, and what is only a subjective judgment, divorced from the facts as they are and informed by prejudice and wishful thinking.

*   *   *

For realism, theory consists in ascertaining facts and giving them meaning through reason. It assumes that the character of a foreign policy can be ascertained only through the examination of the political acts performed and of the foreseeable consequences of these acts. Thus, we can find out what statesmen have actually done, and from the foreseeable consequences of their acts we can surmise what their objectives might have been.

Yet examination of the facts is not enough. To give meaning to the factual raw material of foreign policy, we must approach political reality with a kind of rational outline, a map that suggests to us the possible meanings of foreign policy. In other words, we put ourselves in the position of a statesman who must meet a certain problem of foreign policy under certain circumstances, and we ask ourselves what the rational alternatives are from which a statesman may choose who must meet this problem under these circumstances (presuming always that he acts in a rational manner), and which of these rational alternatives this particular statesman, acting under these circumstances, is likely to choose. It is the testing of this rational hypothesis against the actual facts and their consequences that gives meaning to the facts of international politics and makes a theory of politics possible.

The main signpost that helps political realism to find its way through the landscape of international politics is the concept of interest defined in terms of power. This concept provides the link between reason trying to understand international politics and the facts to be understood. * * *

We assume that statesmen think and act in terms of interest defined as power, and the evidence of history bears that assumption out. That assumption allows us to retrace and anticipate, as it were, the steps a statesman—past, present, or future—has taken or will take on the political scene. We look over his shoulder when he writes his dispatches; we listen in on his conversation with other statesmen; we read and anticipate his very thoughts. Thinking in terms of interest defined as power, we think as he does, and as disinterested observers we understand his thoughts and actions perhaps better than he, the actor on the political scene, does himself.

*   *   *

Political realism is aware of the moral significance of political action. It is also aware of the ineluctable tension between the moral command and the requirements of successful political action. And it is unwilling to gloss over and obliterate that tension and thus to obfuscate both the moral and the political issue by making it appear as though the stark facts of politics were morally more satisfying than they actually are, and the moral law less exacting than it actually is.

Realism maintains that universal moral principles cannot be applied to the actions of states in their abstract universal formulation, but that they must be filtered through the concrete circumstances of time and place. The individual may say for himself: "*Fiat justitia, pereat mundus* (Let justice be done, even if the world perish)," but the state has no right to say so in the name of those who are in its care. Both individual and state must judge political action by universal moral principles, such as that of liberty. Yet while the individual has a moral right to sacrifice himself in defense of such a moral principle, the state has no right to let its moral disapprobation of the infringement of liberty get in the way of successful political action, itself inspired by the moral principle of national survival. There can be no political morality without prudence; that is, without consideration of the political consequences of seemingly moral action. Realism, then, considers prudence—the weighing of the consequences of alternative political actions—to be the supreme virtue in politics. Ethics in the abstract judges action by its conformity with the moral law; political ethics judges action by its political consequences. * * *

Political Power

What Is Political Power?

*   *   *

International politics, like all politics, is a struggle for power. Whatever the ultimate aims of international politics, power is always the immediate aim. Statesmen and peoples may ultimately seek freedom, security, prosperity, or power itself. They may define their goals in terms of a religious, philosophic, economic, or social ideal. They may hope that this ideal will materialize through its own inner force, through divine intervention, or through the natural development of human affairs. They may also try to further its realization through nonpolitical means, such as technical co-operation with other nations or international organizations. But whenever they strive to realize their goal by means of international politics, they do so by striving for power. The Crusaders wanted to free the holy places from domination by the Infidels; Woodrow Wilson wanted to make the world safe for democracy; the Nazis wanted to open Eastern Europe to German colonization, to dominate Europe, and to conquer the world. Since they all chose power to achieve these ends, they were actors on the scene of international politics.

*   *   *

* * * When we speak of power, we mean man's control over the minds and actions of other men.

By political power we refer to the mutual relations of control among the holders of public authority and between the latter and the people at large.

Political power, however, must be distinguished from force in the sense of the actual exercise of physical violence. The threat of physical violence in the form of police action, imprisonment, capital punishment, or war is an intrinsic element of politics. When violence becomes an actuality, it signifies the abdication of political power in favor of military or pseudo-military power. In international politics in particular, armed strength as a threat or a potentiality is the most important material factor making for the political power of a nation. If it becomes an actuality in war, it signifies the substitution of military for political power. The actual exercise of physical violence substitutes for the psychological relation between two minds, which is of the essence of political power, the physical relation between two bodies, one of which is strong enough to dominate the other's movements. It is for this reason that in the exercise of physical violence the psychological element of the political relationship is lost, and that we must distinguish between military and political power.

Political power is a psychological relation between those who exercise it and those over whom it is exercised. It gives the former control over certain actions of the latter through the influence which the former exert over the latter's minds. That influence derives from three sources: the expectation of benefits, the fear of disadvantages, the respect or love for men or institutions. It may be exerted through orders, threats, persuasion, the authority or charisma of a man or of an office, or a combination of any of these.

While it is generally recognized that the interplay of these factors, in ever changing combinations, forms the basis of all domestic politics, the importance of these factors for international politics is less obvious, but no less real. There has been a tendency to reduce political power to the actual application of force or at least to equate it with successful threats of force and with persuasion, to the neglect of charisma. That neglect * * * accounts in good measure for the neglect of prestige as an independent element in international politics. * * *

*   *   *

An economic, financial, territorial, or military policy undertaken for its own sake is subject to evaluation in its own terms. Is it economically or financially advantageous? * * *

When, however, the objectives of these policies serve to increase the power of the nation pursuing them with regard to other nations, these policies and their objectives must be judged primarily from the point of view of their contribution to national power. An economic policy that cannot be justified in purely economic terms might nevertheless be undertaken in view of the political policy pursued. The insecure and unprofitable character of a loan to a foreign nation may be a valid argument against it on purely financial grounds. But the argument is irrelevant if the loan, however unwise it may be from a banker's point of view, serves the political policies of the nation. It may of course be that the economic or financial losses involved in such policies will weaken the nation in its international position to such an extent as to outweigh the political advantages to be expected. On these grounds such policies might be rejected. In such a case, what decides the issue is not purely economic and financial considerations but a comparison of the political changes and risks involved; that is, the probable effect of these policies upon the power of the nation.

The Depreciation of Political Power

The aspiration for power being the distinguishing element of international politics, as of all politics, international politics is of necessity power politics. While this fact is generally recognized in the practice of international affairs, it is frequently denied in the pronouncements of scholars, publicists, and even statesmen. Since the end of the Napoleonic Wars, ever larger groups in the Western world have been persuaded that the struggle for power on the international scene is a temporary phenomenon, a historical accident that is bound to disappear once the peculiar historic conditions that have given rise to it have been eliminated. * * * During the nineteenth century, liberals everywhere shared the conviction that power politics and war were residues of an obsolete system of government, and that with the victory of democracy and constitutional government over absolutism and autocracy international harmony and permanent peace would win out over power politics and war. Of this liberal school of thought, Woodrow Wilson was the most eloquent and most influential spokesman.

In recent times, the conviction that the struggle for power can be eliminated from the international scene has been connected with the great attempts at organizing the world, such as the League of Nations and the United Nations. * * *

* * * [In fact,] the struggle for power is universal in time and space and is an undeniable fact of experience. It cannot be denied that throughout historic time, regardless of social, economic, and political conditions, states have met each other in contests for power. Even though anthropologists have shown that certain primitive peoples seem to be free from the desire for power, nobody has yet shown how their state of mind and the conditions under which they live can be recreated on a world-wide scale so as to eliminate the struggle for power from the international scene.[1] It would be useless and even self-destructive to free one or the other of the peoples of the earth from the desire for power while leaving it extant in others. If the desire for power cannot be abolished everywhere in the world, those who might be cured would simply fall victims to the power of others.

The position taken here might be criticized on the ground that conclusions drawn from the past are unconvincing, and that to draw such conclusions has always been the main stock in trade of the enemies of progress and reform. Though it is true that certain social arrangements and institutions have always existed in the past, it does not necessarily follow that they must always exist in the future. The situation is, however, different when we deal not with social arrangements and institutions created by man, but with those elemental biopsychological drives by which in turn society is created. The drives to live, to propagate, and to dominate are common to all men.[2] Their relative strength is dependent upon social conditions that may favor one drive and tend to repress another, or that may withhold social approval from certain manifestations of these drives while they encourage others. Thus, to take examples only from the sphere of power, most societies condemn killing as a means of attaining power within society, but all societies encourage the killing of enemies in that struggle for power which is called war. * * *

NOTES

1. For an illuminating discussion of this problem, see Malcolm Sharp, "Aggression: A Study of Values and Law," *Ethics*, Vol. 57, No. 4, Part II (July 1947).

2. Zoologists have tried to show that the drive to dominate is found even in animals, such as chickens and monkeys, who create social hierarchies on the basis of the will and the ability to dominate. See e.g., Warder Allee, *Animal Life and Social Growth* (Baltimore: The Williams and Wilkins Company, 1932), and *The Social Life of Animals* (New York: W. W. Norton and Company, Inc., 1938).

MICHAEL W. DOYLE

Liberalism and World Politics

Promoting freedom will produce peace, we have often been told. In a speech before the British Parliament in June of 1982, President Reagan proclaimed that governments founded on a respect for individual liberty exercise "restraint" and "peaceful intentions" in their foreign policy. He then announced a "crusade for freedom" and a "campaign for democratic development" (Reagan, June 9, 1982).

In making these claims the president joined a long list of liberal theorists (and propagandists) and echoed an old argument: the aggressive instincts of authoritarian leaders and totalitarian ruling parties make for war. Liberal states, founded on such individual rights as equality before the law, free speech and other civil liberties, private property, and elected representation are fundamentally against war this argument asserts. When the citizens who bear the burdens of war elect their governments, wars become impossible. Furthermore, citizens appreciate that the benefits of trade can be enjoyed only under conditions of peace. Thus the very existence of liberal states, such as the U.S., Japan, and our European allies, makes for peace.

Building on a growing literature in international political science, I reexamine the liberal claim President Reagan reiterated for us. I look at three distinct theoretical traditions of liberalism, attributable to three theorists: Schumpeter, a brilliant explicator of the liberal pacifism the president invoked; Machiavelli, a classical republican whose glory is an imperialism we often practice; and Kant.

Despite the contradictions of liberal pacifism and liberal imperialism, I find, with Kant and other liberal republicans, that liberalism does leave a co-

From *American Political Science Review* 80, no. 4 (December 1986): 1151–69. The author's notes have been omitted.

herent legacy on foreign affairs. Liberal states are different. They are indeed peaceful, yet they are also prone to make war, as the U.S. and our "freedom fighters" are now doing, not so covertly, against Nicaragua. Liberal states have created a separate peace, as Kant argued they would, and have also discovered liberal reasons for aggression, as he feared they might. I conclude by arguing that the differences among liberal pacifism, liberal imperialism, and Kant's liberal internationalism are not arbitrary but rooted in differing conceptions of the citizen and the state.

Liberal Pacifism

There is no canonical description of liberalism. What we tend to call *liberal* resembles a family portrait of principles and institutions, recognizable by certain characteristics—for example, individual freedom, political participation, private property, and equality of opportunity—that most liberal states share, although none has perfected them all. Joseph Schumpeter clearly fits within this family when he considers the international effects of capitalism and democracy.

Schumpeter's "Sociology of Imperialisms," published in 1919, made a coherent and sustained argument concerning the pacifying (in the sense of nonaggressive) effects of liberal institutions and principles (Schumpeter, 1955; see also Doyle, 1986, pp. 155–59). Unlike some of the earlier liberal theorists who focused on a single feature such as trade (Montesquieu, 1949, vol. 1, bk. 20, chap. 1) or failed to examine critically the arguments they were advancing, Schumpeter saw the interaction of capitalism and democracy as the foundation of liberal pacifism, and he tested his arguments in a sociology of historical imperialisms.

He defines *imperialism* as "an objectless disposition on the part of a state to unlimited forcible expansion" (Schumpeter, 1955, p. 6). Excluding imperialisms that were mere "catchwords" and those that were "object-ful" (e.g., defensive imperialism), he traces the roots of objectless imperialism to three sources, each an atavism. Modern imperialism, according to Schumpeter, resulted from the combined impact of a "war machine," warlike instincts, and export monopolism.

Once necessary, the war machine later developed a life of its own and took control of a state's foreign policy: "Created by the wars that required it, the machine now created the wars it required" (Schumpeter, 1955, p. 25). Thus, Schumpeter tells us that the army of ancient Egypt, created to drive the Hyksos out of Egypt, took over the state and pursued militaristic imperialism. Like the later armies of the courts of absolutist Europe, it fought wars for the sake of glory and booty, for the sake of warriors and monarchs—wars *gratia* warriors.

A warlike disposition, elsewhere called "instinctual elements of bloody primitivism," is the natural ideology of a war machine. It also exists independently; the Persians, says Schumpeter (1955, pp. 25–32), were a warrior nation from the outset.

Under modern capitalism, export monopolists, the third source of modern imperialism, push for imperialist expansion as a way to expand their closed markets. The absolute monarchies were the last clear-cut imperialisms. Nineteenth-century imperialisms merely represent the vestiges of the imperialisms created by Louis XIV and Catherine the Great. Thus, the export monopolists are an atavism of the absolute monarchies, for they depend completely on the tariffs imposed by the monarchs and their militaristic successors for revenue (Schumpeter, 1955, p. 82–83). Without tariffs, monopolies would be eliminated by foreign competition.

Modern (nineteenth century) imperialism, therefore, rests on an atavistic war machine, militaristic attitudes left over from the days of monarchical wars, and export monopolism, which is nothing more than the economic residue of monarchical finance. In the modern era, imperialists gratify their private interests. From the national perspective, their imperialistic wars are objectless.

Schumpeter's theme now emerges. Capitalism and democracy are forces for peace. Indeed, they are antithetical to imperialism. For Schumpeter, the further development of capitalism and democracy means that imperialism will inevitably disappear. He maintains that capitalism produces an unwarlike disposition; its populace is "democratized, individualized, rationalized" (Schumpeter, 1955, p. 68). The people's energies are daily absorbed in production. The disciplines of industry and the market train people in "economic rationalism"; the instability of industrial life necessitates calculation. Capitalism also "individualizes"; "subjective opportunities" replace the "immutable factors" of traditional, hierarchical society. Rational individuals demand democratic governance.

Democratic capitalism leads to peace. As evidence, Schumpeter claims that throughout the capitalist world an opposition has arisen to "war, expansion, cabinet diplomacy"; that contemporary capitalism is associated with peace parties; and that the industrial worker of capitalism is "vigorously anti-imperialist." In addition, he points out that the capitalist world has developed means of preventing war, such as the Hague Court and that the least feudal, most capitalist society—the United States—has demonstrated the least imperialistic tendencies (Schumpeter, 1955, pp. 95–96). An example of the lack of imperialistic tendencies in the U.S., Schumpeter thought, was our leaving over half of Mexico unconquered in the war of 1846–48.

Schumpeter's explanation for liberal pacifism is quite simple: Only war profiteers and military aristocrats gain from wars. No democracy would pursue a minority interest and tolerate the high costs of imperialism. When free trade prevails, "no class" gains from forcible expansion because

> foreign raw materials and food stuffs are as accessible to each nation as though they were in its own territory. Where the cultural backwardness of a region makes normal economic intercourse dependent on colonization it does not matter, assuming free trade, which of the "civilized" nations undertakes the task of colonization. (Schumpeter, 1955, pp. 75–76)

Schumpeter's arguments are difficult to evaluate. In partial tests of quasi-Schumpeterian propositions, Michael Haas (1974, pp. 464–65) discovered a cluster that associates democracy, development, and sustained modernization with peaceful conditions. However, M. Small and J. D. Singer (1976) have discovered that there is no clearly negative correlation between democracy and war in the period 1816–1965—the period that would be central to Schumpeter's argument (see also Wilkenfeld, 1968, Wright, 1942, p. 841).

 * * * A recent study by R. J. Rummel (1983) of "libertarianism" and international violence is the closest test Schumpeterian pacifism has received. "Free" states (those enjoying political and economic freedom) were shown to have considerably less conflict at or above the level of economic sanctions than "nonfree" states. The free states, the partly free states (including the democratic socialist countries such as Sweden), and the nonfree states accounted for 24%, 26%, and 61%, respectively, of the international violence during the period examined.

These effects are impressive but not conclusive for the Schumpeterian thesis. The data are limited, in this test, to the period 1976 to 1980. It includes, for example, the Russo-Afghan War, the Vietnamese invasion of Cambodia, China's invasion of Vietnam, and Tanzania's invasion of Uganda but just misses the U.S., quasi-covert intervention in Angola (1975) and our not so covert war against Nicaragua (1981–). More importantly, it excludes the cold war period, with its numerous interventions, and the long history of colonial wars (the Boer War, the Spanish-American War, the Mexican Intervention, etc.) that marked the history of liberal, including democratic capitalist, states (Doyle, 1983b; Chan, 1984; Weede, 1984).

The discrepancy between the warlike history of liberal states and Schumpeter's pacifistic expectations highlights three extreme assumptions. First, his "materialistic monism" leaves little room for noneconomic objectives, whether espoused by states or individuals. Neither glory, nor prestige, nor ideological justification, nor the pure power of ruling shapes policy. These nonmaterial goals leave little room for positive-sum gains, such as the comparative advantages of trade. Second, and relatedly, the same is true for his states. The political life of individuals seems to have been homogenized at the same time as the individuals were "rationalized, individualized, and democratized." Citizens—capitalists and workers, rural and urban—seek material welfare. Schumpeter seems to presume that ruling makes no difference. He also presumes that no one is prepared to take those measures (such as stirring up foreign quarrels to preserve a domestic ruling coalition) that enhance one's political power, despite deterimental effects on mass welfare. Third, like domestic politics, world politics are homogenized. Materially monistic and democratically capitalist, all states evolve toward free trade and liberty together. Countries differently constituted seem to disappear from Schumpeter's analysis. "Civilized" nations govern "culturally backward" *regions*. These assumptions are not shared by Machiavelli's theory of liberalism.

Liberal Imperialism

Machiavelli argues, not only that republics are not pacifistic, but that they are the best form of state for imperial expansion. Establishing a republic fit for imperial expansion is, moreover, the best way to guarantee the survival of a state.

Machiavelli's republic is a classical mixed republic. It is not a democracy—which he thought would quickly degenerate into a tyranny—but is characterized by social equality, popular liberty, and political participation (Machiavelli, 1950, bk. 1, chap. 2, p. 112; see also Huliung, 1983, chap. 2; Mansfield, 1970; Pocock, 1975, pp. 198–99; Skinner, 1981, chap. 3). The consuls serve as "kings," the senate as an aristocracy managing the state, and the people in the assembly as the source of strength.

Liberty results from "disunion"—the competition and necessity for compromise required by the division of powers among senate, consuls, and tribunes (the last representing the common people). Liberty also results from the popular veto. The powerful few threaten the rest with tyranny, Machiavelli says, because they seek to dominate.

The mass demands not to be dominated, and their veto thus preserves the liberties of the state (Machiavelli, 1950, bk. 1, chap. 5, p. 122). However, since the people and the rulers have different social characters, the people need to be "managed" by the few to avoid having their recklessness overturn or their fecklessness undermine the ability of the state to expand (Machiavelli, 1950, bk. 1, chap. 53, pp. 249–50). Thus the senate and the consuls plan expansion, consult oracles, and employ religion to manage the resources that the energy of the people supplies.

Strength, and then imperial expansion, results from the way liberty encourages increased population and property, which grow when the citizens know their lives and goods are secure from arbitrary seizure. Free citizens equip large armies and provide soldiers who fight for public glory and the common good because these are, in fact, their own (Machiavelli, 1950, bk. 2, chap. 2, pp. 287–90). If you seek the honor of having your state expand, Machiavelli advises, you should organize it as a free and popular republic like Rome, rather than as an aristocratic republic like Sparta or Venice. Expansion thus calls for a free republic.

"Necessity"—political survival—calls for expansion. If a stable aristocratic republic is forced by foreign conflict "to extend her territory, in such a case we shall see her foundations give way and herself quickly brought to ruin"; if, on the other hand, domestic security prevails, "the continued tranquility would enervate her, or provoke internal disensions, which together, or either of them separately, will apt to prove her ruin" (Machiavelli, 1950, bk. 1, chap. 6, p. 129). Machiavelli therefore believes it is necessary to take the constitution of Rome, rather than that of Sparta or Venice, as our model.

Hence, this belief leads to liberal imperialism. We are lovers of glory, Machiavelli announces. We seek to rule or, at least, to avoid being oppressed. In either case, we want more for ourselves and our states than just material welfare (materialistic monism). Because other states with similar aims thereby threaten us, we prepare ourselves for expansion. Because our fellow citizens threaten us if we do not allow them either to satisfy their ambition or to release their political energies through imperial expansion, we expand.

There is considerable historical evidence for liberal imperialism. Machiavelli's (Polybius's) Rome and Thucydides' Athens both were imperial republics in the Machiavellian sense (Thucydides, 1954, bk. 6). The historical record of numerous U.S. interventions in the postwar period supports Machiavelli's argument (* * * Barnet, 1968, chap. 11), but the current record of liberal pacifism, weak as it is, calls some of his insights into question. To the extent that the modern populace actually controls (and thus unbalances) the mixed republic, its diffidence may outweigh elite ("senatorial") aggressiveness.

We can conclude either that (1) liberal pacifism has at least taken over with the further development of capitalist democracy, as Schumpeter predicted it would or that (2) the mixed record of liberalism—pacifism and imperialism—indicates that some liberal states are Schumpeterian democracies while others are Machiavellian republics. Before we accept either conclusion, however, we must consider a third apparent regularity of modern world politics.

Liberal Internationalism

Modern liberalism carries with it two legacies. They do not affect liberal states separately, according to whether they are pacifistic or imperialistic, but simultaneously.

The first of these legacies is the pacification of foreign relations among liberal states. * * *

Beginning in the eighteenth century and slowly growing since then, a zone of peace, which Kant called the "pacific federation" or "pacific union," has begun to be established among liberal societies. More than 40 liberal states currently make up the union. Most are in Europe and North America, but they can be found on every continent, as Appendix 1 indicates.

Here the predictions of liberal pacifists (and President Reagan) are borne out: liberal states do exercise peaceful restraint, and a separate peace exists among them. This separate peace provides a solid foundation for the United States' crucial alliances with the liberal powers, e.g., the North Atlantic Treaty Organization and our Japanese alliance. This foundation appears to be impervious to the quarrels with our allies that bedeviled the Carter and Reagan administrations. It also offers the promise of a continuing peace among liberal states, and as the number of liberal states increases, it announces the possibility of global peace this side of the grave or world conquest.

Of course, the probability of the outbreak of war in any given year between any two given states is low. The occurrence of a war between any two adjacent states, considered over a long period of time, would be more probable. The apparent absence of war between liberal states, whether adjacent or not, for almost 200 years thus may have significance. Similar claims cannot be made for feudal, fascist, communist, authoritarian, or totalitarian forms of rule (Doyle, 1983a, pp. 222), nor for pluralistic or merely similar societies. More significant perhaps is that when states are forced to decide on which side of an impending world war they will fight, liberal states all wind up on the same side despite the complexity of the paths that take them there. These characteristics do not prove that the peace among liberals is statistically significant nor that liberalism is the sole valid explanation for the peace. They do suggest that we consider the possibility that liberals have indeed established a separate peace—but only among themselves.

Liberalism also carries with it a second legacy: international "imprudence" (Hume, 1963, pp. 346–47). Peaceful restraint only seems to work in liberals' relations with other liberals. Liberal states have fought numerous wars with nonliberal states. (For a list of international wars since 1816 see Appendix 2.)

Many of these wars have been defensive and thus prudent by necessity. Liberal states have been attacked and threatened by nonliberal states that do not exercise any special restraint in their dealings with the liberal states. Authoritarian rulers both stimulate and respond to an international po-

litical environment in which conflicts of prestige, interest, and pure fear of what other states might do all lead states toward war. War and conquest have thus characterized the careers of many authoritarian rulers and ruling parties, from Louis XIV and Napoleon to Mussolini's fascists, Hitler's Nazis, and Stalin's communists.

Yet we cannot simply blame warfare on the authoritarians or totalitarians, as many of our more enthusiastic politicians would have us do. Most wars arise out of calculations and miscalculations of interest, misunderstandings, and mutual suspicions, such as those that characterized the origins of World War I. However, aggression by the liberal state has also characterized a large number of wars. Both France and Britain fought expansionist colonial wars throughout the nineteenth century. The United States fought a similar war with Mexico from 1846 to 1848, waged a war of annihilation against the American Indians, and intervened militarily against sovereign states many times before and after World War II. Liberal states invade weak nonliberal states and display striking distrust in dealings with powerful nonliberal states (Doyle, 1983b).

Neither realist (statist) nor Marxist theory accounts well for these two legacies. While they can account for aspects of certain periods of international stability (* * * Russett, 1985), neither the logic of the balance of power nor the logic of international hegemony explains the separate peace maintained for more than 150 years among states sharing one particular form of governance—liberal principles and institutions. Balance-of-power theory expects—indeed is premised upon—flexible arrangements of geostrategic rivalry that include preventive war. Hegemonies wax and wane, but the liberal peace holds. Marxist "ultra-imperialists" expect a form of peaceful rivalry among capitalists, but only liberal capitalists maintain peace. Leninists expect liberal capitalists to be aggressive toward nonliberal states, but they also (and especially) expect them to be imperialistic toward fellow liberal capitalists.

Kant's theory of liberal internationalism helps us understand these two legacies. * * * *Perpetual*

Peace, written in 1795 (Kant, 1970, pp. 93–130), helps us understand the interactive nature of international relations. Kant tries to teach us methodologically that we can study neither the systemic relations of states nor the varieties of state behavior in isolation from each other. Substantively, he anticipates for us the ever-widening pacification of a liberal pacific union, explains this pacification, and at the same time suggests why liberal states are not pacific in their relations with nonliberal states. Kant argues that perpetual peace will be guaranteed by the ever-widening acceptance of three "definitive articles" of peace. When all nations have accepted the definitive articles in a metaphorical "treaty" of perpetual peace he asks them to sign, perpetual peace will have been established.

The First Definitive Article requires the civil constitution of the state to be republican. By *republican* Kant means a political society that has solved the problem of combining moral autonomy, individualism, and social order. A private property and market-oriented economy partially addressed that dilemma in the private sphere. The public, or political, sphere was more troubling. His answer was a republic that preserved juridical freedom—the legal equality of citizens as subjects—on the basis of a representative government with a separation of powers. Juridical freedom is preserved because the morally autonomous individual is by means of representation a self-legislator making laws that apply to all citizens equally, including himself or herself. Tyranny is avoided because the individual is subject to laws he or she does not also administer (Kant, *PP* [*Perpetual Peace*], pp. 99–102 * * *).

Liberal republics will progressively establish peace among themselves by means of the pacific federation, or union (*foedus pacificum*), described in Kant's Second Definitive Article. The pacific union will establish peace within a federation of free states and securely maintain the rights of each state. The world will not have achieved the "perpetual peace" that provides the ultimate guarantor of republican freedom until "a late stage and after many unsuccessful attempts" (Kant, *UH* [*The Idea for a Universal History with a Cosmopolitan Pur-*

pose], p. 47). At that time, all nations will have learned the lessons of peace through right conceptions of the appropriate constitution, great and sad experience, and good will. Only then will individuals enjoy perfect republican rights or the full guarantee of a global and just peace. In the meantime, the "pacific federation" of liberal republics—"an enduring and gradually expanding federation likely to prevent war"—brings within it more and more republics—despite republican collapses, backsliding, and disastrous wars—creating an ever-expanding separate peace (Kant, *PP*, p. 105). Kant emphasizes that

> it can be shown that this idea of federalism, extending gradually to encompass all states and thus leading to perpetual peace, is practicable and has objective reality. For if by good fortune one powerful and enlightened nation can form a republic (which is by nature inclined to seek peace), this will provide a focal point for federal association among other states. These will join up with the first one, thus securing the freedom of each state in accordance with the idea of international right, and the whole will gradually spread further and further by a series of alliances of this kind. (Kant, *PP*, p. 104)

The pacific union is not a single peace treaty ending one war, a world state, nor a state of nations. Kant finds the first insufficient. The second and third are impossible or potentially tyrannical. National sovereignty precludes reliable subservience to a state of nations; a world state destroys the civic freedom on which the development of human capacities rests (Kant, *UH*, p. 50). Although Kant obliquely refers to various classical interstate confederations and modern diplomatic congresses, he develops no systematic organizational embodiment of this treaty and presumably does not find institutionalization necessary (Riley, 1983, chap. 5; Schwarz, 1962, p. 77). He appears to have in mind a mutual nonaggression pact, perhaps a collective security agreement, and the cosmopolitan law set forth in the Third Definitive Article.

The Third Definitive Article establishes a cosmopolitan law to operate in conjunction with the pacific union. The cosmopolitan law "shall be limited to conditions of universal hospitality." In this Kant calls for the recognition of the "right of a foreigner not to be treated with hostility when he arrives on someone else's territory." This "does not extend beyond those conditions which make it possible for them [foreigners] to attempt to enter into relations [commerce] with the native inhabitants" (Kant, *PP*, p. 106). Hospitality does not require extending to foreigners either the right to citizenship or the right to settlement, unless the foreign visitors would perish if they were expelled. Foreign conquest and plunder also find no justification under this right. Hospitality does appear to include the right of access and the obligation of maintaining the opportunity for citizens to exchange goods and ideas without imposing the obligation to trade (a voluntary act in all cases under liberal constitutions).

Perpetual peace, for Kant, is an epistemology, a condition for ethical action, and, most importantly, an explanation of how the "mechanical process of nature visibly exhibits the purposive plan of producing concord among men, even against their will and indeed by means of their very discord" (Kant, *PP*, p. 108; *UH*, pp. 44–45). Understanding history requires an epistemological foundation, for without a teleology, such as the promise of perpetual peace, the complexity of history would overwhelm human understanding (Kant, *UH*, pp. 51–53). Perpetual peace, however, is not merely a heuristic device with which to interpret history. It is guaranteed, Kant explains in the "First Addition" to *Perpetual Peace* ("On the Guarantee of Perpetual Peace"), to result from men fulfilling their ethical duty or, failing that, from a hidden plan. Peace is an ethical duty because it is only under conditions of peace that all men can treat each other as ends, rather than means to an end (Kant, *UH*, p. 50; Murphy, 1970, chap. 3). * * *

In the end, however, our guarantee of perpetual peace does not rest on ethical conduct. * * * The guarantee thus rests, Kant argues, not on the probable behavior of moral angels, but on that of "devils, so long as they possess understanding" (*PP*, p. 112). In explaining the sources of each of

the three definitive articles of the perpetual peace, Kant then tells us how we (as free and intelligent devils) could be motivated by fear, force, and calculated advantage to undertake a course of action whose outcome we could reasonably anticipate to be perpetual peace. Yet while it is possible to conceive of the Kantian road to peace in these terms, Kant himself recognizes and argues that social evolution also makes the conditions of moral behavior less onerous and hence more likely (*CF* [*The Contest of Faculties*], pp. 187–89; Kelly, 1969, pp. 106–13). In tracing the effects of both political and moral development, he builds an account of why liberal states do maintain peace among themselves and of how it will (by implication, has) come about that the pacific union will expand. He also explains how these republics would engage in wars with nonrepublics and therefore suffer the "sad experience" of wars that an ethical policy might have avoided.

* * *

Kant shows how republics, once established, lead to peaceful relations. He argues that once the aggressive interests of absolutist monarchies are tamed and the habit of respect for individual rights engrained by republican government, wars would appear as the disaster to the people's welfare that he and the other liberals thought them to be. The fundamental reason is this:

> If, as is inevitability the case under this constitution, the consent of the citizens is required to decide whether or not war should be declared, it is very natural that they will have a great hesitation in embarking on so dangerous an enterprise. For this would mean calling down on themselves all the miseries of war, such as doing the fighting themselves, supplying the costs of the war from their own resources, painfully making good the ensuing devastation, and, as the crowning evil, having to take upon themselves a burden of debts which will embitter peace itself and which can never be paid off on account of the constant threat of new wars. But under a constitution where the subject is not a citizen, and which is therefore not republican, it is the simplest thing in the world to go to war. For the head of state is not a fellow citizen, but the owner of the state, and war

will not force him to make the slightest sacrifice so far as his banquets, hunts, pleasure palaces and court festivals are concerned. He can thus decide on war, without any significant reason, as a kind of amusement, and unconcernedly leave it to the diplomatic corps (who are always ready for such proposes) to justify the war for the sake of propriety. (Kant, *PP*, p. 100)

Yet these domestic republican restraints do not end war. If they did, liberal states would not be warlike, which is far from the case. They do introduce republican caution—Kant's "hesitation"—in place of monarchical caprice. Liberal wars are only fought for popular, liberal purposes. The historical liberal legacy is laden with popular wars fought to promote freedom, to protect private property, or to support liberal allies against nonliberal enemies. Kant's position is ambiguous. He regards these wars as unjust and warns liberals of their susceptibility to them (Kant, *PP*, p. 106). At the same time, Kant argues that each nation "can and ought to" demand that its neighboring nations enter into the pacific union of liberal states (*PP*, p. 102). * * *

* * *

* * * As republics emerge (the first source) and as culture progresses, an understanding of the legitimate rights of all citizens and of all republics comes into play; and this, now that caution characterizes policy, sets up the moral foundations for the liberal peace. Correspondingly, international law highlights the importance of Kantian publicity. Domestically, publicity helps ensure that the officials of republics act according to the principles they profess to hold just and according to the interests of the electors they claim to represent. Internationally, free speech and the effective communication of accurate conceptions of the political life of foreign peoples is essential to establishing and preserving the understanding on which the guarantee of respect depends. Domestically just republics, which rest on consent, then presume foreign republics also to be consensual, just, and therefore deserving of accommodation. * * * Because nonliberal governments are in a state of aggression with their own people, their foreign relations become for liberal governments deeply suspect. In short, fellow liberals benefit from a presumption of amity; nonliberals suffer from a presumption of enmity. Both presumptions may be accurate; each, however, may also be self-confirming.

Lastly, cosmopolitan law adds material incentives to moral commitments. The cosmopolitan right to hospitality permits the "spirit of commerce" sooner or later to take hold of every nation, thus impelling states to promote peace and to try to avert war. Liberal economic theory holds that these cosmopolitan ties derive from a cooperative international division of labor and free trade according to comparative advantage. Each economy is said to be better off than it would have been under autarky; each thus acquires an incentive to avoid policies that would lead the other to break these economic ties. Because keeping open markets rests upon the assumption that the next set of transactions will also be determined by prices rather than coercion, a sense of mutual security is vital to avoid security-motivated searches for economic autarky. Thus, avoiding a challenge to another liberal state's security or even enhancing each other's security by means of alliance naturally follows economic interdependence.

A further cosmopolitan source of liberal peace is the international market's removal of difficult decisions of production and distribution from the direct sphere of state policy. A foreign state thus does not appear directly responsible for these outcomes, and states can stand aside from, and to some degree above, these contentious market rivalries and be ready to step in to resolve crises. The interdependence of commerce and the international contacts of state officials help create crosscutting transnational ties that serve as lobbies for mutual accommodation. According to modern liberal scholars, international financiers and transnational and transgovernmental organizations create interests in favor of accommodation. Moreover, their variety has ensured that no single conflict sours an entire relationship by setting off a spiral of reciprocated retaliation * * *. Conversely, a sense of suspicion, such as that characterizing relations between liberal and nonliberal governments, can lead to restrictions on the range of contacts between societies, and this can increase the prospect that a single conflict will determine an entire relationship.

No single constitutional, international, or cosmopolitan source is alone sufficient, but together (and only together) they plausibly connect the characteristics of liberal polities and economies with sustained liberal peace. Alliances founded on mutual strategic interest among liberal and nonliberal states have been broken; economic ties between liberal and nonliberal states have proven fragile; but the political bonds of liberal rights and interests have proven a remarkably firm foundation for mutual nonaggression. A separate peace exists among liberal states.

In their relations with nonliberal states, however, liberal states have not escaped from the insecurity caused by anarchy in the world political system considered as a whole. Moreover, the very constitutional restraint, international respect for individual rights, and shared commercial interests that establish grounds for peace among liberal states establish grounds for additional conflict in relations between liberal and nonliberal societies.

Conclusion

Kant's liberal internationalism, Machiavelli's liberal imperialism, and Schumpeter's liberal pacifism rest on fundamentally different views of the nature of the human being, the state, and international relations. Schumpeter's humans are rationalized, individualized, and democratized. They are also homogenized, pursuing material interests "monistically." Because their material interests lie in peaceful trade, they and the democratic state that these fellow citizens control are pacifistic. Machiavelli's citizens are splendidly diverse in their goals but fundamentally unequal in them as well, seeking to rule or fearing being dominated. Extending the rule of the dominant elite or avoiding the political collapse of their state, each calls for imperial expansion.

Kant's citizens, too, are diverse in their goals and individualized and rationalized, but most importantly, they are capable of appreciating the moral equality of all individuals and of treating other individuals as ends rather than as means. The Kantian state thus is governed publicly according to law, as a republic. Kant's is the state that solves the problem of governing individualized equals, whether they are the "rational devils" he says we often find ourselves to be or the ethical agents we can and should become. Republics tell us that

> in order to organize a group of rational beings who together require universal laws for their survival, but of whom each separate individual is secretly inclined to exempt himself from them, the constitution must be so designed so that, although the citizens are opposed to one another in their private attitudes, these opposing views may inhibit one another in such a way that the public conduct of the citizens will be the same as if they did not have such evil attitudes. (Kant, *PP*, p. 113)

Unlike Machiavelli's republics, Kant's republics are capable of achieving peace among themselves because they exercise democratic caution and are capable of appreciating the international rights of foreign republics. These international rights of republics derive from the representation of foreign individuals, who are our moral equals. Unlike Schumpeter's capitalist democracies, Kant's republics—including our own—remain in a state of war with nonrepublics. Liberal republics see themselves as threatened by aggression from nonrepublics that are not constrained by representation. Even though wars often cost more than the economic return they generate, liberal republics also are prepared to protect and promote—sometimes forcibly—democracy, private property, and the rights of individuals overseas against nonrepublics, which, because they do not authentically represent the rights of individuals, have no rights to noninterference. These wars may liberate oppressed individuals overseas; they also can generate enormous suffering.

*   *   *

Perpetual peace, Kant says, is the end point of the hard journey his republics will take. The promise of perpetual peace, the violent lessons of war, and the experience of a partial peace are proof of the need for and the possibility of world peace. They are also the grounds for moral citizens and statesmen to assume the duty of striving for peace.

Appendix 1. Liberal Regimes and the Pacific Union, 1700–1982

Period	Period	Period
18th Century	**1900–1945 (cont.)**	**1945 (cont.)**
Swiss Cantons[a]	Italy, –1922	Iceland, 1944–
French Republic, 1790–1795	Belgium, –1940	France, 1945–
United States,[a] 1776–	Netherlands, –1940	Denmark, 1945
Total = 3	Argentina, –1943	Norway, 1945
	France, –1940	Austria, 1945–
1800–1850	Chile, –1924; 1932–	Brazil, 1945–1954; 1955–
Swiss Confederation	Australia, 1901	1964
United States	Norway, 1905–1940	Belgium, 1946–
France, 1830–1849	New Zealand, 1907–	Luxemburg, 1946–
Belgium, 1830–	Colombia, 1910–1949	Netherlands, 1946–
Great Britain, 1832–	Denmark, 1914–1940	Italy, 1946–
Netherlands, 1848–	Poland, 1917–1935	Philippines, 1946–1972
Piedmont, 1848–	Latvia, 1922–1934	India, 1947–1975; 1977–
Denmark, 1849–	Germany, 1918–1932	Sri Lanka, 1948–1961; 1963–1971;
Total = 8	Austria, 1918–1934	1978–
	Estonia, 1919–1934	Ecuador, 1948–1963; 1979–
1850–1900	Finland, 1919–	Israel, 1949–
Switzerland	Uruguay, 1919–	West Germany, 1949–
United States	Costa Rica, 1919–	Greece, 1950–1967; 1975–
Belgium	Czechosovakia, 1920–1939	Peru, 1950–1962; 1963–1968;
Great Britain	Ireland, 1920–	1980–
Netherlands	Mexico, 1928–	El Salvador, 1950–1961
Piedmont, –1861	Lebanon, 1944–	Turkey, 1950–1960; 1966–1971
Italy, 1861–	Total = 29	Japan, 1951–
Denmark, –1866		Bolivia, 1956–1969; 1982–
Sweden, 1864–	**1945–[b]**	Colombia, 1958–
Greece, 1864–	Switzerland	Venezuela, 1959–
Canada, 1867–	United States	Nigeria, 1961–1964; 1979–1984
France, 1871–	Great Britain	Jamaica, 1962–
Argentina, 1880–	Sweden	Trinidad and Tobago, 1962–
Chile, 1891–	Canada	Senegal, 1963–
Total = 13	Australia	Malaysia, 1963–
	New Zealand	Botswana, 1966–
1900–1945	Finland	Singapore, 1965–
Switzerland	Ireland	Portugal, 1976–
United States	Mexico	Spain, 1978–
Great Britain	Uruguay, –1973	Dominican Republic, 1978–
Sweden	Chile, –1973	Honduras, 1981–
Canada	Lebanon, –1975	Papua New Guinea, 1982–
Greece, –1911; 1928–1936	Costa Rica, –1948; 1953–	Total = 50

Note: I have drawn up this approximate list of "Liberal Regimes" according to the four institutions Kant described as essential: market and private property economies; politics that are externally sovereign; citizens who possess juridical rights; and "republican" (whether republican or parliamentary monarchy), representative government. This latter includes the requirement that the legislative branch have an effective role in public policy and be formally and competitively (either inter- or intra-party) elected. Furthermore, I have taken into account whether male suffrage is wide (i.e., 30%) or, as Kant (*MM* [*The Metaphysics of Morals*], p. 139) would have had it, open by "achievement" to inhabitants of the national or metropolitan territory (e.g., to poll-tax payers or householders). This list of liberal regimes is thus more inclusive than a list of democratic regimes, or polyarchies (Powell, 1982, p. 5). Other conditions taken into account here are that female suffrage is granted within a generation of its being demanded by an extensive female suffrage movement and that representative government is internally sovereign (e.g., including, and especially over military and foreign affairs) as well as stable (in existence for at least three years). Sources for these data are Banks and Overstreet (1983), Gastil (1985), *The Europa Yearbook, 1985* (1985), Langer (1968), U.K. Foreign and Commonwealth Office (1980), and U.S. Department of State (1981). Finally, these lists exclude ancient and medieval "republics," since none appears to fit Kant's commitment to liberal individualism (Holmes, 1979).

ᵃThere are domestic variations within these liberal regimes: Switzerland was liberal only in certain cantons; the United States was liberal only north of the Mason-Dixon line until 1865, when it became liberal throughout.

ᵇSelected list, excludes liberal regimes with populations less than one million. These include all states categorized as "free" by Gastil and those "partly free" (four-fifths or more free) states with a more pronounced capitalist orientation.

Appendix 2. International Wars Listed Chronologically

British-Maharattan (1817–1818)
Greek (1821–1828)
Franco-Spanish (1823)
First Anglo-Burmese (1823–1826)
Javanese (1825–1830)
Russo-Persian (1826–1828)
Russo-Turkish (1828–1829)
First Polish (1831)
First Syrian (1831–1832)
Texas (1835–1836)
First British-Afghan (1838–1842)
Second Syrian (1839–1940)
Franco-Algerian (1839–1847)
Peruvian-Bolivian (1841)
First British-Sikh (1845–1846)
Mexican-American (1846–1848)
Austro-Sardinian (1848–1849)
First Schleswig-Holstein (1848–1849)
Hungarian (1848–1849)
Second British-Sikh (1848–1849)
Roman Republic (1849)
La Plata (1851–1852)
First Turco-Montenegran (1852–1853)
Crimean (1853–1856)
Anglo-Persian (1856–1857)
Sepoy (1857–1859)
Second Turco-Montenegran (1858–1859)
Italian Unification (1859)
Spanish-Moroccan (1859–1860)
Italo-Roman (1860)
Italo-Sicilian (1860–1861)

Franco-Mexican (1862–1867)
Ecuadorian-Colombian (1863)
Second Polish (1863–1864)
Spanish-Santo Dominican (1863–1865)
Second Schleswig-Holstein (1864)
Lopez (1864–1870)
Spanish-Chilean (1865–1866)
Seven Weeks (1866)
Ten Years (1868–1878)
Franco-Prussian (1870–1871)
Dutch-Achinese (1873–1878)
Balkan (1875–1877)
Russo-Turkish (1877–1878)
Bosnian (1878)
Second British-Afghan (1878–1880)
Pacific (1879–1883)
British-Zulu (1879)
Franco-Indochinese (1882–1884)
Mahdist (1882–1885)
Sino-French (1884–1885)
Central American (1885)
Serbo-Bulgarian (1885)
Sino-Japanese (1894–1895)
Franco-Madagascan (1894–1895)
Cuban (1895–1898)
Italo-Ethiopian (1895–1896)
First Philippine (1896–1898)
Greco-Turkish (1897)
Spanish-American (1898)
Second Philippine (1899–1902)
Boer (1899–1902)

Boxer Rebellion (1900)
Ilinden (1903)
Russo-Japanese (1904–1905)
Central American (1906)
Central American (1907)
Spanish-Moroccan (1909–1910)
Italo-Turkish (1911–1912)
First Balkan (1912–1913)
Second Balkan (1913)
World War I (1914–1918)
Russian Nationalities (1917–1921)
Russo-Polish (1919–1920)
Hungarian-Allies (1919)
Greco-Turkish (1919–1922)
Riffian (1921–1926)
Druze (1925–1927)
Sino-Soviet (1929)
Manchurian (1931–1933)
Chaco (1932–1935)
Italo-Ethiopian (1935–1936)
Sino-Japanese (1937–1941)
Changkufeng (1938)
Nomohan (1939)
World War II (1939–1945)
Russo-Finnish (1939–1940)
Franco-Thai (1940–1941)
Indonesian (1945–1946)
Indochinese (1945–1954)

Madagascan (1947–1948)
First Kashmir (1947–1949)
Palestine (1948–1949)
Hyderabad (1948)
Korean (1950–1953)
Algerian (1954–1962)
Russo-Hungarian (1956)
Sinai (1956)
Tibetan (1956–1959)
Sino-Indian (1962)
Vietnamese (1965–1975)
Second Kashmir (1965)
Six Day (1967)
Israeli-Egyptian (1969–1970)
Football (1969)
Bangladesh (1971)
Philippine-MNLF (1972–)
Yom Kippur (1973)
Turco-Cypriot (1974)
Ethiopian-Eritrean (1974–)
Vietnamese-Cambodian (1975–)
Timor (1975–)
Saharan (1975–)
Ogaden (1976–)
Ugandan-Tanzanian (1978–1979)
Sino-Vietnamese (1979)
Russo-Afghan (1979–)
Iran-Iraqi (1980–)

Note: This table is taken from Melvin Small and J. David Singer (1982, pp. 79–80). This is a partial list of international wars fought between 1816 and 1980. In Appendices A and B, Small and Singer identify a total of 575 wars during this period, but approximately 159 of them appear to be largely domestic, or civil wars.

This list excludes covert interventions, some of which have been directed by liberal regimes against other liberal regimes—for example, the United States' effort to destabilize the Chilean election and Allende's government. Nonetheless, it is significant that such interventions are not pursued publicly as acknowledged policy. The covert destabilization campaign against Chile is recounted by the Senate Select Committee to Study Governmental Operations with Respect to Intelligence Activities (1975, *Covert Action in Chile, 1963–73*).

Following the argument of this article, this list also excludes civil wars. Civil wars differ from international wars, not in the ferocity of combat, but in the issues that engender them. Two nations that could abide one another as independent neighbors separated by a border might well be the fiercest of enemies if forced to live together in one state, jointly deciding how to raise and spend taxes, choose leaders, and legislate fundamental questions of value. Notwithstanding these differences, no civil wars that I recall upset the argument of liberal pacification.

REFERENCES

Banks, Arthur, and William Overstreet, eds. 1983. *A Political Handbook of the World; 1982–1983.* New York: McGraw Hill.

Barnet, Richard. 1968. *Intervention and Revolution.* Cleveland: World Publishing Co.

Chan, Steve. 1984. Mirror, Mirror on the Wall . . .: Are Freer Countries More Pacific? *Journal of Conflict Resolution,* 28:617–48.

Doyle, Michael W. 1983a. Kant, Liberal Legacies, and Foreign Affairs: Part 1. *Philosophy and Public Affairs,* 12:205–35.

Doyle, Michael W. 1983b. Kant, Liberal Legacies, and Foreign Affairs: Part 2. *Philosophy and Public Affairs,* 12:323–53.

Doyle, Michael W. 1986. *Empires.* Ithaca: Cornell University Press.

The Europa Yearbook for 1985. 1985. 2 vols. London: Europa Publications.

Gastil, Raymond. 1985. The Comparative Survey of Freedom 1985. *Freedom at Issue,* 82:3–16.

Haas, Michael. 1974. *International Conflict.* New York: Bobbs-Merrill.

Holmes, Stephen. 1979. Aristippus in and out of Athens. *American Political Science Review,* 73:113–28.

Huliung, Mark. 1983. *Citizen Machiavelli.* Princeton: Princeton University Press.

Hume, David. 1963. Of the Balance of Power. *Essays: Moral, Political, and Literary.* Oxford: Oxford University Press.

Kant, Immanuel. 1970. *Kant's Political Writings.* Hans Reiss, ed. H. B. Nisbet, trans. Cambridge: Cambridge University Press.

Kelly, George A. 1969. *Idealism, Politics, and History.* Cambridge: Cambridge University Press.

Langer, William L., ed. 1968. *The Encyclopedia of World History.* Boston: Houghton Mifflin.

Machiavelli, Niccolo. 1950. *The Prince and the Discourses.* Max Lerner, ed. Luigi Ricci and Christian Detmold, trans. New York: Modern Library.

Mansfield, Harvey C. 1970. Machiavelli's New Regime. *Italian Quarterly,* 13:63–95.

Montesquieu, Charles de. 1949. *Spirit of the Laws.* New York: Hafner. (Originally published in 1748.)

Murphy, Jeffrie. 1970. *Kant: The Philosophy of Right.* New York: St. Martins.

Pocock, J. G. A. 1975. *The Machiavellian Moment.* Princeton: Princeton University Press.

Powell, G. Bingham. 1982. *Contemporary Democracies.* Cambridge, MA: Harvard University Press.

Reagan, Ronald. June 9, 1982. Address to Parliament. *New York Times.*

Riley, Patrick. 1983. *Kant's Political Philosophy.* Totowa, NJ: Rowman and Littlefield.

Rummel, Rudolph J. 1983. Libertarianism and International Violence. *Journal of Conflict Resolution,* 27:27–71.

Russett, Bruce. 1985. The Mysterious Case of Vanishing Hegemony. *International Organization,* 39:207–31.

Schumpeter, Joseph. 1955. The Sociology of Imperialism. In *Imperialism and Social Classes.* Cleveland: World Publishing Co. (Essay originally published in 1919.)

Schwarz, Wolfgang. 1962. Kant's Philosophy of Law and International Peace. *Philosophy and Phenomenonological Research,* 23:71–80.

Skinner, Quentin. 1981. *Machiavelli.* New York: Hill and Wang.

Small, Melvin, and J. David Singer. 1976. The War-Proneness of Democratic Regimes. *The Jerusalem Journal of International Relations,* 1(4):50–69.

Small, Melvin, and J. David Singer. 1982. *Resort to Arms.* Beverly Hills: Sage Publications.

Thucydides. 1954. *The Peloponnesian War.* Rex Warner, ed. and trans. Baltimore: Penguin.

U.K. Foreign and Commonwealth Office. 1980. *A Yearbook of the Commonwealth 1980.* London: HMSO.

U.S. Congress. Senate. Select Committee to Study Governmental Operations with Respect to Intelligence Activities. 1975. *Covert Action in Chile, 1963–74.* 94th Cong., 1st sess., Washington, D.C.: U.S. Government Printing Office.

U.S. Department of State. 1981. *Country Reports on Human Rights Practices*. Washington, D.C.: U.S. Government Printing Office.

Weede, Erich. 1984. Democracy and War Involvement. *Journal of Conflict Resolution*, 28:649–64.

Wilkenfeld, Jonathan. 1968. Domestic and Foreign Conflict Behavior of Nations. *Journal of Peace Research*, 5:56–69.

Wright, Quincy. 1942. *A Study of History*. Chicago: Chicago University Press.

ANDRE GUNDER FRANK

The Development of Underdevelopment

We cannot hope to formulate adequate development theory and policy for the majority of the world's population who suffer from underdevelopment without first learning how their past economic and social history gave rise to their present underdevelopment. Yet most historians study only the developed metropolitan countries and pay scant attention to the colonial and underdeveloped lands. For this reason most of our theoretical categories and guides to development policy have been distilled exclusively from the historical experience of the European and North American advanced capitalist nations.

Since the historical experience of the colonial and underdeveloped countries has demonstrably been quite different, available theory therefore fails to reflect the past of the underdeveloped part of the world entirely, and reflects the past of the world as a whole only in part. More important, our ignorance of the underdeveloped countries' history leads us to assume that their past and indeed their present resembles earlier stages of the history of the now developed countries. This ignorance and this assumption lead us into serious misconceptions about contemporary underdevelopment and development. Further, most studies of development and underdevelopment fail to take account of the economic and other relations between the metropolis and its economic colonies throughout the history

of the world-wide expansion and development of the mercantilist and capitalist system. Consequently, most of our theory fails to explain the structure and development of the capitalist system as a whole and to account for its simultaneous generation of underdevelopment in some of its parts and of economic development in others.

It is generally held that economic development occurs in a succession of capitalist stages and that today's underdeveloped countries are still in a stage, sometimes depicted as an original stage of history, through which the now developed countries passed long ago. Yet even a modest acquaintance with history shows that underdevelopment is not original or traditional and that neither the past nor the present of the underdeveloped countries resembles in any important respect the past of the now developed countries. The now developed countries were never *under*developed, though they may have been *un*developed. It is also widely believed that the contemporary underdevelopment of a country can be understood as the product of reflection solely of its own economic, political, social, and cultural characteristics or structure. Yet historical research demonstrates that contemporary underdevelopment is in large part the historical product of past and continuing economic and other relations between the satellite underdeveloped and the now developed metropolitan countries. Furthermore, these relations are an essential part of the structure and development of the capi-

From *Monthly Review* (September 1966): 17–31.

talist system on a world scale as a whole. A related and also largely erroneous view is that the development of these underdeveloped countries and, within them of their most underdeveloped domestic areas, must and will be generated or stimulated by diffusing capital, institutions, values, etc., to them from the international and national capitalist metropoles. Historical perspective based on the underdeveloped countries' past experience suggests that on the contrary in the underdeveloped countries economic development can now occur only independently of most of these relations of diffusion.

Evident inequalities of income and differences in culture have led many observers to see "dual" societies and economies in the underdeveloped countries. Each of the two parts is supposed to have a history of its own, a structure, and a contemporary dynamic largely independent of the other. Supposedly, only one part of the economy and society has been importantly affected by intimate economic relations with the "outside" capitalist world; and that part, it is held, became modern, capitalist, and relatively developed precisely because of this contact. The other part is widely regarded as variously isolated, subsistence-based, feudal, or precapitalist, and therefore more underdeveloped.

I believe on the contrary that the entire "dual society" thesis is false and that the policy recommendations to which it leads will, if acted upon, serve only to intensify and perpetuate the very conditions of underdevelopment they are supposedly designed to remedy.

A mounting body of evidence suggests, and I am confident that future historical research will confirm, that the expansion of the capitalist system over the past centuries effectively and entirely penetrated even the apparently most isolated sectors of the underdeveloped world. Therefore, the economic, political, social, and cultural institutions and relations we now observe there are the products of the historical development of the capitalist system no less than are the seemingly more modern or capitalist features of the national metropoles of these underdeveloped countries. Analogously to

the relations between development and underdevelopment on the international level, the contemporary underdeveloped institutions of the so-called backward or feudal domestic areas of an underdeveloped country are no less the product of the single historical process of capitalist development than are the so-called capitalist institutions of the supposedly more progressive areas. In this paper I should like to sketch the kinds of evidence which support this thesis and at the same time indicate lines along which further study and research could fruitfully proceed.

II

The Secretary General of the Latin American Center for Research in the Social Sciences writes in that Center's journal: "The privileged position of the city has its origin in the colonial period. It was founded by the Conqueror to serve the same ends that it still serves today; to incorporate the indigenous population into the economy brought and developed by that Conqueror and his descendants. The regional city was an instrument of conquest and is still today an instrument of domination."[1] The Instituto Nacional Indigenista (National Indian Institute) of Mexico confirms this observation when it notes that "the mestizo population, in fact, always lives in a city, a center of an intercultural region, which acts as the metropolis of a zone of indigenous population and which maintains with the underdeveloped communities an intimate relation which links the center with the satellite communities."[2] The Institute goes on to point out that "between the mestizos who live in the nuclear city of the region and the Indians who live in the peasant hinterland there is in reality a closer economic and social interdependence than might at first glance appear" and that the provincial metropoles "by being centers of intercourse are also centers of exploitation."[3]

Thus these metropolis-satellite relations are not limited to the imperial or international level but penetrate and structure the very economic, political, and social life of the Latin American colonies and countries. Just as the colonial and national capital and its export sector become the satellite of the Iberian (and later of other) metropoles of the world economic system, this satellite immediately becomes a colonial and then a national metropolis with respect to the productive sectors and population of the interior. Furthermore, the provincial capitals, which thus are themselves satellites of the national metropolis—and through the latter of the world metropolis—are in turn provincial centers around which their own local satellites orbit. Thus, a whole chain of constellations of metropoles and satellites relates all parts of the whole system from its metropolitan center in Europe or the United States to the farthest outpost in the Latin American countryside.

When we examine this metropolis-satellite structure, we find that each of the satellites, including now-underdeveloped Spain and Portugal, serves as an instrument to suck capital or economic surplus out of its own satellites and to channel part of this surplus to the world metropolis of which all are satellites. Moreover, each national and local metropolis serves to impose and maintain the monopolistic structure and exploitative relationship of this system (as the Instituto Nacional Indigenista of Mexico calls it) as long as it serves the interests of the metropoles which take advantage of this global, national, and local structure to promote their own development and the enrichment of their ruling classes.

These are the principal and still surviving structural characteristics which were implanted in Latin America by the Conquest. Beyond examining the establishment of this colonial structure in its historical context, the proposed approach calls for study of the development—and underdevelopment—of these metropoles and satellites of Latin America throughout the following and still continuing historical process. In this way we can understand why there were and still are tendencies in the Latin American and world capitalist structure which seem to lead to the development of the metropolis and the underdevelopment of the satellite and why, particularly, the satellized national, regional, and local metropoles in Latin America find

that their economic development is at best a limited or underdeveloped development.

III

That present [1966] underdevelopment of Latin America is the result of its centuries-long participation in the process of world capitalist development, I believe I have shown in my case studies of the economic and social histories of Chile and Brazil.[4] My study of Chilean history suggests that the Conquest not only incorporated this country fully into the expansion and development of the world mercantile and later industrial capitalist system but that it also introduced the monopolistic metropolis-satellite structure and development of capitalism into the Chilean domestic economy and society itself. This structure then penetrated and permeated all of Chile very quickly. Since that time and in the course of world and Chilean history during the epochs of colonialism, free trade, imperialism, and the present, Chile has become increasingly marked by the economic, social, and political structure of satellite underdevelopment. This development of underdevelopment continues today, both in Chile's still increasing satellization by the world metropolis and through the ever more acute polarization of Chile's domestic economy.

The history of Brazil is perhaps the clearest case of both national and regional development of underdevelopment. The expansion of the world economy since the beginning of the sixteenth century successively converted the Northeast, the Minas Gerais interior, the North, and the Center-South (Rio de Janeiro, São Paulo, and Paraná) into export economies and incorporated them into the structure and development of the world capitalist system. Each of these regions experienced what may have appeared as economic development during the period of its respective golden age. But it was a satellite development which was neither self-generating nor self-perpetuating. As the market or the productivity of the first three regions declined, foreign and domestic economic interest in them waned; and they were left to develop the underdevelopment they live today. In the fourth region, the coffee economy experienced a similar though not yet quite as serious fate (though the development of a synthetic coffee substitute promises to deal it a mortal blow in the not too distant future). All of this historical evidence contradicts the generally accepted theses that Latin America suffers from a dual society or from the survival of feudal institutions and that these are important obstacles to its economic development.

IV

During the First World War, however, and even more during the Great Depression and the Second World War, São Paulo began to build up an industrial establishment which is the largest in Latin America today. The question arises whether this industrial development did or can break Brazil out of the cycle of satellite development and underdevelopment which has characterized its other regions and national history within the capitalist system so far. I believe that the answer is no. Domestically the evidence so far is fairly clear. The development of industry in São Paulo has not brought greater riches to the other regions of Brazil. Instead, it converted them into internal colonial satellites, de-capitalized them further, and consolidated or even deepened their underdevelopment. There is little evidence to suggest that this process is likely to be reversed in the foreseeable future except insofar as the provincial poor migrate and become the poor of the metropolitan cities. Externally, the evidence is that although the initial development of São Paulo's industry was relatively autonomous it is being increasingly satellized by the world capitalist metropolis and its future development possibilities are increasingly restricted.[5] This development, my studies lead me to believe, also appears destined to limited or underdeveloped development as long as it takes place in the present economic, political, and social framework.

We must conclude, in short, that underdevelopment is not due to the survival of archaic institutions and the existence of capital shortage in regions that have remained isolated from the stream of world history. On the contrary, underdevelopment was and still is generated by the very same historical process which also generated economic development: the development of capitalism itself. This view, I am glad to say, is gaining adherents among students of Latin America and is proving its worth in shedding new light on the problems of the area and in affording a better perspective for the formulation of theory and policy.[6]

V

The same historical and structural approach can also lead to better development theory and policy by generating a series of hypotheses about development and underdevelopment such as those I am testing in my current research. The hypotheses are derived from the empirical observation and theoretical assumption that within this world-embracing metropolis-satellite structure the metropoles tend to develop and the satellites to underdevelop. The first hypothesis has already been mentioned above: that in contrast to the development of the world metropolis which is no one's satellite, the development of the national and other subordinate metropoles is limited by their satellite status. It is perhaps more difficult to test this hypothesis than the following ones because part of its confirmation depends on the test of the other hypotheses. Nonetheless, this hypothesis appears to be generally confirmed by the non-autonomous and unsatisfactory economic and especially industrial development of Latin America's national metropoles, as documented in the studies already cited. The most important and at the same time most confirmatory examples are the metropolitan regions of Buenos Aires and São Paulo whose growth only began in the nineteenth century, was therefore largely untrammelled by any colonial heritage, but was and remains a satellite development largely dependent on the outside metropolis, first of Britain and then of the United States.

A second hypothesis is that the satellites experience their greatest economic development and especially their most classically capitalist industrial development if and when their ties to their metropolis are weakest. This hypothesis is almost dia-metrically opposed to the generally accepted thesis that development in the underdeveloped countries follows from the greatest degree of contact with and diffusion from the metropolitan developed countries. This hypothesis seems to be confirmed by two kinds of relative isolation that Latin America has experienced in the course of its history. One is the temporary isolation caused by the crises of war or depression in the world metropolis. Apart from minor ones, five periods of such major crises stand out and seem to confirm the hypothesis. These are: the European (and especially Spanish) Depression of the seventeenth century, the Napoleonic Wars, the First World War, the Depression of the 1930's, and the Second World War. It is clearly established and generally recognized that the most important recent industrial develop-ment—especially of Argentina, Brazil, and Mexico, but also of other countries such as Chile—has taken place precisely during the periods of the two World Wars and the intervening Depression. Thanks to the consequent loosening of trade and investment ties during these periods, the satellites initiated marked autonomous industrialization and growth. Historical research demonstrates that the same thing happened in Latin America during Europe's seventeenth-century depression. Manu-facturing grew in the Latin American countries, and several of them such as Chile became ex-porters of manufactured goods. The Napoleonic Wars gave rise to independence movements in Latin America, and these should perhaps also be interpreted as confirming the development hy-pothesis in part.

The other kind of isolation which tends to con-firm the second hypothesis is the geographic and economic isolation of regions which at one time were relatively weakly tied to and poorly integrated into the mercantilist and capitalist system. My pre-liminary research suggests that in Latin America it was these regions which initiated and experienced the most promising self-generating economic de-velopment of the classical industrial capitalist type. The most important regional cases probably are Tucumán and Asunción, as well as other cities such as Mendoza and Rosario, in the interior of Argentina and Paraguay during the end of the eighteenth and the beginning of the nineteenth centuries. Seventeenth and eighteenth century São Paulo, long before coffee was grown there, is an-other example. Perhaps Antioquia in Colombia and Puebla and Querétaro in Mexico are other ex-amples. In its own way, Chile was also an example since, before the sea route around the Horn was opened, this country was relatively isolated at the end of the long voyage from Europe via Panama. All of these regions became manufacturing centers and even exporters, usually of textiles, during the periods preceding their effective incorporation as satellites into the colonial, national, and world cap-italist system.

Internationally, of course, the classic case of in-dustrialization through non-participation as a satellite in the capitalist world system is obviously that of Japan after the Meiji Restoration. Why, one may ask, was resource-poor but unsatellized Japan able to industrialize so quickly at the end of the century while resource-rich Latin American coun-tries and Russia were not able to do so and the lat-ter was easily beaten by Japan in the War of 1904 after the same forty years of development efforts? The second hypothesis suggests that the funda-mental reason is that Japan was not satellized ei-ther during the Tokugawa or the Meiji period and therefore did not have its development structurally limited as did the countries which were so satel-lized.

VI

A corollary of the second hypothesis is that when the metropolis recovers from its crisis and re-establishes the trade and investment ties which fully re-incorporate the satellites into the system, or when the metropolis expands to incorporate previously isolated regions into the world-wide system, the previous development and industrial-ization of these regions is choked off or channelled into directions which are not self-perpetuating and promising. This happened after each of the five crises cited above. The renewed expansion of trade and the spread of economic liberalism in the eighteenth and nineteenth centuries choked off and reversed the manufacturing development which Latin America had experienced during the seventeenth century, and in some places at the beginning of the nineteenth. After the First World War, the new national industry of Brazil suffered serious consequences from American economic invasion. The increase in the growth rate of Gross National Product and particularly of industrialization throughout Latin America was again reversed and industry became increasingly satellized after the Second World War and especially after the post-Korean War recovery and expansion of the metropolis. Far from having become more developed since then, industrial sectors of Brazil and most conspicuously of Argentina have become structurally more and more underdeveloped and less and less able to generate continued industrialization and/or sustain development of the economy. This process, from which India also suffers, is reflected in a whole gamut of balance-of-payments, inflationary, and other economic and political difficulties, and promises to yield to no solution short of far-reaching structural change.

Our hypothesis suggests that fundamentally the same process occurred even more dramatically with the incorporation into the system of previously unsatellized regions. The expansion of Buenos Aires as a satellite of Great Britain and the introduction of free trade in the interest of the ruling groups of both metropoles destroyed the manufacturing and much of the remainder of the economic base of the previously relatively prosperous interior almost entirely. Manufacturing was destroyed by foreign competition, lands were taken and concentrated into latifundia by the rapaciously growing export economy, intra-regional distribution of income became much more unequal, and the previously developing regions became simple satellites of Buenos Aires and through it of London. The provincial centers did not yield to satellization without a struggle. This metropolis-satellite conflict was much of the cause of the long political and armed struggle between the Unitarists in Buenos Aires and the Federalists in the

provinces, and it may be said to have been the sole important cause of the War of the Triple Alliance in which Buenos Aires, Montevideo, and Rio de Janeiro, encouraged and helped by London, destroyed not only the autonomously developing economy of Paraguay but killed off nearly all of its population which was unwilling to give in. Though this is no doubt the most spectacular example which tends to confirm the hypothesis, I believe that historical research on the satellization of previously relatively independent yeoman-farming and incipient manufacturing regions such as the Caribbean islands will confirm it further.[7] These regions did not have a chance against the forces of expanding and developing capitalism, and their own development had to be sacrificed to that of others. The economy and industry of Argentina, Brazil, and other countries which have experienced the effects of metropolitan recovery since the Second World War are today suffering much the same fate, if fortunately still in lesser degree.

VII

A third major hypothesis derived from the metropolis-satellite structure is that the regions which are the most underdeveloped and feudal-seeming today are the ones which had the closest ties to the metropolis in the past. They are the regions which were the greatest exporters of primary products to and the biggest sources of capital for the world metropolis and which were abandoned by the metropolis when for one reason or another business fell off. This hypothesis also contradicts the generally held thesis that the source of a region's underdevelopment is its isolation and its pre-capitalist institutions.

This hypothesis seems to be amply confirmed by the former super-satellite development and present ultra-underdevelopment of the once sugar-exporting West Indies, Northeastern Brazil, the ex-mining districts of Minas Gerais in Brazil, highland Peru, and Bolivia, and the central Mexican states of Guanajuato, Zacatecas, and others whose names were made world famous centuries ago by their silver. There surely are no major regions in Latin America which are today more cursed by underdevelopment and poverty; yet all of these regions, like Bengal in India, once provided the life blood of mercantile and industrial capitalist development—in the metropolis. These regions' participation in the development of the world capitalist system gave them, already in their golden age, the typical structure of underdevelopment of a capitalist export economy. When the market for their sugar or the wealth of their mines disappeared and the metropolis abandoned them to their own devices, the already existing economic, political, and social structure of these regions prohibited autonomous generation of economic development and left them no alternative but to turn in upon themselves and to degenerate into the ultra-underdevelopment we find there today.

VIII

These considerations suggest two further and related hypotheses. One is that the latifundium, irrespective of whether it appears as a plantation or a hacienda today, was typically born as a commercial enterprise which created for itself the institutions which permitted it to respond to increased demand in the world or national market by expanding the amount of its land, capital, and labor and to increase the supply of its products. The fifth hypothesis is that the latifundia which appear isolated, subsistence-based, and semi-feudal today saw the demand for their products or their productive capacity decline and that they are to be found principally in the above-named former agricultural and mining export regions whose economic activity declined in general. These two hypotheses run counter to the notions of most people, and even to the opinions of some historians and other students of the subject, according to whom the historical roots and socio-economic causes of Latin American latifundia and agrarian institutions are to be found in the transfer of feudal institutions from Europe and/or in economic depression.

The evidence to test these hypotheses is not open to easy general inspection and requires detailed analyses of many cases. Nonetheless, some important confirmatory evidence is available. The growth of the latifundium in nineteenth-century Argentina and Cuba is a clear case in support of the fourth hypothesis and can in no way be attributed to the transfer of feudal institutions during colonial times. The same is evidently the case of the post-revolutionary and contemporary resurgence of latifundia particularly in the North of Mexico, which produce for the American market, and of similar ones on the coast of Peru and the new coffee regions of Brazil. The conversion of previously yeoman-farming Caribbean islands, such as Barbados, into sugar-exporting economies at various times between the seventeenth and twentieth centuries and the resulting rise of the latifundia in these islands would seem to confirm the fourth hypothesis as well. In Chile, the rise of the latifundium and the creation of the institutions of servitude which later came to be called feudal occurred in the eighteenth century and have been conclusively shown to be the result of and response to the opening of a market for Chilean wheat in Lima.[8] Even the growth and consolidation of the latifundium in seventeenth-century Mexico—which most expert students have attributed to a depression of the economy caused by the decline of mining and a shortage of Indian labor and to a consequent turning in upon itself and ruralization of the economy—occurred at a time when urban population and demand were growing, food shortages became acute, food prices skyrocketed, and the profitability of other economic activities such as mining and foreign trade declined.[9] All of these and other factors rendered hacienda agriculture more profitable. Thus, even this case would seem to confirm the hypothesis that the growth of the latifundium and its feudal-seeming conditions of servitude in Latin America has always been and still is the commercial response to increased demand and that it does not represent the transfer or survival of alien institutions that have remained beyond the reach of capitalist development. The emergence of latifundia, which today really are more or less (though not entirely) isolated, might then be attributed to the causes advanced in the fifth hypothesis—i.e., the decline of previously profitable agricultural enterprises whose capital was, and whose currently produced economic surplus still is, transferred elsewhere by owners and merchants who frequently are the same persons or families. Testing this hypothesis requires still more detailed analysis, some of which I have undertaken in a study on Brazilian agriculture.[10]

IX

All of these hypotheses and studies suggest that the global extension and unity of the capitalist system, its monopoly structure and uneven development throughout its history, and the resulting persistence of commercial rather than industrial capitalism in the underdeveloped world (including its most industrially advanced countries) deserve much more attention in the study of economic development and cultural change than they have hitherto received. Though science and truth know no national boundaries, it is probably new generations of scientists from the underdeveloped countries themselves who most need to, and best can, devote the necessary attention to these problems and clarify the process of underdevelopment and development. It is their people who in the last analysis face the task of changing this no longer acceptable process and eliminating this miserable reality.

They will not be able to accomplish these goals by importing sterile stereotypes from the metropolis which do not correspond to their satellite economic reality and do not respond to their liberating political needs. To change their reality they must understand it. For this reason, I hope that better confirmation of these hypotheses and further pursuit of the proposed historical, holistic, and structural approach may help the peoples of the underdeveloped countries to understand the causes and eliminate the reality of their development of underdevelopment and their underdevelopment of development.

NOTES

1. *América Latina*, Año 6, No. 4, October–December 1963, p. 8.
2. Instituto Nacional Indigenista, *Los centros coordinadores indigenistas*, Mexico, 1962, p. 34.
3. *Ibid.*, pp. 33–34, 88.
4. "Capitalist Development and Underdevelopment in Chile" and "Capitalist Development and Underdevelopment in Brazil" in *Capitalism and Underdevelopment in Latin America*, to be published soon by Monthly Review Press.
5. Also see, "The Growth and Decline of Import Substitution," *Economic Bulletin for Latin America*, New York, IX, No. 1, March 1964 * * *.
6. Others who use a similar approach, though their ideologies do not permit them to derive the logically following conclusions, are Aníbal Pinto S.C., *Chile: Un caso de desarrollo frustrado*, Santiago, Editorial Universitaria, 1957; Celso Furtado, *A formaçao económica do Brasil*, Rio de Janeiro, Fundo de Cultura, 1959 (recently translated into English and published under the title *The Economic Growth of Brazil* by the University of California Press) * * *.
7. See for instance Ramón Guerra y Sánchez, * * * *Sugar and Society in the Caribbean*, New Haven, Yale University Press, 1964.
8. Mario Góngora, *Origen de los "inquilinos" de Chile central*, Santiago, Editorial Universitaria, 1960 * * *.
9. Woodrow Borah makes depression the centerpiece of his explanation in "New Spain's Century of Depression," *Ibero-Americana*, Berkeley, No. 35, 1951.
10. "Capitalism and the Myth of Feudalism in Brazilian Agriculture," in *Capitalism and Underdevelopment in Latin America*, cited in footnote 4 above.

J. ANN TICKNER

Man, the State, and War: Gendered Perspectives on National Security

It is not in giving life but in risking life that man is raised above the animal: that is why superiority has been accorded in humanity not to the sex that brings forth but to that which kills.
— *Simone de Beauvoir*

If we do not redefine manhood, war is inevitable.
— *Paul Fussell*

In the face of what is generally perceived as a dangerous international environment, states have ranked national security high in terms of their policy priorities. According to international relations scholar Kenneth Waltz, the state conducts its affairs in the "brooding shadow of violence," and therefore war could break out at any time.[1] In the name of national security, states have justified large defense budgets, which take priority over domestic spending, military conscription of their young adult male population, foreign invasions, and the curtailment of civil liberties. The security of the state is perceived as a core value that is generally supported unquestioningly by most citizens, particularly in time of war. While the role of the state in the twentieth century has expanded to include the provision of domestic social programs, national security often takes precedence over the social security of individuals.

When we think about the provision of national security we enter into what has been, and continues to be, an almost exclusively male domain. While most women support what they take to be legitimate calls for state action in the interests of international security, the task of defining, defend-

ing, and advancing the security interests of the state is a man's affair, a task that, through its association with war, has been especially valorized and rewarded in many cultures throughout history. As Simone de Beauvoir's explanation for male superiority suggests, giving one's life for one's country has been considered the highest form of patriotism, but it is an act from which women have been virtually excluded. While men have been associated with defending the state and advancing its international interests as soldiers and diplomats, women have typically been engaged in the "ordering" and "comforting" roles both in the domestic sphere, as mothers and basic needs providers, and in the caring professions, as teachers, nurses, and social workers.[2] The role of women with respect to national security has been ambiguous: defined as those whom the state and its men are protecting, women have had little control over the conditions of their protection.

*   *   *

A Gendered Perspective on National Security

Morgenthau, Waltz, and other realists claim that it is possible to develop a rational, objective theory of international politics based on universal laws that operate across time and space. In her feminist critique of the natural sciences, Evelyn Fox Keller points out that most scientific communities share the "assumption that the universe they study is directly accessible, represented by concepts shaped not by language but only by the demands of logic and experiment." The laws of nature, according to this view of science, are beyond the relativity of

From J. Ann Tickner, *Gender in International Relations: Feminist Perspectives on Achieving Global Security* (New York: Columbia University Press, 1992), 27–66.

language.[3] Like most contemporary feminists, Keller rejects this positivist view of science that, she asserts, imposes a coercive, hierarchical, and conformist pattern on scientific inquiry. Since most contemporary feminist scholars believe that knowledge is socially constructed, they are skeptical of finding an unmediated foundation for knowledge that realists claim is possible. Since they believe that it is language that transmits knowledge, many feminists suggest that the scholarly claims about the neutral uses of language and about objectivity must continually be questioned.[4]

I shall now investigate the individual, the state, and the international system—the three levels of analysis that realists use in their analysis of war and national security—and examine how they have been constructed in realist discourse. I shall argue that the language used to describe these concepts comes out of a Western-centered historical worldview that draws almost exclusively on the experiences of men. Underneath its claim to universality this worldview privileges a view of security that is constructed out of values associated with hegemonic masculinity.

"POLITICAL MAN"

In his *Politics Among Nations*, a text rich in historical detail, Morgenthau has constructed a world almost entirely without women. Morgenthau claims that individuals are engaged in a struggle for power whenever they come into contact with one another, for the tendency to dominate exists at all levels of human life: the family, the polity, and the international system; it is modified only by the conditions under which the struggle takes place.[5] Since women rarely occupy positions of power in any of these arenas, we can assume that, when Morgenthau talks about domination, he is talking primarily about men, although not all men.[6] His "political man" is a social construct based on a partial representation of human nature abstracted from the behavior of men in positions of public power.[7] Morgenthau goes on to suggest that, while society condemns the violent behavior that can result from this struggle for power within the polity,

it encourages it in the international system in the form of war.

While Morgenthau's "political man" has been criticized by other international relations scholars for its essentializing view of human nature, the social construction of hegemonic masculinity and its opposition to a devalued femininity have been central to the way in which the discourse of international politics has been constructed more generally. In Western political theory from the Greeks to Machiavelli, traditions upon which contemporary realism relies heavily for its analysis, this socially constructed type of masculinity has been projected onto the international behavior of states. The violence with which it is associated has been legitimated through the glorification of war.

*   *   *

THE INTERNATIONAL SYSTEM: THE WAR OF EVERYMAN AGAINST EVERYMAN

According to Richard Ashley, realists have privileged a higher reality called "the sovereign state" against which they have posited anarchy understood in a negative way as difference, ambiguity, and contingency—as a space that is external and dangerous.[8] All these characteristics have also been attributed to women. Anarchy is an actual or potential site of war. The most common metaphor that realists employ to describe the anarchical international system is that of the seventeenth-century English philosopher Thomas Hobbes's depiction of the state of nature. Although Hobbes did not write much about international politics, realists have applied his description of individuals' behavior in a hypothetical precontractual state of nature, which Hobbes termed the war of everyman against everyman, to the behavior of states in the international system.[9]

Carole Pateman argues that, in all contemporary discussions of the state of nature, the differentiation between the sexes is generally ignored, even though it was an important consideration for contract theorists themselves.[10] Although Hobbes did suggest that women as well as men could be free and equal individuals in the state of nature, his description of human behavior in this environment refers to that of adult males whose behavior is taken as constitutive of human nature as a whole by contemporary realist analysis. According to Jane Flax, the individuals that Hobbes described in the state of nature appeared to come to full maturity without any engagement with one another; they were solitary creatures lacking any socialization in interactive behavior. Any interactions they did have led to power struggles that resulted in domination or submission. Suspicion of others' motives led to behavior characterized by aggression, self-interest, and the drive for autonomy.[11] In a similar vein, Christine Di Stephano uses feminist psychoanalytic theory to support her claim that the masculine dimension of atomistic egoism is powerfully underscored in Hobbes's state of nature, which, she asserts, is built on the foundation of denied maternity. "Hobbes' abstract man is a creature who is self-possessed and radically solitary in a crowded and inhospitable world, whose relations with others are unavoidably contractual and whose freedom consists in the absence of impediments to the attainment of privately generated and understood desires."[12]

As a model of human behavior, Hobbes's depiction of individuals in the state of nature is partial at best; certain feminists have argued that such behavior could be applicable only to adult males, for if life was to go on for more than one generation in the state of nature, women must have been involved in activities such as reproduction and child rearing rather than in warfare. Reproductive activities require an environment that can provide for the survival of infants and behavior that is interactive and nurturing.

* * *

* * * [W]ar is central to the way we learn about international relations. * * * War is a time when male and female characteristics become polarized; it is a gendering activity at a time when the discourse of militarism and masculinity permeates the whole fabric of society.[13]

As Jean Elshtain points out, war is an experience to which women are exterior; men have inhabited the world of war in a way that women have

not.[14] The history of international politics is therefore a history from which women are, for the most part, absent. Little material can be found on women's roles in wars; generally they are seen as victims, rarely as agents. While war can be a time of advancement for women as they step in to do men's jobs, the battlefront takes precedence, so the hierarchy remains and women are urged to step aside once peace is restored. When women themselves engage in violence, it is often portrayed as a mob or a food riot that is out of control.[15] Movements for peace, which are also part of our history, have not been central to the conventional way in which the evolution of the Western state system has been presented to us. International relations scholars of the early twentieth century, who wrote positively about the possibilities of international law and the collective security system of the League of Nations, were labeled "idealists" and not taken seriously by the more powerful realist tradition.

Metaphors, such as Hobbes's state of nature, are primarily concerned with representing conflictual relations between great powers. The images used to describe nineteenth-century imperialist projects and contemporary great power relations with former colonial states are somewhat different. Historically, colonial people were often described in terms that drew on characteristics associated with women in order to place them lower in a hierarchy that put their white male colonizers on top. As the European state system expanded outward to conquer much of the world in the nineteenth century, its "civilizing" mission was frequently described in stereotypically gendered terms. Colonized peoples were often described as being effeminate, masculinity was an attribute of the white man, and colonial order depended on Victorian standards of manliness. Cynthia Enloe suggests that the concept of "ladylike behavior" was one of the mainstays of imperialist civilization. Like sanitation and Christianity, feminine respectability was meant to convince colonizers and colonized alike that foreign conquest was right and necessary. Masculinity denoted protection of the respectable lady; she stood for the civilizing mission that justified the colonization of benighted peoples.[16] Whereas the feminine stood for danger and disorder for Machiavelli, the European female, in contrast to her colonial counterpart, came to represent a stable, civilized order in nineteenth-century representations of British imperialism.

An example of the way in which these gender identities were manipulated to justify Western policy with respect to the rest of the world can also be seen in attitudes toward Latin America prevalent in the United States in the nineteenth century. According to Michael Hunt, nineteenth-century American images of Latin society depicted a (usually black) male who was lazy, dishonest, and corrupt. A contrary image that was more positive—a Latin as redeemable—took the form of a fair-skinned senorita living in a marginalized society, yet escaping its degrading effects. Hunt suggests that Americans entered the twentieth century with three images of Latin America fostered through legends brought back by American merchants and diplomats. These legends, perpetuated through school texts, cartoons, and political rhetoric, were even incorporated into the views of policymakers. The three images pictured the Latin as a half-breed brute, feminized, or infantile. In each case, Americans stood superior; the first image permitted a predatory aggressiveness, the second allowed the United States to assume the role of ardent suitor, and the third justified America's need to provide tutelage and discipline. All these images are profoundly gendered: the United States as a civilizing warrior, a suitor, or a father, and Latin America as a lesser male, a female, or a child.[17]

Such images, although somewhat muted, remain today and are particularly prevalent in the thinking of Western states when they are dealing with the Third World. * * *

* * *

Feminist Perspectives on National Security

WOMEN DEFINE SECURITY

It is difficult to find definitions by women of national security. While it is not necessarily the case that women have not had ideas on this subject, they are not readily accessible in the literature of international relations. When women speak or write about national security, they are often dismissed as being naive or unrealistic. An example of this is the women in the United States and Europe who spoke out in the early years of the century for a more secure world order. Addressing the International Congress of Women at the Hague during World War I, Jane Addams spoke of the need for a new internationalism to replace the self-destructive nationalism that contributed so centrally to the outbreak and mass destruction of that war. Resolutions adopted at the close of the congress questioned the assumption that women, and civilians more generally, could be protected during modern war. The conference concluded that assuring security through military means was no longer possible owing to the indiscriminate nature of modern warfare, and it called for disarmament as a more appropriate course for ensuring future security.[18]

At the Women's International Peace Conference in Halifax, Canada, in 1985, a meeting of women from all over the world, participants defined security in various ways depending on the most immediate threats to their survival; security meant safe working conditions and freedom from the threat of war or unemployment or the economic squeeze of foreign debt. Discussions of the meaning of security revealed divisions between Western middle-class women's concerns with nuclear war, concerns that were similar to those of Jane Addams and her colleagues, and Third World women who defined insecurity more broadly in terms of the structural violence associated with imperialism, militarism, racism, and sexism. Yet all agreed that security meant nothing if it was built on others' insecurity.[19]

The final document of the World Conference to Review and Appraise the Achievements of the United Nations Decade for Women, held in Nairobi in 1985, offered a similarly multidimensional definition of security. The introductory chapter of the document defined peace as "not only the absence of war, violence and hostilities at the national and international levels but also the enjoyment of economic and social justice."[20] All these definitions of security take issue with realists' assumptions that security is zero-sum and must therefore be built on the insecurity of others.

*   *   *

CITIZENSHIP REDEFINED

Building on the notion of hegemonic masculinity, the notion of the citizen-warrior depends on a devalued femininity for its construction. In international relations, this devalued femininity is bound up with myths about women as victims in need of protection; the protector/protected myth contributes to the legitimation of a militarized version of citizenship that results in unequal gender relations that can precipitate violence against women. Certain feminists have called for the construction of an enriched version of citizenship that would depend less on military values and more on an equal recognition of women's contributions to society. Such a notion of citizenship cannot come about, however, until myths that perpetuate views of women as victims rather than agents are eliminated.

One such myth is the association of women with peace, an association that has been invalidated through considerable evidence of women's support for men's wars in many societies.[21] In spite of a gender gap, a plurality of women generally support war and national security policies; Bernice Carroll suggests that the association of women and peace is one that has been imposed on women by their disarmed condition.[22] In the West, this association grew out of the Victorian ideology of women's moral superiority and the glorification of motherhood. This ideal was expressed by feminist Charlotte Perkins Gilman whose book *Herland* was first serialized in *The Forerunner* in 1915. Gilman glorified women as caring and nurturing mothers whose private sphere skills could benefit the world at large.[23] Most turn-of-the-century feminists shared Gilman's ideas. But if the implication of this view was that women were disqualified from participating in the corrupt world of political and economic power by virtue of their moral superiority, the result could only be the perpetuation of male dominance. Many contemporary feminists see dangers in the continuation of these essentializing myths that can only result in the perpetuation of women's subordination and reinforce dualisms that serve to make men more powerful. The association of femininity with peace lends support to an idealized masculinity that depends on constructing women as passive victims in need of protection. It also contributes to the claim that women are naive in matters relating to international politics. An enriched, less militarized notion of citizenship cannot be built on such a weak foundation.

While women have often been willing to support men's wars, many women are ambivalent about fighting in them, often preferring to leave that task to men. Feminists have also been divided on this issue; some argue, on the grounds of equality, that women must be given equal access to the military, while others suggest that women must resist the draft in order to promote a politics of peace. * * *

*   *   *

In spite of many women's support for men's wars, a consistent gender gap in voting on defense-related issues in many countries suggests that women are less supportive of policies that rest on the use of direct violence. Before the outbreak of the Persian Gulf war in 1990, women in the United States were overwhelmingly against the use of force and, for the first time, women alone turned the public opinion polls against opting for war.[24] During the 1980s, when the Reagan administration was increasing defense budgets, women were less likely to support defense at the expense of social programs, a pattern that, in the United States, holds true for women's behavior more generally.

Explanations for this gender gap, which in the United States appears to be increasing as time goes on, range from suggestions that women have not been socialized into the practice of violence to claims that women are increasingly voting their own interests. While holding down jobs, millions of women also care for children, the aged, and the sick—activities that usually take place outside the economy. When more resources go to the military, additional burdens are placed on such women as public sector resources for social services shrink. While certain women are able, through access to the military, to give service to their country, many more are serving in these traditional care-giving roles. A feminist challenge to the traditional definition of patriotism should therefore question the meaning of service to one's country.[25] In contrast to a citizenship that rests on the assumption that it is more glorious to die than to live for one's state, Wendy Brown suggests that a more constructive view of citizenship could center on the courage to sustain life.[26] In similar terms, Jean Elshtain asserts the need to move toward a politics that shifts the focus of political loyalty and identity from sacrifice to responsibility.[27] Only when women's contributions to society are seen as equal to men's can these reconstructed visions of citizenship come about.

FEMINIST PERSPECTIVES ON STATES' SECURITY-SEEKING BEHAVIOR

Realists have offered us an instrumental version of states' security-seeking behavior, which, I have argued, depends on a partial representation of human behavior associated with a stereotypical hegemonic masculinity. Feminist redefinitions of citizenship allow us to envisage a less militarized version of states' identities, and feminist theories can also propose alternative models for states' international security-seeking behavior, extrapolated from a more comprehensive view of human behavior.

Realists use state-of-nature stories as metaphors to describe the insecurity of states in an anarchical international system. I shall suggest an alternative story, which could equally be applied to the behavior of individuals in the state of nature. Although frequently unreported in standard historical accounts, it is a true story, not a myth, about a state of nature in early nineteenth-century America. Among those present in the first winter encampment of the 1804–1806 Lewis and Clark expedition into the Northwest territories was Saca-

jawea, a member of the Shoshone tribe. Sacajawea had joined the expedition as the wife of a French interpreter; her presence was proving invaluable to the security of the expedition's members, whose task it was to explore uncharted territory and establish contact with the native inhabitants to inform them of claims to these territories by the United States. Although unanticipated by its leaders, the presence of a woman served to assure the native inhabitants that the expedition was peaceful since the Native Americans assumed that war parties would not include women: the expedition was therefore safer because it was not armed.[28]

This story demonstrates that the introduction of women can change the way humans are assumed to behave in the state of nature. Just as Sacajawea's presence changed the Native American's expectations about the behavior of intruders into their territory, the introduction of women into our state-of-nature myths could change the way we think about the behavior of states in the international system. The use of the Hobbesian analogy in international relations theory is based on a partial view of human nature that is stereotypically masculine; a more inclusive perspective would see human nature as both conflictual and cooperative, containing elements of social reproduction and interdependence as well as domination and separation. Generalizing from this more comprehensive view of human nature, a feminist perspective would assume that the potential for international community also exists and that an atomistic, conflictual view of the international system is only a partial representation of reality. Liberal individualism, the instrumental rationality of the marketplace, and the defector's self-help approach in Rousseau's stag hunt [see p. 248] are all, in analogous ways, based on a partial masculine model of human behavior.[29]

*   *   *

Feminist perspectives on national security take us beyond realism's statist representations. They allow us to see that the realist view of national security is constructed out of a masculinized discourse that, while it is only a partial view of reality, is taken as universal. Women's definitions of security are multilevel and multidimensional. Women have defined security as the absence of violence whether it be military, economic, or sexual. Not until the hierarchical social relations, including gender relations, that have been hidden by realism's frequently depersonalized discourse are brought to light can we begin to construct a language of national security that speaks out of the multiple experiences of both women and men. * * *

NOTES

I owe the title of this chapter to Kenneth Waltz's book *Man, the State, and War.*

De Beauvoir epigraph from *The Second Sex* [New York: Knopf, 1972], p. 72. De Beauvoir's analysis suggests that she herself endorsed this explanation for male superiority; * * * Fussell epigraph quoted by Anna Quindlen in *The New York Times,* February 7, 1991, p. A25.

1. [Kenneth N.] Waltz, *Theory of International Politics* [Boston: Addison-Wesley, 1979], p. 102.
2. While heads of state, all men, discussed the "important" issues in world politics at the Group of Seven meeting in London in July 1991, Barbara Bush and Princess Diana were pictured on the "CBS Evening News" (July 17, 1991) meeting with British AIDS patients.
3. [Evelyn Fox] Keller, *Reflections on Gender and Science* [New Haven: Yale University Press 1985], p. 130.
4. For example, see [Donna] Haraway, *Primate Visions* [New York: Routledge, 1989], ch. 1. Considering scientific practice from the perspective of the way its factual findings are narrated, Haraway provocatively explores how scientific theories produce and are embedded in particular kinds of stories. This allows her to challenge the neutrality and objectivity of scientific facts. She suggests that texts about primates can be read as science fictions about race, gender, and nature.
5. [Hans J.] Morgenthau, *Politics Among Nations* [New York: Knopf, 1973], p. 34.

6. Morgenthau does talk about dominating mothers-in-law, but as feminist research has suggested, it is generally men, legally designated as heads of households in most societies, who hold the real power even in the family and certainly with respect to the family's interaction with the public sphere.
7. For an extended discussion of Morgenthau's "political man," see [J. Ann] Tickner, "Hans Morgenthau's Principles of Political Realism" [*Millennium* 17(3):429–440]. In neorealism's depersonalized structural analysis, Morgenthau's depiction of human nature slips out of sight.
8. [Richard K.] Ashley, "Untying the Sovereign State" [*Millennium* 17(2) (1988)], p. 230.
9. Hobbes, *Leviathan,* part 1, ch. 13, quoted in Vasquez, ed., *Classics of International Relations,* pp. 213–215.
10. [Carole] Pateman, *The Sexual Contract* [Stanford: Stanford University Press, 1988], p. 41.
11. [Jane] Flax, "Political Philosophy and the Patriarchal Unconscious: A Psychoanalytic Perspective on Epistemology and Metaphysics," in Harding and Hintikka, eds., *Discovering Reality* [Dordrecht, Holland: D. Reidel, 1983], pp. 245–281.
12. [Christine] Di Stephano, "Masculinity as Ideology in Political Theory" [Women's Studies International Forum 6(6) (1983):633–644]. Carole Pateman has disputed some of Di Stephano's assumptions about Hobbes's characterizations of women and the family in the state of nature. But this does not deny the fact that Di Stephano's characterization of men is the one used by realists in their depiction of the international system. See Pateman, " 'God Hath Ordained to Man a Helper': Hobbes, Patriarchy, and Conjugal Right."
13. [Margaret Randolph] Higonnet et al., *Behind the Lines* [New Haven: Yale University Press, 1987], introduction.
14. [Jean Bethke] Elshtain, *Women and War* [New York: Basic Books, 1987], p. 194.
15. Ibid., p. 168.
16. [Cynthia] Enloe, *Bananas, Beaches, and Bases*

[Berkeley: University of California Press, 1990], pp. 48–49.

17. [Michael H.] Hunt, *Ideology and U.S. Foreign Policy* [New Haven: Yale University Press, 1987], pp. 58–62.

18. [Jane] Addams et al., *Women at The Hague* [New York: Macmillan, 1916], pp. 150ff.

19. [Anne Sisson] Runyan, "Feminism, Peace, and International Politics" [Ph.D. diss., American University, 1988], ch. 6.

20. "Forward-looking Strategies for the Advancement of Women Towards the Year 2000." Quoted in [Hilkka] Pietilä and [Jeanne] Vickers, *Making Women Matter* [London: Zed Books, 1990], pp. 46–47.

21. See Elshtain, *Women and War*, ch. 3.

22. Carroll, "Feminism and Pacifism: Historical and Theoretical Connections," in [Ruth Roach] Pierson, ed., *Women and Peace* [London: Croom Helm, 1987], pp. 2–28.

23. Margaret Hobbs, "The Perils of 'Unbridled Masculinity': Pacifist Elements in the Feminist and Socialist Thought of Charlotte Perkins Gilman," in Pierson, ed., *Women and Peace*, pp. 149–169.

24. The *New York Times* of December 12, 1990 (p. A35) reported that while men were about evenly split on attacking Iraqi forces in Kuwait, women were 73 percent against and 22 percent in favor.

25. Suzanne Gordon, "Another Enemy," *Boston Globe*, March 8, 1991, p. 15.

26. [Wendy] Brown, *Manhood and Politics* [Totowa, N.J.: Rowman and Littlefield, 1988], p. 206.

27. Elshtain, "Sovereignty, Identity, Sacrifice," in [V. Spike] Peterson, ed., *Gendered States* [Boulder: Lynne Rienner, 1992].

28. I am grateful to Michael Capps, historian at the Lewis and Clark Museum in St. Louis, Missouri, for this information. The story of Sacajawea is told in one of the museum's exhibits.

29. In *Man, the State, and War* [New York: Columbia University Press, 1959], [Kenneth N.] Waltz argues that "in the stag-hunt example, the will of the rabbit-snatcher was rational and predictable from his own point of view" (p. 183), while "in the early state of nature, men were sufficiently dispersed to make any pattern of cooperation unnecessary" (p. 167). Neorealist revisionists, such as Snidal [see "Relative Gains and the Pattern of International Cooperation"] do not question the masculine bias of the stag hunt metaphor. Like Waltz and Rousseau, they also assume the autonomous, adult male (unparented and in an environment without women or children) in their discussion of the stag hunt; they do not question the rationality of the rabbit-snatching defector or the restrictive situational descriptions implied by their payoff matrices. Transformations in the social nature of an interaction are very hard to represent using such a model. Their reformulation of Waltz's position is instead focused on the exploration of different specifications of the game payoff in less conflictual ways (i.e., as an assurance game) and on inferences concerning the likely consequences of relative gain-seeking behavior in a gamelike interaction with more than two (equally autonomous and unsocialized) players.

3 ✦ NEW FRONTIERS IN INTERNATIONAL POLITICAL THEORY

One of the ways to clarify debates about international politics is to express basic concepts as rigorously as possible. The readings in this chapter are very explicit about the social scientific underpinnings of realist, liberal, and other contending perspectives. For careful readers, this provides the advantage of laying bare the underlying logic of these arguments. It also means that these readings deal with abstract concepts. Students with a knack for abstract thinking or a good background in social science will find these readings stimulating. Students who prefer to have concrete examples in mind before they tackle abstract theory might want to look first at the related works suggested below and then return to these more conceptual essays.

Theory of International Politics (1979) by Kenneth Waltz has provoked intense discussion by reformulating the realist notion of the balance of power as an elegantly logical theory. The core of his argument is excerpted below. Although Waltz is a direct descendant of Morgenthau's realist school of thought, he differs from Morgenthau in two essential respects. First, Waltz rejects Morgenthau's notion that conflict among nations stems to a large degree from human nature; instead, Waltz argues that chronic warfare among states can be explained by the situation of international anarchy, which forces each state to depend only on itself to provide for its own security. That is, states fight because there is no overarching authority to compel them to conform to any rules or to keep their promises. Second, Waltz tries to reformulate earlier realist ideas as a formal social scientific theory, with rigorously logical deductions derived from explicit assumptions. He also discusses the need to advance "if, then" hypotheses that can be assessed in the light of evidence, though Waltz's critics have charged that his hypotheses are often stated in an elusive way that makes them hard to refute with concrete data. Given Waltz's statement that his is a "theory of international politics" that explains some recurrent patterns, not a "theory of foreign policy" that explains specific decisions, students should read with an eye to what evidence would prove him wrong.

Readers who like to have theory presented along with many historical exam-

ples may want to read John Mearsheimer's book in the Norton series before tackling this selection from Waltz. Mearsheimer's analysis of international power politics draws on Waltz's theory, but he argues that Waltz underestimates the extent to which the imperatives of international anarchy drive states to behave aggressively in an effort to achieve security. In addition, Mearsheimer argues that realist ideas are no less applicable today than they were during the Cold War era, when Waltz formulated his arguments.

Whereas Waltz and Mearsheimer have portrayed the balance of power as a timeless principle of international anarchy, other scholars assert that long-standing ideas about the nature of international politics need to be reevaluated in light of the end of the Cold War and the increasing domination of world politics by powerful liberal democracies. The theory of the liberal democratic peace, presented in Michael Doyle's essay in chapter 2, plays a major role in these debates. However, the newly emerging constructivist theory of international politics, summarized below in an excerpt from John Ruggie's Constructing the World Polity *(1998), argues that both liberal and realist theories fail to consider how our world is constructed by the ideas we share. This essay, like Waltz's, deals at an abstract level with basic conceptions of social science. But Ruggie has not only been a professor at Columbia and Harvard Universities; he has also served as a top adviser on day-to-day policy issues to U.N. General Secretaries Boutros Boutros-Ghali and Kofi Annan. Putting constructivist theory into action, he has tried to show in practice how new ideas can construct a changed world political system. Those who would like to read an empirical piece using the constructivist approach before reading about its theoretical underpinnings should turn to Margaret E. Keck and Kathryn Sikkink's* Activists Beyond Borders, *a book about the promotion of international human rights, excerpted in chapter 9, below.*

Feminist theory has also been a vibrant approach that has gained increasing prominence in the study of international politics. J. Ann Tickner explains in the 1997 article excerpted below why exchanges between those using mainstream and feminist approaches have been frustrating to both sides. Feminists not only make different arguments than realists and liberals, she says, but they also ask different questions, include a broader range of issues under the heading "international politics," and evaluate evidence using different methods and criteria.

KENNETH N. WALTZ

Political Structures

* * * How can we conceive of international politics as a distinct system? What is it that intervenes between interacting units and the results that their acts and interactions produce? To answer these questions, this chapter first examines the concept of social structure and then defines structure as a concept appropriate for national and for international politics.

* * *

A system is composed of a structure and of interacting units. The structure is the system-wide component that makes it possible to think of the system as a whole. The problem * * * is to contrive a definition of structure free of the attributes and the interactions of units. Definitions of structure must leave aside, or abstract from, the characteristics of units, their behavior, and their interactions. Why must those obviously important matters be omitted? They must be omitted so that we can distinguish between variables at the level of the units and variables at the level of the system. * * *

* * *

A structure is defined by the arrangement of its parts. Only changes of arrangement are structural changes. A system is composed of a structure and of interacting parts. Both the structure and the parts are concepts, related to, but not identical with, real agents and agencies. Structure is not something we see. * * * Since structure is an abstraction, it cannot be defined by enumerating material characteristics of the system. It must instead be defined by the arrangement of the system's parts and by the principle of that arrangement.

From Kenneth N. Waltz, *Theory of International Politics* (New York: McGraw-Hill, 1979), chaps. 5, 6.

* * *

* * * In defining structures, the first question to answer is this: What is the principle by which the parts are arranged?

Domestic politics is hierarchically ordered. The units—institutions and agencies—stand vis-à-vis each other in relations of super- and subordination. * * * [P]olitical actors are formally differentiated according to the degrees of their authority, and their distinct functions are specified. * * *

Within a country one can identify the effects of structure by noticing *differences* of behavior in differently structured parts of the polity. From one country to another, one can identify the effects of structure by noticing *similarities* of behavior in polities of similar structure. * * * Despite cultural and other differences, similar structures produce similar effects.

* * *

I defined domestic political structures first by the principle according to which they are organized or ordered, second by the differentiation of units and the specification of their functions, and third by the distribution of capabilities across units. Let us see how the three terms of the definition apply to international politics.

1. Ordering Principles

Structural questions are questions about the arrangement of the parts of a system. The parts of domestic political systems stand in relations of super- and subordination. Some are entitled to command; others are required to obey. Domestic systems are centralized and hierarchic. The parts of international-political systems stand in relations of coordination. Formally, each is the equal of all the others. None is entitled to command; none is required to obey. International systems are decentralized and anarchic. The ordering principles of the two structures are distinctly different, indeed, contrary to each other. Domestic political structures have governmental institutions and offices as their concrete counterparts. International politics, in contrast, has been called "politics in the absence of government" (Fox 1959, p. 35). International organizations do exist, and in ever-growing numbers. Supranational agents able to act effectively, however, either themselves acquire some of the attributes and capabilities of states, as did the medieval papacy in the era of Innocent III, or they soon reveal their inability to act in important ways except with the support, or at least the acquiescence, of the principal states concerned with the matters at hand. Whatever elements of authority emerge internationally are barely once removed from the capability that provides the foundation for the appearance of those elements. Authority quickly reduces to a particular expression of capability. In the absence of agents with system-wide authority, formal relations of super- and subordination fail to develop.

The first term of a structural definition states the principle by which the system is ordered. Structure is an organizational concept. The prominent characteristic of international politics, however, seems to be the lack of order and of organization. How can one think of international politics as being any kind of an order at all? The anarchy of politics internationally is often referred to. If structure is an organizational concept, the terms "structure" and "anarchy" seem to be in contradiction. If international politics is "politics in the absence of government," what are we in the presence of? In looking for international structure, one is brought face to face with the invisible, an uncomfortable position to be in.

The problem is this: how to conceive of an order without an orderer and of organizational effects where formal organization is lacking. Because these are difficult questions, I shall answer them through analogy with microeconomic theory. Reasoning by analogy is helpful where one can move from a domain for which theory is well developed to one where it is not. Reasoning by analogy is permissible where different domains are structurally similar.

Classical economic theory, developed by Adam Smith and his followers, is microtheory. Political scientists tend to think that microtheory is theory about small-scale matters, a usage that ill accords with its established meaning. The term "micro" in economic theory indicates the way in which the theory is constructed rather than the scope of the matters it pertains to. Microeconomic theory describes how an order is spontaneously formed from the self-interested acts and interactions of individual units—in this case, persons and firms. The theory then turns upon the two central concepts of the economic units and of the market. Economic units and economic markets are concepts, not descriptive realities or concrete entities. This must be emphasized since from the early eighteenth century to the present, from the sociologist Auguste Comte to the psychologist George Katona, economic theory has been faulted because its assumptions fail to correspond with realities (Martineau 1853, II, 51–53; Katona 1953). Unrealistically, economic theorists conceive of an economy operating in isolation from its society and polity. Unrealistically, economists assume that the economic world is the whole of the world. Unrealistically, economists think of the acting unit, the famous "economic man," as a single-minded profit maximizer. They single out one aspect of man and leave aside the wondrous variety of human life. As any moderately sensible economist knows, "economic man" does not exist. Anyone who asks businessmen how they make their decisions will find that the assumption that men are economic maximizers grossly distorts their characters. The assumption that men behave as economic men, which is known to be false as a descriptive statement, turns out to be useful in the construction of theory.

Markets are the second major concept invented by microeconomic theorists. Two general questions must be asked about markets: How are they formed? How do they work? The answer to the first question is this: The market of a decentralized economy is individualist in origin, spontaneously generated, and unintended. The market arises out of the activities of separate units—persons and firms—whose aims and efforts are directed not toward creating an order but rather toward fulfilling their own internally defined interests by whatever means they can muster. The individual unit acts for itself. From the coaction of like units emerges a structure that affects and constrains all of them. Once formed, a market becomes a force in itself, and a force that the constitutive units acting singly or in small numbers cannot control. Instead, in lesser or greater degree as market conditions vary, the creators become the creatures of the market that their activity gave rise to. Adam Smith's great achievement was to show how self-interested, greed-driven actions may produce good social outcomes if only political and social conditions permit free competition. If a laissez-faire economy is harmonious, it is so because the intentions of actors do *not* correspond with the outcomes their actions produce. What intervenes between the actors and the objects of their action in order to thwart their purposes? To account for the unexpectedly favorable outcomes of selfish acts, the concept of a market is brought into play. Each unit seeks its own good; the result of a number of units simultaneously doing so transcends the motives and the aims of the separate units. Each would like to work less hard and price his product higher. Taken together, all have to work harder and price their products lower. Each firm seeks to increase its profit; the result of many firms doing so drives the profit rate downward. Each man seeks his own end, and, in doing so, produces a result that was no part of his intention. Out of the mean ambition of its members, the greater good of society is produced.

The market is a cause interposed between the economic actors and the results they produce. It conditions their calculations, their behaviors, and their interactions. It is not an agent in the sense of *A* being the agent that produces outcome *X*. Rather it is a structural cause. A market constrains the units that comprise it from taking certain actions and disposes them toward taking others. The market, created by self-directed interacting economic units, selects behaviors according to their consequences. The market rewards some with high profits and assigns others to bankruptcy. Since a market is not an institution or an agent in any concrete or palpable sense, such statements become impressive only if they can be reliably inferred from a theory as part of a set of more elaborate expectations. They can be. Microeconomic theory explains how an economy operates and why certain effects are to be expected. It generates numerous "if-then" statements that can more or less easily be checked. Consider, for example, the following simple but important propositions. If the money demand for a commodity rises, then so will its price. If price rises, then so will profits. If profits rise, then capital will be attracted and production will increase. If production increases, then price will fall to the level that returns profits to the producers of the commodity at the prevailing rate. This sequence of statements could be extended and refined, but to do so would not serve my purpose. I want to point out that although the stated expectations are now commonplace, they could not be arrived at by economists working in a pre-theoretic era. All of the statements are, of course, made at an appropriate level of generality. They require an "other things being equal" stipulation. They apply, as do statements inferred from any theory, only to the extent that the conditions contemplated by the theory obtain. They are idealizations, and so they are never fully borne out in practice. Many things—social customs, political interventions—will in fact interfere with the theoretically predicted outcomes. Though interferences have to be allowed for, it is nevertheless extraordinarily useful to know what to expect in general.

International-political systems, like economic markets, are formed by the coaction of self-regarding units. International structures are defined in terms of the primary political units of an era, be they city states, empires, or nations. Structures emerge from the coexistence of states. No state intends to participate in the formation of a structure by which it and others will be constrained. International-political systems, like economic markets, are individualist in origin, spontaneously generated, and unintended. In both systems, structures are formed by the coaction of their units. Whether those units live, prosper, or die depends on their own efforts. Both systems are formed and maintained on a principle of self-help that applies to the units. To say that the two realms are structurally similar is not to proclaim their identity. Economically, the self-help principle applies within governmentally contrived limits. Market economies are hedged about in ways that channel energies constructively. One may think of pure food-and-drug standards, antitrust laws, securities and exchange regulations, laws against shooting a competitor, and rules forbidding false claims in advertising. International politics is more nearly a realm in which anything goes. International politics is structurally similar to a market economy insofar as the self-help principle is allowed to operate in the latter.

In a microtheory, whether of international politics or of economics, the motivation of the actors is assumed rather than realistically described. I assume that states seek to ensure their survival. The assumption is a radical simplification made for the sake of constructing a theory. The question to ask of the assumption, as ever, is not whether it is true but whether it is the most sensible and useful one that can be made. Whether it is a useful assumption depends on whether a theory based on the assumption can be contrived, a theory from which important consequences not otherwise obvious can be inferred. Whether it is a sensible assumption can be directly discussed.

Beyond the survival motive, the aims of states may be endlessly varied; they may range from the ambition to conquer the world to the desire merely to be left alone. Survival is a prerequisite to achieving any goals that states may have, other than the goal of promoting their own disappearance as political entities. The survival motive is taken as the ground of action in a world where the security of states is not assured, rather than as a realistic description of the impulse that lies behind every act of state. The assumption allows for the fact that no state always acts exclusively to ensure its survival. It allows for the fact that some states may persistently seek goals that they value more highly than

survival; they may, for example, prefer amalgamation with other states to their own survival in form. It allows for the fact that in pursuit of its security no state will act with perfect knowledge and wisdom—if indeed we could know what those terms might mean. Some systems have high requirements for their functioning. * * * To keep it going, most, but not all, people have to act as expected. * * * One may behave as one likes to. Patterns of behavior nevertheless emerge, and they derive from the structural constraints of the system.

Actors may perceive the structure that constrains them and understand how it serves to reward some kinds of behavior and to penalize others. But then again they either may not see it or, seeing it, may for any of many reasons fail to conform their actions to the patterns that are most often rewarded and least often punished. To say that "the structure selects" means simply that those who conform to accepted and successful practices more often rise to the top and are likelier to stay there. The game one has to win is defined by the structure that determines the kind of player who is likely to prosper.

Where selection according to behavior occurs, no enforced standard of behavior is required for the system to operate, although either system may work better if some standards are enforced or accepted. Internationally, the environment of states' action, or the structure of their system, is set by the fact that some states prefer survival over other ends obtainable in the short run and act with relative efficiency to achieve that end. States may alter their behavior because of the structure they form through interaction with other states. But in what ways and why? To answer these questions we must complete the definition of international structure.

2. The Character of the Units

The second term in the definition of domestic political structure specifies the functions performed by differentiated units. Hierarchy entails relations of super- and subordination among a system's parts, and that implies their differentiation. In defining domestic political structure the second term, like the first and third, is needed because each term points to a possible source of structural variation. The states that are the units of international-political systems are not formally differentiated by the functions they perform. Anarchy entails relations of coordination among a system's units, and that implies their sameness. The second term is not needed in defining international-political structure, because so long as anarchy endures, states remain like units. International structures vary only through a change of organizing principle or, failing that, through variations in the capabilities of units. Nevertheless I shall discuss these like units here, because it is by their interactions that international-political structures are generated.

Two questions arise: Why should states be taken as the units of the system? Given a wide variety of states, how can one call them "like units"? Questioning the choice of states as the primary units of international-political systems became popular in the 1960s and '70s as it was at the turn of the century. Once one understands what is logically involved, the issue is easily resolved. Those who question the state-centric view do so for two main reasons. First, states are not the only actors of importance on the international scene. Second, states are declining in importance, and other actors are gaining, or so it is said. Neither reason is cogent, as the following discussion shows.

States are not and never have been the only international actors. But then structures are defined not by all of the actors that flourish within them but by the major ones. In defining a system's structure one chooses one or some of the infinitely many objects comprising the system and defines its structure in terms of them. For international-political systems, as for any system, one must first decide which units to take as being the parts of the system. Here the economic analogy will help again. The structure of a market is defined by the number of firms competing. If many roughly equal firms contend, a condition of perfect competition is approximated. If a few firms dominate the market, competition is said to be oligopolistic even though

many smaller firms may also be in the field. But we are told that definitions of this sort cannot be applied to international politics because of the interpenetration of states, because of their inability to control the environment of their action, and because rising multinational corporations and other nonstate actors are difficult to regulate and may rival some states in influence. The importance of nonstate actors and the extent of transnational activities are obvious. The conclusion that the state-centric conception of international politics is made obsolete by them does not follow. That economists and economically minded political scientists have thought that it does is ironic. The irony lies in the fact that all of the reasons given for scrapping the state-centric concept can be restated more strongly and applied to firms. Firms competing with numerous others have no hope of controlling their market, and oligopolistic firms constantly struggle with imperfect success to do so. Firms interpenetrate, merge, and buy each other up at a merry pace. Moreover, firms are constantly threatened and regulated by, shall we say, "nonfirm" actors. Some governments encourage concentration; others work to prevent it. The market structure of parts of an economy may move from a wider to a narrower competition or may move in the opposite direction, but whatever the extent and the frequency of change, market structures, generated by the interaction of firms, are defined in terms of them.

Just as economists define markets in terms of firms, so I define international-political structures in terms of states. If Charles P. Kindleberger were right in saying that "the nation-state is just about through as an economic unit" (1969, p. 207), then the structure of international politics would have to be redefined. That would be necessary because economic capabilities cannot be separated from the other capabilities of states. The distinction frequently drawn between matters of high and low politics is misplaced. States use economic means for military and political ends; and military and political means for the achievement of economic interests.

An amended version of Kindleberger's statement may hold: Some states may be nearly washed up as economic entities, and others not. That poses no problem for international-political theory since international politics is mostly about inequalities anyway. So long as the major states are the major actors, the structure of international politics is defined in terms of them. That theoretical statement is of course borne out in practice. States set the scene in which they, along with nonstate actors, stage their dramas or carry on their humdrum affairs. Though they may choose to interfere little in the affairs of nonstate actors for long periods of time, states nevertheless set the terms of the intercourse, whether by passively permitting informal rules to develop or by actively intervening to change rules that no longer suit them. When the crunch comes, states remake the rules by which other actors operate. Indeed, one may be struck by the ability of weak states to impede the operation of strong international corporations and by the attention the latter pay to the wishes of the former.

*   *   *

States are the units whose interactions form the structure of international-political systems. They will long remain so. The death rate among states is remarkably low. Few states die; many firms do. Who is likely to be around 100 years from now—the United States, the Soviet Union, France, Egypt, Thailand, and Uganda? Or Ford, IBM, Shell, Unilever, and Massey-Ferguson? I would bet on the states, perhaps even on Uganda. But what does it mean to refer to the 150-odd states of today's world, which certainly form a motley collection, as being "like units"? Many students of international politics are bothered by the description. To call states "like units" is to say that each state is like all other states in being an autonomous political unit. It is another way of saying that states are sovereign. But sovereignty is also a bothersome concept. Many believe, as the anthropologist M. G. Smith has said, that "in a system of sovereign states no state is sovereign."[1] The error lies in identifying the sovereignty of states with their ability to do as they wish. To say that states are sovereign is not to say that they can do as they please, that they are free of

others' influence, that they are able to get what they want. Sovereign states may be hardpressed all around, constrained to act in ways they would like to avoid, and able to do hardly anything just as they would like to. The sovereignty of states has never entailed their insulation from the effects of other states' actions. To be sovereign and to be dependent are not contradictory conditions. Sovereign states have seldom led free and easy lives. What then is sovereignty? To say that a state is sovereign means that it decides for itself how it will cope with its internal and external problems, including whether or not to seek assistance from others and in doing so to limit its freedom by making commitments to them. States develop their own strategies, chart their own courses, make their own decisions about how to meet whatever needs they experience and whatever desires they develop. It is no more contradictory to say that sovereign states are always constrained and often tightly so than it is to say that free individuals often make decisions under the heavy pressure of events.

*   *   *

States vary widely in size, wealth, power, and form. And yet variations in these and in other respects are variations among like units. In what way are they like units? How can they be placed in a single category? States are alike in the tasks that they face, though not in their abilities to perform them. The differences are of capability, not of function. * * * The functions of states are similar, and distinctions among them arise principally from their varied capabilities. National politics consists of differentiated units performing specified functions. International politics consists of like units duplicating one another's activities.

3. The Distribution of Capabilities

The parts of a hierarchic system are related to one another in ways that are determined both by their functional differentiation and by the extent of their capabilities. The units of an anarchic system are functionally undifferentiated. The units of such an order are then distinguished primarily by their greater or lesser capabilities for performing similar tasks. * * *

* * * [O]ne may wonder why only *capability* is included in the third part of the definition, and not such characteristics as ideology, form of government, peacefulness, bellicosity, or whatever. The answer is this: Power is estimated by comparing the capabilities of a number of units. Although capabilities are attributes of units, the distribution of capabilities across units is not. The distribution of capabilities is not a unit attribute, but rather a system-wide concept. * * *

*   *   *

In defining international-political structures we take states with whatever traditions, habits, objectives, desires, and forms of government they may have. We do not ask whether states are revolutionary or legitimate, authoritarian or democratic, ideological or pragmatic. We abstract from every attribute of states except their capabilities. Nor in thinking about structure do we ask about the relations of states—their feelings of friendship and hostility, their diplomatic exchanges, the alliances they form, and the extent of the contacts and exchanges among them. We ask what range of expectations arises merely from looking at the type of order that prevails among them and at the distribution of capabilities within that order. We abstract from any particular qualities of states and from all of their concrete connections. What emerges is a positional picture, a general description of the ordered overall arrangement of a society written in terms of the placement of units rather than in terms of their qualities.

*   *   *

Anarchic Orders and Balances of Power

*   *   *

1. Violence at Home and Abroad

The state among states, it is often said, conducts its affairs in the brooding shadow of violence. Because some states may at any time use force, all states must be prepared to do so—or live at the mercy of their militarily more vigorous neighbors. Among states, the state of nature is a state of war. This is meant not in the sense that war constantly occurs but in the sense that, with each state deciding for itself whether or not to use force, war may at any time break out. Whether in the family, the community, or the world at large, contact without at least occasional conflict is inconceivable; and the hope that in the absence of an agent to manage or to manipulate conflicting parties the use of force will always be avoided cannot be realistically entertained. Among men as among states, anarchy, or the absence of government, is associated with the occurrence of violence.

The threat of violence and the recurrent use of force are said to distinguish international from national affairs. But in the history of the world surely most rulers have had to bear in mind that their subjects might use force to resist or overthrow them. If the absence of government is associated with the threat of violence, so also is its presence. A haphazard list of national tragedies illustrates the point all too well. The most destructive wars of the hundred years following the defeat of Napoleon took place not among states but *within* them. Estimates of deaths in China's Taiping Rebellion, which began in 1851 and lasted 13 years, range as high as 20 million. In the American Civil War some 600 thousand people lost their lives. In more recent history, forced collectivization and Stalin's purges eliminated five million Russians, and Hitler exterminated six million Jews. In some Latin American countries, coups d'états and rebellions have been normal features of national life. Between

1948 and 1957, for example, 200 thousand Colombians were killed in civil strife. In the middle 1970s most inhabitants of Idi Amin's Uganda must have felt their lives becoming nasty, brutish, and short, quite as in Thomas Hobbes's state of nature. If such cases constitute aberrations, they are uncomfortably common ones. We easily lose sight of the fact that struggles to achieve and maintain power, to establish order, and to contrive a kind of justice within states, may be bloodier than wars among them.

If anarchy is identified with chaos, destruction, and death, then the distinction between anarchy and government does not tell us much. Which is more precarious: the life of a state among states, or of a government in relation to its subjects? The answer varies with time and place. Among some states at some times, the actual or expected occurrence of violence is low. Within some states at some times, the actual or expected occurrence of violence is high. The use of force, or the constant fear of its use, are not sufficient grounds for distinguishing international from domestic affairs. If the possible and the actual use of force mark both national and international orders, then no durable distinction between the two realms can be drawn in terms of the use or the nonuse of force. No human order is proof against violence.

To discover qualitative differences between internal and external affairs one must look for a criterion other than the occurrence of violence. The distinction between international and national realms of politics is not found in the use or the nonuse of force but in their different structures. But if the dangers of being violently attacked are greater, say, in taking an evening stroll through downtown Detroit than they are in picnicking along the French and German border, what practical difference does the difference of structure make? Nationally as internationally, contact generates conflict and at times issues in violence. The difference between national and international politics lies not in the use of force but in the different modes of organization for doing something about it. A government, ruling by some standard of legitimacy, arrogates to itself the right to use force—

that is, to apply a variety of sanctions to control the use of force by its subjects. If some use private force, others may appeal to the government. A government has no monopoly on the use of force, as is all too evident. An effective government, however, has a monopoly on the *legitimate* use of force, and legitimate here means that public agents are organized to prevent and to counter the private use of force. Citizens need not prepare to defend themselves. Public agencies do that. A national system is not one of self-help. The international system is.

2. Interdependence and Integration

The political significance of interdependence varies depending on whether a realm is organized, with relations of authority specified and established, or remains formally unorganized. Insofar as a realm is formally organized, its units are free to specialize, to pursue their own interests without concern for developing the means of maintaining their identity and preserving their security in the presence of others. They are free to specialize because they have no reason to fear the increased interdependence that goes with specialization. If those who specialize most benefit most, then competition in specialization ensues. Goods are manufactured, grain is produced, law and order are maintained, commerce is conducted, and financial services are provided by people who ever more narrowly specialize. In simple economic terms, the cobbler depends on the tailor for his pants and the tailor on the cobbler for his shoes, and each would be ill-clad without the services of the other. In simple political terms, Kansas depends on Washington for protection and regulation and Washington depends on Kansas for beef and wheat. In saying that in such situations interdependence is close, one need not maintain that the one part could not learn to live without the other. One need only say that the cost of breaking the interdependent relation would be high. Persons and institutions depend heavily on one another because of the different tasks they perform and the different goods they produce and exchange. The parts of a polity bind themselves together by their differences (cf. Durkheim 1893, p. 212).

Differences between national and international structures are reflected in the ways the units of each system define their ends and develop the means for reaching them. In anarchic realms, like units coact. In hierarchic realms, unlike units interact. In an anarchic realm, the units are functionally similar and tend to remain so. Like units work to maintain a measure of independence and may even strive for autarchy. In a hierarchic realm, the units are differentiated, and they tend to increase the extent of their specialization. Differentiated units become closely interdependent, the more closely so as their specialization proceeds. Because of the difference of structure, interdependence within and interdependence among nations are two distinct concepts. So as to follow the logicians' admonition to keep a single meaning for a given term throughout one's discourse, I shall use "integration" to describe the condition within nations and "interdependence" to describe the condition among them.

Although states are like units functionally, they differ vastly in their capabilities. Out of such differences something of a division of labor develops. The division of labor across nations, however, is slight in comparison with the highly articulated division of labor within them. Integration draws the parts of a nation closely together. Interdependence among nations leaves them loosely connected. Although the integration of nations is often talked about, it seldom takes place. Nations could mutually enrich themselves by further dividing not just the labor that goes into the production of goods but also some of the other tasks they perform, such as political management and military defense. Why does their integration not take place? The structure of international politics limits the cooperation of states in two ways.

In a self-help system each of the units spends a portion of its effort, not in forwarding its own good, but in providing the means of protecting itself against others. Specialization in a system of divided labor works to everyone's advantage, though not equally so. Inequality in the expected distribu-tion of the increased product works strongly against extension of the division of labor internationally. When faced with the possibility of cooperating for mutual gain, states that feel insecure must ask how the gain will be divided. They are compelled to ask not "Will both of us gain?" but "Who will gain more?" If an expected gain is to be divided, say, in the ratio of two to one, one state may use its disproportionate gain to implement a policy intended to damage or destroy the other. Even the prospect of large absolute gains for both parties does not elicit their cooperation so long as each fears how the other will use its increased capabilities. Notice that the impediments to collaboration may not lie in the character and the immediate intention of either party. Instead, the condition of insecurity—at the least, the uncertainty of each about the other's future intentions and actions— works against their cooperation.

In any self-help system, units worry about their survival, and the worry conditions their behavior. Oligopolistic markets limit the cooperation of firms in much the way that international-political structures limit the cooperation of states. Within rules laid down by governments, whether firms survive and prosper depends on their own efforts. Firms need not protect themselves physically against assaults from other firms. They are free to concentrate on their economic interests. As economic entities, however, they live in a self-help world. All want to increase profits. If they run undue risks in the effort to do so, they must expect to suffer the consequences. As William Fellner says, it is "impossible to maximize joint gains without the collusive handling of all relevant variables." And this can be accomplished only by "complete disarmament of the firms in relation to each other." But firms cannot sensibly disarm even to increase their profits. This statement qualifies, rather than contradicts, the assumption that firms aim at maximum profits. To maximize profits tomorrow as well as today, firms first have to survive. Pooling all resources implies, again as Fellner puts it, "discounting the future possibilities of all participating firms" (1949, p. 35). But the future cannot be discounted. The relative strength of firms changes over time in ways that cannot be foreseen. Firms are constrained to strike a compromise between maximizing their profits and minimizing the danger of their own demise. Each of two firms may be better off if one of them accepts compensation from the other in return for withdrawing from some part of the market. But a firm that accepts smaller markets in exchange for larger profits will be gravely disadvantaged if, for example, a price war should break out as part of a renewed struggle for markets. If possible, one must resist accepting smaller markets in return for larger profits (pp. 132, 217–18). "It is," Fellner insists, "not advisable to disarm in relation to one's rivals" (p. 199). Why not? Because "the potentiality of renewed warfare always exists" (p. 177). Fellner's reasoning is much like the reasoning that led Lenin to believe that capitalist countries would never be able to cooperate for their mutual enrichment in one vast imperialist enterprise. Like nations, oligopolistic firms must be more concerned with relative strength than with absolute advantage.

A state worries about a division of possible gains that may favor others more than itself. That is the first way in which the structure of international politics limits the cooperation of states. A state also worries lest it become dependent on others through cooperative endeavors and exchanges of goods and services. That is the second way in which the structure of international politics limits the cooperation of states. The more a state specializes, the more it relies on others to supply the materials and goods that it is not producing. The larger a state's imports and exports, the more it depends on others. The world's well-being would be increased if an ever more elaborate division of labor were developed, but states would thereby place themselves in situations of ever closer interdependence. Some states may not resist that. For small and ill-endowed states the costs of doing so are excessively high. But states that can resist becoming ever more enmeshed with others ordinarily do so in either or both of two ways. States that are heavily dependent, or closely interdependent, worry about securing that which they depend on. The high interdependence of states means that the states in question experience, or are subject to, the common vulnerability that high interdependence entails. Like other organizations, states seek to control what they depend on or to lessen the extent of their dependency. This simple thought explains quite a bit of the behavior of states: their imperial thrusts to widen the scope of their control and their autarchic strivings toward greater self-sufficiency.

Structures encourage certain behaviors and penalize those who do not respond to the encouragement. Nationally, many lament the extreme development of the division of labor, a development that results in the allocation of ever narrower tasks to individuals. And yet specialization proceeds, and its extent is a measure of the development of societies. In a formally organized realm a premium is put on each unit's being able to specialize in order to increase its value to others in a system of divided labor. The domestic imperative is "specialize"! Internationally, many lament the resources states spend unproductively for their own defense and the opportunities they miss to enhance the welfare of their people through cooperation with other states. And yet the ways of states change little. In an unorganized realm each unit's incentive is to put itself in a position to be able to take care of itself since no one else can be counted on to do so. The international imperative is "take care of yourself"! Some leaders of nations may understand that the well-being of all of them would increase through their participation in a fuller division of labor. But to act on the idea would be to act on a domestic imperative, an imperative that does not run internationally. What one might want to do in the absence of structural constraints is different from what one is encouraged to do in their presence. States do not willingly place themselves in situations of increased dependence. In a self-help system, considerations of security subordinate economic gain to political interest.

What each state does for itself is much like what all of the others are doing. They are denied the advantages that a full division of labor, political as well as economic, would provide. Defense spending, moreover, is unproductive for all and unavoidable for most. Rather than increased well-being, their reward is in the maintenance of their autonomy. * * *

3. Structures and Strategies

That motives and outcomes may well be disjoined should now be easily seen. Structures cause actions to have consequences they were not intended to have. Surely most of the actors will notice that, and at least some of them will be able to figure out why. They may develop a pretty good sense of just how structures work their effects. Will they not then be able to achieve their original ends by appropriately adjusting their strategies? Unfortunately, they often cannot. To show why this is so I shall give only a few examples; once the point is made, the reader will easily think of others.

If shortage of a commodity is expected, all are collectively better off if they buy less of it in order to moderate price increases and to distribute shortages equitably. But because some will be better off if they lay in extra supplies quickly, all have a strong incentive to do so. If one expects others to make a run on a bank, one's prudent course is to run faster than they do even while knowing that if few others run, the bank will remain solvent, and if many run, it will fail. In such cases, pursuit of individual interest produces collective results that nobody wants, yet individuals by behaving differently will hurt themselves without altering outcomes. These two much used examples establish the main point. Some courses of action I cannot sensibly follow unless you do too, and you and I cannot sensibly follow them unless we are pretty sure that many others will as well. Let us go more deeply into the problem by considering two further examples in some detail.

Each of many persons may choose to drive a private car rather than take a train. Cars offer flexibility in scheduling and in choice of destination; yet at times, in bad weather for example, railway passenger service is a much wanted convenience. Each of many persons may shop in supermarkets rather than at corner grocery stores. The stocks of supermarkets are larger, and their prices lower; yet at times the corner grocery store, offering, say, credit and delivery service, is a much wanted convenience. The result of most people usually driving their own cars and shopping at supermarkets is to reduce passenger service and to decrease the number of corner grocery stores. These results may not be what most people want. They may be willing to pay to prevent services from disappearing. And yet individuals can do nothing to affect the outcomes. Increased patronage *would* do it, but not increased patronage by me and the few others I might persuade to follow my example.

We may well notice that our behavior produces unwanted outcomes, but we are also likely to see that such instances as these are examples of what Alfred E. Kahn describes as "large" changes that are brought about by the accumulation of "small" decisions. In such situations people are victims of the "tyranny of small decisions," a phrase suggesting that "if one hundred consumers choose option x, and this causes the market to make decision X (where X equals 100 x), it is not necessarily true that those same consumers would have voted for that outcome if that large decision had ever been presented for their explicit consideration" (Kahn 1966, p. 523). If the market does not present the large question for decision, then individuals are doomed to making decisions that are sensible within their narrow contexts even though they know all the while that in making such decisions they are bringing about a result that most of them do not want. Either that or they organize to overcome some of the effects of the market by changing its structure—for example, by bringing consumer units roughly up to the size of the units that are making producers' decisions. This nicely makes the point: So long as one leaves the structure unaffected it is not possible for changes in the intentions and the actions of particular actors to produce desirable outcomes or to avoid undesirable ones. Structures may be changed, as just mentioned, by changing the distribution of capabilities across units. Structures may also be changed by imposing requirements where previously people had to decide for themselves. If some merchants sell on Sunday, others may have to do so in order to remain competitive even though most prefer a six-day week. Most are able to do as they please only if all are required to keep comparable hours. The only remedies for strong structural effects are structural changes.

Structural constraints cannot be wished away, although many fail to understand this. In every age and place, the units of self-help systems—nations, corporations, or whatever—are told that the greater good, along with their own, requires them to act for the sake of the system and not for their own narrowly defined advantage. In the 1950s, as fear of the world's destruction in nuclear war grew, some concluded that the alternative to world destruction was world disarmament. In the 1970s, with the rapid growth of population, poverty, and pollution, some concluded, as one political scientist put it, that "states must meet the needs of the political ecosystem in its global dimensions or court annihilation" (Sterling 1974, p. 336). The international interest must be served; and if that means anything at all, it means that national interests are subordinate to it. The problems are found at the global level. Solutions to the problems continue to depend on national policies. What are the conditions that would make nations more or less willing to obey the injunctions that are so often laid on them? How can they resolve the tension between pursuing their own interests and acting for the sake of the system? No one has shown how that can be done, although many wring their hands and plead for rational behavior. The very problem, however, is that rational behavior, given structural constraints, does not lead to the wanted results. With each country constrained to take care of itself, no one can take care of the system.[2]

A strong sense of peril and doom may lead to a clear definition of ends that must be achieved. Their achievement is not thereby made possible. The possibility of effective action depends on the ability to provide necessary means. It depends even more so on the existence of conditions that permit nations and other organizations to follow appropriate policies and strategies. World-shaking problems cry for global solutions, but there is no global agency to provide them. Necessities do not create possibilities. * * *

* * *

Some have hoped that changes in the awareness and purpose, in the organization and ideology, of states would change the quality of international life. Over the centuries states have changed in many ways, but the quality of international life has remained much the same. States may seek reasonable and worthy ends, but they cannot figure out how to reach them. The problem is not in their stupidity or ill will, although one does not want to claim that those qualities are lacking. The depth of the difficulty is not understood until one realizes that intelligence and goodwill cannot discover and act on adequate programs. Early in this century Winston Churchill observed that the British-German naval race promised disaster *and* that Britain had no realistic choice other than to run it. States facing global problems are like individual consumers trapped by the "tyranny of small decisions." States, like consumers, can get out of the trap only by changing the structure of their field of activity. The message bears repeating: The only remedy for a strong structural effect is a structural change.

4. The Virtues of Anarchy

To achieve their objectives and maintain their security, units in a condition of anarchy—be they people, corporations, states, or whatever—must rely on the means they can generate and the arrangements they can make for themselves. Self-help is necessarily the principle of action in an anarchic order. A self-help situation is one of high risk—of bankruptcy in the economic realm and of war in a world of free states. * * *

* * *

If the risks of war are unbearably high, can they be reduced by organizing to manage the affairs of nations? At a minimum, management requires controlling the military forces that are at the disposal of states. Within nations, organizations have to work to maintain themselves. As organizations, nations, in working to maintain themselves, sometimes have to use force against dissident elements and areas. As hierarchical systems, governments nationally or globally are disrupted by the defection of major parts. In a society of states with little coherence, attempts at world government would founder on the inability of an emerging central authority to mobilize the resources needed to create and maintain the unity of the system by regulating and managing its parts. The prospect of world government would be an invitation to prepare for world civil war. * * * States cannot entrust managerial powers to a central agency unless that agency is able to protect its client states. The more powerful the clients and the more the power of each of them appears as a threat to the others, the greater the power lodged in the center must be. The greater the power of the center, the stronger the incentive for states to engage in a struggle to control it.

States, like people, are insecure in proportion to the extent of their freedom. If freedom is wanted, insecurity must be accepted. Organizations that establish relations of authority and control may increase security as they decrease freedom. * * *

Nationally, the force of a government is exercised in the name of right and justice. Internationally, the force of a state is employed for the sake of its own protection and advantage. Rebels challenge a government's claim to authority; they question the rightfulness of its rule. Wars among states cannot settle questions of authority and right; they can only determine the allocation of gains and losses among contenders and settle for a time the question of who is the stronger. Nationally, relations of authority are established. Internationally, only relations of strength result. Nationally, private force used against a government threatens the political system. Force used by a state—a public body—is, from the international perspective, the private use of force; but there is no government to overthrow and no governmental apparatus to capture. * * *

National politics is the realm of authority, of administration, and of law. International politics is the realm of power, of struggle, and of accommodation. The international realm is preeminently a political one. * * *

Whether or not by force, each state plots the course it thinks will best serve its interests. If force is used by one state or its use is expected, the recourse of other states is to use force or be prepared to use it singly or in combination. No appeal can be made to a higher entity clothed with the authority and equipped with the ability to act on its own initiative. Under such conditions the possibility that force will be used by one or another of the parties looms always as a threat in the background. In politics force is said to be the *ultima ratio*. In international politics force serves, not only as the *ultima ratio*, but indeed as the first and constant one. * * * The constant possibility that force will be used limits manipulations, moderates demands, and serves as an incentive for the settlement of disputes. One who knows that pressing too hard may lead to war has strong reason to consider whether possible gains are worth the risks entailed. The threat of force internationally is comparable to the role of the strike in labor and management bargaining. "The few strikes that take place are in a sense," as Livernash has said, "the cost of the strike option which produces settlements in the large mass of negotiations" (1963, p. 430). Even if workers seldom strike, their doing so is always a possibility. The possibility of industrial disputes leading to long and costly strikes encourages labor and management to face difficult issues, to try to understand each other's problems, and to work hard to find accommodations. The possibility that conflicts among nations may lead to long and costly wars has similarly sobering effects.

*   *   *

[The Balance of Power]

How can a theory of international politics be constructed? Just as any theory must be. [F]irst, one must conceive of international politics as a bounded realm or domain; second, one must discover some law-like regularities within it; and third, one must develop a way of explaining the observed regularities. * * * [This c]hapter so far has shown how political structures account for some recurrent aspects of the behavior of states and for certain repeated and enduring patterns. Wherever agents and agencies are coupled by force and competition rather than by authority and law, we expect to find such behaviors and outcomes. They are closely identified with the approach to politics suggested by the rubric, *Realpolitik*. The elements of *Realpolitik*, exhaustively listed, are these: The ruler's, and later the state's, interest provides the spring of action; the necessities of policy arise from the unregulated competition of states; calculation based on these necessities can discover the policies that will best serve a state's interests; success is the ultimate test of policy, and success is defined as preserving and strengthening the state. Ever since Machiavelli, interest and necessity—and *raison d'état*, the phrase that comprehends them—have remained the key concepts of *Realpolitik*. From Machiavelli through Meinecke and Morgenthau the elements of the approach and the reasoning remain constant. Machiavelli stands so clearly as the exponent of *Realpolitik* that one easily slips into thinking that he developed the closely associated idea of balance of power as well. Although he did not, his conviction that politics can be explained in its own terms established the ground on which balance-of-power theory can be built.

Realpolitik indicates the methods by which foreign policy is conducted and provides a rationale for them. Structural constraints explain why the methods are repeatedly used despite differences in the persons and states who use them. Balance-of-power theory purports to explain the result that such methods produce. Rather, that is what the theory should do. If there is any distinctively political theory of international politics, balance-of-power theory is it. And yet one cannot find a statement of the theory that is generally accepted. Carefully surveying the copious balance-of-power literature, Ernst Haas discovered eight distinct meanings of the term, and Martin Wight found nine (1953, 1966). Hans Morgenthau, in his profound historical and analytic treatment of the subject, makes use of four different definitions (1973). Balance of power is seen by some as being akin to a law of nature; by others, as simply an outrage. Some view it as a guide to statesmen; others as a cloak that disguises their imperialist policies. Some believe that a balance of power is the best guarantee of the security of states and the peace of the world; others, that it has ruined states by causing most of the wars they have fought.[3]

To believe that one can cut through such confusion may seem quixotic. I shall nevertheless try. It will help to hark back to several basic propositions about theory. (1) A theory contains at least one theoretical assumption. Such assumptions are not factual. One therefore cannot legitimately ask if they are true, but only if they are useful. (2) Theories must be evaluated in terms of what they claim to explain. Balance-of-power theory claims to explain the results of states' actions, under given conditions, and those results may not be foreshadowed in any of the actors' motives or be contained as objectives in their policies. (3) Theory, as a general explanatory system, cannot account for particularities.

Most of the confusions in balance-of-power theory, and criticisms of it, derive from misunderstanding these three points. A balance-of-power theory, properly stated, begins with assumptions about states: They are unitary actors who, at a minimum, seek their own preservation and, at a maximum, drive for universal domination. States, or those who act for them, try in more or less sensible ways to use the means available in order to achieve the ends in view. Those means fall into two categories: internal efforts (moves to increase economic capability, to increase military strength, to develop clever strategies) and external efforts (moves to strengthen and enlarge one's own alliance or to weaken and shrink an opposing one). The external game of alignment and realignment requires three or more players, and it is usually said that balance-of-power systems require at least that number. The statement is false, for in a two-power system the politics of balance continue, but the way to compensate for an incipient external disequilibrium is primarily by intensifying one's internal efforts. To the assumptions of the theory we then add the condition for its operation: that two or more states coexist in a self-help system, one with no superior agent to come to the aid of states that may be weakening or to deny to any of them the use of whatever instruments they think will serve their purposes. The theory, then, is built up from the assumed motivations of states and the actions that correspond to them. It describes the constraints that arise from the system that those actions produce, and it indicates the expected outcome: namely, the formation of balances of power. Balance-of-power theory is microtheory precisely in the economist's sense. The system, like a market in economics, is made by the actions and interactions of its units, and the theory is based on assumptions about their behavior.

A self-help system is one in which those who do not help themselves, or who do so less effectively than others, will fail to prosper, will lay themselves open to dangers, will suffer. Fear of such unwanted consequences stimulates states to behave in ways that tend toward the creation of balances of power. Notice that the theory requires no assumptions of rationality or of constancy of will on the part of all of the actors. The theory says simply that if some do relatively well, others will emulate them or fall by the wayside. Obviously, the system won't work if all states lose interest in preserving themselves. It will, however, continue to work if some states do, while others do not, choose to lose their political identities, say, through amalgamation. Nor need it be assumed that all of the competing states are striving relentlessly to increase their power. The possibility that force may be used by some states to weaken or destroy others does, however, make it difficult for them to break out of the competitive system.

*   *   *

* * * Balance-of-power theory claims to explain a result (the recurrent formation of balances of power), which may not accord with the intentions of any of the units whose actions combine to produce that result. To contrive and maintain a balance may be the aim of one or more states, but then again it may not be. According to the theory, balances of power tend to form whether some or all states consciously aim to establish and maintain a balance, or whether some or all states aim for universal domination.[4] Yet many, and perhaps most, statements of balance-of-power theory attribute the maintenance of a balance to the separate states as a motive. David Hume, in his classic essay "Of the Balance of Power," offers "the maxim of preserving the balance of power" as a constant rule of prudent politics (1742, pp. 142–44). So it may be, but it has proved to be an unfortunately short step from the belief that a high regard for preserving a balance is at the heart of wise statesmanship to the belief that states must follow the maxim if a balance of power is to be maintained. This is apparent in the first of Morgenthau's four definitions of the term: namely, "a policy aimed at a certain state of affairs." The reasoning then easily becomes tautological. If a balance of power is to be maintained, the policies of states must aim to uphold it. If a balance of power is in fact maintained, we can conclude that their aim was accurate. If a balance of power is not produced, we can say that the theory's assumption is erroneous. Finally, and this completes the drift toward the reification of a concept, if the purpose of states is to uphold a balance, the purpose of the balance is "to maintain the stability of the system without destroying the multiplicity of the elements composing it." Reification has obviously occurred where one reads, for example, of the balance operating "successfully" and of the difficulty that nations have in applying it (1973, pp. 167–74, 202–207).

Reification is often merely the loose use of language or the employment of metaphor to make one's prose more pleasing. In this case, however, the theory has been drastically distorted, and not only by introducing the notion that if a balance is to be formed, somebody must want it and must work for it. The further distortion of the theory arises when rules are derived from the results of states' actions and then illogically prescribed to the actors as duties. A possible effect is turned into a necessary cause in the form of a stipulated rule. Thus, it is said, "the balance of power" can "impose its restraints upon the power aspirations of nations" only if they first "restrain themselves by accepting the system of the balance of power as the common framework of their endeavors." Only if states recognize "the same rules of the game" and play "for the same limited stakes" can the balance of power fulfill "its functions for international stability and national independence" (Morgenthau 1973, pp. 219–20).

The closely related errors that fall under our second proposition about theory are, as we have seen, twin traits of the field of international politics: namely, to assume a necessary correspondence of motive and result and to infer rules for the actors from the observed results of their action. What has gone wrong can be made clear by recalling the economic analogy. In a purely competitive economy, everyone's striving to make a profit drives the profit rate downward. Let the competition continue long enough under static conditions, and everyone's profit will be zero. To infer from that result that everyone, or anyone, is seeking to minimize profit, and that the competitors must adopt that goal as a rule in order for the system to work, would be absurd. And yet in international politics one frequently finds that rules inferred from the results of the interactions of states are prescribed to the actors and are said to be a condition of the system's maintenance. Such errors, often made, are also often pointed out, though seemingly to no avail. S. F. Nadel has put the matter simply: "an orderliness abstracted from behaviour cannot guide behaviour" (Nadel 1957, p. 148; cf. Durkheim 1893, pp. 366, 418; Shubik 1959, pp. 11, 32).

Analytic reasoning applied where a systems approach is needed leads to the laying down of all sorts of conditions as prerequisites to balances of power forming and tending toward equilibrium and as general preconditions of world stability and peace. Some require that the number of great powers exceed two; others that a major power be willing to play the role of balancer. Some require that military technology not change radically or rapidly; others that the major states abide by arbitrarily specified rules. But balances of power form in the absence of the "necessary" conditions, and

since 1945 the world has been stable, and the world of major powers remarkably peaceful, even though international conditions have not conformed to theorists' stipulations. Balance-of-power politics prevail wherever two, and only two, requirements are met: that the order be anarchic and that it be populated by units wishing to survive.

*   *   *

Finally, * * * balance-of-power theory is often criticized because it does not explain the particular policies of states. True, the theory does not tell us why state X made a certain move last Tuesday. To expect it to do so would be like expecting the theory of universal gravitation to explain the wayward path of a falling leaf. A theory at one level of generality cannot answer questions about matters at a different level of generality. Failure to notice this is one error on which the criticism rests. Another is to mistake a theory of international politics for a theory of foreign policy. * * *

Any theory covers some matters and leaves other matters aside. Balance-of-power theory is a theory about the results produced by the uncoordinated actions of states. The theory makes assumptions about the interests and motives of states, rather than explaining them. What it does explain are the constraints that confine all states. The clear perception of constraints provides many clues to the expected reactions of states, but by itself the theory cannot explain those reactions. They depend not only on international constraints but also on the characteristics of states. How will a particular state react? To answer that question we need not only a theory of the market, so to speak, but also a theory about the firms that compose it. What will a state have to react to? Balance-of-power theory can give general and useful answers to that question. The theory explains why a certain similarity of behavior is expected from similarly situated states. The expected behavior is similar, not identical. To explain the expected differences in national responses, a theory would have to show how the different internal structures of states affect their external policies and actions. A theory of foreign policy would not predict the detailed content of policy but instead would lead to different expectations about the tendencies and styles of different countries' policies. Because the national and the international levels are linked, theories of both types, if they are any good, tell us some things, but not the same things, about behavior and outcomes at both levels.

[Testing the Theory]

*   *   *

Before subjecting a theory to tests, one asks whether the theory is internally consistent and whether it tells us some things of interest that we would not know in its absence. That the theory meets those requirements does not mean that it can survive tests. Many people prefer tests that, if flunked, falsify a theory. Some people, following Karl Popper (1934, Chapter 1), insist that theories are tested only by attempting to falsify them. Confirmations do not count because, among other reasons, confirming cases may be offered as proof while consciously or not cases likely to confound the theory are avoided. This difficulty, I suggest later, is lessened by choosing hard cases—situations, for example, in which parties have strong reasons to behave contrary to the predictions of one's theory. Confirmations are also rejected because numerous tests that appear to confirm a theory are negated by one falsifying instance. The conception of theory, however, opens the possibility of devising tests that confirm. If a theory depicts a domain, and displays its organization and the connections among its parts, then we can compare features of the observed domain with the picture the theory has limned (cf. Harris 1970). We can ask whether expected behaviors and outcomes are repeatedly found where the conditions contemplated by the theory obtain.

Structural theories, moreover, gain plausibility if similarities of behavior are observed across realms that are different in substance but similar in structure, and if differences of behavior are observed where realms are similar in substance but different in structure. This special advantage is

won: International-political theory gains credibility from the confirmation of certain theories in economics, sociology, anthropology, and other such nonpolitical fields.

Testing theories, of course, always means inferring expectations, or hypotheses, from them and testing those expectations. Testing theories is a difficult and subtle task, made so by the interdependence of fact and theory, by the elusive relation between reality and theory as an instrument for its apprehension. Questions of truth and falsity are somehow involved, but so are questions of usefulness and uselessness. In the end, one sticks with the theory that reveals most, even if its validity is suspect. I shall say more about the acceptance and rejection of theories elsewhere. Here I say only enough to make the relevance of a few examples of theory testing clear. Others can then easily be thought of. Many are provided in the first part of this chapter and in all parts of the next three, although I have not always labeled them as tests or put them in testable form.

Tests are easy to think up, once one has a theory to test, but they are hard to carry through. Given the difficulty of testing any theory, and the added difficulty of testing theories in such nonexperimental fields as international politics, we should exploit all of the ways of testing I have mentioned—by trying to falsify, by devising hard confirmatory tests, by comparing features of the real and the theoretical worlds, by comparing behaviors in realms of similar and of different structure. Any good theory raises many expectations. Multiplying hypotheses and varying tests are all the more important because the results of testing theories are necessarily problematic. That a single hypothesis appears to hold true may not be very impressive. A theory becomes plausible if many hypotheses inferred from it are successfully subjected to tests.

Knowing a little bit more about testing, we can now ask whether expectations drawn from our theory can survive subjection to tests. What will some of the expectations be? Two that are closely related arise in the above discussion. According to the theory, balances of power recurrently form, and states tend to emulate the successful policies of others. Can these expectations be subjected to tests? In principle, the answer is "yes." Within a given arena and over a number of years, we should find the military power of weaker and smaller states or groupings of states growing more rapidly, or shrinking more slowly, than that of stronger and larger ones. And we should find widespread imitation among competing states. In practice, to check such expectations against historical observations is difficult.

Two problems are paramount. First, though balance-of-power theory offers some predictions, the predictions are indeterminate. Because only a loosely defined and inconstant condition of balance is predicted, it is difficult to say that any given distribution of power falsifies the theory. The theory, moreover, does not lead one to expect that emulation among states will proceed to the point where competitors become identical. What will be imitated, and how quickly and closely? Because the theory does not give precise answers, falsification again is difficult. Second, although states may be disposed to react to international constraints and incentives in accordance with the theory's expectations, the policies and actions of states are also shaped by their internal conditions. The failure of balances to form, and the failure of some states to conform to the successful practices of other states, can too easily be explained away by pointing to effects produced by forces that lie outside of the theory's purview.

In the absence of theoretical refinements that fix expectations with certainty and in detail, what can we do? As I have just suggested * * * we should make tests ever more difficult. If we observe outcomes that the theory leads us to expect even though strong forces work against them, the theory will begin to command belief. To confirm the theory one should not look mainly to the eighteenth-century heyday of the balance of power when great powers in convenient numbers interacted and were presumably able to adjust to a shifting distribution of power by changing partners with a grace made possible by the absence of ideological and other cleavages. Instead, one should seek confir-

mation through observation of difficult cases. One should, for example, look for instances of states allying, in accordance with the expectations the theory gives rise to, even though they have strong reasons not to cooperate with one another. * * * One should, for example, look for instances of states making internal efforts to strengthen themselves, however distasteful or difficult such efforts might be. The United States and the Soviet Union following World War II provide such instances: the United States by rearming despite having demonstrated a strong wish not to by dismantling the most powerful military machine the world had ever known; the Soviet Union by maintaining about three million men under arms while striving to acquire a costly new military technology despite the terrible destruction she had suffered in war.

These examples tend to confirm the theory. We find states forming balances of power whether or not they wish to. They also show the difficulties of testing. Germany and Austria-Hungary formed their Dual Alliance in 1879. Since detailed inferences cannot be drawn from the theory, we cannot say just when other states are expected to counter this move. France and Russia waited until 1894. Does this show the theory false by suggesting that states may or may not be brought into balance? We should neither quickly conclude that it does nor lightly chalk the delayed response off to "friction." Instead, we should examine diplomacy and policy in the 15-year interval to see whether the theory serves to explain and broadly predict the actions and reactions of states and to see whether the delay is out of accord with the theory. Careful judgment is needed. For this, historians' accounts serve better than the historical summary I might provide.

The theory leads us to expect states to behave in ways that result in balances forming. To infer that expectation from the theory is not impressive if balancing is a universal pattern of political behavior, as is sometimes claimed. It is not. Whether political actors balance each other or climb on the bandwagon depends on the system's structure. Political parties, when choosing their presidential candidates, dramatically illustrate both points. When nomination time approaches and no one is established as the party's strong favorite, a number of would-be leaders contend. Some of them form coalitions to check the progress of others. The maneuvering and balancing of would-be leaders when the party lacks one is like the external behavior of states. But this is the pattern only during the leaderless period. As soon as someone looks like the winner, nearly all jump on the bandwagon rather than continuing to build coalitions intended to prevent anyone from winning the prize of power. Bandwagoning, not balancing, becomes the characteristic behavior.[5]

Bandwagoning and balancing behavior are in sharp contrast. Internally, losing candidates throw in their lots with the winner. Everyone wants someone to win; the members of a party want a leader established even while they disagree on who it should be. In a competition for the position of leader, bandwagoning is sensible behavior where gains are possible even for the losers and where losing does not place their security in jeopardy. Externally, states work harder to increase their own strength, or they combine with others, if they are falling behind. In a competition for the position of leader, balancing is sensible behavior where the victory of one coalition over another leaves weaker members of the winning coalition at the mercy of the stronger ones. Nobody wants anyone else to win; none of the great powers wants one of their number to emerge as the leader.

If two coalitions form and one of them weakens, perhaps because of the political disorder of a member, we expect the extent of the other coalition's military preparation to slacken or its unity to lessen. The classic example of the latter effect is the breaking apart of a war-winning coalition in or just after the moment of victory. We do not expect the strong to combine with the strong in order to increase the extent of their power over others, but rather to square off and look for allies who might help them. In anarchy, security is the highest end. Only if survival is assured can states safely seek such other goals as tranquility, profit, and power. Because power is a means and not an end, states prefer to join the weaker of two coalitions. They cannot let power, a possibly useful means, become

the end they pursue. The goal the system encourages them to seek is security. Increased power may or may not serve that end. Given two coalitions, for example, the greater success of one in drawing members to it may tempt the other to risk preventive war, hoping for victory through surprise before disparities widen. If states wished to maximize power, they would join the stronger side, and we would see not balances forming but a world hegemony forged. This does not happen because balancing, not bandwagoning, is the behavior induced by the system. The first concern of states is not to maximize power but to maintain their positions in the system.

Secondary states, if they are free to choose, flock to the weaker side; for it is the stronger side that threatens them. On the weaker side, they are both more appreciated and safer, provided, of course, that the coalition they join achieves enough defensive or deterrent strength to dissuade adversaries from attacking. Thus Thucydides records that in the Peloponnesian War the lesser city states of Greece cast the stronger Athens as the tyrant and the weaker Sparta as their liberator (circa 400 B.C., Book v, Chapter 17). According to Werner Jaeger, Thucydides thought this "perfectly natural in the circumstances," but saw "that the parts of tyrant and liberator did not correspond with any permanent moral quality in these states but were simply masks which would one day be interchanged to the astonishment of the beholder when the balance of power was altered" (1939, I, 397). This shows a nice sense of how the placement of states affects their behavior and even colors their characters. It also supports the proposition that states balance power rather than maximize it. States can seldom afford to make maximizing power their goal. International politics is too serious a business for that.

The theory depicts international politics as a competitive realm. Do states develop the characteristics that competitors are expected to display? The question poses another test for the theory. The fate of each state depends on its responses to what other states do. The possibility that conflict will be conducted by force leads to competition in the arts and the instruments of force. Competition produces a tendency toward the sameness of the competitors. Thus Bismarck's startling victories over Austria in 1866 and over France in 1870 quickly led the major continental powers (and Japan) to imitate the Prussian military staff system, and the failure of Britain and the United States to follow the pattern simply indicated that they were outside the immediate arena of competition. Contending states imitate the military innovations contrived by the country of greatest capability and ingenuity. And so the weapons of major contenders, and even their strategies, begin to look much the same all over the world. Thus at the turn of the century Admiral Alfred von Tirpitz argued successfully for building a battleship fleet on the grounds that Germany could challenge Britain at sea only with a naval doctrine and weapons similar to hers (Art 1973, p. 16).

The effects of competition are not confined narrowly to the military realm. Socialization to the system should also occur. Does it? Again, because we can almost always find confirming examples if we look hard, we try to find cases that are unlikely to lend credence to the theory. One should look for instances of states conforming to common international practices even though for internal reasons they would prefer not to. The behavior of the Soviet Union in its early years is one such instance. The Bolsheviks in the early years of their power preached international revolution and flouted the conventions of diplomacy. They were saying, in effect, "we will not be socialized to this system." The attitude was well expressed by Trotsky, who, when asked what he would do as foreign minister, replied, "I will issue some revolutionary proclamations to the peoples and then close up the joint" (quoted in Von Laue 1963, p. 235). In a competitive arena, however, one party may need the assistance of others. Refusal to play the political game may risk one's own destruction. The pressures of competition were rapidly felt and reflected in the Soviet Union's diplomacy. Thus Lenin, sending foreign minister Chicherin to the Genoa Conference of 1922, bade him farewell with this caution: "Avoid big words" (quoted in Moore 1950,

p. 204). Chicherin, who personified the carefully tailored traditional diplomat rather than the simply uniformed revolutionary, was to refrain from inflammatory rhetoric for the sake of working deals. These he successfully completed with that other pariah power and ideological enemy, Germany.

The close juxtaposition of states promotes their sameness through the disadvantages that arise from a failure to conform to successful practices. It is this "sameness," an effect of the system, that is so often attributed to the acceptance of so-called rules of state behavior. Chiliastic rulers occasionally come to power. In power, most of them quickly change their ways. They can refuse to do so, and yet hope to survive, only if they rule countries little affected by the competition of states. The socialization of nonconformist states proceeds at a pace that is set by the extent of their involvement in the system. And that is another testable statement.

The theory leads to many expectations about behaviors and outcomes. From the theory, one predicts that states will engage in balancing behavior, whether or not balanced power is the end of their acts. From the theory, one predicts a strong tendency toward balance in the system. The expectation is not that a balance, once achieved, will be maintained, but that a balance, once disrupted, will be restored in one way or another. Balances of power recurrently form. Since the theory depicts international politics as a competitive system, one predicts more specifically that states will display characteristics common to competitors: namely, that they will imitate each other and become socialized to their system. In this chapter, I have suggested ways of making these propositions more specific and concrete so as to test them. * * *

NOTES

1. Smith should know better. Translated into terms that he has himself so effectively used, to say that states are sovereign is to say that they are segments of a plural society (1966, p. 122; cf. 1956).

2. Put differently, states face a "prisoners' dilemma." If each of two parties follows his own interest, both end up worse off than if each acted to achieve joint interests. For thorough examination of the logic of such situations, see Snyder and Diesing 1977; for brief and suggestive international applications, see Jervis, January 1978.

3. Along with the explication of balance-of-power theory in the pages that follow, the reader may wish to consult a historical study of balance-of-power politics in practice. The best brief work is Wight (1973).

4. Looking at states over a wide span of time and space. Dowty concludes that in no case were shifts in alliances produced "by considerations of an overall balance of power" (1969, p. 95).

5. Stephen Van Evera suggested using "bandwagoning" to serve as the opposite of "balancing."

BIBLIOGRAPHY

Art, Robert J. (1973). "The influence of foreign policy on seapower: new weapons and Weltpolitik in Wilhelminian Germany." *Sage Professional Paper in International Studies*, vol. 2. Beverly Hills: Sage Publications.

Dowty, Alan (1969). "Conflict in war potential politics: an approach to historical macroanalysis." *Peace Research Society Papers*, vol. 13.

Durkheim, Emile (1893). *The Division of Labor in Society*. Translated by George Simpson, 1933. New York: Free Press, 1964.

Fellner, William (1949). *Competition among the Few*. New York: Knopf.

Fox, William T. R. (1959). "The uses of international relations theory." In Fox (ed.), *Theoretical Aspects of International Relations*. Notre Dame: University of Notre Dame Press.

Haas, Ernst B. (July 1953). "The balance of power: prescription, concept, or propaganda?" *World Politics*, vol. 5.

Harris, Errol E. (1970). *Hypothesis and Perception*. London: Allen and Unwin.

Hume, David (1742). "Of the balance of power." In Charles W. Hendel (ed.), *David Hume's Political Essays*. Indianapolis: Bobbs-Merrill, 1953.

Jaeger, Werner (1939). *Paideia: The Ideals of Greek Culture*, vol. 1. Translated from the second German edition by Gilbert Highet. New York: Oxford University Press.

Jervis, Robert (January 1978). "Cooperation under the security dilemma." *World Politics*, vol. 30.

Kahn, Alfred E. (1966). "The tyranny of small decisions: market failures, imperfections, and the limits of econometrics." In Bruce M. Russett (ed.), *Economic Theories of International Relations*. Chicago: Markham, 1968.

Katona, George (September 1953). "Rational behavior and economic behavior." *Psychological Review*, vol. 60.

Kindleberger, Charles P. (1969). *American Business Abroad*. New Haven: Yale University Press.

Livernash, E. R. (1963). "The relation of power to the structure and process of collective bargaining." In Bruce M. Russett (ed.), *Economic Theories of International Politics*. Chicago: Markham, 1968.

Martineau, Harriet (1853). *The Positive Philosophy of Auguste Comte: Freely Translated and Condensed*, 3rd ed., vol. 2. London: Kegan Paul, Trench, Trubner, 1893.

Moore, Barrington, Jr. (1950). *Soviet Politics: The Dilemma of Power*. Cambridge: Harvard University Press.

Morgenthau, Hans J. (1973). *Politics Among Nations*, 5th ed. New York: Knopf.

Nadel, S. F. (1957). *The Theory of Social Structure*. Glencoe, Ill.: Free Press.

Popper, Karl (1934). *The Logic of Scientific Discovery*. New York: Basic Books, 1959.

Shubik, Martin (1959). *Strategy and Market Structure*. New York: Wiley.

Smith, M. G. (July–December 1956). "On segmentary lineage systems." *Journal of the Royal Anthropological Institute of Great Britain and Ireland*, vol. 86.

———(1966). "A structural approach to comparative politics." In David Easton (ed.), *Varieties* of *Political Theories*. Englewood Cliffs, N.J.: Prentice-Hall.

Snyder, Glenn H. and Paul Diesing (1977). *Conflict among Nations*. Princeton: Princeton University Press.

Sterling, Richard W. (1974). *Macropolitics: International Relations in a Global Society*. New York: Knopf.

Thucydides (c. 400 B.C.). *History of the Peloponnesian War*. Translated by Crawley. New York: Modern Library, Random House, 1951.

Von Laue, Theodore H. (1963). "Soviet diplomacy: G. V. Chicherin, People's Commissar for Foreign Affairs 1918–1930." In Gordon A. Craig and Felix Gilbert (eds.), *The Diplomats 1919–1939*, vol. 1. New York: Atheneum.

Wight, Martin (1966). "The balance of power." In H. Butterfield and Martin Wight (eds.), *Diplomatic Investigations: Essays in the Theory of International Politics*. London: Allen and Unwin.

———(1973). "The balance of power and international order." In Alan James (ed.), *The Bases of International Order*. London: Oxford University Press.

JOHN GERARD RUGGIE

What Makes the World Hang Together? Neo-utilitarianism and the Social Constructivist Challenge

Edward Teller, the nuclear physicist, used to draw overflow crowds to his "physics for poets" course at Berkeley, despite his hawkish views on military matters and unwavering conservative politics. Through a thick Hungarian accent he would announce at the outset: "I will show you what makes the world hang together." And he did just that.

An analogous puzzle has defined my research interests from the start: what makes the world hang together in the international relations sense? Like every IR student of my generation I read, and greatly admired, Kenneth Waltz's classic, *Man, the State, and War*, and understood, as a result, the fundamental force of anarchy, the stag and hare parable, the central role of power and interests. In the stag hunt, as is well known, five individuals agree to cooperate in order to trap a stag but when a hare appears one of the five snags it, satisfies his own hunger, and leaves the other four with nothing but food for thought in return for their folly of trusting one another (Waltz 1959: 167ff.). What can break through this logic of anarchy? Only a superior force, Waltz stated then and elaborated later (1979): a hierarchy of formal authority, which he viewed virtually inconceivable at the international level, or power heavily concentrated in the hands of a few who were both able and willing to override the collective action problems that inhere in anarchy. Amid a delicately poised balance of nuclear terror that seemed, perversely, to deter major-power war, Waltz's argument had a certain, albeit dismal, attraction.

From John Gerard Ruggie, introduction to *Constructing the World Polity: Essays on International Institutionalization* (New York: Routledge, 1998). The author's notes have been omitted.

If Waltz was the leading realist theorist of his day, Ernst Haas was his counterpart on the liberal institutionalist side of the discipline. Haas once quipped about the stag hunt in a graduate seminar: "Those five guys weren't leaders of modern welfare states." His point was that the very fact of the welfare state propels its leaders to cooperate with one another to a greater extent than previous sociopolitical forms did if doing so is necessary to satisfy the everyday needs and demands of their domestic constituents. Haas went on to predict not only more extensive international cooperation than Waltz did but, in the case of Western Europe, economic and even political unification (E. Haas 1958). Whatever else has changed in the discipline since then, these core elements of realism and liberalism endure.

My point of entry into the debate was through a small analytical space these intellectual giants left vacant between them. The question—What makes the world hang together?—deserved a more general answer, I felt, than one that relied on the impact of the welfare state. Furthermore, economic and political unification struck me to be a limiting and perhaps even singular case, not fully representative of broader international processes. At the same time, key features of the stag hunt troubled me deeply: the five individuals just happened upon one another; they did not seem to belong to any organized social collectivity or have any ongoing social relations with each other or anyone else. They had only a rudimentary ability to speak. And they knew that they would go their separate ways again—where to?—once the project of trapping the stag was accomplished (or not, as it turned out). This, it seemed to me, was an unduly and unnecessarily undersocialized view of the world.

* * * International relations, like all social relations, exhibit *some* degree of institutionalization: at minimum, a mutual intelligibility of behavior together with the communicative mechanisms and organizational routines which make that possible. As a rule, international institutionalization is likely to fall far short of integrating the separate units even over the long term, but in real life it will rarely be as low as in the stag hunt. Moreover, institutionalization by definition transforms behavior by channeling it in one direction as opposed to all others that are theoretically possible, although how strong or weak a force it will be in any particular instance is an open, empirical question.

Institutionalization in the international polity takes place on at least two levels. The first is among states as we know them today and comprises the realm of international organization, broadly defined. What are the forms whereby relations among states are institutionalized? What are their determinants and consequences? The second level is the very system of states: that is, the system of states itself constitutes a form of institutionalizing political relations on the planet. How did it get here? What factors sustain it? In what manner and toward what new forms might it be transforming?

*   *   *

* * * Since 1980 or so, realism and liberalism have both produced "neo" variants: neorealism and neoliberal institutionalism (see Baldwin 1993 for an overview). Between them, they now occupy center stage. Over time, they have drawn increasingly close to one another. Indeed, Robert Keohane, a leading figure in neoliberal institutionalism, states that this approach "borrows as much from realism as from liberalism" (1993: 272). But the similarity goes beyond cross-fertilization. Most significantly, they share a view of the world of international relations in utilitarian terms: an atomistic universe of self-regarding units whose identity is assumed given and fixed, and who are responsive largely if not solely to material interests that are stipulated by assumption. The two bodies of theory do differ on the extent to which they believe institutions (and by extension institutionalization) to play a significant role in international relations, with neoliberalism being the more expansive in this regard. But they are alike in depicting institutions in strictly instrumental terms, useful (or not) in the pursuit of individual and typically material interests. Hence, I will refer to theorizing based on these premises as neo-utilitarianism. This approach has produced interesting analytical results, some of which have been subjected to empirical tests. But it also has blind spots and silences.

* * * [My] approach [is m]ore sociological in orientation; it has come to be known as social constructivism. Though I was only dimly aware of it at the time, my constructivist turn precedes neorealism and neoliberalism (see 1975). But since the 1980s my thinking has developed in continuous dialogue with their main premises. * * * At bottom, social constructivism seeks to account for what neo-utilitarianism assumes: the identity and/or interests of actors. It views international politics on the basis of a more "relational ontology," in Carol Gilligan's term (1993: 25–38), than the atomistic framing of neo-utilitarianism. In addition, it attributes to ideational factors, including culture, norms, and ideas, social efficacy over and above any functional utility they may have, including a role in shaping the way in which actors define their identity and interests in the first place (Wendt 1994, 1995; Katzenstein 1996b). Finally, it allows for agency—actors doing things—to be not simply the enactment of preprogrammed scripts, as in neo-utilitarianism, but also reflective acts of social creation, within structured constraints to be sure.

In short, even as one disciplinary debate has narrowed in scope and diminished in intensity, another has begun. The latter is the focus of this chapter. The first section briefly summarizes the immediate antecedents to and the distinguishing features of neorealism and neoliberal institutionalism, and notes how they have converged on neo-utilitarian premises. The second section introduces social constructivism indirectly by discussing some of the key limitations of neo-utilitarianism that social constructivism seeks to avoid or overcome, and by summarizing constructivist efforts to do so. Section three presents a more synoptic sketch of the social constructivist project in international relations today. Finally, the fourth section takes up the issue of paradigmatic (ir)reconcilability, not only between neo-utilitarianism and social constructivism but also among the several subspecies of constructivism itself, the aim being not to vindicate one or another theoretical approach but to deepen our collective understanding of what each has to offer.

The Convergence of the Neos

This section summarizes briefly how postwar realism and liberalism in international relations theory evolved toward their respective "neo" variants and, despite the differences that remain, converged on a common neo-utilitarian analytical foundation.

REALISM AND LIBERALISM

Among pundits, commentators, and academic specialists, the heavy guns in postwar America belonged to the realists: George Kennan, Walter Lippmann, Hans Morgenthau, Reinhold Niebuhr, and later, Arnold Wolfers, Kenneth Waltz, as well as Henry Kissinger—though the last never enjoyed the reputation as a scholar that he was accorded in policy circles. Morgenthau was the academic grandmaster, and *Politics Among Nations*, first published in 1948, the canon. In Morgenthau's pithy phrase, international politics was all about "interest defined as power" (1985: 5). That is to say, whatever the ends that leaders may seek to achieve, their doing so is mediated and constrained by all states deploying their power to pursue their own ends, so that power itself becomes the proximate interest of any state's foreign policy.

Notwithstanding Morgenthau's emphasis on power as the driving force, he saw the world of international politics in socially textured terms. For example, he differentiated between the classical European balance of power, which had existed "under the common roof of shared values and universal standards of action," and the "new," more "mechanical," balance of power which emerged between the United States and the Soviet Union after World War II (1985: 358–359, 388–391; also see Little 1989). And he felt that the latter posed a greater danger due to this difference. Moreover, although he rejected the idea that the international system could rest on law and organization, as prewar idealists hoped, *Politics Among Nations* includes serious discussions of both. Similarly, Inis Claude, who wrote the definitive critique of the idea of collective security (1956), also ascribed to international organizations a non-trivial role in collectively (de)legitimating states' use of force (1966).

Initially, there were no comparable contenders on the liberal side. What the horrors of the Holocaust, World War II, and the outbreak of the cold war created on the ground, E. H. Carr's classic polemic, *The Twenty Years' Crisis* (1946), achieved in the realm of theory: pulverizing the utopian streak in liberal internationalism, which momentarily disoriented and discredited liberal international relations theory more generally. The first new serious social scientific form of liberalism took these new facts of life for granted and, indeed, looked to the rubble and ashes of postwar Western Europe as its point of departure. It went by the name of neofunctionalism, focused on regional and later global integration, and was associated with Ernst Haas and his colleagues (see, for example, Haas 1958, 1961, 1964).

Haas expended little energy quarreling with realism as a description of the historical status quo; but he explored the question of whether it always had to be so. He drew on several strands of the liberal tradition in devising his analytical apparatus: republican liberalism, in the sense of stipulating that a pluralistic polity was a precondition for integration; the liberalism of the welfare state, which raised the salience of domestic economic and social issues in the calculus of decision makers; commercial liberalism, in that trade and other forms of cooperation were one vehicle for achieving domestic welfare aims; and what Joseph Nye (1988) calls sociological liberalism, or the growing and increasingly institutionalized transnational ties and coalitions among governments and actors in civil society, through which integrative politics is played out. Western Europe was the perfect laboratory for the new theory. Neofunctionalists were no more surprised than realists by the defeat of the Pleven plan, which would have established a European Defense Community. Their bets were on the Schuman plan, a more indirect, more gradual, and hence less threatening, step-by-step process toward integration, beginning with the declining coal and steel sectors—an approach associated philosophically with David Mitrany

(1943) and in practice with Jean Monnet (Duchene 1994).

Neofunctionalism did not travel well beyond Western Europe, nor to the global level. Indeed, even within Europe, Haas (1976) came to feel, the theory failed to capture key elements of the integration process, which turned out to be more direct and more politically driven than the circuitous and largely technocratic mechanisms he had specified. As a result, he turned his attention to the study of international interdependence and regimes.

The transition essay between the integration and interdependence literatures was written by Robert Keohane and Joseph Nye (1975), who then went on to produce liberalism's core text for the next decade: *Power and Interdependence* (1977). In it, they ceded to realism primary explanatory efficacy for situations in which power is readily and at relatively low costs translated into pursuing desired outcomes. But they also stipulated several other situations—of power not being easily fungible across issue areas; being conferred or constrained by organizationally specific factors, as in international regimes; or having limited utility due to the high costs of disrupting a relationship—wherein realism, they argued, progressively loses its bite. Insofar as they believed international relations to be increasingly characterized by the condition they described as complex interdependence, they concluded that the future explanatory utility of realism was likely to be more circumscribed than in the past.

In short, the relationship between realism and liberalism had been specifically engaged, and the difference between the two hinged on judgments concerning the utility of force and institutionalized constraints on power.

NEOREALISM AND NEOLIBERAL INSTITUTIONALISM

Rarely has a book so influenced a field of study as Kenneth Waltz's *Theory of International Politics* (1979)—neorealism's foundational text. The model * * * goes like this: the international system is characterized by the structural condition of anarchy, defined as the absence of central rule. As a result, states, the wielders of the ultimate arbiter of force, are its constitutive units. The desire of these units, at a minimum, to survive is assumed. And because no one can be counted on to protect anyone else, all are obliged to fend for themselves as best they can or must. Their doing so triggers corresponding efforts by similarly motivated others. Hence, the tendency to balance power is an inherent by-product of self-help. And the distribution of capabilities among states, therefore, is the most important determinant of outcomes—including the very interdependence that liberalism has viewed as an independent variable, with multipolar systems said to exhibit a higher level of interdependence among the major powers than bipolarity.

Waltz's model is almost entirely indeterminate; it directly predicts little more than that tendencies toward balancing will recur and that the system of states will reproduce itself. Numerous refinements have been made to the basic model by analysts sympathetic to its core premises, often supplementing its sparse formulations with additional factors that have yielded new insights: states do not balance power as raw capabilities so much as the powers that threaten them (Walt 1987); military doctrines reflect and, in turn, affect the degree to which potential adversaries view each other as threats (Jervis 1978; Van Evera 1984; Posen 1984; Snyder 1984); states not only balance but also bandwagon (Walt 1987; Schweller 1994) and "pass the buck" (Christensen and Snyder 1990) or "hide" by seeking neutrality (Schroeder 1994); and so on. Other analysts have extended the model to economic relations, arguing that the desire for relative gains that anarchy imposes limits cooperation even in non-military issue areas like international trade (Grieco 1988, 1990). Lastly, the only institutions that neorealists deem worthy of serious consideration are traditional alliances; otherwise, institutions are viewed as mere emanations of state power, such as the major international economic institutions (Gilpin 1975; Krasner 1978), or as window dressing (Mearsheimer 1995).

Waltz self-consciously distanced himself from classical realism in two critical respects; hence the prefix "neo." First, the earlier generation of realists in varying degrees had based their theory of international politics on some understanding of human nature, most dramatically in the case of Niebuhr's Christian realism, but also Morgenthau's "will to power" (1946). In contrast, Waltz delivered on the premise and promise of his earlier theoretical inquiry (1959): neither man nor the state ultimately accounts for war or any other recurrent outcome in international politics; the structure of anarchy and its effects do. Similarly, Waltz shed all aspects of the "social texture" of international politics, as I termed it above, including "the common roof of shared values" under which Morgenthau contended traditional European power politics had been conducted. Waltz's model was strictly third image (that is, systemic) in orientation, and strictly physicalist in character.

Second, whereas classical realism tended to mix first principles with historical observation and prudential judgment, Waltz explicitly adopted a hypothetico-deductive approach to formulating theory and the "covering law" protocol of explanation that is characteristic of the natural sciences and economics (1979: chap. 1). Indeed, Waltz's model *is* the microeconomic model of the formation of markets transposed into the international political realm. The international system, he stipulated, is individualist in origin, more or less spontaneously generated as a by-product of the actions of its constituent units, "whose aims and efforts are directed not toward creating an order but rather toward fulfilling their own internally defined interests by whatever means they can muster" (1979: 90). Likewise, just as "market structure is defined by counting firms, international-political structure [is defined] by counting states. In the counting, distinctions are made only according to capabilities" (ibid.: 98–99). From that analytical base, Waltz derives some generic features of the international system, and he specifies the key differences between multipolar (oligopolistic) and bipolar (duopolistic) competition.

Finally, Waltz's turn to microeconomics provided a methodologically compatible depiction of the international system for game theoretic models of nuclear deterrence and other aspects of military strategy that dated back to the pioneering work of Thomas Schelling (1960, 1966).

The liberal institutionalist research program was moving in a similar direction. Interestingly, Robert Keohane, who had challenged realism's "state centrism" in the early 1970s (Keohane and Nye 1972) and sought to bracket the utility of force under conditions of complex interdependence in the late 1970s (Keohane and Nye 1977), was among the leading movers (1983, 1984). He now ceded to realism even more than he had before: states are the principal actors in international politics; they are driven by their conceptions of self-interests; a system of self-help prevails; and relative capabilities "remain important" (Keohane 1993: 271). But, he maintained, "*where common interests exist* realism is too pessimistic about the prospects for cooperation and the role of institutions" (ibid.: 277, italics in original). Here the continuity with liberal institutionalisms past is evident; the rest is "neo."

Where Waltz had looked to the microeconomic theory of markets, neoliberal institutionalists were drawn to corresponding theories of the firm, or industrial organization more generally. From Oliver Williamson (1975) came the core insight that "hierarchies" at the margin were often more efficient than "markets" by, for example, reducing transaction costs. Thus, in a pioneering work on international regimes, Keohane (1984) sought to specify the conditions under which and the manner whereby regimes may facilitate agreements among states by reducing transaction costs and producing reliable information about one another's intentions and behavior, relative to states "purchasing" those services in the political market place. And in an important paper written jointly with Robert Axelrod (Axelrod and Keohane 1985), game theory provided the analytical means of specifying when and how institutions may play roles in enhancing cooperation among states by reducing the incentives for defecting from agreements and compensating those who cooperate if others defect.

A mini-avalanche of analytical work followed on these and related issues: the problem of credible commitments, signaling, forms of contracting, shirking, monitoring, enforcement, and the like—in which institutions may be "functional" in the sense of enabling states to achieve benefits that would otherwise elude them. The substantive topics explored through this analytical perspective include international economic regimes (Keohane 1984), patterns of national economic adjustment to international changes (Simmons 1994), central bank cooperation (Simmons 1996), economic sanctions (Martin 1992), colonialism (Frieden 1994), European integration (Garrett 1993; Garrett and Weingast 1993), and environmental protection (P. Haas, Keohane, and Levy 1993), among others. Incursions have also been made into the institutional dimension of military alliances (Duffield 1992, 1994/95; Wallander and Keohane 1995)—which had been a site of microeconomic modeling thirty years earlier (Russett 1968).

In the past, international relations theory was often criticized for being non-cumulative, consisting of one fad after another (see, for example, Strange 1982). Neither neorealism nor neoliberal institutionalism can be dismissed in those terms: they are serious research programs. Each is cumulative and, as we have seen, analytically the two have moved in ever-closer proximity to one another. I now turn to the basis of that proximity.

NEO-UTILITARIANISM

Neorealism and neoliberal institutionalism have been able to converge to the extent that they have because they now share very similar analytical foundations. Both take the existence of international anarchy for granted, though they may differ as to its precise causal force. Both stipulate that states are the primary actors in international politics. Both stipulate further that the identities and interests of states are given, a priori and exogenously—that is to say, external to and unexplained within the terms of their theories. On that basis, both assume that states are rational actors maximizing their own expected utilities, defined in such material terms as power, security, and welfare. And both *must* make assumptions of this sort for their hypothetico-deductive mode of theorizing to work; there is no other way to do that. From this starting point, both go on to explain patterns of interaction as the result of states, so conceived, using their capabilities to act on their preferences.

Analytical differences do remain between these two bodies of theory. Stephen Krasner describes the most significant (1997: 16): "for neorealism the basic issues are survival and distributional conflict while for neoliberalism they involve the resolution of market failures." What Krasner means is that neorealists and neoliberals are likely to stress two different effects of anarchy. Neorealists are likely to focus on the fact that the potential use of force is ever present in international relations and affects the calculus of states; for the same reason, states are obliged to worry about not only how much they gain from cooperation in absolute terms, but also how much they gain relative to others, who may become tomorrow's foe (see Grieco 1988 on this latter point). Neoliberals, on the other hand, are more likely to explore the impediments that anarchy poses to states' reaching and keeping agreements even where common interests to cooperate exist, which may reduce potential benefits all around unless means can be devised to overcome these institutional defects.

But there has been some ambiguity about whether these are differences in emphasis or kind. Grieco originally (1988, 1990) held to the latter position, arguing that in the neorealist world states do not seek to maximize absolute but relative gains, and that they are, therefore, positional, not atomistic in character. Snidal (1991) provided interesting analytical results suggesting that the relative gains issue may be exaggerated, especially beyond dyadic relations. Powell (1991, 1994) pointed out that posing the relative gains issue in terms of preferences, as Grieco (and Waltz before him) had done, implies that different types of units are assumed to exist in the two bodies of theory—one driven by absolute gains, the other by relative—which limits the comparability of the

theories' results. He suggested instead that the difference be recast in terms of the strategic contexts that like units face (Is the use of force plausible, and can the potential of its future use be plausibly attributed to relative gains?). In the end, Keohane (1993) conceded that he may have underestimated the problem of relative gains, Grieco (1993) that he may have overstated it, and both agreed that the units are, indeed, similar and that the impact of relative gains is conditional.

A second difference concerns the role of institutions. Although he is sometimes characterized as a "hyper-realist," John Mearsheimer accurately reflects the neorealist position on this question: "The most powerful states in the system create and shape institutions so that they can maintain their share of world power, or even increase it." Internationally, outcomes are "mainly a function of the balance of power," and institutions at best are "intervening variables" (1994/95: 13). Other neorealists, notably Krasner (1983), have long allowed for "stickiness" of institutional arrangements, however, whereby they continue to function along their original paths even after power relations shift, or even take new departures, so long as they do not drift too far out of line of the underlying power-based structure.

Neoliberalism assigns greater scope to institutions, but their scope is similarly functionally determined—by political market failures, in this case, rather than power relations. As Blyth puts it (1997), "as a result of the 'discovery' that hierarchies at the margin were often more efficient than market exchange, it became possible to describe the existence of institutions in terms of their ability to either reduce or exacerbate transaction costs [or attenuate strategic dilemmas]. Consequently, information, enforcement and monitoring emerge as the central concerns of [neoliberal institutionalism] in the model of institutions they employ." This perspective leads to significantly different empirical expectations (see Keohane and Martin 1995, in response to Mearsheimer 1994/95), but the structure of the two arguments is very similar.

That, in brief, is the current state of the debate. Its tenor is barely a faint echo of the titanic intellectual and moral struggles between realism and liberalism down the centuries—Machiavelli or Hobbes versus Kant, for instance. This is so even if we take as our baseline the post-World War II academic literature, as I have done in this discussion. Convergence has been made possible, as noted, by the similar, neo-utilitarian analytical basis on which the two bodies of theory now rest. Neorealism and neoliberal institutionalism, in David Baldwin's words (1993: 3), "engage one another's arguments directly and [this] results in a more focused and productive debate." Baldwin is right up to a point: not only the debate, but also the empirical research programs based on the two theories, have been productive. But Baldwin is right *only* up to a point, because this productivity has been purchased at a price: by neglecting or misspecifying aspects of international relations that do not fit readily within the two theories' increasingly narrow analytical frame. If it can be shown that important elements of international reality are poorly understood, therefore, or misunderstood, or left unattended altogether, then the cost may be too high. The belief that this is so is the major animating source of social constructivism.

The Emergence of Social Constructivism

Unlike neorealism and neoliberal institutionalism, the constructivist approach has no direct antecedent in international relations theory. To that extent, it is *sui generis*. It is true that neofunctionalism embodied many of the methodological and philosophical precepts that we now recognize to be social constructivist, but it did so largely unconsciously. The so-called English school influenced many constructivists, myself included (Butterfield and Wight 1968; James 1973; Wight 1977; Bull 1977; Bull and Watson 1984; Watson 1992; for useful surveys, see Buzan 1993; Little 1995). It holds that the system of states is embedded in a society of states, which includes sets of values, rules, and institutions that are commonly accepted by states and which make it possible for the system of states to function—the balance of power, for ex-

ample, being viewed as a deliberate institutional contrivance, valued by states because of its contribution to their liberty and to overall stability. But a major analytical objective of the English school has seemed to be to resist the influence of social scientific modes of analysis in international relations, and less to clarify and firm up its own theoretical basis. The actual label of social constructivism may not have been affixed to or by any international relations scholar prior to 1989, when it featured in an analytical study by Nicholas Onuf, *World of Our Making*—though Anthony Giddens' (1979) closely related term "structuration theory" was in use earlier (Ruggie 1983; Dessler 1989; Wendt 1987).

By and large, scholarly interest in the social constructivist approach has grown as certain analytical and empirical limitations of conventional theories have become better understood, most emphatically after their neo-utilitarian turn. Ironically, this was true even in the context of my own work. My first publication (1972) applied the microeconomic theory of collective goods to the problem of international cooperation. I was pleased with the analytical and empirical results, and even more so with having them published in the premier political science journal. But they left me with numerous puzzles that were not likely to be resolved by further work using similar analytical tools: How much, if anything, did the actors have to know about the acts the theory ascribed to them? To the extent that their knowledge was implicated, how much of it had to be mutual for things to work? Where did such mutual knowledge reside? Was it responsive to influence through discourse, or only through signaling based on material factors? Do actors ever accept the explanations of others for wrongful acts? Do social bonds form, and if so, when, where, how, and with what consequences? Come to think of it, how did the actors get here, anyway, and to acquire their current characteristics?

Questions of this sort are inescapable if one's research interests include the origins and possible transformation of the system of states, as mine do. But they were also posed by far more prosaic empirical studies on international economic regimes, where I saw numerous instances of communicative and interpretive dynamics at work. States appeared to employ tacit means for assessing (in)appropriate behavior in monetary and trade relations, for example, understanding some deviations from rules in the dual sense of being able to comprehend them and willing to acquiesce in them. Though I claim no expertise in national security policy, as a lay observer I wondered if there were not important instances there as well. For example, the innovations in nuclear strategy developed by the Kennedy administration were far more complex, and at times counterintuitive, than the "massive retaliation" they replaced—"to blow hell out of them in a hurry if they start anything," as President Eisenhower had once described that (quoted in Gaddis 1982: 150). Was it necessary for the Soviets to understand the new strategies for them to work? If so, how did the Soviets learn to do so? If not, precisely how did the strategies work—and how do we know that they did? Or was nuclear war avoided because an "existential deterrence" came to take effect? But where would such an effect "exist"? And how could one test for it?

My brilliant and supportive colleague, Robert Jervis, has long studied cognitive factors in international security relations (1970, 1976). But his many insights could not be employed directly to resolve my puzzles because they concern individual actors (for which the international analogue is individual states): they take the form of, for example, A's unilateral assessment (accurate or not) of verbal and nonverbal cues from B, which includes A's estimation of B's expectations of A; and so on.

But, in some instances that I explored, more seemed to be at work than ideational attributes of individual states. Just as collectivities of individuals within states hold intersubjective understandings that affect their behavior, so too, it seemed, do collectivities of states. In both cases these understandings appear to differ from the mere aggregation of the individual parts. Following Durkheim (1938), I termed these "social facts"—which John Searle has recently (1995) defined simply as those facts that are produced by virtue of all the relevant actors

agreeing that they exist. Social facts, so defined, include states and their collective institutional practices, my major research interest, and the likes of marriage, money, football, property, and Valentine's Day. Social facts differ from two other kinds of socially relevant facts: "brute" facts, such as warheads, population size, market shares, or mountains, which are true (or not) apart from any shared beliefs that they are true; and (ontologically) "subjective" facts, so designated because their existence depends on being experienced by individual subjects, like an individual actor's perceptions of or preferences about the world—Jervis's studies of perception and misperception deal in facts of this sort. The distinguishing feature of social constructivism is that it concerns itself with the nature, origins, and functioning of social facts, and what if any specific methodological requirements their study may entail.

In light of these interests, I left collective goods theory, initially for Berger and Luckman (1966) and the sociology of organizations; I took periodic forays into the classics of social science (above all, Durkheim and Weber); I found Giddens' work helpful (particularly 1981); and, after exploring some of the extraordinarily creative intellectual outbursts in the humanities that took place in the 1980s, I have more recently found a relatively stable philosophical footing in the work of John Searle (1984, and especially 1995).

Hence, because there is no received theory called social constructivism in international relations, I present the perspective here much as it evolved, by challenging the major limiting features of neo-utilitarianism. Below, I take up four such features, in logical order, not chronologically. Moreover, because the most common criticism of social constructivism by neo-utilitarians is that its arguments are largely metatheoretical, whereas the conventional theories are said to traffic in the empirical stuff of things, wherever possible I allow constructivism to speak through its empirical findings, insights, and concerns, becoming "philosophical" only when it is absolutely necessary for the immediate point at hand.

THE CORE ASSUMPTIONS

It is widely accepted in the social sciences that the appropriate test of a model's efficacy is how fruitful its hypotheses are, not the accuracy of its assumptions. But, in the policy sciences, we also want to be right for the right reasons. For policy *is* the manipulation of initial conditions as well as causal factors all along causal paths in the pursuit of desired ends. Here, if a model misses or distorts significant aspects of the reality it purports to represent, there are grounds for caution or corrective measures.

Neorealism and neoliberal institutionalism, as we saw above, are obliged to treat the identity and interests of their constituent actors as being exogenous and given. Some neorealists claim to "derive" state interests from the condition of anarchy, but anarchy is so slippery a concept and the things one can "derive" from it are so indeterminate (Milner 1991) that interests are, in fact, handled by assumption, notwithstanding some claims to the contrary. The power and elegance of the neo-utilitarian model rests on this point of departure. But so, too, do some of its limitations.

First, neo-utilitarianism provides no answer to the foundational question: how the constituent actors—that is, territorial states—came to acquire their current identity and the interests that are assumed to go along with it. Similarly, any potential present or future change in this identity and in corresponding interests is beyond the scope of the theory. I take up the issue of foundational transformation separately below.

Second, while it is of course true that territorial states have generic identities and interests *qua* states, neo-utilitarianism has no analytical means for dealing with the fact that the specific identities of specific states shape their perceived interests and, thereby, patterns of international outcomes. * * * [T]he world would look very different today if the Soviet Union or Nazi Germany had ended up as its hegemon after World War II. Indeed, important things would have differed even if Great Britain had done so. Accordingly, contra neorealism, I suggest that the fact of *American* hegemony

was every bit as important as the fact of American *hegemony* in shaping the post-World War II international order. And, contra neoliberal institutionalism, I note in several of the essays that the origins of none of the major postwar international institutions—the United Nations, the Bretton Woods institutions, GATT, NATO, and what became the European Union—or of the League of Nations, for that matter, can be accurately rendered in marginal utility terms, though their functioning once in existence and patterns of compliance with the rules they generate may well exhibit elements of that logic.

Counterfactuals are impossible to prove, but there is evidence to suggest that the differences in hegemonic scenarios for the post-World War II international order are the product of not only the leading states' power and/or material interests, but also their identities, which affected their definition of interests. For example, * * * internationally oriented leaders in the United States throughout this century have explicitly drawn on America's sense of exceptionalism in order to achieve and sustain US involvement in the maintenance of a stable international security order. More importantly, * * * after World War II, their doing so produced conceptions of US security interests which were both more inclusive and more extensively institutionalized—*even before the Soviet threat*—than they would have been had they merely followed the dictates of geostrategic logic. The creation of the United Nations and NATO's multilateralized security commitments, I contend, were among the effects of that conception of interests.

Likewise, the identity of the same state can change and pull its interests along. Thus, Thomas Berger (1996) argues that Germany and Japan today differ significantly from their pre-World War II predecessors. Antimilitarism, he maintains, has become integral to their sense of self as nations and is embodied in domestic norms and institutions. Peter Katzenstein (1996b) makes a similar case regarding the police and military in postwar Japan and Germany. Robert Herman (1996) describes the Gorbachev revolution in the Soviet

Union and its international aftermath in terms of identity shifts leading to a radical recalibration of interests. And Thomas Risse-Kappen (1996) suggests that a sense of collective identity within the transatlantic community of democracies specifies norms of appropriate behavior for its members. All remain aware of the possibility that these changes may not be irreversible. But Katzenstein in particular identifies the specific normative and institutional practices in Japan and Germany that any move toward reversal would have to contend with and overcome.

Third, there is growing empirical evidence that normative factors in addition to states' identities shape their interests, or their behavior directly, which neo-utilitarianism similarly does not encompass. Some of these factors are international in origin, others domestic. More research needs to be done on this set of issues, but enough is available to merit serious reflection.

On the international side, the literature that Martha Finnemore (1996b) depicts as "sociological institutionalism," revolving around the work of John Meyer and his colleagues, has documented successive waves in the diffusion of cultural norms among states that differ radically in their circumstances, but which then express identical preferences for national policies and institutional arrangements. These include constitutional forms, educational institutions, welfare policies, human rights conventions, defense ministries in states that face no threat (including navies for landlocked states)—to which Finnemore, in her own work (1996a), adds science ministries in countries that have no scientific capability. The norms diffused are those of rationalized bureaucratic structures and, more generally, standards of what it means to be a modern state, which have spread far more rapidly than the technology or markets that neo-utilitarian explanations would utilize to explain the spread. It must be acknowledged, however, that these norms are diffused from core to periphery in the international system: diffusion results from the core as well as from international organizations "teaching" states in the periphery that to be modern states means to have these things.

Finnemore has extended this research to include the emergence of norms among the core countries, such as the Geneva conventions on warfare (1996a) and the evolution of humanitarian intervention (1996c). Others have addressed normative taboos on the use of chemical weapons (Price 1995) and nuclear weapons (Price and Tannenwald 1996). In a completely different (and far more robust institutional context), Burley and Mattli (1993) show how the European Court of Justice shapes domestic legal practices within the member states of the European Union. All specify logics that depart significantly from neo-utilitarianism, even as they fully appreciate that power and interests are intimately involved in these processes.

On the domestic side, Elizabeth Kier (1995, 1996) and Alistair Johnston (1995, 1996) raise serious questions about neo-utilitarian renderings of the origins of strategic cultures and military doctrines, contending that—at least in the cases of France and China, respectively—they are not simply functionally determined either by external or internal factors, but reflect broader cultural and political considerations.

In an oft-cited remark, Waltz has said that his theory does not pretend to explain everything, but what it does explain is important (1986: 329). He is right on both counts. But the subjects addressed in the studies noted above (and others like them) are hardly unimportant either. Indeed, all are important for precisely those dependent variables that Waltz's theory claims to explain. The same point also holds, correspondingly, for neoliberal institutionalism. More empirical work in the social constructivist vein is necessary, and the origins of identities and other normative factors need to be better theorized. But it is not an undue stretch to conclude even at this point that neo-utilitarianism's assumptions that the identities and interests of states are exogenous and given—in contrast to being treated as endogenous and socially constructed—pose potentially serious distortions and omissions—even as they provide the basis on which neo-utilitarianism's theoretical pay-off rests.

IDEATIONAL CAUSATION

Neo-utilitarianism has a narrowly circumscribed view of the role of ideas in social life. But because neorealism and neoliberal institutionalism differ somewhat in this respect, I discuss them separately.

Waltz's model, as noted above, is physicalist in character. Accordingly, ideational factors make only cameo appearances in it. Take, as an example, his reference to the recurrent normative element in US foreign policy: "England claimed to bear the white man's burden; France spoke of her *mission civilisatrice*. In like spirit, we [the United States] say that we act to make and maintain world order . . . For countries at the top, this is predictable behavior" (1979: 200). And that is Waltz's *sole* reference to the role of norms. Ideational factors enter the picture again briefly in the form of socialization, one of the mechanisms by which states, according to Waltz, learn to conform to the dictates of the system (1979: 127). Numerous critics have been puzzled by the presence of socialization in a physicalist model that disclaims any sociality on the part of its actors and their interactions. But even more disturbing is the fact that Waltz, in this instance as elsewhere in *Theory*, turns what is supposed to be a methodological principle into an ontological one: Waltz has *actual states* become socialized to *his model* of the international system, not to the more variegated world of actual international relations.

Other neorealists have modestly modified Waltz's model. For example, Krasner (1978) has explored the role of ideology in North-South economic negotiations, and more recently he refers to states' "ideational interests" (1997: 3). But neither factor has been fully squared with his enduring neorealist commitments (Ruggie 1980). In addition, following the collapse of the Soviet system several neorealists discovered nationalism, which was previously black-boxed into domestic factors, said to have no role in systemic theory (Mearsheimer 1990; Posen 1993a, 1993b). However, as Lapid and Kratochwil suggest (1997: 113), their interest in nationalism is largely limited to its role as a source of conflict or in affecting the capability of existing or would-be states to wage conflicts, thus "making

it difficult to conceive of a nontautological relationship between 'nation' and 'state'."

Finally, Katzenstein has pointed out (1996c: 26–27) that neorealists who seek to add greater determinative content to the predictions of Waltz's sparse model often do so by importing into it unacknowledged ideational factors, particularly the role of culture as an instrument of social mobilization or in generating threat perceptions.

Generally speaking, neoliberal institutionalism also assigns a limited causal role to ideational factors. In strictly rationalist explanations, Goldstein and Keohane note (1993: 4), "ideas are unimportant or epiphenomenal either because agents correctly anticipate the results of their actions or because some selective process ensures that only agents who behave as if they were rational succeed." Goldstein and Keohane believe otherwise, and present a framework for analyzing the impact of ideas on policy outcomes. It serves as a useful point of reference for our discussion because, even though the framework is posed as a challenge to both neo-utilitarianism and social constructivism, Goldstein and Keohane are quickly drawn back into the neo-utilitarian fold.

One part of the framework consists of three causal pathways through which ideas may influence policy outcomes. The first is by serving as "road maps," a role that "derives from the need of individuals to determine their own preferences or to understand the causal relationship between their goals and alternative political strategies by which to reach those goals" (ibid.: 12). The second is as "focal points" in strategic situations of multiple equilibria, that is, several equally "efficient" outcomes. Here, ideas can help individuals select one from among the set of viable outcomes (ibid.: 17). The third causal pathway is through "institutionalization," whereby ideas, once they have become encrusted in institutions, continue to "specify policy in the absence of innovation" (ibid.: 13).

Goldstein and Keohane also define three types of ideas that may do these things. One they call "world views," which are "entwined with people's conceptions of their identities, evoking deep emotions and loyalties" (ibid.: 8). Another is "principled beliefs," which "specify criteria for distinguishing right from wrong and just from unjust" (ibid.: 9). The last is "causal beliefs," that is, beliefs about cause-effect relations (ibid.: 10), which derive from the shared consensus of recognized authorities.

The framework holds promise, but the pull of neo-utilitarian precepts is stronger. Most significantly, what Goldstein and Keohane call world views are disposed of summarily: "Since all the subjects discussed in this volume [of which theirs is the introductory essay] have been profoundly affected by modern Western world views, and our authors all share this modernist outlook, we can say relatively little about the impact of broad world views on politics" (ibid.: 9). Set aside, thereby, are ideas related to state identities and corresponding interests—the heart of the social constructivist project. Left unexplored, thereby, are ideas of the sort that John F. Kennedy had in mind when he honored Jean Monnet by saying: "you are transforming Europe by a constructive idea" (Duchene 1994: 6). Similarly, Samuel Huntington's "clash of civilizations" (1996) finds no place here. Lastly, it is unclear where ideologies fit, not only those for which an instrumental rationalization can be readily claimed, like the resurgence of neo-laissez faire today, but others, such as the Nazi concept of Aryan superiority or Mao's Great Leap Forward and Cultural Revolution. None of these ideational factors are principled or causal beliefs as we normally understand those terms. So they must be parts of world views, which Goldstein and Keohane treat as though they were transcendent and/or invariant and therefore decline to specify.

But what of principled and causal beliefs? Do they not fare better? From a social constructivist vantage, not much. For the individuals featured in the Goldstein-Keohane story are not born into any system of social relationships that helps shape who they become. They are already fully constituted and we find them poised in a policy-making/problem-solving mode. As a result, neither principled beliefs nor ideas as road maps are intended to tell us much about those individuals, only about how they go about their business. By a

process of elimination, then, the heavy lifting in the Goldstein-Keohane scheme ends up being done by principled and causal beliefs functioning as focal points in multiple equilibria situations, and as sunk costs embedded in institutions—both fully consistent with neo-utilitarian precepts.

What is the social constructivist contribution to the ideational research program? According to Goldstein and Keohane (1993: 6), "without either a well-defined set of propositions about behavior or a rich empirical analysis, the [constructivist] critique remains more an expression of understandable frustration than a working research program." Let us be more precise—and, as a result, also more generous. Social constructivists have sought to understand the full array of systematic roles that ideas play in world politics, rather than specifying a priori roles based on theoretical presuppositions and then testing for those specified roles, as neo-utilitarians do. Because there is no received theory of the social construction of international reality, constructivists have gone about their work partly in somewhat of a barefoot empiricist manner and partly by means of conceptual analysis and thick description—in addition to expressing "understandable frustration." So Goldstein and Keohane may be right about the shortage of well-defined propositions, and this state of affairs should be improved in due course. But empirical and conceptual work is rich and accumulating. Indeed, it has become so large that we cannot summarize it all here. To briefly flag constructivist research on ideational factors, I begin by using Goldstein and Keohane's own typology and then push beyond it.

A core constructivist research concern is what happens *before* the neo-utilitarian model purportedly kicks in. Accordingly, what Goldstein and Keohane call "world views" are of great interest: civilizational constructs, cultural factors, state identities, and the like, together with how they shape states' interests and patterns of outcomes. I identified some of the empirical constructivist work on these subjects in the previous section. In addition, such world views presumably would include changing forms of nationalism in its constitutive and transformative roles, as Ernst Haas has studied it extensively (1986, 1997), and not simply as adjunctive to states and state power. They presumably include the globalization of market rationality and its effects, which has been of particular interest to constructivists who work in the tradition of Gramsci (Gill 1995), Polanyi (Ruggie 1995), and the so-called sociological institutionalists (Finnemore 1996b). And they include emerging bonds of "we-feeling" among nations, such as appear to have taken effect within the transatlantic security community—much as Karl Deutsch predicted forty years ago (1957) and explored more recently by Adler and Barnett (1996)—and, of course, in the European Union.

Constructivist empirical studies documenting the impact of principled beliefs on patterns of international outcomes include, among other subjects, the evolution of the human rights regime (Forsythe 1991; Sikkink 1993), the institutionalization of foreign aid (Lumsdaine 1993), decolonization (Jackson 1993), and international support for the termination of apartheid (Klotz 1995); as well as the already mentioned studies on increasingly nondiscriminatory humanitarian interventions (Finnemore 1996c), the emergence of weapons taboos (Price 1995; Price and Tannenwald 1996), and the role of multilateral norms in stabilizing the consequences of rapid international change. The single most important feature differentiating constructivist from other readings of these and similar phenomena is that they make the case that principled beliefs are not simply "theoretical fillers," to use Blyth's term (1997), invoked to round out or shore up instrumentalist accounts, but that in certain circumstances they lead states to redefine their interests or even their sense of self.

The major venue for constructivist explorations of the impact of causal beliefs has been via "epistemic communities," or transnational networks of knowledge-based experts (P. Haas 1992a). Here the empirical research seeks to relate the roles that such communities play in policymaking processes to the impact of their ideas on resolving particular policy problems, such as ozone depletion (P. Haas 1992b; Litfin 1994); providing operational content to general and sometimes am-

bivalent state interests, as in the Bretton Woods negotiations (Ikenberry 1992); and redefining states' interests, as in the antiballistic missile treaty (Adler 1992) and the pollution control regime for the Mediterranean Sea (P. Haas 1990). Disentangling strictly ideational from institutional impacts is difficult in practice, but that problem is not unique to the epistemic community literature (see Yee 1996; Blyth 1997).

Moreover, the further up one climbs on this impact ladder, the more is "learning" said to come into play (for the most extensive discussion, see E. Haas 1990). On the higher rungs, learning progressively means more than merely adapting to constraints, imitating the successful, or undertaking bounded search processes until a viable solution is identified—its typical meaning in conventional theories. Instead, it becomes second-order learning or, as Haas and some of his associates have termed it, "evolutionary epistemology" (E. Haas 1983a, 1990; Adler 1991, 1992; Adler and P. Haas 1992). This refers to the process whereby actors change not only how they deal with particular policy problems but also their very concept of problem solving—resulting from the recognition that they and other actors face similar conditions, have mutual interests, and share aspirations—by moving toward adopting what neo-utilitarians would describe as interdependent utility functions. That possibility takes us well beyond the Goldstein-Keohane typology.

But when all is said and done, the critical difference between the social constructivist and neo-utilitarian ideational research programs does not lie in empirical issues of the sort we have been looking at, as important as they are. They have to do with the neo-utilitarian misspecification of certain kinds of ideas. Let me explain. Goldstein and Keohane define ideas as "beliefs held by individuals" (1993: 3). It is of course true that, physiologically speaking, only individuals can have ideas or beliefs. But the reverse proposition, that all beliefs are individual beliefs or are reducible to individual beliefs, does not follow. It is the product of the methodological individualism on which neo-utilitarianism rests. Social constructivism, in contrast, also deals in the realm of "intersubjective beliefs," which cannot be reduced to the form "I believe that you believe that I believe," and so on. They are "social facts," and rest on what Searle calls "collective intentionality" (1995: 24–25). The concept of collective intentionality, Searle stresses, does not require "the idea that there exists some Hegelian world spirit, a collective consciousness, or something equally implausible" (ibid.: 25). Why not? Because the intentionality remains in individual heads. But within those individual heads it exists in the form "we intend," and "I intend only as part of our intending" (ibid.: 26).

Constructivists have explored the impact of collective intentionality, so understood, at several levels in the international polity. At the deepest is the question of who counts as a constitutive unit of the international system. The mutual recognition of sovereignty * * * is a precondition for the normal functioning of a system of sovereign states. Sovereignty, like private property or money, can only exist within a social framework that recognizes it to be valid—that is, by virtue of collective intentionality. But its impact is not limited to the one-time designation, "you are in this game, and you are out." Over time, sovereignty has affected patterns of conflict between sovereign states and other types of political formations (Strang 1991). And it continues to empower and provide resources to some states, irrespective of how dysfunctional they may be, that might not otherwise survive (Jackson 1990). Though this is not the place to pursue the issue, constructivists also tend to believe, as a working hypothesis, that insofar as sovereignty is a matter of collective intentionality, in the final analysis, so, too, is its future.

In addition to this constitutive role, collective intentionality also has a deontic function within the system of states—that is, it creates new rights and responsibilities. The process that Claude (1966) called collective legitimation includes an entire class of such functions which, if anything, has expanded since he wrote his classic article (see Barnett 1996). For example, Finnemore (1996c) observes that humanitarian intervention not only is becoming more nondiscriminatory, but that

states increasingly tend to seek the endorsement of international organizations before undertaking such interventions. Searle, viewing the subject through a philosopher's eyes, finds that human rights are "perhaps the most amazing" instance of creating rights through collective intentionality—amazing because it ascribes rights "solely by virtue of being a human being" (1995: 93). Constructivists are equally amazed by the fact it ascribes rights to individuals vis-à-vis their own states.

At the most routine level, collective intentionality creates meaning. [F]or example, * * * the Bretton Woods monetary negotiations and the corresponding negotiations to establish an international trade regime produced more than standards of behavior and rules of conduct. They also established intersubjective frameworks of meaning that included a shared narrative about the conditions that had made these regimes necessary and what they were intended to accomplish, which in turn generated a grammar, as it were, on the basis of which states agreed to interpret the appropriateness of future acts that they could not possibly foresee (for an empirical update, see Ruggie 1996).

Theoretical analysis along these lines is most advanced among German international relations scholars, who are more directly influenced by the work of Juergen Habermas than their American counterparts. One of the key questions is the extent to which Habermas's theory of communicative action (1979, 1984, 1987) can or cannot be reconciled with rational-choice theory and neo-utilitarianism more generally (Mueller 1994; Keck 1995; Risse-Kappen 1995; Schmalz-Bruns 1995; Mueller 1995; also see Kratochwil 1989 and Alker 1990, 1996). The consensus appears to be that accommodating communicative action, including acts of deliberation and persuasion, requires devising a conception of actors who are not only strategically but also discursively competent, a feat that is unlikely to be achieved at least within currently available neo-utilitarian formulations.

There is yet another major difference between social constructivism and neo-utilitarianism on the issue of ideational causation: it concerns how "causation" is understood. Some ideational factors simply do not function causally in the same way as either brute facts or the agentive role that neo-utilitarianism attributes to interests. As a result, the efficacy of such ideational factors is easily underestimated. This is too complex a problem to be resolved here, so I merely acknowledge its existence. Aspirations are one instance, legitimacy is another, and rights a third. They fall into the category of *reasons for actions*, which are not the same as *causes of actions*—so that, for example, the aspiration for a united Europe has not caused European integration but it is the reason the direct causal factors have had their causal capacity (on causal capacity, see Yee 1996).

In sum, by now the constructivist ideational research program adds up to considerably more than "an expression of understandable frustration"—and it includes entire domains of ideational causation that even an expanded neo-utilitarian agenda does not and cannot comprise.

CONSTITUTIVE AND REGULATIVE RULES

Thus far, we have focused largely on the independent variable side of things; we now shift our concern to some critical limits and omissions of neo-utilitarianism in regard to dependent variables, the types of things it does and does not seek to explain. The first has to do with the distinction between constitutive and regulative rules, which goes back at least to a seminal article by John Rawls (1955). But Searle (1995: 27–29) offers an easier point of entry.

Let us begin with a simple illustration. We can readily imagine the act of driving cars existing prior to the rule that specified "drive on the right (left)-hand side of the road." In an account that is perfectly consistent with neo-utilitarianism, the rule would have been instituted as a function of increased traffic and growing numbers of fender-benders. Specifying which side of the road to drive on is an example of a regulative rule; as the term implies, it regulates an antecedently existing activity. To this rule were soon added others, requiring licenses, imposing speed limits, forbidding driving

under the influence of alcohol, yielding at intersections, and so on.

Now imagine a quite different situation: playing the game of chess. "It is not the case," Searle notes sardonically (ibid.: 28), "that there were a lot of people pushing bits of wood around on boards, and in order to prevent them from bumping into each other all the time and creating traffic jams, we had to regulate the activity. Rather, the rules of chess create the very possibility of playing chess. The rules are constitutive of chess in the sense that playing chess is constituted in part by acting in accord with the rules." Regulative rules are intended to have causal effects—getting people to approximate the speed limit, for example. Constitutive rules define the set of practices that make up any particular consciously organized social activity—that is to say, they specify *what counts as* that activity.

This basic distinction permits us to describe a profound limitation of neo-utilitarianism: it lacks any concept of constitutive rules. Its universe of discourse consists entirely of antecedently existing actors and their behavior, and its project is to explain the character and efficacy of regulative rules in coordinating them. This feature accounts for the fact that within the terms of their theories, neorealism and neoliberal institutionalism explain the origins of virtually nothing that is constitutive of the very possibility of conducting international relations: not territorial states, not systems of states, not any concrete international order, nor the whole host of institutional forms that states use, ranging from promises or treaties to multilateral organizing principles. All are assumed to exist already or they are misspecified—as, for example, when the post–World War II international order is attributed to American hegemony, taking the specificity of American identity for granted.

Why is this the case, and is it inherent to the enterprise? The reason is not difficult to decipher: neo-utilitarian models of international relations are imported from economics. The economy, we well know, is embedded in broader social, political, and legal institutional frameworks that make it possible to conduct economic relations—that are *constitutive of* economic relations. Economic actors and economists, appropriately, take their existence for granted. The problem arises because when neo-utilitarian models are imported into other fields they leave those constitutive frameworks behind. This seems not to matter for some (as yet unspecified) range of political phenomena, domestic and international, which has been explored by means of microeconomic models and the microfoundations of which are now better understood than before. But there are certain things that these models are incapable of doing. Accounting for constitutive rules—which they were not responsible for in economics—is among the most important.

Furthermore, this defect cannot be remedied within the neo-utilitarian framework. The terms of a theory cannot explain the conditions that are necessary for that theory to function, because no theory can explain anything until its necessary preconditions hold. Thus, Alexander James Field (1979, 1981, 1984) has demonstrated from within the neoclassical tradition, and Robert Brenner (1977) the neo-Marxist, that market rationality cannot account for the constitutive rules that are required to make market rationality work, as specified by modern economic theory—an insight that Max Weber (1958) had already established at the turn of the century.

Social constructivists in international relations have not yet managed to devise a theory of constitutive rules, but the phenomenon itself is of central concern to them (for general theoretical treatments, see Kratochwil 1989; Onuf 1989 * * *). Take first the very system of states. * * * [T]he concept of the modern state was made possible only when a new rule for differentiating the constituent units within medieval Christendom replaced the rule of heteronomy (interwoven and overlapping jurisdictions, moral and political). * * * [V]arious material and ideational factors * * * interacted to produce the institutional form of exclusive territoriality, by which the new principle of differentiation was instantiated, and which then served as the constitutive rule defining the spatial organization of modern international politics.

Moreover, Hedley Bull (1977) of the English school argued that norms regarding contracting and promise-keeping are constitutive of order in the international realm no less than domestic—in the sense that the institution of contracts or the concept of promises must be recognized and enjoy legitimacy before there can be any talk of regulative rules designed to deal with problems of incomplete contracting or cheating on agreements. Kratochwil (1989) elaborates on these issues fruitfully in an explicitly constructivist vein.

In addition, even as they acknowledge that the specific (as opposed to generic) identities of states are defined primarily internally, constructivists have shown that to some extent such identities are also mutually constituted. Wendt (forthcoming) draws on G. H. Mead's theory of symbolic interactionism to elucidate the process. On the premise that every identity implies a difference, constructivist scholars have also explored the role of "the other"—whether denigrated, feared, or emulated—in the mutual constitution of identities: Neumann and Welsh (1991) on the role of the Ottoman Empire, "the Turk," in consolidating the civilizational construct of Europe; Campbell (1992) on the "old world," the communist menace, as well as various internal "others" in forging America's sense of self; and Der Derian (1987) on the mediating role of diplomacy in sustaining relations among culturally estranged entities.

Lastly, it is necessary to take note of a philosophical point: in some cases, constitutive rules themselves provide the desired explanation. If we are asked to "explain" the game of chess, the appropriate response consists of its constitutive rules. In Searle's simple formulation (1995: 28), constitutive rules are of the type "X [a move] counts as Y [checkmate] in context C [chess]." Because X does not temporally precede and is not independent of Y, it follows that these are noncausal explanations. (A causal explanation is called for in response to questions such as, "Why do I keep losing at chess?") Precisely the same holds for "explaining" modern international politics in contrast to the medieval or classical Greek systems: the relevant answer is provided by their respective constitutive rules. Indeed, it also holds for social constructions that are closer to the surface level of the international system, such as the cold war or the embedded liberalism compromise. The point to note is this: lacking a conception of constitutive rules makes it impossible to provide endogenously the noncausal explanations that constitutive rules embody and which are logically prior to the domain in which causal explanations take effect.

Constitutive rules are the institutional foundation of all social life. No consciously organized realm of human activity is imaginable without them, including international politics—though they may be relatively more "thin" in this than in many other forms of social order. Some constitutive rules, like exclusive territoriality, are so deeply sedimented or reified that actors no longer think of them as rules at all. But their durability remains based in collective intentionality, even if they started with a brute physical act such as seizing a piece of land. The sudden and universally surprising collapse of the Soviet Union's East European empire illuminates vividly what can happen, Searle observes (1995: 92), "when the system of status-functions [assigned by constitutive rules] is no longer accepted"—despite the fact that, in that instance, brute force remained *entirely* on the side of the status quo (see also Koslowski and Kratochwil 1995). A similar erosion of collective intentionality, only partly related to shifts in brute force or material interests, was evidenced in the termination of colonialism and of the slave trade before it. Under certain circumstances, it seems, collective intentionality can "will" the rules of the game to change.

Constructivists do not claim to understand the extraordinarily complex processes regarding constitutive rules fully (or even mostly). But neorealists and neoliberal institutionalists lack even a space for them in their ontology. The scope of their theories, as a result, is confined to regulative rules that coordinate behavior in a pre-constituted world.

TRANSFORMATION

In light of the foregoing discussion, it follows almost axiomatically that neo-utilitarian models of international relations theory would have little to offer on the subject of systemic transformation: doing so would require them to problematize states' identities and interests and to have some concept of constitutive rules. Neoliberal institutionalism did not yet exist when I first noted of Waltz's model that it contained only a reproductive logic, but no transformative logic. While neorealists have made some effort to respond by claiming, in essence, that no theory of transformation is necessary, neoliberal institutionalism has remained relatively silent on the subject.

The neorealist claim that no theory of transformation is necessary takes one of two forms. The first argues that there is no decisive difference between medieval Europe and the modern system of states because conflict groups, striving for advantage, forming alliances, and using force to settle disputes, existed in both and were not visibly affected by whatever common norms that medieval Christendom may have embodied (Fischer 1992). Mearsheimer (1994/95: 45) infers from this claim that "realism . . . appears best to explain international politics in the five centuries of the feudal era"—a claim that will surprise medievalists—and, of course, ever since. Fischer's historiography and selection bias of cases have been challenged by Hall and Kratochwil (1993). But even if Fischer were correct, the point he makes is irrelevant to the issue at hand: the personalized and parcelized structure of political authority relations in feudal society collapsed and was replaced by the completely different institutional system of modern states.

The second neorealist argument is that not enough is happening in the world today to warrant a theory of transformation. This was implied by Waltz (1979), and has been explored extensively by Krasner (1993, 1995/96, 1997). Krasner maintains that the "Westphalian baseline"—the Peace of Westphalia (1648) symbolizing the beginning of the modern state system—was never as clear-cut as some analysts have made it out to be, has been compromised throughout by recurrent forces, and with some exceptions (most notably the European Union) it remains the rough approximation of the international polity that it has always been. Nevertheless, as Krasner acknowledges when he grapples with the elusive concept of sovereignty, even the markers of international transformation are badly underspecified and ill-understood. A deeper theoretical understanding of possible processes of transformation, of course, would go some way toward clarifying its indicators.

Here again, constructivists have not yet managed to devise a fully fledged formulation of their own. They have come at the problem from three sides. The first is a purely theoretical "solution," and rests on Giddens' notion (1978) of the "duality of structure"—that structure both constrains action but is also the medium through which actors act and, in doing so, potentially transform the structure. David Dessler (1989) goes so far as to posit what he calls a "transformational ontology" to subsume neorealism's "positional" one (for a similarly inspired "dialectical" rendering of "agent-structure" relations, see Wendt 1987). These endeavors are thought-provoking, and they help avoid the reification of structures. But as they stand they rely too heavily on the linguistic analogy: any given language precedes its individual speakers and thereby constrains how they communicate; at the same time, their use of that language can change it over time—and so the practice alters the structure. This is all well and good in the realm of language, but linguistic structures, as sociologist William Sewell (1992: 23–24) observes, "are much less implicated in power relations" than most other social structures, and altering a linguistic practice "has minor power consequences" compared to changes in other social structures. It follows that "particularly poor candidates for the linguistic analogy would be state or political structures, which commonly generate and utilize large concentrations of power."

A second constructivist tack is more empirical, albeit in a "jumbo" sense. It consists of attempts to specify the macro-structural dimension of international politics in a manner that shows it to be space-time contingent: that is to say, to make transparent the fact that "structure" is the aggregation of specific social practices that are situated in time and space; to specify what the characteristic forms of those social practices are; and to discern how they may become susceptible to change. * * * [T]he characteristically modern form of organizing political space may be undergoing slow but fundamental change as a result of the sectoral unbundling of territoriality in various functional regimes, together with the emergence of multiperspectival state identities in contrast to identities based strictly on single-point perspective. Both of these processes are most advanced in the European Union, I argue, but are not limited to it.

The third constructivist line of transformational research is to identify, inventory, and specify the consequences of innovative micro-practices in international relations today. Examples include Saskia Sassen's work (1996) on the institutional mechanisms that are reconfiguring global economic geography today, ranging from legal practices and financial instruments to accounting rules and telecommunication standards. Kathryn Sikkink's work on the subject of "advocacy networks" (1993, forthcoming) exemplifies this genre. So too does a host of studies on the growing role of nongovernmental actors and the emergence of transnational civil society (see, for example, Wapner 1995). This approach is most productive when it is linked up with work on macro-structures, to determine which micro-practices are potentially transformative agents.

Finally, * * * the emergence of the modern state was shaped repeatedly and fundamentally by the unanticipated consequences triggered by the behavior of various social actors. That fact makes it difficult to devise any comprehensive theory of transformation, but especially one based on the rationalistic assumptions of neo-utilitarianism.

Let us draw this discussion to a close. Social constructivism in international relations has come into its own during the past decade or so, not only as metatheoretical critique but increasingly in the form of empirical evidence and insights. Constructivism addresses many of the same issues that neoutilitarianism has addressed, though typically from a different angle, but also some that neoutilitarianism treats by assumption, discounts, ignores, or simply cannot apprehend within its ontology and/or epistemology. Constructivists seek to push the empirical and explanatory domains of international relations theory beyond the analytical confines of neorealism and neoliberal institutionalism in all directions: by problematizing states' identities and interests; by broadening the array of ideational factors that affect international outcomes; by introducing the logically prior constitutive rules alongside regulative rules; and by including transformation as a normal feature of international politics that systemic theory should encompass even if its empirical occurrence is episodic and moves on a different time line from everyday life.

There can be little doubt but that subsequent research will show some constructivist claims to be in error, others even misguided. What is more, constructivism is still unable to specify a fully articulated set of propositions and rigorous renderings of the contexts within which they are expected to hold. Indeed, for reasons explored below, it may never be able to do so entirely to the satisfaction of neo-utilitarianism and the epistemological preferences it embodies. But having now described the emergence of social constructivism in international relations, stressing its dialogue and tension with the ascendancy of neo-utilitarianism, we can turn next to developing a more synoptic overview of the main constructivist precepts and practices.

The Social Constructivist Project

*   *   *

In light of our discussion thus far, we can readily dismiss a stereotype one sometimes encounters in the literature, especially among hyper-realists: that constructivists discount the potential for conflict in international politics, and that they believe in the Dorothy principle—that extant reality, as in the Land of Oz, can be changed by closing one's eyes and wishing hard. Emanuel Adler, a constructivist, responds thusly (1997): "If international reality is socially constructed, then World War II, the Holocaust, and the Bosnian conflict must also have

been socially constructed." At bottom, constructivism concerns the issue of human consciousness: the role it plays in international relations, and the implications for the logic and methods of social inquiry of taking it seriously. Constructivists hold the view that the building blocks of international reality are ideational as well as material; that ideational factors have normative as well as instrumental dimensions; that they express not only individual but also collective intentionality; and that the meaning and significance of ideational factors are not independent of time and place.

The most distinctive features of constructivism, then, are in the realm of ontology, the real-world phenomena that are posited by any theory and are invoked by its explanations (for a good discussion of ontology in the context of international relations theory, see Dessler 1989). As summarized in section two of this essay, at the level of individual actors constructivism seeks, first of all, to problematize the identities and interests of states, to show that and how they are socially constructed. Neorealists come close to believing that states' identities and interests are, in fact, given and fixed. For neoliberal institutionalists, this posture is more likely to reflect merely a convenient assumption, designed to permit their analytical apparatus to function. When neoliberal institutionalists are pressed about the origins of either, however, they turn immediately to domestic politics (see, for example, Keohane 1993: 294). Social constructivists, in contrast, argue and have shown that even identities are generated in part by international interactions, both the generic identities of states *qua* states, as well as their specific identities, as in America's sense of difference from the old world or from godless communism. Still at the level of individual actors, constructivism also seeks to map the full array of additional ideational factors that shape actors' outlooks and behavior, ranging from culture and ideology, to aspirations and principled beliefs, on to cause/effect knowledge of specific policy problems.

At the level of the international polity, the concept of structure in social constructivism is suffused with ideational factors. There can be no mutually comprehensible conduct of international relations, constructivists hold, without mutually recognized constitutive rules, resting on collective intentionality. These rules may be more or less "thick" or "thin," depending on the issue area or the international grouping at hand. Similarly, they may be constitutive of conflict or cooperation. But in any event, these constitutive rules prestructure the domains of action within which regulative rules take effect. In some circumstances, collective intentionality includes an interpretive function— as in the case of international regimes, which limit strictly interest-based self-interpretation of appropriate behavior by their members. And in others collective intentionality also includes a deontic function—creating rights and responsibilities in a manner that is not simply determined by the material interests of the dominant powers. In short, constructivists view international structure to be a social structure * * * made up of socially knowledgeable and competent actors who are subject to constraints that are in part material, in part institutional.

These ontological characteristics have implications for the logic and methods of constructivist inquiry. First, constructivism is not itself a theory of international relations, the way balance-of-power theory is, for example, but a theoretically informed approach to the study of international relations. Moreover, constructivism does not aspire to the hypothetico-deductive mode of theory construction. It is by necessity more "realistic," to use Weber's term, or inductive in orientation. Additionally, its concepts in the first instance are intended to tap into and help interpret the meaning and significance that actors ascribe to the collective situation in which they find themselves. It is unlikely that this function could be performed by concepts that represent a priori types derived from some universalizing theory sketch or from purely nominal definitions.

Finally, constructivism differs in its explanatory forms. As discussed previously, for some purposes constitutive rules in themselves provide an appropriate and adequate, albeit non-causal, explanatory account. And in its causal explanations, constructivism, again by necessity, adheres to narrative explanatory protocols, not the nomological-deductive (N-D) model prized by naturalistic monism. The N-D model establishes causality by subsuming the explanandum under a covering law or law-like generalizations. Causality in the narrative explanatory form is established through a process of successive interrogative reasoning between explanans and explanandum, anticipated by Weber with his heuristic use of ideal types, and called "abduction" by the American pragmatist philosopher Charles Peirce (1955: 151–152). At least in these respects, then, constructivism is non- or post-positivist in its epistemology.

These epistemological practices of constructivism have not been well received in the mainstream of the discipline. Part of the problem is that the mainstream has become increasingly narrow in its understanding of what constitutes social science, so that on the dominant conception today Weber might no longer qualify. The other part of the problem is that there are very different strands of constructivism in international relations and they differ precisely on epistemological grounds, not surprisingly creating confusion as a result. * * *

*   *   *

Paradigmatic (Ir)reconcilability

The "great debates" that have swept through the field of international relations over the decades typically have been posed in terms of the alleged superiority of one approach over another. But the fact that these debates recur so regularly offers proof positive that no approach can rightfully claim a monopoly on truth—or even on useful insights. The current encounter between neo-utilitarianism and constructivism exhibits the additional feature that the strength of each approach is also the source of its major weakness. As a result, the issue of any possible relationship between them must be joined.

The strength of neo-utilitarianism lies in its axiomatic structure, which permits a degree of analytical rigor, and in neoliberal institutionalism's case also of theoretical specification, that other approaches cannot match. This is not an aesthetic but a practical judgment. Rigor and specificity are desirable on intellectual grounds because they make cumulative findings more likely, and on policy grounds because they raise the probability that predicted effects will actually materialize. At the same time, neo-utilitarianism's major weakness lies in the foundations of its axiomatic structure, its ontology, which for some purposes is seriously flawed and leads to an incomplete or distorted view of international reality. That problem is particularly pronounced at a time such as today, when states are struggling to redefine stable sets of interests and preferences regarding key aspects of the international order.

The obverse is true of constructivism. It rests on a deeper and broader ontology, thereby providing a richer understanding of some phenomena and shedding light on other aspects of international life that, quite literally, do not exist within the neo-utilitarian rendering of the world polity. At the same time, it lacks rigor and specification—in fact, it is still relatively poor at specifying its own scope conditions, the contexts within which its explanatory features can be expected to make how much difference. Improvements are inevitable as work in the constructivist vein continues to expand, but given the nature of the beast there are inherent limits to the endeavor.

Where do we go from here? Can a systematic relationship between the two approaches be articulated, and if so how? A substantial number of adherents to each is unlikely to be interested in any such effort. Hard-core rational choice theorists, post-modernist constructivists, and most neorealists will reject any need to do so. But even coalitions of the willing may find the going difficult as they discover the analytical boundaries beyond which their respective approaches cannot be pushed.

The first instinct of willing neo-utilitarians is to expand their analytical foundation in the direction of greater sociality. For example, Keohane (1993: 289) states that his version of institutionalist theory "embeds it selectively in a larger framework of neoliberal thought," which also includes commercial, republican, and sociological liberalism. Doing so, Keohane believes, provides a richer and more robust social context for neoliberal institutionalism. Keohane is right up to a point: that point is defined by the boundaries of methodological individualism and instrumental rationality. Commercial liberalism poses few problems in this regard, nor does the transnational bureaucratic politics that comprises one aspect of what he calls sociological liberalism. But republican liberalism? It would be enormously surprising if the ties among democratic societies, especially those in "the West," did not reflect an intersubjective cultural affinity, a sense of "we-feeling," a shared belief of belonging to a common historical project, which fall well beyond the "selectively" expanded foundation of neoliberalism that Keohane proposes.

Indeed, Keohane acknowledges that not even the most fundamental attribute of liberalism, that which distinguishes it from all other views on the nature of humanity, justice, and good government, can be accommodated within his version of neoliberalism. He writes (1990a: 174): "the emphasis of liberalism on liberty and rights only suggests a general orientation toward the moral evaluation of world politics," but it does not lend itself to the analysis of choice under constraints that he wishes to employ. As a result, he finds it "more useful" to put that "emphasis" aside for his analytical purposes. All deontic features of social life go with it.

In short, a selective expansion of neoutilitarianism's core is possible, and it may even be desirable. But we should not expect it to carry us far toward a "social"—ideational and relational—ontology.

The first instinct of the willing constructivist is to incorporate the study of norms, identities, and meaning in the study of international relations with minimum disruption to the field's prevailing epistemological stance, on which hopes for analytical rigor and cumulative knowledge are believed to rest. Typically, this takes the form of maintaining that constructivist concerns are a useful tool in the context of discovery, but that at the end of the day they do not affect the logic of inquiry (see

Neufield 1993 for an extended criticism of this practice). For example, I read the methodological discussions in Katzenstein's edited volume, *The Culture of National Security* (1996b), in this light. The essays in that book, Jepperson, Wendt, and Katzenstein insist (1996: 65), neither advance nor depend on "any special methodology or epistomology . . . When they attempt explanation, they engage in 'normal science,' with its usual desiderata in mind."

Everything hinges, of course, on what is meant by "normal science." On my reading, "normal science" in international relations has a hard time grasping truly intersubjective meanings at the international level, as opposed to aggregations of meanings held by individual units; it lacks the possibility that ideational factors relate to social action in the form of constitutive rules; it is exceedingly uncomfortable with the notion of noncausal explanation, which constitutive rules entail; and even though it is almost never achieved in practice—and in most instances perhaps cannot be achieved—the "normal science" of international relations nevertheless aspires to the deductive-nomological model of causal explanation, while dismissing even rigorous forms of the narrative mode as mere story-telling.

*   *   *

Having said all that, I nevertheless conclude with the conviction that both of these moves are fruitful. In the hope of gaining at once a deeper and clearer understanding of the structure and functioning of the world polity, neo-utilitarians should strive to expand their analytical foundations, and constructivists should strive for greater analytical rigor and specification. The two approaches are not additive, and they are unlikely to meet and merge on some happy middle ground. But by pushing their respective limits in the direction of the other, we are more likely to discover precisely when one approach subsumes the other, when they represent competing explanations of the same phenomenon, and when one complements or supplements the other (for an excellent beginning, see Jepperson, Wendt, and Katzenstein 1996: 68–72).

The stakes are high enough, and the limits of the two approaches inherent and apparent enough, for any claims of universal priority at this point to be entirely unwarranted.

REFERENCES

Adler, E. (1991) "Cognitive evolution: a dynamic approach for the study of international relations and their progress," in E. Adler and B. Crawford (eds) *Progress in Postwar International Relations*, New York: Columbia University Press.

——— (1992) "The emergence of cooperation: national epistemic communities and the international evolution of the idea of nuclear arms control," *International Organization* 46(1): 101–145.

——— (1997) "Seizing the middle ground: constructivism and world politics," *European Journal of International Relations* 3(3) 319–359.

Adler, E. and Barnett, M. N. (1996) "Governing anarchy: a research agenda for the study of security communities," *Ethics and International Affairs* 10: 63–98.

Adler, E. and Haas, P. (1992) "Conclusion: epistemic communities, world order, and the creation of a reflective research program," *International Organization* 46(1): 367–390.

Alker, H. A., Jr. (1990) "Rescuing 'reason' from the 'rationalists': reading Vico, Marx and Weber as reflective institutionalists," *Millennium: Journal of International Studies* 19(2): 161–184.

——— (1996) *Rediscoveries and Reformulations: Humanistic Methodologies for International Studies*, New York: Cambridge University Press.

Axelrod, R. and Keohane, R. O. (1985) "Achieving cooperation under anarchy: strategies and institutions," *World Politics* 38(1): 226–254.

Baldwin, D. A. (ed.) (1993) *Neorealism and Neoliberalism: The Contemporary Debate*, New York: Columbia University Press.

Barnett, M. (1996) "Identity and alliances in the Middle East," in P. J. Katzenstein (ed.) *The Culture of National Security: Norms and Identity in World Politics,* New York: Columbia University Press.

Berger, P. L. and Luckman, T. (1966) *The Social Construction of Reality,* Garden City NY: Doubleday.

Berger, T. U. (1996) "Norms, identity, and national security in Germany and Japan," in P. J. Katzenstein (ed.) *The Culture of National Security: Norms and Identity in World Politics,* New York: Columbia University Press.

Blyth, M. (1997) "Any more good ideas?" *Comparative Politics.*

Brenner, R. (1977) "The origins of capitalist development: a critique of neo-Smithian Marxism," *New Left Review* 104: 25–92.

Bull, H. (1977) *The Anarchical Society: A Study of Order in World Politics,* London: Macmillan.

Bull, H. and Watson, A. (eds) (1984) *The Expansion of European Society,* London: Oxford University Press.

Burley, A. M. and Mattli, W. (1993) "Europe before the court: a political theory of legal integration," *International Organization* 47(1): 41–76.

Butterfield, H. and Wight, M. (1968) *Diplomatic Investigations: Essays in the Theory of International Politics,* London: Allen and Unwin.

Buzan, B. (1993) "From international system to international society: structural realism and regime theory meet the English School," *International Organization* 47(3): 327–352.

Campbell, D. (1992) *Writing Security: United States Foreign Policy and the Politics of Identity,* Minneapolis: University of Minnesota Press.

Carr, E. H. (1946) *The Twenty Years' Crisis 1919–1939,* New York: Harper.

Christensen, T. J. and Snyder, J. (1990) "Chain gangs and passed bucks: predicting alliance patterns in multipolarity," *International Organization* 44(2): 137–168.

Claude, I. L., Jr (1956) *Swords into Plowshares: The Problems and Progress of International Organization,* New York: Random House.

——— (1966) "Collective legitimization as a political function of the United Nations," *International Organization* 20(3): 367–379.

Der Derian, J. (1987) *On Diplomacy,* Oxford: Blackwell.

Dessler, D. (1989) "What's at stake in the agent-structure debate?" *International Organization* 43(3): 441–473.

Deutsch, K. W. et al. (1957) *Political Community and the North Atlantic Area,* Princeton: Princeton University Press.

Duchene, F. (1994) *Jean Monnet: The First Statesman of Interdependence,* New York: Norton.

Duffield, J. S. (1992) "International regimes and alliance behavior," *International Organization* 46(4): 369–388.

——— (1994/5) "NATO's functions after the Cold War," *Political Science Quarterly* 109(5): 763–788.

Durkheim, E. (1938) [1895] *The Rules of Sociological Method,* E. G. Catlin (ed.), New York: Free Press.

Field, A. J. (1979) "On the explanation of rules using rational choice models," *Journal of Economic Issues* 13(1): 49–72.

——— (1981) "The problem with neoclassical institutional economics: a critique with special reference to the North/Thomas Model of pre-1500 Europe," *Explorations in Economic History* 19(2): 174–198.

——— (1984) "Microeconomics, norms, and rationality," *Economic Development and Cultural Change* 32(4): 683–711.

Finnemore, M. (1996a) *National Interests in International Society,* Ithaca: Cornell University Press.

——— (1996b) "Norms, culture, and world politics: insights from sociology's institutionalism," *International Organization* 50(2): 349–347.

——— (1996c) "Constructing norms of humanitarian intervention," in P. J. Katzenstein (ed.) *The Culture of National Security: Norms and Identity in World Politics,* New York: Columbia University Press.

Fischer, M. (1992) "Feudal Europe, 800–1300: communal discourse and conflictual practices," *International Organization* 46(2): 427–466.

Forsythe, D. (1991) *The Internationalization of Human Rights,* Lexington MA: Lexington Books.

Frieden, J. (1994) "International investment and colonial control: a new interpretation," *International Organization* 48(4): 559–593.

Gaddis, J. L. (1982) *Strategies of Containment,* New York: Oxford University Press.

Garrett, G. (1993) "International cooperation and institutional choice: the European Community's internal market," in J. G. Ruggie (ed.) *Multilateralism Matters: The Theory and Praxis of an Institutional Form,* New York: Columbia University Press.

Garrett, G. and Weingast, B. (1993) "Ideas, interests, and institutions: constructing the European Community's internal market," in J. Goldstein and R. O. Keohane (eds) *Ideas and Foreign Policy,* Ithaca: Cornell University Press.

Giddens, A. (1978) *Emile Durkheim,* New York: Penguin.

——— (1979) *Central Problems in Social and Political Theory,* Berkeley/Los Angeles: University of California Press.

——— (1981) *A Contemporary Critique of Historical Materialism,* Berkeley: University of California Press.

Gill, S. (1995) "Globalisation, market civilisation, and disciplinary neoliberalism," *Millennium: Journal of International Studies* 24(3): 399–424.

Gilligan, C. (1993) *In a Different Voice: Psychological Theory and Women's Development,* Cambridge MA: Harvard University Press.

Gilpin, R. (1975) *Power and the Multinational Corporation,* New York: Basic Books.

Goldstein, J. and Keohane, R. O. (eds) (1993) *Ideas and Foreign Policy,* Ithaca NY: Cornell University Press.

Grieco, J. M. (1988) "Anarchy and the limits of cooperation," *International Organization* 42(3): 485–508.

——— (1990) *Cooperation Among Nations,* Ithaca: Cornell University Press.

——— (1993) "Understanding the problem of international cooperation: the limits of neoliberal institutionalism and the future of realist theory," in D. A. Baldwin (ed.) *Neorealism and Neoliberalism: The Contemporary Debate,* New York: Columbia University Press.

Haas, E. B. (1958) *The Uniting of Europe,* Stanford: Stanford University Press.

——— (1961) "International integration: the European and the universal process," *International Organization* 15(3): 366–392.

——— (1964) *Beyond the Nation State,* Stanford: Stanford University Press.

——— (1976) *The Obsolescence of Regional Integration Theory,* Research Monograph no. 25, Berkeley: Institute of International Studies, University of California.

——— (1983a) "Words can hurt you: or, who said what to whom about regimes," in S. D. Krasner (ed.) *International Regimes,* Ithaca NY: Cornell University Press.

——— (1986) "What is nationalism and why should we study it?" *International Organization* 40(3): 707–744.

——— (1990) *When Knowledge is Power,* Berkeley: University of California Press.

——— (1997) *Nationalism, Liberalism, and Progress,* Ithaca: Cornell University Press.

Haas, P. M. (1990) *Saving the Mediterranean,* New York: Columbia University Press.

——— (ed.) (1992a) "Knowledge, power, and international policy coordination," *International Organization* 46 (special issue): 1.

——— (1992b) "Epistemic communities and international policy coordination," *International Organization* 46(1): 1–36.

Haas, P. M., Keohane, R. O., and Levy, M. (eds) (1993) *Institutions for the Earth,* Cambridge MA: MIT Press.

Habermas, J. (1979) *Communication and the Evolution of Society,* Boston: Beacon Press.

——— (1984) *Theory of Communicative Action,* vol. 1, Boston: Beacon Press.

——— (1987) *Theory of Communicative Action,* vol. 2, Boston: Beacon Press.

Hall, B. M. and Kratochwil, F. V. (1993) "Medieval

tales: neorealist 'science' and the abuse of history," *International Organization* 47(3): 479–491.

Herman, R. G. (1996) "Identity, norms, and national security: the Soviet foreign policy revolution and the end of the Cold War," in P. J. Katzenstein (ed.) *The Culture of National Security: Norms and Identity in World Politics*, New York: Columbia University Press.

Huntington, S. (1996) *The Clash of Civilizations and the Remaking of World Order*, New York: Simon and Schuster.

Ikenberry, G. J. (1992) "A world economy restored: expert consensus and the Anglo-American postwar settlement," *International Organization* 46(1): 289–321.

Jackson, R. (1990) *Quasi-States: Sovereignty, International Relations, and the Third World*, Cambridge: Cambridge University Press.

—— (1993) "The weight of ideas in decolonization: normative change in international relations," in J. Goldstein and R. O. Keohane (eds) *Ideas and Foreign Policy*, Ithaca NY: Cornell University Press.

Jakobson, P. V. (1996) "Use and abuse of military threats in Bosnia-Herzegovina: why compellence and deterrence failed," paper prepared for 37th annual convention, International Studies Association, San Diego CA, 16–20 April 1996.

James, A. (ed.) (1973) *The Bases of International Order*, London: Oxford University Press.

Jepperson, R. L., Wendt, A., and Katzenstein, P. J. (1996) "Norms, identity, and culture in national security," in P. J. Katzenstein (ed.) *The Culture of National Security: Norms and Identity in World Politics*, New York: Columbia University Press.

Jervis, R. (1970) *The Logic of Images in International Relations*, Princeton: Princeton University Press.

—— (1976) *Perception and Misperception in International Politics*, Princeton: Princeton University Press.

—— (1978) "Cooperation under the security dilemma," *World Politics* 30(2): 167–214.

Johnston, A. I. (1995) *Cultural Realism: Strategic Culture and Grand Strategy in Chinese History*, Princeton: Princeton University Press.

—— (1996) "Cultural realism and strategy in Maoist China," in P. J. Katzenstein (ed.) *The Culture of National Security: Norms and Identity in World Politics*, New York: Columbia University Press.

Katzenstein, P. J. (1996a) *Cultural Norms and National Security*, Ithaca: Cornell University Press.

—— (ed.) (1996b) *The Culture of National Security: Norms and Identity in World Politics*, New York: Columbia University Press.

—— (1996c) "Introduction: alternative conceptions on national security," in P. J. Katzenstein (ed.) *The Culture of National Security: Norms and Identity in World Politics*, New York: Columbia University Press.

Keck, O. (1995) "Rationales kommunikatives Handeln in den internationalen Beziehungen: Ist eine Verbindung von Rational-Choice-Theorie und Habermas' Theorie des kommunikativen Handelns möglich?" *Zeitschrift für Internationale Beziehungen* 1: 5–48.

Keir, E. (1995) *Imagining War, French and British Military Doctrine Between the Wars*, Princeton: Princeton University Press.

—— (1996) "Culture and French military doctrine before World War II," in P. J. Katzenstein (ed.) *The Culture of National Security: Norms and Identity in World Politics*, New York: Columbia University Press.

Keohane, R. O. (1983a) "The demand for international regimes," in S. D. Krasner (ed.) *International Regimes*, Ithaca NY: Cornell University Press.

—— (1983b) "Associative American development, 1776–1860," in J. G. Ruggie (ed.) *The Antinomies of Interdependence: National Welfare and the International Division of Labor*, New York: Columbia University Press.

—— (1984) *After Hegemony*, Princeton: Princeton University Press.

—— (1990a) "Multilateralism: an agenda for research," *International Journal* 45(4): 731–764.

———— (1993) "Institutional theory and the realist challenge after the Cold War," in D. A. Baldwin (ed.) *Neorealism and Neoliberalism: The Contemporary Debate,* New York: Columbia University Press.

Keohane, R. O. and Nye, J. S. (1971) "Transnational relations and world politics: an introduction," *International Organization* 25(3): 329–350.

———— (eds) (1972) *Transnational Relations and World Politics,* Cambridge MA: Harvard University Press.

———— (1975) "International interdependence and integration," in F. I. Greenstein and N. W. Polsby (eds) *Handbook of Political Science,* vol. 8, Reading MA: Addison-Wesley.

———— (1977) *Power and Interdependence,* Boston: Little, Brown.

Keohane, R. O. and Martin, L. (1995) "The promise of institutionalist theory," *International Security,* 20(1): 39–51.

Klotz, A. (1995) *Protesting Prejudice: Apartheid and the Politics of Norms in International Relations,* Ithaca NY: Cornell University Press.

Koslowski, R. and Kratochwil, F. V. (1995) "Understanding change in international politics: the Soviet empire's demise and the international system," in R. N. Lebow and T. Risse-Kappen (eds) *International Relations Theory and the End of the Cold War,* New York: Columbia University Press.

Krasner, S. D. (1976) "State power and the structure of international trade," *World Politics* 28(2): 317–347.

———— (1978) *Defending the National Interest,* Princeton: Princeton University Press.

———— (ed.) (1983) *International Regimes,* Ithaca NY: Cornell University Press.

———— (1993) "Westphalia and all that," in J. Goldstein and R. O. Keohane (eds) *Ideas and Foreign Policy,* Ithaca NY: Cornell University Press.

———— (1995/96) "Compromising Westphalia," *International Security* 20(3): 115–151.

———— (1997) "Sovereignty and its discontents," Stanford University, unpublished manuscript.

Kratochwil, F. V. (1989) *Rules, Norms and Decisions,* New York: Cambridge University Press.

Lapid, Y. and Kratochwil, F. (1997) "Revising the 'national': toward an identity agenda in neorealism?" in Lapid and Kratochwil (eds) *The Return of Culture and Identity in International Relations Theory,* Boulder CO: Rienner.

Litfin, K. (1994) *Ozone Discourses,* New York: Columbia University Press.

Little, R. (1989) "Deconstructing the balance of power," *Review of International Studies* 15(2): 87–100.

———— (1995) "Neorealism and the English School: a methodological, ontological and theoretical reassessment," *European Journal of International Relations* 1(1): 14–27.

Lumsdaine, D. H. (1993) *Moral Vision in International Politics,* Princeton: Princeton University Press.

Martin, L. (1992) *Coercive Cooperation: Explaining Multilateral Economic Sanctions,* Princeton: Princeton University Press.

Mearsheimer, J. J. (1990) "Back to the future: instability in Europe after the Cold War," *International Security* 15(1):5–56.

———— (1994/5) "The false promise of international institutions," *International Security* 19(3): 5–49.

———— (1995) "A realist reply," *International Security* 20(1): 82–93.

Milner, H. (1991) "The assumption of anarchy in international relations theory," *Review of International Studies* 17(1): 67–85.

Mitrany, D. (1943) *A Working Peace System,* Chicago: Quadrangle Press.

Morgenthau, H. (1946) *Scientific Man vs. Power Politics,* Chicago: University of Chicago Press.

———— (1985) [1948] *Politics Among Nations,* 6th edn, revised by Kenneth W. Thompson, New York: Knopf.

Mueller, H. (1994) "Internationale Beziehungen als Kommunikativen Handeln: Zur Kritik der utilitarischen Handlungstheorien," *Zeitschrift für Internationale Beziehungen* 1(1): 15–44.

———— (1995) "Spielen Hilft Nicht Immer: Die Grenzen des Rational-Choice-Ansatzens under der Platz der Theorie kommunikativen Handelns in der Analyse international Beziehungen," *Zeitschrift für Internationale Beziehungen* 2(2): 371–391.

Neufield, M. (1993) "Interpretation and the 'science' of international relations," *Review of International Studies* 19(1): 39–61.

Neumann, I. B. and Welsh, J. M. (1991) "The other in European self-definition: an addendum to the literature on international society," *Review of International Studies* 17(4): 327–348.

Niebuhr, R. (1944) *The Children of Light and the Children of Darkness,* New York: Scribners.

—— (1953) *Christian Realism and Political Problems,* Fairfield NJ: A. M. Kelley.

Nye, J. S. (1988) "Neorealism and neoliberalism," *World Politics* 40(2): 235–251.

Onuf, N. (1989) *World of Our Making,* Columbia: University of South Carolina Press.

Peirce, C. S. (1955) *Philosophical Writings,* Justus Buchler (ed.), New York: Dover.

Posen, B. (1984) *The Sources of Military Doctrine,* Ithaca NY: Cornell University Press.

—— (1993a) "Nationalism, the mass army, and military power," *International Security* 18(2): 80–124.

—— (1993b) "The security dilemma and ethnic conflict," *Survival* 35(3): 27–47.

Powell, R. (1991) "The problem of absolute and relative gains in international relations theory," *American Political Science Review* 85(4): 1303–1320.

—— (1994) "Anarchy in international relations theory: the neorealist-neoliberal debate," *International Organization* 48(2): 313–334.

Price, R. (1995) "A genealogy of the chemical weapons taboo," *International Organization* 49(1): 73–103.

Price, R. and Tannenwald, N. (1996) "Norms and deterrence: the nuclear and chemical weapons taboos," in P. J. Katzenstein (ed.) *The Culture of National Security: Norms and Identity in World Politics,* New York: Columbia University Press.

Rawls, J. (1955) "Two concepts of justice," *Philosophical Review* 64(1): 3–33.

Risse-Kappen, T. (1995) "Reden ist nicht bilig: Zur Debate um Kommunkation und Rationalität," *Zeitschrift für Internationale Beziehungen* 2(1): 171–184.

—— (1996) "Collective identity in a democratic community: the case of NATO," in P. J. Katzenstein (ed.) *The Culture of National Security: Norms and Identity in World Politics,* New York: Columbia University Press.

Ruggie, J. G. (1972) "Collective goods and future international collaboration," *American Political Science Review* 66(3): 874–893.

—— (1975) "International responses to technology: concepts and trends," *International Organization* 29(3): 557–583; also in S. Jasanoff (ed.) *Comparative Science and Technology Policy,* Cheltenham UK: Edward Elgar (1997).

—— (1980) Review of Stephen D. Krasner, "Defending the national interest: raw materials investments and US foreign policy," *American Political Science Review* 74(1): 296–299.

—— (1983) "Continuity and transformation in the world polity: toward a neorealist synthesis," *World Politics* 35(2): 261–285; also in R. O. Keohane (ed.) *Neorealism and its Critics,* New York: Columbia University Press (1986).

—— (1995) "At home abroad, abroad at home: international liberalization and domestic stability in the new world economy," *Jean Monnet Chair Papers,* 20, Florence: European University Institute; revised version in *Millennium: Journal of International Studies* 24(3): 507–526; excerpted as "Trade, protectionism and the future of welfare capitalism," in *Journal of International Affairs* 48(1): 1–11.

—— (1996) *Winning the Peace: America and World Order in the New Era,* New York: Columbia University Press.

Sassen, S. (1996) *Losing Control? Sovereignty in an Age of Globalization,* New York: Columbia University Press.

Schelling, T. C. (1960) *The Strategy of Conflict,* Cambridge, MA: Harvard University Press.

—— (1966) *Arms and Influence,* New Haven CT: Yale University Press.

Schmalz-Bruns, R. (1995) "Die Theorie kommunikativen Handelns—eine Flaschenpost?" *Zeitschrift für Internationale Beziehungen* 2(2): 347–370.

Schroeder, P. (1994) "Historical reality vs. neorealist theory," *International Security* 19(1): 108–148.

Schweller, R. (1994) "Bandwagoning for profit: bringing the revisionist state back in," *International Security* 19(1): 72–107.

Searle, J. (1984) *Minds, Brains and Science*, Cambridge MA: Harvard University Press.

—— (1995) *The Construction of Social Reality*, New York: Free Press.

Sewell, W. H. (1992) "A theory of structure: duality, agency, and transformation," *American Journal of Sociology* 98(1): 1–29.

Sikkink, K. (1993) "Human rights, principled issue-networks, and sovereignty in Latin America," *International Organization* 47(3): 411–441.

Sikkink, K. and Keck, M. [1998] *Activists Beyond Borders: Advocacy Networks in International Politics*, Ithaca: Cornell University Press.

Simmons, B. (1994) *Who Adjusts? Domestic Sources of Foreign Economic Policy During the Interwar Years*, Princeton: Princeton University Press.

—— (1996) "Rulers of the game: Central Bank independence during the interwar years," *International Organization* 50(3): 407–443.

Snidal, D. (1991) "Relative gains and the pattern of international cooperation," *American Political Science Review* 85(3): 701–726.

Snyder, J. (1984) *The Ideology of the Offensive*, Ithaca NY: Cornell University Press.

Strang, D. (1991) "Anomaly and commonplace in European political expansion: realist and institutionalist accounts," *International Organization* 45(2): 143–162.

Strange, S. (1982) "Still an extraordinary power: America's role in a global monetary system," in R. E. Lombra and W. E. Witte (eds) *Political Economy of International and Domestic Monetary Relations*, Ames: Iowa State University Press.

Van Evera, S. (1984) "Causes of war," PhD dissertation, University of California, Berkeley.

Wallander, C. A. and Keohane, R. O. (1995) "Toward an institutional theory of alliances," paper presented to Annual Meeting of International Studies Association, Chicago IL, 22–25 February 1995.

Walt, S. (1987) *The Origins of Alliances*, Ithaca NY: Cornell University Press.

Waltz, K. N. (1959) *Man, the State, and War*, New York: Columbia University Press.

—— (1979) *Theory of International Politics*, Reading MA: Addison-Wesley.

—— (1986) "Reflections on *Theory of International Politics:* a response to my critics," in R. O. Keohane (ed.) *Neorealism and its Critics*, New York: Columbia University Press.

Wapner, P. (1995) "Politics beyond the state: environmental activism and world civic politics," *World Politics* 47(3): 311–340.

Watson, A. (1992) *The Evolution of International Society*, London: Routledge.

Weber, M. (1958) *The Protestant Ethic and the Spirit of Capitalism*, Talcott Parsons (trans.), New York: Scribners.

Wendt, A. (1987) "The agent-structure problem in international relations theory," *International Organization* 41(3): 335–350.

—— (1994) "Collective identity formation and the international state," *American Political Science Review* 88(2): 384–396.

—— (1995) "Constructing international politics," *International Security* 20(1): 71–81.

Wight, M. (1977) *Systems of States*, Leicester UK: Leicester University Press.

Williamson, O. (1975) *Markets and Hierarchies*, New York: Free Press.

Yee, A. S. (1996) "The causal effects of ideas on policies," *International Organization* 50(1): 69–108.

J. ANN TICKNER

You Just Don't Understand: Troubled Engagements between Feminists and IR Theorists

Since feminist approaches to international relations first made their appearance in the late 1980s, courses on women and world politics and publications in this area have proliferated rapidly, as have panels at professional meetings.[1] Yet, the effect on the mainstream discipline, particularly in the United States, continues to be marginal, and the lack of attention paid to feminist perspectives by other critical approaches has also been disappointing (Sylvester, 1994b:ch. 4). While feminist scholars, as well as a few IR theorists, have called for conversations and dialogue across paradigms (Keohane, 1989; Peterson, 1992b:184), few public conversations or debates have occurred.[2] These continuing silences have led one scholar working in this area to conclude that most women are homeless as far as the canons of IR knowledge are concerned (Sylvester, 1994a:316).

Linguist Deborah Tannen, from whose widely read book the title of this article is taken, asserts that everyday conversations between women and men are cross-cultural and fraught with all the misunderstandings and talking at cross-purposes that cross-cultural communications frequently incur (Tannen, 1990).[3] The lack of sustained dialogue or substantively focused debates between feminists and scholars of international relations is troubling. Could this reluctance to engage in similarly difficult cross-cultural conversations be due to the very different realities and epistemologies with which feminists and international relations scholars are working?

From *International Studies Quarterly* 41 (1997): 611–32. Some of the author's notes have been omitted.

Although critical engagement is rare, evidence of awkward silences and miscommunications can be found in the oral questions and comments IR-trained feminists frequently encounter when presenting their work to IR audiences. Having articulated what seems to her (or him)[4] to be a reasoned feminist critique of international relations, or some suggestions as to the potential benefits of looking at IR through "gender-sensitive" lenses, a feminist scholar is often surprised to find that her audience does not engage with what, to her at least, are the main claims of her presentation. Questioners may assert that her presentation has little to do with the discipline of international relations or the practice of international politics. Prefaced by affirmations that the material presented is genuinely interesting and important, questions such as the following are frequently asked: What does this talk have to do with solving "real-world" problems such as Bosnia, Northern Ireland or nuclear proliferation? Why does gender have anything to do with explaining the behavior of states in the international system? Isn't IR a gender-neutral discipline? More unsettling are comments suggesting that the presentation is personally insulting to the audience, or that the material is more suitable for bedside reading than for serious scholarly discussion.

Furthermore, to scholars trained in conventional scientific methodologies, feminist approaches appear to be atheoretical—merely criticism, devoid of potential for fruitful empirical research. Therefore, they ask: Where is your research program? or: Why can't women just as well be subsumed under established theoretical approaches? Assuming the idealist notion that women are more peaceful than men lurks somewhere behind the presenter's remarks, a questioner may challenge this unasserted claim by referring to Margaret Thatcher or Golda Meier. Believing these questions to be indications of an audience unfamiliar with, or even threatened by, feminist subject matter, a frustrated presenter may well wish to declare: You just don't understand.

These often unsatisfactory oral engagements illustrate a gendered estrangement that inhibits more sustained conversations, both oral and written, between feminists and other international relations scholars. I am not saying that this is an estrangement that pits men against women. A majority of IR women scholars do not work with feminist approaches, and some men do use gender as a category of analysis. Nevertheless, I do believe, and will argue below, that these theoretical divides evidence socially constructed gender differences. Understanding them as such may be a useful entry point for overcoming silences and miscommucations, thus beginning more constructive dialogues.

In this article I explore the implications and apparent presuppositions of some of these frequently asked questions. I will demonstrate that feminists and IR scholars are drawing on very different realities and using different epistemologies when they engage in theorizing about international relations. It is my belief that these differences themselves are gendered, with all the difficulties of cross-cultural communication that this implies.

While misunderstandings occur in both directions, I will focus on feminist responses to questions and comments from conventional IR scholars because these are less familiar to IR audiences. Because I believe it is where the greatest misunderstandings occur, I have chosen to engage with methodologically conventional IR scholars—whom I define as realists, neorealists, neoliberals, peace researchers, behavioralists, and empiricists committed to data-based methods of testing, rather than with recent critical approaches, associated with post-positivist methodologies as defined in the third debate (Lapid, 1989).[5] I realize there are significant differences between these conventional

approaches. However, none of them has used gender as a category of analysis; it is in this sense, as well as in their shared commitment to a scientific methodology, that I have grouped them together.

There are three types of misunderstandings embedded in the questions outlined above: first, misunderstandings about the meaning of gender as manifested in the more personal reactions; second, the different realities or ontologies that feminists and nonfeminists see when they write about international politics, evident in comments that feminist scholars are not engaging the subject matter of IR; third, the epistemological divides that underlie questions as to whether feminists are doing theory at all.

Summarizing some work from a variety of feminist approaches, I will discuss each of these issues in the first part of this article. The second part offers some feminist perspectives on security and suggests how these perspectives might contribute to new ways of understanding contemporary security problems. This is not intended as an extensive feminist analysis of security but, rather, as a more concrete illustration of some of the issues raised in part one—that is, how misunderstandings can occur when feminists analyze IR issues. In conclusion, I will offer some thoughts on how these troubling feminist/nonfeminist IR engagements might be pursued more constructively.

Sources of Misunderstanding

GENDER: IS THE PERSONAL INTERNATIONAL?

Responding to a call to change the name of the International Brotherhood of Teamsters to include a recognition of its 30 percent female membership, James Hoffa asserted that the name should remain because "the definition of brotherhood is that it's neutral" (*New York Times*, 1996). While scholars of international relations, aware of the need to pay attention to gender-sensitive language, would probably want to claim some distance from this statement, it does indicate how, all too often, claims of gender neutrality mask deeply embedded masculinist assumptions which can naturalize or hide gender differences and gender inequalities. As documented above, even amongst the most sophisticated audiences, feminist challenges to these assumptions can often appear threatening, even when "male-bashing" is not intended.[6] Deborah Tannen has suggested that the reason gender differences are more troubling than other cross-cultural differences is that they occur where the home and hearth are: "[W]e enact and create our gender, and our inequality, with every move that we make" (Tannen, 1990:283). Feminist scholars claim that gender differences permeate all facets of public and private life, a socially constructed divide which they take to be problematic in itself; IR scholars, however, may believe that gender is about interpersonal relations between women and men, but not about international politics.

Given that most contemporary feminist scholarship takes gender—which embodies relationships of power inequality—as its central category of analysis, the fact that the meaning of gender is so often misunderstood is, I believe, central to problems of misunderstanding and miscommunication. Almost all feminists who write about international relations use gender in a social constructivist sense, a move that many see not only as necessary for overcoming gender discrimination, but also as a way of opening avenues for communication by avoiding some of the threatened responses illustrated above.

As Sandra Harding (1986:17–8) has suggested, gendered social life is produced through three distinct processes: assigning dualistic gender metaphors to various perceived dichotomies, appealing to these gender dualisms to organize social activity, and dividing necessary social activities between different groups of humans. She refers to these three aspects of gender as gender symbolism, gender structure, and individual gender.

Feminists define gender, in the symbolic sense, as a set of variable but socially and culturally constructed characteristics—such as power, autonomy, rationality, and public—that are stereotypically associated with masculinity. Their opposites—weakness, dependence, emotion, and private—are associated with femininity. There is

evidence to suggest that both women and men assign a more positive value to masculine characteristics. Importantly, definitions of masculinity and femininity are relational and depend on each other for their meaning; in other words, what it means to be a "real man" is not to display "womanly" weaknesses. Since these characteristics are social constructions, it is entirely possible for Margaret Thatcher to act like an iron lady or a "real man"; in fact, many feminists would argue that such behavior is necessary for both women and men to succeed in the tough world of international politics. As Tannen (1990:43) claims, girls and boys grow up in different worlds of words, but gender goes beyond language: it is a symbolic system that shapes many aspects of our culture. As Carol Cohn (1993:229) has suggested, even if real men and women do not fit these gender "ideals," the existence of this system of meaning affects us all—both our interpretations of the world and the way the world understands us.

As Joan Scott (1986:1069) claims, while the forms gender relations take across different cultures may vary, they are almost always unequal; therefore, gender, in the structural sense, is a primary way of signifying relationships of power. Although gender is frequently seen as belonging in the household and, therefore, antithetical to the "real" business of politics, a reason why it is often seen as irrelevant to IR, Scott argues that it is constructed in the economy and the polity through various institutional structures that have the effect of "naturalizing," and even legalizing, women's inferior status. Recent feminist writings that deal with issues of race and class problematize these power relationships still further.[7]

Individual gender relations enter into and are constituent elements in every aspect of human experience (Flax, 1987:624). Jane Flax reminds us that, while feminism is about recovering women's activities, it must also be aware of how these activities are constituted through the social relations in which they are situated. Therefore, gender is not just about women; it is also about men and masculinity, a point that needs to be emphasized if scholars of international relations are to better understand why feminists claim that it is relevant to their discipline and why they believe that a gendered analysis of its basic assumptions and concepts can yield fruitful results.

THEORIZING THE INTERNATIONAL: ARE FEMINISTS REALLY "DOING" IR?

Deborah Tannen (1990:97) claims that women are more comfortable than men with an ethnographic style of individually oriented story-telling typical of anthropology, a difference that fits IR scholarship as well. International relations, particularly after the move toward science in the post–World War II period in the United States, has generally shied away from level-one analysis, preferring a more systemic or state-oriented focus. Coming out of literatures that are centrally concerned with individuals and social relations, and that are more explicitly normative, feminist perspectives, on the other hand, demonstrate a preference for more humanistically oriented methodologies. Although their focus is different, their discomfort with structural IR is similar to that captured in Martin Wight's famous title, "Why Is There No International Theory?"

In "Why Is There No International Theory?" Martin Wight (1995) remarked on the absence of an international theoretical tradition comparable to the very rich historical tradition of Western political philosophy.[8] According to Wight, the reason for this absence can be found in the character of the international system. Theorizing the international would mean speculating about a society or community of states. Since he saw the international system as evidencing the absence of society, a "realm of necessity" characterized by "recurrence and repetition," Wight (1995:32) claimed that there could be no "progressive" international theory, only a "theory of survival" marked by "an intellectual and moral poverty." Wight is, of course, using theory in an explicitly normative sense, not fashionable amongst contemporary, more scientific theoretical approaches. He is postulating a "theory of the good life" (Wight, 1995:32), a progressive theory of social relations that calls for soci-

etal improvements, improvements, Wight claims, that can take place only within a political space such as the state.

While many contemporary feminist theorists would take issue with Wight's views on equating progressive theory with a tradition of Western political thought that has generally either excluded women altogether or treated them as less than fully human (Okin, 1980), his reasons for claiming the poverty of international theory have relevance for problems feminists encounter when theorizing the international. With an ontology based on unitary states operating in an asocial, anarchical international environment, there is little in realist theory that provides an entry point for feminist theories, grounded as they are in an epistemology that takes social relations as its central category of analysis.

As demonstrated above, much of contemporary feminism is also committed to progressive or emancipatory goals, particularly the goal of achieving equality for women through the elimination of unequal gender relations. Drawing on earlier literatures, such as those on women in the military and women and development, feminist writings on international relations have focused on individuals in their social, political, and economic settings, rather than on decontextualized unitary states and anarchical international structures. They investigate how military conflict and the behavior of states in the international system are constructed through, or embedded in, unequal gendered structural relations and how these affect the life chances of individuals, particularly women. These very different foci evoke the kind of questions introduced above about what is the legitimate subject matter of the discipline.

*   *   *

EPISTEMOLOGICAL DIVIDES: WHERE IS YOUR RESEARCH PROGRAM?

International Theory. In his commentary on Wight's piece, discussed earlier, Hans Morgenthau (1995) asserted that international theory could be progressive but in a rather different sense: "[T]he ideal toward which these theories try to progress is ultimately international peace and order to be achieved through scientific precision and predictability in understanding and manipulating international affairs" (Morgenthau, 1995:40). For Morgenthau, the purpose of theory was "to bring order and meaning into a mass of unconnected material and to increase knowledge through the logical development of certain propositions empirically established" (Morgenthau, 1995:46). Unlike Wight, Morgenthau, motivated by countering German fascism of the 1930s, was making the case for a scientific international theory, a type of theory that has strongly influenced mainstream international relations, at least in the United States.[9]

As I shall discuss below, this view of the purposes of theory is one that feminists have found problematic. However, feminists often misunderstand or ignore the rationale for the search for more scientific theories offered by early realists such as Morgenthau. Most of the founding fathers of American realism in the post–World War II period were European intellectuals fleeing from Nazi persecution. Flagrant violations of international law and abuses of human rights in the name of German nationalism motivated Morgenthau, and other early realists, to dissociate the realm of morality and values from the realpolitik of international politics. Painting a gloomy picture of "political man," and the dangers of an anarchic international system, Morgenthau claimed that war was always a possibility. However, he believed that the search for deeper explanations of the laws that govern human action could contribute to lessening the chances that such disasters would recur in the future.[10] Defending science against ideologically charged claims, which he associated with European fascism of the 1930s, Morgenthau believed that only by a more "scientific" understanding of its causes could the likelihood of war be diminished.

According to Stanley Hoffmann (1977), Morgenthau shaped these truths as a guide to those in power; thus, the growth of the discipline cannot be separated from the growing American role in world affairs in the post–World War II era. Speaking to and moving among foreign policy elites, this "American discipline" was, and is, aimed at an audience very different from feminist international relations. This difference—to which I return below—also causes misunderstandings.

The scientific turn in postwar realism was also adopted by behavioralists, neorealists, liberal institutionalists, and some peace researchers, all of whom drew on models from the natural sciences and from economics to build their theories. Seeking scientific respectability, international theorists turned to the natural sciences for their methodologies; many of them were also defending the autonomy of rational inquiry against totalitarian ideologies, this time of postwar Communism. Theories were defined as sets of logically related, ideally causal propositions, to be empirically tested or falsified in the Popperian sense. Scientific research programs were developed from realist assumptions about the international system serving as the "hard core" (Lakatos and Musgrave, 1970). While international theorists never sought the precision of Newton's grand schemes of deterministic laws and inescapable forces, they did claim that the international system is more than the constant and regular behavior of its parts (Hollis and Smith, 1990:50). Popular in the discipline, structural theories account for behavior by searching for causes. These theorists believe that events are governed by the laws of nature; in other words, behavior is generated by structures external to the actors themselves (Hollis and Smith, 1990:3).[11] In all these endeavors, theorists have generally assumed the possibility as well as the desirability of conducting systematic and cumulative scientific research.

Borrowing from economics, game theory and rational choice theory became popular for explaining the choices and optimizing behavior of self-interested states in an anarchical international system as well as a means for interpreting the actions of their foreign policy decision makers. Given the dangers and unpredictability of such a system, theory building was motivated by the desire to control and predict (Waltz, 1979:6).[12] The search for systematic inquiry could, hopefully, contribute to the effort of diminishing the likelihood of future conflict. Broadly defined as positivist, this turn to science represents a view of the creation of knowledge based on four assumptions: first, a belief in the unity of science—that is, the same methodologies can apply in the natural and social worlds; second, that there is a distinction between facts and values, with facts being neutral between theories; third, that the social world has regularities like the natural world; and fourth, that the way to determine the truth of statements is by appeal to neutral facts or an empiricist epistemology (Smith, 1997:168).[13]

Feminist Theory. Since it entered the field of international relations in the late 1980s, feminist theory has often, but not exclusively, been located within the critical voices of the "third debate," a term articulated by Yosef Lapid (1989). Although they are not all postmodern, or even post-Enlightenment, in their normative orientation at least, an assumption sometimes implied by conventional scholars, many contemporary feminist international relations scholars would identify themselves as post-positivists in terms of Lapid's articulation of the term and in terms of the definition of positivism outlined above. While there is no necessary connection between feminist approaches and post-positivism, there is a strong resonance for a variety of reasons including a commitment to epistemological pluralism as well as to certain ontological sensitivities. With a preference for hermeneutic, historically based, humanistic and philosophical traditions of knowledge cumulation, rather than those based on the natural sciences, feminist theorists are often skeptical of empiricist methodologies that claim neutrality of facts. While many feminists do see structural regularities, such as gender and patriarchy, they define them as socially constructed and variable across time, place, and cultures, rather than as universal and natural.

Agreeing with Robert Cox's assertion that theory is always for someone and for some purpose, the goal of feminist approaches is similar to that of critical theory as defined by Cox. While not all historians would accept this link, Cox asserts that critical theory "stands apart from the prevailing order of the world and asks how that order came about":

it can, therefore, be a guide to strategic action for bringing about an alternative order (Cox, 1981: 129–30).

Cox contrasts critical theory with conventional theory which he labels "problem-solving,"—a type of conversation that Tannen associates with men (1990:ch. 2). Problem-solving takes the world as it finds it and implicitly accepts the prevailing order as its framework (Cox, 1981:130). Since feminist theorists believe that the world is characterized by gender hierarchies that are detrimental to women, they would be unlikely to take such an epistemological stance. In the words of one feminist scholar who defines herself as a post-positivist, "postpositivism compels our attention to context and historical process, to contingency and uncertainty, to how we construct, rather than dis-cover, our world(s)" (Peterson, 1992a:57).

In constructing their approaches to international theory, feminists draw on a variety of philosophical traditions and literatures outside international relations and political science within which most IR scholars are trained. While IR feminists are seeking genuine knowledge that can help them to better understand the issues with which they are concerned, the IR training they receive rarely includes such knowledge. Hence, they, like scholars in other critical approaches, have gone outside the discipline to seek what they believe are more appropriate methodologies for understanding the social construction and maintenance of gender heirarchies. This deepens the level of misunderstanding and miscommunication and, unfortunately, often leads to negative stereotyping on all sides of these epistemological divides.

*   *   *

Feminists are arguing for moving beyond knowledge frameworks that construct international theory without attention to gender and for searching deeper to find ways in which gender hierarchies serve to reinforce socially constructed institutions and practices that perpetuate different and unequal role expectations, expectations that have contributed to fundamental inequalities between women and men in the world of international politics. Therefore, including gender as a central category of analysis transforms knowledge in ways that go beyond adding women; importantly, but frequently misunderstood, this means that women cannot be studied in isolation from men.

While most feminists are committed to the emancipatory goal of achieving a more just society, which, for them, includes ending the oppression of women, the Kantian project of achieving this goal through Enlightenment knowledge is problematic because of feminist claims that this type of knowledge is gendered. Feminists assert that dichotomies, such as rational/irrational, fact/value, universal/particular, and public/private, upon which Western Enlightenment knowledge has been built and which they see as gendered, separate the mind (rationality) from the body (nature) and, therefore, diminish the legitimacy of women as "knowers." Susan Heckman has claimed that, "since the Enlightenment, knowledge has been defined in terms of 'man,' the subject, and espouses an epistemology that is radically homocentric." Since Enlightenment epistemology places women in an inferior position, outside the realm of rationality, challenging the priority of "man" in the modern episteme must be fundamental to any feminist program (Heckman, 1990:2). Similarly, Patricia Hill Collins (1989) claims that Black women would be unlikely to subscribe to an epistemology that has, for the most part, excluded Blacks and other minorities. Black women, she claims, prefer, and consider more legitimate, knowledge construction based on concrete experience of everyday lives, stories, and dialogues. These subjective epistemological positions are unsettling for scholars trained in scientific methodologies based on more abstract knowledge claims.

∗   ∗   ∗

Feminists argue, however, that broadening the base from which knowledge is constructed, that is, including the experiences of women, can actually enhance objectivity.[14] Arguing from a modified standpoint position,[15] Sandra Harding explores the question as to whether objectivity and socially situated knowledge is an impossible combination. She concludes that adopting a feminist standpoint actually strengthens standards of objectivity. While it requires acknowledging that all human beliefs are socially situated, it also requires critical evaluation to determine which social situations tend to generate the most objective knowledge claims. Harding argues for what she calls "strong objectivity" which extends the task of scientific research to include a systematic examination of powerful background beliefs and making strange what has hitherto appeared as familiar (Harding, 1991:142, 149).

Likewise, Donna Haraway argues for what she calls "embodied objectivity" or "situated knowledge." For Haraway, situated knowledge does not mean relativism but shared conversations leading to "better accounts of the world" (Haraway, 1988:580).[16] Indeed, feminists frequently use the metaphor of conversation both as a preferred methodology and in their calls for engagement with IR scholars. Since conversational or dialogic methodologies come out of a hermeneutic tradition, conversation is not a metaphor social scientists are likely to employ; indeed, it is one that would appear quite strange as a basis for theory construction.[17]

This brief overview of a variety of feminist epistemologies suggests that they are quite different from those prevailing in conventional international relations. Since all feminist approaches are concerned with social relations, particularly the investigation of the causes and consequences of unequal relationships between women and men, the questions they ask about international relations are likely to be quite different from those of international theorists primarily concerned with the interaction of states in the international system. While feminist theories might fit more comfortably into what Hollis and Smith (1990) term the "inside," or hermeneutical approach, feminists construct their knowledge about international relations not so much from the perspectives of "insiders" but from voices of the disempowered and marginalized not previously heard.[18] The sounds of these unfamiliar voices and the issues they raise sometimes cause conventional scholars to question whether feminists even belong within the same discipline.

As Sandra Harding (1991:123) tells us, an important task of feminist theory is to make strange what has previously appeared familiar, or to challenge us to question what has hitherto appeared as "natural." In international relations, this has involved an examination of the basic assumptions and concepts of the field, taken as unproblematic—and gender-neutral—by conventional international theorists. While critical approaches more generally have often been accused of indulging in criticism rather than producing new research programs (Walt, 1991:223), feminists would argue that a critical examination is necessary because feminist research agendas cannot be built without first exposing and questioning the gender biases of the field. As an example of one such conceptual reexamination and its implications for different kinds of investigations and understandings, I shall now outline some feminist perspectives on security. Rather than attempt to offer a comprehensive analysis of the subject, I use these observations to illustrate more concretely some of the sources of misunderstanding discussed above; this section is also intended to suggest potential feminist research agendas.[19]

Feminist Perspectives on Security

I have chosen to focus on security because it has been central to the discipline of international relations since its inception in the early twentieth century. It is also an important issue for feminists who write about international relations. However, as I have indicated, since feminist perspectives are constructed out of very different ontologies and epistemologies, their definitions of security, explanations of insecurity, and prescriptions for security enhancement are areas where divergence from conventional international theory is significant. Thus, they offer a good illustration of some of the misunderstandings outlined above. I shall begin by defining what certain feminist scholars mean by security and insecurity; I shall outline some of the kinds of empirical evidence feminists use when analyzing security. Then, drawing on some of the feminist approaches discussed earlier, I will illus-

trate some of the types of explanations feminist theories offer for some contemporary insecurities, thereby demonstrating potential avenues for further research. While these research agendas may be different from conventional analyses of security, they too claim to seek greater understanding of "real-world" security issues.

WHAT IS SECURITY?

Scholars in the realist paradigm, within which much of the analysis of security has taken place, define security in political/military terms, as the protection of the boundaries and integrity of the state and its values against the dangers of a hostile international environment, Martin Wight's "realm of necessity" (Wolfers, 1962). In their search for more parsimonious explanations, neorealists emphasize the anarchical structure of the system rather than domestic factors as being the primary determinant of states' insecurities. States are postulated as unitary actors whose internal characteristics, beyond an assessment of their relative capabilities, are not seen as necessary for understanding their vulnerabilities or security-enhancing behavior (Waltz, 1979). States' efforts to increase their power or engage in balance-of-power activities are explained as attempts to improve their security. In the United States, security studies, defined largely in terms of the bipolar nuclear confrontation between the United States and the former Soviet Union, became an important subfield within the discipline. For security specialists, this definition of security remains in place in the post–Cold War era. Security specialists believe that military power remains a central element of international politics and that the traditional agenda of security studies is, therefore, expanding rather than shrinking (Walt, 1991:222).

In the 1980s, a trend toward broadening the definition of security emerged as peace researchers, those concerned with poverty in the South, environmentalists, and certain European policy makers began to define security in economic and environmental as well as political/military terms (Independent Commission, 1982; Ullman, 1983; Mathews,

1989; Buzan, 1991). While this trend continues to gain strength after the end of the Cold War, the issue remains controversial.[20] It is, however, a definition more compatible with most contemporary feminist scholarship that also finds traditional definitions of security too narrow for what they consider to be the security issues of the post–Cold War world. There are, however, important differences between the new security literature and feminist perspectives since very little of the new security literature has paid attention to women or gender.

Many IR feminists define security broadly in multidimensional and multilevel terms—as the diminution of all forms of violence, including physical, structural, and ecological (Tickner, 1992; Peterson and Runyan, 1993). Since women are marginal to the power structures of most states, and since feminist perspectives on security take women's security as their central concern, most of these definitions start with the individual or community rather than the state or the international system. According to Christine Sylvester (1994b), security is elusive and partial and involves struggle and contention; it is a process rather than an ideal in which women must act as agents in the provision of their own security. Speaking from the margins, feminists are sensitive to the various ways in which social hierarchies manifest themselves across societies and history. Striving for security involves exposing these different social hierarchies, understanding how they construct and are constructed by the international order, and working to denaturalize and dismantle them.

These feminist definitions of security grow out of the centrality of social relations, particularly gender relations, for feminist theorizing. Coming out of different literatures and working with definitions based on different ontologies as well as different normative goals, feminist writings on security open themselves up to criticism that their work does not fall within the subject matter of international relations. Feminists would respond by asserting that structural inequalities, which are central contributors to the insecurity of individuals, are built into the historical legacy of the modern state and the international system of which it is a part. Calling into question realist boundaries between anarchy and danger on the outside and order and security on the inside, feminists believe that state-centric or structural analyses miss the interrelation of insecurity across levels of analysis. Since "women's space" inside households has also been beyond the reach of law in most states, feminists are often quite suspicious of boundaries that mark states as security providers. They would argue that Martin Wight's political space, within which theorizing the good life is possible, requires radical restructuring before it can be regarded as offering a safe space for women.[21] I shall now outline some of the evidence feminists draw on when defining the kinds of personal and structural insecurities they believe must be overcome in order to create a more secure world.

Questioning the role of states as adequate security providers leads feminists to analyze power and military capabilities differently from conventional international relations scholars. Rather than seeing military capability as an assurance against outside threats to the state, militaries frequently are seen as antithetical to individuals', particularly women's, security—as winners in the competition for resources for social safety nets on which women depend disproportionately to men, as definers of an ideal type of militarized citizenship, usually denied to women (Tobias, 1990), or as legitimators of a kind of social order that can sometimes even valorize state violence.

Consequently, when analyzing political/military dimensions of security, feminists tend to focus on the consequences of what happens during wars rather than on their causes (Pettman, 1996:87–106). They draw on evidence to emphasize the negative impact of contemporary military conflicts on civilian populations. According to the United Nations' *Human Development Report*, there has been a sharp increase in the proportion of civilian casualties of war—from about 10 percent at the beginning of the century to 90 percent today. While the *Report* does not break down these casualties by sex, it claims that this makes women among the worst sufferers even though they constitute only 2 percent of the world's regular army personnel (United Nations, 1995:45). As mothers, family providers, and care-givers, women are particularly penalized by economic sanctions associated with military conflict, such as the UN boycott put in place against Iraq after the Gulf War. Women and children (about 18 million at the end of 1993) constitute about 80 percent of the total refugee population, a population whose numbers increased from 3 million to 27 million between 1970 and 1994, mainly due to military conflict (United Nations, 1995:14).[22] Feminists also draw attention to issues of rape in war; as illustrated by the Bosnian case, rape is not just an accident of war but is, or can be, a systematic military strategy. Cynthia Enloe (1993:119) has described social structures in place around most army bases where women are often kidnapped and sold into prostitution.

For feminists writing about security, economic dimensions and issues of structural violence have been as important as issues of military conflict.[23] According to the *Human Development Report*, in no country are women doing as well as men. While figures vary from state to state, on an average, women earn three quarters of men's earnings. Of the 1.3 billion people estimated to be in poverty today, 70 percent are women: the number of rural women living in absolute poverty rose by nearly 50 percent over the past two decades (United Nations, 1995:36). Women receive a disproportionately small share of credit from formal banking institutions. For example, in Latin America, women constitute only 7–11 percent of the beneficiaries of credit programs; while women in Africa contribute up to 80 percent of total food production, they receive less than 10 percent of the credit to small farmers and 1 percent of total credit to agriculture (United Nations, 1995:4, 39). While women actually work more hours than men in almost all societies, their work is underremunerated and undervalued because much of it takes place outside the market economy, in households or subsistence sectors. Whether women are gatherers of fuel and firewood or mothers of sick children, their lives are severely impacted by resource shortages and environmental pollution.

These are some of the issues with which feminists writing about security, defined in both political/military and economic terms, are concerned. They are not, however, issues considered relevant to conventional state-centric security concerns. Challenging both the traditional notion of the state as the framework within which security should be defined and analyzed, and the conventional boundaries between security inside and anarchy outside the state, feminists embed their analyses in a system of relations that cross the boundaries. Challenging the notion of discrete levels of analysis, they argue that inequalities between women and men, inequalities that contribute to all forms of insecurity, can only be understood and explained within the framework of a system shaped by patriarchal structures that extend from the household to the global economy. I shall now elaborate on some of the ways feminists explain these persistent inequalities.

EXPLAINING INSECURITY

Feminists claim that inequalities, which decrease individuals', particularly women's, security, cannot be understood using conventional tools of analysis. Theories that construct structural explanations that aspire to universality typically fail to recognize how unequal social structures impact in different ways on the security of different groups. Feminists believe that only by introducing gender as a category of analysis can the differential impact of the state system and the global economy on the lives of women and men be analyzed and understood. Feminists also caution that searching for universal laws may miss the ways in which gender hierarchies manifest themselves in a variety of ways across time and culture; therefore, theories must be sensitive to history, context, and contingency.

Questioning the neutrality of facts and concepts, feminists have challenged international theory's claim that the state can be taken as given in its theoretical investigations. Feminists assert that only by analyzing the evolution of the modern state system and its changing political, economic, and social structures can we begin to understand its limitations as a security provider. The particular insecurities of women cannot be understood without reference to historical divisions between public and private spheres. As Spike Peterson and other feminists have pointed out, at the time of the foundation of the modern Western state, and coincidentally with the beginnings of capitalism, women were not included as citizens but consigned to the private space of the household; thus, they were removed both from the public sphere of politics and the economic sphere of production (Peterson, 1992a:40–4). As a result, women lost much of their existing autonomy and agency, becoming more dependent on men for their economic security.

∗ ∗ ∗ While these issues may appear irrelevant to the conduct of international politics, feminists claim that these gender-differentiated roles actually support and legitimate the international security-seeking behavior of the state.

For example, feminists have argued that unequal gender relations are important for sustaining the military activities of the state. Thus, what goes on in wars is not irrelevant to their causes and outcomes. The notion that (young) males fight wars to protect vulnerable groups such as women and children who cannot be expected to protect themselves has been an important motivator for the recruitment of military forces and support for wars. Feminists have challenged this protector/protected relationship with evidence of the high increase in civilian casualties documented above.[24] As feminists have pointed out, if women are thought to be in need of protection, it is often their protectors who provide the greatest threat. Judith Stiehm (1982) claims that this dependent, asymmetric relationship leads to feelings of low self-esteem and little sense of responsibility on the part of women. For men, the presence of able-bodied, competent adults who are seen as dependent and incapable can contribute to misogyny. Anne Orford (1996) tells us that accounts of sexual assault by peacekeepers have emerged in many UN peacekeeping operations. However, such violence against women is usually dismissed as a "natural" outcome of the right of young soldiers to enjoy themselves. This type of behavior may also be aggravated by the misogynist training of soldiers

who are taught to fight and kill through appeals to their masculinity; such behavior further erodes the notion of protection.

Whereas feminist analysis of military security has focused on the gendered structures of state institutions, issues of economic security and insecurity have emphasized the interrelationship between activities in markets and households. Feminists claim that women's particular economic insecurities can only be understood in the context of patriarchal structures, mediated through race, class, and ethnicity, which have the effect of consigning women to households or low-paying jobs. Public/private boundaries have the effect of naturalizing women's unremunerated work in the home to the detriment of women's autonomy and economic security. Women's disproportionate numbers at the bottom of the socioeconomic scale cannot be explained by market conditions alone; they also require an understanding that certain types of work such as teaching, nursing, and other forms of care-giving are often considered "natural" for women to perform (Peterson and Runyan, 1993:37; Pettman, 1996:165–8). Moreover, the clustering of women in low-paying or non-waged work in subsistence or households cannot be understood by using rational choice models, because women may have internalized the ideas behind traditional systems of discrimination, and thus may themselves view their roles as natural (Nussbaum and Glover, 1995:91). In other words, social expectations having to do with gender roles can reinforce economic inequalities between women and men and exacerbate women's insecurities. Such issues can only be explained by using gender as a category of analysis; since they take them as given, rational actor models miss the extent to which opportunities and choices are constrained by the social relations in which they are embedded.

Many of these issues seem far removed from the concerns of international relations. But, employing bottom-up rather than top-down explanations, feminists claim that the operation of the global economy and states' attempts to secure benefits from it are built on these unequal social relations between women and men which work to the detriment of women's (and certain men's) security. For example, states that successfully compete in attracting multinational corporations often do so by promising them a pool of docile cheap labor consisting of young unmarried women who are not seen as "breadwinners" and who are unlikely to organize to protest working conditions and low wages (Enloe, 1990:151–76). When states are forced to cut back on government spending in order to comply with structural adjustment programs, it is often the expectation that women, by virtue of their traditional role as care-givers, will perform the welfare tasks previously assumed by the state without remuneration. According to Caroline Moser (1991:105), structural adjustment programs dedicated to economic "efficiency" are built on the assumption of the elasticity of women's unpaid labor.

In presenting some feminist perspectives on security and some explanations for insecurity, I have demonstrated how feminists are challenging levels of analysis and boundaries between inside and outside which they see, not as discrete constructs delineating boundaries between anarchy and order, but as contested and mutually constitutive of one another. Through a reexamination of the state, feminists demonstrate how the unequal social relations on which most states are founded both influence their external security-seeking behavior and are influenced by it. Investigating states as gendered constructs is not irrelevant to understanding their security-seeking behaviors as well as whose interests are most served by these behaviors. Bringing to light social structures that support war and "naturalize" the gender inequalities manifested in markets and households is not irrelevant for understanding their causes. Feminists claim that the gendered foundations of states and markets must be exposed and challenged before adequate understandings of, and prescriptions for, women's (and certain men's) security broadly defined can be formulated.

Conclusions

Feminist theorists have rarely achieved the serious engagement with other IR scholars for which they have frequently called. When they have occurred, conversations have often led to misunderstandings and other kinds of miscommunication, such as awkward silences and feminist resistances to suggestions for incorporation into more mainstream approaches. In this article I have tried to reconstruct some typical conversational encounters and to offer some hypotheses as to why estrangement seems so often to be the result. Although I realize that these encounters demonstrate misunderstandings on both sides, I have emphasized some feminist perspectives because they are less likely to be familiar to IR scholars. While it is all too easy to account for these troubled engagements between IR scholars and feminists solely in terms of differences in ontologies and epistemologies, it must be acknowledged that power differences play an important role also. Inequalities in power between mainstream and feminist IR allow for greater ignorance of feminist approaches on the part of the mainstream than is possible for feminists with respect to conventional IR, if they are to be accorded any legitimacy within the profession. Because of this power differential, feminists are suspicious of cooptation or attempts to label certain of their approaches as more compatible than others.

Understanding that all these problems are inherent in calling for one more effort at renewed conversation, I have tried to suggest and analyze reasons for the frequent failures or avoidance of such efforts, comparing these failures to problems of cross-cultural communications. * * *

*   *   *

Feminists often draw on the notion of conversation when pursuing their goal of shareable understandings of the world. Skeptical of the possibility of arriving at one universal truth, they advocate seeking understanding through dialogues across boundaries and cultures in which the voices of others, particularly those on the margins, must be seen as equally valid as one's own.[25] This method of truth-seeking, motivated by the attempt to separate valid knowledge from what feminists see as power-induced distortions, is far removed from more scientific methodologies and from a discipline whose original goal was to better understand the behavior of states in order to offer advice to their policy makers. Therefore, feminists must understand that their preferred methodologies and the issues they raise are alien to the traditional discipline; and IR scholars must realize that speaking from the perspective of the disempowered appears increasingly urgent in a world where the marginalized are the most likely victims of war and the negative effects of economic globalization.

*　　*　　*

Asking the question as to how we open lines of communication, Deborah Tannen (1990:120–1) suggests that men and women must try to take each other on their own terms rather than apply the standards of one group to the behavior of the other. Additionally, she claims that this is not an easy task because all of us tend to look for a single "right" way of doing things. Could this be a model for beginning more productive conversations between feminists and IR theorists?

NOTES

1. In defining this literature as new, I am referring to recent work that is critiquing international relations theory from a variety of feminist perspectives and reconstructing international relations through gender-sensitive lenses. For some examples see Enloe, 1990, Grant and Newland, 1991, Peterson, 1992a, Tickner, 1992, Sylvester, 1994b, and Pettman, 1996. * * *

2. One recent article that does engage in a critique of some feminist literature is Jones (1996). Certain introductory IR texts have begun to incorporate feminist approaches. See for examples Rourke (1993) and Goldstein (1994). As yet, feminist articles in mainstream U.S./IR journals have been rare. There has been some recognition of critical approaches other than feminism by the mainstream; however, they have often been dismissed or assessed quite negatively, particularly postmod-

ernism. For a more constructive engagement see Keohane (1988) and the response by Walker (1989).

3. While *You Just Don't Understand* is a popular, somewhat stereotypical book, it is, I believe, a useful entry point for offering insights into the problems of gendered cross-cultural communications. It comes out of a rich tradition of gender-sensitive discourse analysis many of whose classics are cited in Tannen's bibliography.

4. I am not saying that men cannot engage in feminist or gender analysis; indeed, gender is not just about women. However, it is usually women and feminists who write about gender issues. The main reason for this is that what it means to be human has generally been equated with (often Western elite) men. As feminists point out, women have often been rendered less than fully human, or even invisible, by this move. Revelations of the gender biases of medical research are an important illustration of this.

5. For examples of where I have engaged more systematically with some of these approaches I have defined as conventional see Tickner, 1988, 1992, 1994.

6. Conversely, dangers lurk in the uncritical switch to gender-neutral language when it is used even when the speaker is clearly not speaking for or about women. See Okin, 1989: 10–3, for elaboration of this point.

7. For example, as Bell Hooks (1984) claims, nonwhite women would not subscribe to the feminist goal of making women equal to men who are themselves victims of racist oppression. I am aware of the importance of including class and race differences when defining and analyzing gender and women's oppression. However, I do not believe this should prevent us from making testable, generalizeable claims about the gendering of the discipline of international relations. For a useful discussion of this issue more generally see Martin, 1994.

8. It is interesting to note that certain IR feminists

have expressed some affinity with classical realism and/or more sociological approaches associated with the English School. Whitworth (1989:268) claims that the classical realism of Morgenthau acknowledges that meaning is contingent and socially constructed, thus creating a space, in theory if not in practice, for the analysis of gender. The authors chosen by James Der Derian for his edited volume *International Theory* (1995), which includes Wight's piece, illustrate the link between the English School and some other contemporary critical perspectives. It also includes American scholars of the scientific tradition. I have chosen to cite from this volume, rather than going back to the original sources, for this reason.

9. Just as he was not considered scientific enough by many subsequent international theorists, Morgenthau was himself ambivalent about the turn to science in American international theory. For evidence of this ambivalence see Morgenthau, 1946. For an analysis of the reasons for the preference for scientific methodologies in the U.S. see Hoffmann, 1977.

10. For a feminist critique of Morgenthau's six principles of political realism see Tickner, 1988.

11. Hollis and Smith (1990) identify two traditions in international theory, "inside" and "outside." Since "inside" theories are interpretive or hermeneutical, feminist theories would probably fit more comfortably into this tradition, although it too presents problems for feminists. A tradition constructed out of the beliefs and intentions of human actors has rarely included women as actors.

12. What level of prediction is desirable or possible is a matter of some contention amongst international theorists. Claims that international theorists failed to predict the end of the Cold War has added fuel to this debate (see Gaddis, 1992–93).

13. Not all IR theorists, who associate themselves with the scientific tradition, would agree with all parts of this definition. Few social scientists believe that their work is value-free or that

universally valid generalizations are possible; nevertheless, they would probably agree that these are useful standards to which to aspire. Most would believe, however, that systematic social scientific research is possible and desirable and that methodologies borrowed from the natural sciences can be useful, although some have recognized the problems of applying natural science methods to the social sciences. I am indebted to an anonymous reviewer and to Harvey Starr for these observations.

14. As Sandra Harding (1991:123) emphasizes, women's experiences alone are not a reliable guide for deciding which knowledge claims are preferable because women tend to speak in socially acceptable ways. Nevertheless, Harding believes that women's lives are the place from which feminist research should begin.

15. I use the term *modified* to indicate that Harding takes into consideration postmodern critiques of an essentialized standpoint which, they say, speaks from the position of privileged Western women. Standpoint feminism comes out of Hegel's notion of the master/slave relationship and out of Marxist theory more generally. Hegel and Marxists claim that the slave (or the proletariat) have, by necessity, a more comprehensive understanding of the position of both the master (or the capitalist) *and* the slave.

16. Christine Sylvester's method of emphathetic cooperation draws on this idea of shared conversations (see Sylvester, 1994a, 1994b).

17. Tannen's (1990:ch.3) distinction between "report-talk" and "rapport talk" may be relevant to this discussion of the gendering of scientific methods. According to Tannen, for most men, talk is a means of preserving independence, whereas, for most women, it is a way of establishing connections.

18. It is important to stress that feminists recognize the multiplicity of women's voices mediated by class, race, and cultural positions. Debate on the problems of essentialism is one of the most vital in feminist theory today. For

an elaboration of the issues at stake see Martin, 1994.

19. I have offered a more systematic analysis of security from a feminist perspective in *Gender in International Relations* (Tickner, 1992; see also Peterson, 1992a, and Peterson and Runyan, 1993).

20. Walt (1991) makes a case for continuing to define security narrowly. For a critique of Walt's position see Kolodziej, 1992.

21. I am aware that women's relations to the state vary across race, class, and culture. I am also aware that the state may not be a safe space for men in racially or ethnically divided societies. Mona Harrington (1992) has offered an interesting challenge to feminists' often negative views of the state. Harrington argues for a reformulated "feminist" state which could provide the necessary protection against global capitalism and international institutions which, she argues, increasingly, have no democratic accountability. This challenge seems to have saliency in an era of "globalization" and its negative effects on marginalized populations documented by the *Human Development Report* (United Nations, 1995). I cite the 1995 edition because it focused specifically on women and gender issues. The UN's recent disaggregation of data by sex has significantly advanced the potential for research on women worldwide.

22. Although the majority of refugees in camps are women left alone to care for children and, therefore, acting as heads of households, they usually do not have refugee status in their own right but only as wives within families (Moser, 1991:96).

23. The term *structural violence* was first introduced by Johan Galtung in the 1970s to explain decreased life expectancy of individuals due to structures that cause economic deprivation (see Galtung, 1971).

24. For an extensive analysis of women's relationship to war throughout history see Elshtain, 1987.

25. Jef Huysmans (1995:486) suggests that this dialogic approach, typical of late-modern or postmodern approaches to IR, is inspired by the liberal idea of pluralism and a democratic ethos.

REFERENCES

Benhabib, S. (1987) "The Generalized and the Concrete Other." In *Feminism as Critique: Essays on the Politics of Gender in Late-Capitalist Societies*, edited by S. Benhabib and D. Cornell, pp. 77–95. Cambridge: Polity Press.

Buzan, B. (1991) *People, States and Fear*, 2nd ed. Boulder, CO: Lynne Rienner.

Charlesworth, H., C. Chinkin, and S. Wright (1991) Feminist Approaches to International Law. *American Journal of International Law* 85:613–645.

Cohn, C. (1987) Sex and Death in the Rational World of Defense Intellectuals. *Signs: Journal of Women in Culture and Society* 12(4):687–718.

Cohn, C. (1993) "Wars, Wimps, and Women: Talking Gender and Thinking War." In *Gendering War Talk*, edited by M. Cooke and A. Wollacott, pp. 227–246. Princeton, NJ: Princeton University Press.

Collins, P. H. (1989) The Social Construction of Black Feminist Thought. *Signs: Journal of Women in Culture and Society* 14(4):745–773.

Cox, R. (1981) Social Forces, States and World Orders: Beyond International Theory. *Millennium* 10(2):126–155.

Der Derian, J. (1995) *International Theory: Critical Investigations*. New York: New York University Press.

Elshtain, J. B. (1987) *Women and War*. New York: Basic Books.

Elshtain, J. B. (1990) "The Problem with Peace." In *Women, Militarism and War*, edited by J. B. Elshtain and S. Tobias, pp. 255–266. Savage, MD: Rowman and Littlefield.

Enloe, C. (1990) *Bananas, Beaches and Bases: Making Feminist Sense of International Politics*. Berkeley: University of California Press.

Enloe, C. (1993) *The Morning After: Sexual Politics at the End of the Cold War.* Berkeley: University of California Press.

Flax, J. (1987) Postmodernism and Gender Relations in Feminist Theory. *Signs: Journal of Women in Culture and Society* 12(4):621–643.

Gaddis, J. (1992–93) International Relations Theory and the End of the Cold War. *International Security* 17(3):5–58.

Galtung, J. (1971) A Structural Theory of Imperialism. *Journal of Peace Research* 8:81–117.

Goldstein, J. (1994) *International Relations.* New York: Harper Collins.

Grant, R. (1991) "The Sources of Gender Bias in International Relations Theory." In *Gender and International Relations,* edited by R. Grant and K. Newland, pp. 8–26. Indianapolis: Indiana University Press.

Grant, R., and K. Newland, eds. (1991) *Gender and International Relations.* Indianapolis: Indiana University Press.

Haraway, D. (1988) Situated Knowledges: The Science Question in Feminism and the Privilege of Partial Perspective. *Feminist Studies* 14:575–599.

Harding, S. (1986) *The Science Question in Feminism.* Ithaca, NY: Cornell University Press.

Harding, S. (1987) Introduction: Is There a Feminist Method? In *Feminism and Methodology,* edited by S. Harding, pp. 1–14. Bloomington: Indiana University Press.

Harding, S. (1991) *Whose Science? Whose Knowledge? Thinking from Women's Lives.* Ithaca, NY: Cornell University Press.

Harrington, M. (1992) "What Exactly Is Wrong with the Liberal State as an Agent of Change?" In *Gendered States,* edited by V. S. Peterson, Boulder, CO: Lynne Rienner.

Heckman, S. (1990) *Gender and Knowledge: Elements of a Postmodern Feminism.* Boston: Northeastern University Press.

Hoffmann, S. (1977) An American Social Science: International Relations. *Daedalus* 106(3): 41–60.

Hollis, M., and S. Smith (1990) *Explaining and Understanding International Relations.* Oxford: Oxford University Press.

Hooks, B. (1984) *Feminist Theory: From Margin to Center.* Boston: South End Press.

Huysmans, J. (1995) Post–Cold War Implosion and Globalisation: Liberalism Running Past Itself? *Millennium* 24(3):471–487.

Independent Commission on Disarmament and Security Issues (1982) *Common Security: A Blueprint for Survival.* New York: Simon and Schuster.

Jones, A. (1996) Does "Gender" Make the World Go Round? Feminist Critiques of International Relations. *Review of International Studies* 22:405–429.

Keller, E. F. (1985) *Reflections on Gender and Science.* New Haven, CT: Yale University Press.

Keohane, R. (1988) International Institutions: Two Approaches. *International Studies Quarterly* 32:379–396.

Keohane, R. (1989) International Relations Theory: Contributions of a Feminist Standpoint. *Millennium* 18:245–253.

Kolodziej, E. (1992) Renaissance in Security Studies? Caveat Lector! *International Studies Quarterly* 36:421–438.

Lakatos, I., and A. Musgrave (1970) *Criticism and the Growth of Knowledge.* Cambridge: Cambridge University Press.

Lapid, Y. (1989) The Third Debate: On the Prospects of International Theory in a Post-Positivist Era. *International Studies Quarterly* 33:235–254.

Linklater, A. (1982) *Men and Citizens in the Theory of International Relations.* London: Macmillan.

Martin, J. R. (1994) Methodological Essentialism, False Difference, and Other Dangerous Traps. *Signs: Journal of Women in Culture and Society* 19(3):630–657.

Mathews, J. (1989) Redefining Security. *Foreign Affairs* 68(2):162–177.

Morgenthau, H. (1946) *Scientific Man Vs Power Politics.* Chicago: University of Chicago Press.

Morgenthau, H. (1995) "The Intellectual and Political Functions of Theory." In *International Theory: Critical Investigations,* edited by J. Der Derian, pp. 36–52. New York: New York University Press.

Moser, C. (1991) "Gender Planning in the Third

World: Meeting Practical and Strategic Needs." In *Gender and International Relations,* edited by R. Grant and K. Newland, pp. 83–121. Indianapolis: Indiana University Press.

New York Times (1996) "Cause for Sibling Rivalry at Teamsters," by Peter Kilborn, July 17, p. A16.

Nussbaum, M., and J. Glover, eds. (1995) *Women, Culture and Development: A Study of Human Capabilities.* Oxford: Oxford University Press.

Okin, S. M. (1980) *Women in Western Political Thought.* Princeton, NJ: Princeton University Press.

Okin, S. M. (1989) *Justice, Gender and the Family.* New York: Basic Books.

Orford, A. (1996) The Politics of Collective Security. *Michigan Journal of International Law* 17(2):373–409.

Pateman, C. (1988) *The Sexual Contract.* Stanford, CA: Stanford University Press.

Pateman, C. (1994) The Rights of Man and Early Feminism. *Schweizerisches Jahrbuch für Politische Wissenschaft* 34:19–31.

Peterson, V. S. (1992a) *Gendered States: Feminist (Re)Visions of International Relations Theory.* Boulder, CO: Lynne Rienner.

Peterson, V. S. (1992b) Transgressing Boundaries: Theories of Knowledge, Gender and International Relations, *Millennium* 21(2):183–206.

Peterson, V. S., and A. S. Runyan (1993) *Global Gender Issues.* Boulder, CO: Westview Press.

Pettman, J. (1996) *Worlding Women: A Feminist International Politics.* New York: Routledge.

Rosenberg, E. (1990) Gender. *Journal of American History* 77(1):116–124.

Rourke, J. (1993) *International Politics on the World Stage,* 4th ed. Guilford, CT: Dushkin Publishing Group.

Scott, J. (1986) Gender: A Useful Category of Historical Analysis. *American Historical Review* 91:1053–1075.

Smith, S. (1997) "New Approaches to International Theory." In *The Globalization of World Politics,* edited by J. Baylis and S. Smith, pp. 165–190. Oxford: Oxford University Press.

Stiehm, J. (1982) The Protected, the Protector, the Defender. *Women's Studies International Forum* 5(3/4):367–376.

Sylvester, C. (1987) Some Dangers in Merging Feminist and Peace Projects. *Alternatives* 12(4): 493–509.

Sylvester, C. (1994a) Empathetic Cooperation: A Feminist Method for IR. *Millennium* 23(2): 315–334.

Sylvester, C. (1994b) *Feminist Theory and International Relations in a Postmodern Era.* Cambridge: Cambridge University Press.

Tannen, D. (1990) *You just Don't Understand: Women and Men in Conversation.* New York: William Morrow.

Tickner, J. A. (1988) Hans Morgenthau's Principles of Political Realism: A Feminist Reformulation. *Millennium* 17(3):429–440.

Tickner, J. A. (1992) *Gender in International Relations: Feminist Perspectives on Achieving Global Security.* New York: Columbia University Press.

Tickner, J. A. (1994) "Feminist Perspectives on Peace and World Security in the Post–Cold War Era." In *Peace and World Security Studies: A Curriculum Guide,* 6th ed., edited by M. Klare, pp. 43–54. Boulder, CO: Lynne Rienner.

Tobias, S. (1990) "Shifting Heroisms: The Uses of Military Service in Politics." In *Women, Militarism and War,* edited by J. B. Elshtain and S. Tobias, pp. 163–185. Savage, MD: Rowman and Littlefield.

Tong, R. (1989) *Feminist Thought: A Comprehensive Introduction.* Boulder, CO: Westview Press.

Toulmin, S. (1990) *Cosmopolis: The Hidden Agenda of Modernity.* Chicago: University of Chicago Press.

Tronto, J. (1993) *Moral Boundaries: A Political Argument for an Ethic of Care.* New York: Routledge.

Tuana, N. (1992) "Reading Philosophy as a Woman." In *Against Patriarchal Thinking,* edited by M. Pellikaan-Engel, pp. 47–54. Amsterdam: VU University Press.

Ullman, R. (1983) Redefining Security. *International Security* 8(1):129–153.

United Nations (1995) *Human Development Report.* Oxford: Oxford University Press.

Walker, R. B. J. (1989) History and Structure in the Theory of International Relations. *Millennium* 18(2):163–183.

Walker, R. B. J. (1992) "Gender and Critique in the Theory of International Relations." In *Gendered States,* edited by V. S. Peterson, pp. 179–202. Boulder, CO: Lynne Rienner.

Walt, S. (1991) The Renaissance of Security Studies. *International Studies Quarterly* 35:211–239.

Waltz, K. (1979) *Theory of International Politics,* Reading, MA: Addison-Wesley.

Weber, C. (1994) Good Girls, Little Girls and Bad Girls. *Millennium* 23(2):337–348.

Whitworth, S. (1989) Gender in the Inter-Paradigm Debate. *Millennium* 18(2):265–272.

Wight, M. (1995) "Why Is There No International Theory?" In *International Theory: Critical Investigations,* edited by J. Der Derian, pp. 15–35. New York: New York University Press.

Wolfers, A. (1962) *Discord and Collaboration: Essays on International Politics.* Baltimore, MD: Johns Hopkins University Press.

Yost, D. (1994) Political Philosophy and the Theory of International Relations. *International Affairs* 70(2):263–290.

Zalewski, M. (1995) "Well, What Is the Feminist Perspective on Bosnia?" *International Affairs* 71(2):339–356.

4 ❧ THE INTERNATIONAL SYSTEM

The notion of an international system is critical in both realist and radical thought, as explained in Mingst's Essentials of International Relations. *In liberal thinking, by contrast, the international system is both less central to the theory and, indeed, is itself subject to different interpretations. Drawing upon a rich liberal tradition developed in European thought and practice between the fifteenth and nineteenth centuries, Hedley Bull, in his book* The Anarchical Society *(1977), develops one liberal view of the international system, which he labels "international society." Bull argues that in international society, there have always been common interests among states, and common rules and institutions worked out between them. These commonalities represent elements of order in the international system.*

Realists and radicals disagree about the amount of order found in the international system. The most prominent realist, Hans Morgenthau, writes in Politics Among Nations *that the international system is characterized by the desire of state actors to maximize power. For international stability to be achieved, a balance-of-power system is necessary. In the second selection of this chapter, Morgenthau discusses what states can do to insure the balance. For world-system theorist and sociologist Immanuel Wallerstein, the international system is a capitalist world-system differentiated by three groups of states: core, periphery, and semiperiphery. Utilizing the historical trends developed in his famous book,* The Modern World-System: Capitalist Agriculture and the Origins of the European World-Economy in the Sixteenth Century *(1974), and coming from a radical perspective, Wallerstein traces the evolution of each group. He argues that with each group pursuing its own economic interest, the semiperiphery is the linchpin of the system, both being exploited by the core and exploiting the periphery. Therefore, in both realist and radical visions, the international system is a conflictual one.*

Contemporary theorists offer contrasting interpretations of the international system of the twenty-first century. William C. Wohlforth argues that the contemporary international system is unipolar; U.S. power by all indicators is preponder-

ant. Despite overwhelming power and the absence of a counterhegemon, Wohlforth argues, unipolarity can be peaceful and durable. By contrast, Samuel Huntington predicts that the future international system will be characterized by a clash between the Western and Islamic civilizations. His article and the book that elaborates its thesis, The Clash of Civilizations and the Remaking of World Order *(1996), has been widely discussed and criticized.* The Economist *offers one such critique, the authors arguing that while culture does have an influence on state and individual behavior, it does not play the defining role that Huntington suggests.*

HEDLEY BULL

Does Order Exist in World Politics?

*   *   *

The Idea of International Society

Throughout the history of the modern states system there have been three competing traditions of thought: the Hobbesian or realist tradition, which views international politics as a state of war; the Kantian or universalist tradition, which sees at work in international politics a potential community of mankind; and the Grotian or internationalist tradition, which views international politics as taking place within an international society.[1] Here I shall state what is essential to the Grotian or internationalist idea of international society, and what divides it from the Hobbesian or realist tradition on the one hand, and from the Kantian or universalist tradition on the other. Each of these traditional patterns of thought embodies a description of the nature of international politics and a set of prescriptions about international conduct.

The Hobbesian tradition describes interna-

tional relations as a state of war of all against all, an arena of struggle in which each state is pitted against every other. International relations, on the Hobbesian view, represent pure conflict between states and resemble a game that is wholly distributive or zero-sum: the interests of each state exclude the interests of any other. The particular international activity that, on the Hobbesian view, is most typical of international activity as a whole, or best provides the clue to it, is war itself. Thus peace, on the Hobbesian view, is a period of recuperation from the last war and preparation for the next.

The Hobbesian prescription for international conduct is that the state is free to pursue its goals in relation to other states without moral or legal restrictions of any kind. Ideas of morality and law, on this view, are valid only in the context of a society, but international life is beyond the bounds of any society. If any moral or legal goals are to be pursued in international politics, these can only be the moral or legal goals of the state itself. Either it is held (as by Machiavelli) that the state conducts foreign policy in a kind of moral and legal vacuum, or it is held (as by Hegel and his successors) that moral behaviour for the state in foreign policy lies in its own self-assertion. The only rules or princi-

From Hedley Bull, *The Anarchical Society: A Study of Order in World Politics*, 2d ed. (New York: Columbia University Press, 1977), chap. 2.

ples which, for those in the Hobbesian tradition, may be said to limit or circumscribe the behaviour of states in their relations with one another are rules of prudence or expediency. Thus agreements may be kept if it is expedient to keep them, but may be broken if it is not.

The Kantian or universalist tradition, at the other extreme, takes the essential nature of international politics to lie not in conflict among states, as on the Hobbesian view, but in the trans-national social bonds that link the individual human beings who are the subjects or citizens of states. The dominant theme of international relations, on the Kantian view, is only apparently the relationship among states, and is really the relationship among all men in the community of mankind—which exists potentially, even if it does not exist actually, and which when it comes into being will sweep the system of states into limbo.[2]

Within the community of all mankind, on the universalist view, the interests of all men are one and the same; international politics, considered from this perspective, is not a purely distributive or zero-sum game, as the Hobbesians maintain, but a purely cooperative or non-zero-sum game. Conflicts of interest exist among the ruling cliques of states, but this is only at the superficial or transient level of the existing system of states; properly understood, the interests of all peoples are the same. The particular international activity which, on the Kantian view, most typifies international activity as a whole is the horizontal conflict of ideology that cuts across the boundaries of states and divides human society into two camps—the trustees of the immanent community of mankind and those who stand in its way, those who are of the true faith and the heretics, the liberators and the oppressed.

The Kantian or universalist view of international morality is that, in contrast to the Hobbesian conception, there are moral imperatives in the field of international relations limiting the action of states, but that these imperatives enjoin not coexistence and co-operation among states but rather the overthrow of the system of states and its replacement by a cosmopolitan society. The community of mankind, on the Kantian view, is not only the cen-

tral reality in international politics, in the sense that the forces able to bring it into being are present; it is also the end or object of the highest moral endeavour. The rules that sustain coexistence and social intercourse among states should be ignored if the imperatives of this higher morality require it. Good faith with heretics has no meaning, except in terms of tactical convenience; between the elect and the damned, the liberators and the oppressed, the question of mutual acceptance of rights to sovereignty or independence does not arise.

What has been called the Grotian or internationalist tradition stands between the realist tradition and the universalist tradition. The Grotian tradition describes international politics in terms of a society of states or international society.[3] As against the Hobbesian tradition, the Grotians contend that states are not engaged in simple struggle, like gladiators in an arena, but are limited in their conflicts with one another by common rules and institutions. But as against the Kantian or universalist perspective the Grotians accept the Hobbesian premise that sovereigns or states are the principal reality in international politics; the immediate members of international society are states rather than individual human beings. International politics, in the Grotian understanding, expresses neither complete conflict of interest between states nor complete identity of interest; it resembles a game that is partly distributive but also partly productive. The particular international activity which, on the Grotian view, best typifies international activity as a whole is neither war between states, nor horizontal conflict cutting across the boundaries of states, but trade—or, more generally, economic and social intercourse between one country and another.

The Grotian prescription for international conduct is that all states, in their dealings with one another, are bound by the rules and institutions of the society they form. As against the view of the Hobbesians, states in the Grotian view are bound not only by rules of prudence or expediency but also by imperatives of morality and law. But, as against the view of the universalists, what these imperatives enjoin is not the overthrow of the system of states and its replacement by a universal community of mankind, but rather acceptance of the requirements of coexistence and co-operation in a society of states.

Each of these traditions embodies a great variety of doctrines about international politics, among which there exists only a loose connection. In different periods each pattern of thought appears in a different idiom and in relation to different issues and preoccupations. This is not the place to explore further the connections and distinctions within each tradition. Here we have only to take account of the fact that the Grotian idea of international society has always been present in thought about the states system, and to indicate in broad terms the metamorphoses which, in the last three to four centuries, it has undergone.

CHRISTIAN INTERNATIONAL SOCIETY

In the fifteenth, sixteenth and seventeenth centuries, when the universal political organisation of Western Christendom was still in process of disintegration, and modern states in process of articulation, the three patterns of thought purporting to describe the new international politics, and to prescribe conduct within it, first took shape. On the one hand, thinkers like Machiavelli, Bacon and Hobbes saw the emerging states as confronting one another in the social and moral vacuum left by the receding *respublica Christiana*. On the other hand Papal and Imperialist writers fought a rearguard action on behalf of the ideas of the universal authority of Pope and Emperor. As against these alternatives there was asserted by a third group of thinkers, relying upon the tradition of natural law, the possibility that the princes now making themselves supreme over local rivals and independent of outside authorities were nevertheless bound by common interests and rules. * * *

*   *   *

EUROPEAN INTERNATIONAL SOCIETY

In the eighteenth and nineteenth centuries, when the vestiges of Western Christendom came almost

to disappear from the theory and practice of international politics, when the state came to be fully articulated, first in its dynastic or absolutist phase, then in its national or popular phase, and when a body of modern inter-state practice came to be accumulated and studied, the idea of international society assumed a different form. * * *

The international society conceived by theorists of this period was identified as European rather than Christian in its values or culture. References to Christendom or to divine law as cementing the society of states declined and disappeared, as did religious oaths in treaties. References to Europe took their place, for example in the titles of their books: in the 1740s the Abbe de Mably published his *Droit public de l'Europe*, in the 1770s J. J. Moser his *Versuch des neuesten Europaischen Volkerrechts*, in the 1790s Burke denounced the regicide Directory of France for having violated "the public law of Europe."[4]

As the sense grew of the specifically European character of the society of states, so also did the sense of its cultural differentiation from what lay outside: the sense that European powers in their dealings with one another were bound by a code of conduct that did not apply to them in their dealings with other and lesser societies. * * *

*   *   *

WORLD INTERNATIONAL SOCIETY

*   *   *

In the twentieth century international society ceased to be regarded as specifically European and came to be considered as global or world wide. * * *

Today, when non-European states represent the great majority in international society and the United Nations is nearly universal in its membership, the doctrine that this society rests upon a specific culture or civilisation is generally rejected * * *

In the twentieth century, * * * there has been a retreat from the confident assertions, made in the age of Vattel [France, eighteenth century], that the members of international society were states and nations, towards the ambiguity and imprecision on this point that characterised the era of Grotius [Holland, seventeenth century]. The state as a bearer of rights and duties, legal and moral, in international society today is widely thought to be joined by international organisations, by non-state groups of various kinds operating across frontiers, and—as implied by the Nuremberg and Tokyo War Crimes Tribunals, and by the Universal Declaration of Human Rights—by individuals. There is no agreement as to the relative importance of these different kinds of legal and moral agents, or on any general scheme of rules that would relate them one to another, but Vattel's conception of a society simply of states has been under attack from many different directions.

*   *   *

The twentieth-century emphasis upon ideas of a reformed or improved international society, as distinct from the elements of society in actual practice, has led to a treatment of the League of Nations, the United Nations and other general international organisations as the chief institutions of international society, to the neglect of those institutions whose role in the maintenance of international order is the central one. Thus there has developed the Wilsonian rejection of the balance of power, the denigration of diplomacy and the tendency to seek to replace it by international administration, and a return to the tendency that prevailed in the Grotian era to confuse international law with international morality or international improvement.

*   *   *

THE ELEMENT OF SOCIETY

My contention is that the element of a society has always been present, and remains present, in the modern international system, although only as one of the elements in it, whose survival is sometimes precarious. The modern international system in fact reflects all three of the elements singled out,

respectively, by the Hobbesian, the Kantian and the Grotian traditions: the element of war and struggle for power among states, the element of transnational solidarity and conflict, cutting across the divisions among states, and the element of co-operation and regulated intercourse among states. In different historical phases of the states system, in different geographical theatres of its operation, and in the policies of different states and statesmen, one of these three elements may predominate over the others.

*   *   *

Because international society is no more than one of the basic elements at work in modern international politics, and is always in competition with the elements of a state of war and of transnational solidarity or conflict, it is always erroneous to interpret international events as if international society were the sole or the dominant element. This is the error committed by those who speak or write as if the Concert of Europe, the League of Nations or the United Nations were the principal factors in international politics in their respective times; as if international law were to be assessed only in relation to the function it has of binding states together, and not also in relation to its function as an instrument of state interest and as a vehicle of transnational purposes; as if attempts to maintain a balance of power were to be interpreted only as endeavours to preserve the system of states, and not also as manoeuvres on the part of particular powers to gain ascendancy; as if great powers were to be viewed only as "great responsibles" or "great indispensables," and not also as great predators; as if wars were to be construed only as attempts to violate the law or to uphold it, and not also simply as attempts to advance the interests of particular states or of transnational groups. The element of international society is real, but the elements of a state of war and of transnational loyalties and divisions are real also, and to reify the first element, or to speak as if it annulled the second and third, is an illusion.

Moreover, the fact that international society provides some element of order in international politics should not be taken as justifying an attitude of complacency about it, or as showing that the arguments of those who are dissatisfied with the order provided by international society are without foundation. The order provided within modern international society is precarious and imperfect. To show that modern international society has provided some degree of order is not to have shown that order in world politics could not be provided more effectively by structures of a quite different kind.

NOTES

1. This threefold division derives from Martin Wight. The best published account of it is his "Western Values in International Relations," in *Diplomatic Investigations*, ed. Herbert Butterfield and Martin Wight (London: Allen & Unwin, 1967). The division is further discussed in my "Martin Wight and The Theory of International Relations. The Second Martin Wight Memorial Lecture," *British Journal of International Studies*, vol. II, no. 2 (1976).

2. In Kant's own doctrine there is of course ambivalence as between the universalism of *The Idea of Universal History from a Cosmopolitical Point Of View* (1784) and the position taken up in *Perpetual Peace* (1795), in which Kant accepts the substitute goal of a league of "republican" states.

3. I have myself used the term "Grotian" in two senses: (i) as here, to describe the broad doctrine that there is a society of states; (ii) to describe the solidarist form of this doctrine, which united Grotius himself and the twentieth-century neo-Grotians, in opposition to the pluralist conception of international society entertained by Vattel and later positivist writers. See "The Grotian Conception of International Society," in *Diplomatic Investigations*.

4. See "Third Letter on the Proposals for Peace with the Regicide Directory of France," in *The Works of the Right Honourable Edmund Burke*, ed. John C. Nimmo (London: Bohn's British Classics, 1887).

HANS MORGENTHAU

The Balance of Power[1]

The aspiration for power on the part of several nations, each trying either to maintain or overthrow the status quo, leads of necessity to a configuration that is called the balance of power and to policies that aim at preserving it. We say "of necessity" advisedly. For here again we are confronted with the basic misconception that has impeded the understanding of international poli-

From Hans Morgenthau, *Politics Among Nations: The Struggle for Power and Peace*, 4th ed. (New York: Knopf, 1967), chaps. 11, 12, 14. Some of the author's notes have been omitted.

tics and has made us the prey of illusions. This misconception asserts that men have a choice between power politics and its necessary outgrowth, the balance of power, on the other hand, and a different, better kind of international relations on the other. It insists that a foreign policy based on the balance of power is one among several possible foreign policies and that only stupid and evil men will choose the former and reject the latter.

It will be shown * * * that the international balance of power is only a particular manifestation of a general social principle to which all societies composed of a number of autonomous units owe the autonomy of their component parts; that the balance of power and policies aiming at its preservation are not only inevitable but are an essential stabilizing factor in a society of sovereign nations; and that the instability of the international balance of power is due not to the faultiness of the principle but to the particular conditions under which the principle must operate in a society of sovereign nations.

Social Equilibrium

BALANCE OF POWER AS UNIVERSAL CONCEPT

The concept of "equilibrium" as a synonym for "balance" is commonly employed in many sciences—physics, biology, economics, sociology, and political science. It signifies stability within a system composed of a number of autonomous forces. Whenever the equilibrium is disturbed either by an outside force or by a change in one or the other elements composing the system, the system shows a tendency to re-establish either the original or a new equilibrium. Thus equilibrium exists in the human body. While the human body changes in the process of growth, the equilibrium persists as long as the changes occurring in the different organs of the body do not disturb the body's stability. This is especially so if the quantitative and qualitative changes in the different organs are proportionate to each other. When, however, the body suffers a wound or loss of one of its organs through outside interference, or experiences a malignant growth or a pathological transformation of one of its organs, the equilibrium is disturbed, and the body tries to overcome the disturbance by reestablishing the equilibrium either on the same or a different level from the one that obtained before the disturbance occurred.[2]

The same concept of equilibrium is used in a social science, such as economics, with reference to the relations between the different elements of the economic system, e.g., between savings and investments, exports and imports, supply and demand, costs and prices. Contemporary capitalism itself has been described as a system of "countervailing power."[3] It also applies to society as a whole. Thus we search for a proper balance between different geographical regions, such as the East and the West, the North and the South; between different kinds of activities, such as agriculture and industry, heavy and light industries, big and small businesses, producers and consumers, management and labor, between different functional groups, such as city and country, the old, the middle-aged, and the young, the economic and the political sphere, the middle classes and the upper and lower classes.

Two assumptions are at the foundation of all such equilibriums: first, that the elements to be balanced are necessary for society or are entitled to exist and, second, that without a state of equilibrium among them one element will gain ascendancy over the others, encroach upon their interests and rights, and may ultimately destroy them. Consequently, it is the purpose of all such equilibriums to maintain the stability of the system without destroying the multiplicity of the elements composing it. If the goal were stability alone, it could be achieved by allowing one element to destroy or overwhelm the others and take their place. Since the goal is stability plus the preservation of all the elements of the system, the equilibrium must aim at preventing any element from gaining ascendancy over the others. The means employed to maintain the equilibrium consist in allowing the different elements to pursue their opposing tendencies up to the point where the tendency of one is not so strong as to overcome the tendency of the others, but strong enough to prevent the others from overcoming its own.   * * *

* * *

Different Methods of the
Balance of Power

The balancing process can be carried on either by diminishing the weight of the heavier scale or by increasing the weight of the lighter one.

Divide and Rule

The former method has found its classic manifestation, aside from the imposition of onerous conditions in peace treaties and the incitement to treason and revolution, in the maxim "divide and rule." It has been resorted to by nations who tried to make or keep their competitors weak by dividing them or keeping them divided. The most consistent and important policies of this kind in modern times are the policy of France with respect to Germany and the policy of the Soviet Union with respect to the rest of Europe. From the seventeenth century to the end of the Second World War, it has been an unvarying principle of French foreign policy either to favor the division of the German Empire into a number of small independent states or to prevent the coalescence of such states into one unified nation. * * * Similarly, the Soviet Union from the twenties to the present has consistently opposed all plans for the unification of Europe, on the assumption that the pooling of the divided strength of the European nations into a "Western bloc" would give the enemies of the Soviet Union such power as to threaten the latter's security.

The other method of balancing the power of several nations consists in adding to the strength of the weaker nation. This method can be carried out by two different means: Either B can increase its power sufficiently to offset, if not surpass, the power of A, and vice versa; or B can pool its power with the power of all the other nations that pursue identical policies with regard to A, in which case A will pool its power with all the nations pursuing identical policies with respect to B. The former alternative is exemplified by the policy of compensations and the armament race as well as by disarmament; the latter, by the policy of alliances.

Compensations

Compensations of a territorial nature were a common device in the eighteenth and nineteenth centuries for maintaining a balance of power which had been, or was to be, disturbed by the territorial acquisitions of one nation. The Treaty of Utrecht of 1713, which terminated the War of the Spanish Succession, recognized for the first time expressly the principle of the balance of power by way of territorial compensations. It provided for the division of most of the Spanish possessions, European and colonial, between the Hapsburgs and the Bourbons *"ad conservandum in Europa equilibrium,"* as the treaty put it.

*   *   *

In the latter part of the nineteenth and the beginning of the twentieth century, the principle of compensations was again deliberately applied to the distribution of colonial territories and the delimitation of colonial or semicolonial spheres of influence. Africa, in particular, was during that period the object of numerous treaties delimiting spheres of influence for the major colonial powers. Thus the competition between France, Great Britain, and Italy for the domination of Ethiopia was provisionally resolved * * * by the treaty of 1906, which divided the country into three spheres of influence for the purpose of establishing in that region a balance of power among the nations concerned. * * *

Even where the principle of compensations is not deliberately applied, however, * * * it is nowhere absent from political arrangements, territorial or other, made within a balance-of-power system. For, given such a system, no nation will agree to concede political advantages to another nation without the expectation, which may or may not be well founded, of receiving proportionate advantages in return. The bargaining of diplomatic negotiations, issuing in political compromise, is but the principle of compensations in its most general form, and as such it is organically connected with the balance of power.

Armaments

The principal means, however, by which a nation endeavors with the power at its disposal to maintain or re-establish the balance of power are armaments. The armaments race in which Nation A tries to keep up with, and then to outdo, the armaments of Nation B, and vice versa, is the typical instrumentality of an unstable, dynamic balance of power. The necessary corollary of the armaments race is a constantly increasing burden of military preparations devouring an ever greater portion of the national budget and making for ever deepening fears, suspicions, and insecurity. The situation preceding the First World War, with the naval competition between Germany and Great Britain and the rivalry of the French and German armies, illustrates this point.

It is in recognition of situations such as these that, since the end of the Napoleonic Wars, repeated attempts have been made to create a stable balance of power, if not to establish permanent peace, by means of the proportionate disarmament of competing nations. The technique of stabilizing the balance of power by means of a proportionate reduction of armaments is somewhat similar to the technique of territorial compensations. For both techniques require a quantitative evaluation of the influence that the arrangement is likely to exert on the respective power of the individual nations. The difficulties in making such a quantitative evaluation—in correlating, for instance, the military strength of the French army of 1932 with the military power represented by the industrial potential of Germany—have greatly contributed to the fail-

ure of most attempts at creating a stable balance of power by means of disarmament. The only outstanding success of this kind was the Washington Naval Treaty of 1922, in which Great Britain, the United States, Japan, France, and Italy agreed to a proportionate reduction and limitation of naval armaments. Yet it must be noted that this treaty was part of an over-all political and territorial settlement in the Pacific which sought to stabilize the power relations in that region on the foundation of Anglo-American predominance.

Alliances

The historically most important manifestation of the balance of power, however, is to be found not in the equilibrium of two isolated nations but in the relations between one nation or alliance of nations and another alliance.

*   *   *

Alliances are a necessary function of the balance of power operating within a multiple-state system. Nations A and B, competing with each other, have three choices in order to maintain and improve their relative power positions. They can increase their own power, they can add to their own power the power of other nations, or they can withhold the power of other nations from the adversary. When they make the first choice, they embark upon an armaments race. When they choose the second and third alternatives, they pursue a policy of alliances.

Whether or not a nation shall pursue a policy of alliances is, then, a matter not of principle but of expediency. A nation will shun alliances if it believes that it is strong enough to hold its own unaided or that the burden of the commitments resulting from the alliance is likely to outweigh the advantages to be expected. It is for one or the other or both of these reasons that, throughout the better part of their history, Great Britain and the United States have refrained from entering into peacetime alliances with other nations.

*   *   *

The "Holder" of the Balance

Whenever the balance of power is to be realized by means of an alliance—and this has been generally so throughout the history of the Western world—two possible variations of this pattern have to be distinguished. To use the metaphor of the balance, the system may consist of two scales, in each of which are to be found the nation or nations identified with the same policy of the status quo or of imperialism. The continental nations of Europe have generally operated the balance of power in this way.

The system may, however, consist of two scales plus a third element, the "holder" of the balance or the "balancer." The balancer is not permanently identified with the policies of either nation or group of nations. Its only objective within the system is the maintenance of the balance, regardless of the concrete policies the balance will serve. In consequence, the holder of the balance will throw its weight at one time in this scale, at another time in the other scale, guided only by one consideration—the relative position of the scales. Thus it will put its weight always in the scale that seems to be higher than the other because it is lighter. The balancer may become in a relatively short span of history consecutively the friend and foe of all major powers, provided they all consecutively threaten the balance by approaching predominance over the others and are in turn threatened by others about to gain such predominance. To paraphrase a statement of Palmerston: while the holder of the balance has no permanent friends, it has no permanent enemies either; it has only the permanent interest of maintaining the balance of power itself.

The balancer is in a position of "splendid isolation." It is isolated by its own choice; for, while the two scales of the balance must vie with each other to add its weight to theirs in order to gain the overweight necessary for success, it must refuse to enter into permanent ties with either side. The holder of the balance waits in the middle in watchful detachment to see which scale is likely to sink. Its isolation is "splendid"; for, since its support or lack of support is the decisive factor in the struggle for power, its foreign policy, if cleverly managed, is able to extract the highest price from those whom it supports. But since this support, regardless of the price paid for it, is always uncertain and shifts from one side to the other in accordance with the movements of the balance, its policies are resented and subject to condemnation on moral grounds. Thus it has been said of the outstanding balancer in modern times, Great Britain, that it lets others fight its wars, that it keeps Europe divided in order to dominate the continent, and that the fickleness of its policies is such as to make alliances with Great Britain impossible. "Perfidious Albion" has become a byword in the mouths of those who either were unable to gain Great Britain's support, however hard they tried, or else lost it after they had paid what seemed to them too high a price.

The holder of the balance occupies the key position in the balance-of-power system, since its position determines the outcome of the struggle for power. It has, therefore, been called the "arbiter" of the system, deciding who will win and who will lose. By making it impossible for any nation or combination of nations to gain predominance over the others, it preserves its own independence as well as the independence of all the other nations, and is thus a most powerful factor in international politics.

The holder of the balance can use this power in three different ways. It can make its joining one or the other nation or alliance dependent upon certain conditions favorable to the maintenance or restoration of the balance. It can make its support of the peace settlement dependent upon similar conditions. It can, finally, in either situation see to it that the objectives of its own national policy, apart from the maintenance of the balance of power, are realized in the process of balancing the power of others.

*　　*　　*

Evaluation of the Balance of Power

*   *   *

The Unreality of the Balance of Power

[The] uncertainty of all power calculations not only makes the balance of power incapable of practical application but leads also to its very negation in practice. Since no nation can be sure that its calculation of the distribution of power at any particular moment in history is correct, it must at least make sure that, whatever errors it may commit, they will not put the nation at a disadvantage in the contest for power. In other words, the nation must try to have at least a margin of safety which will allow it to make erroneous calculations and still maintain the balance of power. To that effect, all nations actively engaged in the struggle for power must actually aim not at a balance—that is, equality—of power, but at superiority of power in their own behalf. And since no nation can foresee how large its miscalculations will turn out to be, all nations must ultimately seek the maximum of power obtainable under the circumstances. Only thus can they hope to attain the maximum margin of safety commensurate with the maximum of errors they might commit. The limitless aspiration for power, potentially always present * * * in the power drives of nations, finds in the balance of power a mighty incentive to transform itself into an actuality.

Since the desire to attain a maximum of power is universal, all nations must always be afraid that their own miscalculations and the power increases of other nations might add up to an inferiority for themselves which they must at all costs try to avoid. Hence all nations who have gained an apparent edge over their competitors tend to consolidate that advantage and use it for changing the distribution of power permanently in their favor. This can be done through diplomatic pressure by bringing the full weight of that advantage to bear upon the other nations, compelling them to make the concessions that will consolidate the temporary advantage into a permanent superiority. It can also be done by war. Since in a balance-of-power system all nations live in constant fear lest their rivals deprive them, at the first opportune moment, of their power position, all nations have a vital interest in anticipating such a development and doing unto the others what they do not want the others to do unto them. * * *

NOTES

1. The term "balance of power" is used in the text with four different meanings: (1) as a policy aimed at a certain state of affairs, (2) as an actual state of affairs, (3) as an approximately equal distribution of power, (4) as any distribution of power. Whenever the term is used without qualification, it refers to an actual state of affairs in which power is distributed among several nations with approximate equality. * * *

2. Cf., for instance, the impressive analogy between the equilibrium in the human body and in society in Walter B. Cannon, *The Wisdom of the Body* (New York: W. W. Norton and Company, 1932), pp. 293, 294: "At the outset it is noteworthy that the body politic itself exhibits some indications of crude automatic stabilizing processes. In the previous chapter I expressed the postulate that a certain degree of constancy in a complex system is itself evidence that agencies are acting or are ready to act to maintain that constancy. And moreover, that when a system remains steady it does so because any tendency towards change is met by increased effectiveness of the factor or factors which resist the change. Many familiar facts prove that these statements are to some degree true for society even in its present unstabilized condition. A display of conservatism excites a radical revolt and that in turn is followed by a return to con-

servatism. Loose government and its consequences bring the reformers into power, but
their tight reins soon provoke restiveness and
the desire for release. The noble enthusiasms
and sacrifices of war are succeeded by moral ap-
athy and orgies of self-indulgence. Hardly any
strong tendency in a nation continues to the
stage of disaster; before that extreme is reached
corrective forces arise which check the tendency
and they commonly prevail to such an excessive
degree as themselves to cause a reaction. A
study of the nature of these social swings and

their reversal might lead to valuable understanding and possibly to means of more narrowly limiting the disturbances. At this point,
however, we merely note that the disturbances
are roughly limited, and that this limitation
suggests, perhaps, the early stages of social
homeostasis." (Reprinted by permission of the
publisher. Copyright 1932, 1939, by Walter B.
Cannon.)

3. John K. Galbraith, *American Capitalism, the Concept of Countervailing Power* (Boston: Houghton Mifflin, 1952).

IMMANUEL WALLERSTEIN

The Rise and Future Demise of the World Capitalist System: Concepts for Comparative Analysis

The growth within the capitalist world-economy of the industrial sector of production, the so-called "industrial revolution,"
was accompanied by a very strong current of
thought which defined this change as both a
process of organic development and of progress.
There were those who considered these economic
developments and the concomitant changes in social organization to be some penultimate stage of
world development whose final working out was
but a matter of time. These included such diverse
thinkers as Saint-Simon, Comte, Hegel, Weber,
Durkheim. And then there were the critics, most
notably Marx, who argued, if you will, that the
nineteenth-century present was only an antepenul-

timate stage of development, that the capitalist
world was to know a cataclysmic political revolution
which would then lead in the fullness of time to a final societal form, in this case the classless society.

One of the great strengths of Marxism was that,
being an oppositional and hence critical doctrine,
it called attention not merely to the contradictions
of the system but to those of its ideologists, by appealing to the empirical evidence of historical reality which unmasked the irrelevancy of the models
proposed for the explanation of the social world.
The Marxist critics saw in abstracted models concrete rationalization, and they argued their case
fundamentally by pointing to the failure of their
opponents to analyze the social whole. * * *

*   *   *

We take the defining characteristic of a social system to be the existence within it of a division of la-

From *Comparative Studies in Society and History* 14,
no. 4 (1974): 387–415. Some of the author's notes have
been omitted.

bor, such that the various sectors or areas within are dependent upon economic exchange with others for the smooth and continuous provisioning of the needs of the area. Such economic exchange can clearly exist without a common political structure and even more obviously without sharing the same culture.

A minisystem is an entity that has within it a complete division of labor, and a single cultural framework. Such systems are found only in very simple agricultural or hunting and gathering societies. Such minisystems no longer exist in the world. Furthermore, there were fewer in the past than is often asserted, since any such system that became tied to an empire by the payment of tribute as "protection costs"[1] ceased by that fact to be a "system," no longer having a self-contained division of labor. For such an area, the payment of tribute marked a shift, in Polanyi's language, from being a reciprocal economy to participating in a larger redistributive economy.[2]

Leaving aside the now defunct minisystems, the only kind of social system is a world-system, which we define quite simply as a unit with a single division of labor and multiple cultural systems. It follows logically that there can, however, be two varieties of such world-systems, one with a common political system and one without. We shall designate these respectively as world-empires and world-economies.

It turns out empirically that world-economies have historically been unstable structures leading either towards disintegration or conquest by one group and hence transformation into a world-empire. Examples of such world-empires emerging from world-economies are all the so-called great civilizations of premodern times, such as China, Egypt, Rome (each at appropriate periods of its history). On the other hand, the so-called nineteenth-century empires, such as Great Britain or France, were not world-empires at all, but nation-states with colonial appendages operating within the framework of a world-economy.

World-empires were basically redistributive in economic form. No doubt they bred clusters of merchants who engaged in economic exchange (primarily long distance trade), but such clusters, however large, were a minor part of the total economy and not fundamentally determinative of its fate. * * *

It was only with the emergence of the modern world-economy in sixteenth-century Europe that we saw the full development and economic predominance of market trade. This was the system called capitalism. Capitalism and a world-economy (that is, a single division of labor but multiple polities and cultures) are obverse sides of the same coin. One does not cause the other. We are merely defining the same indivisible phenomenon by different characteristics.

How and why it came about that this particular European world-economy of the sixteenth century did not become transformed into a redistributive world-empire but developed definitively as a capitalist world-economy I have explained elsewhere.[3] The genesis of this world-historical turning point is marginal to the issues under discussion in this paper, which is rather what conceptual apparatus one brings to bear on the analysis of developments within the framework of precisely such a capitalist world-economy.

Let us therefore turn to the capitalist world-economy. * * *

*   *   *

We must start with how one demonstrates the existence of a single division of labor. We can regard a division of labor as a grid which is substantially interdependent. Economic actors operate on some assumption (obviously seldom clear to any individual actor) that the totality of their essential needs—of sustenance, protection, and pleasure—will be met over a reasonable time span by a combination of their own productive activities and exchange in some form. The smallest grid that would substantially meet the expectations of the overwhelming majority of actors within those boundaries constitutes a single division of labor.

The reason why a small farming community whose only significant link to outsiders is the payment of annual tribute does not constitute such a single division of labor is that the assumptions of persons living in it concerning the provision of protection involve an "exchange" with other parts of the world-empire.

This concept of a grid of exchange relationships assumes, however, a distinction between *essential* exchanges and what might be called "luxury" exchanges. This is to be sure a distinction rooted in the social perceptions of the actors and hence in both their social organization and their culture. These perceptions can change. But this distinction is crucial if we are not to fall into the trap of identifying *every* exchange activity as evidence of the existence of a system. Members of a system (a minisystem or a world-system) can be linked in limited exchanges with elements located outside the system, in the "external arena" of the system.

The form of such an exchange is very limited. Elements of the two systems can engage in an exchange of preciosities. That is, each can export to the other what is in *its* system socially defined as worth little in return for the import of what in its system is defined as worth much. This is not a mere pedantic definitional exercise, as the exchange of preciosities *between* world-systems can be extremely important in the historical evolution of a given world-system. The reason why this is so important is that in an exchange of preciosities, the importer is "reaping a windfall" and not obtaining a profit. Both exchange partners can reap windfalls simultaneously but only one can obtain maximum profit, since the exchange of surplus value within a system is a zero-sum game.

We are, as you see, coming to the essential feature of a capitalist world-economy, which is production for sale in a market in which the object is to realize the maximum profit. In such a system production is constantly expanded as long as further production is profitable, and men constantly innovate new ways of producing things that will expand the profit margin. The classical economists tried to argue that such production for the market was somehow the "natural" state of man. But the combined writings of the anthropologists and the Marxists left few in doubt that such a mode of production (these days called "capitalism") was only one of several possible modes.

Since, however, the intellectual debate between the liberals and the Marxists took place in the era of the industrial revolution, there has tended to be a *de facto* confusion between industrialism and capitalism. This left the liberals after 1945 in the dilemma of explaining how a presumably noncapitalist society, the USSR, had industrialized. The most sophisticated response has been to conceive of "liberal capitalism" and "socialism" as two variants of an "industrial society," two variants destined to "converge." * * * But the same confusion left the Marxists, including Marx, with the problem of explaining what was the mode of production that predominated in Europe from the sixteenth to the eighteenth centuries, that is before the industrial revolution. Essentially, most Marxists have talked of a "transitional" stage, which is in fact a blurry non-concept with no operational indicators. This dilemma is heightened if the unit of analysis used is the state, in which case one has to explain why the transition has occurred at different rates and times in different countries.

Marx himself handled this by drawing a distinction between "merchant capitalism" and "industrial capitalism." This I believe is unfortunate teminology, since it leads to such conclusions as that of Maurice Dobb who says of this "transitional" period:

> But why speak of this as a stage of capitalism at all? The workers were generally not proletarianized: that is, they were not separated from the instruments of production, nor even in many cases from occupation of a plot of land. Production was scattered and decentralized and not concentrated. *The capitalist was still predominantly a merchant* [italics mine] who did not control production directly and did not impose his own discipline upon the work of artisan-craftsmen, who both laboured as individual (or family) units and retained a considerable measure of independence (if a dwindling one).[4]

One might well say: why indeed? Especially if one remembers how much emphasis Dobb places a few pages earlier on capitalism as a mode of *production*—how then can the capitalist be primarily a merchant?—on the concentration of such ownership in the hands of a few, and on the fact that capitalism is not synonymous with private owner-ship, capitalism being different from a system in which the owners are "small peasant producers or artisan-producers." Dobb argues that a defining feature of private ownership under capitalism is that some are "obliged to [work for those that own] since [they own] nothing and [have] no access to means of production [and hence] have no other means of livelihood."[5] Given this contradic-tion, the answer Dobb gives to his own question is in my view very weak: "While it is true that at this date the situation was transitional, and capital-to-wage-labour relations were still immaturely devel-oped, the latter were already beginning to assume their characteristic features."[6]

If capitalism is a mode of production, produc-tion for profit in a market, then we ought, I should have thought, to look to whether or not such pro-duction was or was not occurring. It turns out in fact that it was, and in a very substantial form. Most of this production, however, was not indus-trial production. What was happening in Europe from the sixteenth to the eighteenth centuries is that over a large geographical area going from Poland in the northeast westwards and southwards throughout Europe and including large parts of the Western Hemisphere as well, there grew up a world-economy with a single division of labor within which there was a world market, for which men produced largely agricultural products for sale and profit. I would think the simplest thing to do would be to call this agricultural capitalism.

This then resolves the problems incurred by using the pervasiveness of *wage* labor as a defining characteristic of capitalism. An individual is no less a capitalist exploiting labor because the state assists him to pay his laborers low wages (including wages in kind) and denies these laborers the right to change employment. Slavery and so-called "sec-ond serfdom" are not to be regarded as anomalies in a capitalist system. Rather the so-called serf in Poland or the Indian on a Spanish *encomienda* in New Spain in this sixteenth-century world-economy were working for landlords who "paid" them (however euphemistic this term) for cash crop production. This is a relationship in which la-

bor power is a commodity (how could it ever be more so than under slavery?), quite different from the relationship of a feudal serf to his lord in eleventh-century Burgundy, where the economy was not oriented to a world market, and where la-bor power was (therefore?) in no sense bought or sold.

Capitalism thus means labor as a commodity to be sure. But in the era of agricultural capitalism, wage labor is only one of the modes in which labor is recruited and recompensed in the labor market. Slavery, coerced cash-crop production (my name for the so-called "second feudalism"), sharecrop-ping, and tenancy are all alternative modes. It would be too long to develop here the conditions under which differing regions of the world-economy tend to specialize in different agricultural products. * * *

What we must notice now is that this special-ization occurs in specific and differing geographic regions of the world-economy. This regional spe-cialization comes about by the attempts of actors in the market to avoid the normal operation of the market whenever it does not maximize their profit. The attempts of these actors to use non-market de-vices to ensure short-run profits makes them turn to the political entities which have in fact power to affect the market—the nation-states. * * *

In any case, the local capitalist classes—cash-crop landowners (often, even usually, nobility) and merchants—turned to the state, not only to liber-ate them from non-market constraints (as tradi-tionally emphasized by liberal historiography) but to create new constraints on the new market, the market of the European world-economy.

By a series of accidents—historical, ecological, geographic—northwest Europe was better situated in the sixteenth century to diversify its agricultural specialization and add to it certain industries (such as textiles, shipbuilding, and metal wares) than were other parts of Europe. Northwest Europe emerged as the core area of this world-economy, specializing in agricultural production of higher skill levels, which favored (again for reasons too complex to develop) tenancy and wage labor as the modes of labor control. Eastern Europe and the

Western Hemisphere became peripheral areas specializing in export of grains, bullion, wood, cotton, sugar—all of which favored the use of slavery and coerced cash-crop labor as the modes of labor control. Mediterranean Europe emerged as the semiperipheral area of this world-economy specializing in high-cost industrial products (for example, silks) and credit and specie transactions, which had as a consequence in the agricultural arena sharecropping as the mode of labor control and little export to other areas.

The three structural positions in a world-economy—core, periphery, and semiperiphery—had become stabilized by about 1640. How certain areas became one and not the other is a long story.[7] The key fact is that given slightly different starting points, the interests of various local groups converged in northwest Europe, leading to the development of strong state mechanisms, and diverged sharply in the peripheral areas, leading to very weak ones. Once we get a difference in the strength of the state machineries, we get the operation of "unequal exchange"[8] which is enforced by strong states on weak ones, by core states on peripheral areas. Thus capitalism involves not only appropriation of the surplus value by an owner from a laborer, but an appropriation of surplus of the whole world-economy by core areas. * * *

In the early Middle Ages, there was to be sure trade. But it was largely either "local," in a region that we might call the "extended" manor, or "long-distance," primarily of luxury goods. There was no exchange of "bulk" goods, of "staples" across intermediate-size areas, and hence no production for such markets. Later on in the Middle Ages, world-economies may be said to have come into existence, one centering on Venice, a second on the cities of Flanders and the Hanse. For various reasons, these structures were hurt by the retractions (economic, demographic, and ecological) of the period 1300–1450. It is only with the creating of a *European* division of labor after 1450 that capitalism found firm roots.

Capitalism was from the beginning an affair of the world-economy and not of nation-states. It is a misreading of the situation to claim that it is only

in the twentieth century that capitalism has become "world-wide," although this claim is frequently made in various writings, particularly by Marxists. Typical of this line of argument is Charles Bettelheim's response to Arghiri Emmanuel's discussion of unequal exchange:

> The tendency of the capitalist mode of production to become worldwide is manifested not only through the constitution of a group of national economies forming a complex and hierarchical structure, including an imperialist pole and a dominated one, and not only through the antagonistic relations that develop between the different "national economies" and the different states, but also through the constant "transcending" of "national limits" by big capital (the formation of "international big capital," "world firms," etc. . . .).[9]

The whole tone of these remarks ignores the fact that capital has never allowed its aspirations to be determined by national boundaries in a capitalist world-economy, and that the creation of "national" barriers—generically, mercantilism—has historically been a defensive mechanism of capitalists located in states which are one level below the high point of strength in the system. Such was the case of England *vis-à-vis* the Netherlands in 1660–1715, France *vis-à-vis* England in 1715–1815, Germany *vis-à-vis* Britain in the nineteenth century, the Soviet Union *vis-à-vis* the US in the twentieth. In the process a large number of countries create national economic barriers whose consequences often last beyond their initial objectives. At this later point in the process the very same capitalists who pressed their national governments to impose the restrictions now find these restrictions constraining. This is not an "internationalization" of "national" capital. This is simply a new political demand by certain sectors of the capitalist classes who have at all points in time sought to maximize their profits within the real economic market, that of the world-economy.

If this is so, then what meaning does it have to talk of structural positions within this economy and identify states as being in one of these positions? And why talk of three positions, inserting that of "semiperiphery" in between the widely used concepts of core and periphery? The state machineries of the core states were strengthened to meet the needs of capitalist landowners and their merchant allies. But that does not mean that these state machineries were manipulable puppets. Obviously any organization, once created, has a certain autonomy from those who pressed it into existence for two reasons. It creates a stratum of officials whose own careers and interests are furthered by the continued strengthening of the organization itself, however the interests of its capitalist backers may vary. Kings and bureaucrats wanted to stay in power and increase their personal gain constantly. Secondly, in the process of creating the strong state in the first place, certain "constitutional" compromises had to be made with other forces within the state boundaries and these institutionalized compromises limit, as they are designed to do, the freedom of maneuver of the managers of the state machinery. The formula of the state as "executive committee of the ruling class" is only valid, therefore, if one bears in mind that executive committees are never mere reflections of the wills of their constituents, as anyone who has ever participated in any organization knows well.

The strengthening of the state machineries in core areas has as its direct counterpart the decline of the state machineries in peripheral areas. The decline of the Polish monarchy in the sixteenth and seventeenth centuries is a striking example of this phenomenon.[10] There are two reasons for this. In peripheral countries, the interests of the capitalist landowners lie in an opposite direction from those of the local commercial bourgeoisie. Their interests lie in maintaining an open economy to maximize their profit from world-market trade (no restrictions in exports and access to lower-cost industrial products from core countries) and in elimination of the commercial bourgeoisie in favor of outside merchants (who pose no local political threat). Thus, in terms of the state, the coalition which strengthened it in core countries was precisely absent.

The second reason, which has become ever more operative over the history of the modern world-system, is that the strength of the state machinery in core states is a function of the weakness of other state machineries. Hence intervention of outsiders via war, subversion, and diplomacy is the lot of peripheral states.

All this seems very obvious. I repeat it only in order to make clear two points. One cannot reasonably explain the strength of various state machineries at specific moments of the history of the modern world-system primarily in terms of a genetic-cultural line of argumentation, but rather in terms of the structural role a country plays in the world-economy at that moment in time. To be sure, the initial eligibility for a particular role is often decided by an accidental edge a particular country has, and the "accident" of which one is talking is no doubt located in part in past history, in part in current geography. But once this relatively minor accident is given, it is the operations of the world-market forces which accentuate the differences, institutionalize them, and make them impossible to surmount over the short run.

The second point we wish to make about the structural differences of core and periphery is that they are not comprehensible unless we realize that there is a third structural position: that of the semiperiphery. This is not the result merely of establishing arbitrary cutting-points on a continuum of characteristics. Our logic is not merely inductive, sensing the presence of a third category from a comparison of indicator curves. It is also deductive. The semiperiphery is needed to make a capitalist world-economy run smoothly. Both kinds of world-system, the world-empire with a redistributive economy and the world-economy with a capitalist market economy, involve markedly unequal distribution of rewards. Thus, logically, there is immediately posed the question of how it is possible politically for such a system to persist. Why do not the majority who are exploited simply overwhelm the minority who draw disproportionate benefits? The most rapid glance at the historic record shows that these world-systems have been faced rather rarely by fundamental system-wide insurrection. While internal discontent has been eternal, it has usually taken quite long before the accumulation of the erosion of power has led to the decline of a world-system, and as often as not, an external force has been a major factor in this decline.

There have been three major mechanisms that have enabled world-systems to retain relative political stability * * *. One obviously is the concentration of military strength in the hands of the dominant forces. * * *

A second mechanism is the pervasiveness of an ideological commitment to the system as a whole. I do not mean what has often been termed the "legitimation" of a system, because that term has been used to imply that the lower strata of a system feel some affinity with or loyalty towards the rulers, and I doubt that this has ever been a significant factor in the survival of world-systems. I mean rather the degree to which the staff or cadres of the system (and I leave this term deliberately vague) feel that their own well-being is wrapped up in the survival of the system as such and the competence of its leaders. It is this staff which not only propagates the myths; it is they who believe them.

But neither force nor the ideological commitment of the staff would suffice were it not for the division of the majority into a larger lower stratum and a smaller middle stratum. Both the revolutionary call for polarization as a strategy of change and the liberal encomium to consensus as the basis of the liberal polity reflect this proposition. The import is far wider than its use in the analysis of contemporary political problems suggests. It is the normal condition of either kind of world-system to have a three-layered structure. When and if this ceases to be the case, the world-system disintegrates.

In a world-empire, the middle stratum is in fact accorded the role of maintaining the marginally desirable long-distance luxury trade, while the upper stratum concentrates its resources on controlling the military machinery which can collect the tribute, the crucial mode of redistributing surplus. By providing, however, for an access to a limited portion of the surplus to urbanized elements who alone, in premodern societies, could contribute political cohesiveness to isolated clusters of primary producers, the upper stratum effectively buys off the potential leadership of coordinated revolt. And by denying access to political rights for this commercial-urban middle stratum, it makes them constantly vulnerable to confiscatory measures whenever their economic profits become sufficiently swollen so that they might begin to create for themselves military strength.

In a world-economy, such "cultural" stratification is not so simple, because the absence of a single political system means the concentration of economic roles vertically rather than horizontally throughout the system. The solution then is to have three *kinds* of states, with pressures for cultural homogenization within each of them—thus, besides the upper stratum of core states and the lower stratum of peripheral states, there is a middle stratum of semiperipheral ones.

This semiperiphery is then assigned as it were a specific economic role, but the reason is less economic than political. That is to say, one might make a good case that the world-economy as an economy would function every bit as well without a semiperiphery. But it would be far less *politically* stable, for it would mean a polarized world-system. The existence of the third category means precisely that the upper stratum is not faced with the *unified* opposition of all the others because the *middle* stratum is both exploited and exploiter. It follows that the specific economic role is not all that important, and has thus changed through the various historical stages of the modern world-system. * * *

Where then does class analysis fit in all of this? And what in such a formulation are nations, nationalities, peoples, ethnic groups? First of all, without arguing the point now,[11] I would contend that all these latter terms denote variants of a single phenomenon which I will term "ethno-nations."

Both classes and ethnic groups, or status groups, or ethno-nations are phenomena of world-economies and much of the enormous confusion that has surrounded the concrete analysis of their functioning can be attributed quite simply to the fact that they have been analyzed as though they existed within the nation-states of this world-economy, instead of within the world-economy as a whole. This has been a Procrustean bed indeed.

The range of economic activities being far wider in the core than in the periphery, the range of syndical interest groups is far wider there. Thus, it has been widely observed that there does not exist in many parts of the world today a proletariat of the kind which exists in, say, Europe or North America. But this is a confusing way to state the observation. Industrial activity being disproportionately concentrated in certain parts of the world-economy, industrial wage workers are to be found principally in certain geographic regions. Their interests as a syndical group are determined by their collective relationship to the world-economy. Their ability to influence the political functioning of this world-economy is shaped by the fact that they command larger percentages of the population in one sovereign entity than another. The form their organizations take have, in large part, been governed too by these political boundaries. The same might be said about industrial capitalists. Class analysis is perfectly capable of accounting for the political position of, let us say, French skilled workers if we look at their structural position and interests in the world-economy. Similarly with ethno-nations. The meaning of ethnic consciousness in a core area is considerably different from that of ethnic consciousness in a peripheral area precisely because of the different class position such ethnic groups have in the world-economy.[12]

Political struggles of ethno-nations or segments of classes within national boundaries of course are the daily bread and butter of local politics. But their significance or consequences can only be fruitfully analyzed if one spells out the implications of their organizational activity or political demands for the functioning of the world-economy. This also incidentally makes possible more rational assessments of these politics in terms of some set of evaluative criteria such as "left" and "right."

The functioning then of a capitalist world-economy requires that groups pursue their economic interests within a single world market while seeking to distort this market for their benefit by organizing to exert influence on states, some of which are far more powerful than others but none of which controls the world market in its entirety. Of course, we shall find on closer inspection that there are periods where one state is relatively quite powerful and other periods where power is more diffuse and contested, permitting weaker states broader ranges of action. We can talk then of the relative tightness or looseness of the world-system as an important variable and seek to analyze why this dimension tends to be cyclical in nature, as it seems to have been for several hundred years.

*   *   *

* * * We have adumbrated as our basic unit of observation a concept of world-systems that have structural parts and evolving stages. It is within such a framework, I am arguing, that we can fruitfully make comparative analyses—of the wholes and of parts of the whole. Conceptions precede and govern measurements. I am all for minute and sophisticated quantitative indicators. I am all for minute and diligent archival work that will trace a concrete historical series of events in terms of all its immediate complexities. But the point of either is to enable us to see better what has happened and what is happening. For that we need glasses with which to discern the dimensions of difference, we need models with which to weigh significance, we need summarizing concepts with which to create the knowledge which we then seek to communicate to each other. And all this because we are men with hybris and original sin and therefore seek the good, the true, and the beautiful.

Notes

1. See Frederic Lane's discussion of "protection costs" which is reprinted in part 3 of *Venice and History* (Baltimore: Johns Hopkins Press, 1966). For the specific discussion of tribute, see pp. 389–90, 416–20.

2. See Karl Polanyi, "The Economy as Instituted Process," in Karl Polanyi, Conrad M. Arsenberg and Harry W. Pearson (eds.), *Trade and Market in the Early Empire* (Glencoe: Free Press, 1957), pp. 243–70.

3. See my *The Modern World-System: Capitalist Agriculture and the Origins of the European World-Economy in the Sixteenth Century* (New York: Academic Press, 1974).

4. Maurice Dobb, *Capitalism Yesterday and Today* (London: Lawrence and Wishart, 1958), p. 21.

5. *Ibid.*, pp. 6–7.

6. *Ibid.*, p. 21.

7. I give a brief account of this in "Three Paths of National Development in the Sixteenth Century," *Studies in Comparative International Development*, 7: 2 (Summer 1972) 95–101, and below, ch. 2.

8. See Arghiri Emmanuel, *Unequal Exchange* (New York: Monthly Review Press, 1972).

9. Charles Bettelheim, "Theoretical Comments," in Emmanual, *Unequal Exchange*, p. 295.

10. See J. Siemenski, "Constitutional Conditions in the Fifteenth and Sixteenth Centuries," in *Cambridge History of Poland*, vol. 1, W. F. Reddaway *et al.* (eds.), *From the Origins to Sobieski (to 1696)* (Cambridge: University Press, 1950), pp. 416–40; Janusz Tazbir, "The Commonwealth of the Gentry," in Aleksander Gieysztor *et al.*, *History of Poland* (Warszawa: PWN—Polish Scientific Publications, 1968), pp. 169–271.

11. See my fuller analysis in "Social Conflict in Post-Independence Black Africa: The Concepts of Race and Status-Group Reconsidered," in Ernest Q. Campbell (ed.), *Racial Tensions and National Identity* (Nashville: Vanderbilt University Press, 1972), pp. 207–26.

12. See my "The Two Modes of Ethnic Consciousness: Soviet Central Asia in Transition?" in Edward Allworth (ed.), *The Nationality Question in Soviet Central Asia* (New York: Praeger, 1973), pp. 168–75.

WILLIAM C. WOHLFORTH

The Stability of a Unipolar World

The collapse of the Soviet Union produced the greatest change in world power relationships since World War II. With Moscow's headlong fall from superpower status, the bipolar structure that had shaped the security policies of the major powers for nearly half a century vanished, and the United States emerged as the sole surviving superpower. Commentators were quick to recognize that a new "unipolar moment" of unprecedented U.S. power had arrived.[1] In 1992 the Pentagon drafted a new grand strategy designed to preserve unipolarity by preventing the emergence of a global rival.[2] But the draft plan soon ran into controversy, as commentators at home and abroad argued that any effort to preserve unipolarity was quixotic and dangerous.[3] Officials quickly backed away from the idea and now eschew the language of primacy or predominance, speaking instead of the United States as a "leader" or the "indispensable nation."[4]

The rise and sudden demise of an official strategy for preserving primacy lends credence to the widespread belief that unipolarity is dangerous and unstable. While scholars frequently discuss unipolarity, their focus is always on its demise. For neorealists, unipolarity is the least stable of all structures because any great concentration of power threatens other states and causes them to take action to restore a balance.[5] Other scholars

From *International Security* 24, no. 1 (summer 1999): 5–41. The notes to Table 1 have been omitted.

grant that a large concentration of power works for peace, but they doubt that U.S. preeminence can endure.[6] Underlying both views is the belief that U.S. preponderance is fragile and easily negated by the actions of other states. As a result, most analysts argue that unipolarity is an "illusion," a "moment" that "will not last long," or is already "giving way to multipolarity."[7] Indeed, some scholars question whether the system is unipolar at all, arguing instead that it is, in Samuel Huntington's phrase, "uni-multipolar."[8]

Although they disagree vigorously on virtually every other aspect of post–Cold War world politics, scholars of international relations increasingly share this conventional wisdom about unipolarity. Whether they think that the current structure is on the verge of shifting away from unipolarity or that it has already done so, scholars believe that it is prone to conflict as other states seek to create a counterpoise to the overweening power of the leading state. The assumption that unipolarity is unstable has framed the wide-ranging debate over the nature of post–Cold War world politics. Since 1991 one of the central questions in dispute has been how to explain continued cooperation and the absence of old-style balance-of-power politics despite major shifts in the distribution of power.[9]

In this article, I advance three propositions that undermine the emerging conventional wisdom that the distribution of power is unstable and conflict prone. First, the system is unambiguously unipolar. The United States enjoys a much larger margin of superiority over the next most powerful state or, indeed, all other great powers combined than any leading state in the last two centuries. Moreover, the United States is the first leading state in modern international history with decisive preponderance in *all* the underlying components of power: economic, military, technological, and geopolitical.[10] * * *

Second, the current unipolarity is prone to peace. The raw power advantage of the United States means that an important source of conflict in previous systems is absent: hegemonic rivalry over leadership of the international system. No other major power is in a position to follow any policy that depends for its success on prevailing against the United States in a war or an extended rivalry. None is likely to take any step that might invite the focused enmity of the United States. * * *

Third, the current unipolarity is not only peaceful but durable.[11] It is already a decade old, and if Washington plays its cards right, it may last as long as bipolarity. For many decades, no state is likely to be in position to take on the United States in any of the underlying elements of power. * * *

The scholarly conventional wisdom holds that unipolarity is dynamically unstable and that any slight overstep by Washington will spark a dangerous backlash.[12] I find the opposite to be true: unipolarity is durable and peaceful, and the chief threat is U.S. failure to do enough.[13] Possessing an undisputed preponderance of power, the United States is freer than most states to disregard the international system and its incentives. But because the system is built around U.S. power, it creates demands for American engagement. The more efficiently Washington responds to these incentives and provides order, the more long-lived and peaceful the system. * * *

*   *   *

Lonely at the Top: The System Is Unipolar

Unipolarity is a structure in which one state's capabilities are too great to be counterbalanced.[14] Once capabilities are so concentrated, a structure arises that is fundamentally distinct from either multipolarity (a structure comprising three or more especially powerful states) or bipolarity (a structure produced when two states are substantially more powerful than all others). At the same time, capabilities are not so concentrated as to produce a global empire. * * *

Is the current structure unipolar? The crucial first step in answering this question is to compare the current distribution of power with its structural predecessors. The more the current concentration of power in the United States differs from past distributions, the less we should expect post–Cold War world politics to resemble that of earlier epochs. * * *

QUANTITATIVE COMPARISON

To qualify as polar powers, states must score well on *all* the components of power: size of population and territory; resource endowment; economic capabilities; military strength; and "competence," according to Kenneth Waltz.[15] Two states measured up in 1990. One is gone. No new pole has appeared: 2 − 1 = 1. The system is unipolar.

*   *   *

Table 1 shows how U.S. relative power in the late 1990s compares with that of Britain near its peak, as well as the United States itself during the Cold War. The United States' economic dominance is surpassed only by its own position at the dawn of the Cold War—when every other major power's economy was either exhausted or physically destroyed by the recent world war—and its military superiority dwarfs that of any leading state in modern international history. Even the Correlates of War (COW) composite index—which favors states with especially large populations and industrial economies—shows an improvement in the United States' relative position since the mid-1980s.[16] * * *

In short, the standard measures that political scientists traditionally use as surrogates for capabilities suggest that the current system is unipolar.[17] But it takes only a glance at such measures to see that each is flawed in different ways. Economic output misses the salience for the balance of power of militarized states such as Prussia, pre–World

Table 1. Comparing Hegemonies

a. Gross Domestic Product as Percentage of "Hegemon"

Year	United States	Britain	Russia	Japan	Austria	Germany	France	China
1870	108	100	90	n.a.	29	46	75	n.a.
1950	100	24	35	11	n.a.	15	15	n.a.
1985	100	17	39	38	n.a.	21	18	46
1997 (PPP)	100	15	9	38	n.a.	22	16	53
1997 (exchange rate)	100	16	5	50	n.a.	25	17	10

b. Military Expenditures as Percentage of "Hegemon"

Year	United States	Britain	Russia	Japan	Austria	Germany	France	China
1872	68	100	120	n.a.	44	65	113	n.a.
1950	100	16	107	n.a.	n.a.	n.a.	10	n.a.
1985	100	10	109	5	n.a.	8	8	10
1996	100	13	26	17	n.a.	14	17	13

c. Power Capabilities (COW) as Percentage of "Hegemon"

Year	United States	Britain	Russia	Japan	Austria	Germany	France	China
1872	50	100	50	n.a.	27	50	60	n.a.
1950	100	37	103	n.a.	n.a.	3	21	n.a.
1985	100	22	167	56	n.a.	28	22	156
1996	100	14	43	36	n.a.	21	18	118

War II Japan, Nazi Germany, or the Soviet Union, and, in any case, is very hard to measure for some states and in some periods. Military expenditures might conceal gross inefficiencies and involve similar measurement problems. Composite indexes capture the conventional wisdom that states must score well on many underlying elements to qualify as great powers. But any composite index that seems to capture the sources of national power in one period tends to produce patently absurd results for others.

*   *   *

The specific problem with the COW index is its implicit assumption that the wellsprings of national power have not changed since the dawn of the industrial age. Updating such an index to take account of the post–industrial revolution in political economy and military affairs would inevitably be a subjective procedure. By most such "information-age" measures, however, the United States possesses decisive advantages. The United States not only has the largest high-technology economy in the world by far, it also has the greatest concentration in high-technology manufacturing among the major powers.[18] Total U.S. expenditures on research and development (R&D) nearly equal the combined total of the rest of the Group of Seven richest countries (and the G-7 accounts for 90 percent of world spending on R&D). Numerous studies of U.S. technological leadership confirm the country's dominant position in all the key "leading sectors" that are most likely to dominate the world economy into the twenty-first century.[19]

The U.S. combination of quantitative and qualitative material advantages is unprecedented, and it translates into a unique geopolitical position. Thanks to a decades-old policy of harnessing technology to the generation of military power, the U.S. comparative advantage in this area mirrors Britain's naval preeminence in the nineteenth century. At the same time, Washington's current brute share of great power capabilities—its aggregate potential compared with that of the next largest power of all other great powers combined—dwarfs

Britain's share in its day. The United States is the only state with global power projection capabilities; it is probably capable, if challenged, of producing defensive land-power dominance in the key theaters; it retains the world's only truly blue-water navy; it dominates the air; it has retained a nuclear posture that may give it first-strike advantages against other nuclear powers; and it has continued to nurture decades-old investments in military logistics and command, control, communications, and intelligence. * * *

QUALITATIVE COMPARISON

Bringing historical detail to bear on the comparison of today's distribution of power to past systems only strengthens the initial conclusions that emerge from quantitative comparisons. Two major concentrations of power over the last two centuries show up on different quantitative measures of capabilities: the COW measure picks Britain in 1860–70 as an especially powerful actor, and the GDP measure singles out the post–World War II United States. These indicators miss two crucial factors that only historical research can reveal: the clarity of the balance as determined by the events that help decisionmakers define and measure power, and the comprehensiveness of the leader's overall power advantage in each period.[20] Together these factors help to produce a U.S. preponderance that is far less ambiguous, and therefore less subject to challenge, than that of previous leading states.

The end of the Cold War and the collapse of the Soviet Union were much more effective tests of material power relationships than any of the systemic wars of the past two centuries.[21] One reason is simple arithmetic. The greater the number of players, the more difficult it is for any single war or event to clarify relations of power throughout the system. Even very large wars in multipolar systems do not provide unambiguous tests of the relative power of the states belonging to the victorious coalition. And wars often end before the complete defeat of major powers. The systemic wars of the past left several great states standing and ready to argue over their relative power. By contrast, bipolarity was built on two states, and one collapsed with more decisiveness than most wars can generate. The gap between the capabilities of the superpowers, on the one hand, and all other major powers, on the other hand, was already greater in the Cold War than any analogous gap in the history of the European states system. Given that the United States and the Soviet Union were so clearly in a class by themselves, the fall of one from superpower status leaves the other much more unambiguously "number one" than at any other time since 1815.

Moreover, the power gap in the United States' favor is wider than any single measure can capture because the unipolar concentration of resources is *symmetrical*. Unlike previous system leaders, the United States has commanding leads in all the elements of material power: economic, military, technological, and geographical. All the naval and commercial powers that most scholars identify as the hegemonic leaders of the past lacked military (especially land-power) capabilities commensurate with their global influence. Asymmetrical power portfolios generate ambiguity. When the leading state excels in the production of economic and naval capabilities but not conventional land power, it may seem simultaneously powerful and vulnerable. Such asymmetrical power portfolios create resentment among second-tier states that are powerful militarily but lack the great prestige the leading state's commercial and naval advantages bring. At the same time, they make the leader seem vulnerable to pressure from the one element of power in which it does not excel: military capabilities. The result is ambiguity about which state is more powerful, which is more secure, which is threatening which, and which might make a bid for hegemony.

Britain's huge empire, globe-girdling navy, and vibrant economy left strong imprints on nineteenth-century world politics, but because its capabilities were always skewed in favor of naval and commercial power, it never had the aggregate advantage implied by its early industrialization. Indeed, it was not even the international system's unambiguous leader until Russia's defeat in Crimea

in 1856. The Napoleonic Wars yielded *three* potential hegemons: Britain, the decisive naval and financial power; Russia, the preeminent military power on the continent; and France, the state whose military prowess had called forth coalitions involving all the other great states. From 1815 to 1856, Britain had to share leadership of the system with Russia, while the power gap between these two empires and France remained perilously small.[22] Russia's defeat in Crimea punctured its aura of power and established Britain's uncontested primacy. But even after 1856, the gap between London and continental powerhouses such as France, Russia, and Prussia remained small because Britain never translated its early-industrial potential into continental-scale military capabilities. The Crimean victory that ushered in the era of British preeminence was based mainly on *French* land power.[23] And Britain's industrial advantage peaked before industrial capabilities came to be seen as the sine qua non of military power.[24]

The Cold War power gap between the United States and the Soviet Union was much smaller. World War II yielded ambiguous lessons concerning the relative importance of U.S. sea, air, and economic capabilities versus the Soviet Union's proven conventional military superiority in Eurasia.[25] The conflict clearly showed that the United States possessed the greatest military potential in the world—if it could harness its massive economy to the production of military power and deploy that power to the theater in time. Despite its economic weaknesses, however, Stalin's empire retained precisely those advantages that Czar Nicholas I's had had: the ability to take and hold key Eurasian territory with land forces. The fact that Moscow's share of world power was already in Eurasia (and already in the form of an armed fighting force) was decisive in explaining the Cold War. It was chiefly because of its location (and its militarized nature) that the Soviet Union's economy was capable of generating bipolarity. At the dawn of the Cold War, when the United States' economy was as big as those of all other great powers combined, the balance of power was still seen as precarious.[26]

In both the Pax Britannica and the early Cold War, different measures show power to have been concentrated in the leading state to an unusual degree. Yet in both periods, the perceived power gaps were closer than the measures imply. Asymmetrical power portfolios and small power gaps are the norm in modern international history. They are absent from the distribution of power of the late 1990s. Previous postwar hegemonic moments therefore cannot compare with post–Cold War unipolarity. Given the dramatically different power distribution alone, we should expect world politics to work much differently now than in the past.

Unipolarity Is Peaceful

Unipolarity favors the absence of war among the great powers and comparatively low levels of competition for prestige or security for two reasons: the leading state's power advantage removes the problem of hegemonic rivalry from world politics, and it reduces the salience and stakes of balance-of-power politics among the major states. This argument is based on two well-known realist theories: hegemonic theory and balance-of-power theory. Each is controversial, and the relationship between the two is complex.[27] For the purposes of this analysis, however, the key point is that both theories predict that a unipolar system will be peaceful.

HOW TO THINK ABOUT UNIPOLARITY

Hegemonic theory has received short shrift in the debate over the nature of the post–Cold War international system.[28] This omission is unwarranted, for the theory has simple and profound implications for the peacefulness of the post–Cold War international order that are backed up by a formidable body of scholarship. The theory stipulates that especially powerful states ("hegemons") foster international orders that are stable until differential growth in power produces a dissatisfied state with the capability to challenge the dominant state for leadership. The clearer and larger the concentration of power in the leading state, the more peaceful the international order associated with it will be.

The key is that conflict occurs only if the leader and the challenger disagree about their relative power. That is, the leader must think itself capable of defending the status quo at the same time that the number two state believes it has the power to challenge it. The set of perceptions and expectations necessary to produce such conflict is most likely under two circumstances: when the overall gap between the leader and the challenger is small and/or when the challenger overtakes the leader in *some* elements of national power but not others, and the two parties disagree over the relative importance of these elements. Hence both the overall size and the comprehensiveness of the leader's power advantage are crucial to peacefulness. If the system is unipolar, the great power hierarchy should be much more stable than any hierarchy lodged within a system of more than one pole. Because unipolarity is based on a historically unprecedented concentration of power in the United States, a potentially important source of great power conflict—hegemonic rivalry—will be missing.

Balance-of-power theory has been at the center of the debate, but absent so far is a clear distinction between peacefulness and durability. The theory predicts that any system comprised of states in anarchy will evince a tendency toward equilibrium. As Waltz puts it, "Unbalanced power, whoever wields it, is a potential danger to others."[29] This central proposition lies behind the widespread belief that unipolarity will not be durable (a contention I address below). Less often noted is the fact that as long as the system remains unipolar, balance-of-power theory predicts peace. When balance-of-power theorists argue that the post–Cold War world is headed toward conflict, they are not claiming that unipolarity causes conflict. Rather, they are claiming that unipolarity leads quickly to bi- or multipolarity. It is not unipolarity's peacefulness but its durability that is in dispute.

Waltz argued that bipolarity is less war prone than multipolarity because it reduces uncertainty. By the same logic, unpolarity is the least war prone of all structures.[30] For as long as unipolarity obtains, there is little uncertainty regarding alliance choices or the calculation of power. The only options available to second-tier states are to bandwagon with the polar power (either explicitly or implicitly) or, at least, to take no action that could incur its focused enmity. As long as their security policies are oriented around the power and preferences of the sole pole, second-tier states are less likely to engage in conflict-prone rivalries for security or prestige. Once the sole pole takes sides, there can be little doubt about which party will prevail. Moreover, the unipolar leader has the capability to be far more interventionist than earlier system leaders. Exploiting the other states' security dependence as well as its unilateral power advantages, the sole pole can maintain a system of alliances that keeps second-tier states out of trouble.[31]

*   *   *

In sum, both hegemonic theory and balance-of-power theory specify thresholds at which great concentrations of power support a peaceful structure. Balance-of-power theory tells us that smaller is better.[32] Therefore one pole is best, and security competition among the great powers should be minimal. Hegemonic theory tells us that a clear preponderance in favor of a leading state with a comprehensive power portfolio should eliminate rivalry for primacy. Overall, then, unipolarity generates comparatively few incentives for security or prestige competition among the great powers.

*   *   *

Unipolarity does not imply the end of all conflict or that Washington can have its way on all issues all the time. It simply means the absence of two big problems that bedeviled the statesmen of past epochs: hegemonic rivalry and balance-of-power politics among the major powers. It is only by forgetting them that scholars and pundits are able to portray the current period as dangerous and threatening.

*   *   *

Unipolarity Is Durable

Unipolarity rests on two pillars. I have already established the first: the sheer size and comprehensiveness of the power gap separating the United States from other states. This massive power gap implies that any countervailing change must be strong and sustained to produce structural effects. The second pillar—geography—is just as important. In addition to all the other advantages the United States possesses, we must also consider its four truest allies: Canada, Mexico, the Atlantic, and the Pacific. Location matters. The fact that Soviet power happened to be situated in the heart of Eurasia was a key condition of bipolarity. Similarly, the U.S. position as an offshore power determines the nature and likely longevity of unipolarity. Just as the raw numbers could not capture the real dynamics of bipolarity, power indexes alone cannot capture the importance of the fact that the United States is in North America while all the other potential poles are in or around Eurasia. * * *

Because they fail to appreciate the sheer size and comprehensiveness of the power gap and the advantages conveyed by geography, many scholars expect bi- or multipolarity to reappear quickly. They propose three ways in which unipolarity will end: counterbalancing by other states, regional integration, or the differential growth in power. None of these is likely to generate structural change in the policy-relevant future.[33]

*   *   *

* * * A unipolar system is one in which a counterbalance is impossible. When a counterbalance becomes possible, the system is not unipolar. The point at which this structural shift can happen is determined in part by how efficiently alliances can aggregate the power of individual states. Alliances aggregate power only to the extent that they are reliably binding and permit the merging of armed forces, defense industries, R&D infrastructures, and strategic decisionmaking. A glance at international history shows how difficult it is to coordinate counterhegemonic alliances. States are tempted to free ride, pass the buck, or bandwagon in search of favors from the aspiring hegemon. States have to worry about being abandoned by alliance partners when the chips are down or being dragged into conflicts of others' making.[34] The aspiring hegemon, meanwhile, has only to make sure its domestic house is in order. In short, a single state gets more bang for the buck than several states in an alliance. To the extent that alliances are inefficient at pooling power, the sole pole obtains greater power per unit of aggregate capabilities than any alliance that might take shape against it. Right away, the odds are skewed in favor of the unipolar power.

The key, however, is that the countercoalitions of the past—on which most of our empirical knowledge of alliance politics is based—formed against centrally located land powers (France, Germany, and the Soviet Union) that constituted relatively unambiguous security threats to their neighbors. Coordinating a counterbalance against an *offshore* state that has *already* achieved unipolar status will be much more difficult.[35] Even a declining offshore unipolar state will have unusually wide opportunities to play divide and rule. Any second-tier state seeking to counterbalance has to contend with the existing pro-U.S. bandwagon. If things go poorly, the aspiring counterbalancer will have to confront not just the capabilities of the unipolar state, but also those of its other great power allies. All of the aspiring poles face a problem the United States does not: great power neighbors that could become crucial U.S. allies the moment an unambiguous challenge to Washington's preeminence emerges. In addition, in each region there are smaller "pivotal states" that make natural U.S. allies against an aspiring regional power.[36] Indeed, the United States' first move in any counterbalancing game of this sort could be to try to promote such pivotal states to great power status, as it did with China against the Soviet Union in the latter days of the Cold War.

NEW REGIONAL UNIPOLARITIES:
A GAME NOT WORTH THE CANDLE

To bring an end to unipolarity, it is not enough for regional powers to coordinate policies in tradi-

tional alliances. They must translate their aggregate economic potential into the concrete capabilities necessary to be a pole: a defense industry and power projection capabilities that can play in the same league as those of the United States. Thus all scenarios for the rapid return of multipolarity involve regional unification or the emergence of strong regional unipolarities.[37] For the European, Central Eurasian, or East Asian poles to measure up to the United States in the near future, each region's resources need to fall under the de facto control of one state or decisionmaking authority. In the near term, either true unification in Europe and Central Eurasia (the European Union [EU] becomes a de facto state, or Russia recreates an empire) or unipolar dominance in each region by Germany, Russia, and China or Japan, respectively, is a necessary condition of bi- or multipolarity.

The problem with these scenarios is that regional balancing dynamics are likely to kick in against the local great power much more reliably than the global counterbalance works against the United States. Given the neighborhoods they live in, an aspiring Chinese, Japanese, Russian, or German pole would face more effective counterbalancing than the United States itself.

*   *   *

Thus the quick routes to multipolarity are blocked. If states value their independence and security, most will prefer the current structure to a multipolarity based on regional unipolarities. Eventually, some great powers will have the capability to counter the United States alone or in traditional great power alliances that exact a smaller price in security or autonomy than unipolarity does. Even allowing for the differential growth in power to the United States' disadvantage, however, for several decades it is likely to remain more costly for second-tier states to form counterbalancing alliances than it is for the unipolar power to sustain a system of alliances that reinforces its own dominance.

THE DIFFUSION OF POWER

In the final analysis, alliances cannot change the system's structure. Only the uneven growth of power (or, in the case of the EU, the creation of a new state) will bring the unipolar era to an end. Europe will take many decades to become a de facto state—if it ever does. Unless and until that happens, the fate of unipolarity depends on the relative rates of growth and innovation of the main powers.

I have established that the gap in favor of the United States is unprecedented * * *.

* * *

Thus far I have kept the analysis focused squarely on the distribution of material capabilities. Widening the view only slightly to consider key legacies of the Cold War strengthens the case for the robustness of unipolarity. The United States was the leading state in the Cold War, so the status quo already reflects its preferences. Washington thus faces only weak incentives to expand, and the preponderance of power in its control buttresses rather than contradicts the status quo. This reduces the incentives of others to counterbalance the United States and reinforces stability.[38] Another important Cold War legacy is that two prime contenders for polar status—Japan and Germany (or Europe)—are close U.S. allies with deeply embedded security dependence on the United States. This legacy of dependence reduces the speed with which these states can foster the institutions and capabilities of superpower status. Meanwhile, the United States inherits from the Cold War a global military structure that deeply penetrates many allied and friendly states, and encompasses a massive and complex physical presence around the world. These initial advantages raise the barriers to competition far higher than the raw measures suggest. Finally, the Cold War and its end appear to many observers to be lessons against the possibility of successful balancing via increased internal mobilization for war. The prospect that domestic mobilization efforts can extract U.S.-scale military power from a comparatively small or undeveloped economy seems less plausible now than it did three decades ago.

THE BALANCE OF POWER IS NOT WHAT STATES MAKE OF IT

* * *

The advent of unipolarity does not mean the end of all politics among great powers. Elites will not stop resenting overweening U.S. capabilities. Second-tier great powers will not suddenly stop caring about their standing vis-à-vis other states. Rising states presently outside the great power club will seek the prerequisites of membership. We should expect evidence of states' efforts to explore the new structure and determine their place in it. Most of the action since 1991 has concerned membership in the second tier of great powers. Some seek formal entry in the second tier via nuclear tests or a permanent seat on the United Nations Security Council. Existing members fear a devaluation of their status and resist new aspirants. All of this requires careful management. But it affects neither the underlying structure nor the basic great power hierarchy.

The fact that some important states have more room to maneuver now than they did under bipolarity does not mean that unipolarity is already giving way to some new form of multipolarity.[39] The end of the bipolar order has decreased the security interdependence of regions and increased the latitude of some regional powers. But polarity does not refer to the existence of merely regional powers. When the world was bipolar, Washington and Moscow had to think strategically whenever they contemplated taking action anywhere within the system. Today there is no other power whose reaction greatly influences U.S. action across multiple theaters. * * *

* * *

Conclusion: Challenges for Scholarship and Strategy

The distribution of material capabilities at the end of the twentieth century is unprecedented. However we view this venerable explanatory variable, the current concentration of power in the United

States is something new in the world. Even if world politics works by the old rules—even if democracy, new forms of interdependence, and international institutions do not matter—we should not expect a return of balance-of-power politics à la multipolarity for the simple reason that we are living in the modern world's first unipolar system. And unipolarity is not a "moment." It is a deeply embedded material condition of world politics that has the potential to last for many decades.

If unipolarity is so robust, why do so many writers hasten to declare its demise? The answer may lie in the common human tendency to conflate power *trends* with existing relationships. The rush to proclaim the return of multipolarity in the 1960s and 1970s, to pronounce the United States' decline in the 1980s, to herald the rise of Japan or China as superpowers in the 1980s and 1990s, and finally to bid unipolarity adieu after the Cold War are all examples. In each case, analysts changed reference points to minimize U.S. power. In the bipolarity debate, the reference point became the extremely tight alliance of the 1950s, so any disagreement between the United States and Europe was seen as a harbinger of multipolarity. In the 1980s, "hegemony" was defined as "the U.S. position circa 1946," so the recovery of Europe and Japan appeared as fatal threats to the United States' position. Many analysts have come to define unipolarity as an imperial system such as Rome where there is only one great power and all other states are satrapies or dependencies. As a result, each act of defiance of Washington's preferences on any issue comes to be seen as the return of a multipolar world.

One explanation for this tendency to shift reference points is that in each case the extent of U.S. power was inconvenient for the scholarly debate of the day. Scholars schooled in nineteenth-century balance-of-power politics were intellectually primed for their return in the 1960s. In the 1980s, continued cooperation between the United States and its allies was a more interesting puzzle if the era of U.S. hegemony was over. In the 1990s, unipolarity is doubly inconvenient for scholars of international relations. For neorealists, unipolarity contradicts the central tendency of their theory. Its longevity is a testament to the theory's indeterminacy. For liberals and constructivists, the absence of balance-of-power politics among the great powers is a much more interesting and tractable puzzle if the world is multipolar. The debate would be far easier if all realist theories predicted instability and conflict and their competitors predicted the opposite.

Today's distribution of power is unprecedented, however, and power-centric theories naturally expect politics among nations to be different than in past systems. In contrast to the past, the existing distribution of capabilities generates incentives for cooperation. The absence of hegemonic rivalry, security competition, and balancing is not necessarily the result of ideational or institutional change. This is not to assert that realism provides the best explanation for the absence of security and prestige competition. Rather, the conclusion is that it offers an explanation that may compete with or complement those of other theoretical traditions. As a result, evaluating the merits of contending theories for understanding the international politics of unipolarity presents greater empirical challenges than many scholars have acknowledged.

Because the baseline expectations of all power-centric theories are novel, so are their implications for grand strategy. Scholar's main message to policymakers has been to prepare for multipolarity. Certainly, we should think about how to manage the transition to a new structure. Yet time and energy are limited. Constant preparation for the return of multipolarity means not gearing up intellectually and materially for unipolarity. Given that unipolarity is prone to peace and the probability that it will last several more decades at least, we should focus on it and get it right.

The first step is to stop calling this the "post–Cold War world." Unipolarity is nearing its tenth birthday. Our experience with this international system matches what the statesmen and scholars of 1825, 1928, and 1955 had. The key to this system is the centrality of the United States. * * * One power is lonely at the top. Calling the current period the true Pax Americana may offend some, but it reflects reality and focuses attention on the stakes involved in U.S. grand strategy.

Second, doing too little is a greater danger than doing too much. Critics note that the United States is far more interventionist than any previous system leader. But given the distribution of power, the U.S. impulse toward interventionism is understandable. In many cases, U.S. involvement has been demand driven, as one would expect in a system with one clear leader. Rhetoric aside, U.S. engagement seems to most other elites to be necessary for the proper functioning of the system. In each region, cobbled-together security arrangements that require an American role seem preferable to the available alternatives. The more efficiently the United States performs this role, the more durable the system. * * *

Third, we should not exaggerate the costs. The clearer the underlying distribution of power is, the less likely it is that states will need to test it in arms races or crises. Because the current concentration of power in the United States is unprecedentedly clear and comprehensive, states are likely to share the expectation that counterbalancing would be a costly and probably doomed venture. As a result, they face incentives to keep their military budgets under control until they observe fundamental changes in the capability of the United States to fulfill its role. The whole system can thus be run at comparatively low costs to both the sole pole and the other major powers. Unipolarity can be made to seem expensive and dangerous if it is equated with a global empire demanding U.S. involvement in all issues everywhere. In reality, unipolarity is a distribution of capabilities among the world's great powers. It does not solve all the world's problems. Rather, it minimizes two major problems—security and prestige competition—that confronted the great powers of the past. Maintaining unipolarity does not require limitless commitments. It involves managing the central security regimes in Europe and Asia, and maintaining the expectation on the part of other states that any geopolitical challenge to the United States is futile. As long as that is the expectation, states will likely refrain from trying, and the system can be maintained at little extra cost.

The main criticism of the Pax Americana, however, is not that Washington is too interventionist. A state cannot be blamed for responding to systemic incentives. The problem is U.S. reluctance to *pay up*. Constrained by a domestic welfare role and consumer culture that the weaker British hegemon never faced, Washington tends to shrink from accepting the financial, military, and especially the domestic political burdens of sole pole status. At the same time, it cannot escape the demand for involvement. The result is cruise missile hegemony, the search for polar status on the cheap, and a grand global broker of deals for which others pay. The United States has responded to structural incentives by assuming the role of global security manager and "indispensable nation" in all matters of importance. But too often the solutions Washington engineers are weakened by American reluctance to take any domestic political risks.

The problem is that structural pressures on the United States are weak. Powerful states may not respond to the international environment because their power makes them immune to its threat. The smaller the number of actors, the greater the potential impact of internal processes on international politics. The sole pole is strong and secure enough that paying up-front costs for system maintenance is hard to sell to a parsimonious public. As Kenneth Waltz argued, "Strong states . . . can afford not to learn."[40] If that was true of the great powers in multi- or bipolar systems, it is even truer of today's unipolar power. The implication is that instead of dwelling on the dangers of over-involvement and the need to prepare for an impending multipolarity, scholars and policymakers should do more to advertise the attractions of unipolarity.

Despite scholars' expectations, it was not the rise of Europe, Japan, and China that ended bipolarity. The monodimensional nature of the Soviet Union's power and the brittleness of its domestic institutions turned out to be the main threats to bipolar stability. Similarly, a uniting Europe or a rising Japan or China may not become the chief engines of structural change in the early twenty-first century. If the analysis here is right, then the live-for-today nature of U.S. domestic institutions may be the chief threat to unipolar stability. In short, the current world order is characterized not by a looming U.S. threat that is driving other powers toward multipolar counterbalancing, but by a material structure that presupposes and demands U.S. preponderance coupled with policies and rhetoric that deny its existence or refuse to face its modest costs.

NOTES

1. Charles Krauthammer, "The Unipolar Moment," *Foreign Affairs*, Vol. 70, No. 1 (Winter 1990/1991), pp. 23–33.

2. Patrick Tyler, "The Lone Superpower Plan: Ammunition for Critics," *New York Times*, March 10, 1992, p. A12.

3. For the most thorough and theoretically grounded criticism of this strategy, see Christopher Layne, "The Unipolar Illusion: Why New Great Powers Will Arise," *International Security*, Vol. 17, No. 4 (Spring 1993), pp. 5–51; and Layne, "From Preponderance to Offshore Balancing: America's Future Grand Strategy," *International Security*, Vol. 22, No. 1 (Summer 1997), pp. 86–124.

4. The phrase—commonly attributed to Secretary of State Madeleine Albright—is also a favorite of President Bill Clinton's. For example, see the account of his speech announcing the expansion of the North Atlantic Treaty Organization in Alison Mitchell, "Clinton Urges NATO Expansion in 1999," *New York Times*, October 23, 1996, p. A20.

5. Kenneth N. Waltz, "Evaluating Theories," *American Political Science Review*, Vol. 91, No. 4 (December 1997), pp. 915–916; Layne, "Unipolar Illusion"; and Michael Mastanduno, "Preserving the Unipolar Moment: Realist Theories and U.S. Grand Strategy after the Cold War," *International Security*, Vol. 21, No. 4 (Spring 1997), pp. 44–98. Although I differ with Waltz on the stability of unipolarity, the title of this article and much of its contents reflect intellectual debts to his work on system structure and stability. See Waltz, "The Stability of a Bipolar World," *Daedalus*, Vol. 93, No. 3 (Summer 1964), pp. 881–901.

6. See Charles A. Kupchan, "After Pax Americana: Benign Power, Regional Integration, and the Sources of Stable Multipolarity," *International Security*, Vol. 23, No. 3 (Fall 1998), pp. 40–79. Samuel P. Huntington maintained this position in Huntington, "Why International Primacy Matters," *International Security*, Vol. 17, No. 4 (Spring 1993), pp. 63–83, but he has since abandoned it. A more bullish assessment, although still more pessimistic than the analysis here, is Douglas Lemke, "Continuity of History: Power Transition Theory and the End of the Cold War," *Journal of Peace Research*, Vol. 34, No. 1 (February 1996), pp. 203–236.

7. As Glenn H. Snyder puts it, the international system "appears to be unipolar, though incipiently multipolar." Snyder, *Alliance Politics* (Ithaca, N.Y.: Cornell University Press, 1997), p. 18. The quoted phrases in this sentence appear in Charles A. Kupchan, "Rethinking Europe," *National Interest*, No. 56 (Summer 1999); Kupchan, "After Pax Americana," p. 41; Layne, "Unipolar Illusion"; Mastanduno, "Preserving the Unipolar Moment"; and Waltz, "Evaluating Theories," p. 914. Although Charles Krauthammer coined the term "unipolar moment" in his article under that title, he argued that unipolarity had the potential to last a generation.

8. Samuel P. Huntington, "The Lonely Superpower," *Foreign Affairs*, Vol. 78, No. 2 (March/April 1999), p. 36. For similar views of the post–Cold War structure, see Aaron L. Friedberg, "Ripe for Rivalry: Prospects for Peace in a Multipolar Asia," *International Security*, Vol. 18, No. 3 (Winter 1993/94), pp. 5–33; and Josef Joffe, " 'Bismarck' or 'Britain'? Toward an American Grand Strategy after Bipolarity," *International Security*, Vol. 19, No. 4 (Spring 1995), pp. 94–117.

9. The assumption that realism predicts instability after the Cold War pervades the scholarly debate. See, for example, Sean M. Lynn-Jones

and Steven E. Miller, eds., *The Cold War and After: Prospects for Peace—An* International Security *Reader* (Cambridge, Mass.: MIT Press, 1993); and David A. Baldwin, ed., *Neorealism and Neoliberalism: The Contemporary Debate* (New York: Columbia University Press, 1993). For more varied perspectives on realism and unipolarity, see Ethan B. Kapstein and Michael Mastanduno, eds., *Unipolar Politics: Realism and State Strategies after the Cold War* (New York: Columbia University Press, 1999). Explanations for stability despite the balance of power fall roughly into three categories: (1) liberal arguments, including democratization, economic interdependence, and international institutions. For examples, see Bruce M. Russett, *Grasping the Democratic Peace* (Princeton, N.J.: Princeton University Press, 1993); John R. Oneal and Bruce M. Russett, "The Classical Liberals Were Right: Democracy, Interdependence, and Conflict, 1950–1985," *International Studies Quarterly*, Vol. 41, No. 2 (June 1997), pp. 267–294; G. John Ikenberry, "Institutions, Strategic Restraint, and the Persistence of the American Postwar Order," *International Security*, Vol. 23, No. 3 (Winter 1998/99), pp. 43–78. (2) Cultural and ideational arguments that highlight social learning. See John Mueller, *Retreat from Doomsday: The Obsolescence of Major War* (Rochester, N.Y.: University of Rochester Press, 1989); and Alexander Wendt, *Social Theory of International Politics* (Cambridge: Cambridge University Press, 1999), chap. 6. (3) Arguments that highlight systemic and material factors other than the balance of power, such as globalization, the offense-defense balance, or nuclear weapons. See Stephen G. Brooks, "The Globalization of Production and the Changing Benefits of Conquest," *Journal of Conflict Resolution*, Vol. 43, No. 5 (October 1999); and Stephen Van Evera, "Primed for Peace: Europe after the Cold War," in Jones and Miller, *Cold War and After*.

10. I focus on material elements of power mainly because current scholarly debates place a premium on making clear distinctions between ideas and material forces. See Wendt, *Social Theory of International Politics*; and Jeffrey Legro and Andrew Moravscik, "Is Anybody Still a Realist?" *International Security*, Vol. 24, No. 2 (Fall 1999). Many nonmaterial elements of power also favor the United States and strengthen the argument for unipolarity's stability. On "soft power," see Joseph S. Nye, Jr., *Bound to Lead: The Changing Nature of American Power* (New York: Basic Books, 1990).

11. I define "stability" as peacefulness and durability. Kenneth Waltz first conflated these two meanings of stability in "The Stability of a Bipolar World." He later eliminated the ambiguity by defining stability exclusively as durability in *Theory of International Politics* (Reading, Mass.: Addison-Wesley, 1979). I avoid ambiguity by treating peacefulness and durability separately. Durability subsumes another common understanding of stability: the idea of a self-reinforcing equilibrium. To say that an international system is durable implies that it can experience significant shifts in power relations without undergoing fundamental change. See Robert Jervis, *Systems Effects: Complexity in Political and Social Life* (Princeton, N.J.: Princeton University Press, 1997), chap. 3.

12. Because overwhelming preponderance favors both peace and durability, stability is less sensitive to how the United States defines its interests than most scholars assume. In contrast, many realists hold that stability is strictly contingent upon Washington's nonthreatening or status quo stance in world affairs. See Mastanduno, "Preserving the Unipolar Moment." Similarly, Kupchan, "After Pax Americana," argues that the United States' "benign" character explains stability.

13. This was Krauthammer's original argument in "The Unipolar Moment." For a comprehensive review of the debate that reflects the standard scholarly skepticism toward the stability of unipolarity, see Barry R. Posen and Andrew L. Ross, "Competing Visions for U.S. Grand

Strategy," *International Security*, Vol. 21, No. 2 (Winter 1996/97), pp. 5–54.

14. This definition flows from the logic of neorealist balance-of-power theory, but it is consistent with classical balance-of-power thinking. See Layne, "Unipolar Illusion," p. 130 n. 2; Snyder, *Alliance Politics*, chap. 1; Morton Kaplan, *System and Process in International Politics* (New York: Wiley, 1957), pp. 22–36; Harrison Wagner, "What Was Bipolarity?" *International Organization*, Vol. 47, No. 1 (Winter 1993), pp. 77–106; and Emerson M.S. Niou, Peter C. Ordeshook, and Gregory F. Rose, *The Balance of Power: Stability in International Systems* (New York: Cambridge University Press, 1989), p. 76.

15. Waltz, *Theory of International Politics*, p. 131.

16. The COW index combines the following indicators with equal weights: total population, urban population, energy consumption, iron and steel production, military expenditures, and military personnel. As noted in Table 1, 1996 data were compiled by the author from different sources; COW methodology may lead to different results. I include the COW measure not because I think it is a good one but because it has a long history in the field. Quantitative scholars are increasingly critical of all such composite indexes. Gross domestic product (GDP) is becoming the favored indicator, a trend started by A.F.K. Organski in *World Politics*, 2d ed. (New York: Knopf, 1965): pp. 199–200, 211–215, and furthered by Organski and Jacek Kugler in *The War Ledger* (Chicago: University of Chicago Press, 1980). Given its weighting of energy consumption, steel production, and military personnel, for example, the COW Index had the Soviet Union surpassing U.S. power in 1971. Indeed, despite the fact that the Soviet Union produced, at best, one-third of U.S. GDP in the 1980s, it decisively surpassed the United States on *every* composite power indicator. See John R. Oneal, "Measuring the Material Base of the Contemporary East-West Balance of Power," *International Interactions*, Vol. 15, No. 2 (Summer 1989), pp. 177–196.

17. The only major indicator of hegemonic status in which the United States has continued to decline is net foreign indebtedness, which surpassed $1 trillion in 1996. For a strong argument on the importance of this indicator in governing the international political economy, see Robert Gilpin, *The Political Economy of International Relations* (Princeton, N.J.: Princeton University Press, 1987). There are other power indexes—many of which are linked to highly specific theories—that show continued U.S. decline. See George Modelski and William R. Thompson, *Leading Sectors and World Powers: The Coevolution of Global Economics and Politics* (Columbia: University of South Carolina Press, 1996); and Karen A. Rasler and William R. Thompson, *Great Powers and Global Struggle, 1490–1990* (Lexington: University Press of Kentucky, 1994). By most other measures of naval power or industrial competitiveness, however, the U.S. position has improved in the 1990s.

18. OECD, *Science, Technology, and Industry: Scoreboard of Indicators 1997* (Paris: OECD, 1997). By one estimate, the United States accounted for 35.8 percent of total world spending on technology in 1997. Japan accounted for 17.6 percent, Germany 6.6 percent, Britain 5.7 percent, France 5.1 percent, and China 1.6 percent. Mark Landler, "When the Dragon Awakes . . . and Finds That It's Not 1999 Anymore," *New York Times*, May 11, 1999, p. C1.

19. These studies do forecast *future* challenges—as they have since the 1970s. The incentives of nearly all data-gathering agencies are to emphasize U.S. vulnerability, yet as good social scientists, the authors of these studies acknowledge the country's decisive current advantages. See, for example, U.S. Department of Commerce, Office of Technology Policy, *The New Innovators: Global Patenting Trends in Five Sectors* (Washington, D.C.: OTP, 1998). Similarly, according to Valéry, "Innovation in Industry," [*Economist*, February 20, 1999,] p. 27, "By 1998, the Council on Competitiveness, an industry think tank in Washington set up

to fathom the reasons for the country's decline, concluded that America had not only regained its former strengths, but was now far ahead technologically in the five most crucial sectors of its economy."

20. This is based on the neoclassical realist argument that power is important to decisionmakers but very hard to measure. See, for a general discussion, Gideon Rose, "Neoclassical Realism and Theories of Foreign Policy," *World Politics*, Vol. 51, No. 1 (October 1998), pp. 144–172.

21. The relationship between hierarchies of power revealed by systemic wars and the stability of international systems is explored in Robert Gilpin, *War and Change in World Politics* (Cambridge: Cambridge University Press, 1981). On wars as power tests, see Geoffrey Blainey, *The Causes of War* (New York: Free Press, 1973).

22. It goes without saying that the nineteenth-century international system was perceived as multipolar, although Russia and Britain were seen as being in a class by themselves. See R.W. Seton-Watson, *Britain in Europe, 1789–1914: A Survey of Foreign Policy* (Cambridge: Cambridge University Press, 1937). To gain a sense of Russia's power in the period, it is enough to recall Czar Nicholas's dispatch of 400,000 troops to crush the 1848 revolt in Hungary—and his simultaneous offer to send another contingent across Europe to establish order in Paris should it be necessary. On Russia as Europe's hegemon, see M.S. Anderson, *The Rise of Modern Diplomacy, 1450–1919* (London: Longman, 1993); Adam Watson, "Russia in the European States System," in Watson and Hedley Bull, eds., *The Expansion of International Society* (Oxford: Clarendon, 1984). On Russia and Britain as (rivalrous) "cohegemons," see Paul W. Schroeder, *The Transformation of European Politics* (London: Oxford University Press, 1993); and Gordon A. Craig, "The System of Alliances and the Balance of Power," in J.P.T. Bury, ed., *New Cambridge Modern History*, Volume 10: *The Zenith of European Power, 1830–70* (Cambridge: Cam-

bridge University Press 1960). The best, concise discussion of the nature and limitations of British power in this period is Paul Kennedy, *The Rise and Fall of British Naval Mastery* (London: Macmillan, 1983), chap. 6.

23. For an excellent account of the British debate on the lessons of Crimea, see Olive Anderson, *A Liberal State at War: English Politics and Economics during the Crimean War* (New York: St. Martin's, 1967).

24. Thus the COW measure suffers from a hindsight bias that accords importance to industrial capabilities before their military significance was appreciated. Cf. William B. Moul, "Measuring the 'Balance of Power': A Look at Some Numbers," *Review of International Studies*, Vol. 15, No. 2 (April 1989), pp. 101–121. On the conservatism of nineteenth-century military assessments, see B.H. Liddell-Hart, "Armed Forces and the Art of War: Armies," in Bury, *New Cambridge Modern History*. On the slowly growing perceptions of industrialization and its implications for war, see William H. McNeil, *The Pursuit of Power: Technology, Armed Force, and Society since A.D. 1000* (Chicago: University of Chicago Press, 1982); Dennis Showalter, *Railroads and Rifles: Soldiers, Technology, and the Unification of Germany* (Hamden, Conn.: Archer, 1975); Paul Kennedy, *The Rise of the Anglo-German Antagonism, 1860–1914* (London: Allen and Unwin, 1980); and Kennedy, *Rise and Fall of British Naval Mastery*.

25. I discuss these lessons in Wohlforth, *Elusive Balance: Power and Perceptions during the Cold War* (Ithaca, N.Y.: Cornell University Press, 1993). A much fuller analysis is available in recent historical works. For the U.S. side, see Marc Trachtenberg, *A Constructed Peace: The Making of the European Settlement, 1945–1963* (Princeton, N.J.: Princeton University Press, 1999); and Melvyn P. Leffler, *A Preponderance of Power: National Security, the Truman Administration, and the Cold War* (Stanford, Calif.: Stanford University Press, 1992). And for the view from Moscow, see Vladislav M.

Zubok and Constantine Pleshakov, *Inside the Kremlin's Cold War* (Cambridge, Mass.: Harvard University Press, 1996); and Vojtech Mastny, *The Cold War and Soviet Insecurity: The Stalin Years* (New York: Oxford University Press, 1996).

26. As Marc Trachtenberg summarizes the view from Washington in 1948: "The defense of the West rested on a very narrow base. Even with the nuclear monopoly, American power only barely balanced Soviet power in central Europe." See Trachtenberg, *A Constructed Peace*, p. 91. Cf. Leffler, *A Preponderance of Power*, who is more critical of U.S. officials' power assessments. Nevertheless, Leffler's narrative—and the massive documentary evidence it relies on—would not be possible had the Soviet potential to dominate Eurasia not been plausible.

27. For simplicity, I treat only Waltz's neorealist version of balance-of-power theory. By "hegemonic theory," I mean the theory of hegemonic war and change in Gilpin, *War and Change in World Politics*, as well as power transition theory, which is sometimes applied to pairs of states other than hegemon and challenger. In addition to Organski, *World Politics*, and Organski and Kugler, *War Ledger*, see Jacek Kugler and Douglas Lemke, eds., *Parity and War: Evaluation and Extension of the War Ledger* (Ann Arbor: University of Michigan Press, 1996); and the chapters by George Modelski and William R. Thompson, Manus I. Midlarsky, and Jacek Kugler and A.F.K. Organski in Midlarsky, ed., *Handbook of War Studies* (London: Unwin, 1989). Theories of the balance of power and hegemony are often thought to be competing. I maintained this position in *Elusive Balance*, chap. 1. In many instances, however, they are complementary. See Randall L. Schweller and William C. Wohlforth, "Power Test: Updating Realism in Response to the End of the Cold War," *Security Studies* (forthcoming). For an interesting synthesis with some points of contact with the analysis here, see William R. Thompson, "Dehio, Long Cycles, and the Geohistorical Context of Structural Transition," *World Politics*, Vol. 45, No. 1 (October 1992), pp. 127–152; and Rasler and Thompson, *Great Powers and Global Struggle*.

28. Exceptions include Lemke, "Continuity of History"; and Mark S. Sheetz, "Correspondence: Debating the Unipolar Moment," *International Security*, Vol. 22, No. 3 (Winter 1997/1998), pp. 168–174.

29. Waltz, "Evaluating Theories," p. 915.

30. The connection between uncertainty, the number of principal players, and war proneness has been questioned. The key to most recent criticisms of neorealist arguments concerning stability is that the distribution of capabilities alone is insufficient to explain the war proneness of international systems. Ancillary assumptions concerning risk attitudes or preferences for the status quo are necessary. See Levy, "The Causes of War" [*Annual Review of Political Science*, Vol. 1 (1998), pp. 139–165]; Bruce Bueno de Mesquita, "Neorealism's Logic and Evidence: When Is a Theory Falsified?" paper prepared for the Fiftieth Annual Conference of the International Studies Association, Washington, D.C., February 1999; and Robert Powell, "Stability and the Distribution of Power," *World Politics*, Vol. 48, No. 2 (January 1996), pp. 239–267, and sources cited therein. These analyses are right that no distribution of power rules out war if some states are great risk takers or have extreme clashes of interest. The greater the preponderance of power, however, the more extreme the values of other variables must be to produce war, because preponderance reduces the uncertainty of assessing the balance of power.

31. The sole pole's power advantages matter only to the degree that it is engaged, and it is most likely to be engaged in politics among the other major powers. The argument applies with less force to potential security competition between regional powers, or between a second-tier state and a lesser power with which the system leader lacks close ties.

32. Three may be worse than four, however. See Waltz, *Theory of International Politics*, chap. 9;

and Schweller, *Deadly Imbalances* [*Tripolarity and Hitler's Strategy of World Conquest* (New York: Columbia University Press, 1998)].

33. Here I depart from Waltz, *Theory of International Politics*, pp. 161–162, for whom a stable system is one with no "consequential variation" in the number of poles (e.g., changes between multi-, tri-, bi-, or unipolarity). In the European states system, multipolarity obtained for three centuries. While the multipolar structure itself was long lived, however, the identity of its members (the leading states in the system) changed with much greater frequency—a matter of no small consequence for the governments concerned. By this measure (change in the identity, as opposed to the number, of the states that define the structure), bipolarity had a typical life span. See Bueno de Mesquita, "Neorealism's Logic and Evidence." I expect that the unipolar era will be of comparable duration.

34. See Snyder, *Alliance Politics*; and Thomas J. Christensen and Jack Snyder, "Chain Gangs and Passed Bucks: Predicting Alliance Patterns in Multipolarity," *International Organization*, Vol. 44, No. 1 (Winter 1990), pp. 137–168.

35. The key here is that from the standpoint of balance-of-power theory, we are dealing with a structural *fait accompli*. Of the two powers that made up the bipolar order, one collapsed, leaving the other at the center of a unipolar system. A situation has arisen in which the theory's central tendency cannot operate. Many readers will perceive this state of affairs as a testimony to the weakness of balance-of-power theory. I agree. The weaker the theory, the longer our initial expectations of unipolarity's longevity.

36. On "pivotal states," see Robert Chase, Emily Hill, and Paul Kennedy, *The Pivotal States: A New Framework for U.S. Policy in the Developing World* (New York: W.W. Norton, 1999).

37. Kupchan, "Pax Americana," advocates just such a system.

38. A preponderance of power makes other states less likely to oppose the United States, but it could also tempt Washington to demand more of others. Because an overwhelming preponderance of power fosters stability, the clash of interests would have to be extreme to produce a counterbalance. In other words, the United States would have to work very hard to push all the other great powers and many regional ones into an opposing alliance. The point is important in theory but moot in practice. Because the post–Cold War world is already so much a reflection of U.S. interests, Washington is less tempted than another state might be to make additional claims as its relative power increases. The result is a preponderance of power backing up the status quo, a condition theorists of many stripes view as an augury of peace and stability. For different perspectives, see E.H. Carr, *The Twenty Years' Crisis: 1919–1939: An Introduction to the Study of International Relations* (London: Macmillan, 1951); Organski, *World Politics*; Gilpin, *War and Change in World Politics*; Powell, "Stability and the Distribution of Power"; and Randall L. Schweller, "Neorealism's Status Quo Bias: What Security Dilemma?" *Security Studies*, Vol. 5, No. 3 (Spring 1996), pp. 225–258.

39. The enhanced autonomy of many regions compared to the bipolar order has given rise to an important new research agenda. See Etel Solingen, *Regional Orders at Century's Dawn* (Princeton, N.J.: Princeton University Press, 1998); and David A. Lake and Patrick N. Morgan, eds., *Regional Orders: Building Security in a New World* (University Park: Pennsylvania State University Press, 1997). This evidence of new regional security dynamics leads many to view the current structure as a hybrid of unipolarity and multipolarity. See Huntington, "Lonely Superpower"; and Friedberg, "Ripe for Rivalry."

40. Waltz, *Theory of International Politics*, p. 195.

SAMUEL P. HUNTINGTON

The Clash of Civilizations?

The Next Pattern of Conflict

World politics is entering a new phase, and intellectuals have not hesitated to proliferate visions of what it will be—the end of history, the return of traditional rivalries between nation states, and the decline of the nation state from the conflicting pulls of tribalism and globalism, among others. Each of these visions catches aspects of the emerging reality. Yet they all miss a crucial, indeed a central, aspect of what global politics is likely to be in the coming years.

It is my hypothesis that the fundamental source of conflict in this new world will not be primarily ideological or primarily economic. The great divisions among humankind and the dominating source of conflict will be cultural. Nation states will remain the most powerful actors in world affairs, but the principal conflicts of global politics will occur between nations and groups of different civilizations. The clash of civilizations will dominate global politics. The fault lines between civilizations will be the battle lines of the future.

Conflict between civilizations will be the latest phase in the evolution of conflict in the modern world. For a century and a half after the emergence of the modern international system with the Peace of Westphalia, the conflicts of the Western world were largely among princes—emperors, absolute monarchs and constitutional monarchs attempting to expand their bureaucracies, their armies, their mercantilist economic strength and, most important, the territory they ruled. In the process they created nation states, and beginning with the French Revolution the principal lines of conflict were between nations rather than princes. * * * [A]s a result of the Russian Revolution and the reaction against it, the conflict of nations yielded to

From *Foreign Affairs* 72, no. 3 (summer 1993): 22–49.

the conflict of ideologies, first among communism, fascism-Nazism and liberal democracy, and then between communism and liberal democracy. During the Cold War, this latter conflict became embodied in the struggle between the two superpowers, neither of which was a nation state in the classical European sense and each of which defined its identity in terms of its ideology.

* * * With the end of the Cold War, international politics moves out of its Western phase, and its centerpiece becomes the interaction between the West and non-Western civilizations and among non-Western civilizations. In the politics of civilizations, the peoples and governments of non-Western civilizations no longer remain the objects of history as targets of Western colonialism but join the West as movers and shapers of history.

The Nature of Civilizations

During the Cold War the world was divided into the First, Second and Third Worlds. Those divisions are no longer relevant. It is far more meaningful now to group countries not in terms of their political or economic systems or in terms of their level of economic development but rather in terms of their culture and civilization.

What do we mean when we talk of a civilization? A civilization is a cultural entity. Villages, regions, ethnic groups, nationalities, religious groups, all have distinct cultures at different levels of cultural heterogeneity. The culture of a village in southern Italy may be different from that of a village in northern Italy, but both will share in a common Italian culture that distinguishes them from German villages. European communities, in turn, will share cultural features that distinguish them from Arab or Chinese communities. Arabs, Chinese and Westerners, however, are not part of any broader cultural entity. They constitute civilizations. A civilization is thus the highest cultural grouping of people and the broadest level of cultural identity people have short of that which distinguishes humans from other species. It is defined both by common objective elements, such as language, history, religion, customs, institutions, and by the subjective self-identification of people. * * *

* * * Civilizations are nonetheless meaningful entities, and while the lines between them are seldom sharp, they are real. Civilizations are dynamic; they rise and fall; they divide and merge. And, as any student of history knows, civilizations disappear and are buried in the sands of time.

Westerners tend to think of nation states as the principal actors in global affairs. They have been that, however, for only a few centuries. The broader reaches of human history have been the history of civilizations. In *A Study of History*, Arnold Toynbee identified 21 major civilizations; only six of them exist in the contemporary world.

Why Civilizations Will Clash

Civilization identity will be increasingly important in the future, and the world will be shaped in large measure by the interactions among seven or eight major civilizations. These include Western, Confucian, Japanese, Islamic, Hindu, Slavic-Orthodox, Latin American and possibly African civilization. The most important conflicts of the future will occur along the cultural fault lines separating these civilizations from one another.

Why will this be the case?

First, differences among civilizations are not only real; they are basic. Civilizations are differentiated from each other by history, language, culture, tradition and, most important, religion. The people of different civilizations have different views on the relations between God and man, the individual and the group, the citizen and the state, parents and children, husband and wife, as well as differing views of the relative importance of rights and responsibilities, liberty and authority, equality and hierarchy. These differences are the product of centuries. They will not soon disappear. * * *

Second, the world is becoming a smaller place. The interactions between peoples of different civilizations are increasing; these increasing interactions intensify civilization consciousness and awareness of differences between civilizations and commonalities within civilizations. * * *

Third, the processes of economic modernization and social change throughout the world are separating people from longstanding local identities. They also weaken the nation state as a source of identity. In much of the world religion has moved in to fill this gap, often in the form of movements that are labeled "fundamentalist." Such movements are found in Western Christianity, Judaism, Buddhism and Hinduism, as well as in Islam. * * * The "unsecularization of the world," George Weigel has remarked, "is one of the dominant social facts of life in the late twentieth century." * * *

Fourth, the growth of civilization-consciousness is enhanced by the dual role of the West. On the one hand, the West is at a peak of power. At the same time, however, and perhaps as a result, a return to the roots phenomenon is occurring among non-Western civilizations. Increasingly one hears references to trends toward a turning inward and "Asianization" in Japan, the end of the Nehru legacy and the "Hinduization" of India, the failure of Western ideas of socialism and nationalism and hence "re-Islamization" of the Middle East, and now a debate over Westernization versus Russianization in Boris Yeltsin's country. A West at the peak of its power confronts non-Wests that increasingly have the desire, the will and the resources to shape the world in non-Western ways.

*   *   *

Fifth, cultural characteristics and differences are less mutable and hence less easily compromised and resolved than political and economic ones. In the former Soviet Union, communists can become democrats, the rich can become poor and the poor rich, but Russians cannot become Estonians and Azeris cannot become Armenians. * * * Even more than ethnicity, religion discriminates sharply and exclusively among people. A person can be half-French and half-Arab and simultaneously even a citizen of two countries. It is more difficult to be half-Catholic and half-Muslim.

Finally, economic regionalism is increasing. * * * On the one hand, successful economic regionalism will reinforce civilization-consciousness. On the other hand, economic regionalism may succeed only when it is rooted in a common civilization. The European Community rests on the shared foundation of European culture and Western Christianity. The success of the North American Free Trade Area depends on the convergence now underway of Mexican, Canadian and American cultures. Japan, in contrast, faces difficulties in creating a comparable economic entity in East Asia because Japan is a society and civilization unique to itself. * * *

*   *   *

As people define their identity in ethnic and religious terms, they are likely to see an "us" versus "them" relation existing between themselves and people of different ethnicity or religion. The end of ideologically defined states in Eastern Europe and the former Soviet Union permits traditional ethnic identities and animosities to come to the fore. Differences in culture and religion create differences over policy issues, ranging from human rights to immigration to trade and commerce to the environment. * * * Most important, the efforts of the West to promote its values of democracy and liberalism as universal values, to maintain its military predominance and to advance its economic interests engender countering responses from other civilizations. * * *

The clash of civilizations thus occurs at two levels. At the micro-level, adjacent groups along the fault lines between civilizations struggle, often violently, over the control of territory and each other. At the macro-level, states from different civilizations compete for relative military and economic power, struggle over the control of international institutions and third parties, and competitively promote their particular political and religious values.

The Fault Lines between Civilizations

The fault lines between civilizations are replacing the political and ideological boundaries of the Cold War as the flash points for crisis and bloodshed. The Cold War began when the Iron Curtain divided Europe politically and ideologically. The Cold War ended with the end of the Iron Curtain. As the ideological division of Europe has disappeared, the cultural division of Europe between Western Christianity, on the one hand, and Orthodox Christianity and Islam, on the other, has reemerged. The most significant dividing line in Europe, as William Wallace has suggested, may well be the eastern boundary of Western Christianity in the year 1500. This line runs along what are now the boundaries between Finland and Russia and between the Baltic states and Russia, cuts through Belarus and Ukraine separating the more Catholic western Ukraine from Orthodox eastern Ukraine, swings westward separating Transylvania from the rest of Romania, and then goes through Yugoslavia almost exactly along the line now separating Croatia and Slovenia from the rest of Yugoslavia. In the Balkans this line, of course, coincides with the historic boundary between the Hapsburg and Ottoman empires. The peoples to the north and west of this line are Protestant or Catholic; they shared the common experiences of European history—feudalism, the Renaissance, the Reformation, the Enlightenment, the French Revolution, the Industrial Revolution; they are generally economically better off than the peoples to the east; and they may now look forward to increasing involvement in a common European economy and to the consolidation of democratic political systems. The peoples to the east and south of this line are Orthodox or Muslim; they historically belonged to the Ottoman or Tsarist empires and were only lightly touched by the shaping events in the rest of Europe; they are generally less advanced economically; they seem much less likely to develop stable democratic political systems. The Velvet Curtain of culture has replaced the Iron Curtain of ideology as the most significant dividing line in Europe. As the events in Yugoslavia show, it is not only a line of difference; it is also at times a line of bloody conflict.

Conflict along the fault line between Western and Islamic civilizations has been going on for 1,300 years. * * *

*   *   *

This centuries-old military interaction between the West and Islam is unlikely to decline. It could become more virulent. The Gulf War left some Arabs feeling proud that Saddam Hussein had attacked Israel and stood up to the West. It also left many feeling humiliated and resentful of the West's military presence in the Persian Gulf, the West's overwhelming military dominance, and their apparent inability to shape their own destiny. Many Arab countries, in addition to the oil exporters, are reaching levels of economic and social development where autocratic forms of government become inappropriate and efforts to introduce democracy become stronger. Some openings in Arab political systems have already occurred. The principal beneficiaries of these openings have been Islamist movements. * * *

Those relations are also complicated by demography. The spectacular population growth in Arab countries, particularly in North Africa, has led to increased migration to Western Europe. The movement within Western Europe toward minimizing internal boundaries has sharpened political sensitivities with respect to this development. * * *

*   *   *

Historically, the other great antagonistic interaction of Arab Islamic civilization has been with the pagan, animist, and now increasingly Christian black peoples to the south. In the past, this antagonism was epitomized in the image of Arab slave dealers and black slaves. It has been reflected in the on-going civil war in the Sudan between Arabs and blacks, the fighting in Chad between Libyan-supported insurgents and the government, the tensions between Orthodox Christians and Muslims in the Horn of Africa, and the political conflicts, recurring riots and communal violence between Muslims and Christians in Nigeria. The modern-

ization of Africa and the spread of Christianity are likely to enhance the probability of violence along this fault line. Symptomatic of the intensification of this conflict was the Pope John Paul II's speech in Khartoum in February 1993 attacking the actions of the Sudan's Islamist government against the Christian minority there.

On the northern border of Islam, conflict has increasingly erupted between Orthodox and Muslim peoples, including the carnage of Bosnia and Sarajevo, the simmering violence between Serb and Albanian, the tenuous relations between Bulgarians and their Turkish minority, the violence between Ossetians and Ingush, the unremitting slaughter of each other by Armenians and Azeris, the tense relations between Russians and Muslims in Central Asia. * * *

The conflict of civilizations is deeply rooted elsewhere in Asia. The historic clash between Muslim and Hindu in the subcontinent manifests itself now not only in the rivalry between Pakistan and India but also in intensifying religious strife within India between increasingly militant Hindu groups and India's substantial Muslim minority. The destruction of the Ayodhya mosque in December 1992 brought to the fore the issue of whether India wll remain a secular democratic state or become a Hindu one. * * *

*   *   *

Groups or states belonging to one civilization that become involved in war with people from a different civilization naturally try to rally support from other members of their own civilization. * * *

*   *   *

Civilization rallying to date has been limited, but it has been growing, and it clearly has the potential to spread much further. As the conflicts in the Persian Gulf, the Caucasus and Bosnia continued, the positions of nations and the cleavages between them increasingly were along civilizational lines. Populist politicians, religious leaders and the media have found it a potent means of arousing mass support and of pressuring hesitant governments. In the coming years, the local conflicts most likely to escalate into major wars will be those, as in Bosnia and the Caucasus, along the fault lines between civilizations. The next world war, if there is one, will be a war between civilizations.

The West versus the Rest

The West is now at an extraordinary peak of power in relation to other civilizations. Its superpower opponent has disappeared from the map. Military conflict among Western states is unthinkable, and Western military power is unrivaled. Apart from Japan, the West faces no economic challenge. It dominates international political and security institutions and with Japan international economic institutions. Global political and security issues are effectively settled by a directorate of the United States, Britain and France, world economic issues by a directorate of the United States, Germany and Japan, all of which maintain extraordinarily close relations with each other to the exclusion of lesser and largely non-Western countries. Decisions made at the U.N. Security Council or in the International Monetary Fund that reflect the interests of the West are presented to the world as reflecting the desires of the world community. The very phrase "the world community" has become the euphemistic collective noun (replacing "the Free World") to give global legitimacy to actions reflecting the interests of the United States and other Western powers.[1] * * *

* * * *

* * * V. S. Naipaul has argued that Western civilization is the "universal civilization" that "fits all men." At a superficial level much of Western culture has indeed permeated the rest of the world. At a more basic level, however, Western concepts differ fundamentally from those prevalent in other civilizations. Western ideas of individualism, liberalism, constitutionalism, human rights, equality, liberty, the rule of law, democracy, free markets, the separation of church and state often have little resonance in Islamic, Confucian, Japanese, Hindu, Buddhist or Orthodox cultures. Western efforts to propagate such ideas produce instead a reaction

against "human rights imperialism" and a reaffirmation of indigenous values, as can be seen in the support for religious fundamentalism by the younger generation in non-Western cultures. The very notion that there could be a "universal civilization" is a Western idea, directly at odds with the particularism of most Asian societies and their emphasis on what distinguishes one people from another. Indeed, the author of a review of 100 comparative studies of values in different societies concluded that "the values that are most important in the West are least important worldwide."[2] In the political realm, of course, these differences are most manifest in the efforts of the United States and other Western powers to induce other peoples to adopt Western ideas concerning democracy and human rights. Modern democratic government originated in the West. When it has developed in non-Western societies it has usually been the product of Western colonialism or imposition.

The central axis of world politics in the future is likely to be, in Kishore Mahbubani's phrase, the conflict between "the West and the Rest" and the responses of non-Western civilizations to Western power and values.[3] Those responses generally take one or a combination of three forms. At one extreme, non-Western states can, like Burma and North Korea, attempt to pursue a course of isolation, to insulate their societies from penetration or "corruption" by the West, and, in effect, to opt out of participation in the Western-dominated global community. The costs of this course, however, are high, and few states have pursued it exclusively. A second alternative, the equivalent of "bandwagoning" in international relations theory, is to attempt to join the West and accept its values and institutions. The third alternative is to attempt to "balance" the West by developing economic and military power and cooperating with other non-Western societies against the West, while preserving indigenous values and institutions; in short, to modernize but not to Westernize.

* * *

Implications for the West

This article does not argue that civilization identities will replace all other identities, that nation states will disappear, that each civilization will become a single coherent political entity, that groups within a civilization will not conflict with and even fight each other. This paper does set forth the hypotheses that differences between civilizations are real and important; civilization-consciousness is increasing; conflict between civilizations will supplant ideological and other forms of conflict as the dominant global form of conflict; international relations, historically a game played out within Western civilization, will increasingly be de-Westernized and become a game in which non-Western civilizations are actors and not simply objects; successful political, security and economic international institutions are more likely to develop within civilizations than across civilizations; conflicts between groups in different civilizations will be more frequent, more sustained and more violent than conflicts between groups in the same civilization; violent conflicts between groups in different civilizations are the most likely and most dangerous source of escalation that could lead to global wars; the paramount axis of world politics will be the relations between "the West and the Rest"; the elites in some torn non-Western countries will try to make their countries part of the West, but in most cases face major obstacles to accomplishing this; a central focus of conflict for the immediate future will be between the West and several Islamic-Confucian states.

This is not to advocate the desirability of conflicts between civilizations. It is to set forth descriptive hypotheses as to what the future may be like. If these are plausible hypotheses, however, it is necessary to consider their implications for Western policy. These implications should be divided between short-term advantage and long-term accommodation. In the short term it is clearly in the interest of the West to promote greater cooperation and unity within its own civilization, particularly between its European and North American components; to incorporate into the West societies in Eastern Europe and Latin America whose cultures are close to those of the West; to promote and maintain cooperative relations with Russia and Japan; to prevent escalation of local inter-civilization conflicts into major inter-civilization wars; to limit the expansion of the military strength of Confucian and Islamic states; to moderate the reduction of Western military capabilities and maintain military superiority in East and Southwest Asia; to exploit differences and conflicts among Confucian and Islamic states; to support in other civilizations groups sympathetic to Western values and interests; to strengthen international institutions that reflect and legitimate Western interests and values and to promote the involvement of non-Western states in those institutions.

In the longer term other measures would be called for. Western civilization is both Western and modern. Non-Western civilizations have attempted to become modern without becoming Western. To date only Japan has fully succeeded in this quest. Non-Western civilizations will continue to attempt to acquire the wealth, technology, skills, machines and weapons that are part of being modern. They will also attempt to reconcile this modernity with their traditional culture and values. Their economic and military strength relative to the West will increase. Hence the West will increasingly have to accommodate these non-Western modern civilizations whose power approaches that of the West but whose values and interests differ significantly from those of the West. This will require the West to maintain the economic and military power necessary to protect its interests in relation to these civilizations. It will also, however, require the West to develop a more profound understanding of the basic religious and philosophical assumptions underlying other civilizations and the ways in which people in those civilizations see their interests. It will require an effort to identify elements of commonality between Western and other civilizations. For the relevant future, there will be no universal civilization, but instead a world of different civilizations, each of which will have to learn to coexist with the others.

NOTES

1. Almost invariably Western leaders claim they are acting on behalf of "the world community." One minor lapse occurred during the run-up to the Gulf War. In an interview on "Good Morning America," Dec. 21, 1990, British Prime Minister John Major referred to the actions "the West" was taking against Saddam Hussein. He quickly corrected himself and subsequently referred to "the world community." He was, however, right when he erred.

2. Harry C. Triandis, *The New York Times*, Dec. 25, 1990, p. 41, and "Cross-Cultural Studies of Individualism and Collectivism," Nebraska Symposium on Motivation, vol. 37, 1989, pp. 41–133.

3. Kishore Mahbubani, "The West and the Rest," *The National Interest*, Summer 1992, pp. 3–13.

THE ECONOMIST

The Man in the Baghdad Café: Which "Civilisation" You Belong to Matters Less than You Might Think

Goering, it was said, growled that every time he heard the word culture he reached for his revolver. His hand would ache today. Since the end of the cold war, "culture" has been everywhere—not the opera-house or gallery kind, but the sort that claims to be the basic driving force behind human behaviour. All over the world, scholars and politicians seek to explain economics, politics and diplomacy in terms of "culture-areas" rather than, say, policies or ideas, economic interests, personalities or plain cock-ups.

Perhaps the best-known example is the notion that "Asian values" explain the success of the tiger economies of South-East Asia. Other accounts have it that international conflict is—or will be—caused by a clash of civilisations; or that different sorts of business organisation can be explained by how much people in different countries trust one other. These pages review the varying types of cultural explanation. They conclude that culture is so imprecise and changeable a phenomenon that it explains less than most people realise.

To see how complex the issue is, begin by considering the telling image with which Bernard Lewis opens his history of the Middle East. A man sits at a table in a coffee house in some Middle Eastern city, "drinking a cup of coffee or tea, perhaps smoking a cigarette, reading a newspaper, playing a board game, and listening with half an ear to whatever is coming out of the radio or the television installed in the corner." Undoubtedly Arab, almost certainly Muslim, the man would clearly identify himself as a member of these cultural groups. He would also, if asked, be likely to say that "western culture" was alien, even hostile to them.

Look closer, though, and the cultural contrasts blur. This coffee-house man probably wears western-style clothes—sneakers, jeans, a T-shirt. The chair and table at which he sits, the coffee he drinks, the tobacco he smokes, the newspaper he reads, all are western imports. The radio and tele-

From *The Economist*, 9 November 1996.

vision are western inventions. If our relaxing friend is a member of his nation's army, he probably operates western or Soviet weapons and trains according to western standards; if he belongs to the government, both his bureaucratic surroundings and the constitutional trappings of his regime may owe their origins to western influence.

The upshot, for Mr Lewis, is clear enough. "In modern times," he writes, "the dominating factor in the consciousness of most Middle Easterners has been the impact of Europe, later of the West more generally, and the transformation—some would say dislocation—which it has brought." Mr Lewis has put his finger on the most important and least studied aspect of cultural identity: how it changes. It would be wise to keep that in mind during the upsurge of debate about culture that is likely to follow the publication of Samuel Huntington's new book, "The Clash of Civilisations and the Remaking of World Order."

The Clash of Civilisations

A professor of international politics at Harvard and the chairman of Harvard's Institute for Strategic Planning, Mr Huntington published in 1993, in *Foreign Affairs*, an essay which that quarterly's editors said generated more discussion than any since George Kennan's article (under the by-line "x") which argued in July 1947 for the need to contain the Soviet threat. Henry Kissinger, a former secretary of state, called Mr Huntington's book-length version of the article "one of the most important books . . . since the end of the cold war."

The article, "The Clash of Civilisations?," belied the question-mark in its title by predicting wars of culture. "It is my hypothesis," Mr Huntington wrote, "that the fundamental source of conflict in this new world will not be primarily ideological or primarily economic. The great divisions among humankind and the dominating source of conflict will be cultural."

After the cold war, ideology seemed less important as an organising principle of foreign policy. Culture seemed a plausible candidate to fill the gap. So future wars, Mr Huntington claimed,

would occur "between nations and groups of different civilisations"—western, Confucian, Japanese, Islamic, Hindu, Orthodox and Latin American, perhaps African and Buddhist. Their disputes would "dominate global politics" and the battle-lines of the future would follow the fault-lines between these cultures.

No mincing words there, and equally few in his new book:

> Culture and cultural identities . . . are shaping the patterns of cohesion, disintegration and conflict in the post-cold war world . . . Global politics is being reconfigured along cultural lines.

Mr Huntington is only one of an increasing number of writers placing stress on the importance of cultural values and institutions in the confusion left in the wake of the cold war. He looked at the influence of culture on international conflict. Three other schools of thought find cultural influences at work in different ways.

- *Culture and the Economy.* Perhaps the oldest school holds that cultural values and norms equip people—and, by extension, countries—either poorly or well for economic success. The archetypal modern pronouncement of this view was Max Weber's investigation of the Protestant work ethic. This, he claimed, was the reason why the Protestant parts of Germany and Switzerland were more successful economically than the Catholic areas. In the recent upsurge of interest in issues cultural, a handful of writers have returned to the theme.

  It is "values and attitudes—culture," claims Lawrence Harrison, that are "mainly responsible for such phenomena as Latin America's persistent instability and inequity, Taiwan's and Korea's economic 'miracles,' and the achievements of the Japanese." Thomas Sowell offers other examples in "Race and Culture: A World View." "A disdain for commerce and industry," he argues, "has . . . been common for centuries among the Hispanic elite, both in Spain and in Latin America." Academics, though, have played a relatively small part in this debate: the best-known exponent of the thesis that "Asian values"—a kind of Confucian work ethic—aid economic development has been Singapore's former prime minister, Lee Kuan Yew.

- *Culture as Social Blueprint.* A second group of analysts has looked at the connections between cultural factors and political systems. Robert Putnam, another Harvard professor, traced Italy's social and political institutions to its "civic culture," or lack thereof. He claimed that, even today, the parts of Italy where democratic institutions are most fully developed are similar to the areas which first began to generate these institutions in the 14th century. His conclusion is that democracy is not something that can be put on like a coat; it is part of a country's social fabric and takes decades, even centuries, to develop.

Francis Fukuyama, of George Mason University, takes a slightly different approach. In a recent book which is not about the end of history [*Trust: The Social Virtues and the Creation of Prosperity*], he focuses on one particular social trait, "trust." "A nation's well-being, as well as its ability to compete, is conditioned by a single, pervasive cultural characteristic: the level of trust inherent in the society," he says. Mr Fukuyama argues that "low-trust" societies such as China, France and Italy—where close relations between people do not extend much beyond the family—are poor at generating large, complex social institutions like multinational corporations; so they are at a competitive disadvantage compared with "high-trust" nations such as Germany, Japan and the United States.

- *Culture and Decision-Making.* The final group of scholars has looked at the way in which cultural assumptions act like blinkers. Politicians from different countries see the same issue in different ways because of their differing cultural backgrounds. Their elec-

torates or nations do, too. As a result, they claim, culture acts as an international barrier. As Ole Elgstrom puts it: "When a Japanese prime minister says that he will 'do his best' to implement a certain policy," Americans applaud a victory but "what the prime minister really meant was 'no.'" There are dozens of examples of misperception in international relations, ranging from Japanese-American trade disputes to the misreading of Saddam Hussein's intentions in the weeks before he attacked Kuwait.

What Are They Talking About?

All of this is intriguing, and much of it is provocative. It has certainly provoked a host of arguments. For example, is Mr Huntington right to lump together all European countries into one culture, though they speak different languages, while separating Spain and Mexico, which speak the same one? Is the Catholic Philippines western or Asian? Or: if it is true (as Mr Fukuyama claims) that the ability to produce multinational firms is vital to economic success, why has "low-trust" China, which has few such companies, grown so fast? And why has yet-more successful "low-trust" South Korea been able to create big firms?

This is nit-picking, of course. But such questions of detail matter because behind them lurks the first of two fundamental doubts that plague all these cultural explanations: how do you define what a culture is?

In their attempts to define what cultures are (and hence what they are talking about), most "culture" writers rely partly on self definition: cultures are what people think of themselves as part of. In Mr Huntington's words, a civilisation "is the broadest level of identification with which [a person] intensely identifies."

The trouble is that relatively few people identify "intensely" with broad cultural groups. They tend to identify with something narrower: nations or ethnic groups. Europe is a case in point. A poll done last year for the European Commission found that half the people of Britain, Portugal and

Greece thought of themselves in purely national terms; so did a third of the Germans, Spaniards and Dutch. And this was in a part of the world where there is an institution—the EU itself—explicitly devoted to the encouragement of "Europeanness."

The same poll found that in every EU country, 70% or more thought of themselves either purely in national terms, or primarily as part of a nation and only secondly as Europeans. Clearly, national loyalty can coexist with wider cultural identification. But, even then, the narrower loyalty can blunt the wider one because national characteristics often are—or at least are often thought to be—peculiar or unique. Seymour Martin Lipset, a sociologist who recently published a book about national characteristics in the United States, called it "American Exceptionalism." David Willetts, a British Conservative member of Parliament, recently claimed that the policies espoused by the opposition Labour Party would go against the grain of "English exceptionalism." And these are the two components of western culture supposedly most like one another.

In Islamic countries, the balance between cultural and national identification may be tilted towards the culture. But even here the sense of, say, Egyptian or Iraqi or Palestinian nationhood remains strong. (Consider the competing national feelings unleashed during the Iran-Iraq war.) In other cultures, national loyalty seems pre-eminent: in Mr Huntington's classification, Thailand, Tibet and Mongolia all count as "Buddhist." It is hard to imagine that a Thai, a Tibetan and a Mongolian really have that much in common.

So the test of subjective identification is hard to apply. That apart, the writers define a culture in the usual terms: language, religion, history, customs and institutions and so on. Such multiple definitions ring true. As Bernard Lewis's man in the Levantine café suggests, cultures are not singular things: they are bundles of characteristics.

The trouble is that such characteristics are highly ambiguous. Some push one way, some another.

Culture as Muddle

Islamic values, for instance, are routinely assumed to be the antithesis of modernising western ones. In Islam, tradition is good; departure from tradition is presumed to be bad until proven otherwise. Yet, at the same time, Islam is also a monotheistic religion which encourages rationalism and science. Some historians have plausibly argued that it was the Islamic universities of medieval Spain that kept science and rationalism alive during Europe's Dark Ages, and that Islam was a vital medieval link between the ancient world of Greece and Rome and the Renaissance. The scientific-rationalist aspect of Islam could well come to the fore again.

If you doubt it, consider the case of China and the "Confucian tradition" (a sort of proxy for Asian values). China has been at various times the world's most prosperous country and also one of its poorest. It has had periods of great scientific innovation and times of technological backwardness and isolation. Accounts of the Confucian tradition have tracked this path. Nowadays, what seems important about the tradition is its encouragement of hard work, savings and investment for the future, plus its emphasis on co-operation towards a single end. All these features have been adduced to explain why the tradition has helped Asian growth.

To Max Weber, however, the same tradition seemed entirely different. He argued that the Confucian insistence on obedience to parental authority discouraged competition and innovation and hence inhibited economic success. And China is not the only country to have been systematically misdiagnosed in this way. In countries as varied as Japan, India, Ghana and South Korea, notions of cultural determination of economic performance have been proved routinely wrong (in 1945, India and Ghana were expected to do best of the four—partly because of their supposed cultural inheritance).

If you take an extreme position, you could argue from this that cultures are so complicated that they can never be used to explain behaviour accurately. Even if you do not go that far, the lesson must be that the same culture embraces such conflicting features that it can produce wholly different effects at different times.

That is hard enough for the schools of culture to get to grips with. But there is worse to come. For cultures never operate in isolation. When affecting how people behave, they are always part of a wider mix. That mix includes government policies, personal leadership, technological or economic change and so on. For any one effect, there are always multiple causes. Which raises the second fundamental doubt about cultural explanations: how do you know whether it is culture—and not something else—that has caused some effect? You cannot. The problem of causation seems insoluble. The best you can do is work out whether, within the mix, culture is becoming more or less important.

Culture as Passenger

Of the many alternative explanations for events, three stand out: the influence of ideas, of government and what might be called the "knowledge era" (shorthand for globalisation, the growth of service-based industries and so forth). Of these, the influence of ideas as a giant organising principle is clearly not what it was when the cold war divided the world between communists and capitalists. We are all capitalists now. To that extent, it is fair to say that the ideological part of the mix has become somewhat less important—though not, as a few people have suggested, insignificant.

As for the government, it is a central thesis of the cultural writers that its influence is falling while that of culture is rising: cultures are in some ways replacing states. To quote Mr Huntington again, "peoples and countries with similar cultures are coming together. Peoples and countries with different cultures are coming apart."

In several respects, that is counter-intuitive. Governments still control what is usually the single most powerful force in any country, the army. And, in all but the poorest places, governments tax and spend a large chunk of GDP—indeed, a larger chunk, in most places, than 50 years ago.

Hardly surprising, then, that governments in-

fluence cultures as much as the other way around. To take a couple of examples. Why does South Korea (a low-trust culture, remember) have so many internationally competitive large firms? The answer is that the government decided that it should. Or another case: since 1945 German politicians of every stripe have been insisting that they want to "save Germany from itself"—an attempt to assert political control over cultural identity.

South Korea and Germany are examples of governments acting positively to create something new. But governments can act upon cultures negatively: ie, they can destroy a culture when they collapse. Robert Kaplan, of an American magazine *Atlantic Monthly*, begins his book, "The Ends of the Earth," in Sierra Leone: "I had assumed that the random crime and social chaos of West Africa were the result of an already-fragile cultural base." Yet by the time he reaches Cambodia at the end of what he calls "a journey at the dawn of the 21st century" he is forced to reconsider that assumption:

> Here I was . . . in a land where the written script was one thousand two hundred years old, and every surrounding country was in some stage of impressive economic growth. Yet Cambodia was eerily similar to Sierra Leone: with random crime, mosquito-borne disease, a government army that was more like a mob and a countryside that was ungovernable.

His conclusion is that "The effect of culture was more a mystery to me near the end of my planetary journey than at its beginning." He might have gone further: the collapse of governments causes cultural turbulence just as much as cultural turbulence causes the collapse of governments.

Culture as Processed Data

Then there is the "knowledge era." Here is a powerful and growing phenomenon. The culture writers do not claim anything different. Like the Industrial Revolution before it, the knowledge era—in which the creation, storage and use of knowledge becomes the basic economic activity—is generating huge change. Emphasising as it does rapid, even chaotic, transformation, it is anti-traditional and anti-authoritarian.

Yet the cultural exponents still claim that, even in the knowledge era, culture remains a primary engine of change. They do so for two quite different reasons. Some claim that the new era has the makings of a world culture. There is a universal language, English. There are the beginnings of an international professional class that cuts across cultural and national boundaries: increasingly, bankers, computer programmers, executives, even military officers are said to have as much in common with their opposite numbers in other countries as with their next-door neighbours. As Mr Fukuyama wrote in his more famous book [*The End of History and the Last Man*]: the "unfolding of modern natural science . . . guarantees an increasing homogenisation of all human societies." Others doubt that technology and the rest of it are producing a genuinely new world order. To them, all this is just modern western culture.

Either way, the notion that modernity is set on a collision course with culture lies near the heart of several of the culture writers' books. Summing them up is the title of Benjamin Barber's "Jihad versus McWorld." In other words, he argues that the main conflicts now and in future will be between tribal, local "cultural" values (Jihad) and a McWorld of technology and democracy.

It would be pointless to deny that globalisation is causing large changes in every society. It is also clear that such influences act on different cultures differently, enforcing a kind of natural selection between those cultures which rise to the challenge and those which do not.

But it is more doubtful that these powerful forces are primarily cultural or even western. Of course, they have a cultural component: the artefacts of American culture are usually the first things to come along in the wake of a new road, or new television networks. But the disruptive force itself is primarily economic and has been adopted as enthusiastically in Japan, Singapore and China as in America. The world market is not a cultural concept.

Moreover, to suggest that trade, globalisation and the rest of it tend to cause conflict, and then leave the argument there, is not enough. When you boil the argument down, much of it seems to be saying that the more countries trade with each other, the more likely they are to go to war. That seems implausible. Trade—indeed, any sort of link—is just as likely to reduce the potential for violent conflict as to increase it. The same goes for the spread of democracy, another feature which is supposed to encourage civilisations to clash with each other. This might well cause ructions within countries. It might well provoke complaints from dictators about "outside interference." But serious international conflict is a different matter. And if democracy really did spread round the world, it might tend to reduce violence; wealthy democracies, at any rate, are usually reluctant to go to war (though poor or angrily nationalist ones may, as history has shown, be much less reluctant).

In short, the "knowledge era" is spreading economic ideas. And these ideas have three cultural effects, not one. They make cultures rub against each other, causing international friction. They also tie different cultures closer together, which offsets the first effect. And they may well increase tension within a culture-area as some groups accommodate themselves to the new world while others turn their back on it. And all this can be true at the same time because cultures are so varied and ambiguous that they are capable of virtually any transformation.

The conclusion must be that while culture will continue to exercise an important influence on both countries and individuals, it has not suddenly become more important than, say, governments or impersonal economic forces. Nor does it play the all-embracing defining role that ideology played during the cold war. Much of its influence is secondary, ie, it comes about partly as a reaction to the "knowledge era." And within the overall mix of what influences people's behaviour, culture's role may well be declining, rather than rising, squeezed between the greedy expansion of the government on one side, and globalisation on the other.

5 ❧ THE STATE

The state remains the key actor in international relations, although challenges to the state are increasing, as detailed in Essentials of International Relations. *The selections in this chapter examine the new contours of the state.* The Economist *admits that while the nation-state is not what it used to be, it remains a key mechanism for containing conflict—only in Europe is there a real possibility of a post-nation-state system. Anne-Marie Slaughter suggests what a twenty-first-century state might look like and argues that in liberal democracies, the state can best be characterized by transgovernmental interactions. Jeffrey Herbst, by contrast, addresses the various ways the international community can deal with failed states. What happens when states are unable to function? How should the international community respond? Drawing on cases of failed states in Africa, Herbst explores various solutions, including an innovative and controversial decertification process.*

The state is challenged in other ways as well. These include changes in the international political economy that undermine state power and authority, discussed in chapter 8, and the rise of ethnonational movements, covered in chapter 10 of this reader and in Jack Snyder's book in the Norton series, From Voting to Violence. *The state is also confronted with the opportunities and constraints that globalization brings, the ramifications of which are discussed in chapter 12.*

THE ECONOMIST

The Nation-State Is Dead.
Long Live the Nation-State

Readjust Your Expectations of the 21st Century. Neither the Age of Superstates, Nor the End of All States, Is About to Happen

The nation-state is not what it used to be. Ignored by the global money markets, condescended to by great multinational corporations, at the mercy of intercontinental missiles, the poor thing can only look back with nostalgia to its days of glory, a century ago, when everybody knew what John Bull and Marianne and Germania and Uncle Sam stood for. It seems inconceivable that so diminished a creature can much longer continue to be the basic unit of international relations, the entity that signs treaties, joins alliances, defies enemies, goes to war. Surely the nation-state is in the process of being dissolved into something larger, more powerful, more capable of coping with the consequences of modern technology: something that will be the new, stronger, basic unit of tomorrow's world?

No, wait; hold on a minute. As Bertie Wooster said, in telling a tangled story it is fatal to begin by assuming that the customers know how matters got where they are. They will simply raise their eyebrows, and walk out on you. The current argument about the role of the nation-state in world affairs is an excellent example of the danger Bertie was pointing to.

Why It Isn't What It Was

For most people, the world is made up of 185 nation-states, on the current count of the United

From *The Economist*, 23 December 1995–5 January 1996, 15–18.

Nations: some huge, some tiny, some of them democracies, most of them not, but all equal in the eye of the world's law. In fact, a majority of these 185 places are not nation-states in the strict meaning of the term, but survivals of older, cruder forms of political life. Nevertheless, all 185 share two vital characteristics. They each cover separate portions of the earth's surface; and each has a government whose claim to speak for it is recognised by most governments of the other portions of the earth's surface. These are the basic units of geopolitics, the pieces on the international chessboard, the essential components of the fearsome game known as foreign policy.

The trouble is that, over the past half-century or so, these basic units have all, big or small, become less dominant, less independent and, in a way, less separate than they were in their prime. This is because of the arrival in the world of new forces, created by the technological discoveries of the 20th century, which have the power to move things visible and invisible from one part of the globe to another whether any nation-state likes it or not. These forces take three main forms, all of which have to some extent eroded the nation-state's autonomy.

In economics, the growing ease and cheapness of moving goods from one place to another has demolished any lingering belief in national self-sufficiency. Almost every country now buys from abroad a larger proportion of what it consumes than it did 50 years ago, and a far bigger share of the world's capital is owned by multinational companies operating freely across national borders. This process has been accelerated by what electronics has done to the movement of money. The markets' ability to transfer cash anywhere at the push of a button has changed the rules for policy-making, introducing what sometimes seems like a sort of direct international democracy: when a government makes a false move, markets vote against it with ruthless speed.

A more globalised economy is in many ways a more efficient one. Most people in most countries are richer now than their ancestors ever were; and the faster discipline of today's international financial markets makes national governments more careful in the handling of their economies. But, for this article's purpose, that is not the point. The point is that the rise of new global forces has noticeably tamed the nation-state's old feeling of confident independence.

In military matters the change has been even more dramatic. Until about 60 years ago, the only way in which one country could successfully use force to impose its will on another was to defeat its soldiers on the ground. Between two countries of even approximately equal strength that could be a long and hazardous business.

The little Heinkels and Dorniers that flew slowly over the English Channel to drop their tiny bomb-loads on Britain in 1940 were the messengers of a radical change in the nature of war. The use of force was no longer two-dimensional; the third dimension had become available. Only a few years later, the means of imposing defeat from the air had moved from aeroplanes to missiles, and their cargo had changed from a bomb that would knock down a house to one that could obliterate a city.

For at least the first part of the coming century, very few countries—perhaps only America, plus anybody who can shelter under America's protection—will have even the remotest technological hope of acquiring anti-missile defences that can ward off the missiles with nuclear (or chemical or bacteriological) warheads which an enemy can aim at you from anywhere in the globe. Otherwise, the nation-state will be naked to such attacks.

The third technology-based challenge to the old picture of the nation-state is the information revolution. People in different countries now have the means to know far more about each other.

They can see on television how others entertain themselves, or argue about politics, or kill their neighbours; and on the Internet, or on ever-cheaper telephones, they can then exchange opinions about it all. Even if the number of people who make active use of the information revolution is still fairly small, as the sceptics claim, this is a startling contrast with what most Englishmen and Germans knew about each other in the 1930s, let alone most Frenchmen and Englishmen in the 1790s.

Like the new forces of global economics, the globalisation of knowledge is in general an excellent thing. It is always better to know than to be ignorant. But, like those economic forces, this change blurs the sense of national separateness. The similarities between people, as well as the differences, become more apparent; the supposed distinctiveness of nations grows less sharp-edged; one day, perhaps, it may even become harder for tomorrow's equivalent of Serb politicians to persuade their people that tomorrow's Bosnian Muslims are an inferior breed.

Between them, these three challenges to the nation-state look pretty powerful. So is the nation-state, as the tongue-in-cheek first paragraph of this article suggested, inevitably about to be replaced as the basic unit of global politics? The answer is no, for two reasons. None of the possible replacements, when you take a closer look at them, seems to have much real solidity. And the nation-state may have more durability than people realise, because it is still the sole possessor of what is needed to be that basic unit. Take the two points in turn.

Why the Alternatives Won't Work

One dreamy successor to the nation-state is certainly not going to happen. The disappearance of communism has not opened the door to the emergence of a one-world system. Until the final failure of the "world community" in Bosnia in 1995, many people still clung to the belief that, after the cold war, the "end of history"—in Francis Fukuyama's misleading phrase—was at hand. Such people reckoned that most countries would no longer have any serious differences of opinion with each other about politics and economics; that they could therefore, seeing things in broadly the same way, use the United Nations as their instrument for solving minor disputes and so keeping the world tidy; and that in this way the foundations would be laid of an eventual system of global government.

It could not be. Countries have long quarrelled, and will continue to quarrel, about many things besides ideology. Anyway, the end of the cold war's particular clash of ideas was not the end of all ideological argument; consult any ardent Muslim, or any earnest exponent of "Asian values." The world remains explosively divided.

By the end of 1995, almost everybody has come to understand this. That fond post-cold-war illusion was the result of a failure to look clearly either at the lessons of history or at today's observable facts.

Ah, says a sharper-eyed band of optimists, but surely the past year's progress towards freer trade, under the aegis of the new World Trade Organisation, shows that the nation-state can indeed be persuaded to obey a global set of rules. That is true; but only up to a clearly defined point.

Most countries accept the discipline of a free-trade system because they recognise that free trade is beneficial to everybody (which does not stop them bargaining ferociously over the distribution of those benefits). But, in general, countries draw a line between this pooling of economic autonomy and the pooling of political and military power. They want to hold on to the means of being able to decide for themselves, in the last resort, what suits them—including whether it suits them to go on obeying free-trade rules. That is why even the most miraculously smooth-running free-trade regime will not inevitably glide forward into a global political unity.

Nor is there much plausibility in a second suggested alternative to the nation-state. This is the idea that various groups of today's nation-states, wanting to belong to something stronger, will gather together into big new entities, each speaking for the culture or civilisation of its component

parts. The most lucid and provocative version of the theory has been set out by Samuel Huntington of Harvard University, who has worryingly talked of a future "clash of civilisations."

This idea, unlike the one-world dream, does rest on a basis of observable fact. Countries that belong to the same "culture-area"—meaning that they have grown out of a shared body of religious or philosophical beliefs, and a shared experience of history—often behave in similar ways long after the event that originally shaped their culture has passed into history.

The ex-communist countries in the Orthodox Christian part of Europe, for instance, seem to find it harder to become free-market democracies than those in the Protestant-Catholic part, perhaps because the Orthodox area never fully digested the Reformation, that great shaper of western civilisation. And the advocates of "Asian values," with their special respect for authority, almost all come from the background of the Confucian culture. It may well be that, as the world works itself into a new, post-cold-war shape, these cultural connections will be the basis of some formidable alliances; and that the competition between these alliances will be a large element in the geopolitics of the 21st century.

But alliances are alliances, not single units of power. The problem with the civilisation-unit theory is not just that Mr Huntington's list of civilisations includes some rather implausible candidates—does Africa, or Latin America, really seem likely to become an actor on the world stage?—but that the component parts of even the more plausible ones are still profoundly reluctant to surrender their separate identities.

It is striking that the new wave of self-awareness in the Muslim world has not produced any serious move towards a merger of Muslim states. Even the Arab sub-section of the Muslim world, with the advantage of a common language, has, after a series of abortive "unification" schemes, come up with nothing grander than the reunion of the two Yemens. In the Orthodox Christian part of the world, another arguably distinct culture-zone, the recent tendency has been for things to fall apart, not come together; this area now contains more separate states than it did a decade ago.

All the other culture-zones look equally unpromising, with one possible exception. Only in Western Europe is there any seriously conceived plan to dissolve existing nation-states into something bigger—and even this European experiment may now be running into the sands. The world does not, in short, seem to be heading for that fearful-sounding "clash of civilisations."

The only other sort of glue that might bind nation-states together, if the cultural glue proves too weak, is ideology. That may seem an odd thing to say while the dust still swirls from the stunning collapse of the communist edifice. But communism's fall does not mean that ideology has ceased to exist. What demolished the communist idea was the superior strength of a rival body of ideas, free-market democracy, which was powerful enough to hold together the 16 countries of the West's alliance through all the alarms and rigours of the cold war.

Free-market democracy won that fight, but free-market democracy is in turn now challenged by two self-proclaimed rivals. One part of the back-to-basics movement that is sweeping through the Muslim world seems to accept the free-market bit, but believes that democracy is a denial of the principle that God decides what should happen in the world. And the East Asian politicians who talk about "Asian values," though they say they accept democracy, want to run it like a family—with themselves, naturally, as the firm but kindly father—so that it does not succumb to the anarchy they think is caused by too much western individualism.

It is not yet clear whether either of these challenges to the West's picture of the future will endure. The Muslim one is already under attack from more open-minded Islamic revivalists, who insist that there should be a democratic way of deciding what God wants for the world. Advocates of Asian values may come to be judged, by their fellow Asians, as just a bunch of politicians trying to hold on to the pleasures of power. But for now it is plain that arguments of ideology are still helping to

shape the world. They pull people into rival camps, and give them more precise reasons for disagreeing with each other than the mere fact of belonging to different "civilisations."

Unfortunately, ideologies suffer from exactly the same difficulty as culture-zones when they offer themselves as a substitute for the nation-state. Nobody seems to want to join the proposed substitute.

The proponents of Asian values happily go on working inside their existing countries, because that is where they wield the authority they want to preserve. The Islamic anti-democrats in various Muslim countries have made no progress in breaking down the frontiers between those countries; indeed, they do not even seem to talk to each other very much. And, when the communist ideology collapsed, it became painfully clear that its component parts had been kept together by mere force, not by the vigour of an idea.

So the late 21st century's maps will not show a handful of sprawling superstates with names like Democratia, Islamia and Leekuanyewia. Their dotted lines will continue to reveal large numbers of those boringly familiar places, nation-states.

Why It Stumbles On

Why is the nation-state so durable, for all the battering it has taken from 20th-century technology? Partly because, in its true meaning, it is a pretty recent arrival on the political scene, and has the resilience of youth; but mostly because it is still the sole possessor of the magic formula without which it is hard, in today's world, to hold any sort of political structure together.

It was little more than 200 years ago, a blink of history's eye, that men invented the nation-state as a better way of organising the business of government than any way previously available. Before that, the state—a recognisable chunk of territory, recognisably under somebody's control—had generally been one or the other of two things. Call them the brute-force state, and the justification-by-good-works state.

A brute-force state came into existence when

some tough took power by strength of arms and stayed in power by killing or otherwise silencing those who objected. That was how government began in most places, and the species is by no means extinct. You could hardly have a better example of such a state than Saddam Hussein's Iraq.

The trouble with relying on brute force, though, is that however ruthless the ruler may be there will in the end usually be somebody angry and desperate enough to put a sword or a bullet through him. This most primitive form of state-system therefore evolved, except in the unluckiest places, into one in which those who controlled power sought to justify their control of it. The rulers did not ask the ruled for their consent to being ruled. But they did try to keep them happy—or just happy enough—by providing for some of their essential needs.

In the arid empires of the Old Testament world, from Babylon to Persia, one essential need was the provision of a reliable flow of water. Later the Romans, having built their empire by force, sought to justify it by providing the rule of law and a sense of order (the British did much the same in India 1,800 years later). By the Middle Ages, the implicit bargain between governors and governed had become a complicated network of mutual obligations between king, barons and the lower orders.

It was not perfect, but it was better than plain thuggery or chaos. Even now, the world contains many examples of this second system. The Chinese government still seeks to justify its one-party grip on power by a claim to have produced order and good economic statistics; so, less convincingly, do the rulers of assorted Arab countries.

What this system still lacks, of course, is any organic link between government and people. Even the most conscientious prince of the pre-nation-state era assumed power by right of inheritance, not by the will of those he governed. "I am the state," said Louis XIV, that most *de-haut-en-bas* specimen of the old order. A century later, the inventors of the nation-state set out to provide an alternative to the lofty arrogance of his first person singular. As they saw it, a government should be

able to say: "The state gives us our authority."

A nation-state is a place where people feel a natural connection with each other because they share a language, a religion, or something else strong enough to bind them together and make them feel different from others: "we," not "they." The nation-state is the politics of the first person plural. Its government can speak for its people because it is part of the "we." It emerges out of the nation.

There can be arguments about how the government does its emerging, by election or by some more obscure process. At many times in the 200-year history of the nation-state ambitious or obsessed men—Hitler was the worst of all—have claimed the right to power because they said they knew better than anybody else what their nation wanted. But even they were different from Louis XIV. They claimed their authority, truthfully or not, from the will of their people. One way or another, in the past couple of centuries the connection between people and government has become organic. The concept of the nation-state shakes hands with the concept of government by consent.

The sense of being "we" can come from a shared language, as it unitingly does in most European countries, but divisively in places like Quebec; or from a shared religion, as in Ireland or Pakistan; or from the proud ownership of some special political idea, such as direct democracy in four-language Switzerland or the "American idea" in the multi-ethnic United States; or from the memory of a shared horror, as in Israel. Sometimes it comes from a mixture of these things. The hatreds of Bosnia are rooted both in differences of religion and in the memories of long-ago frontier wars between different culture-areas.

However it comes about, it is the necessary foundation for any durable political system. No government, unless it is prepared to rely entirely on brute force, can do its job properly in the modern world if the people it governs do not have a clear-cut sense of identity that they share with the government—unless, in other words, they are both part of the "we."

And it still seems that only the nation-state

possesses this necessary sense of identity. It is nice to learn that you belong to such-and-such a civilisation, or are a believer in this ideology or that; but learning this is not enough, it appears, to pull people across the familiar boundaries of the nation-state and into the creation of some new, bigger sort of political entity.

This may not remain true forever. There was a time when Prussians and Bavarians did not smoothly think of themselves as "we Germans," or Tuscans and Sicilians as "we Italians"; but they got round to it in the end. Perhaps, in the end, Muslims will smoothly be able to think of themselves as citizens of a wider Islamic state; or Chinese-speakers will salute a neo-Confucian flag fluttering over Beijing or Singapore; or, who knows, some pan-African power may rise out of that continent's present rubble. But it is not happening yet; and, until and unless it does happen, nation-states will be the only pieces on the geopolitical chessboard.

So Watch Europe

The chief test of whether this might change will take place in Europe over the next few years. The countries of the European Union have come very close to the line that separates the pooling of their economic life from the merging of their politics. They will soon have to decide whether or not they want to cross that line. To cross it, they would need to be reasonably sure that the new Europe passes the first-person-plural test. They would have to be confident that its people now think of themselves in some serious way not chiefly as Germans or French, or whatever, but as "we Europeans."

Twice in history, Europe, or a large part of it, has felt itself to be such a single place; and on both occasions there were solid grounds for such a sense of identity. The first time was when the Roman empire hammered much of Europe into a single entity that shared the blessings of Roman law, the Latin language and the peace of the legions. This was unquestionably a culture-zone: to the first-person-plural question, its people could reply, *Cives Romani sumus* ["We are Roman citizens"].

The second time began when Charlemagne was crowned as "Emperor of the Catholic Church of Europe" in Rome on Christmas Day 800. The political unity of the Europe created by Charlemagne did not long survive his death. Yet, for another six centuries after Charlemagne, Europeans went on believing, as Muslims believe today, that there ought in principle to be no distinction between God's business and man's business, and that politics should come under God's guidance; and for most of that time they kept in existence institutions which tried to put this principle into practice. This was an ideological Europe. To the question of what "we Europeans" stood for, Charlemagne's descendants would have replied, *Credimus in unum Deum* ["We believe in one God"].

The problem for today's unifiers of Europe is not just that Germany, France and Britain want different things out of a European union. It is that none of their versions of a united Europe would be rooted in a distinctive ideology. The political and economic ideas by which Europe lives are much the same as America's, and indeed America was ahead of most of Europe in making itself a democracy. Nor would it be a unique culture-zone. Europe and America come from the same cultural background; they are, with minor variations, subdivisions of a single civilisation.

The underlying argument of those who now pursue a separate European unity is that Europe either does not want to be, or does not think it can be, part of a wider union with its cultural and ideological cousin across the Atlantic. This is an argument of geography, and a circular one at that. Its answer to the "we" question is: We are Europeans because we are Europeans.

That need not rule it out. Tuscans and Sicilians joined each other to become Italians even though the Italy they created 134 years ago had much in common with the rest of Europe. People sometimes band together simply to be stronger than they were separately. The desire to be strong is a powerful force in politics. But not as powerful as the feeling that "we" are different from "them." That is one reason why a growing question-mark floats over Europe.

The nation-state will last longer than most

people had thought. Only in one part of the world, Europe, is there a possibility that it may give way to a bigger post-nation-state system; and even that possibility now looks fainter than it did a few years ago. Like the natural world, the world of geopoli-tics does not easily change its species. The coming century will still be the home of recognisable beasts; muscular lions and fearful deer, lumbering rhinos and cunning jackals. That may be a pity; but the inhabitants of the jungle have to live with it.

ANNE-MARIE SLAUGHTER

The Real New World Order

The State Strikes Back

Many thought that the new world order pro-claimed by George Bush was the promise of 1945 fulfilled, a world in which international institu-tions, led by the United Nations, guaranteed inter-national peace and security with the active support of the world's major powers. That world order is a chimera. Even as a liberal internationalist ideal, it is infeasible at best and dangerous at worst. It re-quires a centralized rule-making authority, a hier-archy of institutions, and universal membership. Equally to the point, efforts to create such an order have failed. The United Nations cannot function effectively independent of the major powers that compose it, nor will those nations cede their power and sovereignty to an international institution. Ef-forts to expand supranational authority, whether by the U.N. secretary-general's office, the Euro-pean Commission, or the World Trade Organi-zation (WTO), have consistently produced a backlash among member states.

The leading alternative to liberal international-ism is "the new medievalism," a back-to-the-future model of the 21st century. Where liberal interna-tionalists see a need for international rules and institutions to solve states' problems, the new medievalists proclaim the end of the nation-state.

From *Foreign Affairs* 75, no. 5 (September/October 1997): 183–97.

Less hyperbolically, in her article, "Power Shift," in the January/February 1997 *Foreign Affairs*, Jessica T. Mathews describes a shift away from the state—up, down, and sideways—to supra-state, sub-state, and, above all, nonstate actors. These new players have multiple allegiances and global reach.

Mathews attributes this power shift to a change in the structure of organizations: from hierarchies to networks, from centralized compulsion to vol-untary association. The engine of this transforma-tion is the information technology revolution, a radically expanded communications capacity that empowers individuals and groups while diminish-ing traditional authority. The result is not world government, but global governance. If government denotes the formal exercise of power by established institutions, governance denotes cooperative problem-solving by a changing and often uncer-tain cast. The result is a world order in which global governance networks link Microsoft, the Roman Catholic Church, and Amnesty Interna-tional to the European Union, the United Nations, and Catalonia.

The new medievalists miss two central points. First, private power is still no substitute for state power. Consumer boycotts of transnational corpo-rations destroying rain forests or exploiting child labor may have an impact on the margin, but most environmentalists or labor activists would prefer national legislation mandating control of foreign subsidiaries. Second, the power shift is not a zero-sum game. A gain in power by nonstate actors does not necessarily translate into a loss of power for the state. On the contrary, many of these nongovernmental organizations (NGOs) network with their foreign counterparts to apply additional pressure on the traditional levers of domestic politics.

A new world order is emerging, with less fanfare but more substance than either the liberal internationalist or new medievalist visions. The state is not disappearing, it is disaggregating into its separate, functionally distinct parts. These parts—courts, regulatory agencies, executives, and even legislatures—are networking with their counterparts abroad, creating a dense web of relations that constitutes a new, transgovernmental order. Today's international problems—terrorism, organized crime, environmental degradation, money laundering, bank failure, and securities fraud—created and sustain these relations. Government institutions have formed networks of their own, ranging from the Basle Committee of Central Bankers to informal ties between law enforcement agencies to legal networks that make foreign judicial decisions more and more familiar. While political scientists Robert Keohane and Joseph Nye first observed its emergence in the 1970s, today transgovernmentalism is rapidly becoming the most widespread and effective mode of international governance.

Compared to the lofty ideals of liberal internationalism and the exuberant possibilities of the new medievalism, transgovernmentalism seems mundane. Meetings between securities regulators, antitrust or environmental officials, judges, or legislators lack the drama of high politics. But for the internationalists of the 1990s—bankers, lawyers, businesspeople, public-interest activists, and criminals—transnational government networks are a reality. Wall Street looks to the Basle Committee rather than the World Bank. Human rights lawyers are more likely to develop transnational litigation strategies for domestic courts than to petition the U.N. Committee on Human Rights.

Moreover, transgovernmentalism has many virtues. It is a key element of a bipartisan foreign policy, simultaneously assuaging conservative fears of a loss of sovereignty to international institutions and liberal fears of a loss of regulatory power in a globalized economy. While presidential candidate Pat Buchanan and Senator Jesse Helms (R-N.C.) demonize the U.N. and the WTO as supranational bureaucracies that seek to dictate to national governments, Senators Ted Kennedy (D-Mass.) and Paul Wellstone (D-Mich.) inveigh against international capital mobility as the catalyst of a global "race to the bottom" in regulatory standards. Networks of bureaucrats responding to international crises and planning to prevent future problems are more flexible than international institutions and expand the regulatory reach of all participating nations. This combination of flexibility and effectiveness offers something for both sides of the aisle.

Transgovernmentalism also offers promising new mechanisms for the Clinton administration's "enlargement" policy, aiming to expand the community of liberal democracies. Contrary to Samuel Huntington's gloomy predictions in *The Clash of Civilizations and the New World Order* (1996), existing government networks span civilizations, drawing in courts from Argentina to Zimbabwe and financial regulators from Japan to Saudi Arabia. The dominant institutions in these networks remain concentrated in North America and Western Europe, but their impact can be felt in every corner of the globe. Moreover, disaggregating the state makes it possible to assess the quality of specific judicial, administrative, and legislative institutions, whether or not the governments are liberal democracies. Regular interaction with foreign colleagues offers new channels for spreading democratic accountability, governmental integrity, and the rule of law.

An offspring of an increasingly borderless world, transgovernmentalism is a world order ideal in its own right, one that is more effective and potentially more accountable than either of the current alternatives. Liberal internationalism poses the prospect of a supranational bureaucracy answerable to no one. The new medievalist vision appeals equally to states' rights enthusiasts and supranationalists, but could easily reflect the worst of both worlds. Transgovernmentalism, by contrast, leaves the control of government institutions in the hands of national citizens, who must hold their governments as accountable for their transnational activities as for their domestic duties.

Judicial Foreign Policy

Judges are building a global community of law. They share values and interests based on their belief in the law as distinct but not divorced from politics and their view of themselves as professionals who must be insulated from direct political influence. At its best, this global community reminds each participant that his or her professional performance is being monitored and supported by a larger audience.

National and international judges are networking, becoming increasingly aware of one another and of their stake in a common enterprise. The most informal level of transnational judicial contact is knowledge of foreign and international judicial decisions and a corresponding willingness to cite them. The Israeli Supreme Court and the German and Canadian constitutional courts have long researched U.S. Supreme Court precedents in reaching their own conclusions on questions like freedom of speech, privacy rights, and due process. Fledgling constitutional courts in Central and Eastern Europe and in Russia are eagerly following suit. In 1995, the South African Supreme Court, finding the death penalty unconstitutional under the national constitution, referred to decisions from national and supranational courts around the world, including ones in Hungary, India, Tanzania, Canada, and Germany and the European Court of Human Rights. The U.S. Supreme Court has typically been more of a giver than a receiver in this exchange, but Justice Sandra Day O'Connor recently chided American lawyers and judges for their insularity in ignoring foreign law and predicted that she and her fellow justices would find themselves "looking more frequently to the decisions of other constitutional courts."

Why should a court in Israel or South Africa cite a decision by the U.S. Supreme Court in reaching its own conclusion? Decisions rendered by outside courts can have no authoritative value. They carry weight only because of their intrinsic logical power or because the court invoking them seeks to gain legitimacy by linking itself to a larger community of courts considering similar issues. National courts have become increasingly aware that they and their foreign counterparts are often engaged in a common effort to delimit the boundaries of individual rights in the face of an apparently overriding public interest. Thus, the British House of Lords recently rebuked the U.S. Supreme Court for its decision to uphold the kidnapping of a Mexican doctor by U.S. officials determined to bring him to trial in the United States.

Judges also cooperate in resolving transnational or international disputes. In cases involving citizens of two different states, courts have long been willing to acknowledge each other's potential interest and to defer to one another when such deference is not too costly. U.S. courts now recognize that they may become involved in a sustained dialogue with a foreign court. For instance, Judge Guido Calabresi of the Second Circuit recently allowed a French litigant to invoke U.S. discovery provisions without exhausting discovery options in France, reasoning that it was up to the French courts to identify and protest any infringements of French sovereignty. U.S. courts would then respond to such protests.

Judicial communication is not always harmonious, as in a recent squabble between a U.S. judge and a Hong Kong judge over an insider trading case. The U.S. judge refused to decline jurisdiction in favor of the Hong Kong court on grounds that "in Hong Kong they practically give you a medal for doing this sort of thing [insider trading]." In response, the Hong Kong judge stiffly defended the adequacy of Hong Kong law and asserted his willingness to apply it. He also chided his American counterpart, pointing out that any conflict "should be approached in the spirit of judicial comity rather than judicial competitiveness." Such conflict is to be expected among diplomats, but what is striking here is the two courts' view of themselves as quasi-autonomous foreign policy actors doing battle against international securities fraud.

The most advanced form of judicial cooperation is a partnership between national courts and a supranational tribunal. In the European Union (EU), the European Court of Justice works with national courts when questions of European law overlap national law. National courts refer cases up to the European Court, which issues an opinion and sends the case back to national courts; the supranational recommendation guides the national court's decision. This cooperation marshals the power of domestic courts behind the judgment of a supranational tribunal. While the Treaty of Rome provides for this reference procedure, it is the courts that have transformed it into a judicial partnership.

Finally, judges are talking face to face. The judges of the supreme courts of Western Europe began meeting every three years in 1978. Since then they have become more aware of one another's decisions, particularly with regard to each other's willingness to accept the decisions handed down by the European Court of Justice. Meetings between U.S. Supreme Court justices and their counterparts on the European Court have been sponsored by private groups, as have meetings of U.S. judges with judges from the supreme courts of Central and Eastern Europe and Russia.

The most formal initiative aimed at bringing judges together is the recently inaugurated Organization of the Supreme Courts of the Americas. Twenty-five supreme court justices or their designees met in Washington in October 1995 and drafted the OCSA charter, dedicating the organization to "promot[ing] and strengthen[ing] judicial independence and the rule of law among the members, as well as the proper constitutional treatment of the judiciary as a fundamental branch of the state." The charter calls for triennial meetings and envisages a permanent secretariat. It required ratification by 15 supreme courts, achieved in spring 1996. An initiative by judges, for judges, it is not a stretch to say that OCSA is the product of judicial foreign policy.

Champions of a global rule of law have most frequently envisioned one rule for all, a unified legal system topped by a world court. The global community of law emerging from judicial networks will more likely encompass many rules of law, each established in a specific state or region. No high court would hand down definitive global rules. National courts would interact with one another and with supranational tribunals in ways that would accommodate differences but acknowledge and reinforce common values.

The Regulatory Web

The densest area of transgovernmental activity is among national regulators. Bureaucrats charged with the administration of antitrust policy, securities regulation, environmental policy, criminal law enforcement, banking and insurance supervision—in short, all the agents of the modern regulatory state—regularly collaborate with their foreign counterparts.

National regulators track their quarry through cooperation. While frequently ad hoc, such cooperation is increasingly cemented by bilateral and multilateral agreements. The most formal of these are mutual legal assistance treaties, whereby two states lay out a protocol governing cooperation between their law enforcement agencies and courts. However, the preferred instrument of cooperation is the memorandum of understanding, in which two or more regulatory agencies set forth and initial terms for an ongoing relationship. Such memorandums are not treaties; they do not engage the executive or the legislature in negotiations, deliberation, or signature. Rather, they are good-faith agreements, affirming ties between regulatory agencies based on their like-minded commitment to getting results.

"Positive comity," a concept developed by the U.S. Department of Justice, epitomizes the changing nature of transgovernmental relations. Comity of nations, an archaic and notoriously vague term beloved by diplomats and international lawyers, has traditionally signified the deference one nation grants another in recognition of their mutual sovereignty. For instance, a state will recognize another state's laws or judicial judgments based on comity. Positive comity requires more active cooperation. As worked out by the Antitrust Division of the U.S. Department of Justice and the EU's European Commission, the regulatory authorities of both states alert one another to violations within their jurisdiction, with the understanding that the responsible authority will take action. Positive comity is a principle of enduring cooperation between government agencies.

In 1988 the central bankers of the world's major financial powers adopted capital adequacy requirements for all banks under their supervision—a significant reform of the international banking system. It was not the World Bank, the International Monetary Fund, or even the Group of Seven that took this step. Rather, the forum was the Basle Committee on Banking Supervision, an organization composed of 12 central bank governors. The Basle Committee was created by a simple agreement among the governors themselves. Its members meet four times a year and follow their own rules. Decisions are made by consensus and are not formally binding; however, members do implement these decisions within their own systems. The Basle Committee's authority is often cited as an argument for taking domestic action.

National securities commissioners and insurance regulators have followed the Basle Committee's example. Incorporated by a private bill of the Quebec National Assembly, the International Organization of Securities Commissioners has no formal charter or founding treaty. Its primary purpose is to solve problems affecting international securities markets by creating a consensus for enactment of national legislation. Its members have also entered into information-sharing agreements on their own initiative. The International Association of Insurance Supervisors follows a similar model, as does the newly created Tripartite Group, an international coalition of banking, insurance, and securities regulators the Basle Committee created to improve the supervision of financial conglomerates.

Pat Buchanan would have had a field day with the Tripartite Group, denouncing it as a prime example of bureaucrats taking power out of the hands of American voters. In fact, unlike the international bogeymen of demagogic fantasy, transnational regulatory organizations do not aspire to exercise power in the international system independent of their members. Indeed, their main purpose is to help regulators apprehend those who would harm the interests of American voters. Transgovernmental networks often promulgate their own rules, but the purpose of those rules is to enhance the enforcement of national law.

Traditional international law requires states to implement the international obligations they incur through their own law. Thus, if states agree to a 12-mile territorial sea, they must change their domestic legislation concerning the interdiction of vessels in territorial waters accordingly. But this legislation is unlikely to overlap with domestic law, as national legislatures do not usually seek to regulate global commons issues and interstate relations.

Transgovernmental regulation, by contrast, produces rules concerning issues that each nation already regulates within its borders: crime, securities fraud, pollution, tax evasion. The advances in technology and transportation that have fueled globalization have made it more difficult to enforce national law. Regulators benefit from coordinating their enforcement efforts with those of their foreign counterparts and from ensuring that other nations adopt similar approaches.

The result is the nationalization of international law. Regulatory agreements between states are pledges of good faith that are self-enforcing, in the sense that each nation will be better able to enforce its national law by implementing the agreement if other nations do likewise. Laws are binding or coercive only at the national level. Uniformity of result and diversity of means go hand in hand, and the makers and enforcers of rules are national leaders who are accountable to the people.

Bipartisan Globalization

Secretary of State Madeleine Albright seeks to revive the bipartisan foreign policy consensus of the late 1940s. Deputy Secretary of State Strobe Talbott argues that promoting democracy worldwide satisfies the American need for idealpolitik as well as realpolitik. President Clinton, in his second inaugural address, called for a "new government for a new century," abroad as well as at home. But bipartisanship is threatened by divergent responses to globalization, democratization is a tricky business, and Vice President Al Gore's efforts to "reinvent government" have focused on domestic rather than international institutions. Transgovernmentalism can address all these problems.

Globalization implies the erosion of national boundaries. Consequently, regulators' power to implement national regulations within those boundaries declines both because people can easily flee their jurisdiction and because the flows of capital, pollution, pathogens, and weapons are too great and sudden for any one regulator to control. The liberal internationalist response to these assaults on state regulatory power is to build a larger international apparatus. Globalization thus leads to internationalization, or the transfer of regulatory authority from the national level to an international institution. The best example is not the WTO itself, but rather the stream of proposals to expand the WTO's jurisdiction to global competition policy, intellectual property regulation, and other trade-related issues. Liberals are likely to support expanding the power of international institutions to guard against the global dismantling of the regulatory state.

Here's the rub. Conservatives are more likely to favor the expansion of globalized markets without the internationalization that goes with it, since internationalization, from their perspective, equals a loss of sovereignty. According to Buchanan, the U.S. foreign policy establishment "want[s] to move America into a New World Order where the World Court decides quarrels between nations; the WTO writes the rules for trade and settles all disputes; the IMF and World Bank order wealth transfers from continent to continent and country to country; the Law of the Sea Treaty tells us what we may and may not do on the high seas and ocean floor, and the United Nations decides where U.S. military forces may and may not intervene." The rhetoric is deliberately inflammatory, but echoes resound across the Republican spectrum.

Transgovernmental initiatives are a compromise that could command bipartisan support. Regulatory loopholes caused by global forces require a coordinated response beyond the reach of any one country. But this coordination need not come from building more international institutions. It can be achieved through transgovernmental cooperation, involving the same officials who make and implement policy at the national level. The transgovernmental alternative is fast, flexible, and effective.

A leading example of transgovernmentalism in action that demonstrates its bipartisan appeal is a State Department initiative christened the New Transatlantic Agenda. Launched in 1991 under the Bush administration and reinvigorated by Secretary of State Warren Christopher in 1995, the initiative structures the relationship between the United States and the EU, fostering cooperation in areas ranging from opening markets to fighting terrorism, drug trafficking, and infectious disease. It is an umbrella for ongoing projects between U.S. officials and their European counterparts. It reaches ordinary citizens, embracing efforts like the Transatlantic Business Dialogue and engaging individuals through people-to-people exchanges and expanded communication through the Internet.

Democratization, Step by Step

Transgovernmental networks are concentrated among liberal democracies but are not limited to them. Some nondemocratic states have institutions capable of cooperating with their foreign counterparts, such as committed and effective regulatory agencies or relatively independent judiciaries. Transgovernmental ties can strengthen institutions in ways that will help them resist political domination, corruption, and incompetence and build democratic institutions in their countries, step by step. The Organization of Supreme Courts of the Americas, for instance, actively seeks to strengthen norms of judicial independence among its members, many of whom must fend off powerful political forces.

Individuals and groups in nondemocratic countries may also "borrow" government institutions of democratic states to achieve a measure of justice they cannot obtain in their own countries. The court or regulatory agency of one state may be able to perform judicial or regulatory functions for the people of another. Victims of human rights violations, for example, in countries such as Argentina, Ethiopia, Haiti, and the Philippines have sued for redress in the courts of the United States. U.S. courts accepted these cases, often over the objections of the executive branch, using a broad interpretation of a moribund statute dating back to 1789. Under this interpretation, aliens may sue in U.S. courts to seek damages from foreign government officials accused of torture, even if the torture allegedly took place in the foreign country. More generally, a nongovernmental organization seeking to prevent human rights violations can often circumvent their own government's corrupt legislature and politicized court by publicizing the plight of victims abroad and mobilizing a foreign court, legislature, or executive to take action.

Responding to calls for a coherent U.S. foreign policy and seeking to strengthen the community of democratic nations, President Clinton substituted the concept of "enlargement" for the Cold War principle of "containment." Expanding transgovernmental outreach to include institutions from nondemocratic states would help expand the circle of democracies one institution at a time.

A New World Order Ideal

Transgovernmentalism offers its own world order ideal, less dramatic but more compelling than either liberal internationalism or the new medievalism. It harnesses the state's power to find and implement solutions to global problems. International institutions have a lackluster record on such problem-solving; indeed, NGOs exist largely to compensate for their inadequacies. Doing away with the state, however, is hardly the answer. The new medievalist mantra of global governance is "governance without government." But governance without government is governance without power, and government without power rarely works. Many pressing international and domestic problems result from states' insufficient power to establish order, build infrastructure, and provide minimum social services. Private actors may take up some slack, but there is no substitute for the state.

Transgovernmental networks allow governments to benefit from the flexibility and decentralization of nonstate actors. Jessica T. Mathews argues that "businesses, citizens' organizations, ethnic groups, and crime cartels have all readily adopted the network model," while governments "are quintessential hierarchies, wedded to an organizational form incompatible with all that the new technologies make possible." Not so. Disaggregating the state into its functional components makes it possible to create networks of institutions engaged in a common enterprise even as they represent distinct national interests. Moreover, they can work with their subnational and supranational counterparts, creating a genuinely new world order in which networked institutions perform the functions of a world government—legislation, administration, and adjudication—without the form.

These globe-spanning networks will strengthen the state as the primary player in the international system. The state's defining attribute has traditionally been sovereignty, conceived as absolute power in domestic affairs and autonomy in relations with other states. But as Abram and Antonia Chayes observe in *The New Sovereignty* (1995), sovereignty is actually "status—the vindication of the state's existence in the international system." More importantly, they demonstrate that in contemporary international relations, sovereignty has been redefined to mean "membership . . . in the regimes that make up the substance of international life." Disaggregating the state permits the disaggregation of sovereignty as well, ensuring that specific state institutions derive strength and status from participation in a transgovernmental order.

Transgovernmental networks will increasingly provide an important anchor for international organizations and nonstate actors alike. U.N. officials have already learned a lesson about the limits of supranational authority; mandated cuts in the international bureaucracy will further tip the balance of power toward national regulators. The next generation of international institutions is also likely to look more like the Basle Committee, or, more formally, the Organization of Economic Cooperation and Development, dedicated to providing a forum for transnational problem-solving and the harmonization of national law. The disaggregation of the state creates opportunities for domestic institutions, particularly courts, to make common cause with their supranational counterparts against their fellow branches of government. Nonstate actors will lobby and litigate wherever they think they will have the most effect. Many already realize that corporate self-regulation and states' promises to comply with vague international agreements are no substitute for national law.

The spread of transgovernmental networks will depend more on political and professional convergence than on civilizational boundaries. Trust and awareness of a common enterprise are more vulnerable to differing political ideologies and corruption than to cultural differences. Government networks transcend the traditional divide between high and low politics. National militaries, for instance, network as extensively as central bankers with their counterparts in friendly states. Judicial and regulatory networks can help achieve gradual political convergence, but are unlikely to be of much help in the face of a serious economic or military threat. If the coming conflict with China is indeed coming, transgovernmentalism will not stop it.

The strength of transgovernmental networks and of transgovernmentalism as a world order ideal will ultimately depend on their accountability to the world's peoples. To many, the prospect of transnational government by judges and bureaucrats looks more like technocracy than democracy. Critics contend that government institutions engaged in policy coordination with their foreign counterparts will be barely visible, much less accountable, to voters still largely tied to national territory.

Citizens of liberal democracies will not accept any form of international regulation they cannot control. But checking unelected officials is a familiar problem in domestic politics. As national legislators become increasingly aware of transgovernmental networks, they will expand their oversight capacities and develop networks of their own. Transnational NGO networks will develop a similar monitoring capacity. It will be harder to monitor themselves.

Transgovernmentalism offers answers to the most important challenges facing advanced industrial countries: loss of regulatory power with economic globalization, perceptions of a "democratic deficit" as international institutions step in to fill the regulatory gap, and the difficulties of engaging nondemocratic states. Moreover, it provides a powerful alternative to a liberal internationalism that has reached its limits and to a new medievalism that, like the old Marxism, sees the state slowly fading away. The new medievalists are right to emphasize the dawn of a new era, in which information technology will transform the globe. But government networks are government for the information age. They offer the world a blue print for the international architecture of the 21st century.

JEFFREY HERBST

Responding to State Failure in Africa

Failed states in Liberia and Somalia have already caused millions of people to suffer grievously, and there is every indication that the central government apparatus is collapsing in other African countries. The international response to these failed states has focused mainly on how to resurrect them, while limiting the number of people harmed. However, the human tragedies caused by the failure of central institutions and the opportunities provided by profound economic and political changes now occurring throughout the global system compel investigation of other responses to state failure in Africa. The article suggests some alternative strategies to deal with failure in Africa, and elsewhere, that would involve significant changes in international legal and diplomatic practices. The goal is to develop a set of responses to state failure that would be more appropriate to the circumstances of a particular state's demise, and thereby move away from the current fixation on maintaining existing units.

The Paradox of Decolonization

In precolonial Africa, a wide variety of political organizations—villages, city-states, nation-states, empires—rose and fell. However, the formal colonization of Africa and the demarcation of the continent into national states between 1885 and 1902 replaced that diversity of forms with the European model of the national state.[1] After independence, Africa's heterogeneous political heritage was brushed aside in the rush by nationalists to seize the reins of power of the nation-states as defined politically and geographically by their European colonizers. Ironically, even as Kwame Nkrumah, Julius Nyerere, and Sekou Touré [African independence leaders] were proclaiming a break with Europe and the West, they uniformly seized upon that most western of political organizations—the nation-state—to rule.

The African embrace of the nation-state as theorized, designed, and demarcated by Europeans was propelled by several forces. First, many Africans were glad to be rid of the confused mixture of political institutions that characterized the precolonial period. * * * Of course, the leaders themselves had a profound interest in maintaining the nation-states they inherited from the Europeans because there was no guarantee, if they began to experiment with different types of political organization, that they would continue to be in power.

Immediately upon decolonization, the United Nations General Assembly—the gatekeeper to statehood—immediately declared the new countries to be sovereign and ratified their borders. The General Assembly was encouraged to do so by the new states who soon constituted a large percentage of that body, by the excitement generated worldwide as so many states gained their freedom largely through non-violent means and the determination to support those new experiments, and by the considerable anxiety worldwide to avoid the kind of violence that accompanied the division of the Indian subcontinent in the late 1940s. However, the UN grant of sovereignty by administrative fiat, simply because a country had achieved independence, was a revolutionary departure from traditional practices whereby sovereignty had to be earned.[2] Indeed, the central paradox of the international treatment of African states is that although sovereignty was granted simply as a result of decolonization, it was immediately assumed that the new states would take on features that had previously characterized sovereignty, most notably unquestioned physical control over the defined

From *International Security* 21, no. 3 (winter 1996/97): 120–44.

territory, but also an administrative presence throughout the country and the allegiance of the population to the idea of the state. Implicitly, the granting of sovereignty to the new nations also suggested that every country that gained freedom from colonization would be politically and economically viable, despite the fact that most colonies in Africa had been demarcated with the assumption that they would not become separate, independent states. Indeed, the principal criteria for state recognition today are a permanent population, a defined territory, and the ability to enter into relations with other states.[3] The ability to control and administer the territory assigned are irrelevant to the modern conception of sovereignty; the ability to develop ties to the population even more so.

The notion that Africa was ever composed of sovereign states classically defined as having a monopoly on force in the territory within their boundaries is false. Most colonial states did not make any effort to extend the administrative apparatus of government much beyond the capital city. * * *

Although sovereignty was for some countries little more than a legal fiction, it was relatively easy to maintain appearances in the 1960s and 1970s. Most African economies were growing, buoyed by global economic growth and relatively high prices for basic commodities, export of which formed the basis of most of the formal economies. The global strategic competition between the United States and Soviet Union also discouraged threats to the design of states in Africa or elsewhere. One of the implicit rules of the Cold War was that supporting efforts to change boundaries was not part of the game. In fact, where the great powers intervened, it was usually to protect the integrity of existing states (as in Zaire, Chad, and Ethiopia).[4]

Finally, no intellectual challenge was made to the immediate assumption of sovereignty by African states. Decolonization happened so quickly and Africans were so intent on seizing power that there was neither the time nor the motivation to develop new concepts of national political organization. Then, once the dozens of newly indepen-

dent states were created, leaders found that the window of opportunity when they could have instituted revolutionary change in political structures was closing.[5]

The Facade of Sovereignty Overturned

The actual nature of some African countries' sovereignty is now being exposed. The long economic crisis that many African countries have experienced has caused a profound erosion of many governments' revenue bases. Even the most basic agents of the state—agricultural extension agents, tax collectors, census takers—are no longer to be found in many rural areas. As a result, some states are increasingly unable to exercise physical control over their territories. * * *

*   *   *

At the same time, international assistance to many African states is stagnant or declining. As donors redirect their aid from Cold War proxies to countries that are achieving some economic and political reform, countries that are failing spiral further downward. Somalia began to decline more sharply when it could no longer play the United States off against the Soviet Union in order to receive more aid. The decline in aid represents a fundamental break with the practice of the last one hundred years, which saw international actors offer support to the African state system, first through the creation of colonies, then by the enshrinement of sovereignty, and finally by the provision of financial resources without regard to domestic economic or political performance.[6] It is thus hardly surprising that so many African states have failed since the Berlin Wall fell, nor that those that collapsed include a notable number of states that had been richly rewarded by international patrons because of their strategic position during the Cold War but were subsequently cut off when aid donors became more concerned with economic and political performance (e.g., Ethiopia, Liberia, Somalia, Zaire).

As a result of this combination of forces, the centers of some states, notably Liberia and Somalia, collapsed when the contending parties were unable to break a military stalemate. More common are the states that are simply contracting because, while the centers still exist, they cannot extend their power very far over the territory they formally control. Zaire is perhaps the worst case: Mobutu seems intent on controlling whatever remains of the country he has bled dry, and the government has extremely limited control over territory outside the capital, to the point that some provinces no longer accept the national currency as legal scrip.[7] In a number of countries, the state is slowly being merged into a web of informal business associations instituted by rulers who have little interest in carrying out the traditional functions of the state and who do not recognize or respect boundaries while enriching themselves through trade.[8] * * *

Unfortunately, the international community, in its response to state failure in Africa, has refused to acknowledge the structural factors at work, despite mounting evidence that the loss of sovereign control is becoming a pattern in at least parts of Africa. Rather, each state failure is taken as a unique event. * * *

Numerous critiques of the performance of African states also assume that there is no alternative to the status quo. For instance, the North-South Roundtable recognized that "institutional decay is currently of endemic proportion in Africa. In all sectors of the polity, the great institutions of the State have failed woefully. Evidence of institutional crisis abounds: in the political system, in the public service, in the management of the economy and even in the military."[9] Even so, the Roundtable restricted itself to asking how the existing states could be reinvigorated despite the long-term record of failure associated with Africa's extant political institutions. No energy was devoted to exploring alternatives.

*   *   *

Old and New Conceptions of African Sovereignty

Understanding what was lost when the Europeans imposed the territorial nation-state is a first step toward investigating what might be appropriate for Africa today. * * *

Precolonial sovereignty had two features radically different from sovereignty exercised in modern Africa. First, in large parts of precolonial Africa, control tended to be exercised over people rather than land.[10] Land was plentiful and populations thin on the ground. * * *

The second notable aspect of precolonial political practices was that sovereignty tended to be shared. It was not unusual for a community to have nominal obligations and allegiances to more than one political center. As power was not strictly defined spatially, there was much greater confusion over what it meant to control a particular community at any one time. At the same time, communications and technology were so poorly developed that few political centers could hope to wield unquestioned authority, even over the areas that they were thought to control. * * *

In this respect, precolonial Africa was similar to medieval Europe, where shared sovereignty—e.g., between the Church and various political units—was not uncommon.[11] * * *

*   *   *

There was nothing exotic about the precolonial African state system. Where Europe and Africa diverge is in the speed in which they moved from one system to another. The European evolution from the old system of states where territory was not well defined and sovereignty was shared was very slow, taking centuries. While the slow transformation from one system to another made it difficult for states to deal with crises, there were advantages to a state in not being called upon to exercise all aspects of modern sovereignty at once: for instance, in many European countries, local notables were still responsible for arresting criminals and providing social services long after the modern state was created, because the state did not have the capacity to carry out these functions.[12] Thus, in Europe there was time for relatively viable states to develop.

In Africa, however, there was an abrupt discontinuity between the old political order and the new one that essentially began with the Berlin West African Conference in 1885. In the space of a few decades, the facade of the new state system was formed and then, shortly thereafter, the states were given independence. The hard-earned structures of political control and authority that allowed for the exercise of political power in the precolonial period were abruptly cast aside, and there were almost no efforts to resurrect them. Indeed, the demarcation of Africa into colonies differed even from imperial practices in other areas of the world in the speed at which it was done, due to the multitude of countries seeking to rule the same area, and the reliance on force to the exclusion of developing loyalties among the subject population.[13]

*   *   *

Alternatives within the Current International State System

The current unvarying reliance on the states that Europe gave to Africa must give way to a world which at least recognizes the possibility of alternatives. The recognition that reform is possible should be guided by two propositions. First, proposed alternatives must, in the end, come from the Africans themselves. No alternative to the nation-state is going to be forced on Africa, especially given the history of colonialism that began with the Berlin Conference. Second, the aim of any alternative should be to increase the dynamism of state formation, so that stronger national units can emerge and dysfunctional ones do not necessarily have to continue indefinitely. Not only would such dynamism have strong resonance with the African past, it would also be critical to setting the essential foundation for political and economic development. *   *   *

BREAKING THE INTELLECTUAL LOG-JAM

The first step toward developing new alternatives would be to provide the intellectual space necessary for Africans to present alternatives; this could be accomplished by publicly declaring that the international community is not blindly wedded to the current state system. This would be a revolutionary act that might help to break the intellectual log-jam that devotion to the status quo has caused. Given the state of African universities, the international community might have to go further and provide resources for think tanks and individuals who might want to analyze alternatives to the nation-state. Western donors are already providing significant amounts of money for "governance" to aid Africa's new democracies in their political transition. Some of this money could be redirected to the bigger question of whether some countries are presently viable. *   *   *

To date, it is not surprising that few countries have engaged in bold experiments regarding national design, given the skeptical international environment. Perhaps the most intriguing possibility for re-engineering an existing African state, especially in regard to the rights of minority groups, is the new Ethiopian constitution which provides for the possibility of secession based on a two-thirds majority vote. This constitution has been backed by a large number of Western countries despite the fact that it explicitly challenges many of the notions of post–World War II diplomacy, especially as it has evolved in Africa. The logic behind the Ethiopian constitution is much the same as the logic driving the liberalization of capital controls worldwide: if a country has made a credible commitment that groups (or in the case of capital controls, money) can leave the country if the minorities (or owners of capital) are unhappy, this demonstrates a government's confidence that it will adopt policies that will not lead to a ruinous exit. Potential secessionists, understanding that they have considerable leverage *vis-à-vis* the central government, may therefore no longer fear marginalization. *   *   *

To aid further development of alternatives to the current state system, the international community and African countries can also begin to study African problems on a regional basis without regard to country boundaries. Despite seemingly endless rhetoric about the regional nature of many African problems, most reports and analytic works still use the existing nation-states as their unit of analysis. * * *

The relatively few studies not based on existing boundaries are important to note because they suggest the possibilities that are opened when the old framework is discarded. Arguably, the most innovative recent work on African development is the West Africa Long Term Perspective Study published by the Club du Sahel. The study seeks to analyze West Africa as a whole to understand region-wide dynamics, and places rather less emphasis on political boundaries. * * *

*   *   *

Donors can accelerate the process of designing new alternatives by using some of their aid for regional integration to promote alternatives and projects which treat sections of Africa as regions, as opposed to groupings of countries. Under current practices, foreign aid further reifies practices of approaching regional problems by using existing countries as the unit of analysis. * * *

RECOGNIZING NEW NATION-STATES

After thirty years of assuming that the boundaries of even the most dysfunctional African state are inviolable, another important initiative for the international community would be to consider the possibility of allowing for the creation of new sovereign states. Opening the possibility for new states to be created would challenge the basic assumption held by African leaders and the international community that boundaries drawn haphazardly during the scramble for Africa a century ago with little regard to the social, political, economic, or ethnic realities on the ground should continue to be universally respected. At the same time, allowing for more dynamism in the creation of African states would help recapture the element of the precolonial perspective on sovereignty that insisted that political control had to be won, not instituted by administrative fiat.

A criterion for recognition appropriate to the particular circumstances of Africa's failing states could be: does the break-away area provide more political order on its own over a significant period of time (say, five years) than is provided by the central government? By order, I mean functioning military, police, and judicial systems, which are the fundamental prerequisites for political and economic progress. These public goods are precisely what Africa's failing states do not provide. Such a standard would rule out many attempts at secession that were not of the utmost seriousness, and also return, to a degree, to older understandings of sovereignty that are resonant with the African past. * * *

*   *   *

* * * [T]he reality on the ground in some African countries is that sovereign control is not being exercised by the central state in outlying areas, and sub-national groups are already exerting authority in certain regions. By recognizing and legitimating those groups, the international community has the opportunity to ask that they respect international norms regarding human rights and also has a chance to bring them into the international economy. For instance, even during intervention in Somalia, initiated explicitly because the central government apparatus had collapsed in Mogadishu, the World Bank and the International Monetary Fund offered no assistance to Somaliland, although the breakaway government in Hargeisa was at least providing some services to its citizens.[14] A less dogmatic approach to sovereignty would have allowed the international community to begin to help a substantial number of people. If the new sub-national arrangements are ignored, they will continue to be more like institutionalized protection rackets than states that guard the rights of their citizens. Local rulers who are actually exercising elements of sovereign control will focus on informal trade, often involving drugs, guns, and

poached animals, to survive, rather than beginning initiatives to promote economic development that would aid all of the people in their region. The international community thus faces the choice between ignoring successful secessionist movements and thereby forcing them to remain semi-criminal affairs, or trying to help create new state institutions. The fact that some African states will dissolve will be the reality no matter which policy stance is adopted.

Alternatives to the Sovereign State

A far more revolutionary approach would be for at least parts of Africa to be reordered around some organization other than the sovereign state. While such reforms would be a dramatic change for international society, their adoption would be an important acknowledgment of what is actually happening in parts of Africa where many states do not exercise sovereign authority over their territories. * * *

It will primarily be up to the Africans to come up with alternatives to the nation-state. However, the international community can play an important role in signaling that the atmosphere has changed and that there is at least the possibility that alternatives to the sovereign state could be accepted. * * *

MAKING INTERNATIONAL INSTITUTIONS MORE FLEXIBLE

*   *   *

In response to the confused situation in some African countries, the institutional framework governing international organizations could be loosened. It would be particularly useful to encourage the participation by subnational units, be they potential breakaway regions or simply units such as towns or regions that have been largely abandoned by their own central government, in technical meetings, and later directly, in organizations such as the World Health Organization, UN International Children's Emergency Fund, and UN Development Program that provide resources directly for development.

Participation in technical and service delivery organizations by traditional leaders or "warlords," who currently exercise authority and may deliver services but are not sovereign, is appealing because international acceptance could be calibrated to the kind and conditions of power actually being exercised. Thus, if a region's schooling has become largely dependent on the leadership and funds provided by a traditional leader, he might develop some kind of formal relationship with the relevant UN agency. * * *

Making critical international institutions more flexible would be more important than having the General Assembly or other highly political organizations begin to recognize subnational ethnic groups.[15] Because it is the source of sovereignty, highly visible, and political, recognition by the General Assembly is probably the last step for a region or group of people breaking away from their old nation-state. In the indeterminate position that some regions of some African countries will occupy, focusing on service delivery is more important.

The diplomacy of integrating non-state actors into what were previously clubs of sovereign nations would, of course, be difficult. However, in a variety of circumstances, the international community has proved adept at adapting to diplomacy with something other than the traditional sovereign states. * * *

DECERTIFYING FAILED STATES

A further step that the United States, and other countries, can take would be to formally recognize that some states are simply not exercising formal control over parts of their country and should no longer be considered sovereign. For instance, the U.S. government already decertifies countries, effectively reducing their eligibility for American aid, that are not attempting to stop the production and trans-shipment of narcotics. * * *

Decertification would be a strong signal that something fundamental has gone wrong in an African country, and that parts of the international community are no longer willing to continue the myth that every state is always exercising sovereign authority. Concretely, decertification might trigger the initiation of new efforts by other countries, including major donors and neighbors, at finding other leaders who are exercising control in parts of the country. Decertification would remove other privileges of sovereignty, including appointments to the rotating positions on the Security Council. It is paradoxical that the United States strongly opposed Libya's attempt to gain a seat on the Security Council because of its support for international terrorism, but seemingly had no problems with Zaire being on the United Nations' most powerful body despite that country's obvious dysfunctional nature.

Whatever concrete measures are taken, decertification would provide some avenue out of the current impasse, where there is no status to accord a country other than sovereignty irrespective of domestic realities. Decertification should be a rare step that would be used only as a last resort. Indeed, making decertification relatively difficult would also make its signal that much more powerful when it was used. Decertification would also have the advantage of correctly stating that the United States and other important actors understand that some countries are not sovereign, even if it is not clear what they are. * * *

Decertification would require what the United States and other great powers dislike doing: altering the rules by which diplomacy is conducted. Great powers are notoriously conservative when it comes to the structure of the international system: witness the U.S. opposition to the breakup of the Soviet Union. No doubt, many diplomats would raise practical objections to decertification, arguing that it is against current practices of state-to-state relations. That is precisely the point. The situation in parts of Africa, and perhaps elsewhere in the developing world, has now diverged so dramatically from the legal fiction that it would actually be in the long-term interest of the great powers to create a new category for states that really can no longer be considered sovereign. While decertification might apply to a very limited number of countries, those are precisely the countries that will inevitably occupy the time and attention of policymakers across the world who search for a solution to mass human suffering.

The idea that complex humanitarian disasters of the type experienced by Somalia and Liberia must, at some level, be the responsibility of the international community is a new phenomenon in international relations, and is at odds with the post–World War II notion of sovereignty for any territory that can achieve self-rule. Accordingly, new tools must be developed to deal with these problems, and the old practice of simply accepting that all countries must always be sovereign should be rejected. Decertification of some countries that have demonstrated an inability over a long period of time to rule their territories could be part of the new arsenal of techniques needed to address new problems the international community faces.

Conclusion

The international society has yet to acknowledge that some states simply do not work. Indeed, it will require significant effort simply to create an environment where the possibility of alternatives to the current nation-states is admitted. Ending the intellectual log-jam caused by the current insistence on retaining the old nation-states would allow Africans in particular to begin to develop, for the first time in over a century, indigenous plans for their nation-states. Given the extent of the problems in Africa's failing states, it would be incorrect to suggest that any innovation will be low-cost, or will be guaranteed to address the root causes of failure. However, the very magnitude of the problems affecting millions of people also suggests that the current emphasis on resuscitating states that have never demonstrated the capacity to be viable is a mistake.

NOTES

1. See I.M. Lewis, "Pre- and Post-Colonial Forms of Polity in Africa," in I.M. Lewis, ed., *Nationalism and Self Determination in the Horn of Africa* (London: Ithaca Press, 1983), p. 74.

2. Robert H. Jackson, *Quasi-States: Sovereignty, International Relations and the Third World* (Cambridge, U.K.: Cambridge University Press, 1990).

3. John Dugard, *Recognition and the United Nations* (Cambridge, U.K.: Grotius Publications, 1987), p. 7.

4. I have developed this argument in Jeffrey Herbst, "The Challenges to Africa's Boundaries," *Journal of International Affairs*, Vol. 46, No. 1 (Summer 1992), pp. 17–31.

5. This point is made well by Julius K. Nyerere, *Uhuru na Ujamaa* (Oxford, U.K.: Oxford University Press, 1968), pp. 28 and 209.

6. For instance, from 1962 to 1988, six countries—Ethiopia, Kenya, Liberia, Somalia, Sudan, and Zaire—accounted for most U.S. foreign aid to Africa, despite their exceptionally poor economic and political performances. Indeed, all but Kenya can now be considered failed states despite American largesse. Michael Clough, *Free at Last: U.S. Policy toward Africa and the End of the Cold War* (New York: Council on Foreign Relations, 1992), p. 77.

7. Steven Metz, *Reform, Conflict, and Security in Zaire* (Carlisle, Penn.: U.S. Army War College, 1996), pp. 25, 35.

8. William Reno, "War, Markets and the Reconfiguration of West Africa's Weak States," unpublished paper, Florida International University, September 1995, p. 1.

9. North-South Roundtable, *Revitalizing Africa for the 21st Century: An Agenda for Renewal* (Rome: Society for International Development, 1995), p. 15.

10. See Jack Goody, *Technology, Tradition and the State in Africa* (Cambridge, U.K.: Cambridge University Press, 1971), p. 30.

11. F.H. Hinsley, *Sovereignty*, 2nd ed. (Cambridge, U.K.: Cambridge University Press, 1986), p. 60.

12. Joseph R. Strayer, *On the Medieval Origins of the Modern State* (Princeton, N.J.: Princeton University Press, 1970), pp. 105–106.

13. Crawford Young, *The African Colonial State in Comparative Perspective* (New Haven: Yale University Press, 1994), p. 278.

14. John Drysdale, *Whatever Happened to Somalia?* (London: HAAN Associates, 1994), p. 147.

15. This is suggested by Gottlieb, *Nation against State* [New York: Council on Foreign Relations, 1993], p. 39.

6 ❧ THE INDIVIDUAL

While realist and radical theorists pay little attention to individuals in international relations, liberal theorists do. Individuals include not only foreign policy elites—the focus of the so-called great men theory—but also groups of individuals who share common characteristics and nonelite activitists who make a difference in how international issues are addressed. Utilizing psychological concepts, Margaret Hermann and Joe Hagan, political psychologist and political scientist, respectively, sketch out the role elite leaders play in international decision making. They contend that the major issue is not whether leaders matter (they do!), but how such leaders matter and how they balance international and domestic factors when making decisions.

Individuals work in groups and through institutions. One group that has been typically underrepresented in both international and domestic politics is women. Political scientist Jane Jaquette, in a widely cited Foreign Policy *article, provides an analysis of why there has been an upsurge in the number of women officeholders over the last decade. Particular attention is given to the globalization of the women's movement and its impact on getting women elected to domestic public offices. She contends that women bring a different perspective to the political arena. One woman who has made a difference is Lori Wallach, activist director of Public Citizen's Global Trade Watch.* Foreign Policy *editor Moisés Naím conducts an insightful interview with Wallach, detailing her personal background and her view of the global trading rules. An organizer of the anti–World Trade Organization demonstrations in Seattle in 1999, Wallach predicts future activism in the trade movement, giving further evidence that individuals make a difference.*

The notion that individuals matter stands in contrast to John Mearsheimer's contention in his book in the Norton series, The Tragedy of Great Power Politics, *that individuals play virtually no role, except to channel the inherent drive of a state toward ultimate power.*

MARGARET G. HERMANN AND JOE D. HAGAN

International Decision Making: Leadership Matters

When conversations turn to foreign policy and international politics, they often focus on particular leaders and evaluations of their leadership. We grade Bill Clinton's performance abroad; argue about why Benjamin Netanyahu is or is not stalling the Middle East peace process; debate Mohammed Khatami's intentions regarding Iranian relations with the United States; and ponder what will happen in South Africa or Russia when Nelson Mandela or Boris Yeltsin leaves office. In each case, our attention is riveted on individuals whose leadership seems to matter beyond the borders of the countries they lead.

Yet, though many of us find such discussions informative, for the past several decades most scholars of world politics would have discounted them, proposing instead to focus on the international constraints that limit what leaders can do. Their rationale went as follows: Because the systemic imperatives of anarchy or interdependence are so clear, leaders can choose from only a limited range of foreign policy strategies. If they are to exercise rational leadership and maximize their state's movement toward its goals, only certain actions are feasible. Consequently, incorporating leaders and leadership into general theories of international relations is unnecessary since such knowledge adds little to our understanding of the dynamics of conflict, cooperation, and change in international affairs.

In the bipolar international system that characterized the Cold War, such a rationale might have seemed reasonable. But today there is little consensus on the nature of the "new world order" and

From *Foreign Policy*, no. 110 (spring 1998): 124–37.

more room for interpretation, innovation, misunderstanding, and miscommunication. In such an ambiguous environment, the perspectives of the leaders involved in foreign policy making can have more influence on what governments do. Moreover, as international constraints on foreign policy have become more flexible and indeterminate, the importance of domestic political concerns has increased. Scholars of international relations have begun to talk not only about different kinds of states—democracies, transitional democracies, and autocracies—but also about how domestic political pressures can help to define the state—strong, weak; stable, unstable; cohesive, fragmented; satisfied, revisionist. And they have started to emphasize that government leaders have some choice in the roles that their states play in international politics—doves, hawks; involved, isolationist; unilateral, multilateral; regional, global; pragmatists, radicals. These differences preordain different kinds of reactions within the international arena.

Ironically, some of the more interesting illustrations of the effects that leaders and domestic politics can have on world politics have emerged in the very literature that originally dismissed their significance. Researchers have tried to account for why states with similar positions in international affairs have reacted in varied (and often self-defeating) ways. For example, in examining the crises of the 1930s, students of international relations have puzzled over why the democracies of the time reacted in divergent ways to the Great Depression and why they failed to balance against seemingly obvious security threats. Scholars seeking to answer such questions have looked at domestic pressures and leadership arrangements with an eye toward developing a theory of state behavior.

Although interest in leaders and domestic politics has ebbed and flowed, scholars who focus on understanding the foreign policy process have made progress in identifying the conditions under which these factors do matter and in specifying the nature of their effects. Building on the research of Graham Allison, Michael Brecher, Alexander George, Morton Halperin, Ole Holsti, Irving Janis, Robert Jervis, Ernest May, James Rosenau, and Richard Snyder, they have explored how leaders perceive and interpret constraints in their international and domestic environments, make decisions, and manage domestic political pressures on their foreign policy choices. These scholars contend that state leaders play a pivotal role in balancing international imperatives with those arising from, or embedded in, domestic politics. What has emerged is a more nuanced picture of the processes that drive and guide the actions of states in world politics.

The Role Leaders Play

LEADERS PERCEIVE AND INTERPRET CONSTRAINTS

Leaders define states' international and domestic constraints. Based on their perceptions and interpretations, they build expectations, plan strategies, and urge actions on their governments that conform with their judgments about what is possible and likely to maintain them in their positions. Such perceptions help frame governments' orientations to international affairs. Leaders' interpretations arise out of their experiences, goals, beliefs about the world, and sensitivity to the political context.

The view that the world is anarchic—embodied in former secretary of state Henry Kissinger's axiom that "tranquility is not the natural state of the world; peace and security are not the law of nature"—leads to a focus on threats and security, a sense of distrust, and a perceived need for carefully managing the balance of power. Leaders with this view must always remain alert to challenges to their state's power and position in the international system. John Vasquez has argued that the

rise to power of militant hardliners who view the world in such realpolitik terms is a crucial prerequisite for war. Thus, the American road to war in Korea and Vietnam was marked first by the demise of former President Franklin Roosevelt's accommodation of nationalism, then by the fall of George Kennan's selective containment strategy, and ultimately by the rise of former secretary of state Dean Acheson's focus on military containment. Describing the vulnerability of empire, Charles Kupchan has observed that the entrenched belief that one's state is "highly vulnerable" has led the leaders of declining states to appease perceived rising powers (consider British behavior before World War II) and encouraged leaders of rising powers to become overly competitive (Wilhelmine Germany before World War I).

Drawing on a more optimistic view of human nature, scholars such as Bruce Russett have argued that democracies do not fight one another because democratic leaders assume their peers have peaceful intentions, adhere to cooperative norms, and face domestic political constraints on the use of force. Others such as Ido Oren and John Owen have proposed that leaders who follow a liberal ideology interpret the world in this manner and act accordingly—they place a higher degree of trust in the leaders of countries they currently perceive are democratic.

LEADERS OFTEN DISAGREE

But what happens if there is no single dominant leader or no set of leaders who share a common interpretation of the world? What if a government is led, as in the People's Republic of China, by a standing committee whose members range in views along a continuum composed of hardliners and reformers? Or what if there is a coalition government such as the one Prime Minister Netanyahu must lead in Israel, composed of leaders with different interests and constituencies and, as a result, various perspectives on what is at stake in the peace process?

Before action is possible, leaders must achieve consensus on how to interpret the problem, what options are feasible, what further information is needed and from whom, who gets to participate in decision making, and where implementation will occur. If consensus is highly unlikely, dealing with the problem will probably be postponed until a decision is forced or the decision unit can be reconstituted.

At issue are the rules of aggregation that facilitate consensus building when disagreement exists among those who must make policy. Ideas derived from studies of group dynamics, bureaucratic politics, and coalition building have proved useful in understanding the factors that influence the shift from individual to collective decisions. Thus, scholars have found that excessive group cohesion can produce "groupthink" and premature closure around options preferred by the more powerful policymakers; bureaucratic interests generally only yield to compromise; the possession of some "idiosyncrasy credit"—be it vital information, control over a critical resource, expertise, or charisma—can lead that party's position to prevail; the lack, or failure, of "rules of the game" usually means deadlock and a politically unstable situation; logrolling provokes overcommitment and overextension.

So how can we determine whose positions count in foreign policy? During an international crisis, when the values of the state are threatened and time for decision making is short, authority tends to concentrate among those persons or groups that bear ultimate responsibility for maintaining the government in power. How these individuals, cabinets, juntas, or standing committees interpret the problem will dominate the state's reactions. Little outside input is sought or tolerated. The experiences, fears, interests, and expectations of these decision makers remain unfettered and affect any action that is chosen. Consider the British cabinet during the Falkland Islands crisis or the Bush administration during the Gulf War. In both cases, the tendency was to close ranks and insulate policymakers from both domestic and international influences. Each group recognized that its government would rise or fall depending on its decisions, and that an overly participatory

decision-making process could mean dangerous delays.

The nature of the foreign policy problem can also help to dictate whose positions count. Economic, security, environmental, and human rights issues, for example, may all be handled by different parts of the government or by different sets of actors, each brought together to interpret what is happening and make judgments about policy. These actors may not be at the apex of power but are often given ultimate authority to make foreign policy decisions for the government because of their expertise, past experience, particular point of view, or official position. The recent threat of the U.S. Federal Maritime Commission to detain Japanese–flag liner vessels in American ports over questions of market access is an extreme example of a well-documented fact: The power to negotiate—and then ratify—trade agreements is generally dispersed across ministries, legislatures, and interest groups.

Another crucial factor is the extent to which rivalries exist within a domestic political system. When authority becomes fragmented and competition for power turns fierce, an unstable situation is likely to ensue, with each person, group, or organization acting on its own in an uncoordinated fashion. Witness the disparate actions in Iran of radical students, relatively moderate politicians in the Provisional Revolutionary Government, hardline clerics dominating the Revolutionary Council, and Ayatollah Ruhollah Khomeini following the 1979 seizure of the U.S. embassy in Tehran. Until Khomeini consolidated his power and coordinated action, a coherent Iranian foreign policy was impossible. When authority is dispersed but little competition for power exists, the result is an oligarchy like that of the Soviet Politburo during the late 1960s and early 1970s: Building consensus among these leaders took time since no one wanted to concede any authority. The current [1998] division in the U.S. government between a Democratic administration and a Congress dominated by Republicans serves as an example of what happens when consolidated authority is combined with strong competition for power—each side questions the other's foreign policy record and often attempts to block the other's initiatives.

LEADERS AND DOMESTIC OPPOSITION

In addition to interpreting potential constraints in the international arena, leaders must also respond effectively to domestic pressures. As Robert Putnam and Andrew Moravcsik have observed, leaders are the "central strategic actors" in the "two-level game" that links domestic politics and international bargaining. In the domestic political game, they face the dual challenge of building a coalition of supporters to retain their authority while contending with opposition forces to maintain their legitimacy.

An appreciation of the alternative strategies that leaders use to respond to domestic opposition is key to understanding how domestic politics affects foreign policy. Leaders who prefer to avoid controversy at home often seek to accommodate the opposition by granting concessions on foreign policy. The result is frequently a policy that is largely unresponsive to international pressures and involves little risk. Note, for example, how nationalistic feelings in both Russia and Japan have precluded the leaders of these countries from resolving ownership issues over the islands that constitute Japan's "Northern Territories," despite the likely diplomatic and economic benefits of a peace treaty and normalized relations. Leaders can also seek to consolidate their domestic position by pushing a foreign policy that mobilizes new support, logrolls with complementary interests, or undercuts the opposition. By this logic, the political attraction of NATO expansion for the Clinton administration is that it garners support from two otherwise contentious groups—liberal internationalists, who favor the spread of democracy; and conservative internationalists, who worry about resurgent threats. Another strategy is to insulate foreign policy from domestic pressures altogether by coopting, suppressing, or ignoring opposition. Leaders of nondemocracies can more easily insulate their foreign policies from domestic pressures than their counterparts in democracies. Leaders in transitional democracies are learning this the hard way as they face the unfamiliar challenge of having their agendas scrutinized by an inquisitive press and elected legislatures.

Bridging Tomorrow's Gaps

As Alexander George has observed, practitioners find it difficult to use academic approaches that "assume that all state actors are alike and can be expected to behave in the same way in given situations." Instead, policymakers prefer to work with "actor-specific models that grasp the different internal structures and behavioral patterns of each state and leader with which they must deal."

Today, scholars who study the dynamics of foreign policy decision making recognize the need to bridge the gap between theory and practice. In particular, skeletal theoretical frameworks must be fleshed out with nuanced detail. Here, the issue of context looms large. What type of state is being examined? Citizens in advanced democracies have different wants and expectations than those in transitional states, poor economies, or states involved in ethnic conflicts. They will be attracted to different kinds of leaders to push for their agendas. How do the leaders who are selected view their state's place in the world? Do they view their state as participating in a cooperative international system or as struggling to maintain ascendancy in an anarchic world? Do they view it as part of a regional (Europe), cultural (Arab), ideological (socialist), religious (Hindu), or ethnic (Serbian) grouping?

Which leaders' interpretations prevail in the formulation of foreign policy depends on the nature of the decision unit and who is ultimately responsible for making a decision. Is an individual (for example, Deng Xiaoping), a single group (such as the junta in Burma), or a coalition of actors (much like the Israeli Labor-Likud coalition cabinet of the 1980s) in charge? When one predominant leader makes the decisions, the focus is on theories that explore political cognition, political socialization, and leadership—what is that person like, and how does he or she view the world and interact with others? When the decision unit is a single group, the focus shifts to theories growing out of group dynamics, bureaucratic politics, and public administration—where does member loyalty lie, and is there a shared view of the problem? If the decision unit is a coalition of contending actors, then attention must turn to theories of bargaining and negotiation, political stability, and institution building—is one actor more pivotal than others, and is compromise possible?

Determining the nature of the decision unit is not always as obvious as it would seem. A ruling oligarchy might be dominated by a single personality. A leader whose authority appears unchallenged might be answerable in reality to a coalition that helps keep him or her in power. Who, for instance, is currently in charge of foreign policy in Iran? President Khatami raised eyebrows in the West when he called recently for improved relations with the United States. But Iran's spiritual leader, Ayatollah Ali Khamenei, who controls its security services and enjoys the support of the conservative Majlis, has openly ruled out any dialogue with the "Great Satan."

Also consider the Japanese government. As Peter Katzenstein has pointed out, some scholars view Japan's government as a highly centralized state bureaucracy, as evidenced by the Liberal Democratic Party's ability to remain in power with few interruptions for 40 years. Haruhiro Fukui and others, however, have suggested that Japanese governments are best described as corporatist systems that grow out of a deeply embedded political norm that requires consensus building across party factions and business interests. Iran and Japan serve as reminders that understanding a government's formal structure is less important than understanding whose positions actually count at a particular point in time.

THE ORIGINS OF PREFERENCES

To what extent are leaders the products of their cultures, genders, and domestic political systems? Samuel Huntington, J. Ann Tickner, and Bruce Russett would have us believe that these ties are quite strong. Socialization into Christian, democratic, or male-dominated cultures, they would argue, imbues people with certain predispositions and expectations. In sharp contrast, James David Barber has pointed out that the leadership styles of American presidents often derive from the same techniques that helped them achieve their initial political successes. Ronald Reagan, who was president of the Screen Actors' Guild when that organization fought off a communist takeover, learned from his experience that the United States could only negotiate with the Soviet Union from a position of strength.

Other scholars have shown that the worldviews of leaders are shaped in large part by the generation that they happened to be born into—specifically, by what critical political events they and their cohorts have faced during their lifetimes. Yet, we have also observed leaders who appear to have undergone substantial changes in their perspectives. Consider former Egyptian president Anwar el-Sadat and his journey to Jerusalem, former Israeli prime minister Yitzhak Rabin and his pursuit of the Oslo accords, and ex-president Richard Nixon and his decision to open U.S. relations with China. Arguments abound as to whether these leaders themselves changed or whether they were merely responding to changes in the international scene, their own domestic arenas, or perceived opportunities to attain goals that might previously have been foreclosed to others.

Underlying this debate is the question concerning the extent to which leaders shape their own preferences. On the one hand, we have leaders—such as former British prime minister Margaret Thatcher and Cuban president Fidel Castro—who are crusaders or ideologues, highly insensitive to information and constituencies unless these can help further their causes or spread their worldviews. These leaders are interested in persuading others, not in being persuaded. On the other hand, we have leaders—former Iranian president Ali Akbar Hashemi Rafsanjani among them—who appear chameleon-like, their views mirroring whatever other important players are saying or doing at the moment. They seek cues from their environment to help them choose whichever position is likely to prevail. In between these two extremes, we find leaders—such as Syrian president Hafez al-Assad—who take a more strategic approach; they know where they want to go but proceed with incremental steps, forever testing the waters to see if the time is right for action. Thus, preferences tend to be more fixed for crusaders and more fluid for pragmatic and strategic leaders.

BALANCING FOREIGN AND DOMESTIC PRESSURES

At times, governments can seem nearly oblivious to the international arena, focusing instead on matters at home. Consider the Cultural Revolution in China, the Botha regime in South Africa, and former president Lyndon Johnson's inner circle of advisers, the "Tuesday Lunch Group." In each case, domestic conditions isolated the state's leadership from full participation in world politics. During the Cultural Revolution, no one was effectively in charge of China. All attention had to be directed toward the return of political stability. Former president P. W. Botha was a crusader for apartheid and intent on maintaining it regardless of world opinion and sanctions. And the Tuesday Lunch Group suppressed its skepticism and doubt about U.S. involvement in Vietnam rather than lose favor with the president. With their attention captured by events at home, these decision units turned their focus inward, intent on maintaining their authority and legitimacy on the domestic front. But the opposite also proves true at times. Decision units may decide to use foreign policy to help them domestically.

Knowledge about the inner workings of decision units can offer clues as to whether their efforts will be internally or externally oriented. The current literature suggests that the leadership focuses on domestic pressures when its opposition sits close to the centers of power, controls many of the resources needed to deal with the problem, challenges domestic political order, or has legitimacy of its own—in other words, when the leadership feels vulnerable domestically. Consider how Netanyahu's current [1998] resistance to international pressure for greater Israeli cooperation in the peace process reflects not only his own hardline convictions but the Likud-led coalition's tenuous majority in the Knesset, his dependence on cabinet hardliners holding key ministries, and, more generally, the realignment of Israeli party politics in the 1990s.

There can be a time lag, however, before certain decision units respond to such domestic pressures. The crusading predominant leader or the highly cohesive, loyal ruling group may try to suppress the opposition or opt to engage in several diversionary foreign activities before realizing the seriousness of the domestic situation. In coalitions where minority parties have a veto—as when Fourth Republic France stalled over the question of granting independence to Algeria or when Dutch cabinets deadlocked over accepting NATO cruise missiles—foreign policy may be paralyzed as the different parties work to preserve a government.

STRATEGIC ATTRIBUTION

Much of what goes on in world politics revolves around interactions between governments—two or more states trying to gauge the rationales behind the other's actions and anticipate its next moves. Here, the critical issue is how leaders assess the intentions and attitudes of their foreign counterparts. Are these assessments derived from personal interactions with the leaders of the other state, are they filtered through other peoples' lenses, or are they hunches and guesses based on the past behavior of that state, a shared identity, or national interests? Leaders tend to extrapolate from their own perspectives in solving problems when they have had little or no contact with their counterparts on the other side. But even with contact, a decision unit led by a crusading leader, for example, will see what that leader wants to see. When leaders make incorrect assessments, the consequences can be serious. Nikita Khrushchev's attempted deployment of Soviet missiles to Cuba in 1962 is one example of how strategies can backfire if there is confusion as to what the other side's leadership is doing.

Adding to the complexity is the realization that leaders must not only engage in this two-level game of balancing their own perceived domestic and international pressures, but must simultaneously try to comprehend the nature of the balancing act in which their counterparts are engaged. Such comprehension is critical in today's multipolar world, where leaders vary in their interpretations of how international politics should work and face increased pressure from constituents at home who clamor for an ever improving quality of life. Moreover, governments are becoming aware of the importance of knowing whose positions count in other states and toward which side of the internal-external debate these individuals are likely to lean. Without such information, it is difficult to predict which decision makers will take the stability of international relations for granted and retreat from international affairs to deal with domestic ones, which will stand their ground and take bold initiatives, and which will engage in behavior that could cause their states to implode.

Understanding Leadership

The leaders who dominated the world stage at the beginning of the Cold War—Stalin, Churchill, De Gaulle, and Truman—often seem upon reflection to have been larger than life. Today, with the collapse of the Soviet Union and the expansion of market democracies, it is hard to imagine such leaders coming to power with the same kind of authority. In fact, much of contemporary international relations theory would contend that with the end of the Cold War we have merely exchanged one set of constraints for another. Leaders are said to be as limited now as they were when superpower rivalry defined their actions. The key systematic constraints no longer center on security issues but on economic and environmental ones.

Yet, even in today's multipolar world, leadership still matters. Leaders are called on to interpret and frame what is happening in the international arena for their constituencies and governments. In addition, more leaders are becoming involved in the regional and international regimes defining the rules and norms that will guide the international system into the twenty-first century. Thus, for example, Clinton must convince a skeptical public and a recalcitrant Congress that it is in their best interests to free up funds for the United Nations and the International Monetary Fund's bailout of Asia, as well as try to strike a bargain with congressional Democrats that will grant him fast-track authority.

Rather than proceed with the debate over whether or not leaders matter, it is essential to continue the study of how leaders work to balance what they see as the important international factors impinging on their countries with what they believe are their domestic imperatives. The lesson to be learned so far is that international constraints only have policy implications when they are perceived as such by the leaders whose positions count in dealing with a particular problem. Whether and how such leaders judge themselves constrained depends on the nature of the domestic challenges to their leadership, how the leaders are organized, and what they are like as people. To chart the shape of any future world, we need to be able to demarcate which leaders and leadership groups will become more caught up in the flow of events, and thus perceive external forces as limiting their parameters for action, and which will instead challenge the international constraints they see in their path.

JANE S. JAQUETTE

Women in Power:
From Tokenism to Critical Mass

Never before have so many women held so much power. The growing participation and representation of woman in politics is one of the most remarkable developments of the late twentieth century. For the first time, women in all countries and social classes are becoming politically active, achieving dramatic gains in the number and kind of offices they hold. Why is political power, off limits for so long, suddenly becoming accessible to women! And what are the implications of this trend for domestic and foreign policy?

Women have been gaining the right to vote and run for office since New Zealand became the first country to authorize women's suffrage in 1893. By 1920, the year the United States amended the Constitution to allow women to vote, 10 countries had already granted women the franchise. Yet many European countries did not allow women to vote until after World War II, including France, Greece, Italy, and Switzerland. In Latin America, Ecuador was the first to recognize women's political rights, in 1929; but women could not vote in Mexico until 1953. In Asia, women voted first in Mongolia, in 1923; then, with the U.S. occupation after 1945, women secured the right to vote in Japan and South Korea. The former European colonies in Africa and Asia enfranchised women when they gained independence, from the late 1940s into the 1970s.

Historically, women began to demand the right to vote by claiming their equality: If all men are created equal, why not women? The American and British suffrage movements inspired "women's emancipation" efforts among educated female (and sometimes male) élites worldwide, and most

contemporary feminist movements trace their roots to these stirrings at the turn of the century. The nineteenth-century European movements had a strong influence on the thinking of Friedrich Engels, who made gender equality a central tenet of socialist doctrine. A similar movement among the Russian intelligentsia ensured that the equality of women in political and economic life would be an important goal of the Soviet state—and subsequently of its Central and Eastern European satellites.

But if the logic existed to support women's claims to political equality, the facts on the ground did not. As educated women mobilized to demand the right to vote, men in all countries largely resisted, with the result that most of the world's women gained this basic right of citizenship only in the last 50 years. Before women could vote, they organized to influence legislation, from the marriage and property rights acts of the mid-nineteenth century to the early twentieth century wave of Progressive legislation in the United States and Western Europe's generous maternal and protective labor laws.

However, the vote itself did not bring women into politics. On the contrary, some countries gave women the right to vote but not to run for office. In virtually every nation, women who tried to enter politics were subject to popular ridicule. Political parties routinely excluded women from decision-making positions, resisted nominating them as candidates, and denied their female candidates adequate campaign support.

Cultural factors partially explain the varying degrees of women's representation from region to region and country to country. Predictably, women in the Nordic and northern European

From *Foreign Policy*, no. 108 (fall 1997): 23–37.

countries, with long traditions of gender equality, have been the most successful in breaking through traditional resistance and increasing their representation. In contrast, those in Arab countries, with curbs against women in public life and contemporary pressures to abandon secular laws for religious rules, have consistently registered the lowest levels of female participation (and the lowest levels of democratization).

But "culture" does not fully explain why women in the United States and Great Britain, which rank high on various measures of gender equality, accounted for less than 7 percent of all parliamentarians as late as 1987. Nor have women been excluded from politics in all Islamic nations. The legislatures of Syria and Indonesia, while decidedly undemocratic, are composed of 10 to 12 percent women. Former prime ministers Benazir Bhutto of Pakistan and Khaleda Zia of Bangladesh have wielded major power in Muslim societies.

Historically, a country's level of development has not been a reliable indicator of women's representation. Of the 32 most developed countries that reported electoral data in 1975, 19 had fewer than 10 percent female legislators and 11 had fewer than 5 percent. In France, Greece, and Japan—all developed, industrialized countries—female members accounted for 2 percent or less of their legislatures.

Although more women than ever are working for wages, even an increase in female participation in the work force does not necessarily translate into greater political clout for women. In recent years, for example, much of the growth in participation has been in low-wage labor. And although women's managerial participation has increased dramatically in many countries, from New Zealand to Peru, women are still rarely found at the highest levels of corporate management and ownership. Their underrepresentation in top management limits the number of private sector women invited to enter government as high-level appointees; women's lower salaries, in turn, restrict an important source of financial support for female candidates.

One can, however, discern significant worldwide increases in female representation beginning in 1975, the year in which the United Nations held its first international women's conference. From 1975 to 1995, the number of women legislators doubled in the developed West; the global average rose from 7.4 percent to nearly 11 percent.

Between 1987 and 1995 in particular, women's representation registered a dramatic increase in the developed countries, Africa, and Latin America. Of the 32 women who have served as presidents or prime ministers during the twentieth century, 24 were in power in the 1990s. In the United States, women now make up 11.2 percent of Congress, about one-third the proportion in Nordic countries, but substantially higher than the 5 percent in

Percent of Women in National Legislatures, by region, 1975–97

	1975	1987	1997*
Arab States	3.5	2.8	3.3
Asia	8.4	9.7	13.4
(Asia excluding China, Mongolia, N. Korea, Vietnam)†	(3.8)	(6.2)	(6.3)
Central and Eastern Europe and Former Soviet Union	23.3	23.1	11.5
Developed countries (excluding East Asia)	5.1	9.6	14.7
Latin America and the Caribbean	6.0	6.9	10.5
Nordic Countries	16.1	28.8	36.4

*1997 statistics for lower houses and single house systems. (Mongolia excluded.)

†women's representation under party control

Sources: *Democracy Still in the Making: A World Comparative Study* (Geneva: Inter-Parliamentary Union, 1997) and *The World's Women, 1970–1990: Trends and Statistics* (New York: United Nations, 1991).

1987. And although only 23 women won seats in the Diet in Japan's 1996 elections, an unprecedented 153 women ran for office. In 1997, the Inter-Parliamentary Union reported only nine countries with no women in their legislatures. From 1987 to 1995, the number of countries without any women ministers dropped from 93 to 47, and 10 countries reported that women held more than 20 percent of all ministerial-level positions, although generally in "female" portfolios like health, education, and environment rather than the "power ministries" like finance and defense.

The only exception to the global acceleration in women's representation during the past decade is in the New Independent States of the former Soviet Union and the former members of the Eastern bloc. Here, representation has dropped from earlier highs under communist rule of 25 to 35 percent women (although they exercised little real power) to around 8 to 15 percent today, and numbers are lower in the largely Muslim states of Central Asia. Where women's representation is still under Communist Party control, as in China, North Korea, and Vietnam, women still account for about 20 percent of the national legislators.

The Globalization of the Women's Movement

Why the surge in women officeholders in the last 10 years?

Three interconnected reasons seem to stand out: First, the rise of women's movements worldwide has heightened women's awareness of their political potential and developed new issues for which women are ready to mobilize. Second, a new willingness by political parties and states to ease the constraints on women's access to politics, from increasing their recruitment pools to modifying electoral systems and adopting quotas. And third, as social issues supplant security concerns in the post–Cold War political environment, opportunities have opened for new styles of leadership and have reordered political priorities.

The recent wave of female mobilization is a response to a series of political and economic crises—and opportunities—over the last two decades. On the political front, women's groups like the Madres de la Plaza de Mayo (Argentine mothers who demonstrated on behalf of their "disappeared" husbands and children) helped to inspire the defense of human rights in Latin America and beyond. Women were also recognized as valued participants in the opposition to authoritarian rule in the former Soviet bloc, where they took up the cause of human rights when their husbands and sons were arrested—dissident Andrei Sakharov's wife, Yelena Bonner, is just one example. In Africa and Asia, women are increasingly regarded as important opposition figures. In South Africa, for example, women were among prominent anti-apartheid leaders and have helped to lead the new government-sponsored effort to develop a women's charter for the post-apartheid period. In Iran, women have played an important role in defining electoral outcomes, despite the conventional wisdom that they are powerless.

On the economic front, the widespread adoption of market-oriented reforms, often accompanied by austerity programs, has had a severe impact on many women, who in turn have organized against price rises and the loss of health care and other public services. Women created communal kitchens in Chile and Peru to help feed their communities. Other small-scale, self-help programs like the Grameen Bank in Bangladesh and the Self-Employed Women's Association in India were developed to meet women's needs for credit. The war in Bosnia put an international spotlight on rape as a weapon of war and led to the demand that "women's rights" be considered "human rights" rather than some different or lesser category of concern.

These efforts were reinforced by international connections, many of which were created by the U.N. Decade for Women (1976–85). Three times during the decade (in 1975, 1980, and 1985) and again in 1995, the United Nations convened official delegations from member countries to report on the status of women and to commit governments to remedy women's lack of access to political, economic, and educational resources. Not only women's issues were geared to the U.N. agenda, which in the 1970s focused on the creation of a "new international economic order" and a more equitable sharing of resources between North and South. By the mid-1980s, however, attention had shifted from integrating women into world development efforts to enhancing roles for women in the promotion of market economics and democracy. The turn toward democracy made it easier for women to seek explicitly political goals, and the footdragging by the U.N. and its member countries on implementing their international pledges helped to stimulate women's interest in increasing their political power.

Breaking the Political Glass Ceiling

Since some of the public policies holding women back from greater political power—particularly women's access to education—have been easing rapidly, attention has turned to other barriers. Chief among them have been the constraints on the pool of women available to run for office. Although women constitute a growing proportion of the rank and file in political parties, unions, and civil services, they still account for only a small proportion of the higher echelons that provide a springboard to higher political office.

Although women participate more actively in local government than they do at the national level, many more men make the jump from local to national leadership. One problem has been a lack of campaign funds. In the United States, women began to address that obstacle in the 1980s through innovative fund-raising strategies. In other countries, women have organized voting blocs to support female candidates. Yet there is only one women's political party, in Iceland, that has succeeded over time in electing women to office. By the mid-1990s, the European-based Inter-Parliamentary Union was holding meetings twice a year for female parliamentarians aimed at improving their electoral skills as well as their abilities to perform more effectively in office. In another innovative effort, a group called Women of Russia organized to stem the decline in women's repre-

did these conferences encourage a flurry of local and national organizing, but they produced parallel meetings of nongovernmental organizations (NGOs), including the nearly 30,000 women who participated in the NGO conference in Beijing in 1995.

The Decade for Women originally meant that

sentation under the new democratic electoral rules. Women of Russia surprised everyone by gathering over 100,000 signatures and winning 8 percent of the vote in the 1993 Duma elections, but in the 1995 elections they failed to maintain the minimum level of support necessary under Russian electoral rules. As a result of Women in Russia's initial success, however, other Russian parties are nominating more women.

Research has shown that different kinds of voting systems can dramatically affect women's chances of election. The widely accepted explanation for the relatively low numbers of female legislators in the United States and Britain is their "single-member district" electoral systems. When each district elects only one candidate, minority votes are lost. Significantly more women are elected in countries with electoral systems based on proportional representation (in which candidates are elected from party lists according to the percentage of total votes the party receives) or on at-large districts ("multi-member constituencies"). Several countries have experimented with different electoral systems, including mixed single-member and multi-member district systems, to improve the participation of underrepresented groups, particularly women.

The surest way to achieve an increased number of women in national legislatures is to adopt a quota system that requires a certain percentage of women to be nominated or elected. Although the issue of quotas is scarcely open to debate in the United States—where Lani Guinier's nomination for U.S. attorney general in 1993 was torpedoed by detractors' interpretations of essays she had written in support of "group" representation—many political parties (especially on the Left) and national legislatures around the world are experimenting with gender quotas. Quotas account for the high levels of female representation in the Nordic countries and for the recent doubling (to 18 percent) of the number of women in the House of Commons in Britain when the Labour Party swept the election. A quota law in Argentina increased the women in its house of representatives from 4 percent in 1991 to over 16 percent in 1993

and 28 percent in 1995. In Brazil, when quotas were used in the 1997 congressional elections, the number of women legislators increased by nearly 40 percent since the last elections.

Quotas are used in Taiwan, by some of the political parties in Chile, and are under active discussion in Costa Rica, Ecuador, Paraguay, South Korea, and several other countries. The Indian constitution now mandates that one-third of the seats in local government bodies be "reserved" for women, and Pakistan is debating a similar measure. In Mexico, the Institutional Revolutionary Party (PRI) and its leftist opposition have adopted quotas, while the right-of-center party accepts the goal but maintains that it can promote women as effectively without them. Japan has adopted measures to ensure that more women are appointed to ministerial posts, and Bangladesh, among other countries, is experimenting with quotas for top civil service jobs.

It is obvious that quotas increase the number of women officeholders, but why are they being adopted now? Even where quotas are not seen to violate fundamental notions of democracy, as they appear to be in the United States, there are powerful arguments against them. Some insist that they will ghettoize women legislators and their issues. Others object that quotas lead to "proxy" representation, where women legislators run as "fronts" for their husbands or other male interests. In India, for example, there are many anecdotal cases of this phenomenon, and in Argentina there are complaints that many of the women nominated by the majority Peronist Party (which pushed through the quota law) have been chosen because of their unquestioning loyalty to President Carlos Saúl Menem rather than because of their qualifications as candidates—as if only women could be considered party hacks.

Despite the controversy quotas raise, they have become popular not only because women have organized to push for them, but—importantly—because more men have become convinced that quotas serve useful political goals in a more democratic environment. A sea change in attitudes about women in public office is occurring at a time when the number of countries under some form of democratic governance is expanding rapidly, giving new salience to the question of whether national legislatures are truly representative of pluralistic societies. Adequate representation of all groups could strengthen the consolidation of democracies that are open and responsive—and thus make them more durable.

What Do Women Want?

The post–Cold War shift in national priorities from defense and security concerns to social and environmental issues also plays to women's strong suits. So do the negative impacts of economic globalization and structural adjustment policies, which have put the need for effective social safety nets high on domestic agendas. Many observers argue that the rejection of "unbridled capitalism" and the desire to retain social welfare policies explain the victories of the Labour Party in Britain, the socialists in France, and the electoral loss of the PRI in Mexico last July [1997]. Rightly or wrongly, many voters also associate market reforms with a rise in corruption. Despite accusations of corruption against leaders such as Pakistan's Bhutto and Tansu Ciller in Turkey, women's perceived "purity" and their status as outsiders, once considered political weaknesses, are now seen as strengths. In the last 10 years, it is not so much the case that women have come to politics; rather, politics has come to women.

If the trend continues, quotas will soon produce a quantum leap in women's political power. For the first time, women will form a "critical mass" of legislators in many countries, able to set new agendas and perhaps create new styles of leadership. How will women use their growing political influence?

One way to predict the direction of change is to look at how the political attitudes of women differ from those of men. Surveys show that one of the most persistent gender differences regards attitudes toward peace and war: Women are more pacifistic than men, less likely to favor defense spending, or to support aggressive policies abroad.

Recent interviews of women heads of state show that most believe that they are more committed to peace than their male counterparts. Historically and today, women and women leaders are more interested in the so-called "soft" issues, including the environment and social welfare. On some measures, women are more conservative than men: They are less likely to vote for the parties on the Left, and rather than pursue their own self-interests, they more often mobilize for defensive reasons—namely to protect the interests of the family. As a result, these tendencies will probably place more focus on policies to support the family and to strengthen local communities.

But women are far from conservative in one important sense: Women are more likely than men to support state regulation of business to protect the consumer and the environment and to assure that the needs of society's weakest members are addressed. Because women are often more skeptical than men about the effectiveness of market reforms, the election of more women may signal a softening of some of reform's harsher aspects. The market's continued dominance in global politics will reinforce women's efforts to improve their access to the resources that count, from education and credit to the ownership of land and housing.

Women who find themselves experiencing real power for the first time may decide to try out blanket initiatives in areas that they believe male leaders have traditionally neglected: declarations banning war and legislation on children's rights and social or political morality.

However, radical change is unlikely. Predictions that women will act as a bloc have never been borne out in the past. Like their male counterparts, female officeholders come from all parts of the ideological spectrum and depend on the support of diverse and often divided constituencies. Women leaders are not necessarily pacifists or environmentally oriented. While former prime minister Gro Harlem Brundtland of Norway or Ireland's president Mary Robinson may support the "soft" issues, Indira Gandhi or Margaret Thatcher is capable of using force to achieve her ends.

Further, few of the initiatives on those social issues mobilizing women today directly confront male power. Global support for efforts to stem violence against women is an important exception. Antidiscrimination legislation has been developed at the international level through the U.N. Convention on the Elimination of All Forms of Discrimination Against Women—which has been ratified by 160 countries, but not the United States. The implementation of the instrument by signatories, however, lags far behind. And women leaders themselves disagree on many of the issues affecting women most, from reproductive rights and family law to genital mutilation.

Today, women are recruited aggressively into politics not to right past inequities or to recognize their equal citizenship—but to bring a different, explicitly female perspective to the political arena and to appeal to the women's vote. Whether the rationale for increasing female representation is equality or difference, women will have an unprecedented opportunity to put their stamp on politics and to increase the range of alternatives available to policymakers across the globe.

FOREIGN POLICY

Lori's War

Meet Lori Wallach, Leader of the Anti-WTO Protests in Seattle. Find Out Who She Is, How She Works, and What She Plans to Do Next

Not many people have heard of Lori Wallach. But millions of people around the world saw the results of her work in organizing massive protests against the meeting of the World Trade Organization (WTO) last November in Seattle. In 1997, many people were similarly ignorant about the Multilateral Agreement on Investment—a set of rules about international investment then being negotiated by representatives of the world's largest economies in the Organisation for Economic Co-operation and Development. But after Wallach and her collaborators started their campaign against the treaty, many government ministers came to wish that they had never heard of it either.

These are just two of the battles that the 36-year-old Wallach has won in the war she has been waging for more than a decade against what she

From *Foreign Policy*, no. 118 (spring 2000): 28–55.

disdainfully calls "the system of corporate-managed trade." While most of her Harvard Law classmates were making the big money at white-shoe investment banks and law firms, Wallach started her career working with Public Citizen, the public interest group founded by consumer advocate Ralph Nader. While lobbying the U.S. Congress on consumer protection issues, she realized that many of her legislative causes conflicted with the international commitments that the United States had undertaken as a member of the General Agreement on Tariffs and Trade, the international body then in charge of setting and enforcing the rules governing trade among nations. This realization led her to focus on reforming trade's rules and institutions and, eventually, to become the director of Public Citizen's Global Trade Watch.

Wallach is widely regarded as an intelligent, well-informed, and media-savvy political organizer. She is also highly controversial. One senior WTO official told *Foreign Policy* that dealing with her is nearly impossible because "her criticisms and attacks on the WTO constitute a subtle blend of legitimate concerns, deliberate or partly deliberate misinformation, and populist rhetoric." Her supporters instead view her as an indispensable leader with a unique vision.

Wallach's achievements illustrate the dilemmas and opportunities created by globalization. While she crusades against the current system of international trade and investment, the sharp drops in the costs of communication and transportation produced by technology and economic liberalization have dramatically increased her influence and effectiveness. Her informal, decentralized, and non-hierarchical network of committed activists has proven more nimble and effective than the bureaucratic, centralized, and unwieldy institutions that she opposes. Indeed, even as globalization has endowed some nations and organizations with unprecedented power, it has also allowed the emergence of leaders like Lori Wallach, who do more than just talk about bending the will of these powerful entities—they succeed in forcing them to change their ways. Recently, *Foreign Policy*'s editor, Moisés Naím, sat down with Wallach to have the first of what we hope will be many dialogues with people you may not know but should. What follows is an edited and abbreviated version of their conversation, which took place on January 24, 2000.

The Making of a Global Activist

Moisés Naím: Tell us about some things that are not in your curriculum vitae—things that are not well known about you, that can help us understand who you are.

Lori Wallach: Well, I guess one thing that's relevant when I think about how I got here is that I grew up in a small town in northern Wisconsin, as one of the only Jewish kids for about two hours in any direction. Fighting for one's principles became a necessity the moment we went to school and started getting picked on for being Jewish. My father was in small business, and my grandfather came here fleeing the Nazis and really sort of started over from scratch.

I think my upbringing gave me a combination of what Ralph Nader calls an early learned

scrappiness from just defending myself, and the notion of being able to accomplish almost anything you really feel is worth fighting for. I remember, at one point, coming home after a fight at school, and my mom said, kick your enemies and pick your friends; no one should feel neutral about you. Your friends should love you, and your enemies should think you're a major pain.

*   *   *

MN: What are the high points in your career? Can you point to three moments when you savored victory and felt good about what you were doing?

LW: Well, one great moment, certainly, was the failure of U.S. fast-track legislation in Congress in November 1997, when ultimately we achieved what we had not been able to achieve in the case of the North American Free Trade Agreement (NAFTA). Congressional district by congressional district, we had built permanent, educated movements of people who were not willing to take any more NAFTA expansion, any more of fast track.

And as important as winning that battle was realizing that the better part of a decade of grass-roots organizing—very tedious, painstaking, district by district, small town by small town, educating rooms of people, 50 at a time—had actually come to critical mass.

Another very important time was when we found out that the Organization for Economic Co-operation and Development (OECD) had pulled the plug on the Multilateral Agreement on Investment (MAI), a deal that was negotiated largely in secret, and was 90 percent done, when we heisted it out of the OECD's copy rooms, scanned it into our Web site, and made sure the whole world knew it existed.

The third great moment was in Seattle. The time of all times was to see so many Americans educated enough to take time off and come to Seattle on their own dollar, with all of the chaos and confusion of trying to find a place to stay, simply to have their own word. It wasn't the actual announcement that the trade round was stalled, but rather to see that years and years of work had resulted in 40,000 educated people dropping everything to say, "No more of the same."

MN: What about low points?

LW: Certainly one of the key down periods was the year and a half I spent in the very early '90s, going to Geneva to meet with officials on the General Agreement on Tariffs and Trade (GATT). At that point, I was not much of an activist or organizer, but much more a policy wonk and trade lawyer with my reams of paper explaining how to change the draft text of the technical barriers agreement, to add due process into the dispute resolution agreement, and any number of other, if you will, reformist proposals that were promptly sent by paper airplane out the door right after me. There was no openness, and the level of arrogance was amazing. As disheartening as it was, it was also a motivating factor for an enormous amount of political organizing.

*   *   *

MN: Why can you now claim the influence to stop a new round of world trade talks when your previous trips to Geneva to persuade the GATT staff to make minor reforms were fruitless? What has empowered you?

LW: Two things. First, I would say 70 percent of it is the actual track record of NAFTA and the World Trade Organization (WTO). Second, the years and years of work, to make ourselves politically organized and relevant.

MN: What about the Internet?

LW: It's a tool like anything else. The real organizing for the "No New Round Turnaround" campaign culminating in Seattle was face to face. It's people I've been meeting with three to four times a year, from around the world, since 1992.

MN: So you think you could have achieved almost the same outcome without the Internet?

LW: Well, the Internet certainly made it a lot easier, and faster. For instance, when we were working on the Uruguay Round in 1992, we finally liberated a copy of the text. It was on Christmas Eve; I got someone to take it out of the copier room at the GATT headquarters, put it on KLM. They flew it to Dulles International Airport, outside of Washington; I drove to Dulles, I drove back to Capitol Hill. I sent it to the Kinko's copy shop on Pennsylvania Avenue, they made me 30 copies, I ran it to Federal Express—because it was Christmas Eve—and I sent it to my coalition partner in Japan, who also was responsible for getting it to Thailand, just as the guy in Malaysia was supposed to get it to Indonesia, and the person in France should have gotten it to Spain and Portugal, etc., all by mail. So there was this whole *meshugas* of trying to mechanically make copies of an 800-page text and mail it, at $50 a pop. It took a week and a half before anyone had it in their hands, by the time all the running around and Christmas happened.

MN: Contrast that with the experience with the OECD's Multilateral Agreement on Investment.

LW: The text came in a brown paper bag. I will not say anything more detailed about how we got it, and we scanned it onto the Internet.

MN: Came to whom?

LW: Public Citizen. It was delivered by a stork. It was not supposed to be liberated; it was secret, had been secret for three years. We scanned it into a computer, cleaned up the text, and had it turned around and posted on the World Wide Web, with, by the way, our analysis, because while other people were scrubbing the text, I was explaining what it meant—and we had the whole thing out in about three days, and the whole world got it.

Rewriting Globalization's Rules

MN: Let's move on to your worldview. If all of your efforts, and those of your colleagues, were successful, how would the world be different from the way it is now?

LW: There would be a global regime of rules that more than anything create the political space for the kinds of value decisions that mechanisms like the WTO now make, at a level where people living with the results can hold the decision makers accountable. Right now, there are decisions, value-subjective decisions, being shifted into totally unaccountable, international realms where, if the decision is wrong, there's no way to fix it. If the decision makers are self-interested, and as a result themselves need to be changed, there's no way to change them.

MN: Who should make the rules about international trade?

LW: Those kind of rules should be made at a level where people who are going to live with the results can hold decision makers accountable. So, for instance, I believe, as do many of my colleagues, that India can have a rule that says no patenting of critical basic medicines. As long as they don't give intellectual property protection to domestic producers of those goods, they should be able to treat imported goods the same way. It's their decision.

MN: Mike Moore, the head of the World Trade Organization, says that he detects "a potentially dangerous rise" in isolationist nationalism. That, for example, there is the need to have some homogeneity in the world trading system. He says: "The setback faced by the WTO has far-reaching consequences, which go beyond the multilateral trading system and should be a concern to all international organizations."

LW: Well, but to challenge your basic principle, the diversity that you see as a lack of homogeneity, and thus somehow identify with nationalism—we see that diversity as a result of democracy, as a blessing. The United States is nuts about cancer. So our food safety regulations have this benchmark of zero risk of cancer. Europe, on the other hand, for who knows what historical reasons, worries about genetic birth defects.

MN: What are the implications of this difference for international trade?

LW: The United States allows additives and colors that are banned in Europe. They have no risk of cancer, but they could give you a three-headed child. In Europe, they are drinking Diet Coke that has a bunch of stuff that will give you, theo-

LORI WALLACH'S GLOBAL IMPACT

The last major pieces of trade legislation approved by the U.S. Congress were the North American Free Trade Agreement in 1993, creating a trade and investment region among Canada, the United States, and Mexico, and the General Agreement on Tariffs and Trade Uruguay Round in 1994, which created the World Trade Organization (WTO). Wallach and her global coalition opposed these initiatives and were defeated. Since then, however, she has played a leading role in three campaigns that achieved major victories.

"Fast-track" trade authority was finally shelved in November 1997, after almost four years of White House dithering over whether to propose the legislation or not. "Fast track" is the legislative legerdemain under which Congress allows the president to negotiate trade agreements that are then voted on without amendments. Without it, the White House has no guarantee that lawmakers will not seek to change the terms of trade agreements reached after lengthy trade talks.

Negotiations were taking place among the nations belonging to the Organisation for Economic Co-operation and Development (OECD) on the **Multilateral Agreement on Investment**, which proponents called the new world constitution on the rights and rules of investment. Opponents obtained a copy of the draft agreement and placed it on the World Wide Web, launching a public campaign that led, in some countries, to parliamentary hearings and initiatives that eroded governmental support for the agreement. Shortly afterwards, the OECD countries failed to reach an accord and decided to table the issue. Corporate and political leaders still insist on the need to establish rules to protect investments, but there is no sign that negotiations will be relaunched.

The WTO planned to launch the so-called **Millenium Round** of trade talks that would encompass issues including agriculture and trade in services during a four-day meeting (November 29–December 3, 1999) held in Seattle. But public protests, including marches and street riots, delayed the opening ceremonies and poisoned the atmosphere. The talks broke down. Many see the Seattle events as a symbol of the beginning of a backlash against free trade and globalization in general. In February 2000, the WTO announced that it had decided to launch a new round of trade negotiations scheduled to begin this spring.

—FP

retically, according to the U.S. rules, cancer, but they don't care as much. It's their decision, it's their life. And similarly, if India believes, at its stage of development, that it is more important—as, by the way, the United States did in heisting European technology when we were a developing country—to take care of the health of its people, and thus have access to pharmaceuticals, as a principle more important than protecting the intellectual property rights of foreign pharmaceutical companies through compulsory licensing, then it should have the right to do so. That's a democratic decision in which governments, which can be elected and replaced by the people who will live with the results, are the ones setting priorities aimed at those people's needs.

MN: You're referring to the idea of democratic deficits in multilateral organizations, namely, that these organizations are run in ways that you say lack democracy, transparency, accountability, and so on. Some people argue that nongovernmental organizations (NGOs) like yours also have a democratic deficit—that you also lack democracy, transparency, and accountability. Who elected you to represent the people in Seattle, and why are you more influential than the elected officials, or, for that matter, the appointed officials, from elected governments?

LW: Who elected Mr. Moore? Who elected Charlene Barshefsky? Who elected any of them?

*　　*　　*

MN: * * * Describe the alternative system that you would propose.

LW: Well, a main feature of it is to prune back the WTO. There need to be international rules, no doubt—again, we're not calling for autarky, but to have rules about food safety protection, to have rules on how to balance the need of people to have access to medicine with the interests of the pharmaceutical industry. That is not the kind of decision you want made at an institution that was designed for the purpose of expanding trade, and whose staff has an agenda that does

not include the array of interests and issues that are implicated, much less the expertise.

So for instance, if I could redesign it overnight, it would be on many levels. Some of it would be domestic changes, mind you. But in terms of international institutions, I would call for the pruning back of much of what happened in the Uruguay Round.

I would keep the notion of national treatment, the notion of competition between countries without discrimination based on where something is made, but I would eliminate all these subjective decisions that have been patched onto the trade system.

MN: Such as?

LW: I would take intellectual property rules and revert them to the World Intellectual Property Organization, for instance. And I wouldn't impose a worldwide 20-year monopoly on patents on every single country, regardless of level of development or other domestic interests and values. I would maintain a global regime of trading, because I would have the tariff and quota rules, which need to be tweaked.

And I would have international rules in other fora that would be given treatment equal to those commercial rules of the WTO. Alternatively, I would have some system of adjudicating between those sets of rules made by different multilateral bodies.

*　　*　　*

MN: So essentially your answer is that the WTO needs to be shrunk—depowered, you called it— with some of its powers pruned, and some of its powers transferred to organizations like the ILO [International Labor Organization]. Are you therefore in favor of creating a global organization to deal with environmental issues?

LW: I think that there are merits to that.

MN: If Lori Wallach had her way, would she like the United States to pull out of the WTO?

LW: Well, I speak for a whole coalition of people, where we're talking about that very question for all of their countries, not just the United States . . . and I think that half of the people think the

WTO is not fixable. From my perspective, it has given every indication that it is an institution that will break itself by its inability to bend.

I hope that's not how it is, but that's how it has looked to me. Either it is going to be something that everyone gets out of—and half of the international activists are for that right now—or it's going to have to be transformed. And where the international activists, the network that brought you Seattle, is going, on consensus, is to say all right, Seattle was the wake-up call of all time.

For 10 years, they should have been paying attention and they didn't. But okay, Seattle really woke them up. Between now and the next meeting of the world's trade ministers, there is a list of things the WTO must do—not talk about, like they did for five years about transparency, and nothing happened. Things that must be accomplished, that are concrete changes, in the World Trade Organization, both in its substantive rules and its own procedures.

And if those changes aren't made at the end of those 18 months or so before the next ministerial, then, not only should the United States get out, but, in fact, all of the country-based campaigns, and there are 30 of them at least, will launch campaigns either to get their countries out or to withdraw their funding. Because at that point, if they don't change, the institution will have been thoroughly proved to be unredeemable.

Making Trade Work

*   *   *

MN: Let's talk also about NAFTA. You have been very critical of NAFTA, and you have said that the track record of NAFTA now has helped you persuade people to support you. What do you say to people who tell you that NAFTA has been a success, both for Mexico and for the United States, that lost employment to NAFTA in the United States is minimal, compared with the impact of technology, for example.

LW: Well, I don't think anyone argues that anymore. I mean, it's hard to do that with a straight face. Even the greatest boosters of NAFTA, unless they are super-NAFTA ideologues, have basically just given up on trying to say it was a success. The Clinton administration documents call it a wash that's been overdramatized and didn't really do much of anything either in creating or destroying jobs. I think that's an understatement of its damage. It's pretty accurate about its benefits. The bottom-line answer is this: Show me the data. In 1996, when we filed a Freedom of Information Act (FOIA) request for data by the Commerce Department documenting job creation, it was the most amusing government document I have ever gotten under FOIA. Literally, there are about 800 jobs that you could see were created.

MN: The framing of NAFTA as a job issue was probably wrong, and the evaluation of NAFTA mostly in terms of job creation or job losses is also wrong. NAFTA is about the economic integration of three countries.

LW: Right. The question, though, is under what rules and with what incentives and outcomes? And although you can't show job creation in the United States under NAFTA, what you can show is that despite an enormous, long economic recovery, you only now have real wages starting to grow at all. And they're still below the levels of 1972. The real effect jobwise of NAFTA is on wages. It's on the quality of jobs, more than the number of jobs. So typically, when someone in the Clinton administration tries to say, "All right—NAFTA, we oversold it. But you know something? Even if NAFTA's had some downsides, the overall economy as we've managed it has created so many jobs, how upset can you be?" And I say, excuse me, the Labor Department says the top areas of job creation are janitorial, waiters and waitresses, retail clerks and cashiers. What kind of jobs are those that we are creating?

When you talk about the recovery in Mexico, in macroeconomic terms there is growth, there are increased exports. But in terms of what the real measure of an economy is, which is the standard of living of the majority of the people there, actually Mexico has gotten it the worst under NAFTA, by far.

MN: You have also opposed the initiative by the United States to give trade preferences to Africa. You called it NAFTA with Africa. Why is it so bad to help African economies export more to the United States?

LW: The issue is not so much market access to the United States. The issue is Section Four of that legislation, which was a set of conditionalities. African countries only got favorable access to the United States market if they were certified by the U.S. president each year as meeting a set of conditions. And those conditions read like the investment and intellectual property chapters of NAFTA. African countries had to, for instance, set up monopoly-style intellectual property rules. There were a variety of different rules that had to do with what they could do with agriculture. They were specifically required to make domestic budget cuts in the name of stimulating macroeconomic growth, etc.

MN: Let's go back to the effects of the trading system. The world is enjoying a huge surge in trade. In the year 2000, global trade is likely to grow beyond 7 percent. Those who believe that trade boosts growth, and that growth creates jobs, regardless of other conditions, see this as a positive trend. You, instead, do not see a boost in trade as something to celebrate. So is achieving 7 percent global growth something to be very worried about?

LW: The issue is not so much the rate of growth, or the volume of trade. The question is, what is going on in real measures of well-being? So, while the volume, the flow of goods, may be up, and in some countries gross national product may be up, those macroeconomic indicators don't represent what's happening for the day-to-day standard of living for an enormous number of people in the world. That gets to one of the biggest critiques of the WTO in its first five years, which is that while the overall global flow of trade continues to grow, the share of trade

flows held by developing countries has declined steadily. Similarly, over that five-year period, while the macroeconomic indicators have often looked good, real wages in many countries have declined, and wage inequality has increased both within and between countries. And you also have to reckon with a variety of social and environmental damage that is related to trade—everything from the loss of indigenous knowledge and culture to commodification of, for instance, plants for medical usage and the patenting of seeds.

*   *   *

Getting to No

MN: Let's talk about Seattle. There are people who say that you or your coalition allies exaggerate the influence you had in derailing the Seattle ministerial meeting. That Seattle was, in fact, dead from the beginning because of a lack of preparation, due to the absence of a WTO director general for so long. That the agenda covered too many issues. That developing countries, for example, were still trying to implement some of the provisions coming out of the last round. That Seattle was the wrong place to hold the WTO ministerial. That it was a mistake to have it in the United States given the election-year political climate . . .

LW: And particularly, there was the issue that God had heartburn that day. I mean, these are ridiculous, *post hoc*, revisionist spins of people who lost. All of those "facts" are contributing factors. So let's say there's a 30 percent karma factor that takes into account all of that stuff. I mean, the jinx of not being able to get a director general, or the choice of Seattle—the day Seattle was picked, the same people who are now saying that holding it in Seattle was really stupid were saying Seattle, what a great idea! Home of the new economy, a big export engine, a coastal city attached to the Pacific Rim. The fact is that more important than anything that happened in Seattle was a yearlong campaign conducted by 30 multisectoral coalitions like the one we have in the United States. And it was the No New Round Turnaround campaign.

MN: You have put together a very odd coalition of labor, Greens, environmentalists, Gray Panthers, progressives . . .

LW: Church groups, Tibetan monks, small businesses . . .

MN: What holds that coalition together?

LW: I would say two things. One, philosophically, the notion that the democracy deficit in the global economy is neither necessary nor acceptable. The second is that they're all directly damaged by the actual outcomes of the status quo, in different ways. And so you have family farmers, for instance, who've seen a huge increase in the volume of exports of U.S. agricultural commodities, in the exact same decade that farm income has crashed.

MN: How many countries are members of this coalition?

LW: Well, there are country-based campaigns, and there are basically 30 of them, 25 of which are really quite operational.

MN: You had a year of preparation or more?

LW: Yeah, it wasn't the week on the ground, it was the work that happened beforehand. Perhaps there was an enzymatic effect, where all of the work to that point was cooked, ultimately, by some reaction that was sparked by what was going on on the ground. But that was just the final stop. As soon as the European Union and Japan announced their agreement in 1999 to push for a millennium round, the NGOs around the world that had been working together since the Uruguay Round negotiations, and that certainly had just come out of the campaign against the Multilateral Agreement on Investment, basically said, "Listen, we sort of thought maybe the MAI would send the message that we are not going down that road anymore." But it's like that shell game in a carnival. With the MAI, we smashed the shell that was the OECD. So they just took the pea and put it in another shell. And now it's in the WTO shell, and we're going to just have to smash that one.

MN: Let's go back to how you organize a rally like this. Walk us through the mechanics, the actual logistics, of organizing Seattle.

LW: Well, the logistics of it are at two levels. To do the yearlong campaign on No New Round Turnaround involved meeting with all of our coalition partners, key coalition partners, from around the world, in person, at the end of '98 and the beginning of '99, to sketch out a campaign plan. Even though the Internet is used to share information, the real deep planning and organizing is still done person to person.

MN: What was your strategy?

LW: Well, there were two phases. There was the actual international campaigning, which involved each of us in our different countries, working our own government systems, to try and hold our negotiators accountable. So for the first time, when they got to Seattle and to the WTO ministerial behind closed doors, they each had a pinkie toe, at least, glued to the floor of accountability on some important thing they could not give away. And that made it much harder to play footsie in the middle, once the door shut. So the European NGOs made sure that their countries' negotiators would not support a new biotechnology WTO market access agreement. In the United States, we got the administration to commit to Congress that it would not allow the European push to put the MAI into the WTO.

MN: So your multilateral system of NGOs worked better and had a higher level of synchronicity and organization than the world's governments?

LW: Well, I would say it's because we have a much more common philosophy, which is, we're looking at the public interest, and trying to balance that against the corporate interests. All these governments are basically fronts for their corporate interests, but they also have a mercantilist streak that looks at what's in their national interest.

MN: How much did your protest in Seattle cost?

LW: Well, the international campaigning cost the price of a dreadfully expensive conference call, every three weeks for a whole year. I mean, it wasn't so bad, relatively speaking; it was like a $20,000 phone bill.

MN: How did you organize the logistics in Seattle?

LW: The day we heard Seattle was announced, we literally maxed out the personal credit cards of every individual staff member, and most of our mothers and fathers, to save every hotel room we could get locked up, so that we had 400 hotel rooms pinned down before the U.S. chair made their first call. We knew it was going to be San Diego, Honolulu, or Seattle, so I already had a list of the most centrally located, cheap hotels in each of these cities.

We opened an office in Seattle in March of 1999, in a storefront, like a campaign office downtown, and started signing up volunteers, and having volunteer speakers' pools to go into local colleges, and PTAs, and Rotary Clubs, and neighborhood groups, to teach people about the WTO and also get them involved in Seattle. All of our critics think that somehow we raised millions of dollars because the corporations raised millions of dollars to put on their whole thing. In fact, we raised very little money, because almost everything was done by public citizens, people with a day job, but with a passion about these issues, who volunteered. We ended up putting over 2,000 people into families' homes. So when people said, how did you pay for all of your developing country coalition partners to stay for 10 days in the United States? We didn't pay at all; they were staying in the guest room of some family who drove them around, and had dinner with them every night, and I mean, we had a car pool system of volunteers, of 100 cars. We had walkie-talkies—that was one of the few things we actually paid money for—to help coordinate all the volunteers. But, on the ground in Seattle, we had four paid staff and about 600 volunteers. The four paid staff basically coordinated the volunteers. Probably the entire operation cost a lot less than the bar tab for the opening ceremony of the corporate event.

The Next Targets

MN: What is the next shell to smash?

LW: Well, I think there are two in the United States. One is a continuing fight to stop any further expansion of the WTO. I mean, the folks who wanted to expand the WTO's agenda have now shifted to wanting to expand the WTO's membership. And the biggest country that is missing, the biggest economy, is China.

MN: You want to prevent China from joining the WTO?

LW: No. Basically, our goal is to prevent the granting by the United States of permanent most-favored-nation trading status to China.

MN: Why?

LW: Because we believe that the U.S. Congress needs to have its annual review of China's conduct in a whole array of issues, particularly after eight years of the Clinton administration's constructive engagement strategy toward China, which was the notion that increasing liberalization of the economy would bring about liberalization in human rights, increased democracy, etc. This strategy has been a total bust. This year, the State Department in its annual human rights report noted that conditions in China have deteriorated yet further. This year, they have finally certified that basically every Chinese democracy activist and labor activist is either in jail or in exile. And so during this period when the free market would allegedly enhance their freedoms, we've seen the opposite. And ironically, during that same period, we've seen the economics of the relationship deteriorate as well. First, with a trade deficit that has literally quadrupled during that period, but also with China more and more not following its obligations under bilateral agreements, the intellectual property agreement, the insurance agreement, the auto parts agreement.

MN: What would you consider to be a sensible U.S. policy toward China?

LW: I would describe it as principle-based reciprocity. There would be a bilateral agreement between the two sovereign nations that would go to the terms of trade between those countries, that would include some basic rules of the road about prison labor, about basic human rights, political right to organize, freedom of religious expression, freedom of communications, access to information—the things that you really need to make a capitalistic society work in the long term.

MN: What is a second campaign that you have in mind?

LW: The second campaign we're going to run is called the "WTO: Fix It or Nix It" campaign. The WTO No New Round Turnaround campaign was successful. There was no new round, but the status quo itself is unacceptable. So the second part of our original campaign was the turnaround part—basically, to give the WTO, if you will, its last chance to show itself to be an international organization for the next century. There will be a list of specific things that must concretely be accomplished before the next ministerial, which we are discussing among all of these broad-based coalitions.

MN: Do you have any other campaigns planned?

LW: Well, we're still working with a coalition of African American ministers who are passionately opposed to the NAFTA for Africa bill. And so we're also working with them, to support their work, to make sure the U.S. Congress doesn't pass the NAFTA for Africa.

MN: Are many of your criticisms of the WTO also applicable to the International Monetary Fund (IMF) and the World Bank?

LW: Yes.

MN: You would also like to see the World Bank and the IMF shrunk in their scope of activity, essentially transferring some of the power they have now to governments and states?

LW: Yeah, well, that's one approach. I've not worked on those institutions very much at all. My colleagues from around the world who have are arguing at this point that those institutions are really not reformable and should just be abolished. Jim Wolfensohn has done some things as president of the World Bank, but when the rubber hits the road, a lot of it has just been basically to mollify the critics instead of to make fundamental changes. And the IMF has just been an unmitigated disaster, to the point where you have U.S. Treasury Secretary Larry Sum-

mers saying, hmm, maybe we should look at what it was meant for. It wasn't supposed to be giving out long-term loans with conditionalities to all of its potential poor-country beneficiaries, or to organize a one-size-fits-all solution for their economies.

MN: Are you planning a march or a rally at the annual meetings of the WTO and the World Bank in the fall in Prague?

LW: The place where an interesting set of protests will occur is at the April 16 meetings of the World Bank and the IMF in Washington.

MN: What are you planning for that?

LW: Well, nothing on the scale of Seattle. I think that there will be a lot of church-based groups, some of whom were involved in the WTO effort and are incredibly serious about debt relief. They see the World Bank and the IMF as not just failed and flawed institutions, but literally as immoral ones. The faith-based groups are planning a lot of protest events. Smaller scale, but I think quite passionate.

MN: When you are in these kinds of fights, you sometimes need to envision who your worst enemies are, whether people or institutions. Who embodies the forces that you are trying to bend, that you're trying to modify?

LW: Well, the rules we're trying to modify, but some of these individuals need to be flattened altogether. Some of these individuals are not modifiable. The rules are what we want to modify.

MN: But who embodies, in your mind, the forces you're trying to overcome?

LW: Well, when it comes down to nuts and bolts, the real power pushing this particular system is a handful of big multinational corporations. So people like the CEOs of Monsanto and some other particularly egregious corporations frequently come to mind.

MN: Who else?

LW: For different countries, different people. In the United States, for example, Phil Knight, the CEO of Nike. Bill Gates gets an enormous amount of attention. But also, you know, there are individuals in government who so typify the sort of arrogance and lack of attention to the public interest. Like Larry Summers, who is just the poster child. And Charlene Barshefsky is someone whom I think a lot of people think just deeply doesn't get it. It is not even so much like Carla Hills, who was evil; Charlene just doesn't get it.

And then, you know, there are individuals who get the foot-in-the-mouth award. We cried many a tear when Renato Ruggiero resigned as the head of the WTO, because he was a one-man public relations operation for us. I mean, some of the things he said were so revealingly honest. And he had these attacks of candor at the most useful times—for instance, after the WTO released its big report on the environment saying, oh, it's not mutually, you know, incompatible. He gave a speech then where he said basically that any attempt to modify anything in the trade system to preserve the environment can only result in failure of the global trading system, which obviously is more important than the environment.

Then there is the *New York Times'* Tom Friedman, who inevitably ends up getting hooted at as just the most uninformed . . . I must have 40 e-mails saved of you-have-to-laugh-out-loud, almost-wet-your-pants things that he's said, that are just so ignorant and out of touch with political reality. So much of the so-called mainstream media has religiously avoided dealing with any of these issues, except in the most boosterish, noninformative, non-open-minded way. Until Seattle.

MN: Anything that we missed in this conversation?

LW: Well, we didn't miss it, but I think I'd just reiterate my vision of where I'd like things to go. I don't have a plan of how to get from A to B, because there are a lot of foibles that have to do with accountability and democracy.

But people of good faith who want to work on transforming the system into something more broadly acceptable, both the critics of the status quo and the proponents, need to just fess up to certain problems. An inherent systematic problem is how to have international standards that are of a scope that is appropriate to international corporations and international capital, and yet still have democratic accountability for those decisions, particularly when they're not objective decisions, but rather subjective. And that is a really hard question. How do you have democratic accountability in governance, and enforceable international standards? Either we'll have international rules about that, or we're just going to do it ourselves. That's it.

7 ～ WAR AND STRIFE

Warfare and military intervention continue to be central problems of international relations. In Essentials of International Relations, *Mingst examines how the adherents of the contending approaches to international relations attempt to explain how states manage insecurity. She explains why wars occur and presents a typology of different kinds of warfare.*

*Two readings in this chapter address a core issue: the relationship between the use of force and politics. Excerpts from classic books by Carl von Clausewitz (*On War, *originally published in the 1830s) and Thomas Schelling (*Arms and Influence, *published in 1966) remind us that warfare is not simply a matter of brute force; war needs to be understood as a continuation of political bargaining. In the most influential treatise on warfare ever written, the Prussian general Clausewitz reminded the generation that followed the devastating Napoleonic Wars that armed conflict should not be considered a blind, all-out struggle governed by the logic of military operations. Rather, he said, the conduct of war had to be subordinated to its political objectives. These ideas resonated strongly with American strategic thinkers of Schelling's era, who worried that military plans for total nuclear war would outstrip the ability of political leaders to control them. Schelling, a Harvard professor who also spent time at the RAND Corporation advising the U.S. Air Force on its nuclear weapons strategy, explained that political bargaining and risk taking, not military victory, lay at the heart of the use and threat of force in the nuclear era.*

Like Schelling, Robert Jervis drew on mathematical game theory and theories of bargaining in his influential 1978 article on the "security dilemma," which explains how war can arise even among states that seek only to defend themselves. Like the realists, these analysts are interested in studying how states' strategies for survival can lead to tragic results. However, they go beyond the realists in examining how differences in bargaining tactics and perceptions can intensify or mitigate the struggle for security.

Even more optimistic about the prospects for avoiding war is John Mueller, whose 1988 article excerpted below argues that extremely costly major wars such as World Wars I and II have now become obsolete. Though if this view turns out to be correct, it still cannot be ignored that war and military competition continue to engulf many parts of the developing world. An excerpt from Michael Doyle's Ways of War and Peace *(1997) shows the relevance of the realist, liberal, and Marxist perspectives to understanding the practical and ethical dilemmas of military intervention in such conflicts.*

Of course, ethical issues of international security may look different from different vantage points. Jaswant Singh, adviser to the Indian prime minister and member of Parliament for the Bharatiya Janata Party, explains why India felt it had the need and the right to develop nuclear weapons to protect itself in a world of nuclear-armed competitors. For a more general discussion of the pros and cons of nuclear proliferation, readers should look at the debate between Kenneth Waltz and Scott Sagan in their book, The Spread of Nuclear Weapons: A Debate *(1995). Finally, military analyst Edward Luttwak reminds us that a decisive military victory sometimes provides a more reliable basis for a lasting peace than does the attempt to maintain an indefinite stalemate with the help of ineffective peace-keeping forces.*

John Mearsheimer's book in the Norton Series in World Politics provides a starkly realist view of the causes of war and the role of military force in international politics. Among the targets of his "offensive realist" argument are Robert Jervis and other "defensive realists," who contend that the security dilemma between states can be mitigated through arms control agreements or by unilaterally adopting measures of self-defense that do not threaten the security of other states. The series book by John Oneal and Bruce Russett differs even more fundamentally with Mearsheimer about the possibility of eliminating the causes of war. Extending Doyle's argument about the "democratic peace" (excerpted in chapter 2), they argue that the mutually reinforcing trinity of democracy, international organizations, and international trade can establish and lock in incentives for a durable peace that will overcome the security dilemma in anarchy that so concerns the realists.

CARL VON CLAUSEWITZ

War as an Instrument of Policy

*   *   *

* * * *War is only a part of political intercourse, therefore by no means an independent thing in itself.*

We know, certainly, that War is only called forth through the political intercourse of Governments and Nations; but in general it is supposed that such intercourse is broken off by War, and that a totally different state of things ensues, subject to no laws but its own.

We maintain, on the contrary, that War is nothing but a continuation of political intercourse, with a mixture of other means. We say mixed with other means in order thereby to maintain at the same time that this political intercourse does not cease by the War itself, is not changed into something quite different, but that, in its essence, it continues to exist, whatever may be the form of the means which it uses, and that the chief lines on which the events of the War progress, and to which they are attached, are only the general features of policy which run all through the War until peace takes place. And how can we conceive it to be otherwise? Does the cessation of diplomatic notes stop the political relations between different Nations and Governments? Is not War merely another kind of writing and language for political thoughts? It has certainly a grammar of its own, but its logic is not peculiar to itself.

Accordingly, War can never be separated from political intercourse, and if, in the consideration of the matter, this is done in any way, all the threads of the different relations are, to a certain extent, broken, and we have before us a senseless thing without an object.

This kind of idea would be indispensable even if War was perfect War, the perfectly unbridled element of hostility, for all the circumstances on which it rests, and which determine its leading features, viz. our own power, the enemy's power, Allies on both sides, the characteristics of the people and their Governments respectively, etc.—are they not of a political nature, and are they not so intimately connected with the whole political intercourse that it is impossible to separate them? But this view is doubly indispensable if we reflect that real War is no such consistent effort tending to an extreme, as it should be according to the abstract idea, but a half-and-half thing, a contradiction in itself; that, as such, it cannot follow its own laws, but must be looked upon as a part of another whole—and this whole is policy.

Policy in making use of War avoids all those rigorous conclusions which proceed from its nature; it troubles itself little about final possibilities, confining its attention to immediate probabilities. If such uncertainty in the whole action ensues therefrom, if it thereby becomes a sort of game, the policy of each Cabinet places its confidence in the belief that in this game it will surpass its neighbour in skill and sharp-sightedness.

Thus policy makes out of the all-overpowering element of War a mere instrument, changes the tremendous battle-sword, which should be lifted with both hands and the whole power of the body to strike once for all, into a light handy weapon, which is even sometimes nothing more than a rapier to exchange thrusts and feints and parries.

Thus the contradictions in which man, naturally timid, becomes involved by War may be solved, if we choose to accept this as a solution.

If War belongs to policy, it will naturally take its character from thence. If policy is grand and powerful, so also will be the War, and this may be carried to the point at which War attains to *its absolute form.*

In this way of viewing the subject, therefore, we

From Carl von Clausewitz, *On War* (Harmondsworth: Penguin Books, 1968), bk. 5, chap. 6. The author's notes have been omitted.

need not shut out of sight the absolute form of War, we rather keep it continually in view in the background.

Only through this kind of view War recovers unity; only by it can we see all Wars as things of *one* kind; and it is only through it that the judgement can obtain the true and perfect basis and point of view from which great plans may be traced out and determined upon.

It is true the political element does not sink deep into the details of War. Vedettes are not planted, patrols do not make their rounds from political considerations; but small as is its influence in this respect, it is great in the formation of a plan for a whole War, or a campaign, and often even for a battle.

For this reason we were in no hurry to establish this view at the commencement. While engaged with particulars, it would have given us little help, and, on the other hand, would have distracted our attention to a certain extent; in the plan of a War or campaign it is indispensable.

There is, upon the whole, nothing more important in life than to find out the right point of view from which things should be looked at and judged of, and then to keep to that point; for we can only apprehend the mass of events in their unity from *one* standpoint; and it is only the keeping to one point of view that guards us from inconsistency.

If, therefore, in drawing up a plan of a War, it is not allowable to have a two-fold or three-fold point of view, from which things may be looked at, now with the eye of a soldier, then with that of an administrator, and then again with that of a politician, etc., then the next question is, whether *policy* is necessarily paramount and everything else subordinate to it.

That policy unites in itself, and reconciles all the interests of internal administrations, even those of humanity, and whatever else are rational subjects of consideration is presupposed, for it is nothing in itself, except a mere representative and exponent of all these interests towards other States. That policy may take a false direction, and may promote unfairly the ambitious ends, the private interests, the vanity of rulers, does not concern us here; for, under no circumstances can the Art of War be regarded as its preceptor, and we can only look at policy here as the representative of the interests generally of the whole community.

The only question, therefore, is whether in framing plans for a War the political point of view should give way to the purely military (if such a point is conceivable), that is to say, should disappear altogether, or subordinate itself to it, or whether the political is to remain the ruling point of view and the military to be considered subordinate to it.

That the political point of view should end completely when War begins is only conceivable in contests which are Wars of life and death, from pure hatred: as Wars are in reality, they are, as we before said, only the expressions or manifestations of policy itself. The subordination of the political point of view to the military would be contrary to common sense, for policy has declared the War; it is the intelligent faculty, War only the instrument, and not the reverse. The subordination of the military point of view to the political is, therefore, the only thing which is possible.

If we reflect on the nature of real War, and call to mind what has been said, *that every War should be viewed above all things according to the probability of its character, and its leading features as they are to be deduced from the political forces and proportions*, and that often—indeed we may safely affirm, in our days, *almost* always—War is to be regarded as an organic whole, from which the single branches are not to be separated, in which therefore every individual activity flows into the whole, and also has its origin in the idea of this whole, then it becomes certain and palpable to us that the superior standpoint for the conduct of the War, from which its leading lines must proceed, can be no other than that of policy.

From this point of view the plans come, as it were, out of a cast; the apprehension of them and the judgement upon them become easier and more natural, our convictions respecting them gain in force, motives are more satisfying and history more intelligible.

At all events from this point of view there is no longer in the nature of things a necessary conflict between the political and military interests, and where it appears it is therefore to be regarded as imperfect knowledge only. That policy makes demands on the War which it cannot respond to, would be contrary to the supposition that it knows the instrument which it is going to use, therefore, contrary to a natural and indispensable supposition. But if policy judges correctly of the march of military events, it is entirely its affair to determine what are the events and what the direction of events most favourable to the ultimate and great end of the War.

In one word, the Art of War in its highest point of view is policy, but, no doubt, a policy which fights battles instead of writing notes.

According to this view, to leave a great military enterprise or the plan for one, to *a purely military judgement and decision* is a distinction which cannot be allowed, and is even prejudicial; indeed, it is an irrational proceeding to consult professional soldiers on the plan of a War, that they may give a *purely military opinion* upon what the Cabinet ought to do; but still more absurd is the demand of Theorists that a statement of the available means of War should be laid before the General, that he may draw out a purely military plan for the War or for a campaign in accordance with those means. Experience in general also teaches us that notwithstanding the multifarious branches and scientific character of military art in the present day, still the leading outlines of a War are always determined by the Cabinet, that is, if we would use technical language, by a political not a military organ.

This is perfectly natural. None of the principal plans which are required for a War can be made without an insight into the political relations; and, in reality, when people speak, as they often do, of the prejudicial influence of policy on the conduct of a War, they say in reality something very different to what they intend. It is not this influence but the policy itself which should be found fault with. If policy is right, that is, if it succeeds in hitting the object, then it can only act with advantage on the War. If this influence of policy causes a divergence from the object, the cause is only to be looked for in a mistaken policy.

It is only when policy promises itself a wrong effect from certain military means and measures, an effect opposed to their nature, that it can exercise a prejudicial effect on War by the course it prescribes. Just as a person in a language with which he is not conversant sometimes says what he does not intend, so policy, when intending right, may often order things which do not tally with its own views.

This has happened times without end, and it shows that a certain knowledge of the nature of War is essential to the management of political intercourse.

But before going further, we must guard ourselves against a false interpretation of which this is very susceptible. We are far from holding the opinion that a War Minister smothered in official papers, a scientific engineer, or even a soldier who has been well tried in the field, would, any of them, necessarily make the best Minister of State where the Sovereign does not act for himself; or, in other words, we do not mean to say that this acquaintance with the nature of War is the principal qualification for a War Minister; elevation, superiority of mind, strength of character, these are the principal qualifications which he must possess; a knowledge of War may be supplied in one way or the other. * * *

*   *   *

We shall now conclude with some reflections derived from history.

In the last decade of the past century, when that remarkable change in the Art of War in Europe took place by which the best Armies found that a part of their method of War had become utterly unserviceable, and events were brought about of a magnitude far beyond what any one had any previous conception of, it certainly appeared that a false calculation of everything was to be laid to the charge of the Art of War. * * *

*   *   *

But is it true that the real surprise by which men's minds were seized was confined to the conduct of

War, and did not rather relate to policy itself? That is: Did the ill success proceed from the influence of policy on the War, or from a wrong policy itself?

The prodigious effects of the French Revolution abroad were evidently brought about much less through new methods and views introduced by the French in the conduct of War than through the changes which it wrought in state-craft and civil administration, in the character of Governments, in the condition of the people, etc. That other Governments took a mistaken view of all these things; that they endeavoured, with their ordinary means, to hold their own against forces of a novel kind and overwhelming in strength—all that was a blunder in policy.

Would it have been possible to perceive and mend this error by a scheme for the War from a purely military point of view? Impossible. For if there had been a philosophical strategist, who merely from the nature of the hostile elements had foreseen all the consequences, and prophesied remote possibilities, still it would have been practically impossible to have turned such wisdom to account.

If policy had risen to a just appreciation of the forces which had sprung up in France, and of the new relations in the political state of Europe, it might have foreseen the consequences which must follow in respect to the great features of War, and it was only in this way that it could arrive at a correct view of the extent of the means required as well as of the best use to make of those means.

We may therefore say, that the twenty years' victories of the Revolution are chiefly to be ascribed to the erroneous policy of the Governments by which it was opposed.

It is true these errors first displayed themselves in the War, and the events of the War completely disappointed the expectations which policy entertained. But this did not take place because policy neglected to consult its military advisers. That Art of War in which the politician of the day could believe, namely, that derived from the reality of War at that time, that which belonged to the policy of the day, that familiar instrument which policy had hitherto used—*that* Art of War, I say, was naturally involved in the error of policy, and therefore could not teach it anything better. It is true that War itself underwent important alterations both in its nature and forms, which brought it nearer to its absolute form; but these changes were not brought about because the French Government had, to a certain extent, delivered itself from the leading-strings of policy; they arose from an altered policy, produced by the French Revolution, not only in France, but over the rest of Europe as well. This policy had called forth other means and other powers, by which it became possible to conduct War with a degree of energy which could not have been thought of otherwise.

Therefore, the actual changes in the Art of War are a consequence of alterations in policy; and, so far from being an argument for the possible separation of the two, they are, on the contrary, very strong evidence of the intimacy of their connexion.

Therefore, once more: War is an instrument of policy; it must necessarily bear its character, it must measure with its scale: the conduct of War, in its great features, is therefore policy itself, which takes up the sword in place of the pen, but does not on that account cease to think according to its own laws.

THOMAS C. SCHELLING

The Diplomacy of Violence

The usual distinction between diplomacy and force is not merely in the instruments, words or bullets, but in the relation between adversaries—in the interplay of motives and the role of communication, understandings, compromise, and restraint. Diplomacy is bargaining: it seeks outcomes that, though not ideal for either party, are better for both than some of the alternatives. In diplomacy each party somewhat controls what the other wants, and can get more by compromise, exchange, or collaboration than by taking things in his own hands and ignoring the other's wishes. The bargaining can be polite or rude, entail threats as well as offers, assume a status quo or ignore all rights and privileges, and assume mistrust rather than trust. But whether polite or impolite, constructive or aggressive, respectful or vicious, whether it occurs among friends or antagonists and whether or not there is a basis for trust and goodwill, there must be some common interest, if only in the avoidance of mutual damage, and an awareness of the need to make the other party prefer an outcome acceptable to oneself.

With enough military force a country may not need to bargain. Some things a country wants it can take, and some things it has it can keep, by sheer strength, skill and ingenuity. It can do this *forcibly*, accommodating only to opposing strength, skill, and ingenuity and without trying to appeal to an enemy's wishes. Forcibly a country can repel and expel, penetrate and occupy, seize, exterminate, disarm and disable, confine, deny access, and directly frustrate intrusion or attack. It can, that is, if it has enough strength. "Enough" depends on how much an opponent has.

There is something else, though, that force can

From Thomas C. Schelling, *Arms and Influence* (New Haven: Yale University Press, 1966), chap. 1. Some of the author's notes have been omitted.

do. It is less military, less heroic, less impersonal, and less unilateral; it is uglier, and has received less attention in Western military strategy. In addition to seizing and holding, disarming and confining, penetrating and obstructing, and all that, military force can be used *to hurt*. In addition to taking and protecting things of value it can *destroy* value. In addition to weakening an enemy militarily it can cause an enemy plain suffering.

Pain and shock, loss and grief, privation and horror are always in some degree, sometimes in terrible degree, among the results of warfare; but in traditional military science they are incidental, they are not the object. If violence can be done incidentally, though, it can also be done purposely. The power to hurt can be counted among the most impressive attributes of military force.

Hurting, unlike forcible seizure or self-defense, is not unconcerned with the interest of others. It is measured in the suffering it can cause and the victims' motivation to avoid it. Forcible action will work against weeds or floods as well as against armies, but suffering requires a victim that can feel pain or has something to lose. To inflict suffering gains nothing and saves nothing directly; it can only make people behave to avoid it. The only purpose, unless sport or revenge, must be to influence somebody's behavior, to coerce his decision or choice. To be coercive, violence has to be anticipated. And it has to be avoidable by accommodation. The power to hurt is bargaining power. To exploit it is diplomacy—vicious diplomacy, but diplomacy.

The Contrast of Brute Force with Coercion

There is a difference between taking what you want and making someone give it to you, between fend-ing off assault and making someone afraid to assault you, between holding what people are trying to take and making them afraid to take it, between losing what someone can forcibly take and giving it up to avoid risk or damage. It is the difference between defense and deterrence, between brute force and intimidation, between conquest and blackmail, between action and threats. It is the difference between the unilateral, "undiplomatic" recourse to strength, and coercive diplomacy based on the power to hurt.

The contrasts are several. The purely "military" or "undiplomatic" recourse to forcible action is concerned with enemy strength, not enemy interests; the coercive use of the power to hurt, though, is the very exploitation of enemy wants and fears. And brute strength is usually measured relative to enemy strength, the one directly opposing the other, while the power to hurt is typically not reduced by the enemy's power to hurt in return. Opposing strengths may cancel each other, pain and grief do not. The willingness to hurt, the credibility of a threat, and the ability to exploit the power to hurt will indeed depend on how much the adversary can hurt in return; but there is little or nothing about an adversary's pain or grief that directly reduces one's own. Two sides cannot both overcome each other with superior strength; they may both be able to hurt each other. With strength they can dispute objects of value; with sheer violence they can destroy them.

And brute force succeeds when it is used, whereas the power to hurt is most successful when held in reserve. It is the *threat* of damage, or of more damage to come, that can make someone yield or comply. It is *latent* violence that can influence someone's choice—violence that can still be withheld or inflicted, or that a victim believes can be withheld or inflicted. The threat of pain tries to structure someone's motives, while brute force tries to overcome his strength. Unhappily, the power to hurt is often communicated by some performance of it. Whether it is sheer terroristic violence to induce an irrational response, or cool premeditated violence to persuade somebody that you mean it and may do it again, it is not the pain and damage itself but its influence on somebody's behavior that matters. It is the expectation of *more* violence that gets the wanted behavior, if the power to hurt can get it at all.

To exploit a capacity for hurting and inflicting damage one needs to know what an adversary treasures and what scares him and one needs the adversary to understand what behavior of his will cause the violence to be inflicted and what will cause it to be withheld. The victim has to know what is wanted, and he may have to be assured of what is not wanted. The pain and suffering have to appear *contingent* on his behavior; it is not alone the threat that is effective—the threat of pain or loss if he fails to comply—but the corresponding assurance, possibly an implicit one, that he can avoid the pain or loss if he does comply. The prospect of certain death may stun him, but it gives him no choice.

Coercion by threat of damage also requires that our interests and our opponent's not be absolutely opposed. If his pain were our greatest delight and our satisfaction his greatest woe, we would just proceed to hurt and to frustrate each other. It is when his pain gives us little or no satisfaction compared with what he can do for us, and the action or inaction that satisfies us costs him less than the pain we can cause, that there is room for coercion. Coercion requires finding a bargain, arranging for him to be better off doing what we want—worse off not doing what we want—when he takes the threatened penalty into account.

It is this capacity for pure damage, pure violence, that is usually associated with the most vicious labor disputes, with racial disorders, with civil uprisings and their suppression, with racketeering. It is also the power to hurt rather than brute force that we use in dealing with criminals; we hurt them afterward, or threaten to, for their misdeeds rather than protect ourselves with cordons of electric wires, masonry walls, and armed guards. Jail, of course, can be either forcible restraint or threatened privation; if the object is to keep criminals out of mischief by confinement, success is measured by how many of them are gotten behind bars, but if the object is to *threaten* privation, success will be measured by how few have to be put behind bars and success then depends on the subject's understanding of the consequences. Pure damage is what a car threatens when it tries to hog the road or to keep its rightful share, or to go first through an intersection. A tank or a bulldozer can force its way regardless of others' wishes; the rest of us have to threaten damage, usually mutual damage, hoping the other driver values his car or his limbs enough to give way, hoping he sees us, and hoping he is in control of his own car. The threat of pure damage will not work against an unmanned vehicle.

This difference between coercion and brute force is as often in the intent as in the instrument. To hunt down Comanches and to exterminate them was brute force; to raid their villages to make them behave was coercive diplomacy, based on the power to hurt. The pain and loss to the Indians might have looked much the same one way as the other; the difference was one of purpose and effect. If Indians were killed because they were in the way, or somebody wanted their land, or the authorities despaired of making them behave and could not confine them and decided to exterminate them, that was pure unilateral force. If *some* Indians were killed to make *other* Indians behave, that was coercive violence—or intended to be, whether or not it was effective. The Germans at Verdun perceived themselves to be chewing up hundreds of thousands of French soldiers in a gruesome "meat-grinder." If the purpose was to eliminate a military obstacle—the French infantryman, viewed as a military "asset" rather than as a warm human being—the offensive at Verdun was a unilateral exercise of military force. If instead the object was to make the loss of young men—not of impersonal "effectives," but of sons, husbands, fathers, and the pride of French manhood—so anguishing as to be unendurable, to make surrender a welcome relief and to spoil the foretaste of an Allied victory, then it was an exercise in coercion, in applied violence, intended to offer relief upon accommodation. And of course, since any use of force tends to be brutal, thoughtless, vengeful, or plain obstinate, the motives themselves can be mixed and confused. The

fact that heroism and brutality can be either coercive diplomacy or a contest in pure strength does not promise that the distinction will be made, and the strategies enlightened by the distinction, every time some vicious enterprise gets launched.

The contrast between brute force and coercion is illustrated by two alternative strategies attributed to Genghis Khan. Early in his career he pursued the war creed of the Mongols: the vanquished can never be the friends of the victors, their death is necessary for the victor's safety. This was the unilateral extermination of a menace or a liability. The turning point of his career, according to Lynn Montross, came later when he discovered how to use his power to hurt for diplomatic ends. "The great Khan, who was not inhibited by the usual mercies, conceived the plan of forcing captives— women, children, aged fathers, favorite sons—to march ahead of his army as the first potential victims of resistance."[1] Live captives have often proved more valuable than enemy dead; and the technique discovered by the Khan in his maturity remains contemporary. North Koreans and Chinese were reported to have quartered prisoners of war near strategic targets to inhibit bombing attacks by United Nations aircraft. Hostages represent the power to hurt in its purest form.

Coercive Violence in Warfare

This distinction between the power to hurt and the power to seize or hold forcibly is important in modern war, both big war and little war, hypothetical war and real war. For many years the Greeks and the Turks on Cyprus could hurt each other indefinitely but neither could quite take or hold forcibly what they wanted or protect themselves from violence by physical means. The Jews in Palestine could not expel the British in the late 1940s but they could cause pain and fear and frustration through terrorism, and eventually influence somebody's decision. The brutal war in Algeria was more a contest in pure violence than in military strength; the question was who would first find the pain and degradation unendurable. The French troops preferred—indeed they continually tried—to make it a contest of strength, to pit military force against the nationalists' capacity for terror, to exterminate or disable the nationalists and to screen off the nationalists from the victims of their violence. But because in civil war terrorists commonly have access to victims by sheer physical propinquity, the victims and their properties could not be forcibly defended and in the end the French troops themselves resorted, unsuccessfully, to a war of pain.

Nobody believes that the Russians can take Hawaii from us, or New York, or Chicago, but nobody doubts that they might destroy people and buildings in Hawaii, Chicago, or New York. Whether the Russians can conquer West Germany in any meaningful sense is questionable; whether they can hurt it terribly is not doubted. That the United States can destroy a large part of Russia is universally taken for granted; that the United States can keep from being badly hurt, even devastated, in return, or can keep Western Europe from being devastated while itself destroying Russia, is at best arguable; and it is virtually out of the question that we could conquer Russia territorially and use its economic assets unless it were by threatening disaster and inducing compliance. It is the power to hurt, not military strength in the traditional sense, that inheres in our most impressive military capabilities at the present time [1966]. We have a Department of *Defense* but emphasize *retaliation*— "to return evil for evil" (synonyms: requital, reprisal, revenge, vengeance, retribution). And it is pain and violence, not force in the traditional sense, that inheres also in some of the least impressive military capabilities of the present time—the plastic bomb, the terrorist's bullet, the burnt crops, and the tortured farmer.

War appears to be, or threatens to be, not so much a contest of strength as one of endurance, nerve, obstinacy, and pain. It appears to be, and threatens to be, not so much a contest of military strength as a bargaining process—dirty, extortionate, and often quite reluctant bargaining on one side or both—nevertheless a bargaining process.

The difference cannot quite be expressed as one between the *use* of force and the *threat* of force. The actions involved in forcible accomplishment, on the one hand, and in fulfilling a threat, on the other, can be quite different. Sometimes the most effective direct action inflicts enough cost or pain on the enemy to serve as a threat, sometimes not. The United States threatens the Soviet Union with virtual destruction of its society in the event of a surprise attack on the United States; a hundred million deaths are awesome as pure damage, but they are useless in stopping the Soviet attack— especially if the threat is to do it all afterward anyway. So it is worth while to keep the concepts distinct—to distinguish forcible action from the threat of pain—recognizing that some actions serve as both a means of forcible accomplishment and a means of inflicting pure damage, some do not. Hostages tend to entail almost pure pain and damage, as do all forms of reprisal after the fact. Some modes of self-defense may exact so little in blood or treasure as to entail negligible violence; and some forcible actions entail so much violence that their threat can be effective by itself.

The power to hurt, though it can usually accomplish nothing directly, is potentially more versatile than a straightforward capacity for forcible accomplishment. By force alone we cannot even lead a horse to water—we have to drag him— much less make him drink. Any affirmative action, any collaboration, almost anything but physical exclusion, expulsion, or extermination, requires that an opponent or a victim *do* something, even if only to stop or get out. The threat of pain and damage may make him want to do it, and anything he can do is potentially susceptible to inducement. Brute force can only accomplish what requires no collaboration. The principle is illustrated by a technique of unarmed combat: one can disable a man by various stunning, fracturing, or killing blows, but to take him to jail one has to exploit the man's own efforts. "Come-along" holds are those that threaten pain or disablement, giving relief as long as the victim complies, giving him the option of using his own legs to get to jail.

We have to keep in mind, though, that what is pure pain, or the threat of it, at one level of decision can be equivalent to brute force at another level. Churchill was worried, during the early bombing raids on London in 1940, that Londoners might panic. Against people the bombs were pure violence, to induce their undisciplined evasion; to Churchill and the government, the bombs were a cause of inefficiency, whether they spoiled transport and made people late to work or scared people and made them afraid to work. Churchill's decisions were not going to be coerced by the fear of a few casualties. Similarly on the battlefield: tactics that frighten soldiers so that they run, duck their heads, or lay down their arms and surrender represent coercion based on the power to hurt; to the top command, which is frustrated but not coerced, such tactics are part of the contest in military discipline and strength.

The fact that violence—pure pain and damage—can be used or threatened to coerce and to deter, to intimidate and to blackmail, to demoralize and to paralyze, in a conscious process of dirty bargaining, does not by any means imply that violence is not often wanton and meaningless or, even when purposive, in danger of getting out of hand. Ancient wars were often quite "total" for the loser, the men being put to death, the women sold as slaves, the boys castrated, the cattle slaughtered, and the buildings leveled, for the sake of revenge, justice, personal gain, or merely custom. If an enemy bombs a city, by design or by carelessness, we usually bomb his if we can. In the excitement and fatigue of warfare, revenge is one of the few satisfactions that can be savored; and justice can often be construed to demand the enemy's punishment, even if it is delivered with more enthusiasm than justice requires. When Jerusalem fell to the Crusaders in 1099 the ensuing slaughter was one of the bloodiest in military chronicles. "The men of the West literally waded in gore, their march to the church of the Holy Sepulcher being gruesomely likened to 'treading out the wine press' . . . . ," reports Montross (p. 138), who observes that these excesses usually came at the climax of the capture of a fortified post or city. "For long the assailants have endured more punishment than they were able to inflict; then once the walls are breached, pent up emotions find an outlet in murder, rape and plunder, which discipline is powerless to prevent." The same occurred when Tyre fell to Alexander after a painful siege, and the phenomenon was not unknown on Pacific islands in the Second World War. Pure violence, like fire, can be harnessed to a purpose; that does not mean that behind every holocaust is a shrewd intention successfully fulfilled.

But if the occurrence of violence does not always bespeak a shrewd purpose, the absence of pain and destruction is no sign that violence was idle. Violence is most purposive and most successful when it is threatened and not used. Successful threats are those that do not have to be carried out. By European standards, Denmark was virtually unharmed in the Second World War; it was violence that made the Danes submit. Withheld violence—successfully threatened violence—can look clean, even merciful. The fact that a kidnap victim is returned unharmed, against receipt of ample ransom, does not make kidnapping a nonviolent enterprise. * * *

*   *   *

The Strategic Role of Pain and Damage

Pure violence, nonmilitary violence, appears most conspicuously in relations between unequal countries, where there is no substantial military challenge and the outcome of military engagement is not in question. Hitler could make his threats contemptuously and brutally against Austria; he could make them, if he wished, in a more refined way against Denmark. It is noteworthy that it was Hitler, not his generals, who used this kind of language; proud military establishments do not like to think of themselves as extortionists. Their favorite job is to deliver victory, to dispose of opposing military force and to leave most of the civilian violence to politics and diplomacy. But if there is no room for doubt how a contest in strength will come out, it may be possible to bypass the military stage altogether and to proceed at once to the coercive bargaining.

A typical confrontation of unequal forces occurs at the *end* of a war, between victor and vanquished. Where Austria was vulnerable before a shot was fired, France was vulnerable after its military shield had collapsed in 1940. Surrender negotiations are the place where the threat of civil violence can come to the fore. Surrender negotiations are often so one-sided, or the potential violence so unmistakable, that bargaining succeeds and the violence remains in reserve. But the fact that most of the actual damage was done during the military stage of the war, prior to victory and defeat, does not mean that violence was idle in the aftermath, only that it was latent and the threat of it successful.

Indeed, victory is often but a prerequisite to the exploitation of the power to hurt. When Xenophon was fighting in Asia Minor under Persian leadership, it took military strength to disperse enemy soldiers and occupy their lands; but land was not what the victor wanted, nor was victory for its own sake.

> Next day the Persian leader burned the villages to the ground, not leaving a single house standing, so as to strike terror into the other tribes to show them what would happen if they did not give in. . . . He sent some of the prisoners into the hills and told them to say that if the inhabitants did not come down and settle in their houses to submit to him, he would burn up their villages too and destroy their crops, and they would die of hunger.[2]

Military victory was but the *price of admission*. The payoff depended upon the successful threat of violence.

*   *   *

The Nuclear Contribution to Terror and Violence

Man has, it is said, for the first time in history enough military power to eliminate his species from the earth, weapons against which there is no conceivable defense. War has become, it is said, so destructive and terrible that it ceases to be an instrument of national power. "For the first time in human history," says Max Lerner in a book whose title, *The Age of Overkill*, conveys the point, "men have bottled up a power . . . which they have thus far not dared to use."[3] And Soviet military authorities, whose party dislikes having to accommodate an entire theory of history to a single technological event, have had to reexamine a set of principles that had been given the embarrassing name of "permanently operating factors" in warfare. Indeed, our era is epitomized by words like "the first time in human history," and by the abdication of what was "permanent."

For dramatic impact these statements are splendid. Some of them display a tendency, not at all necessary, to belittle the catastrophe of earlier wars. They may exaggerate the historical novelty of deterrence and the balance of terror. More important, they do not help to identify just what is new about war when so much destructive energy can be packed in warheads at a price that permits advanced countries to have them in large numbers. Nuclear warheads are incomparably more devastating than anything packaged before. What does that imply about war?

It is not true that for the first time in history man has the capability to destroy a large fraction, even the major part, of the human race. Japan was defenseless by August 1945. With a combination of bombing and blockade, eventually invasion, and if necessary the deliberate spread of disease, the United States could probably have exterminated the population of the Japanese islands without nuclear weapons. It would have been a gruesome, expensive, and mortifying campaign; it would have taken time and demanded persistence. But we had the economic and technical capacity to do it; and, together with the Russians or without them, we could have done the same in many populous parts of the world. Against defenseless people there is not much that nuclear weapons can do that cannot be done with an ice pick. And it would not have strained our Gross National Product to do it with ice picks.

It is a grisly thing to talk about. We did not do it and it is not imaginable that we would have done it. We had no reason; if we had had a reason, we would not have the persistence of purpose, once the fury of war had been dissipated in victory and we had taken on the task of executioner. If we and our enemies might do such a thing to each other now, and to others as well, it is not because nuclear weapons have for the first time made it feasible.

*   *   *

* * * In the past it has usually been the victors who could do what they pleased to the enemy. War has often been "total war" for the loser. With deadly monotony the Persians, Greeks, or Romans "put to death all men of military age, and sold the women and children into slavery," leaving the defeated territory nothing but its name until new settlers arrived sometime later. But the defeated could not do the same to their victors. The boys could be castrated and sold only after the war had been won, and only on the side that lost it. The power to hurt could be brought to bear only after military strength had achieved victory. The same sequence characterized the great wars of this century; for reasons of technology and geography, military force has usually had to penetrate, to exhaust, or to collapse opposing military force—to achieve military victory—before it could be brought to bear on the enemy nation itself. The Allies in World War I could not inflict coercive pain and suffering directly on the Germans in a decisive way until they could defeat the German army; and the Germans could not coerce the French people with bayonets unless they first beat the Allied troops that stood in their way. With two-dimensional warfare, there is a tendency for troops to confront each other, shielding their own lands while attempting to press into each other's. Small penetrations could not do major damage to the people; large penetrations were so destructive of military organization that they usually ended the military phase of the war.

Nuclear weapons make it possible to do monstrous violence to the enemy without first achieving victory. With nuclear weapons and today's means of delivery, one expects to penetrate an enemy homeland without first collapsing his military force. What nuclear weapons have done, or appear to do, is to promote this kind of warfare to first place. Nuclear weapons threaten to make war less military, and are responsible for the lowered status of "military victory" at the present time. *Victory is no longer a prerequisite for hurting the enemy.* And it is no assurance against being terribly hurt. One need not wait until he has won the war before inflicting "unendurable" damages on his enemy. One need not wait until he has lost the war. There was a time when the assurance of victory—false or genuine assurance—could make national leaders not just willing but sometimes enthusiastic about war. Not now.

Not only *can* nuclear weapons hurt the enemy before the war has been won, and perhaps hurt decisively enough to make the military engagement academic, but it is widely assumed that in a major war that is *all* they can do. Major war is often discussed as though it would be only a contest in national destruction. If this is indeed the case—if the destruction of cities and their populations has become, with nuclear weapons, the primary object in an all-out war—the sequence of war has been reversed. Instead of destroying enemy forces as a prelude to imposing one's will on the enemy nation, one would have to destroy the nation as a means or a prelude to destroying the enemy forces. If one cannot disable enemy forces without virtually destroying the country, the victor does not even have the option of sparing the conquered nation. He has already destroyed it. Even with blockade and strategic bombing it could be supposed that a country would be defeated before it was destroyed, or would elect surrender before annihilation had gone far. In the Civil War it could be hoped that the South would become too weak to fight before it became too weak to survive. For "all-out" war, nuclear weapons threaten to reverse this sequence.

So nuclear weapons do make a difference, marking an epoch in warfare. The difference is not just in the amount of destruction that can be accomplished but in the role of destruction and in the decision process. Nuclear weapons can change the speed of events, the control of events, the sequence of events, the relation of victor to vanquished, and the relation of homeland to fighting front. Deterrence rests today on the threat of pain and extinction, not just on the threat of military defeat. We may argue about the wisdom of announcing "unconditional surrender" as an aim in the last major war, but seem to expect "unconditional destruction" as a matter of course in another one.

Something like the same destruction always *could* be done. With nuclear weapons there is an expectation that it *would* be done. It is not "overkill" that is new; the American army surely had enough 30 caliber bullets to kill everybody in the world in 1945, or if it did not it could have bought them without any strain. What is new is plain "kill"—the idea that major war might be just a contest in the killing of countries, or not even a contest but just two parallel exercises in devastation.

That is the difference nuclear weapons make. At least they *may* make that difference. They also may not. If the weapons themselves are vulnerable to attack, or the machines that carry them, a successful surprise might eliminate the opponent's means of retribution. That an enormous explosion can be packaged in a single bomb does not by itself guarantee that the victor will receive deadly punishment. Two gunfighters facing each other in a Western town had an unquestioned capacity to kill one another; that did not guarantee that both would die in a gunfight—only the slower of the two. Less deadly weapons, permitting an injured one to shoot back before he died, might have been more conducive to a restraining balance of terror, or of caution. The very efficiency of nuclear weapons could make them ideal for starting war, if they can suddenly eliminate the enemy's capability to shoot back.

And there is a contrary possibility: that nuclear weapons are not vulnerable to attack and prove not to be terribly effective against each other, posing no need to shoot them quickly for fear they will be destroyed before they are launched, and with no task available but the systematic destruction of the enemy country and no necessary reason to do it

fast rather than slowly. Imagine that nuclear destruction *had* to go slowly—that the bombs could be dropped only one per day. The prospect would look very different, something like the most terroristic guerilla warfare on a massive scale. It happens that nuclear war does not have to go slowly; but it may also not have to go speedily. The mere existence of nuclear weapons does not itself determine that everything must go off in a blinding flash, any more than that it must go slowly. Nuclear weapons do not simplify things quite that much.

*   *   *

War no longer looks like just a contest of strength. War and the brink of war are more a contest of nerve and risk-taking, of pain and endurance. Small wars embody the threat of a larger war; they are not just military engagements but "crisis diplomacy." The threat of war has always been somewhere underneath international diplomacy, but for Americans it is now much nearer the surface. Like the threat of a strike in industrial relations, the threat of divorce in a family dispute, or the threat of bolting the party at a political convention, the threat of violence continuously circumscribes international politics. Neither strength nor goodwill procures immunity.

Military strategy can no longer be thought of, as it could for some countries in some eras, as the science of military victory. It is now equally, if not more, the art of coercion, of intimidation and deterrence. The instruments of war are more punitive than acquisitive. Military strategy, whether we like it or not, has become the diplomacy of violence.

NOTES

1. Lynn Montross, *War Through the Ages* (3d ed. New York, Harper and Brothers, 1960), p. 146.
2. Xenophon, *The Persian Expedition*, Rex Warner, transl. (Baltimore, Penguin Books, 1949), p. 272. "The 'rational' goal of the threat of violence," says H. L. Nieburg, "is an accommodation of interests, not the provocation of actual

violence. Similarly the 'rational' goal of actual violence is demonstration of the will and capability of action, establishing a measure of the credibility of future threats, not the exhaustion

of that capability in unlimited conflict." "Uses of Violence," *Journal of Conflict Resolution,* 7 (1963), 44.

3. New York, Simon and Schuster, 1962, p. 47.

ROBERT JERVIS

Cooperation under the Security Dilemma

I. Anarchy and the Security Dilemma

The lack of an international sovereign not only permits wars to occur, but also makes it difficult for states that are satisfied with the status quo to arrive at goals that they recognize as being in their common interest. Because there are no institutions or authorities that can make and enforce international laws, the policies of cooperation that will bring mutual rewards if others cooperate may bring disaster if they do not. Because states are aware of this, anarchy encourages behavior that leaves all concerned worse off than they could be, even in the extreme case in which all states would like to freeze the status quo. This is true of the men in Rousseau's "Stag Hunt." If they cooperate to trap the stag, they will all eat well. But if one person defects to chase a rabbit—which he likes less than stag—none of the others will get anything. Thus, all actors have the same preference order, and there is a solution that gives each his first choice: (1) cooperate and trap the stag (the international analogue being cooperation and disarmament); (2) chase a rabbit while others remain at their posts (maintain a high level of arms while others are disarmed); (3) all chase rabbits (arms competition and high risk of war); and (4) stay at the original position while another chases a rabbit (being disarmed while others are armed). Unless

From *World Politics* 30, no. 2 (January 1978): 167–214. Some of the author's notes have been omitted.

each person thinks that the others will cooperate, he himself will not. And why might he fear that any other person would do something that would sacrifice his own first choice? The other might not understand the situation, or might not be able to control his impulses if he saw a rabbit, or might fear that some other member of the group is unreliable. If the person voices any of these suspicions, others are more likely to fear that he will defect, thus making them more likely to defect, thus making it more rational for him to defect. Of course in this simple case—and in many that are more realistic—there are a number of arrangements that could permit cooperation. But the main point remains: although actors may know that they seek a common goal, they may not be able to reach it.

Even when there is a solution that is everyone's first choice, the international case is characterized by three difficulties not present in the Stag Hunt. First, to the incentives to defect given above must be added the potent fear that even if the other state now supports the status quo, it may become dissatisfied later. No matter how much decision makers are committed to the status quo, they cannot bind themselves and their successors to the same path. Minds can be changed, new leaders can come to power, values can shift, new opportunities and dangers can arise.

The second problem arises from a possible solution. In order to protect their possessions, states often seek to control resources or land outside their own territory. Countries that are not self-sufficient must try to assure that the necessary supplies will continue to flow in wartime. This was part of the explanation for Japan's drive into China and Southeast Asia before World War II. If there were an international authority that could guarantee access, this motive for control would disappear. But since there is not, even a state that would prefer the status quo to increasing its area of control may pursue the latter policy.

When there are believed to be tight linkages between domestic and foreign policy or between the domestic politics of two states, the quest for security may drive states to interfere pre-emptively in the domestic politics of others in order to provide an ideological buffer zone. * * *

More frequently, the concern is with direct attack. In order to protect themselves, states seek to control, or at least to neutralize, areas on their borders. But attempts to establish buffer zones can alarm others who have stakes there, who fear that undesirable precedents will be set, or who believe that their own vulnerability will be increased. When buffers are sought in areas empty of great powers, expansion tends to feed on itself in order to protect what is acquired * * *.

Though this process is most clearly visible when it involves territorial expansion, it often operates with the increase of less tangible power and influence. The expansion of power usually brings with it an expansion of responsibilities and commitments; to meet them, still greater power is required. The state will take many positions that are subject to challenge. It will be involved with a wide range of controversial issues unrelated to its core values. And retreats that would be seen as normal if made by a small power would be taken as an index of weakness inviting predation if made by a large one.

The third problem present in international politics but not in the Stag Hunt is the security dilemma: many of the means by which a state tries to increase its security decrease the security of others. In domestic society, there are several ways to increase the safety of one's person and property without endangering others. One can move to a safer neighborhood, put bars on the windows, avoid dark streets, and keep a distance from suspicious-looking characters. Of course these measures are not convenient, cheap, or certain of success. But no one save criminals need be alarmed if a person takes them. In international politics, however, one state's gain in security often inadvertently threatens others. In explaining British policy on naval disarmament in the interwar period to the Japanese, Ramsey MacDonald said that "Nobody wanted Japan to be insecure."[1] But the problem was not with British desires, but with the consequences of her policy. In earlier periods, too, Britain had needed a navy large enough to keep the shipping lanes open. But such a navy could not avoid being a menace to any other state with a coast that could be raided, trade that could be interdicted, or colonies that could be isolated. When Germany started building a powerful navy before World War I, Britain objected that it could only be an offensive weapon aimed at her. As Sir Edward Grey, the Foreign Secretary, put it to King Edward VII: "If the German Fleet ever becomes superior to ours, the German Army can conquer this country. There is no corresponding risk of this kind to Germany; for however superior our Fleet was, no naval victory could bring us any nearer to Berlin." The English position was half correct: Germany's navy was an anti-British instrument. But the British often overlooked what the Germans knew full well: "in every quarrel with England, German colonies and trade were . . . hostages for England to take." Thus, whether she intended it or not, the British Navy constituted an important instrument of coercion.[2]

II. What Makes Cooperation More Likely?

Given this gloomy picture, the obvious question is, why are we not all dead? Or, to put it less starkly, what kinds of variables ameliorate the impact of anarchy and the security dilemma? The working of several can be seen in terms of the Stag Hunt or repeated plays of the Prisoner's Dilemma.[3] The Prisoner's Dilemma differs from the Stag Hunt in that there is no solution that is in the best interests of all the participants; there are offensive as well as defensive incentives to defect from the coalition with the others; and, if the game is to be played only once, the only rational response is to defect. But if the game is repeated indefinitely, the latter characteristic no longer holds and we can analyze the game in terms similar to those applied to the Stag Hunt. It would be in the interest of each actor to have others deprived of the power to defect; each would be willing to sacrifice this ability if others were similarly restrained. But if the others are not, then it is in the actor's interest to retain the power to defect.[4] The game theory matrices for these two situations are given below, with the numbers in the boxes being the order of the actor's preferences.

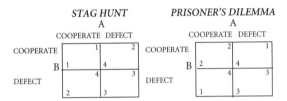

We can see the logical possibilities by rephrasing our question: "Given either of the above situations, what makes it more or less likely that the players will cooperate and arrive at CC?" The chances of achieving this outcome will be increased by: (1) anything that increases incentives to cooperate by increasing the gains of mutual cooperation (CC) and/or decreasing the costs the actor will pay if he cooperates and the other does not (CD); (2) anything that decreases the incentives for defecting by decreasing the gains of taking advantage of the other (DC) and/or increasing the costs of mutual noncooperation (DD); (3) anything that increases each side's expectation that the other will cooperate.[5]

THE COSTS OF BEING EXPLOITED (CD)

The fear of being exploited (that is, the cost of CD) most strongly drives the security dilemma; one of the main reasons why international life is not more nasty, brutish, and short is that states are not as vulnerable as men are in a state of nature. People are easy to kill, but as Adam Smith replied to a friend who feared that the Napoleonic Wars would ruin England, "Sir, there is a great deal of ruin in a nation."[6] The easier it is to destroy a state, the greater the reason for it either to join a larger and more secure unit, or else to be especially suspicious of others, to require a large army, and, if conditions are favorable, to attack at the slightest provocation rather than wait to be attacked. If the failure to eat that day—be it venison or rabbit—means that he will starve, a person is likely to defect in the Stag Hunt even if he really likes venison and has a high level of trust in his colleagues. (Defection is especially likely if the others are also starving or if they know that he is.) By contrast, if the costs of CD are lower, if people are well-fed or states are resilient, they can afford to take a more relaxed view of threats.

A relatively low cost of CD has the effect of transforming the game from one in which both players make their choices simultaneously to one in which an actor can make his choice after the other has moved. He will not have to defect out of fear that the other will, but can wait to see what the other will do. States that can afford to be cheated in a bargain or that cannot be destroyed by a surprise attack can more easily trust others and need not act at the first, and ambiguous, sign of menace. Because they have a margin of time and error, they need not match, or more than match, any others' arms in peacetime. They can mobilize in the prewar period or even at the start of the war itself, and still survive. For example, those who opposed a crash program to develop the H-bomb felt that the U.S. margin of safety was large enough so that even if Russia managed to gain a lead in the race, America would not be endangered. The program's advocates disagreed: "If we let the Russians get the super first, catastrophe becomes all but certain."[7]

When the costs of CD are tolerable, not only is security easier to attain but, what is even more important here, the relatively low level of arms and relatively passive foreign policy that a status-quo power will be able to adopt are less likely to threaten others. Thus it is easier for status-quo states to act on their common interests if they are hard to conquer. All other things being equal, a world of small states will feel the effects of anarchy much more than a world of large ones. Defensible borders, large size, and protection against sudden attack not only aid the state, but facilitate cooperation that can benefit all states.

Of course, if one state gains invulnerability by being more powerful than most others, the problem will remain because its security provides a base from which it can exploit others. When the price a state will pay for DD is low, it leaves others with few hostages for its good behavior. Others who are more vulnerable will grow apprehensive, which will lead them to acquire more arms and will reduce the chances of cooperation. The best situation is one in which a state will not suffer greatly if others exploit it, for example, by cheating on an arms control agreement (that is, the costs of CD are low); but it will pay a high long-run price if cooperation with the others breaks down—for example, if agreements cease functioning or if there is a long war (that is, the costs of DD are high). The state's invulnerability is then mostly passive; it provides some protection, but it cannot be used to menace others. As we will discuss below, this situation is approximated when it is easier for states to defend themselves than to attack others, or when mutual deterrence obtains because neither side can protect itself.

The differences between highly vulnerable and less vulnerable states are illustrated by the contrasting policies of Britain and Austria after the Napoleonic Wars. Britain's geographic isolation and political stability allowed her to take a fairly relaxed view of disturbances on the Continent. Minor wars and small changes in territory or in the distribution of power did not affect her vital interests. An adversary who was out to overthrow the system could be stopped after he had made his intentions clear. And revolutions within other states were no menace, since they would not set off unrest within England. Austria, surrounded by strong powers, was not so fortunate; her policy had to be more closely attuned to all conflicts. By the time an aggressor-state had clearly shown its colors, Aus-

tria would be gravely threatened. And foreign revolutions, be they democratic or nationalistic, would encourage groups in Austria to upset the existing order. So it is not surprising that Metternich propounded the doctrine summarized earlier, which defended Austria's right to interfere in the internal affairs of others, and that British leaders rejected this view. Similarly, Austria wanted the Congress system to be a relatively tight one, regulating most disputes. The British favored a less centralized system. In other words, in order to protect herself, Austria had either to threaten or to harm others, whereas Britain did not. For Austria and her neighbors the security dilemma was acute; for Britain it was not.

The ultimate cost of CD is of course loss of sovereignty. This cost can vary from situation to situation. The lower it is (for instance, because the two states have compatible ideologies, are similar ethnically, have a common culture, or because the citizens of the losing state expect economic benefits), the less the impact of the security dilemma; the greater the costs, the greater the impact of the dilemma. Here is another reason why extreme differences in values and ideologies exacerbate international conflict.

*   *   *

Subjective Security Demands.   Decision makers act in terms of the vulnerability they feel, which can differ from the actual situation; we must therefore examine the decision makers' subjective security requirements. Two dimensions are involved. First, even if they agree about the objective situation, people can differ about how much security they desire—or, to put it more precisely, about the price they are willing to pay to gain increments of security. The more states value their security above all else (that is, see a prohibitively high cost in CD), the more they are likely to be sensitive to even minimal threats, and to demand high levels of arms. And if arms are positively valued because of pressures from a military-industrial complex, it will be especially hard for status-quo powers to cooperate. By contrast, the security dilemma will not operate as strongly when pressing domestic concerns increase the opportunity costs of armaments. In this case, the net advantage of exploiting the other (DC) will be less, and the costs of arms races (that is, one aspect of DD) will be greater; therefore the state will behave as though it were relatively invulnerable.

The second aspect of subjective security is the perception of threat (that is, the estimate of whether the other will cooperate). A state that is predisposed to see either a specific other state as an adversary, or others in general as a menace, will react more strongly and more quickly than a state that sees its environment as benign. Indeed, when a state believes that another not only is not likely to be an adversary, but has sufficient interests in common with it to be an ally, then it will actually welcome an increase in the other's power.

*   *   *

GEOGRAPHY, COMMITMENTS, BELIEFS, AND SECURITY
THROUGH EXPANSION

* * * Situations vary in the ease or difficulty with which all states can simultaneously achieve a high degree of security. The influence of military technology on this variable is the subject of the next section. Here we want to treat the impact of beliefs, geography, and commitments (many of which can be considered to be modifications of geography, since they bind states to defend areas outside their homelands). In the crowded continent of Europe, security requirements were hard to mesh. Being surrounded by powerful states, Germany's problem—or the problem created by Germany—was always great and was even worse when her relations with both France and Russia were bad, such as before World War I. In that case, even a status-quo Germany, if she could not change the political situation, would almost have been forced to adopt something like the Schlieffen Plan. Because she could not hold off both of her enemies, she had to be prepared to defeat one quickly and then deal with the other in a more leisurely fashion. If France or Russia stayed out of a war between the other

state and Germany, they would allow Germany to dominate the Continent (even if that was not Germany's aim). They therefore had to deny Germany this ability, thus making Germany less secure. Although Germany's arrogant and erratic behavior, coupled with the desire for an unreasonably high level of security (which amounted to the desire to escape from her geographic plight), compounded the problem, even wise German statesmen would have been hard put to gain a high degree of security without alarming their neighbors.

*   *   *

III. Offense, Defense, and the Security Dilemma

Another approach starts with the central point of the security dilemma—that an increase in one state's security decreases the security of others—and examines the conditions under which this proposition holds. Two crucial variables are involved: whether defensive weapons and policies can be distinguished from offensive ones, and whether the defense or the offense has the advantage. The definitions are not always clear, and many cases are difficult to judge, but these two variables shed a great deal of light on the question of whether status-quo powers will adopt compatible security policies. All the variables discussed so far leave the heart of the problem untouched. But when defensive weapons differ from offensive ones, it is possible for a state to make itself more secure without making others less secure. And when the defense has the advantage over the offense, a large increase in one state's security only slightly decreases the security of the others, and status-quo powers can all enjoy a high level of security and largely escape from the state of nature.

OFFENSE-DEFENSE BALANCE

When we say that the offense has the advantage, we simply mean that it is easier to destroy the other's army and take its territory than it is to defend one's own. When the defense has the advantage, it is easier to protect and to hold than it is to move forward, destroy, and take. If effective defenses can be erected quickly, an attacker may be able to keep territory he has taken in an initial victory. Thus, the dominance of the defense made it very hard for Britain and France to push Germany out of France in World War I. But when superior defenses are difficult for an aggressor to improvise on the battlefield and must be constructed during peacetime, they provide no direct assistance to him.

The security dilemma is at its most vicious when commitments, strategy, or technology dictate that the only route to security lies through expansion. Status-quo powers must then act like aggressors; the fact that they would gladly agree to forego the opportunity for expansion in return for guarantees for their security has no implications for their behavior. Even if expansion is not sought as a goal in itself, there will be quick and drastic changes in the distribution of territory and influence. Conversely, when the defense has the advantage, status-quo states can make themselves more secure without gravely endangering others.[8] Indeed, if the defense has enough of an advantage and if the states are of roughly equal size, not only will the security dilemma cease to inhibit status-quo states from cooperating, but aggression will be next to impossible, thus rendering international anarchy relatively unimportant. If states cannot conquer each other, then the lack of sovereignty, although it presents problems of collective goods in a number of areas, no longer forces states to devote their primary attention to self-preservation. Although, if force were not usable, there would be fewer restraints on the use of nonmilitary instruments, these are rarely powerful enough to threaten the vital interests of a major state.

Two questions of the offense-defense balance can be separated. First, does the state have to spend more or less than one dollar on defensive forces to offset each dollar spent by the other side on forces that could be used to attack? If the state has one dollar to spend on increasing its security, should it put it into offensive or defensive forces? Second, with a given inventory of forces, is it better to attack or to defend? Is there an incentive to strike first or to absorb the other's blow? These two aspects are often linked: if each dollar spent on offense can overcome each dollar spent on defense, and if both sides have the same defense budgets, then both are likely to build offensive forces and find it attractive to attack rather than to wait for the adversary to strike.

These aspects affect the security dilemma in different ways. The first has its greatest impact on arms races. If the defense has the advantage, and if the status-quo powers have reasonable subjective security requirements, they can probably avoid an arms race. Although an increase in one side's arms and security will still decrease the other's security, the former's increase will be larger than the latter's decrease. So if one side increases its arms, the other can bring its security back up to its previous level by adding a smaller amount to its forces. And if the first side reacts to this change, its increase will also be smaller than the stimulus that produced it. Thus a stable equilibrium will be reached. Shifting from dynamics to statics, each side can be quite secure with forces roughly equal to those of the other. Indeed, if the defense is much more potent than the offense, each side can be willing to have forces much smaller than the other's, and can be indifferent to a wide range of the other's defense policies.

The second aspect—whether it is better to attack or to defend—influences short-run stability. When the offense has the advantage, a state's reaction to international tension will increase the chances of war. The incentives for pre-emption and the "reciprocal fear of surprise attack" in this situation have been made clear by analyses of the dangers that exist when two countries have first-strike capabilities.[9] There is no way for the state to increase its security without menacing, or even attacking, the other. Even Bismarck, who once called preventive war "committing suicide from fear of death," said that "no government, if it regards war as inevitable even if it does not want it, would be so foolish as to leave to the enemy the choice of time and occasion and to wait for the moment which is most convenient for the enemy."[10] In another arena, the same dilemma applies to the policeman in a dark alley confronting a suspected criminal who appears to be holding a weapon. Though racism may indeed be present, the security dilemma can account for many of the tragic shootings of innocent people in the ghettos.

Beliefs about the course of a war in which the offense has the advantage further deepen the security dilemma. When there are incentives to strike first, a successful attack will usually so weaken the other side that victory will be relatively quick, bloodless, and decisive. It is in these periods when conquest is possible and attractive that states consolidate power internally—for instance, by destroying the feudal barons—and expand externally. There are several consequences that decrease the chance of cooperation among status-quo states. First, war will be profitable for the winner. The costs will be low and the benefits high. Of course, losers will suffer; the fear of losing could induce states to try to form stable cooperative arrangements, but the temptation of victory will make this particularly difficult. Second, because wars are expected to be both frequent and short, there will be incentives for high levels of arms, and quick and strong reaction to the other's increases in arms. The state cannot afford to wait until there is unambiguous evidence that the other is building new weapons. Even large states that have faith in their economic strength cannot wait, because the war will be over before their products can reach the army. Third, when wars are quick, states will have to recruit allies in advance.[11] Without the opportunity for bargaining and re-alignments during the opening stages of hostilities, peacetime diplomacy loses a degree of the fluidity that facilitates balance-of-power policies. Because alliances must be secured during peacetime, the international system is more likely to become bipolar. It is hard to say whether war therefore becomes more or less likely, but this bipolarity increases tension between the two camps and makes it harder for status-quo states to gain the benefits of cooperation. Fourth, if wars are frequent, statesmen's perceptual thresholds will be adjusted accordingly and they will be quick to perceive ambiguous evidence as indicating that others are aggressive. Thus, there will be more cases of status-quo powers arming against each other in the incorrect belief that the other is hostile.

When the defense has the advantage, all the foregoing is reversed. The state that fears attack does not pre-empt—since that would be a wasteful use of its military resources—but rather prepares to receive an attack. Doing so does not decrease the security of others, and several states can do it simultaneously; the situation will therefore be stable, and status-quo powers will be able to cooperate. * * *

More is involved than short-run dynamics. When the defense is dominant, wars are likely to become stalemates and can be won only at enormous cost. Relatively small and weak states can hold off larger and stronger ones, or can deter attack by raising the costs of conquest to an unacceptable level. States then approach equality in what they can do to each other. Like the .45-caliber pistol in the American West, fortifications were the "great equalizer" in some periods. Changes in the status quo are less frequent and cooperation is more common wherever the security dilemma is thereby reduced.

Many of these arguments can be illustrated by the major powers' policies in the periods preceding the two world wars. Bismarck's wars surprised statesmen by showing that the offense had the advantage, and by being quick, relatively cheap, and quite decisive. Falling into a common error, observers projected this pattern into the future. The resulting expectations had several effects. First, states sought semi-permanent allies. In the early stages of the Franco-Prussian War, Napoleon III had thought that there would be plenty of time to recruit Austria to his side. Now, others were not going to repeat this mistake. Second, defense budgets were high and reacted quite sharply to increases on the other side. * * * Third, most decision makers thought that the next European war would not cost much blood and treasure.[12] That is one reason why war was generally seen as inevitable and why mass opinion was so bellicose. Fourth, once war seemed likely, there were strong pressures to pre-empt. Both sides believed that whoever moved first could penetrate the other deep enough to disrupt mobilization and thus gain an insurmountable advantage. (There was no such belief about the use of naval forces. Although Churchill made an ill-advised speech saying that if German ships "do not come out and fight in time of war they will be dug out like rats in a hole,"[13] everyone knew that submarines, mines, and coastal fortifications made this impossible. So at the start of the war each navy prepared to defend itself rather than attack, and the short-run destabilizing forces that launched the armies toward each other did not operate.)[14] Furthermore, each side knew that the other saw the situation the same way, thus increasing the perceived danger that the other would attack, and giving each added reasons to precipitate a war if conditions seemed favorable. In the long and the short run, there were thus both offensive and defensive incentives to strike. This situation casts light on the common question about German motives in 1914: "Did Germany unleash the war deliberately to become a world power or did she support Austria merely to defend a weakening ally," thereby protecting her own position?[15] To some extent, this question is misleading. Because of the perceived advantage of the offense, war was seen as the best route both to gaining expansion and to avoiding drastic loss of influence. There seemed to be no way for Germany merely to retain and safeguard her existing position.

Of course the war showed these beliefs to have been wrong on all points. Trenches and machine guns gave the defense an overwhelming advantage. The fighting became deadlocked and produced horrendous casualties. It made no sense for the combatants to bleed themselves to death. If they had known the power of the defense beforehand, they would have rushed for their own trenches rather than for the enemy's territory. Each side could have done this without increasing the other's incentives to strike. War might have broken out anyway, * * * but at least the pressures of time and the fear of allowing the other to get the first blow would not have contributed to this end. And, had both sides known the costs of the war, they would have negotiated much more seriously. The

obvious question is why the states did not seek a negotiated settlement as soon as the shape of the war became clear. Schlieffen had said that if his plan failed, peace should be sought.[16] The answer is complex, uncertain, and largely outside of the scope of our concerns. But part of the reason was the hope and sometimes the expectation that breakthroughs could be made and the dominance of the offensive restored. Without that hope, the political and psychological pressures to fight to a decisive victory might have been overcome.

The politics of the interwar period were shaped by the memories of the previous conflict and the belief that any future war would resemble it. Political and military lessons reinforced each other in ameliorating the security dilemma. Because it was believed that the First World War had been a mistake that could have been avoided by skillful conciliation, both Britain and, to a lesser extent, France were highly sensitive to the possibility that interwar Germany was not a real threat to peace, and alert to the danger that reacting quickly and strongly to her arms could create unnecessary conflict. And because Britain and France expected the defense to continue to dominate, they concluded that it was safe to adopt a more relaxed and non-threatening military posture.[17] Britain also felt less need to maintain tight alliance bonds. The Allies' military posture then constituted only a slight danger to Germany; had the latter been content with the status quo, it would have been easy for both sides to have felt secure behind their lines of fortifications. Of course the Germans were not content, so it is not surprising that they devoted their money and attention to finding ways out of a defense-dominated stalemate. *Blitzkrieg* tactics were necessary if they were to use force to change the status quo.

The initial stages of the war on the Western Front also contrasted with the First World War. Only with the new air arm were there any incentives to strike first, and these forces were too weak to carry out the grandiose plans that had been both dreamed and feared. The armies, still the main instrument, rushed to defensive positions. Perhaps the allies could have successfully attacked while the

Germans were occupied in Poland.[18] But belief in the defense was so great that this was never seriously contemplated. Three months after the start of the war, the French Prime Minister summed up the view held by almost everyone but Hitler: on the Western Front there is "deadlock. Two Forces of equal strength and the one that attacks seeing such enormous casualties that it cannot move without endangering the continuation of the war or of the aftermath."[19] The Allies were caught in a dilemma they never fully recognized, let alone solved. On the one hand, they had very high war aims; although unconditional surrender had not yet been adopted, the British had decided from the start that the removal of Hitler was a necessary condition for peace.[20] On the other hand, there were no realistic plans or instruments for allowing the Allies to impose their will on the other side. The British Chief of the Imperial General Staff noted, "The French have no intention of carrying out an offensive for years, if at all"; the British were only slightly bolder.[21] So the Allies looked to a long war that would wear the Germans down, cause civilian suffering through shortages, and eventually undermine Hitler. There was little analysis to support this view—and indeed it probably was not supportable—but as long as the defense was dominant and the numbers on each side relatively equal, what else could the Allies do?

To summarize, the security dilemma was much less powerful after World War I than it had been before. In the later period, the expected power of the defense allowed status-quo states to pursue compatible security policies and avoid arms races. Furthermore, high tension and fear of war did not set off short-run dynamics by which each state, trying to increase its security, inadvertently acted to make war more likely. The expected high costs of war, however, led the Allies to believe that no sane German leader would run the risks entailed in an attempt to dominate the Continent, and discouraged them from risking war themselves.

Technology and Geography. Technology and geography are the two main factors that determine whether the offense or the defense has the advantage.

As Brodie notes, "On the tactical level, as a rule, few physical factors favor the attacker but many favor the defender. The defender usually has the advantage of cover. He characteristically fires from behind some form of shelter while his opponent crosses open ground."[22] Anything that increases the amount of ground the attacker has to cross, or impedes his progress across it, or makes him more vulnerable while crossing, increases the advantage accruing to the defense. When states are separated by barriers that produce these effects, the security dilemma is eased, since both can have forces adequate for defense without being able to attack. * * *

Oceans, large rivers, and mountain ranges serve the same function as buffer zones. Being hard to cross, they allow defense against superior numbers. The defender has merely to stay on his side of the barrier and so can utilize all the men he can bring up to it. The attacker's men, however, can cross only a few at a time, and they are very vulnerable when doing so. If all states were self-sufficient islands, anarchy would be much less of a problem. A small investment in shore defenses and a small army would be sufficient to repel invasion. Only very weak states would be vulnerable, and only very large ones could menace others. As noted above, the United States, and to a lesser extent Great Britain, have partly been able to escape from the state of nature because their geographical positions approximated this ideal.

Although geography cannot be changed to conform to borders, borders can and do change to conform to geography. Borders across which an attack is easy tend to be unstable. States living within them are likely to expand or be absorbed. Frequent wars are almost inevitable since attacking will often seem the best way to protect what one has. This process will stop, or at least slow down, when the state's borders reach—by expansion or contraction—a line of natural obstacles. Security without attack will then be possible. Furthermore, these lines constitute salient solutions to bargaining problems and, to the extent that they are barriers to migration, are likely to divide ethnic groups, thereby raising the costs and lowering the incentives for conquest.

Attachment to one's state and its land reinforce one quasi-geographical aid to the defense. Conquest usually becomes more difficult the deeper the attacker pushes into the other's territory. Nationalism spurs the defenders to fight harder; advancing not only lengthens the attacker's supply lines, but takes him through unfamiliar and often devastated lands that require troops for garrison duty. These stabilizing dynamics will not operate, however, if the defender's war materiel is situated near its borders, or if the people do not care about their state, but only about being on the winning side. * * *

*   *   *

The other major determinant of the offense-defense balance is technology. When weapons are highly vulnerable, they must be employed before they are attacked. Others can remain quite invulnerable in their bases. The former characteristics are embodied in unprotected missiles and many kinds of bombers. (It should be noted that it is not vulnerability *per se* that is crucial, but the location of the vulnerability. Bombers and missiles that are easy to destroy only after having been launched toward their targets do not create destabilizing dynamics.) Incentives to strike first are usually absent for naval forces that are threatened by a naval attack. Like missiles in hardened silos, they are usually well protected when in their bases. Both sides can then simultaneously be prepared to defend themselves successfully.

In ground warfare under some conditions, forts, trenches, and small groups of men in prepared positions can hold off large numbers of attackers. * * *

*   *   *

Concerning nuclear weapons, it is generally agreed that defense is impossible—a triumph not of the offense, but of deterrence. Attack makes no sense, not because it can be beaten off, but because the attacker will be destroyed in turn. In terms of the questions under consideration here, the result is the equivalent of the primacy of the defense. First, security is relatively cheap. Less than one percent of the G.N.P. is devoted to deterring a direct attack on the United States; most of it is spent on acquiring redundant systems to provide a lot of insurance against the worst conceivable contingencies. Second, both sides can simultaneously gain security in the form of second-strike capability. Third, and related to the foregoing, second-strike capability can be maintained in the face of wide variations in the other side's military posture. There is no purely military reason why each side has to react quickly and strongly to the other's increases in arms. Any spending that the other devotes to trying to achieve first-strike capability can be neutralized by the state's spending much smaller sums on protecting its second-strike capability. Fourth, there are no incentives to strike first in a crisis.

*   *   *

OFFENSE-DEFENSE DIFFERENTIATION

The other major variable that affects how strongly the security dilemma operates is whether weapons and policies that protect the state also provide the capability for attack. If they do not, the basic postulate of the security dilemma no longer applies. A state can increase its own security without decreasing that of others. The advantage of the defense can only ameliorate the security dilemma. A differentiation between offensive and defensive stances comes close to abolishing it. Such differentiation does not mean, however, that all security problems will be abolished. If the offense has the advantage, conquest and aggression will still be possible. And if the offense's advantage is great enough, status-quo powers may find it too expensive to protect themselves by defensive forces and decide to procure offensive weapons even though this will menace others. Furthermore, states will still have to worry that even if the other's military posture shows that it is peaceful now, it may develop aggressive intentions in the future.

Assuming that the defense is at least as potent as the offense, the differentiation between them allows status-quo states to behave in ways that are clearly different from those of aggressors. Three beneficial consequences follow. First, status-quo powers can identify each other, thus laying the foundations for cooperation. Conflicts growing out of the mistaken belief that the other side is expansionist will be less frequent. Second, status-quo states will obtain advance warning when others plan aggression. Before a state can attack, it has to develop and deploy offensive weapons. If procurement of these weapons cannot be disguised and takes a fair amount of time, as it almost always does, a status-quo state will have the time to take countermeasures. It need not maintain a high level of defensive arms as long as its potential adversaries are adopting a peaceful posture. * * *

* * *

* * * [I]f all states support the status quo, an obvious arms control agreement is a ban on weapons that are useful for attacking. As President Roosevelt put it in his message to the Geneva Disarmament Conference in 1933: "If all nations will agree wholly to eliminate from possession and use the weapons which make possible a successful attack, defenses automatically will become impregnable, and the frontiers and independence of every nation will become secure."[23] The fact that such treaties have been rare * * * shows either that states are not always willing to guarantee the security of others, or that it is hard to distinguish offensive from defensive weapons.

* * *

IV. Four Worlds

The two variables we have been discussing—whether the offense or the defense has the advantage, and whether offensive postures can be distinguished from defensive ones—can be combined to yield four possible worlds.

The first world is the worst for status-quo states. There is no way to get security without menacing others, and security through defense is terribly difficult to obtain. Because offensive and defensive postures are the same, status-quo states acquire the same kind of arms that are sought by aggressors. And because the offense has the advantage over the defense, attacking is the best route to protecting what you have; status-quo states will therefore behave like aggressors. The situation will be unstable. Arms races are likely. Incentives to strike first will turn crises into wars. Decisive victories and conquests will be common. States will grow and shrink rapidly, and it will be hard for any state to maintain its size and influence without trying to increase them. Cooperation among status-quo powers will be extremely hard to achieve.

	Offense Has the Advantage	Defense Has the Advantage
Offensive Posture Not Distinguishable from Defensive One	1 Doubly dangerous	2 Security dilemma, but security requirements may be compatible.
Offensive Posture Distinguishable from Defensive One	3 No security dilemma, but aggression possible. Status-quo states can follow different policy than aggressors. Warning given.	4 Doubly stable

There are no cases that totally fit this picture, but it bears more than a passing resemblance to Europe before World War I. Britain and Germany, although in many respects natural allies, ended up as enemies. Of course much of the explanation lies in Germany's ill-chosen policy. And from the perspective of our theory, the powers' ability to avoid war in a series of earlier crises cannot be easily explained. Nevertheless, much of the behavior in this period was the product of technology and beliefs that magnified the security dilemma. Decision makers thought that the offense had a big advantage and saw little difference between offensive and defensive military postures. The era was characterized by arms races. And once war seemed likely, mobilization races created powerful incentives to strike first.

In the nuclear era, the first world would be one in which each side relied on vulnerable weapons that were aimed at similar forces and each side understood the situation. In this case, the incentives to strike first would be very high—so high that status-quo powers as well as aggressors would be sorely tempted to pre-empt. And since the forces could be used to change the status quo as well as to preserve it, there would be no way for both sides to increase their security simultaneously. Now the familiar logic of deterrence leads both sides to see the dangers in this world. Indeed, the new understanding of this situation was one reason why vulnerable bombers and missiles were replaced. Ironically, the 1950's would have been more hazardous if the decision makers had been aware of the dangers of their posture and had therefore felt greater pressure to strike first. This situation could be recreated if both sides were to rely on MIRVed ICBM's.

In the second world, the security dilemma operates because offensive and defensive postures cannot be distinguished; but it does not operate as strongly as in the first world because the defense has the advantage, and so an increment in one side's strength increases its security more than it decreases the other's. So, if both sides have reasonable subjective security requirements, are of roughly equal power, and the variables discussed earlier are favorable, it is quite likely that status-quo states can adopt compatible security policies. * * *

This world is the one that comes closest to matching most periods in history. Attacking is usually harder than defending because of the strength of fortifications and obstacles. But purely defensive postures are rarely possible because fortifications are usually supplemented by armies and mobile guns which can support an attack. In the nuclear era, this world would be one in which both sides relied on relatively invulnerable ICBM's and believed that limited nuclear war was impossible. * * *

In the third world there may be no security dilemma, but there are security problems. Because states can procure defensive systems that do not threaten others, the dilemma need not operate. But because the offense has the advantage, aggression is possible, and perhaps easy. If the offense has enough of an advantage, even a status-quo state

may take the initiative rather than risk being attacked and defeated. If the offense has less of an advantage, stability and cooperation are likely because the status-quo states will procure defensive forces. They need not react to others who are similarly armed, but can wait for the warning they would receive if others started to deploy offensive weapons. But each state will have to watch the others carefully, and there is room for false suspicions. The costliness of the defense and the allure of the offense can lead to unnecessary mistrust, hostility, and war, unless some of the variables discussed earlier are operating to restrain defection.

* * *

The fourth world is doubly safe. The differentiation between offensive and defensive systems permits a way out of the security dilemma; the advantage of the defense disposes of the problems discussed in the previous paragraphs. There is no reason for a status-quo power to be tempted to procure offensive forces, and aggressors give notice of their intentions by the posture they adopt. Indeed, if the advantage of the defense is great enough, there are no security problems. The loss of the ultimate form of the power to alter the status quo would allow greater scope for the exercise of nonmilitary means and probably would tend to freeze the distribution of values.

* * *

NOTES

1. Quoted in Gerald Wheeler, *Prelude to Pearl Harbor* (Columbia: University of Missouri Press 1963), 167.
2. Quoted in Leonard Wainstein, "The Dreadnought Gap," in Robert Art and Kenneth Waltz, eds., *The Use of Force* (Boston: Little, Brown 1971), 155 * * *.
3. In another article, Jervis says: "International politics sometimes resembles what is called a Prisoner's Dilemma (PD). In this scenario, two men have been caught red-handed com-

mitting a minor crime. The district attorney knows that they are also guilty of a much more serious offense. He tells each of them separately that if he confesses and squeals on his buddy, he will go free and the former colleague will go to jail for thirty years. If both of them refuse to give any information, they will be prosecuted for the minor crime and be jailed for thirty days; if they both squeal, plea-bargaining will get them ten years. In other words, as long as each criminal cares only about himself, he will confess to the more serious crime no matter what he thinks his colleague will do. If he confesses and his buddy does not, he will get the best possible outcome (freedom); if he confesses and his buddy also does so, the outcome will not be good (ten years in jail), but it will be better than keeping silent and going to jail for thirty years. Since both can see this, both will confess. Paradoxically, if they had both been irrational and kept quiet, they would have gone to jail for only a month." (Robert Jervis, "A Political Science Perspective on the Balance of Power and the Concert," *American Historical Review* 97, no. 3 (June 1992): 720.)

4. Experimental evidence for this proposition is summarized in James Tedeschi, Barry Schlenker, and Thomas Bonoma, *Conflict, Power, and Games* (Chicago: Aldine 1973), 135–41.

5. The results of Prisoner's Dilemma games played in the laboratory support this argument. See Anatol Rapoport and Albert Chammah, *Prisoner's Dilemma* (Ann Arbor: University of Michigan Press 1965), 33–50. Also see Robert Axelrod, *Conflict of Interest* (Chicago: Markham 1970), 60–70.

6. Quoted in Bernard Brodie, *Strategy in the Missile Age* (Princeton: Princeton University Press 1959), 6.

7. Herbert York, *The Advisors: Oppenheimer, Teller, and the Superbomb* (San Francisco: Freemar, 1976), 56–60.

8. Thus, when Wolfers, [*Discord and Collaboration* (Baltimore: Johns Hopkins Press 1962),] 126, argues that a status-quo state that settles for rough equality of power with its adversary, rather than seeking preponderance, may be able to convince the other to reciprocate by showing that it wants only to protect itself, not menace the other, he assumes that the defense has an advantage.

9. Schelling, [*The Strategy of Conflict* (New York: Oxford University Press 1963),] chap. 9.

10. Quoted in Fritz Fischer, *War of Illusions* (New York: Norton 1975), 377, 461.

11. George Quester, *Offense and Defense in the International System* (New York: John Wiley 1977), 105–06; Sontag [*European Diplomatic History, 1871–1932* (New York: Appleton-Century-Crofts 1933)], 4–5.

12. Some were not so optimistic. Gray's remark is well-known: "The lamps are going out all over Europe; we shall not see them lit again in our life-time." The German Prime Minister, Beth-mann Hollweg, also feared the consequences of the war. But the controlling view was that it would certainly pay for the winner.

13. Quoted in Martin Gilbert, *Winston S. Churchill*, III, *The Challenge of War, 1914–1916* (Boston: Houghton Mifflin 1971), 84.

14. Quester (fn. 33), 98–99. Robert Art, *The Influence of Foreign Policy on Seapower*, II (Beverly Hills: Sage Professional Papers in International Studies Series, 1973), 14–18, 26–28.

15. Konrad Jarausch, "The Illusion of Limited War: Chancellor Bethmann Hollweg's Calculated Risk, July 1914," *Central European History*, II (March 1969), 50.

16. Brodie (fn. 6), 58.

17. President Roosevelt and the American delegates to the League of Nations Disarmament Conference maintained that the tank and mobile heavy artillery had re-established the dominance of the offensive, thus making disarmament more urgent (Boggs, [*Attempts to Define and Limit "Aggressive" Armament in Diplomacy and Strategy* (Columbia: University of Missouri Studies, XVI, No. 1, 1941)], pp. 31, 108), but this was a minority position and may not even have been believed by the Amer-

icans. The reduced prestige and influence of the military, and the high pressures to cut government spending throughout this period also contributed to the lowering of defense budgets.

18. Jon Kimche, *The Unfought Battle* (New York: Stein 1968); Nicholas William Bethell, *The War Hitler Won: The Fall of Poland, September 1939* (New York: Holt 1972); Alan Alexandroff and Richard Rosecrance, "Deterrence in 1939," *World Politics,* XXIX (April 1977), 404–24.

19. Roderick Macleod and Denis Kelly, eds., *Time Unguarded: The Ironside Diaries, 1937–1940* (New York: McKay 1962), 173.

20. For a short time, as France was falling, the British Cabinet did discuss reaching a negotiated peace with Hitler. The official history ignores this, but it is covered in P.M.H. Bell, *A Certain Eventuality* (Farnborough, England: Saxon House 1974), 40–48.

21. Macleod and Kelly (fn. 19), 174. In flat contradiction to common sense and almost everything they believed about modern warfare, the Allies planned an expedition to Scandinavia to cut the supply of iron ore to Germany and to aid Finland against the Russians. But the dominant mood was the one described above.

22. Brodie (fn. 6), 179.

23. Quoted in Merze Tate, *The United States and Armaments* (Cambridge: Harvard University Press 1948), 108.

JOHN MUELLER

The Essential Irrelevance of Nuclear Weapons: Stability in the Postwar World

I t is widely assumed that, for better or worse, the existence of nuclear weapons has profoundly shaped our lives and destinies. Some find the weapons supremely beneficial. Defense analyst Edward Luttwak says, "we have lived since 1945 without another world war precisely because rational minds . . . extracted a durable peace from the very terror of nuclear weapons."[1] And Robert Art and Kenneth Waltz conclude, "the probability of war between America and Russia or between NATO and the Warsaw Pact is practically nil precisely because the military planning and deployments of each, together with the fear of escalation to general nuclear war, keep it that way."[2] Others argue that, while we may have been lucky so far, the continued existence of the weapons promises eventual calamity: The doomsday clock on the cover of the *Bulletin of the Atomic Scientists* has been pointedly hovering near midnight for over 40 years now, and in his influential bestseller, *The Fate of the Earth,* Jonathan Schell dramatically concludes that if we do not "rise up and cleanse the earth of nuclear weapons," we will "sink into the final coma and end it all."[3]

This article takes issue with both of these points of view and concludes that nuclear weapons neither crucially define a fundamental stability nor threaten severely to disturb it.

The paper is in two parts. In the first it is argued that, while nuclear weapons may have substantially influenced political rhetoric, public discourse, and defense budgets and planning, it is not at all clear that they have had a significant im-

From *International Security* 13, no. 2 (fall 1988): 55–79. Some of the author's notes have been omitted.

pact on the history of world affairs since World War II. They do not seem to have been necessary to deter World War III, to determine alliance patterns, or to cause the United States and the Soviet Union to behave cautiously.

In the second part, these notions are broadened to a discussion of stability in the postwar world. It is concluded that there may be a long-term trend away from war among developed countries and that the long peace since World War II is less a peculiarity of the nuclear age than the logical conclusion of a substantial historical process. Seen broadly, deterrence seems to be remarkably firm; major war—a war among developed countries, like World War II or worse—is so improbable as to be obsolescent; imbalances in weapons systems are unlikely to have much impact on anything except budgets; and the nuclear arms competition may eventually come under control not so much out of conscious design as out of atrophy born of boredom.

The Impact of Nuclear Weapons

The postwar world might well have turned out much the same even in the absence of nuclear weapons. Without them, world war would have been discouraged by the memory of World War II, by superpower contentment with the postwar status quo, by the nature of Soviet ideology, and by the fear of escalation. Nor do the weapons seem to have been the crucial determinants of Cold War developments, of alliance patterns, or of the way the major powers have behaved in crises.

DETERRENCE OF WORLD WAR

It is true that there has been no world war since 1945 and it is also true that nuclear weapons have been developed and deployed in part to deter such a conflict. It does not follow, however, that it is the weapons that have prevented the war—that peace has been, in Winston Churchill's memorable construction, "the sturdy child of [nuclear] terror." To assert that the ominous presence of nuclear weapons has prevented a war between the two

power blocs, one must assume that there would have been a war had these weapons not existed. This assumption ignores several other important war-discouraging factors in the postwar world.

The Memory of World War II. A nuclear war would certainly be vastly destructive, but for the most part nuclear weapons simply compound and dramatize a military reality that by 1945 had already become appalling. Few with the experience of World War II behind them would contemplate its repetition with anything other than horror. Even before the bomb had been perfected, world war had become spectacularly costly and destructive, killing some 50 million worldwide. As former Secretary of State Alexander Haig put it in 1982: "The catastrophic consequences of another world war—with or without nuclear weapons—make deterrence our highest objective and our only rational military strategy."[4]

Postwar Contentment. For many of the combatants, World War I was as destructive as World War II, but its memory did not prevent another world war. Of course, as will be discussed more fully in the second half of this article, most nations *did* conclude from the horrors of World War I that such an event must never be repeated. If the only nations capable of starting World War II had been Britain, France, the Soviet Union, and the United States, the war would probably never have occurred. Unfortunately other major nations sought direct territorial expansion, and conflicts over these desires finally led to war.

Unlike the situation after World War I, however, the only powers capable of creating another world war since 1945 have been the big victors, the United States and the Soviet Union, each of which has emerged comfortably dominant in its respective sphere. As Waltz has observed, "the United States, and the Soviet Union as well, have more reason to be satisfied with the status quo than most earlier great powers had."[5] (Indeed, except for the dismemberment of Germany, even Hitler might have been content with the empire his arch-enemy Stalin controlled at the end of the war.) While there have been many disputes since the war, neither power has had a grievance so essential as to make a world war—whether nuclear or not—an attractive means for removing the grievance.

Soviet Ideology.   Although the Soviet Union and international communism have visions of changing the world in a direction they prefer, their ideology stresses revolutionary procedures over major war. The Soviet Union may have hegemonic desires as many have argued but, with a few exceptions (especially the Korean War) to be discussed below, its tactics, inspired by the cautiously pragmatic Lenin, have stressed subversion, revolution, diplomatic and economic pressure, seduction, guerrilla warfare, local uprising, and civil war—levels at which nuclear weapons have little relevance. The communist powers have never—before or after the invention of nuclear weapons—subscribed to a Hitler-style theory of direct, Armageddon-risking conquest, and they have been extremely wary of provoking Western powers into large-scale war. Moreover, if the memory of World War II deters anyone, it probably does so to an extreme degree for the Soviets. Officially and unofficially they seem obsessed by the memory of the destruction they suffered. In 1953 Ambassador Averell Harriman, certainly no admirer of Stalin, observed that the Soviet dictator "was determined, if he could avoid it, never again to go through the horrors of another protracted world war."[6]

The Belief in Escalation.   Those who started World Wars I and II did so not because they felt that costly wars of attrition were desirable, but because they felt that escalation to wars of attrition could be avoided. In World War I the offensive was believed to be dominant, and it was widely assumed that conflict would be short and decisive.[7] In World War II, both Germany and Japan experienced repeated success with bluster, short wars in peripheral areas, and blitzkrieg, aided by the counterproductive effects of their opponents' appeasement and inaction.[8]

World war in the post-1945 era has been prevented not so much by visions of nuclear horror as by the generally-accepted belief that conflict can easily escalate to a level, nuclear or not, that the essentially satisfied major powers would find intolerably costly.

To deal with the crucial issue of escalation, it is useful to assess two important phenomena of the early post-war years: the Soviet preponderance in conventional arms and the Korean War.

First, it has been argued that the Soviets would have been tempted to take advantage of their conventional strength after World War II to snap up a prize like Western Europe if its chief defender, the United States, had not possessed nuclear weapons. As Winston Churchill put it in 1950, "nothing preserves Europe from an overwhelming military attack except the devastating resources of the United States in this awful weapon."[9]

This argument requires at least three questionable assumptions: (1) that the Soviets really think of Western Europe as a prize worth taking risks for; (2) that, even without the atomic bomb to rely on, the United States would have disarmed after 1945 as substantially as it did; and (3) that the Soviets have actually ever had the strength to be quickly and overwhelmingly successful in a conventional attack in Western Europe.[10]

However, even if one accepts these assumptions, the Soviet Union would in all probability still have been deterred from attacking Western Europe by the enormous potential of the American war machine. Even if the USSR had the ability to blitz Western Europe, it could not have stopped the United States from repeating what it did after 1941: mobilizing with deliberate speed, putting its economy onto a wartime footing, and wearing the enemy down in a protracted conventional major war of attrition massively supplied from its unapproachable rear base.

The economic achievement of the United States during the war was astounding. While holding off one major enemy, it concentrated with its allies on defeating another, then turned back to the first. Meanwhile, it supplied everybody. With 8 million of its ablest men out of the labor market, it increased industrial production 15 percent per year and agricultural production 30 percent overall. Before the end of 1943 it was producing so much that some munitions plants were closed down, and even so it ended the war with a substantial surplus of wheat and over $90 billion in surplus war goods. (National governmental expenditures in the first peacetime year, 1946, were only about $60 billion.) As Denis Brogan observed at the time, "to the Americans war is a business, not an art."[11]

If anyone was in a position to appreciate this, it was the Soviets. By various circuitous routes the United States supplied the Soviet Union with, among other things, 409,526 trucks; 12,161 combat vehicles (more than the Germans had in 1939); 32,200 motorcycles; 1,966 locomotives; 16,000,000 pairs of boots (in two sizes); and over one-half pound of food for every Soviet soldier for every day of the war (much of it Spam).[12] It is the kind of feat that concentrates the mind, and it is extremely difficult to imagine the Soviets willingly taking on this somewhat lethargic, but ultimately hugely effective juggernaut. That Stalin was fully aware of the American achievement—and deeply impressed by it—is clear. Adam Ulam has observed that Stalin had "great respect for the United States' vast economic and hence military potential, quite apart from the bomb," and that his "whole career as dictator had been a testimony to his belief that production figures were a direct indicator of a given country's power."[13] As a member of the Joint Chiefs of Staff put it in 1949, "if there is any single factor today which would deter a nation seeking world domination, it would be the great industrial capacity of this country rather than its armed strength."[14] Or, as Hugh Thomas has concluded, "if the atomic bomb had not existed, Stalin would still have feared the success of the U.S. wartime economy."[15]

After a successful attack on Western Europe the Soviets would have been in a position similar to that of Japan after Pearl Harbor: they might have gains aplenty, but they would have no way to stop the United States (and its major unapproachable allies, Canada and Japan) from eventually gearing up for, and then launching, a war of attrition. * * *

Second, there is the important issue of the Ko-

rean War. Despite the vast American superiority in atomic weapons in 1950, Stalin was willing to order, approve, or at least acquiesce in an outright attack by a communist state on a non-communist one, and it must be assumed that he would have done so at least as readily had nuclear weapons not existed. The American response was essentially the result of the lessons learned from the experiences of the 1930s: comparing this to similar incursions in Manchuria, Ethiopia, and Czechoslovakia (and partly also to previous Soviet incursions into neighboring states in East Europe and the Baltic area), Western leaders resolved that such provocations must be nipped in the bud. If they were allowed to succeed, they would only encourage more aggression in more important locales later. Consequently it seems likely that the Korean War would have occurred in much the same way had nuclear weapons not existed.

For the Soviets the lessons of the Korean War must have enhanced those of World War II: once again the United States was caught surprised and under-armed, once again it rushed hastily into action, once again it soon applied itself in a forceful way to combat—in this case for an area that it had previously declared to be of only peripheral concern. If the Korean War was a limited probe of Western resolve, it seems the Soviets drew the lessons the Truman administration intended. Unlike Germany, Japan, and Italy in the 1930s, they were tempted to try no more such probes: there have been no Koreas since Korea. It seems likely that this valuable result would have come about regardless of the existence of nuclear weapons, and it suggests that the Korean War helped to delimit vividly the methods the Soviet Union would be allowed to use to pursue its policy.[16]

It is conceivable that the USSR, in carrying out its ideological commitment to revolution, might have been tempted to try step-by-step, Hitler-style military probes if it felt these would be reasonably cheap and free of risk. The policy of containment, of course, carrying with it the threat of escalation, was designed precisely to counter such probes. * * *

*   *   *

COLD WAR AND CRISIS

If nuclear weapons have been unnecessary to prevent world war, they also do not seem to have crucially affected other important developments, including * * * the * * * behavior of the superpowers in crisis.

*   *   *

Crisis Behavior.   Because of the harrowing image of nuclear war, it is sometimes argued, the United States and the Soviet Union have been notably more restrained than they might otherwise have been, and thus crises that might have escalated to dangerous levels have been resolved safely at low levels.[17]

There is, of course, no definitive way to refute this notion since we are unable to run the events of the last forty years over, this time without nuclear weapons. And it is certainly the case that decision-makers are well aware of the horrors of nuclear war and cannot be expected to ignore the possibility that a crisis could lead to such devastation.

However, this idea—that it is the fear of nuclear war that has kept behavior restrained—looks far less convincing when its underlying assumption is directly confronted: that the major powers would have allowed their various crises to escalate if all they had to fear at the end of the escalatory ladder was something like a repetition of World War II. Whatever the rhetoric in these crises, it is difficult to see why the unaugmented horror of repeating World War II, combined with considerable comfort with the status quo, wouldn't have been enough to inspire restraint.

Once again, escalation is the key: what deters is the belief that escalation to something intolerable will occur, not so much what the details of the ultimate unbearable punishment are believed to be. Where the belief that the conflict will escalate is absent, nuclear countries *have* been militarily challenged with war—as in Korea, Vietnam, Afghanistan, Algeria, and the Falklands.

To be clear: None of this is meant to deny that the sheer horror of nuclear war is impressive and mind-concentratingly dramatic, particularly in the speed with which it could bring about massive destruction. Nor is it meant to deny that decision-makers, both in times of crisis and otherwise, are fully conscious of how horribly destructive a nuclear war could be. It is simply to stress that the sheer horror of repeating World War II is not all that much *less* impressive or dramatic, and that powers essentially satisfied with the status quo will strive to avoid anything that they feel could lead to *either* calamity. World War II did not cause total destruction in the world, but it did utterly annihilate the three national regimes that brought it about. It is probably quite a bit more terrifying to think about a jump from the 50th floor than about a jump from the 5th floor, but anyone who finds life even minimally satisfying is extremely unlikely to do either.

Did the existence of nuclear weapons keep the Korean conflict restrained? As noted, the communist venture there seems to have been a limited probe—though somewhat more adventurous than usual and one that got out of hand with the massive American and Chinese involvement. As such, there was no particular reason—or meaningful military opportunity—for the Soviets to escalate the war further. In justifying *their* restraint, the Americans continually stressed the danger of escalating to a war with the Soviet Union—something of major concern whether or not the Soviets possessed nuclear weapons.

Nor is it clear that the existence of nuclear weapons has vitally influenced other events. For example, President Harry Truman was of the opinion that his nuclear threat drove the Soviets out of Iran in 1946, and President Dwight Eisenhower, that his nuclear threat drove the Chinese into productive discussions at the end of the Korean War in 1953. McGeorge Bundy's reassessment of these events suggests that neither threat was very well communicated and that, in any event, other occurrences—the maneuverings of the Iranian government in the one case and the death of Stalin in the other—were more important in determining the outcome.[18] But even if we assume the threats *were* important, it is not clear why the threat had to be peculiarly *nuclear*—a threat to commit destruction on the order of World War II would also have been notably unpleasant and dramatic.

Much the same could be said about other instances in which there was a real or implied threat that nuclear weapons might be brought into play: the Taiwan Straits crises of 1954–55 and 1958, the Berlin blockade of 1948–49, the Soviet-Chinese confrontation of 1969, the Six-day War in 1967, the Yom Kippur War of 1973, Cold War disagreements over Lebanon in 1958, Berlin in 1958 and 1961, offensive weapons in Cuba in 1962. All were resolved, or allowed to dissipate, at rather low rungs on the escalatory ladder. While the horror of a possible nuclear war was doubtless clear to the participants, it is certainly not apparent that they would have been much more casual about escalation if the worst they had to visualize was a repetition of World War II.[19]

Of course nuclear weapons add new elements to international politics: new pieces for the players to move around the board (missiles in and out of Cuba, for example), new terrors to contemplate. But in counter to the remark attributed to Albert Einstein that nuclear weapons have changed everything except our way of thinking, it might be suggested that nuclear weapons have changed little except our way of talking, gesturing, and spending money.

*   *   *

Notes

1. Edward N. Luttwak, "Of Bombs and Men," *Commentary,* August 1983, p. 82.

2. Robert J. Art and Kenneth N. Waltz, "Technology, Strategy, and the Uses of Force," in Robert J. Art and Kenneth N. Waltz, eds., *The Use of Force* (Lanham, Md.: University Press of America, 1983), p. 28. See also Klaus Knorr, "Controlling Nuclear War," *International Security,* Vol. 9, No. 4 (Spring 1985), p. 79; John J. Mearsheimer, "Nuclear Weapons and Deterrence in Europe," *International Security,* Vol. 9, No. 3 (Winter 1984/85), pp. 25–26; Robert

Gilpin, *War and Change in World Politics* (Cambridge: Cambridge University Press, 1981), pp. 213–219.

3. Jonathan Schell, *The Fate of the Earth* (New York: Knopf, 1982), p. 231.

4. *New York Times,* April 7, 1982. * * *

5. Kenneth N. Waltz, *Theory of International Politics* (Reading, Mass.: Addison-Wesley, 1979), p. 190. * * *

6. *Newsweek,* March 16, 1953, p. 31. The Soviets presumably picked up a few things from World War I as well; as Taubman notes, they learned the "crucial lesson . . . that world war . . . can destroy the Russian regime." Taubman, *Stalin's American Policy* [New York: Norton, 1982], p. 11.

7. Jack Snyder, *The Ideology of the Offensive* (Ithaca: Cornell University Press, 1984); Stephen Van Evera, "Why Cooperation Failed in 1914," *World Politics,* Vol. 38, No. 1 (October 1985), pp. 80–117. * * *

8. Hitler, however, may have anticipated (or at any rate, was planning for) a total war once he had established his expanded empire—a part of his grand scheme he carefully kept from military and industrial leaders who, he knew, would find it unthinkable: see R.J. Overy, "Hitler's War and the German Economy," *Economic History Review,* Vol. 35, No. 2 (May 1982), pp. 272–291. The Japanese did not want a major war, but they were willing to risk it when their anticipated short war in China became a lengthy, enervating one, and they were forced to choose between wider war and the abandonment of the empire to which they were ideologically committed. See Robert J.C. Butow, *Tojo and the Coming of the War* (Stanford, Calif.: Stanford University Press, 1961), ch. 11.

9. Matthew A. Evangelista, "Stalin's Postwar Army Reappraised," *International Security,* Vol. 7, No. 3 (Winter 1982/83), p. 110.

10. This assumption is strongly questioned in Evangelista, "Stalin's Postwar Army Reappraised," pp. 110–138. * * *

11. Despite shortages, rationing, and tax sur-

charges, American consumer spending increased by 12 percent between 1939 and 1944. Richard R. Lingeman, *Don't You Know There's a War On?* (New York: Putnam, 1970), pp. 133, 357, and ch. 4; Alan S. Milward, *War, Economy and Society 1939–1945* (Berkeley and Los Angeles: University of California Press, 1977), pp. 63–74, 271–275; Mercedes Rosebery, *This Day's Madness* (New York: Macmillan, 1944), p. xii.

12. John R. Deane, *The Strange Alliance* (New York: Viking, 1947), pp. 92–95; Robert Huhn Jones, *The Roads to Russia* (Norman: University of Oklahoma Press, 1969), Appendix A. Additional information from Harvey De-Weerd.

13. Adam Ulam, *The Rivals: America and Russia Since World War II* (New York: Penguin, 1971), pp. 95 and 5. * * *

14. Samuel P. Huntington, *The Common Defense* (New York: Columbia University Press, 1961), p. 46. * * *

15. Thomas, *Armed Truce* [*The Beginnings of the Cold War, 1945–46* (New York: Atheneum, 1986)], p. 548.

16. Soviet military intervention in Afghanistan in 1979 was an effort to prop up a faltering pro-Soviet regime. As such it was not like Korea, but more like American escalation in Vietnam in 1965 or like the Soviet interventions in Hungary in 1956 or Czechoslovakia in 1968. * * *

17. John Lewis Gaddis, *The Long Peace* (New York: Oxford University Press, 1987), pp. 229–232. * * *

18. McGeorge Bundy, "The Unimpressive Record of Atomic Diplomacy," in Gwyn Prins, ed., *The Nuclear Crisis Reader* (New York: Vintage, 1984), pp. 44–47. For the argument that Truman never made a threat, see James A. Thorpe, "Truman's Ultimatum to Stalin in the Azerbaijan Crisis: The Making of a Myth," *Journal of Politics,* Vol. 40, No. 1 (February 1978), pp. 188–195. See also Gaddis, [*The*] *Long Peace* [New York: Oxford University Press, 1987], pp. 124–129; and Richard K. Betts, *Nuclear Blackmail and Nuclear Balance* (Washington, D.C.: Brookings, 1987), pp. 42–47.

19. Interestingly, even in the great "nuclear" crisis over Cuba in 1962, Khrushchev seems to have been affected as much by his memories of World War I and II as by the prospect of thermonuclear destruction. See Graham T. Allison, *Essence of Decision* (Boston: Little, Brown, 1971), p. 221. * * *

MICHAEL W. DOYLE

International Intervention

How might the principles of political independence and territorial integrity be justified? Nonintervention, the dominant norm of international law designed to protect those principles, has been justified by straightforward appeals to law and order that rest on the value of having rules of the road that reduce the probability of conflicts between those actors who prefer some coordination. But abstract ethical considerations such as those fail to include the purposes for which a state engages in or avoids conflict. Nor does ethics give us enough information about who the actors are, their interests, values, environment, and capacities. Political philosophies aim to fill in those blanks. They provide contingent justification for nonintervention but also permit intervention, though for differing reasons.

Principles of nonintervention and intervention have been justified, though in differing ways, by Realists, by Socialists, by Liberals. Although these principles never have been formally justified as a single treaty according to set of philosophical precepts, they nonetheless throughout time have been justified by scholars, by politicians, by citizens who have sought to provide for us good reasons why we should abide by these conventional principles of classic international law and good reasons why we should, as Vattel suggests, sometimes override them.[1] * * *

Principles of Nonintervention and Intervention

REALISTS

In many respects the principles of nonintervention can be seen as a summary of the sort of principles

From Michael Doyle, *Ways of War and Peace* (New York: W. W. Norton, 1997), chap. 11. Some of the author's notes have been omitted.

that a cautious or "soft" Realist would most want to have govern the international system. For example, Hobbes demanded that his sovereigns seek peace wherever they safely could. Rousseau, commenting on the peace plan of the Abbé de St-Pierre, argued that responsible statesmen, particularly, of course, those who were democratic, would not want to engage in wars of aggression but instead would merely seek the security of their own state. In a speech in 1994 U.S. Senator Richard Lugar suggested how a moderate definition of national ambitions can limit interventionism. "The American people," he declared, "are not convinced that we have vital interests in invading Haiti, despite immigration, which we believe might continue even if Mr. Aristide was restored. . . . And we've really not had a policy of forcing democracy on a country, however despicable that regime might be."[2]

But if we probe deeper, we can see that these justifications are extremely contingent from an overall Realist point of view. Doubting the efficacy of international law and morality as foundations for an obligation of nonintervention, Realists tend to see all states as caught in a state of war in which the only source of security is self-help. Security drives states then to focus on relative capabilities and a consequent search for predominance that is unrestrained by any factor but prudence.

Thucydides noted a first challenge to nonintervention coming from what we can describe as a "hard" Realist view, a view espoused by the Athenian generals Cleomedes and Tisias in command of the blockade of Melos.[3] The generals say that rules are fit only for relations among equals. Among unequals, when the strong confront the weak, the only rules that hold are the will of the strong and the obedience of the weak. And so the generals tell the Melians that they should not hope to be saved by the Spartans, their allies, or be saved by rules that would restrict the aggressive actions of states. Instead they have to confront the hard face of power, which is the Athenian fleet blockading the island. The generals add that for Athens this conquest is important. Melos may be a small island, but if a small island can successfully resist the might of Athens, other islands might be tempted to engage in similar rebellions. If this challenge were then to spread, Athens would lose its power. In order to deter challenges and enhance Athenian prestige, the generals claim that the Melian borders have to be overridden; the Melians must surrender or be destroyed.

Even though conquering Melos may have seemed the right thing to do in the view of the two Athenian generals, there's good reason for us to believe that this was not necessarily Thucydides's own view. He seemed to think the Athenian disaster in Sicily was its just consequence. His own view on intervention was more evident in an earlier debate on the fate of Mytilene, a subordinate ally of Athens. There a group of rebels against the Athenian empire sought to establish a self-determining, independent state. When they did so, they came up against the might of Athens.[4]

In the Athenian Assembly, Cleon, a hard-liner, lines up against Diodotus, a soft-liner and they debate the fate of the Mytileneans. What form of punishment, Cleon asks, is the correct fate for those who rebel against the alliance and law of Athens? He says the punishment must fit the crime: They seek to destroy Athens's power, on which its security, indeed, survival rests. The rebels must be killed—men, women, and children—in order to teach a lesson to all others who might be tempted to imitate them. Diodotus corrects Cleon's demands for vengeance and responds as the better Realist, regretting Cleon's harsh conclusion. Diodotus says that thinking about international politics as a matter of right and wrong, as a matter of just and unjust, legal and unlawful, confuses politics with a court of law and interferes with what should be a matter of prudence and rational self-interest. International politics should cover no more than the prudent calculation of long-run security. We have to think of what sort of message, we, the Athenians, send if we slaughter all of them as Cleon urges. Diodotus warns that we may intimidate the subject cities but we also will stir up resistance elsewhere in the empire or with potential allies. Thus Diodotus argues for a softer course. The soft course is not too soft—it involves the death of about a thousand Mytilinean rebels—but he advocates sparing the rest of the island in hopes of a future of imperial reconciliation and imperial stability.

In addition to considerations of prestige and imperial stability, preventive war provides a third reason to override the nonintervention principle. The great English polymath Francis Bacon, in his essay "Of Empire," provided this rationale and drew the policy implications with eloquence and force, urging "that princes do keep due sentinel that none of their neighbors do overgrow so (by increase of territory, by embracing trade, by approaches, or the like) as they become more able to annoy them than they were. . . . [F]or there is no question but a justfear of an imminent danger, though no blow be given, is a lawful cause of war."[5]

Principles of nonintervention seem to have a thin foundation in Realist ethics, which finds them valuable only to the extent they are useful from a national point of view. One cannot abide by the rules of sovereign equality, sovereign nonintervention, when security is at stake. Rousseau thought that security need not be at stake if statesmen isolated themselves from one another, as should an ideal Corsica. Cleon and the Athenian generals at Melos had an expansive notion of security that included the merest threat to prestige. Bacon included any threats to the relative balance of power. Diodotus had a less but still-expansive notion of security, including as it did the stability of the empire.

Today, for example, some Israelis argue that the occupied West Bank—a form of long-term intervention against the Palestinians—is Israel's biblical heritage. Others, Liberals, argue that Israel must respect the right to self-determination of the Palestinians and return authority over the land to the people who inhabit it. Realism enters the debate when arguments focus on holding the West Bank as a necessary measure for Israel's security.

But other Israelis of course think Realism calls for a recognition that occupation provokes more regional hostility, and thus danger, than it assuages. Realist arguments, whether hard or soft, shape a debate either when their underlying assumptions are widely shared or when actions force two sides into a state of war. For when a debate becomes a matter only of "them or us," the Realists say and usually convince us that the answer has to be "us."

SOCIALISTS

Socialists tend to regard international politics, particularly international law, as a mere reflection of the much more fundamental class interests that truly govern international society. International society, according to Socialists, is akin to international civil war, where capitalists line up against workers, both domestically and internationally. State borders among nations are semifictions and not the fundamental dividing blocks of world politics. Nonetheless, national borders can and have played a progressive role in history. Marx himself saw reasons to support the development of the working class within a national framework. For that development to be successful, one had to appreciate the value of national sovereignty and therefore the value of national defense. So he hesitates only very rarely to condemn aggressive wars as he sees them occurring in his own times.[6]

When Marx considers a doctrine that should guide Socialists in their own choices for world politics, he wants to remind them that even though they have a duty to advance to the greatest extent that they can, the processes of Socialism on a worldwide front, this does not include a duty to crusade for Socialism. He warns that the liberation of the working class can be achieved only by the working class. One cannot create revolutions for others by prematurely attempting to put a working-class or union movement in political power. Socialist crusades would create the grounds for an enormous amount of suffering, a great deal of instability, and the defeat of that particular working class at the hands of social forces, capitalist and others, that it has not yet historically been able to master. Therefore, Marxists of the Second International, the pre-1914 Marxists and the post-1914 social democrats, often lined up in favor of the principle of nonintervention.

Leninism and Stalinism, by contrast, came to perceive the role of international revolution as an important tool not just in the promotion of Socialism worldwide but also in the defense of the one Communist state that was the Soviet Union. In the early revolutionary phase, Bolsheviks enthusiastically adopted an expansive program of revolutionary intervention. The Soviet soldiers who conquered Armenia hailed their achievement from the balcony of the Armenian parliament building with these cheers: "Long live Soviet Armenia! Long live Soviet Azerbaijan! Long live Soviet Russia! Georgia will soon be a Soviet, too. Turkey will follow. Our Red Armies will sweep across Europe. . . . Long live the Third International!"[7]

In order to defend Socialism in one country,

Views on Intervention

		Egalitarian								Libertarian
Nationalism	M		R	E	A	L	I	S	T	S
	A	Classic			International					Law
	R				LIBERALS					
	X				National Liberals					
	I		(Walzer)							
	S				(Mill)					
	T		Left Cosmopolitans				Right Cosmopolitans			
Cosmopolitanism	S		(Luban)				(Arkes)			

Lenin and Stalin thought it necessary to adopt two contradictory policies. The first was to weaken the inherently aggressive forces of capitalism directed at the Socialist state. So Lenin on a number of occasions—and Stalin after him—interfered aggressively in the domestic politics of other states, not so much with armed force as with attempts at subversion. Some of the strategies adopted were justifiable in Marxist terms, such as the financial aid that the Soviets provided for the British workers in the General Strike of 1926. On the other hand, Soviet state and party interests sometimes precluded a revolutionary strategy, such as the Comintern's targeting of German Socialists, whose appeals for help against the growing Nazi movement were rejected by the Soviets.[8]

Once the Soviet Union acquired great power of its own after World War Two, interventionism became a practice that then turned into doctrine, the Brezhnev Doctrine. Following the forcible "Stalinization" of East European states after 1948 and then the interventions in Germany in 1953, Hungary in 1956, and Czechoslovakia in 1968, Brezhnev declared that the Soviet Union stood in a particularly privileged position as the guardian of the collective interest of the working class worldwide and particularly, of course, within the Soviet bloc. The Communist Party of the Soviet Union thus claimed to act in the name of the worldwide working class in intervening against governments that it claimed were about to "betray" the interests of the working class.

LIBERALS: FOR AND AGAINST

Nonintervention has been a particularly important and occasionally disturbing principle for liberal political philosophers. On the one hand, Liberals have provided some of the very strongest reasons to abide by a strict form of the nonintervention doctrine, and on the other hand, those very same principles when applied in different contexts have provided justifications for overriding the principle of nonintervention.

Liberal Nonintervention. Although the principle emerged historically as a practice among the monarchical sovereigns of Europe, when democratic and Liberal governments came to power, they too adopted it. The Liberals contributed two new justifications for nonintervention.

The most important value they saw in the principle was that it reflected and protected human *rights*. Nonintervention enabled citizens to determine their own way of life without outside interference. If democratic rights and liberal freedoms were to mean something, they had to be worked out among those who shared them and were making them through their own participation. The first precondition of democratic government is self-government by one's own people. Kant's "Perpetual Peace" made a strong case for respecting the right of nonintervention because it afforded a polity the necessary territorial space and political independence in which free and equal citizens could work out what their way of life would be.[9]

John Stuart Mill provides a second argument for nonintervention, one focusing on likely *consequences*, when he explains in his famous 1859 essay "A Few Words on Nonintervention" that it would be a great mistake to export freedom to a foreign people that was not in a position to win it on its own.[10] A people given freedom by a foreign intervention would not, he argues, be able to hold on to it. It's only by winning and holding on to freedom through local effort that one acquires a true sense of its value. Moreover, it is only by winning freedom that one acquires the political capacities to defend it adequately against threats both at home and abroad. If, on the other hand, Liberal government were to be introduced into a foreign society, in the "knapsack," so to speak, of a conquering Liberal army, the local Liberals placed in power would find themselves immediately in a difficult situation. Not having been able to win political power on their own, they would have few domestic supporters and many non-Liberal domestic enemies. They then would wind up doing one of three different things:

They would (1) begin to rule as did previous governments—that is, repress their opposition. The intervention would have done no good; it simply would have created another oppressive government. Or they would (2) simply collapse in an ensuing civil war. Intervention therefore, would have produced not freedom and progress but a civil war with all its attendant violence. Or (3) the intervenors would have continually to send in foreign support. Rather than having set up a free government, one that reflected the participation of the citizens of the state, the intervention would have set up a puppet government, one that would reflect the wills and interests of the intervening, the truly sovereign state.[11]

*   *   *

Liberal Intervention.   Liberal arguments in favor of overriding nonintervention fall into two camps depending on what value they attach to national distinctiveness and on how confident the intervenors are that foreigners can truly understand the circumstances of another people.

The *cosmopolitan* Liberals are radically skeptical of the principle of nonintervention, almost as much as are the Realists, though of course for different reasons. The other group, the *national* Liberals, are firm defenders of nonintervention but would override the principle in certain exceptional circumstances.

The cosmopolitan position portrays nonintervention as a derivative or instrumental value. It holds only where it seems to protect principles believed to be more fundamental. We can divide these more fundamental principles into right-wing libertarian cosmopolitan principles and left-wing, egalitarian cosmopolitan principles. But both sets share a confident reading of the moral world, a "flat" world, where all is or should be the same, where we can clearly interpret the meaning and priority others attach to values and interest, such that we can directly judge for others just as we judge for ourselves. We can therefore know what are the justifiable ends and means—here, there, and everywhere.

A Comparison of Policy on Empire and Intervention

	Empire (Long-term)	Intervention (Short-term)
Realists	For national interest—security, prestige, profit—with prudence	
Hard	x	x
Soft		x
Marxists	When "progressive" or "international class war"	
Leninists		x
Stalinists	x ("Brezhnev Doctrine")	x

Liberal Justifications for Intervention

	Empire	Pro-dem Civil Lib.	Basic Rts. Social Rts.	Protracted Civil War	Cold War	National Liberation	Counter-interven.	Humanitarian
Rt. Cosmo. (Arkes)		x	x			x	x	x
Lt. Cosmo. (Luban)			x			x	x	x
Mill	x			x	x	x	x	x
Nat. Lib. (Walzer)						x	x	x

Articulating just such a flat, confident moral universe, right-wing cosmopolitans hold that a morally adequate recognition of equal human freedom requires freedom from torture, free speech, privacy rights, and private property. It also demands democratic elections and an independent judiciary and, as a safeguard, a right of emigration. The entire package goes together, as Hadley Arkes has eloquently argued.[12] The third right, emigration, serves as an obvious safety valve. The second group of political rights—democratic elections and an independent judiciary—serves to protect the basic rights of free speech, privacy, and private property. Free governments are governments that protect all the basic rights and all the political rights. Totalitarian governments violate all those rights. They violate free speech, privacy, private property, democracy, and the independence of the judiciary. Authoritarian governments are not quite as bad as the totalitarians. They nonetheless violate the political rights of democratic elections and a free independent judiciary, while managing to preserve (partially) the rights of privacy and private property.[13]

The rights of cosmopolitan freedom are valuable everywhere for all people. Any violation of them should be resisted whenever and wherever it occurs, provided that we can do so proportionally, without causing more harm than we seek to avoid.[14] Applying these views to the history of American interventionism, Arkes says we justly fought in Vietnam to prevent the takeover of a flawed South Vietnamese democracy by totalitarian North Vietnamese communism. We justly fought, he says, for good ends and used good means, and our only fault was in not sticking it out to protect South Vietnam, Cambodia, and Laos from the terror of oppression that accompanied the communist victories.

Equally cosmopolitan but at the other end of the Liberal political spectrum is the left cosmopolitan view. David Luban argues powerfully that we can make an equally clear judgment about basic rights, but his basic rights are different.[15] Basic rights include both subsistence rights—that is, rights to food and shelter and clothing—and security rights—that is, rights to be free from arbitrary killing, from torture, and from assault. We all have a duty to protect these socially basic rights. They are the rights held by humanity and claimable by all against all human beings.

In international politics, this means that states that fail to protect those rights do not have the right to be free from intervention. The most complete form of nonintervention thus is claimable only by states that do not violate basic rights. Moreover, all states have a duty to protect and to intervene, if an intervention is necessary, in order to provide subsistence needs held by all human beings. Both these considerations are subject to standard proportionality: We should never do something that would cause more harm than it saves. One implication of this principle is that if 500 individuals were to die of torture in country X this year and we could militarily or otherwise intervene at a cost of 499 lives or less, intervention would be the right thing to do, and we would have a duty to do it. Correspondingly, if the only way that Haitians could provide subsistence for themselves is by sailing a boat to Florida, the United States has no right to stop them.

National Liberals, a third group of Liberals, reject both cosmopolitan worldviews. They favor a revision and not a radical revolution in the principle of nonintervention. For Michael Walzer, who builds on the argument of John Stuart Mill, the moral world is not flat and clearly interpretable by all but a series of moral hills and valleys. The particular values the national community develops are hard for foreigners to perceive. They are the product not of abstract philosophic judgment but of complicated historical compromises.[16] If they are contracts, they are Burkean contracts among the dead, the living, the yet to be born. We cannot freely unpack the compromises that they have made between principle and stability, between justice and security, nor do we as nonparticipants in those packings, in those historical contracts, have a clear right to do so.

J. S. Mill argued on those grounds that for "civilized" nations, his principles of consequentialist nonintervention hold. Interventions do more harm than good, with three now unusual exceptions.

First, reflecting the imperial metropolitan values of nineteenth-century Britain, Mill does not think that all peoples are sufficiently "civilized" to be fit for national independence. Some societies are not, he claims, capable of the "reciprocity" on which all legal equality rests partly because of political chaos, partly because these peoples (like children) are incapable of postponing gratification. Moreover, they would benefit from the tutelage and commercial development imperial rule could provide. The only rights such peoples have are the right to be properly educated and the right to become a nation.[17]

Second, some civil wars become so protracted and so seemingly unresolvable by local struggle that a common sense of humanity and sympathy for the suffering of the populations calls for an outside intervention to halt the fighting in order to see if some negotiated solution might be achieved under the aegis of foreign arms. Mill here cites the success of outsiders in calling a halt to and helping settle the protracted mid-century Portuguese civil war.

Third, in a system-wide internationalized civil war, a "cold war," such as that waged between Protestantism and Catholicism in the sixteenth century, nonintervention can neglect vital transnational sources of national security. If one side intervenes to spread its ideology, the other has a defensive right to do the same.

Mill's last three exceptions have been the most influential and have been adopted and developed by Michael Walzer, who, like Mill, acknowledges that sovereignty and nonintervention ultimately depend upon consent. If the people welcome an intervention or refuse to resist, something less than aggression has occurred.[18] But we cannot make those judgments reliably in advance. We should assume, he suggests, that foreigners will be resisted, that nationals will protect their state from foreign aggression. For even if the state is not just, it's their state, not ours. We have no standing to decide what their state should be. We do not happen to be engaged full-time, as they are, in the national historical project of creating it.

All the injustices, therefore, that do justify a domestic revolution do not always justify a foreign intervention. Following Mill, Walzer says that domestic revolutions need to be left to domestic citizens. Foreign interventions to achieve a domestic revolution are inauthentic, ineffective, and likely to cause more harm than they eliminate.

But there are some injustices that do justify foreign intervention, for sometimes the national self-determination that nonintervention protects and the harms that nonintervention tries to avoid are overwhelmed by the domestic oppression and suffering that borders permit. Building on John Stuart Mill's classic essay, Walzer offers us three cases in which intervention serves the underlying purposes that nonintervention was designed to uphold.[19]

The first case occurs when too many nations contest one piece of territory. When an imperial government opposes the independence of a subordinate nation or when there are two distinct peoples, one attempting to crush the other, then national self-determination cannot be a reason to shun intervention. Here foreigners can intervene to help the liberation of the oppressed people, once that people has demonstrated through its own "arduous struggle" that it truly is another nation. Then decolonization is the principle that should rule, allowing a people to form its own destiny. One model of this might be the American Revolution against Britain; another in Mill's time was the 1848–49 Hungarian rebellion against Austria, and in our time the many anticolonial movements in Africa and Asia that quickly won recognition and, in a few cases, support from the international community.

The second instance in which the principle against intervention should be overridden is counterintervention in a civil war. A civil war should be left to the combatants. When conflicting factions of one people are struggling to define what sort of society and government should rule, only *that* struggle, not foreigners, should decide the outcome. But when an external power intervenes on behalf of one of the participants in a civil war, then another foreign power can counterintervene to balance the first intervention. This second intervention serves the purposes of self-determination, which the first intervention sought to undermine. Even if, Mill argues, the Hungarian rebellion was not clearly a national rebellion against "a foreign yoke," it was clearly the case that Russia should not have intervened to assist Austria in its suppression. By doing so, Russia gave others a right to counter-intervene.

Third—and perhaps the most controversial case—one can intervene for humanitarian purposes, to halt what appears to be a gross violation of the rights to survival of a population. When we see a pattern of massacres, the development of a campaign of genocide, the institutionalization of slavery—violations so horrendous that in the classical phrase they "shock the conscience of mankind"—one has good ground to question whether there is any national connection between the population and the state that is so brutally oppressing it. Under those circumstances, outsiders can intervene. But the intervenor should have a morally defensible motive and share the purpose of ending the slaughter and establishing a self-determining people. (Solely self-serving interventions promote imperialism.) Furthermore, intervenors should act only as a "last resort," after exploring peaceful resolution. They should then act only when it is clear that they will save more lives than the intervention itself will almost inevitably wind up costing, and even then with minimum necessary force. It makes no moral sense to rescue a village and start World War III or to destroy a village in order to save it. Thus, even though one often finds humanitarian intervention abused, Michael Walzer suggests that a reasonable case can be made that the Indian invasion of East Pakistan in 1971, designed to save the people of what became Bangladesh from the massacre that was being inflicted upon them by their own government (headquartered in West Pakistan), is a case of legitimate humanitarian intervention. It allowed the people of East Pakistan to survive and form their own state.

A right to intervene does not, however, establish a duty to intervene. States retain the duty to weigh the lives of their own citizens as a special responsibility. If an intervention could be costless, then there might be a strong obligation to intervene. But rarely is that so, and statesmen have an obligation not to volunteer their citizens in causes those citizens do not want to undertake. This is the basis of the right of neutrality in most wars. National interests invariably will come into play and should do so to justify an intervention to the citizens whose sons and daughters are likely to bear the casualties. In contradistinction to the Realists, Liberals hold that national interests should not govern when to intervene, just whether a nation should intervene when it has a right to do so.

*   *   *

Conclusions

Realists, Socialists, and Liberals each defend and each override the principle of nonintervention. The Realists do so to promote the national interest and especially national security; the Marxist, to promote Socialist revolution; the Liberals, to protect and promote human rights. Each of the differing types of Liberal—right-wing cosmopolitan, left-wing cosmopolitan, and national—justifies intervention using the same logic and arguments (with sign reversed) that it uses to justify when states should uphold nonintervention. Right-wing cosmopolitans want to protect from intervention democratic capitalist states; left-wing cosmopolitans want to protect from intervention all states that guarantee the basic rights of their citizens. The right-wing cosmopolitans justify interventions against any state that violates civil and economic liberties, including radical democratic (non-Liberal, democratic anticapitalist) states; the left-wing cosmopolitans, against those states that violate the basic social welfare rights of their citizens, whether Liberal, capitalist, or democratic or all three. The national Liberals raise the hurdles somewhat higher, leaving much more room for national struggle, variation, and oppression. They insist that revolutions are matters for domestic citizens. But when one people struggles to be free of the oppression inflicted by another, when a second state has already intervened in an ongoing civil war (and one needs to intervene to right the balance), and when a state turns against its own citizens and makes all notion of a national community ridiculous through its acts of slaughter or slavery, then the principle of nonintervention needs to be overridden in order to achieve the very purposes of national self-determination that the rule is designed to protect.

* * *

When, for the Realists, national survival is threatened either by or by not intervening, Realists give simple answers. Liberals tend to agree with them, with the proviso and presumption that no fellow Liberal state could pose such a threat. But where survival is not at stake, Realist arguments tend to rest on contingent assessments of alternative policy outcomes and nebulous estimates of prestige. * * * Liberals then will strongly disagree if the intervention violates their principles.

When, for the Liberals, nations need to be liberated from foreign yoke, foreign intervention, or genocide, all Liberals respond clearly and together. Realists tend to disagree; those are none of their concerns. When Liberals face powerful oppressors, such as was the USSR or is China, the differences among Liberals disappear. A cosmopolitan intervention to promote democracy or basic human rights is unlikely to be proportional except when the authoritarian oppression has led to genocide, and even then it may be so costly as to preclude anything but symbolic action or economic sanctions. When faced with a weak oppressor, Liberal differences in policy expand. Proportionality allows more room for choice because the costs of intervention are low. * * * [R]escues by democratic appeal should constitute another broad Liberal exception to nonintervention. Indeed this exception seems now to be emerging as a standard of international law, but only when interventions are approved by multilateral consent.

* * *

NOTES

1. An insightful study of the historical context of the doctrine of nonintervention is John Vincent, *Nonintervention and International Order* [Princeton, N.J.: Princeton University Press, 1974]. For valuable overviews, see Gerald Graham, "The Justice of Intervention," *Review of International Studies* 13 (1987), pp. 133–46, and Jefferson McMahan, "The Ethics of International Intervention," in Kenneth Kipnis and Diana Meyers, eds., *Political Realism and International Morality* (Boulder, Colo.: Westview Press, 1987), pp. 75–101.

2. Quoted in the *New York Times*, September 1, 1994. For more on the role of prudence in limiting Realist intervention, see Hoffmann, *Duties beyond Borders* [Syracuse, N.Y.: Syracuse University Press, 1981] and Smith, *Realist Thought from Weber to Kissinger* [Baton Rouge, La.: Louisiana State University Press, 1986], chap. 9.

3. Thucydides, *The Peloponnesian War*, V, para. 87–116. For a valuable and more general discussion of Realist ethics, see J. E. Hare and Carey Joynt, *Ethics and International Affairs* (New York: St. Martin's Press, 1982), chap. 3.

4. Thucydides, 3:1–50.

5. Francis Bacon, "Of Empire," in *The Works of Francis Bacon*, ed. J. Spedding (London: 1870), vol. 6, pp. 420–421.

6. See pp. 64–66 of Walzer, *Just and Unjust Wars* [New York: Basic Books, 1977] for a complicated account of Marx's motives.

7. Reported by Oliver Baldwin, *Six Prisons and Two Revolutions* (London: 1925), quoted in Lord Kinross, *Ataturk: The Birth of a Nation* (London: Weidenfeld, 1993), p. 280.

8. R. Craig Nation, *Black Earth, Red Star* (Ithaca: Cornell University Press, 1992), pp. 60–67. On p. 70, he notes that the Comintern "encouraged division on the left."

9. See Immanuel Kant, "Perpetual Peace," particularly the preliminary articles of a perpetual peace in which he spells out the rights of non-

intervention that he hopes will hold among all states even in the state of war. These rights take on an absolute character within the pacific union of republican states.

10. John Stuart Mill, "A Few Words on Nonintervention," in *Essays on Politics and Culture,* ed. Gertrude Himmelfarb (Gloucester: Peter Smith, 1973), pp. 368–84.

11. A good discussion of consequentialist issues can be found in Anthony Ellis, "Utilitarianism and International Ethics," in Terry Nardin and David Mapel, eds., *Traditions of International Ethics* (Cambridge: Cambridge University Press, 1992), pp. 158–79. * * *

12. Hadley Arkes, *First Things* (Princeton: Princeton University Press, 1986), esp. chaps. 11–13. Transformed in a political and expediential way, these views relate to those adopted by the Reagan administration in its defense of global "freedom fighters." See a valuable discussion of this by Charles Beitz, "The Reagan Doctrine in Nicaragua," in Steven Luper-Foy, ed., *Problems of International Justice* (Boulder, Colo.: Westview Press, 1988), pp. 182–95.

13. This distinction has been developed by Jeane Kirkpatrick in "Dictatorships and Double Standards," [in Gettleman, Marvin E., Patrick Lacefield, Louis Menashe, and David Mermelstein, eds., *El Salvador: Central America in the New Cold War* (New York: Grove Press, 1987), pp. 14–35,] but it also appears in traditional Liberal discourse.

14. The best discussion of the practical applications of the proportionality issue that I have seen is Richard Ullman, "Human Rights and Economic Power: The United States versus Idi Amin," *Foreign Affairs* 56, 3 (April 1978), pp. 529–43. The author explains how carefully targeting sanctions on the government and bypassing the people could put pressure on the murderous Amin government.

15. David Luban, "Just War and Human Rights," *Philosophy and Public Affairs* 9, 2 (Winter 1980), reprinted in Charles Beitz, ed., *International Ethics* (Princeton: Princeton University Press, 1985), pp. 195–216.

16. These compromises are part of the "thick" texture of moral and political life that each nation forms for itself. Beyond the "thin" foundation of basic human rights that all nations should share, these "thick" moralities cover such issues as form of government, distributions of income, family law, education, and the status of religious practices. See Michael Walzer, *Thick and Thin: Moral Argument at Home and Abroad* (Notre Dame: University of Notre Dame Press, 1994).

17. Mill, "Nonintervention," p. 376.

18. Michael Walzer, "The Moral Standing of States: A Response to Four Critics," in Bertz, ed., *International Ethics*, ed., p. 221, n. 7.

19. Walzer, *Just and Unjust Wars*, pp. 106–08, 339–42.

JASWANT SINGH

Against Nuclear Apartheid

The Case for India's Tests

While the end of the Cold War transformed the political landscape of Europe, it did little to ameliorate India's security concerns. The rise of China and continued strains with Pakistan made the 1980s and 1990s a greatly troubling period for India. At the global level, the nuclear weapons states showed no signs of moving decisively toward a world free of atomic danger. Instead, the nuclear nonproliferation treaty (NPT) was extended indefinitely and unconditionally in 1995, perpetuating the existence of nuclear weapons in the hands of five countries busily modernizing their nuclear arsenals. In 1996, after they had conducted over 2,000 tests, a Comprehensive Test Ban Treaty (CTBT) was opened for signature, following two and a half years of negotiations in which India participated actively. This treaty, alas, was neither comprehensive nor related to disarmament but rather devoted to ratifying the nuclear status quo. India's options had narrowed critically.

India had to ensure that its nuclear option, developed and safeguarded over decades, was not eroded by self-imposed restraint. Such a loss would place the country at risk. Faced with a difficult decision, New Delhi realized that its lone touchstone remained national security. The nuclear tests it conducted on May 11 and 13 were by then not only inevitable but a continuation of policies from almost the earliest years of independence. India's nuclear policy remains firmly committed to a basic tenet: that the country's national security in a world of nuclear proliferation lies either in global disarmament or in exercise of the principle of equal and legitimate security for all.

From *Foreign Affairs* 77, no. 5 (September/October 1998): 41–52.

The Tests of May

In 1947, when a free India took its rightful place in the world, both the nuclear age and the Cold War had already dawned. Instead of aligning with either bloc, India rejected the Cold War paradigm and chose the more difficult path of nonalignment. From the very beginning, India's foreign policy was based on its desire to attain an alternative global balance of power that, crucially, was structured around universal, nondiscriminatory disarmament.

Nuclear technology had already transformed global security. Nuclear weapons, theorists reasoned, are not actually weapons of war but, in effect, military deterrents and tools of possible diplomatic coercion. The basis of Indian nuclear policy, therefore, remains that a world free of nuclear weapons would enhance not only India's security but the security of all nations. In the absence of universal disarmament, India could scarcely accept a regime that arbitrarily divided nuclear haves from have-nots. India has always insisted that all nations' security interests are equal and legitimate. From the start, therefore, its principles instilled a distaste for the self-identified and closed club of the five permanent members of the U.N. Security Council.

During the 1950s, nuclear weapons were routinely tested above ground, making the mushroom cloud the age's symbol. Even then, when the world had witnessed only a few dozen tests, India took the lead in calling for an end to all nuclear weapons testing, but the calls of India's first prime minister, Jawaharlal Nehru, went unheeded.

In the 1960s, India's security concerns deepened. In 1962, China attacked India on its Himalayan border. The nuclear age entered India's neighborhood when China became a nuclear power in October 1964. From then on, no responsible Indian leader could rule out the option of following suit.

With no international guarantees of Indian security forthcoming, nuclear abstinence by India alone seemed increasingly worrisome. With the 1962 war with China very much on his mind, Indian Prime Minister Lal Bahadur Shastri began tentatively investigating a subterranean nuclear explosion project. A series of Indian nonproliferation initiatives had scant impact. In 1965, to make matters worse, the second war between India and Pakistan broke out. Shastri died in 1966 and was succeeded by Indira Gandhi, who continued the fruitless search for international guarantees. In 1968, India reaffirmed its commitment to disarmament but decided not to sign the NPT. In 1974, it conducted its first nuclear test, Pokharan I.

The first 50 years of Indian independence reveal that the country's moralistic nuclear policy and restraint paid no measurable dividends, except resentment that India was being discriminated against. Disarmament seemed increasingly unrealistic politics. If the permanent five's possession of nuclear weapons increases security, why would India's possession of nuclear weapons be dangerous? If the permanent five continue to employ nuclear weapons as an international currency of force and power, why should India voluntarily devalue its own state power and national security? Why admonish India after the fact for not falling in line behind a new international agenda of discriminatory nonproliferation pursued largely due to the internal agendas or political debates of the nuclear club? If deterrence works in the West—as it so obviously appears to, since Western nations insist on continuing to possess nuclear weapons—by what reasoning will it not work in India? Nuclear weapons powers continue to have, but preach to the have-nots to have even less. India counters by suggesting either universal, nondiscriminatory disarmament or equal security for the entire world.

India is alone in the world in having debated the available nuclear options for almost the last 35 years. No other country has deliberated so carefully and, at times, torturously over the dichotomy between its sovereign security needs and global disarmament instincts, between a moralistic approach and a realistic one, and between a covert nuclear policy and an overt one. May 11, 1998, changed all that. India successfully carried out three underground nuclear tests, followed on May 13 by two more underground, sub-kiloton tests. These five tests, ranging from the sub-kiloton and fission variety to a thermonuclear device, amply demonstrated India's scientific, technical, and organizational abilities, which until then had only been vaguely suspected. A fortnight later, on May 28 and 30, neighboring Pakistan predictably carried out its own tests in the bleak fastness of the Chagai Hills in Baluchistan, near the Afghan border. Suddenly the strategic equipoise of the post–Cold War world was rattled. The entire nonproliferation regime and the future of disarmament were at the forefront of international agendas.

The Failure of the Old Regime

Since independence, India has consistently advocated global nuclear disarmament, convinced that a world without nuclear weapons will enhance both global and Indian security. India was the first to call for a ban on nuclear testing in 1954, for a nondiscriminatory treaty on nonproliferation in 1965, for a treaty on nonuse of nuclear weapons in 1978, for a nuclear freeze in 1982, and for a phased program for complete elimination of nuclear weapons in 1988. Unfortunately, most of these initiatives were rejected by the nuclear weapons states, who still consider these weapons essential for their own security. What emerged, in consequence, has been a discriminatory and flawed nonproliferation regime that damages India's security. For years India conveyed its apprehensions to other countries, but this did not improve its security environment. This disharmony and disjunction between global thought and trends in Indian thought about nuclear weapons is, unfortunately, the objective reality of the world. Nuclear weapons remain a key indicator of state power. Since this currency is operational in large parts of the globe, India was left with no choice but to update and validate the capability that had been demonstrated 24 years ago in the nuclear test of 1974.

India's May 1998 tests violated no international treaty obligations. The CTBT, to which India does not subscribe, permits parties to withdraw if they believe their supreme national interests to be jeopardized. Moreover, the forcing of an unconditional and indefinite extension of the NPT on the international community made 1995 a watershed in the evolution of the South Asian situation. India was left with no option but to go in for overt nuclear weaponization. The Sino-Pakistani nuclear weapons collaboration—a flagrant violation of the NPT—made it obvious that the NPT regime had collapsed in India's neighborhood. Since it is now argued that the NPT is unamendable, the legitimization of nuclear weapons implicit in the unconditional and indefinite extension of the NPT is also irreversible. India could have lived with a nuclear option but without overt weaponization in a world where nuclear weapons had not been formally legitimized. That course was no longer viable in the post-1995 world of legitimized nuclear weapons. Unfortunately, the full implications of the 1995 NPT extension were debated neither in India nor abroad. This fatal setback to nuclear disarmament and to progress toward delegitimization of nuclear weapons was thoughtlessly hailed by most peace movements abroad as a great victory.

Nor was the CTBT helpful. In negotiations on the CTBT in 1996, India for the first time stated that the nuclear issue is a national security concern for India and advanced that as one reason why India was unable to accede to the CTBT. Presumably this persuaded the nuclear hegemons to introduce a clause at the last minute pressing India, along with 43 other nations, to sign the treaty to bring it into force. This coercive clause violates the Vienna Convention on Treaties, which stipulates that a nation not willing to be a party to a treaty cannot have obligations arising out of that treaty imposed on it. Even more galling, this clause was introduced at the insistence of China—the provider of nuclear technology to Pakistan. When the international community approved the coercive CTBT,

India's security environment deteriorated significantly.

India's plight worsened as the decade wore on. In 1997 more evidence surfaced on the proliferation between China and Pakistan and about U.S. permissiveness on this issue. During Chinese President Jiang Zemin's recent visit to Washington, the United States insisted on a separate agreement with China on Chinese proliferation to Iran and Pakistan, which the Chinese signed instead of professing their innocence. Both the U.S. unease and the Chinese signature attest to Chinese proliferation as a threat to India's security. After all these assurances, China continued to pass missile technology and components to Pakistan. Despite this, the Clinton administration was still willing to certify that China was not proliferating or—even worse for India—that the United States was either unable or unwilling to restrain China. As the range of options for India narrowed, so, too, did the difficulties of taking corrective action.

A Fine Balance

Today India is a nuclear weapons state. This adds to its sense of responsibility as a nation committed to the principles of the U.N. Charter and to promoting regional peace and stability. During the past 50 years, India made its nuclear decisions guided only by its national interest * * *.

* * *

The first and perhaps principal obstacle in understanding India's position lies in the failure to recognize the country's security needs; of the need in this nuclearized world for a balance between the rights and obligations of all nations; of restraint in acquisition of nuclear weaponry; of ending today's unequal division between nuclear haves and have-nots. No other country in the world has demonstrated the restraint that India has for the nearly quarter-century after the first Pokharan test in 1974.

Now, as the century turns, India faces critical choices. India had witnessed decades of international unconcern and incomprehension as its security environment, both globally and in Asia, deteriorated. The end of the Cold War created the appearance of American unipolarity but also led to the rise of additional power centers. The fulcrum of the international balance of power shifted from Europe to Asia. Asian nations began their process of economic resurgence. The Asia-Pacific as a trade and security bloc became a geopolitical reality. But the rise of China led to new security strains that were not addressed by the existing nonproliferation regime. The 1995 indefinite extension of the NPT—essentially a Cold War arms control treaty with a heretofore fixed duration of 25 years—legitimized in perpetuity the existing nuclear arsenals and, in effect, an unequal nuclear regime. Even as the nations of the world acceded to the treaty, the five acknowledged nuclear weapons powers—Britain, China, France, Russia, and the United States—stood apart; the three undeclared nuclear weapons states—India, Israel, and Pakistan—were also unable to subscribe. Neither the world nor the nuclear powers succeeded in halting the transfer of nuclear weapons technology from declared nuclear weapons powers to their preferred clients. The NPT notwithstanding, proliferation in India's back yard spread.

Since nuclear powers that assist or condone proliferation are subject to no penalty, the entire nonproliferation regime became flawed. Nuclear technologies became, at worst, commodities of international commerce and, at best, lubricants of diplomatic fidelity. Chinese and Pakistani proliferation was no secret. Not only did the Central Intelligence Agency refer to it but, indeed, from the early 1990s on the required U.S. presidential certification of nonproliferation could not even be provided. India is the only country in the world sandwiched between two nuclear weapons powers.

Today most nations are also the beneficiaries of a nuclear security paradigm. From Vancouver to Vladivostok stretches a club: a security framework in which four nuclear weapons powers, as partners in peace, provide extended deterrent protection. The Americas are under the U.S. nuclear deterrent as members of the Organization of American States. South Korea, Japan, and Australasia are also under the U.S. umbrella. China is, of course, a major nuclear power. Only Africa and southern Asia remain outside this new international nuclear paradigm where nuclear weapons and their role in international conduct are paradoxically legitimized. These differentiated standards of national security—a sort of international nuclear apartheid—are not simply a challenge to India but demonstrate the inequality of the entire nonproliferation regime.

In the aftermath of the Cold War, an Asian balance of power is emerging with new alignments and new vacuums. India, in exercise of its supreme national interests, has acted in a timely fashion to correct an imbalance and fill a potentially dangerous vacuum. It endeavors to contribute to a stable balance of power in Asia, which it holds will further the advance of democracy. A more powerful India will help balance and connect the oil-rich Gulf region and the rapidly industrializing countries of Southeast Asia.

*   *   *

Faced as India was with a legitimization of nuclear weapons by the haves, a global nuclear security paradigm from which it was excluded, trends toward disequilibrium in the Asian balance of power, and a neighborhood in which two nuclear weapons countries act in concert, India had to protect its future by exercising its nuclear option. By so doing, India has brought into the open the nuclear reality that had remained clandestine for at least the past 11 years. India could not accept a flawed nonproliferation regime as the international norm when all realities conclusively demanded the contrary.

*   *   *

Join the Club

India is now a nuclear weapons state, as is Pakistan. That reality can neither be denied nor wished away. This category of "nuclear weapons state" is not, in actuality, a conferment. Nor is it a status for others to grant. It is, rather, an objective reality. India's strengthened nuclear capability adds to its sense of responsibility—the obligation of power.

India, mindful of its international duties, is committed to not using these weapons to commit aggression or to mount threats against any country. These are weapons of self-defense, to ensure that India, too, is not subjected to nuclear coercion.

India has reiterated its desire to enter into a no-first-use agreement with any country, either negotiated bilaterally or in a collective forum. India shall not engage in an arms race, nor, of course, shall it subscribe to or reinvent the sterile doctrines of the Cold War. India remains committed to the basic tenet of its foreign policy—a conviction that global elimination of nuclear weapons will enhance its security as well as that of the rest of the world. It will continue to urge countries, particularly other nuclear weapons states, to adopt measures that would contribute meaningfully to such an objective. This is the defining difference. It is also the cornerstone of India's nuclear doctrine.

*　　*　　*

After the tests, India stated that it will henceforth observe a voluntary moratorium and refrain from conducting underground nuclear test explosions. It has also indicated a willingness to move toward a de jure formalization of this declaration. The basic obligation of the CTBT is thus met: to undertake no more nuclear tests. Since India already subscribes to the substance of the test ban treaty, all that remains is its actual signature.

India has also expressed readiness to participate in negotiations in the Conference on Disarmament in Geneva on a fissile material cut-off treaty. The basic objective of this pact is to prohibit future production of fissile materials for use in nuclear weapons. India's approach in these negotiations will be to ensure that this treaty is universal, nondiscriminatory, and backed by an effective verification mechanism. That same constructive approach will underlie India's dialogue with countries that need to be persuaded of India's serious intent. The challenge to Indian statecraft remains to reconcile India's security imperatives with valid international concerns regarding nuclear weapons.

Let the world move toward finding more realistic solutions and evolving a universal security paradigm for the entire globe. Since nuclear weapons are not really usable, the dilemma lies, paradoxically, in their continuing deterrent value. This paradox further deepens the concern of statesmen. How are they to employ state power in the service of national security and simultaneously address international concerns? How can they help the world create an order that ensures a peaceful present and an orderly future? How are they to reconcile the fact that nuclear weapons have a deterrent value with the objective global reality that some countries have this value and others do not? How can a lasting balance be founded? While humanity is indivisible, national security interests, as expressions of sovereignty, are not. What India did in May was to assert that it is impossible to have two standards for national security—one based on nuclear deterrence and the other outside of it.

The end of the Cold War did not result in the end of history. The great thaw that began in the late 1980s only melted down the ancient animosities of Europe. We have not entered a unipolar order. India still lives in a rough neighborhood. It would be a great error to assume that simply advocating the new mantras of globalization and the market makes national security subservient to global trade. The 21st century will not be the century of trade. The world still has to address the unfinished agenda of the centuries.

EDWARD N. LUTTWAK

Give War a Chance

Premature Peacemaking

An unpleasant truth often overlooked is that although war is a great evil, it does have a great virtue: it can resolve political conflicts and lead to peace. This can happen when all belligerents become exhausted or when one wins decisively. Either way the key is that the fighting must continue until a resolution is reached. War brings peace only after passing a culminating phase of violence. Hopes of military success must fade for accommodation to become more attractive than further combat.

Since the establishment of the United Nations and the enshrinement of great-power politics in its Security Council, however, wars among lesser powers have rarely been allowed to run their natural course. Instead, they have typically been interrupted early on, before they could burn themselves out and establish the preconditions for a lasting settlement. Cease-fires and armistices have frequently been imposed under the aegis of the Security Council in order to halt fighting. NATO's intervention in the Kosovo crisis follows this pattern.

But a cease-fire tends to arrest war-induced exhaustion and lets belligerents reconstitute and rearm their forces. It intensifies and prolongs the struggle once the cease-fire ends—and it does usually end. This was true of the Arab-Israeli war of 1948–49, which might have come to closure in a matter of weeks if two cease-fires ordained by the Security Council had not let the combatants recuperate. It has recently been true in the Balkans. Imposed cease-fires frequently interrupted the fighting between Serbs and Croats in Krajina, between the forces of the rump Yugoslav federation and the Croat army, and between the Serbs,

From *Foreign Affairs* 78, no. 4 (July/August 1999): 36–44.

Croats, and Muslims in Bosnia. Each time, the opponents used the pause to recruit, train, and equip additional forces for further combat, prolonging the war and widening the scope of its killing and destruction. Imposed armistices, meanwhile—again, unless followed by negotiated peace accords—artificially freeze conflict and perpetuate a state of war indefinitely by shielding the weaker side from the consequences of refusing to make concessions for peace.

The Cold War provided compelling justification for such behavior by the two superpowers, which sometimes collaborated in coercing less-powerful belligerents to avoid being drawn into their conflicts and clashing directly. Although imposed cease-fires ultimately did increase the total quantity of warfare among the lesser powers, and armistices did perpetuate states of war, both outcomes were clearly lesser evils (from a global point of view) than the possibility of nuclear war. But today, neither Americans nor Russians are inclined to intervene *competitively* in the wars of lesser powers, so the unfortunate consequences of interrupting war persist while no greater danger is averted. It might be best for all parties to let minor wars burn themselves out.

The Problems of Peacekeepers

Today cease-fires and armistices are imposed on lesser powers by multilateral agreement—not to avoid great-power competition but for essentially disinterested and indeed frivolous motives, such as television audiences' revulsion at harrowing scenes of war. But this, perversely, can *systematically* prevent the transformation of war into peace. The Dayton accords are typical of the genre: they have condemned Bosnia to remain divided into three rival armed camps, with combat suspended momentarily but a state of hostility prolonged indefinitely.

Since no side is threatened by defeat and loss, none has a sufficient incentive to negotiate a lasting settlement; because no path to peace is even visible, the dominant priority is to prepare for future war rather than to reconstruct devastated economies and ravaged societies. Uninterrupted war would certainly have caused further suffering and led to an unjust outcome from one perspective or another, but it would also have led to a more stable situation that would have let the postwar era truly begin. Peace takes hold only when war is truly over.

A variety of multilateral organizations now make it their business to intervene in other peoples' wars. The defining characteristic of these entities is that they insert themselves in war situations while refusing to engage in combat. In the long run this only adds to the damage. If the United Nations helped the strong defeat the weak faster and more decisively, it would actually enhance the peacemaking potential of war. But the first priority of U.N. peacekeeping contingents is to avoid casualties among their own personnel. Unit commanders therefore habitually appease the *locally* stronger force, accepting its dictates and tolerating its abuses. This appeasement is not strategically purposeful, as siding with the stronger power overall would be; rather, it merely reflects the determination of each U.N. unit to avoid confrontation. The final result is to prevent the emergence of a coherent outcome, which requires an imbalance of strength sufficient to end the fighting.

Peacekeepers chary of violence are also unable to effectively protect civilians who are caught up in the fighting or deliberately attacked. At best, U.N. peacekeeping forces have been passive spectators to outrages and massacres, as in Bosnia and Rwanda; at worst, they collaborate with it, as Dutch U.N. troops did in the fall of Srebenica by helping the Bosnian Serbs separate the men of military age from the rest of the population.

The very presence of U.N. forces, meanwhile, inhibits the normal remedy of endangered civilians, which is to escape from the combat zone. Deluded into thinking that they will be protected, civilians in danger remain in place until it is too late to flee. During the 1992–94 siege of Sarajevo, appeasement interacted with the pretense of protection in an especially perverse manner: U.N. personnel inspected outgoing flights to prevent the escape of Sarajevo civilians in obedience to a cease-fire agreement negotiated with the locally dominant Bosnian Serbs—who habitually violated that deal. The more sensible, realistic response to a raging war would have been for the Muslims to either flee the city or drive the Serbs out.

Institutions such as the European Union, the Western European Union, and the Organization for Security and Cooperation in Europe lack even the U.N.'s rudimentary command structure and personnel, yet they too now seek to intervene in warlike situations, with predictable consequences. Bereft of forces even theoretically capable of combat, they satisfy the interventionist urges of member states (or their own institutional ambitions) by sending unarmed or lightly armed "observer" missions, which have the same problems as U.N. peacekeeping missions, only more so.

Military organizations such as NATO or the West African Peacekeeping Force (ECOMOG, recently at work in Sierra Leone) are capable of stopping warfare. Their interventions still have the destructive consequence of prolonging the state of war, but they can at least protect civilians from its consequences. Even that often fails to happen, however, because multinational military commands engaged in disinterested interventions tend to avoid any risk of combat, thereby limiting their effectiveness. U.S. troops in Bosnia, for example, repeatedly failed to arrest known war criminals passing through their checkpoints lest this provoke confrontation.

Multinational commands, moreover, find it difficult to control the quality and conduct of member states' troops, which can reduce the performance of all forces involved to the lowest common denominator. This was true of otherwise fine British troops in Bosnia and of the Nigerian marines in Sierra Leone. The phenomenon of troop degradation can rarely be detected by external observers, although its consequences are abundantly visible in the litter of dead, mutilated, raped, and tortured victims that attends such interventions. The true state of affairs is illuminated by the rare exception, such as the vigorous Danish tank battalion in Bosnia that replied to any attack on it by firing back in full force, quickly stopping the fighting.

The First "Post-Heroic" War

All prior examples of disinterested warfare and its crippling limitations, however, have been cast into shadow by NATO's current intervention against Serbia for the sake of Kosovo. The alliance has relied on airpower alone to minimize the risk of NATO casualties, bombing targets in Serbia, Montenegro, and Kosovo for weeks without losing a single pilot. This seemingly miraculous immunity from Yugoslav anti-aircraft guns and missiles was achieved by multiple layers of precautions. First, for all the noise and imagery suggestive of a massive operation, very few strike sorties were actually flown during the first few weeks. That reduced the risks to pilots and aircraft but of course also limited the scope of the bombing to a mere fraction of NATO's potential. Second, the air campaign targeted air-defense systems first and foremost, minimizing present and future allied casualties, though at the price of very limited destruction and the loss of any shock effect. Third, NATO avoided most anti-aircraft weapons by releasing munitions not from optimal altitudes but from an ultra-safe 15,000 feet or more. Fourth, the alliance greatly restricted its operations in less-than-perfect weather conditions. NATO officials complained that dense clouds were impeding the bombing campaign, often limiting nightly operations to a few cruise-missile strikes against fixed targets of known location. In truth, what the cloud ceiling prohibited was not all bombing—low-altitude attacks could easily have taken place—but rather perfectly safe bombing.

On the ground far beneath the high-flying planes, small groups of Serb soldiers and police in armored vehicles were terrorizing hundreds of thousands of Albanian Kosovars. NATO has a panoply of aircraft designed for finding and destroying such vehicles. All its major powers have anti-tank helicopters, some equipped to operate without base support. But no country offered to send them into Kosovo when the ethnic cleansing began—after all, they might have been shot down. When U.S. Apache helicopters based in Germany were finally ordered to Albania, in spite of the vast expenditure devoted to their instantaneous "readiness" over the years, they required more than three weeks of "predeployment preparations" to make the journey. Six weeks into the war, the Apaches had yet to fly their first mission, although two had already crashed during training. More than mere bureaucratic foot-dragging was responsible for this inordinate delay: the U.S. Army insisted that the Apaches could not operate on their own, but would need the support of heavy rocket barrages to suppress Serb anti-aircraft weapons. This created a much larger logistical load than the Apaches alone, and an additional, evidently welcome delay.

Even before the Apache saga began, NATO already had aircraft deployed on Italian bases that could have done the job just as well: U.S. A-10 "Warthogs" built around their powerful 30 mm antitank guns and British Royal Air Force Harriers ideal for low-altitude bombing at close range. Neither was employed, again because it could not be done in perfect safety. In the calculus of the NATO democracies, the immediate possibility of saving thousands of Albanians from massacre and hundreds of thousands from deportation was obviously not worth the lives of a few pilots. That may reflect unavoidable political reality, but it demonstrates how even a large-scale disinterested intervention can fail to achieve its ostensibly humanitarian aim. It is worth wondering whether the Kosovars would have been better off had NATO simply done nothing.

Refugee Nations

The most disinterested of all interventions in war—and the most destructive—are humanitarian relief activities. The largest and most protracted is the United Nations Relief and Works Agency (UNRWA). It was built on the model of its predecessor, the United Nations Relief and Rehabilitation Agency (UNRRA), which operated displaced-person's camps in Europe immediately after World War II. The UNRWA was established immediately after the 1948–49 Arab-Israeli war to feed, shelter, educate, and provide health services for Arab refugees who had fled Israeli zones in the former territory of Palestine.

By keeping refugees alive in spartan conditions that encouraged their rapid emigration or local resettlement, the UNRRA's camps in Europe had assuaged postwar resentments and helped disperse revanchist concentrations of national groups. But UNRWA camps in Lebanon, Syria, Jordan, the West Bank, and the Gaza Strip provided on the whole a higher standard of living than most Arab villagers had previously enjoyed, with a more varied diet, organized schooling, superior medical care, and no backbreaking labor in stony fields. They had, therefore, the opposite effect, becoming desirable homes rather than eagerly abandoned transit camps. With the encouragement of several Arab countries, the UNRWA turned escaping civilians into lifelong refugees who gave birth to refugee children, who have in turn had refugee children of their own.

During its half-century of operation, the UNRWA has thus perpetuated a Palestinian refugee nation, preserving its resentments in as fresh a condition as they were in 1948 and keeping the first bloom of revanchist emotion intact. By its very existence, the UNRWA dissuades integration into local society and inhibits emigration. The concentration of Palestinians in the camps, moreover, has facilitated the voluntary or forced enlistment of refugee youths by armed organizations that fight both Israel and each other. The UNRWA has contributed to a half-century of Arab-Israeli violence and still retards the advent of peace.

If each European war had been attended by its own postwar UNRWA, today's Europe would be filled with giant camps for millions of descendants of uprooted Gallo-Romans, abandoned Vandals, defeated Burgundians, and misplaced Visigoths—not to speak of more recent refugee nations such as post-1945 Sudeten Germans (three million of whom were expelled from Czechoslovakia in 1945). Such a Europe would have remained a mosaic of warring tribes, undigested and unreconciled in their separate feeding camps. It might have assuaged consciences to help each one at each remove, but it would have led to permanent instability and violence.

The UNRWA has counterparts elsewhere, such as the Cambodian camps along the Thai border, which incidentally provided safe havens for the mass-murdering Khmer Rouge. But because the United Nations is limited by stingy national contributions, these camps' sabotage of peace is at least localized.

That is not true of the proliferating, feverishly competitive non-governmental organizations (NGOs) that now aid war refugees. Like any other institution, these NGOs are interested in perpetuating themselves, which means that their first priority is to attract charitable contributions by being seen to be active in high-visibility situations. Only the most dramatic natural disasters attract any significant mass-media attention, and then only briefly; soon after an earthquake or flood, the cameras depart. War refugees, by contrast, can win sustained press coverage if kept concentrated in reasonably accessible camps. Regular warfare among well-developed countries is rare and offers few opportunities for such NGOs, so they focus their efforts on aiding refugees in the poorest parts of the world. This ensures that the food, shelter, and health care offered—although abysmal by Western standards—exceeds what is locally available to non-refugees. The consequences are entirely predictable. Among many examples, the huge refugee camps along the Democratic Republic of Congo's border with Rwanda stand out. They sustain a Hutu nation that would otherwise have been dispersed, making the consolidation of Rwanda impossible and providing a base for radicals to launch more Tutsi-killing raids across the border. Humanitarian intervention has worsened the chances of a stable, long-term resolution of the tensions in Rwanda.

To keep refugee nations intact and preserve their resentments forever is bad enough, but inserting material aid into ongoing conflicts is even worse. Many NGOs that operate in an odor of sanctity routinely supply active combatants. Defenseless, they cannot exclude armed warriors from their feeding stations, clinics, and shelters. Since refugees are presumptively on the losing side, the warriors among them are usually in retreat. By intervening to help, NGOs systematically impede the progress of their enemies toward a decisive victory that could end the war. Sometimes NGOs, impartial to a fault, even help both sides, thus preventing mutual exhaustion and a resulting settlement. And in some extreme cases, such as Somalia, NGOs even pay protection money to local war bands, which use those funds to buy arms. Those NGOs are therefore helping prolong the warfare whose consequences they ostensibly seek to mitigate.

Make War to Make Peace

Too many wars nowadays become endemic conflicts that never end because the transformative effects of both decisive victory and exhaustion are blocked by outside intervention. Unlike the ancient problem of war, however, the compounding of its evils by disinterested interventions is a new malpractice that could be curtailed. Policy elites should actively resist the emotional impulse to intervene in other people's wars—not because they are indifferent to human suffering but precisely because they care about it and want to facilitate the advent of peace. The United States should dissuade multilateral interventions instead of leading them. New rules should be established for U.N. refugee relief activities to ensure that immediate succor is swiftly followed by repatriation, local absorption, or emigration, ruling out the establishment of permanent refugee camps. And although it may not be possible to constrain interventionist NGOs, they should at least be neither officially encouraged nor funded. Underlying these seemingly perverse measures would be a true appreciation of war's paradoxical logic and a commitment to let it serve its sole useful function: to bring peace.

8 ✑ INTERNATIONAL POLITICAL ECONOMY

Within international political economy there is a plethora of different issues critical to understanding international relations in the twenty-first century. To understand these issues, Essentials of International Relations *presents the contending theoretical approaches to international political economy and shows how contemporary policy debates are embedded in these contending approaches. In the first selection of this chapters, excerpted from* U.S. Power and the Multinational Corporation *(1975) and now considered a classic, Robert Gilpin clearly and concisely discusses the relationship between economics and politics. He examines the three basic conceptions of political economy (liberalism, Marxism, and mercantilism), comparing them along a number of dimensions, including their perspective on the nature, actors, and goals of economic relations; their theories of change; and how they characterize the relationship between economics and politics. In the second selection, Stephen D. Krasner, writing in the same decade, explicitly uses the international political theory of realism to explain international economic affairs. In particular, he addresses the relationship between the power of major states and trade openness. Based on an analysis of historical data, he argues that a hegemon (or leading state) is critical for the creation and maintenance of free trade.*

The two other selections in this chapter move away from an explicitly theoretical orientation and address contemporary political economy issues. Of all the words used to describe the international political economy, "inequality" is clearly the most accurate. Nancy Birdsall, executive vice president of the Inter-American Development Bank, shows poignantly the extent of this inequality, outlines the basic causes, and proposes some "tempting and dangerous" remedies. Several international institutions have been designed to address the problems of international inequality. The International Monetary Fund has assumed the new duties of managing the debt crisis and advocating structural reform. In the final section, Devesh Kapur discusses changes in the IMF in light of its management of the Latin American and Asian financial crises. He makes substantive suggestions concerning how the IMF and debtor countries should change.

Additional articles included in this reader address international economic is-sues. "Lori's War," in chapter 6, contains a perspective on the World Trade Organi-zation, and three articles in chapter 12 address aspects of economic globalization.

For readers who want to look further into the ways states cooperate to influ-ence the global economy, the Norton series will soon offer a more extensive study from Stephen Krasner. Also, Robert Bates's Prosperity and Violence *shows how the growth of the modern, coercive state was crucial in fomenting investment, innova-tion, and trade.*

ROBERT GILPIN

The Nature of Political Economy

The international corporations have evidently de-clared ideological war on the "antiquated" nation state. . . . The charge that materialism, moderniza-tion and internationalism is the new liberal creed of corporate capitalism is a valid one. The implication is clear: the nation state as a political unit of demo-cratic decision-making must, in the interest of "progress," yield control to the new mercantile mini-powers.[1]

While the structure of the multinational corporation is a modern concept, designed to meet the require-ments of a modern age, the nation state is a very old-fashioned idea and badly adapted to serve the needs of our present complex world.[2]

These two statements—the first by Kari Levitt, a Canadian nationalist, the second by George Ball, a former United States undersecretary of state—express a dominant theme of contemporary writings on international relations. International society, we are told, is increasingly rent between its economic and its political organization. On the one hand, powerful economic and technological forces are creating a highly interdependent world

From Robert Gilpin, *U.S. Power and the Multinational Corporation* (New York: Basic Books, 1975), chap. 1.

economy, thus diminishing the traditional signifi-cance of national boundaries. On the other hand, the nation-state continues to command men's loy-alties and to be the basic unit of political decision making. As one writer has put the issue, "The con-flict of our era is between ethnocentric nationalism and geocentric technology."[3]

Ball and Levitt represent two contending posi-tions with respect to this conflict. Whereas Ball ad-vocates the diminution of the power of the nation-state in order to give full rein to the pro-ductive potentialities of the multinational corpora-tion, Levitt argues for a powerful nationalism which could counterbalance American corporate domination. What appears to one as the logical and desirable consequence of economic rationality seems to the other to be an effort on the part of American imperialism to eliminate all contending centers of power.

Although the advent of the multinational corpo-ration has put the question of the relationship be-tween economics and politics in a new guise, it is an old issue. In the nineteenth century, for example, it was this issue that divided classical liberals like John Stuart Mill from economic nationalists, represented by Georg Friedrich List. Whereas the former gave primacy in the organization of society to economics and the production of wealth, the latter emphasized the political determination of economic relations. As this issue is central both to the contemporary debate on the multinational corporation and to the argument of this study, this chapter analyzes the three major treatments of the relationship between economics and politics—that is, the three major ideologies of political economy.

The Meaning of Political Economy

The argument of this study is that the relationship between economics and politics, at least in the modern world, is a reciprocal one. On the one hand, politics largely determines the framework of economic activity and channels it in directions intended to serve the interests of dominant groups; the exercise of power in all its forms is a major determinant of the nature of an economic system. On the other hand, the economic process itself tends to redistribute power and wealth; it transforms the power relationships among groups. This in turn leads to a transformation of the political system, thereby giving rise to a new structure of economic relationships. Thus, the dynamics of international relations in the modern world is largely a function of the reciprocal interaction between economics and politics.

First of all, what do I mean by "politics" or "economics"? Charles Kindleberger speaks of economics and politics as two different methods of allocating scarce resources: the first through a market mechanism, the latter through a budget.[4] Robert Keohane and Joseph Nye, in an excellent analysis of international political economy, define economics and politics in terms of two levels of analysis: those of structure and of process.[5] Politics is the domain "having to do with the establishment of an order of relations, a structure. . . ."[6] Economics deals with "short-term allocative behavior (i.e., holding institutions, fundamental assumptions, and expectations constant). . . ."[7] Like Kindleberger's definition, however, this definition tends to isolate economic and political phenomena except under certain conditions, which Keohane and

Nye define as the "politicization" of the economic system. Neither formulation comes to terms adequately with the dynamic and intimate nature of the relationship between the two.

In this study, the issue of the relationship between economics and politics translates into that between wealth and power. According to this statement of the problem, economics takes as its province the creation and distribution of wealth; politics is the realm of power. I shall examine their relationship from several ideological perspectives, including my own. But what is wealth? What is power?

In response to the question, What is wealth?, an economist-colleague responded, "What do you want, my thirty-second or thirty-volume answer?" Basic concepts are elusive in economics, as in any field of inquiry. No unchallengeable definitions are possible. Ask a physicist for his definition of the nature of space, time, and matter, and you will not get a very satisfying response. What you will get is an *operational* definition, one which is usable: it permits the physicist to build an intellectual edifice whose foundations would crumble under the scrutiny of the philosopher.

Similarly, the concept of wealth, upon which the science of economics ultimately rests, cannot be clarified in a definitive way. Paul Samuelson, in his textbook, doesn't even try, though he provides a clue in his definition of economics as "the study of how men and society *choose* . . . to employ *scarce* productive resources . . . to produce various commodities . . . and distribute them for consumption."[8] Following this lead, we can say that wealth is anything (capital, land, or labor) that can generate future income; it is composed of physical assets and human capital (including embodied knowledge).

The basic concept of political science is power. Most political scientists would not stop here; they would include in the definition of political science the purpose for which power is used, whether this be the advancement of the public welfare or the domination of one group over another. In any case, few would dissent from the following statement of Harold Lasswell and Abraham Kaplan:

The concept of power is perhaps the most fundamental in the whole of political science: the political process is the shaping, distribution, and exercise of power (in a wider sense, of all the deference values, or of influence in general.)[9]

Power as such is not the sole or even the principal goal of state behavior. Other goals or values constitute the objectives pursued by nation-states: welfare, security, prestige. But power in its several forms (military, economic, psychological) is ultimately the necessary means to achieve these goals. For this reason, nation-states are intensely jealous of and sensitive to their relative power position. The distribution of power is important because it profoundly affects the ability of states to achieve what they perceive to be their interests.

The nature of power, however, is even more elusive than that of wealth. The number and variety of definitions should be an embarrassment to political scientists. Unfortunately, this study cannot bring the intradisciplinary squabble to an end. Rather, it adopts the definition used by Hans Morgenthau in his influential *Politics Among Nations*: "man's control over the minds and actions of other men."[10] Thus, power, like wealth, is the capacity to produce certain results.

Unlike wealth, however, power can not be quantified; indeed, it cannot be overemphasized that power has an important psychological dimension. Perceptions of power relations are of critical importance; as a consequence, a fundamental task of statesmen is to manipulate the perceptions of other statesmen regarding the distribution of power. Moreover, power is relative to a specific situation or set of circumstances; there is no single hierarchy of power in international relations. Power may take many forms—military, economic, or psychological—though, in the final analysis, force is the ultimate form of power. Finally, the inability to predict the behavior of others or the outcome of events is of great significance. Uncertainty regarding the distribution of power and the ability of the statesmen to control events plays an important role in international relations. Ultimately, the determination of the distribution of power can be made only in retrospect as a consequence of war. It is precisely for this reason that war has had, unfortunately, such a central place in the history of international relations. In short, power is an elusive concept indeed upon which to erect a science of politics.

*   *   *

The distinction * * * between economics as the science of wealth and politics as the science of power is essentially an analytical one. In the real world, wealth and power are ultimately joined. This, in fact, is the basic rationale for a political economy of international relations. But in order to develop the argument of this study, wealth and power will be treated, at least for the moment, as analytically distinct.

To provide a perspective on the nature of political economy, the next section of the chapter will discuss the three prevailing conceptions of political economy: liberalism, Marxism, and mercantilism. Liberalism regards politics and economics as relatively separable and autonomous spheres of activities; I associate most professional economists as well as many other academics, businessmen, and American officials with this outlook. Marxism refers to the radical critique of capitalism identified with Karl Marx and his contemporary disciples; according to this conception, economics determines politics and political structure. Mercantilism is a more questionable term because of its historical association with the desire of nation-states for a trade surplus and for treasure (money). One must distinguish, however, between the specific form mercantilism took in the seventeenth and eighteenth centuries and the general outlook of mercantilistic thought. The essence of the mercantilistic perspective, whether it is labeled economic nationalism, protectionism, or the doctrine of the German Historical School, is the subservience of the economy to the state and its interests—interests that range from matters of domestic welfare to those of international security. It is this more general meaning of mercantilism that is implied by the use of the term in this study.

*   *   *

Three Conceptions of Political Economy

The three prevailing conceptions of political economy differ on many points. Several critical differences will be examined in this brief comparison. (See Table)

THE NATURE OF ECONOMIC RELATIONS

The basic assumption of liberalism is that the nature of international economic relations is essentially harmonious. Herein lay the great intellectual innovation of Adam Smith. Disputing his mercantilist predecessors, Smith argued that international economic relations could be made a positive-sum game; that is to say, everyone could gain, and no one need lose, from a proper ordering of economic relations, albeit the distribution of these gains may not be equal. Following Smith, liberalism assumes that there is a basic harmony between true national interest and cosmopolitan economic interest. Thus, a prominent member of this school of thought has written, in response to a radical critique, that the economic efficiency of the sterling standard in the nineteenth century and that of the dollar standard in the twentieth century serve "the cosmopolitan interest in a national form."[11]

Although Great Britain and the United States gained the most from the international role of their respective currencies, everyone else gained as well.

Liberals argue that, given this underlying identity of national and cosmopolitan interests in a free market, the state should not interfere with economic transactions across national boundaries. Through free exchange of commodities, removal of restrictions on the flow of investment, and an international division of labor, everyone will benefit in the long run as a result of a more efficient utilization of the world's scarce resources. The national interest is therefore best served, liberals maintain, by a generous and cooperative attitude regarding economic relations with other countries. In essence, the pursuit of self-interest in a free, competitive economy achieves the greatest good for the greatest number in international no less than in the national society.

Both mercantilists and Marxists, on the other hand, begin with the premise that the essence of economic relations is conflictual. There is no underlying harmony; indeed, one group's gain is another's loss. Thus, in the language of game theory, whereas liberals regard economic relations as a non-zero-sum game, Marxists and mercantilists view economic relations as essentially a zero-sum game.

Comparison of the Three Conceptions of Political Economy

	Liberalism	*Marxism*	*Mercantilism*
Nature of economic relations	Harmonious	Conflictual	Conflictual
Nature of the actors	Households and firms	Economic classes	Nation-states
Goal of economic activity	Maximization of global welfare	Maximization of class interests	Maximization of national interest
Relationship between economics and politics	Economics *should* determine politics	Economics *does* determine politics	Politics determines economics
Theory of change	Dynamic equilibrium	Tendency toward` disequilibrium	Shifts in the distribution of power

THE GOAL OF ECONOMIC ACTIVITY

For the liberal, the goal of economic activity is the optimum or efficient use of the world's scarce resources and the maximization of world welfare. While most liberals refuse to make value judgments regarding income distribution, Marxists and mercantilists stress the distributive effects of economic relations. For the Marxist the distribution of wealth among social classes is central; for the mercantilist it is the distribution of employment, industry, and military power among nation-states that is most significant. Thus, the goal of economic (and political) activity for both Marxists and mercantilists is the redistribution of wealth and power.

THE STATE AND PUBLIC POLICY

These three perspectives differ decisively in their views regarding the nature of the economic actors. In Marxist analysis, the basic actors in both domestic and international relations are economic classes; the interests of the dominant class determine the foreign policy of the state. For mercantilists, the real actors in international economic relations are nation-states; national interest determines foreign policy. National interest may at times be influenced by the peculiar economic interests of classes, elites, or other subgroups of the society; but factors of geography, external configurations of power, and the exigencies of national survival are primary in determining foreign policy. Thus, whereas liberals speak of world welfare and Marxists of class interests, mercantilists recognize only the interests of particular nation-states.

Although liberal economists such as David Ricardo and Joseph Schumpeter recognized the importance of class conflict and neoclassical liberals analyze economic growth and policy in terms of national economies, the liberal emphasis is on the individual consumer, firm, or entrepreneur. The liberal ideal is summarized in the view of Harry Johnson that the nation-state has no meaning as an economic entity.[12]

Underlying these contrasting views are differing conceptions of the nature of the state and public policy. For liberals, the state represents an aggregation of private interests: public policy is but the outcome of a pluralistic struggle among interest groups. Marxists, on the other hand, regard the state as simply the "executive committee of the ruling class," and public policy reflects its interests. Mercantilists, however, regard the state as an organic unit in its own right: the whole is greater than the sum of its parts. Public policy, therefore, embodies the national interest or Rousseau's "general will" as conceived by the political elite.

THE RELATIONSHIP BETWEEN ECONOMICS AND POLITICS; THEORIES OF CHANGE

Liberalism, Marxism, and mercantilism also have differing views on the relationship between economics and politics. And their differences on this issue are directly relevant to their contrasting theories of international political change.

Although the liberal ideal is the separation of economics from politics in the interest of maximizing world welfare, the fulfillment of this ideal would have important political implications. The classical statement of these implications was that of Adam Smith in *The Wealth of Nations*.[13] Economic growth, Smith argued, is primarily a function of the extent of the division of labor, which in turn is dependent upon the scale of the market. Thus he attacked the barriers erected by feudal principalities and mercantilistic states against the exchange of goods and the enlargement of markets. If men were to multiply their wealth, Smith argued, the contradiction between political organization and economic rationality had to be resolved in favor of the latter. That is, the pursuit of wealth should determine the nature of the political order.

Subsequently, from nineteenth-century economic liberals to twentieth-century writers on economic integration, there has existed "the dream . . . of a great republic of world commerce, in which national boundaries would cease to have any great economic importance and the web of trade would bind all the people of the world in the prosperity of peace."[14] For liberals the long-term trend is toward world integration, wherein functions, authority, and loyalties will be transferred from "smaller units to larger ones; from states to federalism; from federalism to supranational unions and from these to superstates."[15] The logic of economic and technological development, it is argued, has set mankind on an inexorable course toward global political unification and world peace.

In Marxism, the concept of the contradiction between economic and political relations was enacted into historical law. Whereas classical liberals—although Smith less than others—held that the requirements of economic rationality *ought* to determine political relations, the Marxist position was that the mode of production does in fact determine the superstructure of political relations. Therefore, it is argued, history can be understood as the product of the dialectical process—the contradiction between the evolving techniques of production and the resistant sociopolitical system.

Although Marx and Engels wrote remarkably little on international economics, Engels, in his famous polemic, *Anti-Duhring*, explicitly considers whether economics or politics is primary in determining the structure of international relations.[16] E. K. Duhring, a minor figure in the German Historical School, had argued, in contradiction to Marxism, that property and market relations resulted less from the economic logic of capitalism than from extraeconomic political factors: "The basis of the exploitation of man by man was an historical act of force which created an exploitative economic system for the benefit of the stronger man or class."[17] Since Engels, in his attack on Duhring, used the example of the unification of Germany through the Zollverein or customs union of 1833, his analysis is directly relevant to this discussion of the relationship between economics and political organization.

Engels argued that when contradictions arise between economic and political structures, political power adapts itself to the changes in the balance of economic forces; politics yields to the

dictates of economic development. Thus, in the case of nineteenth-century Germany, the requirements of industrial production had become incompatible with its feudal, politically fragmented structure. "Though political reaction was victorious in 1815 and again in 1848," he argued, "it was unable to prevent the growth of large-scale industry in Germany and the growing participation of German commerce in the world market."[18] In summary, Engels wrote, "German unity had become an economic necessity."[19]

In the view of both Smith and Engels, the nation-state represented a progressive stage in human development, because it enlarged the political realm of economic activity. In each successive economic epoch, advances in technology and an increasing scale of production necessitate an enlargement of political organization. Because the city-state and feudalism restricted the scale of production and the division of labor made possible by the Industrial Revolution, they prevented the efficient utilization of resources and were, therefore, superseded by larger political units. Smith considered this to be a desirable objective; for Engels it was an historical necessity. Thus, in the opinion of liberals, the establishment of the Zollverein was a movement toward maximizing world economic welfare;[20] for Marxists it was the unavoidable triumph of the German industrialists over the feudal aristocracy.

Mercantilist writers from Alexander Hamilton to Frederick List to Charles de Gaulle, on the other hand, have emphasized the primacy of politics; politics, in this view, determines economic organization. Whereas Marxists and liberals have pointed to the production of wealth as the basic determinant of social and political organization, the mercantilists of the German Historical School, for example, stressed the primacy of national security, industrial development, and national sentiment in international political and economic dynamics.

In response to Engels's interpretation of the unification of Germany, mercantilists would no doubt agree with Jacob Viner that "Prussia engineered the customs union primarily for political reasons, in order to gain hegemony or at least influence over the lesser German states. It was largely in order to make certain that the hegemony should be Prussian and not Austrian that Prussia continually opposed Austrian entry into the Union, either openly or by pressing for a customs union tariff lower than highly protectionist Austria could stomach."[21] In pursuit of this strategic interest, it was "Prussian might, rather than a common zeal for political unification arising out of economic partnership, (that) . . . played the major role."[22]

In contrast to Marxism, neither liberalism nor mercantilism has a developed theory of dynamics. The basic assumption of orthodox economic analysis (liberalism) is the tendency toward equilibrium; liberalism takes for granted the existing social order and given institutions. Change is assumed to be gradual and adaptive—a continuous process of dynamic equilibrium. There is no necessary connection between such political phenomena as war and revolution and the evolution of the economic system, although they would not deny that misguided statesmen can blunder into war over economic issues or that revolutions are conflicts over the distribution of wealth; but neither is inevitably linked to the evolution of the productive system. As for mercantilism, it sees change as taking place owing to shifts in the balance of power; yet, mercantilist writers such as members of the German Historical School and contemporary political realists have not developed a systematic theory of how this shift occurs.

On the other hand, dynamics is central to Marxism; indeed Marxism is essentially a theory of social *change*. It emphasizes the tendency toward *dis*equilibrium owing to changes in the means of production, and the consequent effects on the everpresent class conflict. When these tendencies can no longer be contained, the sociopolitical system breaks down through violent upheaval. Thus war and revolution are seen as an integral part of the economic process. Politics and economics are intimately joined.

WHY AN INTERNATIONAL ECONOMY?

From these differences among the three ideologies, one can get a sense of their respective explanations for the existence and functioning of the international economy.

An interdependent world economy constitutes the normal state of affairs for most liberal economists. Responding to technological advances in transportation and communications, the scope of the market mechanism, according to this analysis, continuously expands. Thus, despite temporary setbacks, the long-term trend is toward global economic integration. The functioning of the international economy is determined primarily by considerations of efficiency. The role of the dollar as the basis of the international monetary system, for example, is explained by the preference for it among traders and nations as the vehicle of international commerce.[23] The system is maintained by the mutuality of the benefits provided by trade, monetary arrangements, and investment.

A second view—one shared by Marxists and mercantilists alike—is that every interdependent international economy is essentially an imperial or hierarchical system. The imperial or hegemonic power organizes trade, monetary, and investment relations in order to advance its own economic and political interests. In the absence of the economic and especially the political influence of the hegemonic power, the system would fragment into autarkic economies or regional blocs. Whereas for liberalism maintenance of harmonious international market relations is the norm, for Marxism and mercantilism conflicts of class or national interests are the norm.

*   *   *

NOTES

1. Kari Levitt, "The Hinterland Economy," *Canadian Forum* 50 (July–August 1970): 163.
2. George W. Ball, "The Promise of the Multinational Corporation," *Fortune*, June 1, 1967, p. 80.

3. Sidney Rolfe, "Updating Adam Smith," *Interplay* (November 1968): 15.

4. Charles Kindleberger, *Power and Money: The Economics of International Politics and the Politics of International Economics* (New York: Basic Books, 1970), p. 5.

5. Robert Keohane and Joseph Nye, "World Politics and the International Economic System," in *The Future of the International Economic Order: An Agenda for Research,* ed. C. Fred Bergsten (Lexington, Mass.: D. C. Heath, 1973), p. 116.

6. Ibid.

7. Ibid., p. 117.

8. Paul Samuelson, *Economics: An Introductory Analysis* (New York: McGraw-Hill, 1967), p. 5.

9. Harold Lasswell and Abraham Kaplan, *Power and Society: A Framework for Political Inquiry* (New Haven: Yale University Press, 1950), p. 75.

10. Hans Morgenthau, *Politics Among Nations* (New York: Alfred A. Knopf), p. 26. For a more complex but essentially identical view, see Robert Dahl, *Modern Political Analysis* (Englewood Cliffs, N.J.: Prentice-Hall, 1963).

11. Kindleberger, *Power and Money,* p. 227.

12. For Johnson's critique of economic nationalism, see Harry Johnson, ed., *Economic Nationalism in Old and New States* (Chicago: University of Chicago Press, 1967).

13. Adam Smith, *The Wealth of Nations* (New York: Modern Library, 1937).

14. J. B. Condliffe, *The Commerce of Nations* (New York: W. W. Norton, 1950), p. 136.

15. Amitai Etzioni, "The Dialectics of Supranational Unification" in *International Political Communities* (New York: Doubleday, 1966), p. 147.

16. The relevant sections appear in Ernst Wangerman, ed., *The Role of Force in History: A Study of Bismarck's Policy of Blood and Iron,* trans. Jack Cohen (New York: International Publishers, 1968).

17. Ibid., p. 12.

18. Ibid., p. 13.

19. Ibid., p. 14.

20. Gustav Stopler, *The German Economy* (New York: Harcourt, Brace and World, 1967), p. 11.

21. Jacob Viner, *The Customs Union Issue,* Studies in the Administration of International Law and Organization, no. 10 (New York: Carnegie Endowment for International Peace, 1950), pp. 98–99.

22. Ibid., p. 101.

23. Richard Cooper, "Eurodollars, Reserve Dollars, and Asymmetrics in the International Monetary System," *Journal of International Economics* 2 (September 1972): 325–44.

STEPHEN D. KRASNER

State Power and the Structure of International Trade

Introduction

In recent years, students of international relations have multinationalized, transnationalized, bureaucratized, and transgovernmentalized the state until it has virtually ceased to exist as an analytic construct. Nowhere is that trend more apparent than in the study of the politics of international economic relations. The basic conventional assumptions have been undermined by assertions that the state is trapped by a transnational society created not by sovereigns, but by nonstate actors. Interdependence is not seen as a reflection of state policies and state choices (the perspective of balance-of-power theory), but as the result of elements beyond the control of any state or a system created by states.

This perspective is at best profoundly misleading. It may explain developments within a particular international economic structure, but it cannot explain the structure itself. That structure has many institutional and behavioral manifestations. The central continuum along which it can be described is openness. International economic structures may range from complete autarky (if all states prevent movements across their borders), to complete openness (if no restrictions exist). In this paper I will present an analysis of one aspect of the international economy—the structure of international trade; that is, the degree of openness for the movement of goods as opposed to capital, labor, technology, or other factors of production.

Since the beginning of the nineteenth century, this structure has gone through several changes. These can be explained, albeit imperfectly, by a state-power theory: an approach that begins with

From *World Politics* (April 1976): 317–47.

the assumption that the structure of international trade is determined by the interests and power of states acting to maximize national goals. The first step in this argument is to relate four basic state interests—aggregate national income, social stability, political power, and economic growth—to the degree of openness for the movement of goods. The relationship between these interests and openness depends upon the potential economic power of any given state. Potential economic power is operationalized in terms of the relative size and level of economic development of the state. The second step in the argument is to relate different distributions of potential power, such as multipolar and hegemonic, to different international trading structures. The most important conclusion of this theoretical analysis is that a hegemonic distribution of potential economic power is likely to result in an open trading structure. * * *

The Causal Argument: State Interests, State Power, and International Trading Structures

Neoclassical trade theory is based upon the assumption that states act to maximize their aggregate economic utility. This leads to the conclusion that maximum global welfare and Pareto optimality are achieved under free trade. While particular countries might better their situations through protectionism, economic theory has generally looked askance at such policies. * * * Neoclassical theory recognizes that trade regulations can also be used to correct domestic distortions and to promote infant industries,[1] but these are exceptions or temporary departures from policy conclusions that lead logically to the support of free trade.

STATE PREFERENCES

Historical experience suggests that policy makers are dense, or that the assumptions of the conventional argument are wrong. Free trade has hardly been the norm. Stupidity is not a very interesting analytic category. An alternative approach to explaining international trading structures is to assume that states seek a broad range of goals. At least four major state interests affected by the structure of international trade can be identified. They are: political power, aggregate national income, economic growth, and social stability. The way in which each of these goals is affected by the degree of openness depends upon the potential economic power of the state as defined by its relative size and level of development.

Let us begin with aggregate national income because it is most straightforward. Given the exceptions noted above, conventional neoclassical theory demonstrates that the greater the degree of openness in the international trading system, the greater the level of aggregate economic income. This conclusion applies to all states regardless of their size or relative level of development. The static economic benefits of openness are, however, generally inversely related to size. Trade gives small states relatively more welfare benefits than it gives large ones. Empirically, small states have higher ratios of trade to national product. They do not have the generous factor endowments or potential for national economies of scale that are enjoyed by larger—particularly continental—states.

The impact of openness on social stability runs in the opposite direction. Greater openness exposes the domestic economy to the exigencies of the world market. That implies a higher level of factor movements than in a closed economy, because domestic production patterns must adjust to changes in international prices. Social instability is thereby increased, since there is friction in moving factors, particularly labor, from one sector to another. The impact will be stronger in small states than in large, and in relatively less developed than in more developed ones. Large states are less involved in the international economy: a smaller percentage of their total factor endowment is affected by the international market at any given level of openness. More developed states are better able to adjust factors: skilled workers can more easily be moved from one kind of production to another than can unskilled laborers or peasants. Hence social stability is, *ceteris paribus*, inversely related to openness, but the deleterious consequences of exposure to the international trading system are mitigated by larger size and greater economic development.

The relationship between political power and the international trading structure can be analyzed in terms of the relative opportunity costs of closure for trading partners.[2] The higher the relative cost of closure, the weaker the political position of the state. Hirschman has argued that this cost can be measured in terms of direct income losses and the adjustment costs of reallocating factors.[3] These will be smaller for large states and for relatively more developed states. Other things being equal, utility costs will be less for large states because they generally have a smaller proportion of their economy engaged in the international economic system. Reallocation costs will be less for more advanced states because their factors are more mobile. Hence a state that is relatively large and more developed will find its political power enhanced by an open system because its opportunity costs of closure are less. The large state can use the threat to alter the system to secure economic or noneconomic objectives. Historically, there is one important exception to this generalization—the oil-exporting states. The level of reserves for some of these states, particularly Saudi Arabia, has reduced the economic opportunity costs of closure to a very low level despite their lack of development.

The relationship between international economic structure and economic growth is elusive. For small states, economic growth has generally been empirically associated with openness.[4] Exposure to the international system makes possible a much more efficient allocation of resources. Openness also probably furthers the rate of growth of large countries with relatively advanced technologies because they do not need to protect infant industries and can take advantage of expanded world markets. In the long term, however, openness for capital and technology, as well as goods, may hamper the growth of large, developed countries by diverting resources from the domestic economy, and by providing potential competitors with the knowledge needed to develop their own industries. Only by maintaining its technological lead and continually developing new industries can even a very large state escape the undesired consequences of an entirely open economic system. For medium-size states, the relationship between international trading structure and growth is impossible to specify definitively, either theoretically or empirically. On the one hand, writers from the mercantilists through the American protectionists and the German historical school, and more recently analysts of *dependencia*, have argued that an entirely open system can undermine a state's effort to develop, and even lead to underdevelopment.[5] On the other hand, adherents of more conventional neoclassical positions have maintained that exposure to international competition spurs economic transformation.[6] The evidence is not yet in. All that can confidently be said is that openness furthers the economic growth of small states and of large ones so long as they maintain their technological edge.

FROM STATE PREFERENCES TO INTERNATIONAL
TRADING STRUCTURES

The next step in this argument is to relate particular distributions of potential economic power, defined by the size and level of development of individual states, to the structure of the international trading system, defined in terms of openness.

Let us consider a system composed of a large number of small, highly developed states. Such a system is likely to lead to an open international trading structure. The aggregate income and economic growth of each state are increased by an open system. The social instability produced by exposure to international competition is mitigated by the factor mobility made possible by higher levels of development. There is no loss of political power

from openness because the costs of closure are symmetrical for all members of the system.

Now let us consider a system composed of a few very large, but unequally developed states. Such a distribution of potential economic power is likely to lead to a closed structure. Each state could increase its income through a more open system, but the gains would be modest. Openness would create more social instability in the less developed countries. The rate of growth for more backward areas might be frustrated, while that of the more advanced ones would be enhanced. A more open structure would leave the less developed states in a politically more vulnerable position, because their greater factor rigidity would mean a higher relative cost of closure. Because of these disadvantages, large but relatively less developed states are unlikely to accept an open trading structure. More advanced states cannot, unless they are militarily much more powerful, force large backward countries to accept openness.

Finally, let us consider a hegemonic system—one in which there is a single state that is much larger and relatively more advanced than its trading partners. The costs and benefits of openness are not symmetrical for all members of the system. The hegemonic state will have a preference for an open structure. Such a structure increases its aggregate national income. It also increases its rate of growth during its ascendency—that is, when its relative size and technological lead are increasing. Further, an open structure increases its political power, since the opportunity costs of closure are least for a large and developed state. The social instability resulting from exposure to the international system is mitigated by the hegemonic power's relatively low level of involvement in the international economy, and the mobility of its factors.

What of the other members of a hegemonic system? Small states are likely to opt for openness because the advantages in terms of aggregate income and growth are so great, and their political power is bound to be restricted regardless of what they do. The reaction of medium-size states is hard to predict; it depends at least in part on the way in

Chart I. Probability of an Open Trading Structure with Different Distributions of Potential Economic Power

Size of States

| | | RELATIVELY EQUAL | | VERY UNEQUAL |
		SMALL	*LARGE*	
Level of Development of States	EQUAL	Moderate–High	Low–Moderate	High
	UNEQUAL	Moderate	Low	Moderate–High

which the hegemonic power utilizes its resources. The potentially dominant state has symbolic, economic, and military capabilities that can be used to entice or compel others to accept an open trading structure.

At the symbolic level, the hegemonic state stands as an example of how economic development can be achieved. Its policies may be emulated, even if they are inappropriate for other states. Where there are very dramatic asymmetries, military power can be used to coerce weaker states into an open structure. Force is not, however, a very efficient means for changing economic policies, and it is unlikely to be employed against medium-size states.

Most importantly, the hegemonic state can use its economic resources to create an open structure. In terms of positive incentives, it can offer access to its large domestic market and to its relatively cheap exports. In terms of negative ones, it can withhold foreign grants and engage in competition, potentially ruinous for the weaker state, in third-country markets. The size and economic robustness of the hegemonic state also enable it to provide the confidence necessary for a stable international monetary system, and its currency can offer the liquidity needed for an increasingly open system.

In sum, openness is most likely to occur during periods when a hegemonic state is in its ascendency. Such a state has the interest and the resources to create a structure characterized by lower tariffs, rising trade proportions, and less regionalism. There are other distributions of potential

power where openness is likely, such as a system composed of many small, highly developed states. But even here, that potential might not be realized because of the problems of creating confidence in a monetary system where adequate liquidity would have to be provided by a negotiated international reserve asset or a group of national currencies. Finally, it is unlikely that very large states, particularly at unequal levels of development, would accept open trading relations.

These arguments, and the implications of other ideal typical configurations of potential economic power for the openness of trading structures, are summarized in the [above] chart.

The Dependent Variable: Describing the Structure of the International Trading System

The structure of international trade has both behavioral and institutional attributes. The degree of openness can be described both by the *flow* of goods and by the *policies* that are followed by states with respect to trade barriers and international payments. The two are not unrelated, but they do not coincide perfectly.

In common usage, the focus of attention has been upon institutions. Openness is associated with those historical periods in which tariffs were substantially lowered: the third quarter of the nineteenth century and the period since the Second World War.

Tariffs alone, however, are not an adequate indicator of structure. They are hard to operationalize quantitatively. Tariffs do not have to be high to be effective. If cost functions are nearly identical, even low tariffs can prevent trade. Effective tariff rates may be much higher than nominal ones. Non-tariff barriers to trade, which are not easily compared across states, can substitute for duties. An undervalued exchange rate can protect domestic markets from foreign competition. Tariff levels alone cannot describe the structure of international trade.[7]

A second indicator, and one which is behavioral rather than institutional, is trade proportions—the ratios of trade to national income for different states. Like tariff levels, these involve describing the system in terms of an agglomeration of national tendencies. A period in which these ratios are increasing across time for most states can be described as one of increasing openness.

A third indicator is the concentration of trade within regions composed of states at different levels of development. The degree of such regional encapsulation is determined not so much by comparative advantage (because relative factor endowments would allow almost any backward area to trade with almost any developed one), but by political choices or dictates. Large states, attempting to protect themselves from the vagaries of a global system, seek to maximize their interests by creating regional blocs. Openness in the global economic system has in effect meant greater trade among the leading industrial states. Periods of closure are associated with the encapsulation of certain advanced states within regional systems shared with certain less developed areas.

A description of the international trading system involves, then, an exercise that is comparative rather than absolute. A period when tariffs are falling, trade proportions are rising, and regional trading patterns are becoming less extreme will be defined as one in which the structure is becoming more open.

TARIFF LEVELS

The period from the 1820's to 1879 was basically one of decreasing tariff levels in Europe. The trend began in Great Britain in the 1820's, with reductions of duties and other barriers to trade. In 1846 the abolition of the Corn Laws ended agricultural protectionism. France reduced duties on some intermediate goods in the 1830's, and on coal, iron, and steel in 1852. The *Zollverein* established fairly low tariffs in 1834. Belgium, Portugal, Spain, Piedmont, Norway, Switzerland, and Sweden lowered imposts in the 1850's. The golden age of free trade began in 1860, when Britain and France signed the Cobden-Chevalier Treaty, which virtually eliminated trade barriers. This was followed by a series of bilateral trade agreements between virtually all European states. It is important to note, however, that the United States took little part in the general movement toward lower trade barriers.[8]

The movement toward greater liberality was reversed in the late 1870's. Austria-Hungary increased duties in 1876 and 1878, and Italy also in 1878; but the main breach came in Germany in 1879. France increased tariffs modestly in 1881, sharply in 1892, and raised them still further in 1910. Other countries followed a similar pattern. Only Great Britain, Belgium, the Netherlands, and Switzerland continued to follow free-trade policies through the 1880's. Although Britain did not herself impose duties, she began establishing a system of preferential markets in her overseas Empire in 1898.[9] The United States was basically protectionist throughout the nineteenth century. The high tariffs imposed during the Civil War continued with the exception of a brief period in the 1890's. There were no major duty reductions before 1914.

During the 1920's, tariff levels increased further. Western European states protected their agrarian sectors against imports from the Danube region, Australia, Canada, and the United States, where the war had stimulated increased output. Great Britain adopted some colonial preferences in 1919, imposed a small number of tariffs in 1921, and extended some wartime duties. The successor states of the Austro-Hungarian Empire imposed duties to achieve some national self-sufficiency. The British dominions and Latin America protected industries nurtured by wartime demands. In the United States the Fordney-McCumber Tariff Act of 1922 increased protectionism. The October Revolution removed Russia from the Western trading system.[10]

Dramatic closure in terms of tariff levels began with the passage of the Smoot-Hawley Tariff Act in the United States in 1930. Britain raised tariffs in 1931 and definitively abandoned free trade at the Ottawa Conference of 1932, which introduced extensive imperial preferences. Germany and Japan established trading blocs within their own spheres of influence. All other major countries followed protectionist policies.[11]

Significant reductions in protection began after the Second World War; the United States had foreshadowed the movement toward greater liberality with the passage of the Reciprocal Trade Agreements Act in 1934. Since 1945 there have been seven rounds of multilateral tariff reductions. The first, held in 1947 at Geneva, and the Kennedy Round, held during the 1960's, have been the most significant. They have substantially reduced the level of protection.[12]

*   *   *

In sum, after 1820 there was a general trend toward lower tariffs (with the notable exception of the United States), which culminated between 1860 and 1879; higher tariffs from 1879 through the interwar years, with dramatic increases in the 1930's; and less protectionism from 1945 through the conclusion of the Kennedy Round in 1967.

TRADE PROPORTIONS

With the exception of one period, ratios of trade to aggregate economic activity followed the same general pattern as tariff levels. Trade proportions increased from the early part of the nineteenth century to about 1880. Between 1880 and 1900 there was a decrease, sharper if measured in current prices than constant ones, but apparent in both statistical series for most countries. Between 1900 and 1913—and here is the exception from the tariff pattern—there was a marked increase in the ratio of trade to aggregate economic activity. This

trend brought trade proportions to levels that have generally not been reattained. During the 1920's and 1930's the importance of trade in national economic activity declined. After the Second World War it increased.

There are considerable differences in the movement of trade proportions among states. They hold more or less constant for the United States; Japan, Denmark, and Norway are unaffected by the general decrease in the ratio of trade to aggregate economic activity that takes place after 1880. The pattern does, however, hold for Great Britain, France, Sweden, Germany, and Italy.

Because of the boom in commodity prices that occurred in the early 1950's, the ratio of trade to gross domestic product was relatively high for larger states during these years, at least in current prices. It then faltered or remained constant until about 1960. From the early 1960's through 1972, trade proportions rose for all major states except Japan. Data for 1973 and 1974 show further increases. For smaller countries the trend was more erratic, with Belgium showing a more or less steady increase, Norway vacillating between 82 and 90 per cent, and Denmark and the Netherlands showing higher figures for the late 1950's than for more recent years. There is then, in current prices, a generally upward trend in trade proportions since 1960, particularly for larger states. This movement is more pronounced if constant prices are used.[13]

REGIONAL TRADING PATTERNS

The final indicator of the degree of openness of the global trading system is regional bloc concentration. There is a natural affinity for some states to trade with others because of geographical propinquity or comparative advantage. In general, however, a system in which there are fewer manifestations of trading within given blocs, particularly among specific groups of more and less developed states, is a more open one. Over time there have been extensive changes in trading patterns between particular areas of the world whose relative factor endowments have remained largely the same.

Richard Chadwick and Karl Deutsch have collected extensive information on international trading patterns since 1890. Their basic datum is the relative acceptance indicator (RA), which measures deviations from a null hypothesis in which trade between a pair of states, or a state and a region, is precisely what would be predicted on the basis of their total share of international trade.[14] When the null hypothesis holds, the RA indicator is equal to zero. Values less than zero indicate less trade than expected, greater than zero more trade than expected. For our purposes the critical issue is whether, over time, trade tends to become more concentrated as shown by movements away from zero, or less as shown by movements toward zero.

[F]igures for the years 1890, 1913, 1928, 1938, 1954, and 1958 through 1968, the set collected by Chadwick and Deutsch, [are considered] for the following pairs of major states and regions: Commonwealth-United Kingdom; United States-Latin America; Russia-Eastern Europe; and France-French speaking Africa. The region's percentage of exports to the country, and the country's percentage of imports from the region, are included along with RA indicators to give some sense of the overall importance of the particular trading relationship.

There is a general pattern. In three of the four cases, the RA value closest to zero—that is the least regional encapsulation—occurred in 1890, 1913, or 1928; in the fourth case (France and French West Africa), the 1928 value was not bettered until 1964. In every case there was an increase in the RA indicator between 1928 and 1938, reflecting the breakdown of international commerce that is associated with the depression. Surprisingly, the RA indicator was higher for each of the four pairs in 1954 than in 1938, an indication that regional patterns persisted and even became more intense in the postwar period. With the exception of the Soviet Union and Eastern Europe, there was a general trend toward decreasing RA's for the period after 1954. They still, however, show fairly high values even in the late 1960's.

If we put all three indicators—tariff levels,

trade proportions, and trade patterns—together, they suggest the following periodization.

Period I (1820–1879): Increasing openness —tariffs are generally lowered; trade proportions increase. Data are not available for trade patterns. However, it is important to note that this is not a universal pattern. The United States is largely unaffected: its tariff levels remain high (and are in fact increased during the early 1860's) and American trade proportions remain almost constant.

Period II (1879–1900): Modest closure— tariffs are increased; trade proportions decline modestly for most states. Data are not available for trade patterns.

Period III (1900–1913): Greater openness— tariff levels remain generally unchanged; trade proportions increase for all major trading states except the United States. Trading patterns become less regional in three out of the four cases for which data are available.

Period IV (1918–1939): Closure—tariff levels are increased in the 1920's and again in the 1930's; trade proportions decline. Trade becomes more regionally encapsulated.

Period V (1945–c. 1970): Great openness— tariffs are lowered; trade proportions increase, particularly after 1960. Regional concentration decreases after 1960. However, these developments are limited to non-Communist areas of the world.

The Independent Variable: Describing the Distribution of Potential Economic Power Among States

Analysts of international relations have an almost pro forma set of variables designed to show the distribution of potential power in the international *political* system. It includes such factors as gross national product, per capita income, geographical position, and size of armed forces. A similar set of indicators can be presented for the international *economic* system.

Statistics are available over a long time period

for per capita income, aggregate size, share of world trade, and share of world investment. They demonstrate that, since the beginning of the nineteenth century, there have been two first-rank economic powers in the world economy—Britain and the United States. The United States passed Britain in aggregate size sometime in the middle of the nineteenth century and, in the 1880's, became the largest producer of manufactures. America's lead was particularly marked in technologically advanced industries turning out sewing machines, harvesters, cash registers, locomotives, steam pumps, telephones, and petroleum.[15] Until the First World War, however, Great Britain had a higher per capita income, a greater share of world trade, and a greater share of world investment than any other state. The peak of British ascendance occurred around 1880, when Britain's relative per capita income, share of world trade, and share of investment flows reached their highest levels. Britain's potential dominance in 1880 and 1900 was particularly striking in the international economic system, where her share of trade and foreign investment was about twice as large as that of any other state.

It was only after the First World War that the United States became relatively larger and more developed in terms of all four indicators. This potential dominance reached new and dramatic heights between 1945 and 1960. Since then, the relative position of the United States has declined, bringing it quite close to West Germany, its nearest rival, in terms of per capita income and share of world trade. The devaluations of the dollar that have taken place since 1972 are reflected in a continuation of this downward trend for income and aggregate size.

*   *   *

In sum, Britain was the world's most important trading state from the period after the Napoleonic Wars until 1913. Her relative position rose until about 1880 and fell thereafter. The United States became the largest and most advanced state in economic terms after the First World War, but did not equal the relative share of world trade and investment achieved by Britain in the 1880's until after the Second World War.

Testing the Argument

The contention that hegemony leads to a more open trading structure is fairly well, but not perfectly, confirmed by the empirical evidence presented in the preceding sections. The argument explains the periods 1820 to 1879, 1880 to 1900, and 1945 to 1960 * * *

*   *   *

1945–1960. [One] period that is neatly explained by the argument that hegemony leads to an open trading structure is the decade and a-half after the Second World War, characterized by the ascendancy of the United States. During these years the structure of the international trading system became increasingly open. Tariffs were lowered; trade proportions were restored well above interwar levels. Asymmetrical regional trading patterns did begin to decline, although not until the late 1950's. America's bilateral rival, the Soviet Union, remained—as the theory would predict—encapsulated within its own regional sphere of influence.

Unlike Britain in the nineteenth century, the United States after World War II operated in a bipolar political structure. Free trade was preferred, but departures such as the Common Market and Japanese import restrictions were accepted to make sure that these areas remained within the general American sphere of influence.[16] Domestically the Reciprocal Trade Agreements Act, first passed in 1934, was extended several times after the war. Internationally the United States supported the framework for tariff reductions provided by the General Agreement on Tariffs and Trade. American policy makers used their economic leverage over Great Britain to force an end to the imperial preference system.[17] The monetary system established at Bretton Woods was basically an American creation. In practice, liquidity was provided by the American deficit; confidence by the size of the American economy. Behind the economic veil stood American military protection for other industrialized market economies—an overwhelming incentive for them to accept an open system, particularly one which was in fact relatively beneficial.

The argument about the relationship between hegemony and openness is not as satisfactory for the years 1900 to 1913, 1919 to 1939, and 1960 to the present.

*   *   *

1960–present. The final period not adequately dealt with by a state-power explanation is the last decade or so. In recent years, the relative size and level of development of the U.S. economy has fallen. This decline has not, however, been accompanied by a clear turn toward protectionism. The Trade Expansion Act of 1962 was extremely liberal and led to the very successful Kennedy Round of multilateral tariff cuts during the mid-sixties. The protectionist Burke-Hartke Bill did not pass. The 1974 Trade Act does include new protectionist aspects, particularly in its requirements for review of the removal of non-tariff barriers by Congress and for stiffer requirements for the imposition of countervailing duties, but it still maintains the mechanism of presidential discretion on tariff cuts that has been the keystone of postwar reductions. While the Voluntary Steel Agreement, the August 1971 economic policy, and restrictions on agricultural exports all show a tendency toward protectionism, there is as yet no evidence of a basic turn away from a commitment to openness.

In terms of behavior in the international trading system, the decade of the 1960's was clearly one of greater openness. Trade proportions increased, and traditional regional trade patterns became weaker. A state-power argument would predict a downturn or at least a faltering in these indicators as American power declined.

In sum, although the general pattern of the structure of international trade conforms with the predictions of a state-power argument—two periods of openness separated by one of closure—corresponding to periods of rising British and American hegemony and an interregnum, the whole pattern is out of phase. British commitment to openness continued long after Britain's position had declined. American commitment to openness did not begin until well after the United States had become the world's leading economic power and has continued during a period of relative American decline. The state-power argument needs to be amended to take these delayed reactions into account.

Amending the Argument

The structure of the international trading system does not move in lockstep with changes in the distribution of potential power among states. Systems are initiated and ended, not as a state-power theory would predict, by close assessments of the interests of the state at every given moment, but by external events—usually cataclysmic ones. The closure that began in 1879 coincided with the Great Depression of the last part of the nineteenth century. The final dismantling of the nineteenth-century international economic system was not precipitated by a change in British trade or monetary policy, but by the First World War and the Depression. * * *

Once policies have been adopted, they are pursued until a new crisis demonstrates that they are no longer feasible. States become locked in by the impact of prior choices on their domestic political structures. * * *

Institutions created during periods of rising ascendancy remained in operation when they were no longer appropriate. * * * The British state was unable to free itself from the domestic structures that its earlier policy decisions had created, and continued to follow policies appropriate for a rising hegemony long after Britain's star had begun to fall.

Similarly, earlier policies in the United States begat social structures and institutional arrangements that trammeled state policy. After protecting import-competing industries for a century, the United States was unable in the 1920's to opt for more open policies, even though state interests would have been furthered thereby. Institutionally, decisions about tariff reductions were taken primarily in congressional committees, giving virtually any group seeking protection easy access to the decision-making process. When there were conflicts among groups, they were resolved by raising the levels of protection for everyone. It was only after the cataclysm of the depression that the decision-making processes for trade policy were changed. The Presidency, far more insulated from the entreaties of particular societal groups than congressional committees, was then given more power.[18] * * *

Having taken the critical decisions that created an open system after 1945, the American Government is unlikely to change its policy until it confronts some external event that it cannot control, such as a worldwide deflation, drought in the great plains, or the malicious use of petrodollars. * * *

The structure of international trade changes in fits and starts; it does not flow smoothly with the redistribution of potential state power. Nevertheless, it is the power and the policies of states that create order where there would otherwise be chaos or at best a Lockian state of nature. The existence of various transnational, multinational, transgovernmental, and other nonstate actors that have riveted scholarly attention in recent years can only be understood within the context of a broader structure that ultimately rests upon the power and interests of states, shackled though they may be by the societal consequences of their own past decisions.

Notes

1. See, for instance, Everett Hagen, "An Economic Justification of Protectionism," *Quarterly Journal of Economics*, Vol. 72 (November 1958), 496–514; Harry Johnson, "Optimal Trade Intervention in the Presence of Domestic Distortions," in Robert Baldwin and others, *Trade, Growth and the Balance of Payments: Essays in Honor of Gottfried Haberler* (Chicago: Rand McNally 1965), 3–34; and Jagdish Bhag-

wati, *Trade, Tariffs, and Growth* (Cambridge: MIT Press 1969), 295–308.

2. This notion is reflected in Albert O. Hirschman, *National Power and the Structure of Foreign Trade* (Berkeley: University of California Press 1945); Robert W. Tucker, *The New Isolationism: Threat or Promise?* (Washington: Potomac Associates 1972); and Kenneth Waltz, "The Myth of Interdependence," in Charles P. Kindleberger, ed., *The International Corporation* (Cambridge: MIT Press 1970), 205–23.

3. Hirschman (fn. 2), 13–34.

4. Simon Kuznets, *Modern Economic Growth: Rate, Structure, and Spread* (New Haven: Yale University Press 1966), 302.

5. See David P. Calleo and Benjamin Rowland, *America and the World Political Economy* (Bloomington: Indiana University Press 1973), Part II, for a discussion of American thought; Eli Heckscher, *Mercantilism* (New York: Macmillan 1955); and D. C. Coleman, ed., *Revisions in Mercantilism* (London: Methuen 1969), for the classic discussion and a collection of recent articles on mercantilism; Andre Gunder Frank, *Latin America: Underdevelopment or Revolution* (New York: Monthly Review 1969); Arghiri Emmanuel, *Unequal Exchange: A Study of the Imperialism of Trade* (New York: Monthly Review 1972); and Johan Galtung, "A Structural Theory of Imperialism," *Journal of Peace Research*, VIII, No. 2 (1971), 81–117, for some representative arguments about the deleterious effects of free trade.

6. See Gottfried Haberler, *International Trade and Economic Development* (Cairo: National Bank of Egypt 1959); and Carlos F. Diaz-Alejandro, "Latin America: Toward 2000 A.D.," in Jagdish Bhagwati, ed., *Economics and World Order from the 1970s to the 1990s* (New York: Macmillan 1972), 223–55, for some arguments concerning the benefits of trade.

7. See Harry Johnson, *Economic Policies Toward Less Developed Countries* (New York: Praeger 1967), 90–94, for a discussion of nominal versus effective tariffs; Bela Belassa, *Trade Liberal-*

ization among Industrial Countries (New York: McGraw-Hill 1967), chap. 3, for the problems of determining the height of tariffs; and Hans O. Schmitt, "International Monetary System: Three Options for Reform," *International Affairs*, L (April 1974), 200, for similar effects of tariffs and undervalued exchange rates.

8. Charles P. Kindleberger, "The Rise of Free Trade in Western Europe 1820–1875," *The Journal of Economic History*, XXXV (March 1975), 20–55; Sidney Pollard, *European Economic Integration 1815–1970* (London: Thames and Hudson 1974), 117; J. B. Condliffe, *The Commerce of Nations* (New York: Norton 1950), 212–23, 229–30.

9. Charles P. Kindleberger, "Group Behavior and International Trade," *Journal of Political Economy*, Vol. 59 (February 1951), 33; Condliffe (fn. 8), 498: Pollard (fn. 8), 121; and Peter A. Gourevitch, "International Trade, Domestic Coalitions, and Liberty: Comparative Responses to the Great Depression of 1873–1896," paper delivered at the International Studies Association Convention, Washington, 1973.

10. Charles P. Kindleberger, *The World in Depression* (Berkeley: University of California Press 1973), 171; Condliffe (fn. 8), 478–81.

11. Condliffe (fn. 8), 498; Robert Gilpin, "The Politics of Transnational Economic Relations," *International Organization*, XXV (Summer 1971), 407; Kindleberger (fn. 10), 132, 171.

12. John W. Evans, *The Kennedy Round in American Trade Policy* (Cambridge: Harvard University Press 1971), 10–20.

13. Figures are available in United Nations, *Yearbook of National Account Statistics*, various years.

14. Richard I. Savage and Karl W. Deutsch, "A Statistical Model of the Gross Analysis of Transaction Flows," *Econometrica*, XXVIII (July 1960), 551–72. Richard Chadwick and Karl W. Deutsch, in "International Trade and Economic Integration: Further Developments in Trade Matrix Analysis," *Comparative Political Studies*, VI (April 1973), 84–109, make some amendments to earlier methods of calculation when regional groupings are being analyzed. * * *

15. League of Nations, *Industrialization and Foreign Trade* (1945, II.A.10), 13; Mira Wilkins, *The Emergence of Multinational Enterprise* (Cambridge: Harvard University Press 1970), 45–65.

16. Raymond Aron, *The Imperial Republic* (Englewood Cliffs, N.J.: Prentice-Hall 1973), 191; Gilpin (fn. 11), 409–12; Calleo and Rowland (fn. 5), chap. 3.

17. Lloyd Gardner, *Economic Aspects of New Deal Diplomacy* (Madison: University of Wisconsin Press 1964), 389; Gilpin (fn. 11), 409.

18. This draws from arguments made by Theodore Lowi, particularly his "Four Systems of Policy, Politics and Choice," *Public Administration Review*, XXXII (July–August 1972), 298–310. See also E. E. Schattschneider, *Politics, Pressures and the Tariff: A Study of Free Enterprise in Pressure Politics as Shown in the 1929–1930 Revision of the Tariff* (New York: Prentice-Hall 1935).

NANCY BIRDSALL

Life Is Unfair: Inequality in the World

Exactly 150 years after publication of the *Communist Manifesto*, inequality looms large on the global agenda. In the United States, the income of the poorest 20 percent of households has declined steadily since the early 1970s. Meanwhile, the income of the richest 20 percent has increased by 15 percent and that of the top 1 percent by more than 100 percent. In Asia, the high concentrations of wealth and power produced by strong growth have been given a new label: crony capitalism. In Russia and Eastern Europe, the end of communism has brought huge income gaps. In Latin America, wealth and income gaps—already the highest in the world in the 1970s—widened dramatically in the 1980s, a decade of no growth and high inflation, and have continued to increase even with the resumption of growth in the 1990s.

At the global level, it seems that the old saw is still correct: The rich get richer and the poor get children. The ratio of average income of the richest country in the world to that of the poorest has risen from about 9 to 1 at the end of the nineteenth century to at least 60 to 1 today. That is, the average family in the United States is 60 times richer than the average family in Ethiopia. Since 1950, the portion of the world's population living in poor countries grew by about 250 percent, while in rich countries the population increased by less than 50 percent. Today, 80 percent of the world's population lives in countries that generate only 20 percent of the world's total income (see charts [on page 310]).

Ironically, inequality is growing at a time when the triumph of democracy and open markets was supposed to usher in a new age of freedom and opportunity. In fact, both developments seem to be having the opposite effect. At the end of the twentieth century, Karl Marx's screed against capitalism has metamorphosed into post-Marxist angst about an integrated global market that creates a new divide between well-educated élite workers and their vulnerable unskilled counterparts, gives capital an apparent whip hand over labor, and pushes governments to unravel social safety nets. Meanwhile, the spread of democracy has made more visible the problem of income gaps, which can no longer be blamed on poor politics—not on communism in Eastern Europe and the former Soviet Union nor on military authoritarianism in Latin America. Regularly invoked as the handmaiden of open markets, democracy looks more and more like their accomplice in a vicious circle of inequality and injustice.

Technology plays a central role in the drama of inequality, and it seems to be making the situation worse, not better. The television and the airplane made income gaps more visible, but at least the falling costs and increasing accessibility of communication and transportation reduced actual differences in living standards. The computer, however, represents a whole new production process and creates a world in which the scarce commodities commanding the highest economic returns are information and skills. As information technology spreads, will some fundamental transformation take place that permanently favors an agile and educated minority? Or are we simply in the midst of a prolonged transition, analogous to the one that fooled Marx, to a postindustrial world with an expanded information age middle class?

In fact, postwar progress toward free trade and free politics has been dominated by the expectation of "convergence"—that those now lagging behind, whether nations or groups within nations, will inevitably catch up. But what happens if that expectation fails to materialize? How would the end of

From *Foreign Policy*, no. 111 (summer 1998): 76–93.

convergence affect conduct among nations? Can open and democratic societies endure the strains of high inequality? Will inequality become a lightning rod for dangerous populist rhetoric and self-defeating isolation? Even as we talk of disappearing national borders, is the worldwide phenomenon of inequality creating instead a new set of global rifts?

What Are The Facts?

In the United States, where the impact of global integration and the information revolution is probably the most widespread, the facts are sobering. Income inequality in the United States is increasing, not only because of gains at the top, but more disturbingly, because of losses at the bottom. The average wage of white male high-school graduates fell 15 percent from 1973 to 1993, and the number of men aged 25 to 54 years earning less than $10,000 a year grew. Possibly for the first time in the nation's history, educational gains may be reinforcing rather than offsetting income inequality: Higher education has become a prerequisite for economic success, but because access to it depends on family income, the poor are at a distinct disadvantage.

Elsewhere, the forces of change—whether the spread of capitalism and global integration, or simply the march of technological progress—have at best reinforced, or at worst exacerbated, high inequality. In Latin America, the ratio of income of the top 20 percent of earners to the bottom is about 16 to 1 (almost 25 to 1 in Brazil, probably the world's most unequal country, compared with about 10 to 1 in the United States and about 5 to 1 in Western Europe). The wage gap between the skilled and the unskilled increased in this decade by more than 30 percent in Peru, 20 percent in Colombia, and nearly 25 percent in Mexico. Ironically, these were the countries with the greatest wage increases.

The situation is less clear but no more heartening in other parts of the world. In China, the liberalization of agricultural and other markets has spurred growth, yet large segments of the population have been left behind. In the affluent countries of northern Europe, increases in poor immigrant populations, growing unemployment, and the stricter fiscal demands of the Maastricht Treaty are undermining the historic commitment of these nations to address inequality.

Economic growth (and for that matter lack of growth) in the postwar era has seemed everywhere to be accompanied by persistent, often high, and sometimes worsening, inequality within countries. The few exceptions include Hong Kong, Korea, Malaysia, Singapore, Taiwan, and Thailand in East Asia—where several decades of extraordinarily high growth saw low and even declining levels of inequality. Even when income distribution does improve, it does so painfully slowly. A study that examined income distribution in 45 countries found that only eight, including Japan and three European nations, showed any improvement in income distribution over any time period, and this progress was minimal.

The idea of convergence of income across countries—that poor countries will ultimately catch up to the rich—has also gone by the wayside. China and India illustrate the difficulties of arguing for the eventual convergence in income of poor and rich countries. For the last 15 years, these two nations have experienced faster income growth than the rich countries, yet it would take them almost a century of constant growth at rates higher than those in today's industrialized countries just to reach current U.S. income levels.

What Makes the World Unfair?

Inequality is nobody's fault and cannot be fixed in our lifetime. Understanding its causes helps us determine what can be done about it and what might actually make it worse. But what are the causes of inequality, across and within countries?

HISTORY

Inequality begets inequality. Therefore, history matters. Consider Latin America. The combination of mineral wealth, soils and climate suitable for sugar production, and imported slave labor, or

While Rich Nations Get Richer . . .

(Estimated GDP in 1980 dollars)

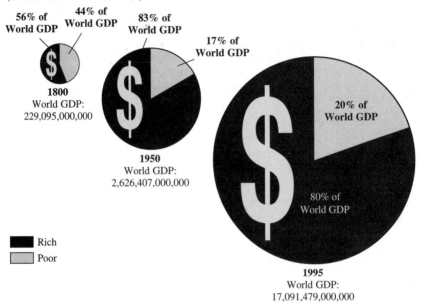

. . . the Poor Population Continues to Grow.

(World Population)

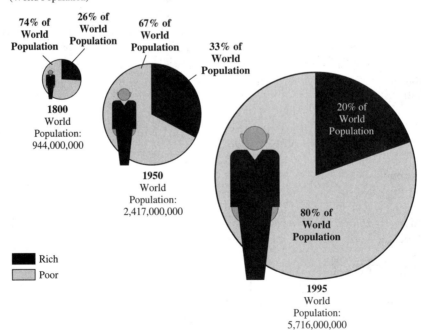

Sources: *1984 World Development Report* (Washington, D.C.: World Bank, 1984), *UN World Population Prospects, The 1994 Revision* (New York: United Nations, 1994), and author's calculations.

conquered indigenous labor, helped produce two castes: large landowners and politically unarmed workers. In 1950, just 1.5 percent of farm owners in Latin America accounted for 65 percent of all agricultural land; unequal land distribution, then the highest in the world, has risen since. Wealth in natural resources invited concentration of income. History and politics subsequently conspired to produce economic and institutional arrangements that have perpetuated that concentration.

THE POOR'S RATIONAL DECISIONS

A source of some inequality lies in predictable human behavior. Because the rich and educated marry each other, as do the poor and uneducated, family income gaps widen. Rational differences in human behavior between the rich and the poor also add to inequality. In many countries, the poor are members of ethnic or racial groups. If they suffer discrimination in the labor market, their gains from schooling and job skills are small, prompting them to respond by investing little in these income-producing assets. But by handicapping their children economically, the sum of these parents' sensible decisions can lock society as a whole into another generation of inequality.

The same happens with fertility. For good reasons, the poor and the less educated tend to have more children. As is to be expected in these poor households, spending per child on nutrition, health, and education declines with the number of children. Less spending on the children of the poor creates a new generation in which the number of unskilled workers grows faster than skilled workers, bringing down wages for the former and thus perpetuating the cycle. In societies with high population growth (Africa, for example), the education levels of mothers are a major determinant of fertility rates. As poorly educated mothers have many more children than their well-educated sisters, the cycle of high fertility and poor opportunities for their children continues, helping perpetuate inequality in their societies.

East Asia provides an example of how fertility change can break this vicious cycle. A dramatic decline in infant mortality in the region after World War II was followed in the early 1960s by an equally dramatic, and very rapid, decline in fertility—which spread quickly to the poor and less educated. These changes had major demographic consequences: In Korea, for example, the percent of the population in the prime working ages of 25 to 59 rose from less than 35 percent to close to 50 percent between 1965 and 1990, while the percent of children between ages 0 and 14 fell. With this demographic growth in the work force came dramatic increases in savings and investment (from about 15 to 35 percent in Korea and Indonesia) that helped fuel growth. Compared with those of other regions, East Asia's private and household savings and investment rates were especially high—including among poor households that invested heavily in the more affordable education of their fewer children.

PROSPERITY

Prosperity can produce inequality—an outcome that, within limits, may be economically justifiable. After all, some inequality may encourage innovation and hard work. Newfound inequality in China and in the economies of Eastern Europe may simply mean that new economic incentives are not only inducing growth but also creating opportunities for some individuals to excel and profit.

But the market reforms that bring prosperity also may not give all players an equal shot at the prize. In the short run, privatization and public-sector downsizing will penalize some workers; and open trade, because it hurts formerly protected industries and makes their inefficiencies unsustainable, can lead to wage reductions and higher unemployment. If corruption infects the privatization process, as in Russia, such reforms will provide windfalls to insiders. More insidious for the poor over the long run are the effects of reforms on the value of assets. During the Latin American debt crisis of the 1980s, many high-income citizens of indebted countries were able to store most of their financial assets abroad, even as their governments (and thus, their fellow taxpayers) assumed the bad debts incurred by enterprises either owned or controlled by the rich. Today's lower inflation and more realistic exchange rates mean dollar accounts held abroad can now buy more at home. Similarly, well-connected individuals in emerging markets who had previously profited from cheap credit, subsidized prices for hard foreign currency, or government regulatory exceptions (say, on the use of urban land) benefited again, as economic reforms raised the market value of assets that they had been able to acquire at low cost.

BAD ECONOMIC POLICY

The most avoidable and thus most disappointing source of inequality are policies that hamper economic growth and fuel inflation—the most devastating outcome of all for the poor. Most populist programs designed to attract the political support of the working class hurt workers in the long run. When financed by unsustainable fiscal largesse, they bring the inflation or high interest rates that exacerbate inequality. Inflation worsens inequality because the poor are forced to hold money and cannot acquire the debts that inflation devalues. High interest rates, driven by unsustainable public debt, crowd out investments and jobs in small and medium enterprises, while encouraging easy gains in government bonds for those with plenty of money. Price controls, usually imposed on the products most consumed by the poor, often lead to their disappearance from stores, as they are hoarded and resold at higher prices. The imposition of a minimum wage temporarily benefits those who have formal jobs but makes it harder for the unemployed to find work. Finally, regulatory privileges, trade protection, and special access to cheap credit and foreign exchange—all bad economic policies—will inevitably increase the profits of a wealthy minority. For all these reasons, IMF-style reforms, often attacked for hurting the poor majority, are key to ending corrupt practices that usually benefit only a few.

Bad policy also includes what governments fail to do. Failure to invest in the education and skills of the poor is a fundamental cause of inequality.

When adequate education does not reach enough of any population, educated workers become scarce, and employers compete for them by offering higher wages. The widening wage gap between college graduates and others in the United States indicates that the demand for graduates still exceeds the supply, feeding inequality. In Brazil, during the 1970s, the salaries of scarce university graduates rose rapidly, worsening wage inequality. In contrast, wage differences in Korea between those with university education and their less-educated colleagues fell, as more and more students completed secondary school and attended universities. In fact, above-average spending on education characterizes each of the few countries that have managed high growth with low inequality in the postwar period.

Tempting and Dangerous Remedies

Paradoxically, the rhetoric of fairness can encourage policies that worsen global and local inequalities. Some examples of these self-defeating policies include:

PROTECTIONISM

Protection from global competition is a dangerous nonremedy, whether it involves import barriers, high import tariffs, or currency controls. Developing countries that have been most open to trade have had the fastest growth, reducing global inequality; those least integrated into global markets, such as many African economies, have remained among the world's poorest. Historically, the same pattern holds. Those countries that aggressively sought commercial links to the outside world—Japan, beginning in the Meiji Era, and the East Asian countries after World War II—whether via technology licensing, openness to foreign investment or an export push, have had the fastest growth. Trade (along with mass migration) explains most of the convergence in income among the countries of Europe and between them and the United States in the late nineteenth century. Convergence of incomes in Europe stalled as economic links disintegrated from 1914 to 1950 and then re-sumed in force in the postwar period, when European economies became more integrated.

But does global integration create worsening inequality within countries, rich and poor alike? The growing wage gap in the United States coincides with increasing imports from developing countries that have large pools of unskilled labor. But most research shows that technology is more to blame than trade for most of the U.S. wage gap: Few U.S. workers (probably less than 5 percent) are in industries competing with low-wage goods from developing countries, and the wages of workers without a high-school diploma have fallen as much if not more in nontrade as in trade industries. True, more subtle forces are also at play—for example, the ability of firms to threaten to move jobs overseas may be undermining American unions. But a recourse to protectionism would almost surely hurt poor consumers more than it would help low-skilled workers.

Growing wage inequality is associated with increased trade and integration into global markets even in developing countries. One reason: Foreign capital inflows and higher domestic capital investment create new jobs for skilled workers, and skilled workers' wages then rise faster than average wages. But the bottom line is that international trade and open markets are less of a problem than worldwide changes in the technology of production that favor skilled workers everywhere.

Indeed, increases in trade and economic integration in poor countries, though associated with high wage inequality, may actually reduce inequality of income and consumption. There are two possible reasons: First, as obstacles to imports fall and price competition intensifies, prices drop—a boon for the poor, who use most of their income for consumption. Second, trade liberalization and open markets in general weaken the unfair advantages enjoyed by the rich and connected, undermining the economic privileges and monopolies (reflected in wealth not wage gaps) that otherwise perpetuate high inequality.

SPECIAL WORKER ENTITLEMENTS

President Franklin Roosevelt's New Deal legislation set countrywide wage rates and labor standards for U.S. workers during the 1930s depression. Could a global minimum wage and global labor standards force up wages of the unskilled in poor countries, reducing in-country and worldwide wage gaps?

Advocates of a global New Deal have a point: Property rights remain elaborately protected in the complex codes of international trade agreements, while labor rights remain unacknowledged. Almost all countries can agree on some standards of behavior: the prohibition of slavery and debt bondage, assurance of a reasonable measure of safety in the workplace, a guarantee of rights to collective bargaining. The problem is that in developing countries, even standards that look noncontroversial (the prohibition of child labor, for example) may hurt those they are meant to protect. Most standards, including collective bargaining rights, which might increase wages in some firms, would affect only the usually small proportion of workers in the formal urban sector, thus increasing the gap between them and the majority of workers in rural and informal jobs. This result might do little harm if it helped a few without hurting others. But harm to many is likely because higher labor costs would then induce employers to invest in labor-saving technologies. The loss of new jobs would hurt mostly the poor and unskilled, whose main asset, after all, is their own labor.

Weaker infrastructure, unreliable judicial and regulatory regimes, and less education mean workers in developing countries produce less—even in well-equipped export firms. A global New Deal will only work when it is no longer needed: that is, when development progress in poor countries brings worker productivity—now as low as one-third the U.S. level—much closer to rich country levels. Only with convergence of worker productivity (and worker pay) across and within nations—as was the case across the United States in Roosevelt's time—could global rules on workers' rights help rather than hurt those now worse off.

UNDERPRICING PUBLIC SERVICES

For decades, governments have monopolized delivery of such public services as water, sanitation, electricity, and health care. They have also charged industries and households much less for these services than they actually cost—all in the name of helping the poor. Mountains of evidence demonstrate two virtually universal results:

First, in the face of any scarcity at all, prices that are too low reduce public supply of the underpriced service. India's public resources will never be sufficient to cover hospital care for its entire population. Short of privatization and adequate meter-based customer charges, electricity services in cities such as Lagos and Karachi will never catch up to demand, and "brownouts" (scheduled times without electricity) will continue.

Second, in the face of any kind of rationing, the poor will be last in line. The guarantee of free university education in Egypt and France, for example, is a false entitlement: Low-income families cannot afford the secondary schooling and tutoring needed to pass the university admissions test. In the Philippines, cheap electricity and water are available to powerful industrial interests, while the poor in the slums rely on jerrybuilt connections and buy bottled water at high prices from private trucks. In Mexico, for decades, general food subsidies benefited the urban middle class and created the incentives for food producers to bribe the politicians and government officials who controlled allocation of these subsidies. Meanwhile, the poor in rural areas and indigenous communities received little if any benefit.

LAISSEZ-FAIRE ECONOMICS

Because trade protection, worker rights, and cheap public services can in fact hurt the poor does not mean the inequality problem can be left to the market. It is one mistake for government to restrict and distort market activity, reducing competition and perpetuating privileges; it is another to assume that market forces will automatically create opportunities for those at the margin.

Every society has some interest in avoiding the worst forms of inequality and injustice. That means in every society there is a role for government—not only to avoid the creation of unfair advantages for the rich and powerful, but to guarantee equal opportunities that market forces will naturally neglect, especially for those individuals who will otherwise be left on the sidelines. But this brings us to the question of what does work.

What Does Work

The false remedies have short-run political appeal. Unfortunately, what does work takes time and patience.

WORKER-BASED GROWTH

Economic growth that is based on the intensive use of labor reduces income inequality—within as well as across countries. Oil-rich countries such as Venezuela and Nigeria have grown quickly at times, but the advantages of oil, bauxite, copper, and other mineral wealth can be short-lived. An abundance of natural resources invites concentration of income and discourages reliance on people, technology, and skills. Lack of natural resources, meanwhile, can be a hidden blessing, as the sustained and equitable growth of Switzerland and Hong Kong show. The labor-using growth of Taiwan and Singapore has reduced income gaps in those economies and propelled their convergence toward industrial-country income levels over the last three decades.

Worker-based growth is best encouraged by avoiding the wrong policies—those that directly or indirectly raise employers' cost of labor. In countries such as Costa Rica and Ghana, where agriculture is labor-using and generates exports, the correction of overvalued exchange rates (which make imports cheaper for urban consumers) has increased rural jobs and income. In England, and now in Venezuela, relaxation of onerous severance-pay rules has encouraged hiring, inducing employers to substitute people and skills for energy and environmentally costly production inputs. The United States could also encourage more hiring of unskilled workers by reducing payroll tax rates and raising the threshold at which these rates are applied.

EDUCATION: THE PEOPLE'S ASSET

In the increasingly service-oriented global economy, education and skills represent a kind of wealth. They are key assets—and once acquired cannot be taken away, even from those who are otherwise powerless. Moreover, as education is shared more broadly, other assets such as land, stocks, or money will become less important.

It should be no surprise that the best predictor of a child's education is her parents' education and income. The poor, especially in developing countries, are last in line for education, as well as other publicly financed services. (Among 13 industrialized countries studied, only in Sweden and the Netherlands have educational opportunities become less stratified by socioeconomic class during this century.) So without a jump-start from public policy, the rich will become educated and stay rich, and the poor will not, perpetuating the inequality of assets and income across generations. In the United States, Europe, and in today's poor developing countries, the single best weapon against income inequality is educating the poor.

Other mechanisms to distribute and redistribute assets, including land reform and microcredit programs, can also improve the pattern by which income is distributed. Pension reforms in Chile, Mexico, Peru, and elsewhere in Latin America have the potential to reduce the disequalizing characteristics of traditional pay-as-you-go systems and to create stakeholders in a market economy among those once excluded from its benefits. In the United States, the current arguments against "privatizing" social security reflect in part the myth that traditional systems are highly redistributive. Much evidence suggests that this is not necessarily true.

DEMOCRACY

Relatively low levels of income inequality in China, Cuba, and the former Soviet Union seem to suggest that authoritarian politics can at least produce equality. But in fact, it is the Western democracies that have over time generated sustained and equalizing economic growth. In economically unequal societies, the one-person, one-vote system can offset the ability of the economically powerful to perpetuate their privileges by buying political power. Perhaps this is why the market today sees greater risk of social disorder fed by political privilege in Indonesia than in its more democratic neighbors, such as Thailand and Korea. In today's global market, good politics is good for equalizing growth.

OPPORTUNITIES, NOT TRANSFERS

Although transfers and income subsidies to help the poor or reduce inequality make sense on paper, they are not long-run solutions. As declining spending on income-tied welfare programs in the United States shows, transfers and subsidies tied to low income are politically difficult to sustain. In fact, because the poor tend to be less organized and politically effective, redistributive programs often respond to more vocal entrenched interests, transforming these initiatives into a regressive tax rather than a safety net. For example, Senegal's program to cushion the effects of its economic reforms channeled state money to privileged groups within the system (civil servants and university graduates), while doing nothing to protect the urban and rural poor from rising consumer prices and unemployment. Often, even those subsidies originally meant for the poor are quickly captured by the middle class and the rich, as ample public spending on university education in California suggests. Finally, the taxes that pay for large transfer programs are increasingly regressive. Because global competition puts pressure on governments to reduce taxes on footloose capital and highly mobile skilled labor, workers and consumers must bear more of the tax burden associated with redistributive transfers, mainly in the form of growing payroll and sales taxes.

Public spending for the poor is more effective in the long run and politically more attractive when it enhances opportunities. But for such public spending to be effective, two rules must prevail: First, spending should concentrate on programs that reach everyone but benefit the poor most—in the United States, secondary education, child care, and immunizations. Second, the poor's access to opportunities should be improved not by directly providing services, but by giving them tax breaks and vouchers for school, health, and housing, which would help them become effective consumers. In Chile, public spending on universal services and on voucher-like programs ensures that more than 80 percent of all public health-care services and 60 percent of all education services go to the poorest 40 percent of households—raising the total income of the poorest one-fifth of households by nearly 50 percent.

STRENGTHEN DOMESTIC POLICIES FOR GLOBAL INTEGRATION

It bears repeating that the poorest countries of the world are those least integrated into global markets; the facts are so obvious that most poor developing countries have joined the bandwagon of unilateral trade opening. Since global markets reward skilled over unskilled labor, poor countries are adjusting to their growing wage inequality by increasing spending on education and training.

Then again, industrial countries are highly integrated among themselves but still relatively closed to poor country products and services. Rich countries could significantly ease global inequality by lifting their barriers to imports of agriculture and manufactured textiles. But progress against protection often implies visible short-run costs to communities and workers. Programs to retrain those workers hurt by opening markets in rich countries, and to top up their wages if they accept a lower-paying job, would reduce income inequality at home and indirectly around the world.

Learning to Live with Inequality

Any hopes for a quick fix to inequality are misplaced. Belying Marx, the biggest story of the last 150 years has been the emergence in the West of a prosperous and stable middle class. But it took time. During a long transition from agriculture to industry, changes in production and in the structure of employment caused wrenching inequality. Much inequality today may be the natural outcome of what is an analogous transition from an industrial to an information age.

Still, there is no reason to despair. Some inequality is healthy and will speed the transition. The rapidly growing wages of the educated and skilled are making education and training much more attractive personal investments. As more people get greater access to education, their relative income advantage over the unskilled will decline. Meanwhile, the high cost of skilled workers should eventually induce technological change that relies more on unskilled labor, increasing the demand for workers with less training.

More fundamentally, people may care less about their current ranking in a static picture of global income distribution than about just and fair access to a better future, especially for their children. In an unequal world, good opportunities represent fair rules and matter at least as much as current status. Greater opportunities—which can be delivered today—are a better guarantee of a socially coherent global community than improved distribution tomorrow.

The real danger is that growing inequality may become a lightning rod for populist rhetoric and self-defeating isolation. It would be unfortunate if such tempting but false remedies eclipsed the more promising policies—international and domestic— that can help the world manage the long transition to a less-divided postindustrial future.

DEVESH KAPUR

The IMF: A Cure or a Curse?

In November 1996, an International Monetary Fund (IMF) publication reporting on an IMF-sponsored conference in Jakarta trumpeted, "ASEAN's Sound Fundamentals Bode Well for Sustained Growth." The central message of the conference, it stressed, was that "the region is poised to extend its success into the twenty-first century and that governments still have a major role in driving this process. . . . Participants' confidence . . . was rooted in the region's strong macroeconomic fundamentals; in ASEAN's (Association of Southeast Asian Nations) tradition of, and commitment to, efficient allocation of investment; and in the widespread belief that the external environment will continue to be supportive."

If the IMF was publicly confident about the strength of Asia's "fundamentals," it was even more enamored with the virtues of the international capital movements that were helping fuel the region's remarkable growth. Even as Asia's ongoing economic crisis began to unfold in the summer of 1997, the IMF was strongly pressing its members to amend its charter (for just the fourth time in its 53-year history) to make the liberalization of capital accounts a specific goal of the fund, and to give it "appropriate jurisdiction" over capital movements.

It took less than a year for the IMF to decry Asia's "fundamentals" as severely wanting. The crisis, it argued, was "mostly homegrown." Instead of urging the prompt dissolution of capital controls, IMF managing director Michel Camdessus began calling for "orderly, properly sequenced and cautious" liberalization of government controls on money flows in and out of countries.

The mistakes of the past, however, did not deter the IMF from intervening in Asia's crisis

countries with unprecedented zeal. But if the IMF's predictions about Asia were so wrong, why should its prescriptions be any better? Do they flow from a technocratic diagnosis? Or do they merely mask the institution's own interests and those of its controlling owners? For that matter, just exactly whose interests does the IMF represent? Its actions during the Asian financial crisis not only cast the answers to these questions in sharp and disturbing relief, but also raise serious doubts about the soundness of the institutional architecture for global governance in general, and for international economic and financial management in particular.

Letting the Record Speak

If the IMF had a dollar for every criticism of its purpose and role by the Right, the Left, and the Center, it would perhaps never again have to approach its shareholders for more money to sustain its operations. Countless *Wall Street Journal* editorials have denounced the institution's "bailouts" and tax-raising proposals as efforts to prop up "bloated" states. Left wingers claim that the fund's policies are a not-so-thinly-disguised wedge for capitalist interests—a view underscored by former U.S. trade representative Mickey Kantor's colorful rendering of the institution as a "battering ram" for U.S. interests. A more banal interpretation portrays the IMF as a hapless Wizard of Oz figure, "a mythologized contraption through which weak human beings speak," to use one observer's words, whose effects are far more limited than its champions and its critics would have us believe.

The IMF's actual record is helpful in sorting out these many overblown and conflicting claims. Founded in 1944 (see box on next page), the institution played a modest but important role in

From *Foreign Policy*, no. III (summer 1998): 114–29.

maintaining stable exchange rates in its first two decades. This raison d'être collapsed after 1971, when the major currencies moved to a floating exchange rate system. Since then (and especially after 1978, when the second amendment to the IMF's charter formally ratified the move to floating exchange rates), its engagement with industrialized countries has been largely pro forma. By the beginning of the 1980s, with commercial bank lending in high gear, the IMF's clientele had shrunk to those poor countries to which no commercial bank was willing to lend.

Until the mid-1980s, fund programs in these poor countries were relatively narrow and generally of short duration. Loan conditions focused on currency devaluations, budget cuts, higher taxes, and curbs on the supply of credit in the economy. Naturally, however, there was no shortage of criticism. Nationalists of all hues lamented the loss of sovereignty entailed by the requirements of IMF programs. More tellingly, critics questioned the fund's single-minded attention to budget deficits, particularly its tendency to ignore the political realities that led governments to cut politically expedient expenditures (funds for primary education, for example), while protecting more politically powerful interests (those of the military and university students). By the same token, governments desperate to meet IMF-mandated targets often chose to impose tax increases that followed the path of least political resistance—raising sales taxes instead of property taxes, for example.

In short, criticisms of fund programs frequently served to mask the actions of the same politicians and policymakers who were largely responsible for their countries' predicaments. Despite the IMF's best intentions, the realities of local politics often resulted in outcomes that were socially regressive, economically myopic, and only modestly able to put a country back on a sustainable growth path. A burst of IMF programs in Africa at the end of the 1970s, for example, proved singularly ill-advised for a continent whose economic problems stemmed from deep-rooted political and social causes. Then again, fund programs significantly helped countries that had viable institutional infrastructures and were willing to implement tough decisions (such as India, Indonesia, South Korea, and Thailand in the 1970s and 1980s).

How the IMF Works

The International Monetary Fund (IMF) and the World Bank—known as the Bretton Woods institutions—were established in 1944. The purpose of the IMF was to promote international monetary cooperation, exchange rate stability, and the expansion of international trade by acting as a lender of last resort when a member country faced an economic crisis.

In principle, the IMF has a structure akin to a financial cooperative. A member country's contributions to the IMF (called "quotas") are based on its weight in the global economy. This weight also determines its voting power and borrowing capacity (called "drawings"). Quotas amount to an exchange of assets with little direct cost to taxpayers. For instance, in the case of the United States, its contributions entitle it to an equal amount of U.S. claims on other currencies. That is, just as other countries can draw U.S. dollars from the IMF in times of need (such as pressures on the U.S. dollar), the United States can draw their currencies (be it the Japanese yen or the German mark) for itself. In fact, the United States has drawn on the IMF on 28 different occasions, most recently a $3 billion drawing in 1978.

By approaching the IMF, a member country facing a financial crisis has access to the fund's resources and advice. As a country's drawings become larger relative to its quotas, it must meet more exacting standards or "conditionalities," which typically mean significant changes in economic policies to ensure that the country's domestic and external deficits are drastically lowered or even eliminated. Failure to meet those conditions results in suspension, renegotiation, or even cancellation of the program.

Although the total size of the IMF's quotas increased from about $9 billion at its creation to nearly $200 billion in 1997, it has declined relative to almost all relevant global economic indicators, whether the size of world trade, international reserves, or international financial flows.

—D.K.

The Debt Crisis: A Historical Pivot

The advent of the Latin American debt crisis in 1982 marked a major turning point for the IMF's fortunes. Navigating skillfully through uncharted waters, the fund helped to forestall the dangers posed by the crisis to the global financial system. But its role in the debt crisis also had two important long-term consequences for the institution. First, it became the equivalent of a debt collector for commercial banks. Second, the IMF expanded its mandate to promote structural reforms.

THE "CREDITOR COMMUNITY'S ENFORCER"

Although both debtors and creditors shared blame for the 1980s debt crisis, the costs of adjustment were borne asymmetrically by debtor countries, which suffered their worst economic decline since the Great Depression. Even as the fund's programs grew in number, its net lending shrank. Particularly embarassing for the IMF was the contrast between the late-1980s increase in repayments by Latin nations and the further contraction of their economies. Describing the IMF as the "creditor community's enforcer," former Columbia University professor Karin Lissakers (now the U.S. executive director at the IMF) noted that the behavior of "a political organization" such as the IMF "raises the question of which way will its biases go" when placed between debtors and creditors. Denunciations by MIT professor Stanley Fischer (currently the IMF's first deputy managing director) of the institution's "mistaken no-debt-relief strategy" were seconded by Jacques Polak, a respected former research director and later the Dutch executive director, who complained that the institution was "being used by the commercial banks in the collection of their debts."

This debt-collector role inevitably undermined the institution's credibility. Its economic projections, for example, became malleable to major shareholder pressure. As former Federal Reserve chairman Paul Volcker once bluntly said of the IMF's numbers in the debt crisis, they were "negotiated" numbers, embracing in some instances what former IMF research director Jacob Frenkel called "considerations other than purely analytical ones." Indeed, if "the record shows that frank and open debate does not take place in official and banking circles" (to use Fischer's 1989 characterization of the Bretton Woods institutions' behavior in the debt crisis), a decline in client trust is inevitable.

THE ADVENT OF STRUCTURAL REFORMS

A second consequence of the debt crisis was that the IMF, chastened by the modest results of its programs and pressed by its critics, reformulated its approach. Rather than focus just on the size of budget deficits and the magnitude of revenue increases and the expenditure cuts needed to correct them, the fund began to demand specific cuts and increases—for example, pressing some countries to protect social programs and prune military spending. As the economic travails of Africa—and the IMF's very limited success then—became evident, fund programs became even more detailed. To counter criticisms that its policies hurt the poor, or its bias toward austerity and exports encouraged environmental destruction, the fund added poverty alleviation and governance-related issues (such as corruption) to its agenda—a trend reinforced by the East European countries joining the fund at the end of the 1980s. In many cases, the IMF devised loan conditions at the behest of borrowers, whether local officials who felt powerless to sway their political leaders or politicians who used the IMF to shield themselves from popular rejection of policies that they too recognized as essential.

Although there was more rhetoric than reality to these changes in the fund's approach, its loan conditions were clearly moving beyond merely requiring fiscal and monetary adjustments. An equally clear and more troubling trend implicit in the IMF's mission creep was its growing hubris. Spurred on by the demands of its principal owners and the internal activism of its technocrat managers, the fund began to assume that all that was deemed good for a country should also be part of its mandate. As a result, its overlap with its Bretton Woods sister, the World Bank, grew. And with the major powers holding a "very pro-Fund view" relative to the World Bank (again, to use Fischer's words), the advice emanating from the Bretton Woods institutions began to have an increasing IMF flavor.

Mexico 1994: A Model Crashes

The aftermath of the 1980s debt crisis led to a consensus among policymakers that less developed countries (LDCs) should place greater reliance on market forces. When coupled with sound macroeconomic policies (especially low budget deficits), liberalized financial markets would produce stronger growth and enable the self-correcting mechanisms of market discipline to work. Countries such as Mexico, which sharply reduced their budget deficits, privatized state-owned enterprises, and welcomed foreign investment, were praised and rewarded by the fund and Wall Street as star pupils who could do no wrong. Evidence to the contrary was ignored or pooh-poohed by an IMF determined to uphold and spread its model of economic reform. So when financial crisis hit Mexico in December 1994, the IMF (not to mention Wall Street, the media, and most academic analysts) was, to put it mildly, caught offguard.

The massive $40 billion financial package that the IMF organized for Mexico in 1995—at the time its largest package ever—was only possible because Mexico borders the IMF's largest shareholder. The package prevented a default and allowed Mexico to regain access to financial markets, while limiting the impact of the crisis on other countries in the region. But it also set a precedent. At the very least, it held out the likelihood that foreign creditors could expect to be bailed out in similar situations. And although several recent commentaries have hailed the IMF's intervention as a "success," such a characterization glosses over the somber reality that real wages in Mexico are still one-quarter below their pre-crisis levels of more than three years ago.

The IMF's postmortem of the Mexican crisis concluded not that the fund was wrong, but that it lacked the wherewithal to be right. It identified a generic problem afflicting LDCs—a lack of transparency—and asked its shareholders for additional policing powers and resources to correct it. Persuading nations to make more financial information available to international institutions such as the IMF (and to the public) would doubtless help avert or defuse crises. But there are limits to this approach. Even if the IMF had more relevant information, it would have to remain discreet in the face of an emerging problem, since financial markets have a tendency to make even not-so-dire predictions by such institutions self-fulfilling. And the more information that the IMF asks for, the less countries are likely to be able to provide it, at least within the rapid time frame that markets move, and especially when global money managers sense looming problems. Finally, it is not the availability of information that matters per se, but its interpretation. There are none so blind as those who will not see; and staring at the proverbial pot of gold can be blinding.

A more curious response to the peso crisis was the fund's enthusiasm for unfettered global financial markets. That global financial markets bring high risks and high rewards is well established. But since the poor have less capacity to bear risk, the IMF might have been expected to move cautiously in integrating poor countries into global financial markets, despite the high potential rewards. As Larry Summers put it when he was chief economist at the World Bank, in banking as in nuclear plants, "free entry is not sensible." But arguing that the benefits of free capital movements were substantial, the fund began its campaign to bring the promotion of capital account liberalization under its mandate and jurisdiction barely a year and a half after the Mexico crisis. Of course, another factor behind the fund's views may have been the sentiment subsequently expressed by Summers in his current capacity as deputy secretary of the U.S. Treasury: namely, that "financial liberalization, both domestically and internationally is a critical part of the U.S. agenda."

Asia 1998: Déjà Vu with a Difference

The consequences of the IMF's experience in earlier crises are manifest in its unfolding role in the Asian crisis. As before, the fund's diagnosis has emphasized the internal roots of the problem: the failure to control large balance-of-payments deficits; the explosion in property and financial markets; mismanaged exchange rate regimes; rapidly expanding financial systems that were poorly regulated; and an unwillingness to act decisively once confidence was lost.

But, as in the past, the fund's focus on in-country factors has deflected attention from both its earlier firm endorsement of these countries' policies and its unbridled cheerleading on removing the barriers impeding globalization. Indonesia, Korea, Malaysia, and Thailand had thrived for years, despite weak financial systems and numerous destabilizing external events, including the oil shocks of the 1970s and the soaring dollar of the early 1980s. And, yes, crony capitalism had thrived as well—if anything, in a rather transparent way. Now the IMF and international capital markets claimed they were shocked, just shocked, to find that the regime's impressive economic achievements were built on such dodgy foundations.

The countries did make egregious mistakes—perhaps the worst was their overconfidence that their success was somehow uniquely based on quasi-magical "Asian values." In reality, their economies were undone not by visible internal flaws, but by the unforeseen impact of the global capital flows that the IMF sought to set free. The conventional macroeconomic indicators of the Asian crisis countries were well within prudential norms. These were not profligate governments whose policies yielded large deficits and inflation. Current account deficits in Thailand were extremely high, but that was hardly a secret. In hindsight, there were cracks in exchange rate regimes, especially in Korea and Thailand; yet they were not apparent at the time, and exchange rates were not excessively overvalued. But the combination of huge capital inflows with high domestic savings rates tempted inexperienced business executives and corrupt and incompetent politicians, particularly when the state implicitly stood behind the financial speculations of private institutions.

When a domestic asset bubble bursts, the consequences can be painful. Capital flight severely amplifies the pain. In the case of the Asian crisis, a vicious circle set in. As capital flooded out, exchange rates collapsed, and a wave of bankruptcies by firms unable to pay their foreign debts engulfed the private sector, leaving the countries at the mercy of panic-stricken private lenders and obdurate official ones.

The IMF assembled a mammoth financial package—$17 billion for Thailand, $43 billion for Indonesia, and $57 billion for Korea—with resources drawn from the IMF itself, together with the World Bank, the Asian Development Bank, and leading governments. Despite the poor judgment shown by financial markets (differences in interest rates between Asian and U.S. sovereign debt, a measure of the relative risks that markets attached to these countries, had continued to narrow until the first half of 1997, shortly before the crisis), resources disbursed by fund programs have been used by the crumbling Asian economies to pay off foreign creditors.

But the disbursements were linked to the countries' meeting a range of conditions that seem to go well beyond the IMF's mandate. Two decades ago, fund programs typically imposed a dozen or so requirements or strictures. But the Asian countries have had to sign agreements that look more like Christmas trees than contracts, with anywhere from 50 to 80 detailed conditions covering everything from the deregulation of garlic monopolies to taxes on cattle feed and new environmental laws.

Many of the objectives underlying these conditions are laudable. Unfortunately, they also reflect a troubling lack of institutional self-restraint. According to fund sources, conditions such as the one asking Korea to speed up the opening of its automobile and financial sectors reflected pressures from major shareholders (Japan and the United

States). In Indonesia, detailed conditions related to the banking sector were imposed despite the fund's limited expertise in this area. In November 1997, the Indonesian government shut 16 banks at the IMF's insistence without providing firm assurances that the government would stand behind those banks that remained. The resulting bank run almost dragged down the entire Indonesian banking sector. By the IMF's own admission, a fragile system was pushed over the brink—a tragic illustration of the folly of institutional overreach.

Restoring the Balance

Against the backdrop of the IMF's history of the last 50 years, the Asian financial crisis suggests four conclusions:

The first and most evident conclusion is that, as Federal Reserve chairman Alan Greenspan remarked recently, the global financial system seems to facilitate "the transmission of financial disturbances far more effectively than ever before." Many analysts now share the view that foreign financial flows should be regulated in some way. The question is how to make openness to the world's capital markets less perilous. Although LDCs undoubtedly need to open up to the world's capital markets, they would be well advised to do so at a pace commensurate with their capacity to develop sound regulatory and institutional structures. In particular, tighter limits on short-term foreign borrowing—especially by banks—may well be essential.

This need for greater prudence on the part of LDCs is underscored by the failure of various proposals designed to protect nations from the full force of global financial flows (such as a tax on international financial transactions or financier George Soros's suggestion for a publicly funded international insurance organization). In theory, when a financial crisis does occur, there should be an international equivalent of domestic bankruptcy codes that would create a legal venue for creditors and debtors to resolve their differences, and allow both sides to avert financial panics and

to stop shirking their responsibilities. But the major actors in international financial markets dislike the idea. Perhaps this is because they are aware that more pressure can be brought onto LDCs through the IMF than through a judicial "due process." Barring much greater losses in major industrialized countries, support for any of these proposals is unlikely.

A second conclusion is that "moral hazard"—the propensity in both borrowing countries and creditors to take excessive risks because of the implicit insurance offered by bailouts—applies to the IMF as well as to borrowers and creditors.

In the case of borrowers, costs to their citizens and politics vastly exceed financial inflows from the bailouts. Thus, to say that borrowing countries will misbehave in hopes of being "bailed out" is to miss the point. The hazard (moral or otherwise) is that LDC leaders will use the IMF and other external forces to steer domestic discontent away from their own machinations. There is perhaps greater "moral hazard" among creditors, particularly in the banking segment of the financial sector—a subject much commented on in recent years.

More worrisome is a certain moral hazard on the part of the IMF and its major shareholders. The steady expansion of institutional objectives (and loan conditions) has occurred because borrowing countries bear a disproportionate share of the political, economic, and financial risks of IMF programs. There is little downside to these programs for the fund's major shareholders, its management, or staff. Financially, IMF-led bailouts impose few net costs on the industrialized countries, since the fund has always been repaid (with the exception of Sudan, arrears to the IMF exist only in the case of countries that have imploded). The damage resulting from the IMF's mishandling of the Indonesian banking sector was entirely borne by the country—not by the IMF or the board that had signed onto these conditions. The IMF's apex role among multilateral financial institutions means that it is the first to go into crisis countries—but also the first to get out—further reducing its financial risks. Instead of underscoring the fund's limitations, the various crises that have afflicted LDCs have enlarged its resources and mandate, an aggrandizement driven by the bogeyman of "systemic" threats to the world's financial system.

If the financial risks are few for the IMF, the political risks are even fewer. The fund is largely irrelevant to managing economic relations among major economic powers. As a result, its member countries are divided into "structural" creditors and debtors, with the latter group comprising LDCs and, more recently, countries making the transition from central planning to market economies. With this division, the essence of the institution as a cooperative has dwindled. Knowing that they were unlikely to borrow from the IMF, the major economic powers have had fewer qualms about continually expanding its power and role. For example, many European members of the IMF signed on to conditions calling for greater labor market flexibility in Asia without pausing to reflect on the situation in their own countries, where extremely rigid labor markets have resulted in soaring unemployment. This contradiction has less to do with an apparent double standard than with the unlikelihood of many European nations ever being subject to IMF strictures.

A third conclusion is that the continued expansion of the IMF's power and mandate is bad for debtor nations, for the global financial system, and, ultimately, for the IMF itself. The increasing scope of loan conditions implies that during a financial crisis, the IMF should take over more and more of a country's decision-making process, without any commensurate increase in accountability. Put in a different way, the absence of risk sharing means that these conditions amount to a form of political taxation without representation.

Moreover, in today's financially rooted economic crises, expanding the IMF's agenda (and its associated loan conditions) can be self-defeating. Unlike the slow burning "old style" economic crises caused by macroeconomic imbalances, financial crises can spread globally like wildfire.

Quick and decisive action is necessary to bring them under control. The widening of loan conditions invariably results in a loss of precious time, whether during negotiation or implementation, making a bad situation worse.

The long-term damage to the IMF itself should also not be underestimated. In the absence of rules designed to ensure self-restraint, its staff—like that of any other bureaucracy—will always push the fund toward policy prescriptions that give them greater prominence and influence. Observers of governmental bureaucracies have long recognized that a multiplicity of missions impairs bureaucratic effectiveness and erodes institutional autonomy. The IMF's widening agenda has made it both less effective and more vulnerable to politicization, thus tarnishing the technocratic reputation that is essential to the credibility of its prescriptions. As its goals increase, the criteria for "success" become more elusive, leading the institution to tout its own "achievements" ever more ardently—with discrediting results, as demonstrated by the debt crisis in the 1980s, and again by the 1994–95 Mexican peso crash.

The final conclusion is that by placing the onus of adjustment solely on debtor countries, the fund's actions relieve any pressure on creditor countries to change the status quo, whether the creaky architecture of international organizations set up 50 years ago, an exchange rate regime whose gyrations trap weaker countries, or the increasingly ineffective regulation of international finance. Today, the principles for which the IMF claims to stand are increasingly at odds with the way in which it conducts its own affairs. It promotes the virtues of democracy—while deeming them impractical, if not downright dangerous, for multilateral governance. It derides and discourages state intervention in economic affairs—while insisting on its right to restructure from top to bottom the economies of the LDCs. And it rejects the need for international controls on capital as invidious—while asserting the need for those on labor to be obvious.

This welter of contradictions serves to highlight the corrosive impact of a long series of ad hoc solutions on an increasingly dilapidated system of global governance. Ultimately, the limitations of multilateral institutions such as the IMF reflect the limitations of those nation-states that created them. And, if as a normative principle power should go hand-in-hand with responsibility, then those states with the most power in these institutions must bear the blame for their failings and assume the greatest responsibility for their rejuvenation.

9 ⟋ QUEST FOR GLOBAL GOVERNANCE

There are many pieces to the global governance puzzle. One prominent piece of that puzzle is the United Nations. The first selection of this chapter, from The Economist, *suggests how this institution may be reformed and explains the difficulties in the process. Another piece of the puzzle is the array of rules and norms found in international law. In the light of these rules and norms, the actions taken by the international community in particular international crises may be illegal, but just. In the second selection, Michael J. Glennon examines the trade-off between legality and justice in the case of NATO's bombing of Kosovo. Global governance also involves nongovernmental organizations (NGOs) and transnational advocacy networks. Using a constructivist approach, Margaret E. Keck and Kathryn Sikkink, in a selection from their award-winning book,* Activists Beyond Borders: Advocacy Networks in International Politics *(1998), show how such networks develop and operate by "building new links among actors in civil societies, states, and international organizations." In their series book,* Triangulating Peace, *Bruce Russett and John Oneal build upon Keck and Sikkink's discussion, arguing that layering bonds of trade and democracy upon the ties of international organizations effectively increases the chances of a sustainable peace.*

John Mearsheimer, the quintessential realist, is openly skeptical about the impact of international institutions. In the final excerpt of this chapter, he carefully delineates the flaws of liberal institutionalist theory and concludes that policies based on these theories are bound to fail. Mearsheimer's book for the Norton series expands and supports with historical material his argument that states are ultimately free from restraints imposed by international institutions.

THE ECONOMIST

Reforming the United Nations: Pope Kofi's Unruly Flock

Kofi Annan Is the Most Respected Leader of the United Nations for a Generation. Can He Push through the Revolution the Organisation Needs?

The job of secretary-general at the United Nations is not unlike that of a medieval pope. In one sense, you are the leader of Christendom. Yet, at the same time, your power is limited: you have no battalions of your own (all those peacekeeping troops are only on loan); your own organisation is a hotch-potch of feuding bishoprics, most of whom feel more loyalty to temporal rulers than to you; and you are normally broke.

In such a job much depends on character and momentum. Kofi Annan has shown that he has plenty of the former. The softly spoken Ghanaian is not just more affable than his predecessor, Boutros Boutros-Ghali, but also more politically astute, especially in dealing with America. Since becoming secretary-general in January 1997, Mr Annan has quieted criticism in Congress, won $1 billion from Ted Turner, started holding meetings with the private sector, and made a series of encouraging appointments, including Louise Fréchette as his deputy. Mr Boutros-Ghali would never appoint a deputy for fear that he (never mind she) might start elbowing him out of his job.

Until recently Mr Annan also seemed to have momentum on his side. But his successful diplomatic crusade in Iraq at the beginning of the year is in the sad process of unravelling. Over the past few weeks the UN's monitors have been hustled out of Congo and the hard-won peace in Angola is at vanishing point. The United Nations High Com-

missioner for Refugees (UNHCR), one of the better-run UN fiefs, faces unexpected allegations of corruption.

Such setbacks reflect more basic flaws. The UN remains a place where a senior official can still compare the bureaucracy unfavourably with that of the old Soviet Union; where discord between "the South" (as less-developed nations are known) and the North paralyses decision-making; where America still owes nearly $1.5 billion in dues; and where the current budget was agreed only after a demeaning haggling session in which favoured secretariat posts and perks were auctioned off by a moderator using a tin of potato crisps as a gavel.

These failings are largely attributable to the membership, not to Mr Annan. Yet they underline his fundamental challenge. Over the past two decades, virtually every large commercial organisation and most big governmental ones have gone through a process in which they have had to answer the question: "What can I do that other people cannot?" The result: takeovers and lay-offs in the corporate world and privatisation in the public sector. Despite several committees pondering its future, the UN has so far shirked most of the big questions.

The UN is an enormous body that, among other things, buys half the world's children's vaccines, protects 22m refugees, is host to 7,500 meetings a year in Geneva alone and is the world's biggest purchaser of condoms. This diversity is complicated by a structure that bewilders even its own staff. It is fairly easy, for instance, to find officials in Geneva who believe that the World Trade Organisation is part of the UN (it is not, though its staff are part of the pension scheme). There are at least five big UN centres—New York, Geneva, Vienna, Rome and Nairobi—and countless smaller ones.

From *The Economist*, 8 August 1998, 19–21.

The UN's parliament is the General Assembly, which meets from September to December each year. It includes all 185 members (each with an equal vote). Most of the UN's political operations, including peacekeeping, answer to the Security Council, which has five permanent members (Britain, China, France, Russia and the United States). A much larger Economic and Social Council supervises the development work that accounts for around 60% of the UN's budget.

The operational side of the UN can be divided a little crudely into three levels:

- The secretariat, run by Mr Annan.
- The funds and programmes, which include the UNHCR and the United Nations Children's Fund (UNICEF). Many of these institutions raise their money from outside sources though, in most cases, Mr Annan has the right to appoint the chief executive.
- The specialised agencies, a group that includes everything from the Bretton Woods financial organisations, such as the IMF and the World Bank, to the World Health Organisation and the World Meteorological Organisation, all of which have their own governing bodies, financial backers and (often contradictory) points of view.

The agencies, alongside all the funds and programmes, attend the twice-yearly meetings of the Administrative Committee on Co-ordination (ACC). The diversity of the conferees make these slightly bizarre affairs, where as one person points out, "discussing issues like the security of UN personnel in war zones is a little lost on the man from the World Intellectual Property Organisation."

The structure makes for patchy results and little accountability. Most agencies regard their membership of the UN as accidental. Staff at the International Labour Organisation and the International Telecommunication Union point out that their institutions both predate the UN. The president of the World Bank, Jim Wolfensohn, has taken to calling Mr Annan "my boss" in public; if Mr Annan had any real power over him, he might not be so chummy.

Called to Account

Last year, Mr Annan began what he likes to call his "quiet revolution." Part of this meant letting Joseph Connor, the UN's administrative chief (and an ex-chairman of Price Waterhouse), continue his work of slimming down the central bureaucracy. Having reduced the headcount by 14% since 1994 to 8,800 (almost entirely through attrition, partly

The UN's Scattered Family

Selected Activities

New York	Washington	Rome	London	Geneva	Gaza
Secretariat	IMF*	Food†	Maritime*	Disarmament	Palestine
Children*	World Bank*	Food and		Health*	refugees
Development†		agriculture*	**Paris**	Human rights†	
	Montreal		Education*	Intellectual	**Nairobi**
Jamaica	Civil aviation*	**Vienna**		property*	Environment†
Seabed		Atomic energy	**The Hague**	Labour*	
		Drugs†	Justice	Population†	**Tokyo**
		Industry*		Refugees†	University

Source: *The UN Handbook*

*Specialised agencies

†Funds and programmes

because, thanks to American non-payments, the UN is too broke to pay redundancy money), Mr Connor now wants to cut back the administrative portion of the central budget from 38% to 25%; the money saved, some $200m, should go to front-line economic development.

Mr Annan has also tried to streamline the chain-of-command, while creating what he calls "a more collegial approach." Acting on a report by Maurice Strong, a Canadian businessman, he has marshalled the central part of the UN into five "executive groups," and then formed these departmental heads into a cabinet that takes most of the important decisions. He has also promoted the idea of UN houses in various countries to bring together the different agencies and programmes—and encourage them to talk to each other.

The reformers had hoped to knock out more layers. But Mr Annan backed off, after a row with UNICEF. Mr Strong argues loyally that Mr Annan has done as much as could be expected. Insiders

Some Get Off Lightly

United Nations Assessment, 1998–2000, Selected Countries

Rank by contribution	UN regular budget %	GDP* 1996 % of world	GDP* 1996 $ per person
1 United States†	25.0	20.8	28,020
2 Japan	18.0	8.3	23,420
3 Germany	9.6	4.8	21,110
4 France†	6.5	3.5	21,510
5 Italy	5.4	3.2	19,890
6 Britain†	5.1	3.3	19,960
7 Russia†	2.9	1.7	4,190
8 Canada	2.8	1.8	21,380
16 Mexico	0.9	2.0	7,660
18 China†	0.9	11.3	3,330
23 Saudi Arabia	0.6	0.5	9,700
38 Malaysia	0.2	0.6	10,390
39 Singapore	0.2	0.2	26,910

Sources: UN; World Bank

*At PPP exchange rates

†Permanent members of the Security Council

say that the cabinet does indeed seem to have increased coordination at the top of the UN; and there are some signs of "a common service approach" between agencies in the field. Yet, overall, there is plainly not enough co-ordination and too much administration.

This is not Mr Connor's fault (nor for that matter Mr Annan's): most of the duplication occurs among the various funds, programmes and agencies where they have little power. The UN could save a small fortune if its various bits bought the paper for their reports in bulk (it could save even more if they agreed to have only one report on each subject). Mr Connor hopes a new, much delayed computer system will simplify the UN's famously complex (and chronically overstaffed) personnel system—but already some UN bodies have refused to take parts of it.

UNICEF is one of those that have opted to be choosy. Carol Bellamy, the fund's chief, is plainly not just being difficult for the sake of it: she points out that her agency has already paid $3m to adapt the personnel part of the new system to its own needs; taking the rest would have cost much more. Similarly, she supports the idea of UN houses—but not in countries where it is cheaper to stick to the current system. Volunteers at UNICEF insist that one of its strengths is its *esprit de corps*: its workers resent being bundled in with other, less effective bodies, such as UNESCO.

In both New York and Geneva, there is a feeling that Mr Annan has done enough—for the moment. The reforms have been largely restricted to the few parts of the UN he controls; those that fall under the jurisdiction of the assembly or the various governing bodies of the agencies remain untouched. Last month the assembly held a brief plenary meeting that "deferred further consideration" of Mr Annan's proposal to set sunset times for new committees and commitments of funds. The assembly has also messed around with Mr Connor's plan to transfer $200m in administrative savings to field operations—and stopped several fairly painless reforms, such as transferring the decolonisation unit from the prestigious political department to the more lowly services one.

The World Changes, the UN Stays Still

Most outsiders would argue that the real question is whether the UN should have a decolonisation unit at all. Indeed, the real issue for both Mr Annan and the assembly is whether his quiet revolution went far enough in the first place. A bit like a struggling country, the UN often makes the mistake of measuring reforms by its own historical standards, rather than against those of the world outside its walls.

That world is changing fast. The UN remains a governmental organisation that devotes most of its time and money to development. Yet at best the public sector (including the UN) now accounts for only 5% of the money flowing to the developing world. The rest comes from private companies and from non-governmental organisations, such as Save the Children. There are nearly 1,700 NGOs based in Geneva alone. Usually leaner and more dynamic, the NGOs are not only competing for dollars that might otherwise go to UN bodies, but often assuming its role. It was, as Mr Annan readily concedes, the NGOs that pushed for the recent treaty to ban anti-personnel landmines and for the new world criminal court.

Last year, Mr Annan held a secret summit at the Rockefeller estate near New York city, where business leaders, such as Percy Barnevik, tried to explain this new world to the UN's top brass. Since then, Mr Annan has initiated an overdue "dialogue with the private sector." But education counts only for so much. Sooner or later, more radical change will be demanded by the 15 or so richer countries that pay virtually all the UN's budget.

In particular, the UN will have to change from a body that tries to do everything everywhere into the "narrower, deeper organisation" reformers have always wished it would be. What should it concentrate on? One answer would be global problems that nobody else can tackle. In general, the UN's core political activities pass this test more easily than its economic and social ones (they also stand more easily with its original charter).

Taking responsibility for refugees and peace-keeping is something the UN should be able to do. It is also a natural forum for debates on global problems, from asteroid collisions to drug-trafficking. Indeed, the extremely controversial idea of the UN having a small standing army (so that it can put peacekeepers on the ground quickly) fits much more neatly into the concept of a narrower, deeper UN than, say, financing environmental research (which is waved through every year).

Mr Annan's supporters point out that the secretariat cannot destroy even the smallest committee; that has to be done by the membership. Richard Sklar, who represents America on questions of reform and debt payment, says that reform does not always have to be a top-down process. He cites WIPO as being the only part of the UN that is a "results-based organisation." The intellectual property agency recently cut its 31 programmes down to 19, because these were the only useful ones.

A Louder Revolution?

Mr Annan is nervous about the idea of a much narrower UN: "governments are always demanding that something must be done, and that something always ends up at the UN." But he has in theory left the door open for another more fundamental wave of reform. Last year he persuaded the General Assembly to give him permission to examine several things, including the agency system. He would also dearly love to bully the assembly into reorganising its currently chaotic agenda.

Why not be bolder? Conventional wisdom within the UN is that reform must be gradual. "You have to remember," Ms Fréchette says, "that this is a universal organisation that has to reflect its members' wishes." Many members see Mr Annan as more of a secretary than a general. Most clubs dislike change. In the assembly's case, the subject of reform scratches all four of its deepest wounds.

The first wound is the chasm between South and North. Virtually any sensible rethink of the UN would involve the organisation concentrating more on political projects than economic and social ones. But the latter is the part of the UN that three-quarters of its members hold most dear. Ms Fréchette, who may have to tackle this problem, is already suspect as a "northern" woman, put in by the UN's paymasters, to balance the southern Mr Annan.

Two southern institutions are particularly hostile to change. One is the "Group of 77" previously non-aligned countries which holds a lock over many appointments. The other is the Fifth Committee, which deals with the budget—and has become home to the group of young obstructionists who were responsible for the tawdry potato-crisp auction last year.

The second wound is America's non-payment. "Reforming the UN" is the excuse that Congress gives for delaying payment of its dues. It is difficult to overestimate the disgust with the United States, ever among its allies, at the UN. "They have poisoned the well," says one senior ambassador. Many doubt that America really wants to see a more efficient UN—just a smaller one. Last year, Mr Annan's quiet revolution received a boost when Congress broke its promise to settle the debt (up to that point the assembly had not wanted to be seen to be doing America's bidding).

The third awkwardness is the Security Council and the relentless politicking about its anachronistic composition. One of the most difficult countries when it comes to almost all reform issues is Pakistan. The reason? Any meaningful debate about reform would include a proposal to widen the permanent membership of the council, probably bringing in India, which Pakistan does not want (just as the Italians do not want the Germans and the Argentines do not want the Brazilians).

The fourth tender area is the way that the budget is parcelled out. Ten countries pay more than three-quarters of the current $1.3 billion budget. Although nobody begrudges the fact that the world's poorest nations contribute only $13,000 each, many fairly prosperous countries escape lightly. China, which pays just 0.9% of the total (less than Belgium), is understandably no great proponent of reform.

If the UN does eventually bicker itself into oblivion, the central responsibility will lie with its members not its secretary-general. Even those governments that support reform have no clear policy towards the UN. One senior UN official, involved in the ACC, points out that the central UN has "no real political constituency." In governments around the world, there are labour ministers to plead the ILO's case and health officials to defend the WHO. But the UN itself has no dedicated spokesman.

On the other hand, the excuse that Mr Annan is purely the club secretary does not wash. As the late Dag Hammarskjold, the Swede who was the only outstanding secretary-general so far, stressed repeatedly, the post is not just about fulfilling mandates, but also representing the world's broader interests. That surely includes a healthy UN. Put another way, if he wants to change the UN, the diplomatic Mr Annan will have to try to force his club members to accept changes that most of them do not want.

How Mr Annan decides to launch this crusade is a matter of tactics. Many would counsel waiting until the Americans have paid up. Mr Annan seems to be holding back his ammunition for a special Millennium Assembly in 2000. That might present a chance to go back to the UN's original charter, using that as the basis for a comprehensive reform plan that included the agencies, the Security Council and the budget dues. So far there has not been much action—other than talk about yet another report.

Mr Annan says with a wry smile that "the UN is not a house in which revolutionaries flourish." But he is probably in a stronger position than he realises. The fact that nobody else has any clear policy about the UN's future gives him a chance to set the agenda. Moreover, some individual reforms might be easier to push through if they are part of a wider plan. For instance, if Mr Annan proposes merging the UN's three food agencies (all of which are located in Rome), the Italians will probably object; put such a reform into a wider package, where other governments lost favoured perks, and the Italians might be more co-operative. Having seen the way that Mr Strong's proposals were gradually watered down, one reformer says: "A big bang solution is the only way anything fundamental will happen."

The parallel with the medieval papacy should both inspire and frighten Mr Annan. On the one hand, by using their bully pulpit effectively, some strong popes did manage to lead Christendom, regardless of their lack of battalions. On the other, the failure by most popes to face up to the abuses within their own organisation opened up the way to reformation of a more devastating type. Or as one insider puts it: "If the UN's friends do not reform it, its enemies will."

MICHAEL J. GLENNON

The New Interventionism: The Search for a Just International Law

As the twentieth century fades away, so too does the international consensus on when to get involved in another state's affairs. The United States and NATO—with little discussion and less fanfare—have effectively abandoned the old U.N. Charter rules that strictly limit international intervention in local conflicts. They have done so in favor of a vague new system that is much more tolerant of military intervention but has few hard and fast rules. What rules do exist seem more the product of after-the-fact rationalization by the West than of deliberation and pre-agreement.

The death of the restrictive old rules on peacekeeping and peacemaking—under which most bloody conflicts were simply ignored as "domestic matters"—should not be mourned. Events since the end of the Cold War starkly show that the anti-interventionist regime has fallen out of sync with modern notions of justice. The crisis in Kosovo illustrates this disjunction and America's new willingness to do what it thinks right—international law notwithstanding. The horror of ethnic cleansing in the Serbian province was well publicized. As Slobodan Milošević thumbed his nose at the international community, pressure built to use force

From *Foreign Affairs* 78, no. 3 (May/June 1999): 2–7.

against him, whether the U.N. Charter allowed it or not. Thus when the Western allies launched air strikes, the move was largely popular. It was not, however, technically legal under the old regime. After all, Kosovo is still part of Yugoslavia. No cross-border attack—the one circumstance where the charter allows an international military response—had occurred, and the Security Council had never authorized NATO military measures.

Thus in Kosovo, justice (as it is now understood) and the U.N. Charter seemed to collide. But it is not only that the U.N. Charter prohibits intervention where enlightened states now believe it to be just—its problems run even deeper. For the charter is grounded on a premise that is simply no longer valid—the assumption that the core threat to international security still comes from interstate violence. This assumption is no longer true. Moreover, thanks to Cold War deadlock and the veto power held by the five permanent members of the Security Council, the old rules never prevented such interstate violence in the first place (witness Afghanistan, Vietnam, etc.).

Whether the cost of abandoning the old anti-interventionist structure will be offset by the benefits of the newly emerging one remains to be seen. Replacing a formal system with a set of vague, half-formed, ad hoc principles can be dangerous.

Untested rules may have unexpected consequences, and justice formed on the fly may come to be resented. The failings of the old system were so disastrous, however, that little will be lost in the attempt to forge a new one.

Crisis (Mis-)management

Just as generals too often refight the last war, when the drafters of the U.N. Charter set its limits on state power, they responded to the crises precipitating World War II, without anticipating those that would follow it. They devised a legal regime they hoped would govern the use of force for generations to come—recognizing all states as sovereign equals, prohibiting interference in their internal affairs, and permitting the nondefensive use of force only when authorized by the U.N. Security Council, and then only in limited circumstances (when provoked by "any threat to the peace, breach of the peace or act of aggression"). Reflecting the mindset of its makers, the charter's core prohibitions are directed at invasion, the paradigm being the 1939 German takeover of Poland. The transcendent problem, it was thought in 1945, was interstate conflict. But the recurrent problem today is intrastate violence, which is not addressed effectively by the charter. Thus in Haiti, Somalia, and Rwanda—all conflicts within a single country—when the international community stepped in to halt the slaughter of civilians, it did so without the blessing of international law. Although intervention was authorized by the Security Council, its consent flew in the face of the constraints of the charter and 40 years of U.N. precedent that virtually ignored civil war and instability. The charter regards internal violence as a question of "domestic jurisdiction" only—that is, beyond official international concern.

To the extent that interstate violence persists in 1999, it does so in a form to which the charter is oblivious: state-sponsored terrorism. The two Libyans indicted for the 1988 bombing of Pan Am flight 103 over Lockerbie, Scotland, have yet to be brought to justice (although talks are ongoing), despite the efforts of their victims' families and fruit-

less U.N. sanctions. Although Chile's intelligence chief was finally imprisoned in that country in 1995 for ordering the 1976 assassination of Orlando Letelier in Washington, this was due largely to unilateral pressure from the United States—no sanction was ever imposed on Chile by the United Nations. When American embassies were bombed in Kenya and Tanzania last August [1998], world attention focused entirely on the propriety of American air strikes against perpetrators allegedly ensconced in Afghanistan and Sudan; the idea that the United Nations might actually do something to combat such bombings was never even raised, so conditioned had observers become to expect it to do nothing.

Had it ever been effective in curbing interstate violence, the charter's anachronistic focus on such conflicts might be tolerable. But it was not. The charter generated no formal international response to Soviet intervention in Hungary, Czechoslovakia, or Afghanistan, none to American intervention in the Dominican Republic, Grenada, Panama, or Nicaragua, and none to that of India in Goa, Indonesia in East Timor, China in Tibet, Argentina in the Falklands, or Vietnam in Cambodia, or to the countless other cross-border military excursions since 1945. Diplomatic historians have yet to identify a single instance of interstate violence that was actually stopped by the United Nations.

The organization's paralysis in such crises has often been due to abuse of the Security Council veto, a power exclusive to the body's five permanent members. Originally meant as a check on unilateral power, the veto was transformed over time into a tool for reallocating it from stronger states to weaker ones. Since the Soviet Union's collapse, the requirement of unanimity among the council's five permanent members has provided a lever for France, Russia, and China to pry their way into a disproportionately powerful diplomatic position not otherwise afforded them by their economic or military power. When last year the United States threatened force to curb Iraqi misbehavior, for example, these states exploited their vetoes by stalling the process for their own diplomatic gain. The charter served the strategic objective of France,

Russia, and China—to transform a unipolar post–Cold War world into a multipolar one—far better than it did that of the United States or much of the rest of the world.

Having analyzed the many problems in the current regime and NATO's new willingness to circumvent it, discussion often grinds to a halt. This is understandable, since those who cherish the rule of law are loath to counsel law-breaking in any form, no matter how disfunctional the status quo has become. It is far easier to paper over problems in the current system than to admit that it no longer works. But challenging a law is not synonymous with challenging the rule of law. Quite the contrary: challenging an unjust law (as NATO has done with the charter) can actually reinforce the legal regime. Openly breaking the law is much less dangerous than only pretending to comply with it, since disingenuous, disguised violations undermine the open debate on which legal reform and the law's legitimacy depend.

A Just World Order

If the costs of abandoning the old anti-interventionist regime would be minimal, what of the benefits of adopting a new one? The calculus is difficult, since the contours of the new regime have only dimly emerged and many questions about its implementation remain (for example, will the U.N. Charter need revision?). Nonetheless, some general observations can be made.

The West's new rules of thumb on intervention accord less deference to the old idea of sovereign equality—the erstwhile notion that all countries, large or small, are equal in the eyes of the law. The new posture recognizes the hollowness of this concept, accepting that all states are not in fact the same in their power, wealth, or commitment to human rights or peace. The new system acknowledges something else the U.N. Charter overlooks: that the major threats to stability and well-being now come from internal violence as or more often than they do from cross-border fighting—and that to be effective, international law needs to stop the former as well as the latter. As before, the new

regime allows that domestic order is the primary and initial responsibility of the state; the difference now is that intervention has been deemed appropriate where the humanitarian costs of failing to intervene are too high (as in cases of genocide). Intervention on a pretext—toppling a government in the name of international law just because its political or economic philosophy is objectionable to some other state—is still prohibited. How this will be policed remains unclear (as do many details of the new system), but as a safety measure, the new regime favors multilateral intervention over unilateral action. The hope is that building a multinational coalition will filter out the worst forms of national self-interest and keep them from playing a leading role in international intervention.

Still, the new regime will not represent the true rule of law. Like the counterinterventionist norms of the U.N. Charter, it too will replicate existing power dynamics. For many of the same reasons that the international community was unable in 1945 to establish a true global legal system, the effort to do so today is almost surely doomed. States continue to distrust concentrations of state power, and rightly so. The risks posed by a universal system that provides no escape from lawfully centralized coercion remain greater than the risks of a system that lacks coercive enforcement mechanisms. No one, as yet, has devised safeguards sufficient to guarantee that power will not be abused by the strong, that coercion will not be misdirected to undermine the values that it was established to protect. Until such safeguards are devised, the global rule of law will remain a dream.

But what of justice? Can it be achieved in the meantime? That a new interventionist regime might not at the outset be a legal one does not mean that enhanced global justice need remain a fantasy. International justice can in fact be pursued ad hoc, without a fully functioning legal system. This evidently is what NATO and the United States have recently set out to do. And they have achieved some success: A child saved from ethnic cleansing in Kosovo by NATO's intervention is no less alive because the intervention was impromptu rather than part of a formal system. Even so, the long-term systemic consequences of such interventions must be considered when the system is established. If they are not, the risk arises that the old regime might be scrapped in favor of one that undermines, rather than enhances, justice.

The question, then, is how the long-term systemic consequences are best assessed. Would it be better to rethink collectively and comprehensively when intervention ought to be expected, rather than to make decisions on the fly in a melee of international violence? The issue, as the political scientist Thomas C. Schelling has put it, is whether "some collective and formally integrated attack on [global] issues can do a better job than coping piecemeal, ad hoc, unilaterally, opportunistically." By making no choice, by resolving intervention issues case-by-case with respect to Iraq, Kosovo, and earlier crises, the United States and NATO have endorsed the latter option.

Improvising Intervention

There is, of course, ample precedent for the ad hoc, opportunistic approach. The Peace of Westphalia, signed to conclude the Thirty Years' War in 1648, legitimated the notion of sovereignty and the modern state system. The treaty's drafters sought to balance one equal, independent state or group of states against another, in the belief that the resulting *principe d'équilibre* would secure a stable, lasting peace. Following the Napoleonic Wars, the 1815 Congress of Vienna re-established that equilibrium for about 40 years, until percolating nationalism and liberalism proved uncontrollable.

Ever since Athens founded the Delian League in 478 B.C., however, humanity has striven to establish a structure for truly lasting peace, before conflict erupts—not after. Recent hopes have focused on joining states together into international organizations with supranational force. This reflects the prevailing belief that the balance of power, however skillfully the scaffolding of state sovereignty might be aligned, cannot last. Something more is needed. The 1919 Treaty of Versailles represented the first effort to establish an alternative, an activist international peacekeeping mechanism: namely, the League of Nations. The 1945 U.N. Charter sought to perfect the collective enforcement model by establishing a supranational authority, the U.N. Security Council, to deal with miscreant states.

Both systems—balance of power and the integrative model—represented efforts at imposing the rule of law, albeit in profoundly different versions, to check interstate violence. Each, in its own way, failed.

The question therefore remains open as to which approach better maintains world order. Neither can claim superiority in purely utilitarian terms. A treaty approach, however, presents a distinct advantage over improvisation: greater legitimacy.

In 1999, written texts appear more legitimate than customary norms. The history of international law in this century has been a history of codification, a process in which one custom after another—diplomatic immunity, treaty law, use of force—has been committed to paper. Codification lessens the risk of error and promotes reliance. Enhanced predictability and more regularized behavior result. The old rules of the charter have been accorded the dignity of a solemnly negotiated text; anything less formal would produce new rules of lesser stature.

It is therefore dangerous for NATO to unilaterally rewrite the rules by intervening in domestic conflicts on an irregular, case-by-case basis. The test of the new interventionism is not whether it can be contrived to generate immediate popular support. Of course it can, at least in influential Western publics, in ways known to all military planners and their publicists: with smart-bomb strikes portrayed in the media as being undertaken only after patience has run out. Such attacks are a swift, short, and successful method of punishing a demon and vindicating international honor. They produce few (CNN-reported) civilian deaths and still fewer Western casualties. The script for successful military spinning is no state secret.

But that script is not the best way to give a new interventionist regime long-term acceptance. The real test of a new system will be whether succeeding generations throughout the community of nations—not simply in centers of wealth and power—believe the system and the actions it prescribes to be just. Case-by-case decisions to use force, made by the users alone, are not likely to generate such support. Even if the purposes are widely approved of, sooner or later the exclusionary decision-making process is likely to create resentment, particularly as inevitable foul-ups occur and lives are lost through error and oversight. Justice, it turns out, requires legitimacy; without widespread acceptance of intervention as part of a formal justice system, the new interventionism will appear to be built on neither law nor justice, but on power alone. It will then be only a matter of time before the meddling of the illegitimate interventionist regime is rejected just as roundly as was the one it replaced.

The new interventionists must reconcile the need for broad acceptance of their regime with the resistance of the defiant, the indolent, and the miscreant. Proponents of the new regime must assess whether the cost of alienating the disorderly outweighs whatever benefits can be wrought in the form of a more orderly world. Ultimately, the question will be empirical; unless a critical mass of nations accepts the solution that NATO and the United States stand ready to offer, that solution will soon be resented. But the new interventionists should not be daunted by fears of destroying some lofty, imagined temple of law enshrined in the U.N. Charter's anti-interventionist proscriptions. The higher, grander goal that has eluded humanity for centuries—the ideal of justice backed by power—should not be abandoned so easily. Achieving justice is the hard part; revising international law to reflect it can come afterward. If power is used to do justice, law will follow.

MARGARET E. KECK AND KATHRYN SIKKINK

Transnational Advocacy Networks in International Politics: Introduction

World politics at the end of the twentieth century involves, alongside states, many nonstate actors that interact with each other, with states, and with international organizations. These interactions are structured in terms of networks, and transnational networks are increasingly visible in international politics. [Networks are forms of organization characterized by voluntary,

From Margaret E. Keck and Kathryn Sikkink, *Activists Beyond Borders: Advocacy Networks in International Politics* (Ithaca, N.Y.: Cornell University Press, 1998), chaps. 1, 3.

reciprocal, and horizontal patterns of communication and exchange.] Some involve economic actors and firms. Some are networks of scientists and experts whose professional ties and shared causal ideas underpin their efforts to influence policy.[1] Others are networks of activists, distinguishable largely by the centrality of principled ideas or values in motivating their formation.[2] We will call these *transnational advocacy networks*. [A transnational advocacy network includes those relevant actors working internationally on an issue who are bound together by shared values, a common discourse, and dense exchanges of information and services.]

Advocacy networks are significant transnationally and domestically. By building new links among actors in civil societies, states, and international organizations, they multiply the channels of access to the international system. In such issue areas as the environment and human rights, they also make international resources available to new actors in domestic political and social struggles. By thus blurring the boundaries between a state's relations with its own nationals and the recourse both citizens and states have to the international system, advocacy networks are helping to transform the practice of national sovereignty.

*   *   *

Transnational advocacy networks are proliferating, and their goal is to change the behavior of states and of international organizations. Simultaneously principled and strategic actors, they "frame" issues to make them comprehensible to target audiences, to attract attention and encourage action, and to "fit" with favorable institutional venues.[3] Network actors bring new ideas, norms, and discourses into policy debates, and serve as sources of information and testimony. * * *

They also promote norm implementation, by pressuring target actors to adopt new policies, and by monitoring compliance with international standards. Insofar as is possible, they seek to maximize their influence or leverage over the target of their actions. In doing so they contribute to changing perceptions that both state and societal actors may have of their identities, interests, and preferences, to transforming their discursive positions, and ultimately to changing procedures, policies, and behavior.[4]

Networks are communicative structures. To influence discourse, procedures, and policy, activists may engage and become part of larger policy communities that group actors working on an issue from a variety of institutional and value perspectives. Transnational advocacy networks must also be understood as political spaces, in which differently situated actors negotiate—formally or informally—the social, cultural, and political meanings of their joint enterprise.

*   *   *

Major actors in advocacy networks may include the following: (1) international and domestic nongovernmental research and advocacy organizations; (2) local social movements; (3) foundations; (4) the media; (5) churches, trade unions, consumer organizations, and intellectuals; (6) parts of regional and international intergovernmental organizations; and (7) parts of the executive and/or parliamentary branches of governments. Not all these will be present in each advocacy network. Initial research suggests, however, that international and domestic NGOs play a central role in all advocacy networks, usually initiating actions and pressuring more powerful actors to take positions. NGOs introduce new ideas, provide information, and lobby for policy changes.

Groups in a network share values and frequently exchange information and services. The flow of information among actors in the network reveals a dense web of connections among these groups, both formal and informal. The movement of funds and services is especially notable between foundations and NGOs, and some NGOs provide services such as training for other NGOs in the same and sometimes other advocacy networks. Personnel also circulate within and among networks, as relevant players move from one to another in a version of the "revolving door."

*   *   *

We cannot accurately count transnational advocacy networks to measure their growth over time, but one proxy is the increase in the number of international NGOs committed to social change. Because international NGOs are key components of any advocacy network, this increase suggests broader trends in the number, size, and density of advocacy networks generally. Table 1 suggests that the number of international nongovernmental social change groups has increased across all issues, though to varying degrees in different issue areas. There are five times as many organizations working primarily on human rights as there were in 1950, but proportionally human rights groups have remained roughly a quarter of all such

Table 1. International Nongovernmental Social Change Organizations
(categorized by the major issue focus of their work)

Issue area (N)	1953 (N=110)	1963 (N=141)	1973 (N=183)	1983 (N=348)	1993 (N=631)
Human rights	33 30.0%	38 27.0%	41 22.4%	79 22.7%	168 26.6%
World order	8 7.3	4 2.8	12 6.6	31 8.9	48 7.6
International law	14 12.7	19 13.4	25 13.7	26 7.4	26 4.1
Peace	11 10.0	20 14.2	14 7.7	22 6.3	59 9.4
Women's rights	10 9.1	14 9.9	16 8.7	25 7.2	61 9.7
Environment	2 1.8	5 3.5	10 5.5	26 7.5	90 14.3
Development	3 2.7	3 2.1	7 3.8	13 3.7	34 5.4
Ethnic unity/Group rts.	10 9.1	12 8.5	18 9.8	37 10.6	29 4.6
Esperanto	11 10.0	18 12.8	28 15.3	41 11.8	54 8.6

Source: Union of International Associations, *Yearbook of International Organizations* (1953, 1963, 1973, 1983, 1993). We are indebted to Jackie Smith, University of Notre Dame, for the use of her data from 1983 and 1993, and the use of her coding form and codebook for our data collection for the period 1953–73.

groups. Similarly, groups working on women's rights accounted for 9 percent of all groups in 1953 and in 1993. Transnational environmental organizations have grown most dramatically in absolute and relative terms, increasing from two groups in 1953 to ninety in 1993, and from 1.8 percent of total groups in 1953 to 14.3 percent in 1993. The percentage share of groups in such issue areas as international law, peace, ethnic unity, and Esperanto, has declined.[5]

*   *   *

How Do Transnational Advocacy Networks Work?

Transnational advocacy networks seek influence in many of the same ways that other political groups or social movements do. Since they are not powerful in a traditional sense of the word, they must use the power of their information, ideas, and strategies to alter the information and value contexts within which states make policies. The bulk of what networks do might be termed persuasion or socialization, but neither process is devoid of conflict. Persuasion and socialization often involve not just reasoning with opponents, but also bringing pressure, arm-twisting, encouraging sanctions, and shaming. * * *

Our typology of tactics that networks use in their efforts at persuasion, socialization, and pressure includes (1) *information politics*, or the ability to quickly and credibly generate politically usable information and move it to where it will have the most impact; (2) *symbolic politics*, or the ability to call upon symbols, actions, or stories that make sense of a situation for an audience that is frequently far away;[6] (3) *leverage politics*, or the ability to call upon powerful actors to affect a situation where weaker members of a network are unlikely to have influence; and (4) *accountability politics*, or the effort to hold powerful actors to their previously stated policies or principles.

A single campaign may contain many of these elements simultaneously. For example, the human rights network disseminated information about human rights abuses in Argentina in the period 1976–83. The Mothers of the Plaza de Mayo marched in circles in the central square in Buenos Aires wearing white handkerchiefs to draw symbolic attention to the plight of their missing children. The network also tried to use both material and moral leverage against the Argentine regime, by pressuring the United States and other governments to cut off military and economic aid, and by efforts to get the UN and the Inter-American Commission on Human Rights to condemn Argentina's human rights practices. Monitoring is a variation on information politics, in which activists use information strategically to ensure accountability with public statements, existing legislation and international standards.

*   *   *

Network members actively seek ways to bring issues to the public agenda by framing them in innovative ways and by seeking hospitable venues. Sometimes they create issues by framing old problems in new ways; occasionally they help transform other actors' understanding of their identities and their interests. Land use rights in the Amazon, for example, took on an entirely different character and gained quite different allies viewed in a deforestation frame than they did in either social justice or regional development frames. In the 1970s and 1980s many states decided for the first time that promotion of human rights in other countries was a legitimate foreign policy goal and an authentic expression of national interest. This decision came in part from interaction with an emerging global human rights network. We argue that this represents not the victory of morality over self-interest, but a

transformed understanding of national interest, possible in part because of structured interactions between state components and networks. * * *

*   *   *

Under What Conditions Do Advocacy Networks Have Influence?

To assess the influence of advocacy networks we must look at goal achievement at several different levels. We identify the following types or stages of network influence: (1) issue creation and agenda setting; (2) influence on discursive positions of states and international organizations; (3) influence on institutional procedures; (4) influence on policy change in "target actors" which may be states, international organizations like the World Bank, or private actors like the Nestlé Corporation; and (5) influence on state behavior.

Networks generate attention to new issues and help set agendas when they provoke media attention, debates, hearings, and meetings on issues that previously had not been a matter of public debate. Because values are the essence of advocacy networks, this stage of influence may require a modification of the "value context" in which policy debates takes place. The UN's theme years and decades, such as International Women's Decade and the Year of Indigenous Peoples, were international events promoted by networks that heightened awareness of issues.

Networks influence discursive positions when they help persuade states and international organizations to support international declarations or to change stated domestic policy positions. The role environmental networks played in shaping state positions and conference declarations at the 1992 "Earth Summit" in Rio de Janeiro is an example of this kind of impact. They may also pressure states to make more binding commitments by signing conventions and codes of conduct.

The targets of network campaigns frequently respond to demands for policy change with changes in procedures (which may affect policies in the future). The multilateral bank campaign is largely responsible for a number of changes in internal bank directives mandating greater NGO and local participation in discussions of projects. It also opened access to formerly restricted information, and led to the establishment of an independent inspection panel for World Bank projects. Procedural changes can greatly increase the opportunity for advocacy organizations to develop regular contact with other key players on an issue, and they sometimes offer the opportunity to move from outside to inside pressure strategies.

A network's activities may produce changes in policies, not only of the target states, but also of other states and/or international institutions. Explicit policy shifts seem to denote success, but even here both their causes and meanings may be elusive. We can point with some confidence to network impact where human rights network pressures have achieved cutoffs of military aid to repressive regimes, or a curtailment of repressive practices. Sometimes human rights activity even affects regime stability. But we must take care to distinguish between policy change and change in behavior; official policies regarding timber extraction in Sarawak, Malaysia, for example, may say little about how timber companies behave on the ground in the absence of enforcement.

We speak of stages of impact, and not merely types of impact, because we believe that increased attention, followed by changes in discursive positions, make governments more vulnerable to the claims that networks raise. (Discursive changes can also have a powerfully divisive effect on networks themselves, splitting insiders from outsiders, reformers from radicals.[7]) A government that claims to be protecting indigenous areas or ecological reserves is potentially more vulnerable to charges that such areas are endangered than one that makes no such claim. At that point the effort is not to make governments change their position but to hold them to their word. Meaningful policy change is thus more likely when the first three types or stages of impact have occurred.

Both issue characteristics and actor characteristics are important parts of our explanation of how networks affect political outcomes and the conditions under which networks can be effective. Issue characteristics such as salience and resonance within existing national or institutional agendas can tell us something about where networks are likely to be able to insert new ideas and discourses into policy debates. Success in influencing policy also depends on the strength and density of the network and its ability to achieve leverage. * * *

*   *   *

Toward a Global Civil Society?

Many other scholars now recognize that "the state does not monopolize the public sphere,"[8] and are seeking, as we are, ways to describe the sphere of international interactions under a variety of names: transnational relations, international civil society, and global civil society.[9] In these views, states no longer look unitary from the outside. Increasingly dense interactions among individuals, groups, actors from states, and international institutions appear to involve much more than representing interests on a world stage.

We contend that the advocacy network concept cannot be subsumed under notions of transnational social movements or global civil society. In particular, theorists who suggest that a global civil society will inevitably emerge from economic globalization or from revolutions in communication and transportation technologies ignore the issues of agency and political opportunity that we find central for understanding the evolution of new international institutions and relationships.

*   *   *

We lack convincing studies of the sustained and specific processes through which individuals and organizations create (or resist the creation of) something resembling a global civil society. Our research leads us to believe that these interactions involve much more agency than a pure diffusionist perspective suggests. Even though the implications of our findings are much broader than most political scientists would admit, the findings themselves do not yet support the strong claims about an emerging global civil society.[10] We are much more comfortable with a conception of transnational civil society as an arena of struggle, a fragmented and contested area where "the politics of transnational civil society is centrally about the way in which certain groups emerge and are legitimized (by governments, institutions, and other groups)."[11]

*   *   *

Human Rights Advocacy Networks in Latin America

ARGENTINA

Even before the military coup of March 1976, international human rights pressures had influenced the Argentine military's decision to cause political opponents to "disappear," rather than imprisoning them or executing them publicly.[12] (The technique led to the widespread use of the verb "to disappear" in a transitive sense.) The Argentine military believed they had "learned" from the international reaction to the human rights abuses after the Chilean coup. When the Chilean military executed and imprisoned large numbers of people, the ensuing uproar led to the international isolation of the regime of Augusto Pinochet. Hoping to maintain a moderate international image, the Argentine military decided to secretly kidnap, detain, and execute its victims, while denying any knowledge of their whereabouts.[13]

Although this method did initially mute the international response to the coup, Amnesty International and groups staffed by Argentine political exiles eventually were able to document and condemn the new forms of repressive practices. To counteract the rising tide of criticism, the Argentina junta invited AI for an on-site visit in 1976. In March 1977, on the first anniversary of the military coup, AI published the report on its visit, a well-documented denunciation of the abuses of the regime with emphasis on the problem of the disappeared. Amnesty estimated that the regime had taken six thousand political prisoners, most without specifying charges, and had abducted between two and ten thousand people. The report helped demonstrate that the disappearances were part of a deliberate government policy by which the military and the police kidnapped perceived opponents, took them to secret detention centers where they tortured, interrogated, and killed them, then secretly disposed of their bodies.[14] Amnesty International's denunciations of the Argentine regime were legitimized when it won the Nobel Peace Prize later that year.

Such information led the Carter administration and the French, Italian, and Swedish governments to denounce rights violations by the junta. France, Italy, and Sweden each had citizens who had been victims of Argentine repression, but their concerns extended beyond their own citizens. Although the Argentine government claimed that such attacks constituted unacceptable intervention in their internal affairs and violated Argentine sovereignty, U.S. and European officials persisted. In 1977 the U.S. government reduced the planned level of military aid for Argentina because of human rights abuses. Congress later passed a bill eliminating all military assistance to Argentina, which went into effect on 30 September 1978.[15] A number of high-level U.S. delegations met with junta members during this period to discuss human rights.

Early U.S. action on Argentina was based primarily on the human rights documentation provided by AI and other NGOs, not on information received through official channels at the embassy or the State Department.[16] For example, during a 1977 visit, Secretary of State Cyrus Vance carried a list of disappeared people prepared by human rights NGOs to present to members of the junta.[17] When Patricia Derian met with junta member Admiral Emilio Massera during a visit in 1977, she brought up the navy's use of torture. In response to Massera's denial, Derian said she had seen a rudimentary map of a secret detention center in the Navy Mechanical School, where their meeting was being held, and asked whether perhaps under their feet someone was being tortured. Among Derian's key sources of information were NGOs and especially the families of the disappeared, with whom she met frequently during her visits to Buenos Aires.[18]

Within a year of the coup, Argentine domestic human rights organizations began to develop significant external contacts. Their members traveled frequently to the United States and Europe, where they met with human rights organizations, talked to the press, and met with parliamentarians and government officials. These groups sought foreign contacts to publicize the human rights situation, to fund their activities, and to help protect themselves from further repression by their government, and they provided evidence to U.S. and European policymakers. Much of their funding came from European and U.S.-based foundations.[19]

Two key events that served to keep the case of Argentine human rights in the minds of U.S. and European policymakers reflect the impact of transnational linkages on policy. In 1979 the Argentine authorities released Jacobo Timerman, whose memoir describing his disappearance and torture by the Argentine military helped human rights organizations, members of the U.S. Jewish community, and U.S. journalists to make his case a cause célèbre in U.S. policy circles.[20] Then in 1980 the Nobel Peace Prize was awarded to an Argentine human rights activist, Adolfo Pérez Esquivel. Peace and human rights groups in the United States and Europe helped sponsor Pérez Esquivel's speaking tour to the United States exactly at the time that the OAS was considering the IACHR report on Argentina and Congress was debating the end of the arms embargo to Argentina.

The Argentine military government wanted to avoid international human rights censure. Scholars have long recognized that even authoritarian regimes depend on a combination of coercion and consent to stay in power. Without the legitimacy conferred by elections, they rely heavily on claims about their political efficancy and on nationalism.[21] Although the Argentine military mobilized nationalist rhetoric against foreign criticism, a sticking point was that Argentines, especially the groups that most supported the military regime, thought of themselves as the most European of Latin American countries. The military junta claimed to be carrying out the repression in the name of "our Western and Christian civilization."[22] But the military's intent to integrate Argentina more fully into the liberal global economic order was being jeopardized by deteriorating relations with countries most identified with that economic order, and with "Western and Christian civilization."

The junta adopted a sequence of responses to international pressures. From 1976 to 1978 the military pursued an initial strategy of denying the legitimacy of international concern over human rights in Argentina. At the same time it took actions that appear to have contradicted this strategy, such as permitting the visit of the Amnesty International mission to Argentina in 1976. The "failure" of the Amnesty visit, from the military point of view, appeared to reaffirm the junta's resistance to human rights pressures. This strategy was most obvious at the UN, where the Argentine government worked to silence international condemnation in the UN Commission on Human Rights. Ironically, the rabidly anticommunist Argentine regime found a diplomatic ally in the Soviet Union, an importer of Argentine wheat, and the two countries collaborated to block UN consideration of the Argentine human rights situation.[23] Concerned states circumvented this blockage by creating the UN Working Group on Disappearances in 1980. Human rights NGOs provided information, lobbied government delegations, and pursued joint strategies with sympathetic UN delegations.

By 1978 the Argentine government recognized that something had to be done to improve its international image in the United States and Europe, and to restore the flow of military and economic aid.[24] To these ends the junta invited the Inter-American Commission on Human Rights for an on-site visit, in exchange for a U.S. commitment to release Export-Import Bank funds and otherwise improve U.S.-Argentine relations.[25] During 1978 the human rights situation in Argentina improved significantly. [T]he practice of disappearance as a tool of state policy was curtailed only after 1978, when the government began to take the "international variable" seriously.[26]

The value of the network perspective in the Argentine case is in highlighting the fact that international pressures did not work independently, but rather in coordination with national actors. Rapid change occurred because strong domestic human rights organizations documented abuses and protested against repression, and international pressures helped protect domestic monitors and open spaces for their protest. International groups amplified both information and symbolic politics of domestic groups and projected them onto an international stage, from which they echoed back into Argentina. This classic boomerang process was executed nowhere more skillfully than in Argentina, in large part due to the courage and ability of domestic human rights organizations.

Some argue that repression stopped because the military had finally killed all the people that they thought they needed to kill. This argument disregards disagreements within the regime about the size and nature of the "enemy." International pressures affected particular factions within the military regime that had differing ideas about how much repression was "necessary." Although by the military's admission 90 percent of the *armed* opposition had been eliminated by April 1977, this did not lead to an immediate change in human rights practices.[27] By 1978 there were splits within the military about what it should do in the future. One faction was led by Admiral Massera, a right-wing populist, another by Generals Carlos Suarez Mason and Luciano Menéndez, who supported indefinite military dictatorship and unrelenting war against the left, and a third by Generals Jorge Videla and Roberto Viola, who hoped for eventual political liberalization under a military president. Over time, the Videla-Viola faction won out, and by late 1978 Videla had gained increased control over the Ministry of Foreign Affairs, previously under the influence of the navy.[28] Videla's ascendancy in the fall of 1978, combined with U.S. pressure, helps explain his ability to deliver on his promise to allow the Inter-American Commission on Human Rights visit in December.

The Argentine military government thus moved from initial refusal to accept international human rights interventions, to cosmetic cooperation with the human rights network, and eventually to concrete improvements in response to increased international pressures. Once it had invited IACHR and discovered that the commission could not be co-opted or confused, the government ended the practice of disappearance, released political prisoners, and restored some semblance of political participation. Full restoration of human rights in Argentina did not come until after the Malvinas War and the transition to democracy in 1983, but after 1980 the worst abuses had been curtailed.

In 1985, after democratization, Argentina tried the top military leaders of the juntas for human rights abuses, and a number of key network members testified: Theo Van Boven and Patricia Derian spoke about international awareness of the Argentine human rights situation, and a member of the IACHR delegation to Argentina discussed the OAS report. Clyde Snow and Eric Stover provided information about the exhumation of cadavers from mass graves. Snow's testimony, corroborated by witnesses, was a key part of the prosecutor's success in establishing that top military officers were guilty of murder.[29] A public opinion poll taken during the trials showed that 92 percent of Argentines were in favor of the trials of the military juntas.[30] The tribunal convicted five of the nine defendants, though only two—ex-president Videla, and Admiral Massera—were given life sentences. The trials were the first of their kind in Latin America, and among the very few in the world ever to try former leaders for human rights abuses during their rule. In 1990 President Carlos Menem pardoned the former officers. By the mid-1990s, however, democratic rule in Argentina was firmly entrenched, civilian authority over the military was well established, and the military had been weakened by internal disputes and severe cuts in funding.[31]

The Argentine case set important precedents for other international and regional human rights action, and shows the intricate interactions of groups and individuals within the network and the repercussions of these interactions. The story of the Grandmothers of the Plaza de Mayo is an exemplar of network interaction and unanticipated effects. The persistence of the Grandmothers helped create a new profession—what one might call "human rights forensic science." (The scientific skills existed before, but they had never been put to the service of human rights.) Once the Argentine case had demonstrated that forensic science could illuminate mass murder and lead to convictions, these skills were diffused and legitimized. Eric Stover, Clyde Snow, and the Argentine forensic anthropology team they helped create were the prime agents of international diffusion. The team later carried out exhumations and training in Chile, Bolivia, Brazil, Venezuela, and Guatemala.[32] Forensic science is being used to prosecute mass murderers in El Salvador, Honduras, Rwanda, and Bosnia. By 1996 the UN International Criminal Tribunal for the former Yugoslavia had contracted with two veterans of the Argentine forensic experiment, Stover and Dr. Robert Kirschner, to do forensic investigations for its war crimes tribunal. " 'A war crime creates a crime scene,' said Dr. Kirschner, 'That's how we treat it. We recover forensic evidence for prosecution and create a record which cannot be successfully challenged in court.' "[33]

*   *   *

[Conclusions]

A realist approach to international relations would have trouble attributing significance either to the network's activities or to the adoption and implementation of state human rights policies. Realism offers no convincing explanation for why relatively weak nonstate actors could affect state policy, or why states would concern themselves with the internal human rights practices of other states even when doing so interferes with the pursuit of other goals. For example, the U.S. government's pressure on Argentina on human rights led Argentina to defect from the grain embargo of the Soviet Union. Raising human rights issues with Mexico could have undermined the successful completion of the free trade agreement and cooperation with Mexico on antidrug operations. Human rights pressures have costs, even in strategically less important countries of Latin America.

In liberal versions of international relations theory, states and nonstate actors cooperate to realize joint gains or avoid mutually undesirable outcomes when they face problems they cannot resolve alone. These situations have been characterized as cooperation or coordination games with particular payoff structures.[34] But human rights issues are not easily modeled as such. Usually states can ignore the internal human rights practices of other states without incurring undesirable economic or security costs.

In the issue of human rights it is primarily principled ideas that drive change and cooperation. We cannot understand why countries, organizations, and individuals are concerned about human rights or why countries respond to human rights pressures without taking into account the role of norms and ideas in international life. Jack Donnelly has argued that such moral interests are as real as material interests, and that a sense of moral interdependence has led to the emergence of human rights regimes.[35] For human rights * * * the primary movers behind this form of principled international action are international networks.

NOTES

1. Peter Haas has called these "knowledge-based" or "epistemic communities." See Peter Haas, "Introduction: Epistemic Communities and International Policy Coordination," *Knowledge, Power and International Policy Coordination*, special issue, *International Organization* 46 (Winter 1992), pp. 1–36.

2. Ideas that specify criteria for determining whether actions are right and wrong and whether outcomes are just or unjust are shared principled beliefs or values. Beliefs about cause-effect relationships are shared casual beliefs. Judith Goldstein and Robert Keohane, eds., *Ideas and Foreign Policy: Beliefs, Institutions, and Political Change* (Ithaca: Cornell University Press, 1993), pp. 8–10.

3. David Snow and his colleagues have adapted Erving Goffman's concept of framing. We use it to mean "conscious strategic efforts by groups of people to fashion shared understandings of the world and of themselves that legitimate and motivate collective action." Definition from Doug McAdam, John D. McCarthy, and Mayer N. Zald, "Introduction," *Comparative Perspectives on Social Movements: Political Opportunities, Mobilizing Structures, and Cultural Framings*, ed. McAdam, McCarthy, and Zald (New York: Cambridge University Press, 1996), p. 6. See also Frank Baumgartner and Bryan Jones, "Agenda Dynamics and Policy Subsystems," *Journal of Politics* 53:4 (1991): 1044–74.

4. With the "constructivists" in international relations theory, we take actors and interests to be constituted in interaction. See Martha Finnemore, *National Interests in International Society* (Ithaca: Cornell University Press, 1996), who argues that "states are embedded in dense networks of transnational and international social relations that shape their perceptions of the world and their role in that world. States are *socialized* to want certain things by the international society in which they and the people in them live" (p. 2).

5. Data from a collaborative research project with Jackie G. Smith. We thank her for the use of her data from the period 1983–93, whose results are presented in Jackie G. Smith, "Characteristics of the Modern Transnational Social Movement Sector," in Jackie G. Smith, et al., eds. *Transnational Social Movements and World Politics: Solidarity beyond the State* (Syracuse: Syracuse University Press, forthcoming 1997), and for permission to use her coding form and codebook for our data collection for the period 1953–73. All data were coded from Union of International Associations, *The Yearbook of International Organizations*, 1948–95 (published annually).

6. Alison Brysk uses the categories "information politics" and "symbolic politics" to discuss strategies of transnational actors, especially networks around Indian rights. See "Acting Globally: Indian Rights and International Politics in Latin America," in *Indigenous Peoples and Democracy in Latin America*, ed. Donna Lee Van Cott (New York: St. Martin's Press/Inter-American Dialogue, 1994), pp. 29–51; and "Hearts and Minds: Bringing Symbolic Politics Back In," *Polity* 27 (Summer 1995): 559–85.

7. We thank Jonathan Fox for reminding us of this point.

8. M. J. Peterson, "Transnational Activity, International Society, and World Politics," *Millennium* 21:3 (1992): 375–76.

9. See, for example, Ronnie Lipschutz, "Reconstructing World Politics: The Emergence of Global Civil Society," *Millennium* 21:3 (1992): 389–420; Paul Wapner, "Politics beyond the State: Environmental Activism and World Civic Politics," *World Politics* 47 (April 1995): 311–40; and the special issue of *Millennium* on social movements and world politics, 23:3 (Winter 1994).

10. Sidney Tarrow, *Power in Movement: Social Movements and Contentious Politics*, rev. ed. (Cambridge: Cambridge University Press, forthcoming 1998), Chapter 11. An earlier version appeared as "Fishnets, Internets and

Catnets: Globalization and Transnational Collective Action," Instituto Juan March de Estudios e Investigaciones, Madrid: Working Papers 1996/78, March 1996; and Peterson, "Transnational Activity."

11. Andrew Hurrell and Ngaire Woods, "Globalisation and Inequality," *Millennium* 24:3 (1995), p. 468.

12. This section draws upon some material from an earlier co-authored work: Lisa L. Martin and Kathryn Sikkink, "U.S. Policy and Human Rights in Argentina and Guatemala, 1973–1980," in *Double-Edged Diplomacy: International Bargaining and Domestic Politics*, ed., Peter B. Evans, Harold K. Jacobson, and Robert D. Putnam (Berkeley: University of California Press, 1993), pp. 330–62.

13. See Emilio Mignone, *Derechos humanos y sociedad: el caso argentino* (Buenos Aires: Ediciones del Pensamiento Nacional and Centro de Estudios Legales y Sociales, 1991), p. 66; Claudio Uriarte, *Almirante Cero: Biografía No Autorizada de Emilio Eduardo Massera* (Buenos Aires: Planeta, 1992), p. 97; and Carlos H. Acuña and Catalina Smulovitz, "Adjusting the Armed Forces to Democracy: Successes, Failures, and Ambiguities in the Southern Cone," in *Constructing Democracy: Human Rights, Citizenship, and Society in Latin America*, ed. Elizabeth Jelin and Eric Hershberg (Boulder, Colo.: Westview, 1993), p. 15.

14. Amnesty International, *Report of an Amnesty International Mission to Argentina* (London: Amnesty International, 1977).

15. Congressional Research Service, Foreign Affairs and National Defense Division, *Human Rights and U.S. Foreign Assistance: Experiences and Issues in Policy Implementation (1977–1978)*, report prepared for U.S. Senate Committee on Foreign Relations, November 1979, p. 106.

16. After the 1976 coup, Argentine political exiles set up branches of the Argentine Human Rights Commission (CADHU) in Paris, Mexico, Rome, Geneva, and Washington, D.C. In October two of its members testified on human rights abuses before the U.S. House Subcommittee on Human Rights and International Organization. Iain Guest, *Behind the Disappearances: Argentina's Dirty War against Human Rights and the United Nations* (Philadelphia: University of Pennsylvania Press, 1990), pp. 66–67.

17. Interview with Robert Pastor, Wianno, Massachusetts, 28 June 1990.

18. Testimony given by Patricia Derian to the National Criminal Appeals Court in Buenos Aires during the trials of junta members. "Massera sonrió y me dijo: Sabe qué pasó con Poncio Pilatos . . . ?" *Diario del Juicio*, 18 June 1985, p. 3; Guest, *Behind the Disappearances*, pp. 161–63. Later it was confirmed that the Navy Mechanical School was one of the most notorious secret torture and detention centers. *Nunca Más: The Report of the Argentine National Commission for the Disappeared* (New York: Farrar Straus & Giroux, 1986), pp. 79–84.

19. The Mothers of the Plaza de Mayo received grants from Dutch churches and the Norwegian Parliament, and the Ford Foundation provided funds for the Center for Legal and Social Studies (CELS) and the Grandmothers of the Plaza de Mayo.

20. Jacobo Timerman, *Prisoner without a Name, Cell without a Number* (New York: Random House, 1981).

21. See Guillermo O'Donnell, "Tensions in the Bureaucratic Authoritarian State and the Question of Democracy," in *The New Authoritarianism in Latin America*, ed. David Collier (Princeton: Princeton University Press, 1979), pp. 288, 292–94.

22. Daniel Frontalini and Maria Cristina Caiati, *El Mito de la Guerra Sucia* (Buenos Aires: Centro de Estudios Legales y Sociales, 1984), p. 24.

23. Guest, *Behind the Disappearances*, pp. 118–19, 182–83.

24. *Carta Política*, a news magazine considered to reflect the junta's views concluded in 1978 that "the principal problem facing the Argentine State has now become the international siege (cerco internacional)." "Cuadro de Situación," *Carta Política* 57 (August 1978):8.

25. Interviews with Walter Mondale, Minneapolis, Minnesota, 20 June 1989, and Ricardo Yofre, Buenos Aires, 1 August 1990.

26. See Asamblea Permanente por los Derechos Humanos, *Las Cifras de la Guerra Sucia* (Buenos Aires, 1988), pp. 26–32.

27. According to a memorandum signed by General Jorge Videla, the objectives of the military government "go well beyond the simple defeat of subversion." The memorandum called for a continuation and intensification of the "general offensive against subversion," including "intense military action." "Directivo 504," 20 April 1977, in "La orden secreta de Videla," *Diario del Juicio* 28 (3 December 1985): 5–8.

28. David Rock, *Argentina, 1516–1987: From Spanish Colonization to Alfonsín* (Berkeley: University of California Press, 1985), pp. 370–71; Timerman, *Prisoner without a Name*, p. 163.

29. *Diario del Juicio* 1 (27 May 1985), and 9 (23 July 1985).

30. *Diario del Juicio* 25 (12 November 1985).

31. Acuña and Smulovitz, "Adjusting the Armed Forces to Democracy," pp. 20–21.

32. Cohen Salama, *Tumbas anónimas [informe sobre la identificación de restos de víctimas de la represión* (Buenos Aires: Catálogos Editora, 1992)], p. 275.

33. Mike O'Connor, "Harvesting Evidence in Bosnia's Killing Fields," *New York Times*, 7 April 1996, p. E3.

34. See, e.g., Arthur A. Stein, "Coordination and Collaboration: Regimes in an Anarchic World," *International Organization* 36:2 (Spring 1982): 299–324.

35. Donnelly, *Universal Human Rights [in Theory and Practice* (Ithaca: Cornell University Press, 1989)], pp. 211–12.

JOHN J. MEARSHEIMER

The False Promise of International Institutions

*   *   *

What Are Institutions?

There is no widely-agreed upon definition of institutions in the international relations literature.[1] The concept is sometimes defined so broadly as to encompass all of international relations, which gives it little analytical bite.[2] For example, defining institutions as "recognized patterns of behavior or practice around which expectations converge" allows the concept to cover almost every regularized pattern of activity between states, from war to tar-

From *International Security* 19, no. 3 (winter 1994/95): 5–49.

iff bindings negotiated under the General Agreement on Tariffs and Trade (GATT), thus rendering it largely meaningless.[3] Still, it is possible to devise a useful definition that is consistent with how most institutionalist scholars employ the concept.

I define institutions as a set of rules that stipulate the ways in which states should cooperate and compete with each other.[4] They prescribe acceptable forms of state behavior, and proscribe unacceptable kinds of behavior. These rules are negotiated by states, and according to many prominent theorists, they entail the mutual acceptance of higher norms, which are "standards of behavior defined in terms of rights and obligations."[5] These rules are typically formalized in international agreements, and are usually embodied in organizations with their own personnel and budgets.[6] Although rules are usually incorporated into a formal international organization, it is not the organization *per se* that compels states to obey the rules. Institutions are not a form of world government. States themselves must choose to obey the rules they created. Institutions, in short, call for the "decentralized cooperation of individual sovereign states, without any effective mechanism of command."[7]

*   *   *

INSTITUTIONS IN A REALIST WORLD

Realists * * * recognize that states sometimes operate through institutions. However, they believe that those rules reflect state calculations of self-interest based primarily on the international distribution of power. The most powerful states in the system create and shape institutions so that they can maintain their share of world power, or even increase it. In this view, institutions are essentially "arenas for acting out power relationships."[8] For realists, the causes of war and peace are mainly a function of the balance of power, and institutions largely mirror the distribution of power in the system. In short, the balance of power is the independent variable that explains war; institutions are merely an intervening variable in the process.

NATO provides a good example of realist thinking about institutions. NATO is an institution, and it certainly played a role in preventing World War III and helping the West win the Cold War. Nevertheless, NATO was basically a manifestation of the bipolar distribution of power in Europe during the Cold War, and it was that balance of power, not NATO *per se*, that provided the key to maintaining stability on the continent. NATO was essentially an American tool for managing power in the face of the Soviet threat. Now, with the collapse of the Soviet Union, realists argue that NATO must either disappear or reconstitute itself on the basis of the new distribution of power in Europe.[9] NATO cannot remain as it was during the Cold War.

*   *   *

LIBERAL INSTITUTIONALISM

Liberal institutionalism does not directly address the question of whether institutions cause peace, but instead focuses on the less ambitious goal of explaining cooperation in cases where state interests are not fundamentally opposed.[10] Specifically, the theory looks at cases where states are having difficulty cooperating because they have "mixed" interests; in other words, each side has incentives both to cooperate and not to cooperate.[11] Each side can benefit from cooperation, however, which liberal institutionalists define as "goal-directed behavior that entails mutual policy adjustments so that all sides end up better off than they would otherwise be."[12] The theory is of little relevance in situations where states' interests are fundamentally conflictual and neither side thinks it has much to gain from cooperation. In these circumstances, states aim to gain advantage over each other. They think in terms of winning and losing, and this invariably leads to intense security competition, and sometimes war. But liberal institutionalism does not deal directly with these situations, and thus says little about how to resolve or even ameliorate them.

Therefore, the theory largely ignores security issues and concentrates instead on economic and, to a lesser extent, environmental issues.[13] In fact, the theory is built on the assumption that international politics can be divided into two realms—security and political economy—and that liberal institutionalism mainly applies to the latter, but not the former. * * *

*   *   *

According to liberal institutionalists, the principal obstacle to cooperation among states with mutual interests is the threat of cheating.[14] The famous "prisoners' dilemma," which is the analytical centerpiece of most of the liberal institutionalist literature, captures the essence of the problem that states must solve to achieve cooperation.[15] Each of two states can either cheat or cooperate with the other. Each side wants to maximize its own gain, but does not care about the size of the other side's gain; each side cares about the other side only so far as the other side's chosen strategy affects its own prospects for maximizing gain. The most attractive strategy for each state is to cheat and hope the other state pursues a cooperative strategy. In other words, a state's ideal outcome is to "sucker" the other side into thinking it is going to cooperate, and then cheat. But both sides understand this logic, and therefore both sides will try to cheat the other. Consequently, both sides will end up worse off than if they had cooperated, since mutual cheating leads to the worst possible outcome. Even though mutual cooperation is not as attractive as suckering the other side, it is certainly better than the outcome when both sides cheat.

The key to solving this dilemma is for each side to convince the other that they have a collective interest in making what appear to be short-term sacrifices (the gain that might result from successful cheating) for the sake of long-term benefits (the substantial payoff from mutual long-term cooperation). This means convincing states to accept the second-best outcome, which is mutual collaboration. The principal obstacle to reaching this cooperative outcome will be fear of getting suckered, should the other side cheat. This, in a nutshell, is the problem that institutions must solve.

To deal with this problem of "political market failure," institutions must deter cheaters and protect victims.[16] Three messages must be sent to potential cheaters: you will be caught, you will be punished immediately, and you will jeopardize future cooperative efforts. Potential victims, on the other hand, need early warning of cheating to avoid serious injury, and need the means to punish cheaters.

Liberal institutionalists do not aim to deal with cheaters and victims by changing fundamental norms of state behavior. Nor do they suggest transforming the anarchical nature of the international system. They accept the assumption that states operate in an anarchic environment and behave in a self-interested manner.[17] * * * Liberal institutionalists instead concentrate on showing how

rules can work to counter the cheating problem, even while states seek to maximize their own welfare. They argue that institutions can change a state's calculations about how to maximize gains. Specifically, rules can get states to make the short-term sacrifices needed to resolve the prisoners' dilemma and thus to realize long-term gains. Institutions, in short, can produce cooperation.

Rules can ideally be employed to make four major changes in "the contractual environment."[18] First, rules can increase the number of transactions between particular states over time.[19] This *institutionalized iteration* discourages cheating in three ways. It raises the costs of cheating by creating the prospect of future gains through cooperation, thereby invoking "the shadow of the future" to deter cheating today. A state caught cheating would jeopardize its prospects of benefiting from future cooperation, since the victim would probably retaliate. In addition, iteration gives the victim the opportunity to pay back the cheater: it allows for reciprocation, the tit-for-tat strategy, which works to punish cheaters and not allow them to get away with their transgression. Finally, it rewards states that develop a reputation for faithful adherence to agreements, and punishes states that acquire a reputation for cheating.[20]

Second, rules can tie together interactions between states in different issue areas. *Issue-linkage* aims to create greater interdependence between states, who will then be reluctant to cheat in one issue area for fear that the victim—and perhaps other states as well—will retaliate in another issue area. It discourages cheating in much the same way as iteration: it raises the costs of cheating and provides a way for the victim to retaliate against the cheater.

Third, a structure of rules can increase the amount of *information* available to participants in cooperative agreements so that close monitoring is possible. Raising the level of information discourages cheating in two ways: it increases the likelihood that cheaters will be caught, and more importantly, it provides victims with early warning of cheating, thereby enabling them to take protective measures before they are badly hurt.

Fourth, rules can reduce the *transaction costs* of individual agreements.[21] When institutions perform the tasks described above, states can devote less effort to negotiating and monitoring cooperative agreements, and to hedging against possible defections. By increasing the efficiency of international cooperation, institutions make it more profitable and thus more attractive for self-interested states.

Liberal institutionalism is generally thought to be of limited utility in the security realm, because fear of cheating is considered a much greater obstacle to cooperation when military issues are at stake.[22] There is the constant threat that betrayal will result in a devastating military defeat. This threat of "swift, decisive defection" is simply not present when dealing with international economics. Given that "the costs of betrayal" are potentially much graver in the military than the economic sphere, states will be very reluctant to accept the "one step backward, two steps forward" logic which underpins the tit-for-tat strategy of conditional cooperation. One step backward in the security realm might mean destruction, in which case there will be no next step—backward or forward.[23]

* * * There is an important theoretical failing in the liberal institutionalist logic, even as it applies to economic issues. The theory is correct as far as it goes: cheating can be a serious barrier to cooperation. It ignores, however, the other major obstacle to cooperation: relative-gains concerns. As Joseph Grieco has shown, liberal institutionalists assume that states are not concerned about relative gains, but focus exclusively on absolute gains.[24] * * *

This oversight is revealed by the assumed order of preference in the prisoners' dilemma game: each state cares about how its opponent's strategy will affect its own (absolute) gains, but not about how much one side gains relative to the other. In other words, each side simply wants to get the best deal for itself, and does not pay attention to how well the other side fares in the process.[25] Nevertheless, liberal institutionalists cannot ignore relative-gains considerations, because they assume that states are self-interested actors in an anarchic system, and they recognize that military power matters to states. A theory that explicitly accepts realism's core assumptions—and liberal institutionalism does that—must confront the issue of relative gains if it hopes to develop a sound explanation for why states cooperate.

One might expect liberal institutionalists to offer the counterargument that relative-gains logic applies only to the security realm, while absolute-gains logic applies to the economic realm. Given that they are mainly concerned with explaining economic and environmental cooperation, leaving relative-gains concerns out of the theory does not matter.

There are two problems with this argument. First, if cheating were the only significant obstacle to cooperation, liberal institutionalists could argue that their theory applies to the economic, but not the military realm. In fact, they do make that argument. However, once relative-gains considerations are factored into the equation, it becomes impossible to maintain the neat dividing line between economic and military issues, mainly because military might is significantly dependent on economic might. The relative size of a state's economy has profound consequences for its standing in the international balance of military power. Therefore, relative-gains concerns must be taken into account for security reasons when looking at the economic as well as military domain. The neat dividing line that liberal institutionalists employ to specify when their theory applies has little utility when one accepts that states worry about relative gains.[26]

Second, there are non-realist (i.e., nonsecurity) logics that might explain why states worry about relative gains. Strategic trade theory, for example, provides a straightforward economic logic for why states should care about relative gains.[27] It argues that states should help their own firms gain comparative advantage over the firms of rival states, because that is the best way to insure national economic prosperity. There is also a psychological logic, which portrays individuals as caring about how well they do (or their state does) in a cooperative agreement, not for material reasons, but because it is human nature to compare one's progress with that of others.[28]

Another possible liberal institutionalist counterargument is that solving the cheating problem renders the relative-gains problem irrelevant. If states cannot cheat each other, they need not fear each other, and therefore, states would not have to worry about relative power. The problem with this argument, however, is that even if the cheating problem were solved, states would still have to worry about relative gains because gaps in gains can be translated into military advantage that can be used for coercion or aggression. And in the international system, states sometimes have conflicting interests that lead to aggression.

There is also empirical evidence that relative-gains considerations mattered during the Cold War even in economic relations among the advanced industrialized democracies in the Organization for Economic Cooperation and Development (OECD). One would not expect realist logic about relative gains to be influential in this case: the United States was a superpower with little to fear militarily from the other OECD states, and those states were unlikely to use a relative-gains advantage to threaten the United States.[29] Furthermore, the OECD states were important American allies during the Cold War, and thus the United States benefited strategically when they gained substantially in size and strength.

Nonetheless, relative gains appear to have mattered in economic relations among the advanced industrial states. Consider three prominent studies. Stephen Krasner considered efforts at cooperation in different sectors of the international communications industry. He found that states were remarkably unconcerned about cheating but deeply worried about relative gains, which led him to conclude that liberal institutionalism "is not relevant for global communications." Grieco examined American and EC efforts to implement, under the auspices of GATT, a number of agreements relating to non-tariff barriers to trade. He found that the level of success was not a function of concerns about cheating but was influenced primarily by concern about the distribution of gains. Similarly, Michael Mastanduno found that concern about relative gains, not about cheating, was an important factor in shaping American policy towards Japan in three cases: the FSX fighter aircraft, satellites, and high-definition television.[30]

I am not suggesting that relative-gains considerations make cooperation impossible; my point is simply that they can pose a serious impediment to cooperation and must therefore be taken into account when developing a theory of cooperation among states. This point is apparently now recognized by liberal institutionalists. Keohane, for example, acknowledges that he "did make a major mistake by underemphasizing distributive issues and the complexities they create for international cooperation."[31]

Can Liberal Institutionalism Be Repaired? Liberal institutionalists must address two questions if they are to repair their theory. First, can institutions facilitate cooperation when states seriously care about relative gains, or do institutions only matter when states can ignore relative-gains considerations and focus instead on absolute gains? I find no evidence that liberal institutionalists believe that institutions facilitate cooperation when states care deeply about relative gains. They apparently concede that their theory only applies when relative-gains considerations matter little or hardly at all.[32] Thus the second question: when do states not worry about relative gains? The answer to this question would ultimately define the realm in which liberal institutionalism applies.

Liberal institutionalists have not addressed this important question in a systematic fashion, so any assessment of their efforts to repair the theory must be preliminary. * * *

* * *

Problems with the Empirical Record. Although there is much evidence of cooperation among states, this alone does not constitute support for liberal institutionalism. What is needed is evidence of cooperation that would not have occurred in the absence of institutions because of fear of cheating, or its actual presence. But scholars have provided little evidence of cooperation of that sort, nor of cooperation failing because of cheating. Moreover, as discussed above, there is considerable evidence that states worry much about relative gains not only in security matters, but in the economic realm as well.

This dearth of empirical support for liberal institutionalism is acknowledged by proponents of that theory.[33] The empirical record is not completely blank, however, but the few historical cases that liberal institutionalists have studied provide scant support for the theory. Consider two prominent examples.

Keohane looked at the performance of the International Energy Agency (IEA) in 1974–81, a period that included the 1979 oil crisis.[34] This case does not appear to lend the theory much support. First, Keohane concedes that the IEA failed outright when put to the test in 1979: "regime-oriented efforts at cooperation do not always succeed, as the fiasco of IEA actions in 1979 illustrates."[35] He claims, however, that in 1980 the IEA had a minor success "under relatively favorable conditions" in responding to the outbreak of the Iran-Iraq War. Although he admits it is difficult to specify how much the IEA mattered in the 1980 case, he notes that "it seems clear that 'it [the IEA] leaned in the right direction'," a claim that hardly constitutes strong support for the theory.[36] Second, it does not appear from Keohane's analysis that either fear of cheating or actual cheating hindered cooperation in the 1979 case, as the theory would predict. Third, Keohane chose the IEA case precisely because it involved relations among advanced Western democracies with market economies, where the prospects for cooperation were excellent.[37] The modest impact of institutions in this case is thus all the more damning to the theory.

Lisa Martin examined the role that the European Community (EC) played during the Falklands War in helping Britain coax its reluctant allies to continue economic sanctions against Argentina after military action started.[38] She concludes that the EC helped Britain win its allies' cooperation by lowering transaction costs and facilitating issue linkage. Specifically, Britain made concessions on the EC budget and the Common Agricultural Policy (CAP); Britain's allies agreed in return to keep sanctions on Argentina.

This case, too, is less than a ringing endorsement for liberal institutionalism. First, British efforts to maintain EC sanctions against Argentina were not impeded by fears of possible cheating, which the theory identifies as the central impediment to cooperation. So this case does not present an important test of liberal institutionalism, and thus the cooperative outcome does not tell us much about the theory's explanatory power. Second, it was relatively easy for Britain and her allies to strike a deal in this case. Neither side's core interests were threatened, and neither side had to make significant sacrifices to reach an agreement. Forging an accord to continue sanctions was not a difficult undertaking. A stronger test for liberal institutionalism would require states to cooperate when doing so entailed significant costs and risks. Third, the EC was not essential to an agreement. Issues could have been linked without the EC, and although the EC may have lowered transaction costs somewhat, there is no reason to think these costs were a serious impediment to striking a deal.[39] It is noteworthy that Britain and America were able to cooperate during the Falklands War, even though the United States did not belong to the EC.

There is also evidence that directly challenges liberal institutionalism in issue areas where one would expect the theory to operate successfully. The studies discussed above by Grieco, Krasner, and Mastanduno test the institutionalist argument in a number of different political economy cases, and each finds the theory has little explanatory power. More empirical work is needed before a final judgment is rendered on the explanatory power of liberal institutionalism. Nevertheless, the evidence gathered so far is unpromising at best.

In summary, liberal institutionalism does not provide a sound basis for understanding international relations and promoting stability in the post–Cold War world. It makes modest claims about the impact of institutions, and steers clear of war and peace issues, focusing instead on the less ambitious task of explaining economic cooperation. Furthermore, the theory's causal logic is flawed, as proponents of the theory now admit. Having overlooked the relative-gains problem, they are now attempting to repair the theory, but their initial efforts are not promising. Finally, the available empirical evidence provides little support for the theory.

＊   ＊   ＊

Conclusion

＊   ＊   ＊

The attraction of institutionalist theories for both policymakers and scholars is explained, I believe, not by their intrinsic value, but by their relationship to realism, and especially to core elements of American political ideology. Realism has long been and continues to be an influential theory in the United States.[40] Leading realist thinkers such as George Kennan and Henry Kissinger, for example, occupied key policymaking positions during the Cold War. The impact of realism in the academic world is amply demonstrated in the institutionalist literature, where discussions of realism are pervasive.[41] Yet despite its influence, Americans who think seriously about foreign policy issues tend to dislike realism intensely, mainly because it clashes with their basic values. The theory stands opposed to how most Americans prefer to think about themselves and the wider world.[42]

There are four principal reasons why American elites, as well as the American public, tend to regard realism with hostility. First, realism is a pessimistic theory. It depicts a world of stark and harsh competition, and it holds out little promise of making that world more benign. Realists, as Hans Morgenthau wrote, are resigned to the fact that "there is no escape from the evil of power, regardless of what one does."[43] Such pessimism, of course, runs up against the deep-seated American belief that with time and effort, reasonable individuals can solve important social problems. Americans regard progress as both desirable and possible in politics, and they are therefore uncomfortable with realism's claim that

security competition and war will persist despite our best efforts to eliminate them.[44]

Second, realism treats war as an inevitable, and indeed sometimes necessary, form of state activity. For realists, war is an extension of politics by other means. Realists are very cautious in their prescriptions about the use of force: wars should not be fought for idealistic purposes, but instead for balance-of-power reasons. Most Americans, however, tend to think of war as a hideous enterprise that should ultimately be abolished. For the time being, however, it can only justifiably be used for lofty moral goals, like "making the world safe for democracy"; it is morally incorrect to fight wars to change or preserve the balance of power. This makes the realist conception of warfare anathema to many Americans.

Third, as an analytical matter, realism does not distinguish between "good" states and "bad" states, but essentially treats them like billiard balls of varying size. In realist theory, all states are forced to seek the same goal: maximum relative power.[45] A purely realist interpretation of the Cold War, for example, allows for no meaningful difference in the motives behind American and Soviet behavior during that conflict. According to the theory, both sides must have been driven by concerns about the balance of power, and must have done what was necessary to try to achieve a favorable balance. Most Americans would recoil at such a description of the Cold War, because they believe the United States was motivated by good intentions while the Soviet Union was not.[46]

Fourth, America has a rich history of thumbing its nose at realism. For its first 140 years of existence, geography and the British navy allowed the United States to avoid serious involvement in the power politics of Europe. America had an isolationist foreign policy for most of this period, and its rhetoric explicitly emphasized the evils of entangling alliances and balancing behavior. Even as the United States finally entered its first European war in 1917, Woodrow Wilson railed against realist thinking. America has a long tradition of anti-realist rhetoric, which continues to influence us today.

Given that realism is largely alien to American culture, there is a powerful demand in the United States for alternative ways of looking at the world, and especially for theories that square with basic American values. Institutionalist theories nicely meet these requirements, and that is the main source of their appeal to policymakers and scholars. Whatever else one might say about these theories, they have one undeniable advantage in the eyes of their supporters: they are not realism. Not only do institutionalist theories offer an alternative to realism, but they explicitly seek to undermine it. Moreover, institutionalists offer arguments that reflect basic American values. For example, they are optimistic about the possibility of greatly reducing, if not eliminating, security competition among states and creating a more peaceful world. They certainly do not accept the realist stricture that war is politics by other means. Institutionalists, in short, purvey a message that Americans long to hear.

There is, however, a downside for policymakers who rely on institutionalist theories: these theories do not accurately describe the world, hence policies based on them are bound to fail. The international system strongly shapes the behavior of states, limiting the amount of damage that false faith in institutional theories can cause. The constraints of the system notwithstanding, however, states still have considerable freedom of action, and their policy choices can succeed or fail in protecting American national interests and the interests of vulnerable people around the globe. The failure of the League of Nations to address German and Japanese aggression in the 1930s is a case in point. The failure of institutions to prevent or stop the war in Bosnia offers a more recent example. These cases illustrate that institutions have mattered rather little in the past; they also suggest that the false belief that institutions matter has mattered more, and has had pernicious effects. Unfortunately, misplaced reliance on institutional solutions is likely to lead to more failures in the future.

NOTES

1. Regimes and institutions are treated as synonymous concepts in this article. They are also used interchangeably in the institutionalist literature. See Robert O. Keohane, "International Institutions: Two Approaches," *International Studies Quarterly*, Vol. 32, No. 4 (December 1988), p. 384; Robert O. Keohane, *International Institutions and State Power: Essays in International Relations Theory* (Boulder, Colo.: Westview Press, 1989), pp. 3–4; and Oran R. Young, *International Cooperation: Building Regimes for Natural Resources and the Environment* (Ithaca, N.Y.: Cornell University Press, 1989), chaps. 1 and 8. The term "multilateralism" is also virtually synonymous with institutions. To quote John Ruggie, "the term 'multilateral' is an adjective that modifies the noun 'institution.' Thus, multilateralism depicts a *generic institutional form* in international relations. . . . [Specifically,] multilateralism is an institutional form which coordinates relations among three or more states on the basis of 'generalized' principles of conduct." Ruggie, "Multilateralism [The Anatomy of an Institution]," [*International Organization*, Vol. 46, No. 3 (Summer 1992),] pp. 570–571.

2. For discussion of this point, see Arthur A. Stein, *Why Nations Cooperate: Circumstance and Choice in International Relations* (Ithaca, N.Y.: Cornell University Press, 1990), pp. 25–27. Also see Susan Strange, "*Cave! Hic Dragones:* A Critique of Regime Analysis," in Stephen D. Krasner, ed., *International Regimes,* special issue of *International Organization,* Vol. 36, No. 2 (Spring 1982), pp. 479–496.

3. Oran R. Young, "Regime Dynamics: The Rise and Fall of International Regimes," in Krasner, *International Regimes,* p. 277.

4. See Douglass C. North and Robert P. Thomas, "An Economic Theory of the Growth of the Western World," *The Economic History Review,* 2nd series, Vol. 23, No. 1 (April 1970), p. 5.

5. Krasner, *International Regimes,* p. 186. Non-realist institutions are often based on higher norms, while few, if any, realist institutions are

based on norms. The dividing line between norms and rules is not sharply defined in the institutionalist literature. See Robert O. Keohane, *After Hegemony: Cooperation and Discord in the World Political Economy* (Princeton, N.J.: Princeton University Press, 1984), pp. 57–58. For example, one might argue that rules, not just norms, are concerned with rights and obligations. The key point, however, is that for many institutionalists, norms, which are core beliefs about standards of appropriate state behavior, are the foundation on which more specific rules are constructed. This distinction between norms and rules applies in a rather straightforward way in the subsequent discussion. Both collective security and critical theory challenge the realist belief that states behave in a self-interested way, and argue instead for developing norms that require states to act more altruistically. Liberal institutionalism, on the other hand, accepts the realist view that states act on the basis of self-interest, and concentrates on devising rules that facilitate cooperation among states.

6. International organizations are public agencies established through the cooperative efforts of two or more states. These administrative structures have their own budget, personnel, and buildings. John Ruggie defines them as "palpable entities with headquarters and letterheads, voting procedures, and generous pension plans." Ruggie, "Multilateralism," p. 573. Once rules are incorporated into an international organization, "they may seem almost coterminous," even though they are "distinguishable analytically." Keohane, *International Institutions and State Power*, p. 5.

7. Charles Lipson, "Is the Future of Collective Security Like the Past?" in George W. Downs, ed., *Collective Security beyond the Cold War* (Ann Arbor: University of Michigan Press), p. 114.

8. Tony Evans and Peter Wilson, "Regime Theory and the English School of International Relations: A Comparison," *Millennium: Journal of International Studies*, Vol. 21, No. 3 (Winter 1992), p. 330.

9. See Gunther Hellmann and Reinhard Wolf,

"Neorealism Neoliberal Institutionalism, and the Future of NATO," *Security Studies*, Vol. 3, No. 1 (Autumn 1993), pp. 3–43.

10. Among the key liberal institutionalist works are: Robert Axelrod and Robert O. Keohane, "Achieving Cooperation under Anarchy: Strategies and Institutions," *World Politics*, Vol. 38, No. 1 (October 1985), pp. 226–254; Keohane, *After Hegemony*; Keohane, "International Institutions: Two Approaches," pp. 379–396; Keohane, *International Institutions and State Power*, chap. 1; Charles Lipson, "International Cooperation in Economic and Security Affairs," *World Politics*, Vol. 37, No. 1 (October 1984), pp. 1–23; Lisa L. Martin, "Institutions and Cooperation: Sanctions During the Falkland Islands Conflict," *International Security*, Vol. 16, No. 4 (Spring 1992), pp. 143–178; Lisa L. Martin, *Coercive Cooperation: Explaining Multilateral Economic Sanctions* (Princeton, N.J.: Princeton University Press, 1992); Kenneth A. Oye, "Explaining Cooperation Under Anarchy: Hypotheses and Strategies," *World Politics*, Vol. 38, No. 1 (October 1985), pp. 1–24; and Stein, *Why Nations Cooperate*.

11. Stein, *Why Nations Cooperate*, chap. 2. Also see Keohane, *After Hegemony*, pp. 6–7, 12–13, 67–69.

12. Milner, "International Theories of Cooperation [among Nations: Strengths and Weaknesses]," [*World Politics*, Vol. 44, No. 3 (April 1992),] p. 468.

13. For examples of the theory at work in the environmental realm, see Peter M. Haas, Robert O. Keohane, and Marc A. Levy, eds., *Institutions for the Earth: Sources of Effective International Environmental Protection* (Cambridge, Mass.: MIT Press, 1993), especially chaps. 1 and 9. Some of the most important work on institutions and the environment has been done by Oran Young. See, for example, Young, *International Cooperation*. The rest of my discussion concentrates on economic, not environmental issues, for conciseness, and also because the key theoretical works in the liberal institutionalist literature focus on economic rather than environmental matters.

14. Cheating is basically a "breach of promise." Oye, "Explaining Cooperation Under Anarchy," p. 1. It usually implies unobserved non-compliance, although there can be observed cheating as well. Defection is a synonym for cheating in the institutionalist literature.

15. The centrality of the prisoners' dilemma and cheating to the liberal institutionalist literature is clearly reflected in virtually all the works cited in footnote 10. As Helen Milner notes in her review essay on this literature: "The focus is primarily on the role of regimes [institutions] in solving the defection [cheating] problem." Milner, "International Theories of Cooperation," p. 475.

16. The phrase is from Keohane, *After Hegemony*, p. 85.

17. Kenneth Oye, for example, writes in the introduction to an issue of *World Politics* containing a number of liberal institutionalist essays: "Our focus is on non-altruistic cooperation among states dwelling in international anarchy." Oye, "Explaining Cooperation Under Anarchy," p. 2. Also see Keohane, "International Institutions: Two Approaches," pp. 380–381; and Keohane, *International Institutions and State Power*, p. 3.

18. Haas, Keohane, and Levy, *Institutions for the Earth*, p. 11. For general discussions of how rules work, which inform my subsequent discussion of the matter, see Keohane, *After Hegemony*, chaps. 5–6; Martin, "Institutions and Cooperation," pp. 143–178; and Milner, "International Theories of Cooperation," pp. 474–478.

19. See Axelrod and Keohane, "Achieving Cooperation Under Anarchy," pp. 248–250; Lipson, "International Cooperation," pp. 4–18.

20. Lipson, "International Cooperation," p. 5.

21. See Keohane, *After Hegemony*, pp. 89–92.

22. This point is clearly articulated in Lipson, "International Cooperation," especially pp. 12–18. The subsequent quotations in this paragraph are from ibid. Also see Axelrod and Keohane, "Achieving Cooperation Under Anarchy," pp. 232–233.

23. See Roger B. Parks, "What if 'Fools Die'? A Comment on Axelrod," Letter to *American Political Science Review*, Vol. 79, No. 4 (December 1985), pp. 1173–1174.

24. See Grieco, "Anarchy and the Limits of Cooperation [A Realist Critique of the Newest Liberal Institutionalism,]" [*International Organization*, Vol. 42, No. 3 (Summer 1988)]. Other works by Grieco bearing on the subject include: Joseph M. Grieco, "Realist Theory and the Problem of International Cooperation: Analysis with an Amended Prisoner's Dilemma Model," *The Journal of Politics*, Vol. 50, No. 3 (August 1988), pp. 600–624; Grieco, *Cooperation among Nations: Europe, America, and Non-Tariff Barriers to Trade* (Ithaca, N.Y.: Cornell University Press, 1990); and Grieco, "Understanding the Problem of International Cooperation: The Limits of Neoliberal Institutionalism and the Future of Realist Theory," in Baldwin, [ed.,] *Neorealism and Neoliberalism* [*The Contempory Debate* (New York: Columbia University Press, 1993)], pp. 301–338. The telling effect of Grieco's criticism is reflected in ibid., which is essentially organized around the relative gains vs. absolute gains debate, an issue given little attention before Grieco raised it in his widely cited 1988 article. The matter was briefly discussed by two other scholars before Grieco. See Joanne Gowa, "Anarchy, Egoism, and Third Images: *The Evolution of Cooperation and International Relations*," *International Organization*, Vol. 40, No. 1 (Winter 1986), pp. 172–179; and Oran R. Young, "International Regimes: Toward a New Theory of Institutions," *World Politics*, Vol. 39, No. 1 (October 1986), pp. 118–119.

25. Lipson writes: "The Prisoner's Dilemma, in its simplest form, involves two players. Each is assumed to be a self-interested, self-reliant maximizer of his own utility, an assumption that clearly parallels the Realist conception of sovereign states in international politics." Lipson, "International Cooperation," p. 2. Realists, however, do not accept this conception of international politics and, not surprisingly, have

questioned the relevance of the prisoners' dilemma (at least in its common form) for explaining much of international relations. See Gowa, "Anarchy, Egoism, and Third Images"; Grieco, "Realist Theory and the Problem of International Cooperation"; and Stephen D. Krasner, "Global Communications and National Power: Life on the Pareto Frontier," *World Politics*, Vol. 43, No. 3 (April 1991), pp. 336–366.

26. My thinking on this matter has been markedly influenced by Sean Lynn-Jones, in his June 19, 1994, correspondence with me.

27. For a short discussion of strategic trade theory, see Robert Gilpin, *The Political Economy of International Relations* (Princeton, N.J.: Princeton University Press, 1987), pp. 215–221. The most commonly cited reference on the subject is Paul R. Krugman, ed., *Strategic Trade Policy and the New International Economics* (Cambridge, Mass.: MIT Press, 1986).

28. See Robert Axelrod, *The Evolution of Cooperation* (New York: Basic Books, 1984), pp. 110–113.

29. Grieco maintains in *Cooperation among Nations* that realist logic should apply here. Robert Powell, however, points out that "in the context of negotiations between the European Community and the United States . . . it is difficult to attribute any concern for relative gains to the effects that a relative loss may have on the probability of survival." Robert Powell, "Absolute and Relative Gains in International Relations Theory," *American Political Science Review*, Vol. 85, No. 4 (December 1991), p. 1319, footnote 26. I agree with Powell. It is clear from Grieco's response to Powell that Grieco includes non-military logics like strategic trade theory in the realist tent, whereas Powell and I do not. See Grieco's contribution to "The Relative-Gains Problem for International Relations," *American Political Science Review*, Vol. 87, No. 3 (September 1993), pp. 733–735.

30. Krasner, "Global Communications and National Power," pp. 336–366; Grieco, *Cooperation among Nations*; and Michael Mastanduno, "Do Relative Gains Matter? America's Response to Japanese Industrial Policy," *Interna-*

tional Security, Vol. 16, No. 1 (Summer 1991), pp. 73–113. Also see Jonathan B. Tucker, "Partners and Rivals: A Model of International Collaboration in Advanced Technology," *International Organization*, Vol. 45, No. 1 (Winter 1991), pp. 83–120.

31. Keohane, "Institutional Theory and the Realist Challenge," [in Baldwin, *Neorealism and Neoliberalism*,] p. 292.

32. For example, Keohane wrote after becoming aware of Grieco's argument about relative gains: "Under specified conditions—where mutual interests are low and relative gains are therefore particularly important to states— neoliberal theory expects neorealism to explain elements of state behavior." Keohane, *International Institutions and State Power*, pp. 15–16.

33. For example, Lisa Martin writes that "scholars working in the realist tradition maintain a well-founded skepticism about the empirical impact of institutional factors on state behavior. This skepticism is grounded in a lack of studies that show precisely how and when institutions have constrained state decision-making." According to Oran Young, "One of the more surprising features of the emerging literature on regimes [institutions] is the relative absence of sustained discussions of the significance of . . . institutions, as determinants of collective outcomes at the international level." Martin, "Institutions and Cooperation," p. 144; Young, *International Cooperation*, p. 206.

34. Keohane, *After Hegemony*, chap. 10.

35. Ibid., p. 16.

36. Ibid., p. 236. A U.S. Department of Energy review of the IEA's performance in the 1980 crisis concluded that it had "failed to fulfill its promise." Ethan B. Kapstein, *The Insecure Alliance: Energy Crises and Western Politics Since 1944* (New York: Oxford University Press, 1990), p. 198.

37. Keohane, *After Hegemony*, p. 7.

38. Martin, "Institutions and Cooperation." Martin looks closely at three other cases in *Coercive Cooperation* to determine the effect of institu-

tions on cooperation. I have concentrated on the Falklands War case, however, because it is, by her own admission, her strongest case. See ibid., p. 96.

39. Martin does not claim that agreement would not have been possible without the EC. Indeed, she appears to concede that even without the EC, Britain still could have fashioned "separate bilateral agreements with each EEC member in order to gain its cooperation, [although] this would have involved much higher transaction costs." Martin, "Institutions and Cooperation," pp. 174–175. However, transaction costs among the advanced industrial democracies are not very high in an era of rapid communications and permanent diplomatic establishments.

40. See Michael J. Smith, *Realist Thought from Weber to Kissinger* (Baton Rouge: Lousiana State University Press, 1986), chap. 1.

41. Summing up the autobiographical essays of 34 international relations scholars, Joseph Kruzel notes that "Hans Morgenthau is more frequently cited than any other name in these memoirs." Joseph Kruzel, "Reflections on the Journeys," in Joseph Kruzel and James N. Rosenau, eds., *Journeys through World Politics: Autobiographical Reflections of Thirty-four Academic Travelers* (Lexington, Mass.: Lexington Books, 1989), p. 505. Although "Morgenthau is often cited, many of the references in these pages are negative in tone. He seems to have inspired his critics even more than his supporters." Ibid.

42. See Keith L. Shimko, "Realism, Neorealism, and American Liberalism," *Review of Politics*, Vol. 54, No. 2 (Spring 1992), pp. 281–301.

43. Hans J. Morgenthau, *Scientific Man vs. Power Politics* (Chicago: University of Chicago Press, 1974), p. 201. Nevertheless, Keith Shimko convincingly argues that the shift within realism, away from Morgenthau's belief that states are motivated by an unalterable will to power,

and toward Waltz's view that states are motivated by the desire for security, provides "a residual, though subdued optimism, or at least a possible basis for optimism [about international politics]. The extent to which this optimism is stressed or suppressed varies, but it is there if one wants it to be." Shimko, "Realism, Neorealism, and American Liberalism," p. 297. Realists like Stephen Van Evera, for example, point out that although states operate in a dangerous world, they can take steps to dampen security competition and minimize the danger of war. See Van Evera, *Causes of War* [Vol. II: *National Misperception and the Origins of War*, forthcoming].

44. See Reinhold Niebuhr, *The Children of Light and The Children of Darkness: A Vindication of Democracy and a Critique of Its Traditional Defense* (New York: Charles Scribner's, 1944), especially pp. 153–190. See also Samuel P. Huntington, *The Soldier and the State: The Theory and Politics of Civil-Military Relations* (New York: Vintage Books, 1964).

45. It should be emphasized that many realists have strong moral preferences and are driven by deep moral convictions. Realism is not a normative theory, however, and it provides no criteria for moral judgment. Instead, realism merely seeks to explain how the world works. Virtually all realists would prefer a world without security competition and war, but they believe that goal is unrealistic given the structure of the international system. See, for example, Robert G. Gilpin, "The Richness of the Tradition of Political Realism," in Keohane, [ed.,] *Neorealism and Its Critics*, [New York: Columbia University Press, 1986] p. 321.

46. Realism's treatment of states as billiard balls of different sizes tends to raise the hackles of comparative politics scholars, who believe that domestic political and economic factors matter greatly for explaining foreign policy behavior.

10 ∾ NATIONALISM

The 1990s were a decade of bloody ethnic conflicts in several of the post-Communist states, Africa, and other societies undergoing rapid political change. Although the news media blamed many of these on "ancient hatreds," Susanne Hoeber Rudolph and Lloyd I. Rudolph point out that even the conflicts that seem the most ancient, such as the one dividing India's Hindus and Muslims, are actually spurred by very modern developments in an era of mass politics. Jack Snyder's book in the Norton series, From Voting to Violence: Democratization and Nationalist Conflict, *elaborates further on the role played by persuasive elites in promoting nationalist and ethnic conflict in societies that are undergoing a transition to democratic politics.*

Stephen Van Evera, spearheading a renewed interest in the study of nationalism and ethnic conflict among security studies scholars in the 1990s, offers a wealth of hypotheses on the conditions under which nationalism does and does not lead to war. Some of his hypotheses are realist, focusing for example on whether military balances favor dissatisfied ethnic groups. Other hypotheses, however, are grounded in liberalism, considering for example whether the troublemaking rhetoric of nationalist mythmakers is held to strict accountability in an effective, democratic marketplace of ideas. Barry Posen shows how realist theories of conflict in anarchy, long used by scholars to understand the dynamics of international wars, can also illuminate the strategic incentives that intensify ethnic rivalries when states or empires collapse. Both Van Evera and Posen were students of Waltz and draw heavily on the seminal ideas in Jervis's "security dilemma" article (see chapter 7). This shows how fundamental theoretical concepts, grounded in a powerful logical framework, can serve as general-purpose tools to be adapted to new practical problems as the current agenda of international issues changes.

SUSANNE HOEBER RUDOLPH AND LLOYD I. RUDOLPH

Modern Hate

On Inauguration Day, Bill Clinton told the country and the world a story about how "a generation raised in the shadows of the cold war assumes new responsibilities in a world warmed by the sunshine of freedom but threatened still by ancient hatreds." The new president seemed to have in mind such things as ethnic cleansing and religious fundamentalism, the first a deceptive metaphor invented by extreme nationalist Serbs, the second a ubiquitous term that relieves politicians, news anchors and policy intellectuals from thinking about the complexities of the "other."

One event that fed the country's growing preoccupation with ancient hatreds occurred last December, when "Hindu fundamentalists" tore down a mosque built in the sixteenth century by the first Mughal emperor, Babur, in Ayodhya, a small town in eastern Uttar Pradesh, India's most populous state. Its destruction was the climax of three tumultuous years during which the Hindu nationalist Bharatiya Janata Party piqued emotions over the mosque. It held that Babur had destroyed a temple on Lord Rama's birthsite in order to build what came to be known as the Babri Masjid (Babur's Mosque); thus, Hindus should reclaim their heritage by building a new temple to Lord Rama on the site of the mosque. More than 2,500 people were killed in the retaliatory violence that followed the destruction of the Babri Masjid. In January violence erupted again in Bombay, where the police openly abetted burning and vandalism. At the end of February, the BJP attempted to hold a mass rally in New Delhi to bring down the Congress party government.

But recent news accounts that depict the violence as an outgrowth of old animosities are misleading. Hindus and Muslims in India under the Mughal emperor Akbar, the nationalistic leadership of Mahatma Gandhi and the Congress governments of Jawaharlal Nehru have gotten along more often than they have gone for each other's throats. So did Serbs, Croats and Muslims under Tito in Yugoslavia. Clinton and others too easily invoke "ancient hatreds" to explain what are really contemporary conflicts. The question, in other words, is not why old conflicts are flaring up anew, but rather why traditionally harmonious mosaics have been shattered.

Before Christmas, the Hanukkah card section of the University of Chicago bookstore featured a seasonal card depicting two Santas, one with a white beard, one with a brown one, the first carrying the regulation Santa bag, the second carrying a menorah. A scholar of India looks at that card and says, "How Indian!" St. Nicholas integrated into a Jewish festival! Societies with a plurality of religions can and often do work out symbolic settlements. Until recently, the ability to reach such settlements was the dominant theme in Indian history and in its postindependence politics. Friendships are as "ancient" as hatreds. The face we see depends on what human agents cause us to see.

Looking at that Hanukkah card, we were reminded of a friend of ours, an observant Muslim, one of the numerous South Asian diaspora in Chicago. As a child in India, she was once asked to participate in a small community drama about the life of Lord Krishna. Krishna is the blue "Hindu" god adored by shepherdesses, who dance for his pleasure. They exemplify through their human passion the quest of the devout soul for the lord. Not exactly a Muslim monotheist's theme. She was invited to dance as a shepherdess with other

From *The New Republic*, 22 March 1993, 24–29.

schoolgirls. Her father forbade it: Muslims don't dance. In that case, said the drama's director, we will cast you as Krishna. All you have to do is stand there in the usual Krishna pose, a flute at your mouth. Her father consented. She played Krishna.

Line-crossing seemed as natural to that Krishna-playing child as it did to Mahatma Gandhi. In his autobiography, *The Story of My Experiments with Truth*, he recalls that his devout mother regularly visited the tomb of a Muslim *pir* and followed Jain ideas about self-suffering and nonviolence. Her un-self-conscious ecumenism was common in Gandhi's birthplace, Kathiawad, a cosmopolitan entrepôt area bordering the Arabian sea. Gandhi began his historic career in South Africa, working for migrant Muslim businessmen from the same region.

With about 110 million Muslim citizens, India is the second-largest Muslim country in the world, after Indonesia. Islam takes many forms, from the most severe monotheism to a Sufi mysticism and devotion that features worship of saints and their relics—practices repugnant to a more austere orthodoxy. Sufi *pirs* and their magnificent tombs attract Hindu as well as Muslim pilgrims from all parts of the subcontinent. None is more renowned than the Dargah at Ajmer, the burial place of Kwaja Nuin-ud-din-Chisti, founder in the twelfth century of a family of saints and courtiers, a shrine second only to Mecca in the eyes of South Asian Muslims. Cultural practices mingle and mix. Hindu practices persist among converts to Islam— dietary laws are followed, marriage boundaries observed, festivals celebrated. Aristocratic north Indian culture, its language and manners, its music and cuisine, remained distinctively Persian at least until the time of Nehru, embodying the idioms of Mughal court culture. The region's leading performers of Hindu devotional music, the Dagar brothers, are Muslims. Village Muslims, like their urban brothers, share in local or neighborhood *Ramayana* performances and watch as eagerly as the rest of the nation when Doordarshan, Indian state-run television, airs the eighteen-month-long megaseries on the ("Hindu") *Ramayana* and *Mahabharata*.

But not all practices promote a composite culture and unity in diversity. Hindu and Muslim religious sensibilities have vacillated between tendencies to naturalize and demonize differences. Political language in the nationalist era sometimes used religious symbols to make politics meaningful to common people for whom religion was a natural idiom. Religious language, however, is capable of many different forms of expression.

Some nationalists used Hindu religious symbolism that excluded Muslims. B. G. Tilak, India's most influential popular leader before Mahatma Gandhi, led the way in inventing "communalism," the term Indians use for community exclusivism and chauvinism. In the 1890s, keen to build a mass following, he revived a Maharashtrian festival commemorating the birth of Shiva's elephant-headed son, Ganesh, Hinduism's most beloved deity. For ten days each year villagers poured into cities and towns to celebrate and hear recitations of Hindu epic poetry. Ganapati festivals became occasions for clashes with Muslims when paramilitary. "Ganesh guards" directed noisy parades past mosques at prayer time. Muslims began to retaliate by acts of profanation and desacralization, "killing cows" and cutting auspicious peepul trees. Bengali nationalists wrote plays and songs that alienated Muslims by using the theme of opposition to Muslim kings as a surrogate for opposition to British rule.

Secular nationalism took different forms: Nehru maintained that science should ask and answer all questions; Gandhi believed that spiritual truth could be found in all religions. At Gandhi's prayer meetings, the Gita, the Koran and the Bible were read. He favored a national language— Hindustani—which could accommodate Urdu, the language of North Indian Muslims, and Hindi, the language of North Indian Hindus.

"Ancient hatreds" are thus made as much as they are inherited. To call them ancient is to pretend they are primordial forces, outside of history and human agency, when often they are merely synthetic antiques. Intellectuals, writers, artists and politicians "make" hatreds. Films and videos, texts and textbooks, certify stories about the past, the collective memories that shape perceptions and attitudes.

Before democracy, modernization and the nation-state, Hinduism was loose, open and diverse, a web of local and regional sectarian groupings defined by a sacred geography of places and events, deities and temples. The very term "Hinduism" was an abstraction, a word used by outsiders to describe a place and a people, not an institutionalized religion. Travelers—Hsuan Tsang, the seventh-century Chinese Buddhist pilgrim, and Alberuni, the eleventh-century Arab savant accompanying Mahmud of Ghazni—designated trans-Indus peoples as Hindus.

Instead of Hindus, there were followers of saints (*sants*): Kabir followers and Dadu followers, Vaishnavites in Gujarat and Bengal, Lingayats in Karnataka and Shivites in Tamilnadu, pursuing distinctive doctrines and practices. It is a truism to say Hinduism had no church. There was no pope, no ecclesia, no bishops to enunciate what was orthodox and heterodox, much less heretical or blasphemous. Great debates at Banaras reverberated through the centuries. Great teachers such as Shankara in the eighth century and Ramanuja in the twelfth were revered. But there was no all-India, transhistorical authority. Even today a local religious teacher in Jaipur or Bangalore is likely to be the person of greatest authority for her followers; no one is in a position to discipline her or to question her doctrine or ritual practices.

If there was no standard version of Hinduism until yesterday, then when and how did the day before yesterday end? How did it happen that the Bharatiya Janata Party was able to hijack Hinduism, replacing its diversity, multivocality and generativity with a monotheistic Ram cult? An answer can be found in the history of storytelling. The ancient legend of Ram, the virtuous god-king, incarnation of Vishnu, who wandered in exile for twelve years with his wife Sita before vanquishing the Southern demon Ravana, can be found all over India. It is a moral tale, exemplifying what right

conduct should be between a king and his subjects and among generations, genders and relatives. Ram was an intimate deity, his representations infinitely diverse by region and locale. He was the subject of thousands of *Ramayana*s in many languages, of village drama cycles, of stories told by grandmothers, and today of epic comic books.

In time, Ram stories became consolidated. In *The Life of a Text: Performing the Ramcaritmanas of Tulsidas*, Philip Lutgendorf writes that this sixteenth-century *Ramayana* was regarded "not merely as the greatest modern Indian epic, but as something like a living sum of Indian culture." Lutgendorf details how during the nineteenth century the recitations of the *Ramayana* became the vehicle for the "rise of the eternal religion" and how, through the *manas*, Hindus became a "people of the book." In 1984 the vastly popular recitals of the text, boxed in a set of eight audiocassettes, was the "hottest-selling recording in the thriving cassette stalls of Banaras," hotter even than the immensely popular cassettes of Hindi film music.

In January 1987 an eighteen-month-long serial of the *Ramayana* based on the *manas* began airing at 9:30 a.m., prime time, on state-run T.V. *Ramayana* episodes quickly became the most popular program ever shown, attracting an estimated 100 million viewers, roughly the size of the audience for presidential debates in America. On Sundays streets were deserted throughout India. Everyone was watching, even knots of cycle rickshaw drivers crowded in front of T.V. store windows.

The *Ramayana* "megaseries" took advantage of a new space for religious discourse in India, Pakistan, Iran, Oman and elsewhere, a public space outside the private arenas of family and village, temple and mosque. In this space a new public culture is being created and consumed. Distant persons, strangers, create representations of public culture for anonymous viewers. Values and symbols, meaning systems and metaphors, can be standardized for national consumption.

And what did the series do to grandmother's

version of the Rama tale? Or to the village performance? In Gatiali, located in the state of Rajasthan, the local village production of *Ramayana* wasn't performed in 1989. Village leaders who watched the television version had been impressed. The local version seemed to them amateurish by comparison. Why take the trouble and expense to put on an unworthy, moth-eaten version? Other Hinduish megaseries followed—such as the great epic *Mahabharata, Chanakya,* a Hindu nationalist reinvention of the Mauryan empire's cunning prime minister. Together they helped stamp out diversity and localism, replacing them with a national, standardized version of Hinduism, what historian and social critic Romila Thapar has characterized as syndicated, semitized Hinduism, a Hinduism of one God, one book, one place, one people, a religion resembling exclusivist versions of Judaism, Christianity and Islam.

Ten months after the *Ramayana* megaseries, the Vishua Hindu Parishad (World Hindu Council) called on Hindus throughout India to make holy bricks, inscribed with Rama's name, for use at Ayodhya. There, at the site of Rama's birth, and on the place of the Babri Masjid, they would build a temple to Rama. Construction was deferred during the national elections of 1989. The Bharatiya Janata Party, which had captured only two seats with 8 percent of the vote in 1984, now garnered eighty-six seats with 11 percent. Its modest 3 percentage point increase in electoral votes suggests that the party gained eighty-four seats more by virtue of making electoral alliances than by an increase in popular support, but its electoral gains put religion in the political spotlight. After another two years the BJP emerged from the May-June 1991 election as India's second-largest party, its vote share bounding upward from 11 percent to 20 percent and its seats in Parliament increasing from eighty-six to 118. L. K. Advani told India's electorate that if the countries of Western Europe and the United States can call themselves Christian, India should be free to call itself Hindu.

One of the ways to think about the recent savaging of the Babri Masjid by young Hindu men is to see it as a renegotiation of political and economic power and status, or rather as a sign of the pathology of renegotiation. The youths we saw standing on the domes of the doomed mosque were wearing city clothes, shirts and trousers, not the *kurta* and *dhotis* of villagers or the urban poor. They looked like clerks, boys from urban lower-middle-class families. They are the educated unemployed, not the poor and illiterate. Frustrated by the lack of good jobs and opportunities, they are victims of modernization, seeking to victimize others—like "pampered" Muslims. In an India where, despite its problems, the number of persons under the poverty line has been declining and entrepreneurship expanding exponentially, their expectations have run well ahead of available opportunities.

Social mobility in India has become a widespread phenomenon. Liberalization and economic growth have enormously expanded the opportunities for many Indians. The '80s witnessed the highest economic growth rates of the last five decades. Green revolutionaries have grown prosperous on high-yielding varieties of wheat; doctors and engineers educated at government expense find public sector jobs; craftspeople who have parleyed workshops into lucrative enterprises supply large manufacturers. Such mobility is unhinging a severely hierarchical society, creating social stress bred of envy and resentment. Old, established Hindu middle classes, mostly from the upper literate and landed castes, suddenly see a whole range of Johnny-come-latelies at their side who only yesterday were their inferiors in status and income, both low-caste folk and Muslims. The hatred that led Nathuram Godse to kill Mahatma Gandhi was bred in the resentment of upper castes on the way down. Gandhi had mobilized the periphery against the center, the lower castes and village poor against Brahmanical orthodoxy. These are conflicts generated by individuals using the opportunities of recent history.

The short-lived Janata party government of 1990, under V.P. Singh, recognized the political implications of the emergence into politics and social power of these new forces, forging an alliance of the "Backward Classes" (a *raj* euphemism for the disadvantaged lower castes) and Muslims. The Backward Classes, many of them agricultural castes who have profited from the green revolution, have been demanding quotas in government jobs and education for decades. Their demands threaten the position of urban upper castes who respond to an appeal to Hindu identity, whose long traditions of literacy have given them the advantage in merit-based competitions, and who disproportionately control such jobs.

How is that relevant to the position of Muslims? They do not have such quotas, either in government jobs or in education. The main "privilege" they have in independent India is immunity for their religiously based family law, which allows "privileges" such as multiple marriages for men and easy divorce. Muslims also have had tacit guarantees, imperfectly enforced, from state and federal governments to be represented in Cabinet and party posts. These may not be substantial privileges, but to the upper castes in the midst of backlash against their slipping position, it is easier to resent minority "privileges" for Muslims than for other minorities. At 11 percent, Muslims are a more vulnerable target than the proportionately more numerous and politically more powerful "Backwards."

North India's Muslim population was decapitated at independence in 1947, when Muslim landowners and educated professionals, many descendants of Mughal court families, went to Pakistan. They left behind silk weavers in Banaras, gem cutters in Jaipur, poor cultivators and unskilled laborers, hewers of wood and drawers of water. But in recent years Muslims have found new opportunities through migratory labor to the Middle East.

A major component of India's foreign exchange has come from remittances of guest workers in the Gulf, Iraq and other Middle East countries. When several hundred thousand fled the Gulf war in early 1991, the precipitous fall in remittances that followed triggered a foreign exchange crisis that drove India into the arms of the International Monetary Fund and the World Bank. A large proportion of India's guest workers were

(and are again) Muslims. For years they sent their earnings home to poor relatives scattered all over India. Their relatives built fancy houses and mosques cheek by jowl with the ostentatious homes and temples of newly rich Hindu neighbors. As Muslim youths joined the sons of green revolution farmers in sporting jeans and sunglasses, as their parents joined Hindu traders in wearing terry-cotton bush suits and driving Rajiv Gandhi's car of choice, the "Gypsy" off-road vehicle, newly rich Muslims elbowed their way ahead rather than lagging respectfully behind.

Prosperity has also bred resentment and anger among those in North India, Kerala and Bombay accustomed to Muslim invisibility and deference. Hindu professionals and businessmen expect Muslims to serve them as tailors and bakers. Industrial and office workers seeking jobs, better pay or promotions expect them to stick to their traditional occupations—weaving, gem cutting, brass tooling. Hindus often respond to Muslim mobility and wealth by challenging Nehru-style secularism that offers special protection to Islam and Muslims. They decry it as privileging Muslim communalism and stigmatizing Hindu communalism. The Hindu backlash to minority protectionism asks, whose country is this anyway? In Bombay in early January, a month after the destruction of the Babri Masjid, the militantly Hindu, Muslim-hating Shiv Sena acted out the fiery images and language of its campaign videos by torching Muslim homes and shops. The Bombay elite's sense of being in charge and safe in India's most cosmopolitan city was shattered when roving bands searched for Muslim names in elegant apartments along hitherto sacrosanct Marine Drive, Club Road and Malabar Hill.

The prospect that the aspiring poor might receive yet another boost from government action helped precipitate the Ayodhya crisis. In August 1990 Prime Minister Singh's minority government implemented the Mandal Commission report. The report recommended "reservations"—quotas—in federal government employment for Backward Classes. Singh, who had campaigned on the issue, announced that 27 percent of federal jobs were to be reserved for Backward Classes. Together with the current 15 percent for untouchables (those at the bottom of the caste system) and the 7 percent for tribals, roughly their proportions of the population, reservations now totaled 49 percent, a ceiling set by the Supreme Court to maintain the credibility of the equal opportunity clause of the constitution.

Singh's minority government had been held in place by support from a number of left and right parties, including the Hindu-oriented BJP. The BJP leaders, who had not been consulted on the implementation, thought that Singh was ditching their party's support with a view to holding a midterm election that would give him a clear majority. He would appeal to the "minorities"—untouchables, lower castes, Muslims, tribals who together constituted some 60 percent of India's population. The BJP set out to trump Singh's social justice platform, which pitted the disadvantaged against the advantaged, with a Hindu communal unity appeal.

Indian politics began to polarize around *mandir* (temple) versus Mandal. Within a week, anti-Mandal, anti-reservation violence backed by the Congress Party and the BJP began in New Delhi and spread throughout northern India. Upper-caste students, fearful of lost job opportunities, protested the job reservations by blocking traffic, burning buses, forcing shopkeepers to close their businesses and staging immolation rituals that sometimes ended in tragedy. Building on the discontents, BJP president L. K. Advani set out on a 10,000-kilometer chariot pilgrimage to arrive at Ayodhya for the proposed construction of a Ram temple. The country was convulsed as pro- and anti-pilgrimage violence joined anti-reservation violence and refocused attention from Mandal to *mandir*. Advani was arrested on October 23, 1990, and the BJP formally withdrew its support of Singh's government, which fell on November 7. Advani had succeeded in polarizing Indian politics on communal rather than caste-class lines.

The Babri Masjid destruction and the ensuing violence tells us something about the making of "ancient" hatreds: that they are being made in Lebanon, Bosnia, the republics of the former Soviet Union, Iraq, Israel, South-Central Los Angeles and Crown Heights—all those places where neighbors and friends have turned into foreigners and enemies. The enlightenment's vision prophesied human progress, modernization predicted affluence with equality and democracy promised fellow feeling and shared citizenship. Together they foretold a world in which Santa Claus would join the menorah in Hanukkah cards, WASPs eat pizza and Anglos tacos, Muslim performers sing Hindu devotional music and Colin Powell could be chairman of the Joint Chiefs of Staff.

Thinking people are less sanguine about rationality, modernization and democracy reducing ethnic and religious solidarities to harmless dietary differences. Religion has not retreated with increasing media exposure and political participation. The reverse seems to be the case. Religion is on the rise everywhere, from the religious right in Colorado Springs to Islamic fundamentalism in Tehran. It exhibits benign enthusiasm, spiritual exaltation and neo-communitarianism on the one hand, exclusionary and even deadly intolerance on the other. As political ideology recedes with the collapse of communism, the politics of identity and community, of religion, ethnicity and gender have begun to occupy the space vacated by political ideology. Directly and indirectly, religion, ethnicity and gender increasingly define what politics is about, from the standing of Muslim personal law and monuments in India to Muslim and Christian Serbs and Croats sharing sovereignty in Bosnia to the Clinton administration's effort to appoint a government that "looks like America."

Which identities become relevant for politics is not predetermined by some primordial ancientness. They are crafted in benign and malignant ways in print and electronic media, in textbooks and advertising, in India's T.V. megaseries and America's talk shows, in campaign strategies, in all the places and all the ways that self and other, us and them, are represented in an expanding public culture. The struggle in India between Mandal and *mandir*, between quota government and Hindu nationalism, reminds us that in America too the politics of interest is being overtaken by cultural politics, the politics of gender, family values, race and sexual orientation. When T.V. talking heads and op-ed contributors portray "mobs" as "frenzied" and believers as "fanatic," they have given up the task of discerning the human inducements and political calculations that make politics happen. They have given up making motives visible and showing

how they are transformed. "Ancient hatreds" function like the "evil empire." That term too was a projection on a scrim, obscuring the motives and practice that lay behind it. The doctrine of ancient hatreds may become the post-cold war's most robust mystification, a way of having an enemy and knowing evil that deceives as it satisfies. The hatred is modern, and may be closer than we think.

STEPHEN VAN EVERA

Hypotheses on Nationalism and War

Scholars have written widely on the causes of nationalism[1] but said little about its effects, especially its effects on international politics. Most strikingly, the impact of nationalism on the risk of war has barely been explored. Most authors take the war-causing character of nationalism for granted, assuming it without proof or explanation.[2] Factors that govern the size of the dangers posed by nationalism are neglected. What types of nationalism are most likely to cause war? What background conditions catalyze or dampen this causal process? These questions are largely undiscussed, hence the causal nexus between nationalism and war presents an important unsolved riddle.

This article explores that nexus, I define nationalism as a political movement having two characteristics: (1) individual members give their primary loyalty to their own ethnic or national community;[3] this loyalty supersedes their loyalty to other groups, e.g., those based on common kinship or political ideology; and (2) these ethnic or national communities desire their own independent state.[4] I leave the origins of nationalism unexplored, instead focusing on its effects on the risk of

war. Seven questions are addressed: Does nationalism cause war? If so, what types of nationalism are most likely to cause war? How and why do they cause war? What causes these war-causing nationalisms? Under what conditions are they most dangerous? How, if at all, can the war-causing attributes of nationalism be suppressed or neutralized? How large are the risks to peace posed by nationalism in today's Europe, and how can these risks be minimized? In answer I offer unproven hypotheses that I leave untested for now. Our stock of hypotheses on the consequences of nationalism is meager, hence our first order of business should be to expand it. This can set the stage for empirical inquiry by others.

Causes of war or peace can be classified as proximate (causes that directly affect the odds of war) or remote (causes of these proximate causes, or background conditions required for their activation.) I explore proximate causes first, then turn to remote causes. Specifically, the next section of this article identifies varieties of nationalism that are most likely to cause war (including both civil and inter-state war). The section that follows it identifies the causes of these dangerous varieties of nationalism and the conditions that govern the size of the dangers they produce. Twenty-one hypotheses are proposed in all—nine main hypotheses and

From *International Security* 18, no. 4 (spring 1994): 5–39. Most of the author's notes have been omitted.

twelve sub-hypotheses. Some focus on the impact of the environment that surrounds nationalist movements; this environment can incline the movement toward peaceful or toward warlike behavior. Others focus on the impact of the movement's internal character, especially its ideology and vision of history; this, too, can incline the movement toward peace or war. These hypotheses are highlighted because they are deductively sound, survive plausibility probes, and in some cases generate policy prescriptions. They are summarized in Table 1. Viewed together, they suggest that the effects of nationalism are highly varied: some types of nationalism are far more dangerous than other types, all types of nationalism are more dangerous under some conditions than under others, and nationalism can even dampen the risk of war under some conditions.

If accepted, these hypotheses provide a checklist for assessing the dangers posed by a given nationalist movement or by the spread of nationalism in a given region. To illustrate, I use them in the concluding section to assess the risks that nationalism now poses in Europe, because Europe is a region in flux whose future is much debated. This exercise suggests that nationalism poses very little danger of war in Western Europe, but poses large dangers in the East, especially in the former Soviet Union. Current Western European nationalisms are benign, and the conditions required for a return to the malignant nationalisms of 1870–1945 are almost wholly absent. In contrast, many Eastern nationalisms have many (though not all) of the attributes that I argue make nationalism dangerous; hence the risk of large-scale violence stemming from the now-rising tide of Eastern nationalism is substantial.

What prescriptions follow? The character and consequences of nationalism are not written in stone. The Western powers have some capacity to influence the character and consequences of Eastern nationalist movements, and should try to channel it in benign directions. Most importantly, the Western powers should promote full respect for minority rights, democracy, and official respect for historical truth; if Eastern nationalisms adopt these programs, the risks they pose will sharply diminish.

Varieties of Nationalism: Which Cause War?

Four primary attributes of a nationalist movement determine whether it has a large or small potential to produce violence. These are: (1) The movement's political status: is statehood attained or unattained? (2) The movement's stance toward its national diaspora (if it has one): if the movement has a national state, but some members of the nation are dispersed or entrapped beyond the state's borders, does the nation accept continued separation from this diaspora, or does it seek to incorporate the diaspora in the national state? And if it seeks the diaspora's incorporation, will it accomplish this by immigration or by territorial expansion? (3) The movement's stance toward other nations: does it respect or deny other nationalities' right to national independence? (4) The movement's treatment of its own minorities: are these minorities respected or abused?

IS NATIONAL STATEHOOD ATTAINED OR UNATTAINED?

Nationalist movements without states raise greater risks of war because their accommodation requires greater and more disruptive change. Their struggle for national freedom can produce wars of secession, which in turn can widen to become international wars. Their freedom struggle can also injure the interests of other groups, displacing populations whose new grievances sow the seeds of future conflict, as Zionism's displacement of the Palestinian Arabs in 1948 sowed the seeds of later Arab-Israeli wars. Finally, the appearance of new states creates a new, less mature regional international system that lacks "rules of the game" defining the rights and obligations of its members toward one another, and norms of international conduct; these rights, obligations, and norms can take years to define, raising the risk of crises and collisions in the meantime.

The international system tolerates change

Table 1. Hypotheses on Nationalism and War: Summary

I. Immediate Causes

1. The greater the proportion of state-seeking nationalities that are stateless, the greater the risk of war.
2. The more that nationalities pursue the recovery of national diasporas, and the more they pursue annexationist strategies of recovery, the greater the risk of war.
3. The more hegemonistic the goals that nationalities pursue toward one another, the greater the risk of war.
4. The more severely nationalities oppress minorities living in their states, the greater the risk of war.

II. Causes of the Immediate Causes and Conditions Required for Their Operation

Structural Factors:

1. Stateless nationalisms pose a greater risk of war if they have the strength to plausibly reach for freedom, and the central state has the will to resist their attempt.
2. The more densely nationalities are intermingled, the greater the risk of war.
   a. The risks posed by intermingling are larger the more local (house-by-house) rather than regional (province-by-province) the pattern of intermingling.
   b. The risks posed by intermingling are larger if the rescue of diasporas by homelands is difficult but possible; smaller if rescue is either impossible or easy.
3. The greater the defensibility and legitimacy of borders, and the greater the correspondence between these political borders and communal boundaries, the smaller the risk of war.
   a. The less secure and defensible the borders of emerging nation-states, the greater the risk of war.
   b. The greater the international legitimacy of the borders of emerging nation-states, the smaller ther risk of war.
   c. The more closely the boundaries of emerging nation-states follow ethnic boundaries, the smaller the risk of war.

Political/Environmental Factors:

4. The greater the past crimes committed by nationalities toward one another, the greater the risk of war.
   a. The better these crimes are remembered by the victims, the greater the risk of war.
   b. The more that responsibility for past crimes can be attached to groups still on the scene, the greater the risk of war.
   c. The less contrition and repentance shown by the guilty groups, the greater the risk of war.
   d. The greater the coincidence of power and victimhood, the greater the risk of war.
5. The more severely nationalities oppress minorities now living in their states, the greater the risk of war. (This restates Hypothesis No. I.4; I list it twice because it operates as both a direct and a remote cause of war.)

Perceptual Factors:

6. The more divergent are the beliefs of nationalities about their mutual history and their current conduct and character, the greater the risk of war.
   a. The less legitimate the governments or leaders of nationalist movements, the greater their propensity to purvey mythical nationalist beliefs, hence the greater the risk of war.
   b. The more the state must demand of its citizens, the greater its propensity to purvey mythical nationalist beliefs, hence the greater the risk of war.
   c. If economic conditions deteriorate, publics become more receptive to scapegoat myths, hence such myths are more widely believed, hence war is more likely.
   d. If independent evaluative institutions are weak or incompetent, myths will more often prevail, hence war is more likely.

poorly, but the accommodation of new nationalist movements requires it. Thus the first measure of the risks to the peace of a region posed by nationalism is found in the proportion of its nationalist movements that remain unfulfilled in statehood, a factor expressed in the nation-to-state ratio. Are the supply of and demand for states in equilibrium or disequilibrium? Peace in a region is more likely the more closely a supply/demand equilibrium is approached.[5] Modern nationalism disrupted peace over the past two centuries partly because so many of the world's current nationalist movements were stateless at the outset, requiring vast change to accommodate their emergence. Nationalism still threatens peace because its full accommodation would require vast additional change: the number of states in the world has more than tripled since World War II (up from the 50 signers of the UN Charter in 1945, to 180-odd states today), but many nationalities remain stateless; the world has some 6000 language groups,[6] many of which have dormant or manifest aspirations for statehood.

In Western Europe the transition of nations to statehood is largely behind us: that region's remaining stateless nationalities are relatively few and weak. In Eastern Europe and the former Soviet Union, the problem is more serious because the transition to statehood, while largely fulfilled, is still incomplete. The bulk of these stateless nationalities are found in the former Soviet Union; 15 of the 104 nationalities in the former USSR have attained states, but the other 89 have not; these stateless nationalities total 25.6 million people, comprising 10 percent of the former USSR's total population.[7] Most of these nationalities are not potential candidates for statehood (e.g., the Jews) but some might be (e.g., the Tatars, Chechen, Ingush, and Ossetians), and their reach for statehood could sow future friction.

ATTITUDE TOWARD THE NATIONAL DIASPORA: IS PARTIAL OR TOTAL NATIONAL UNITY PURSUED? ARE IMMIGRATIONIST OR EXPANSIONIST TACTICS USED?

Does the nationalist ideology posit that all or only a part of the national ethnic community must be incorporated in the national state? And if the whole nationality must be incorporated, will this be accomplished by immigration (bringing the diaspora to the state) or by territorial expansion (bringing the state to the diaspora)?

These questions suggest a distinction among three types of nationalism: "diaspora-accepting," "immigrationist," and "diaspora-annexing." Some nationalisms (the diaspora-accepting variety) are content with partial union (e.g., Chinese nationalism);[8] such nationalisms are less troublesome because they make fewer territorial demands on their neighbors. Some nationalisms (the immigrationist type) seek to incorporate their diasporas in the national state, but are content to pursue union by seeking immigration of the diaspora (current German nationalism and Zionist Jewish nationalism.) Such immigrationist nationalisms are also easy to accommodate. Finally, some nationalisms seek to incorporate their diasporas by means of territorial expansion (pre-1914 Pan-Germanism and current Pan-Serbianism are examples.) Such diaspora-annexing nationalisms are the most dangerous of the three, since their goals and tactics produce the greatest territorial conflict with others. Thus one scenario for war in the former Soviet Union lies in the possible appearance of a Pan-Russian nationalism that would seek to reincorporate by force the vast Russian diaspora now living in the non-Russian republics. This diaspora includes some 24 million Russians, or 17 percent of all Russians.[9] The future hinges heavily on whether Russian nationalism accepts separation from this diaspora (or seeks to ingather it by immigration), or instead forcibly seeks to annex it.

ATTITUDE TOWARD OTHER INDEPENDENT NATIONALITIES: TOLERANT OR HEGEMONISTIC?

Does the ideology of the nationalism incorporate respect for the freedom of other nationalities, or does it assume a right or duty to rule them? In other words, is the national ideology symmetrical (all nationalities deserve states) or asymmetrical (only our nationality deserves statehood; others should be denied it)?

Hegemonistic, or asymmetrical, nationalism is both the rarest and the most dangerous variety of nationalism. Interwar Nazi nationalism in Germany, fascist nationalism in Mussolini's Italy, and militarist nationalism in imperial Japan illustrate such hegemonistic nationalism; the wars they caused illustrate its results. No European nationalism today displays such hegemonism, but the vast trouble that it caused in the past advises alertness to its possible reappearance in Europe or elsewhere.

THE DEGREE OF NATIONAL RESPECT FOR MINORITY RIGHTS: HIGH OR LOW?

Is the nationalism minority-respecting, or minority-oppressing? A minority-respecting nationalism grants equal rights to other nationalities lying within the boundaries of its claimed state; it may even grant their right to secede and establish their own state. A minority-oppressing nationalism denies such rights to these other nationalities, subjugating them instead. Many of the nationalisms of immigrant nations (American, Anglo-Canadian) have been relatively minority-respecting (in the Canadian case this includes a tacit right to secession, which the Quebecois may soon exercise.) Non-immigrant nationalisms often display far less tolerance for their minorities: prominent current examples include Iraq's and Turkey's oppression of their Kurdish minorities, Bulgaria's oppression of its Turks, China's cruelties in Tibet, Croatia's intolerance toward its Serb minority, and Serbian oppression of its Slavic Moslem and Albanian minorities. Nazi German nationalism was an extreme case of a minority-oppressing nationalism.

The first three attributes—is statehood attained? attitude toward diaspora? attitude toward other independent nationalities?—define the scope of a nationalist movement's claims against others; conversely, the fourth attribute—policy toward minorities?—helps determine the scope of others' claims against the movement. The larger these others' goals become, the more they will collide with the movement's goals, raising the risk of war. Minority-oppressing nationalism can cause war in

two ways: (1) by provoking violent secessions by its captive nations; or (2) by spurring the homelands of these captive nations to move forcefully to free their oppressed co-nationals (as Croatian threats against the Serb minority in Croatia helped spawn the Serb attack on Croatia in 1991). Minority-oppressing nationalism is most dangerous if the oppressed minorities have nearby friends who have the capacity to protect the oppressed nation by force. (The Serbo-Croat war exploded partly because Croatia's Serbs had such a friend in Serbia). The attitude of many nationalisms in Eastern Europe and the former Soviet Union toward their minorities remains undefined, and the future hinges on whether they evolve toward minority respect or oppression.

These four attributes can be used to create a nationalism "danger-scale," expressing the level of danger posed by a given nationalism, or by the spread of nationalism in a given region. If all four attributes are benign, the nationalism poses little danger of war, and may even bolster peace. Specifically, a nationalism is benign if it has achieved statehood; has limited unity goals (i.e., accepts the existence of any unincorporated diaspora) or adopts an immigrationist strategy for ingathering its diaspora; posits no claim to rule other nationalities living beyond its national territory; and respects the rights of minorities found in this territory. Multiplied, such nationalisms may even dampen the risk of war, by making conquest more difficult: where these nationalisms are prevalent, conquest is harder because nation-states are among the most difficult type of state to conquer (since nationalism provides an inspirational liberation doctrine that can be used to mobilize strong popular resistance to conquest).[10] As a result strong states will be deterred from reaching for regional or global hegemony, and will also be less fearful that others might achieve it; hence all states will compete less fiercely with one another. In contrast, a nationalism is bound to collide with others if all four attributes are malign: If the nationalism has no state, the risk of civil war arising from its struggle for national independence is increased; this also raises the risk of inter-state war, since civil war can widen to engulf nearby states. If, after achieving statehood, the nationalism seeks to incorporate a diaspora by force, oppresses minorities found in its claimed national territory, and seeks hegemony over nationalities lying beyond that territory, violence between the nationalism and its neighbors is inevitable.

Causes and Conditions for War-Causing Nationalism

What factors determine whether these four variables will have benign or malignant values? What conditions are required for malignant values to have malignant effects? The deciding factors and conditions are grouped below into three broad families: structural (those arising from the geographic and demographic arrangement of a nation's people); political-environmental (those arising from the past or present conduct of a people's neighbors); and perceptual (those arising from the nationalist movement's self-image and its images of others, including its images of both sides' past and present conduct and character).

STRUCTURAL FACTORS: THE GEOGRAPHIC, DEMOGRAPHIC, AND MILITARY SETTING

The size of the risks posed by nationalism is influenced by the balance of power and of will between stateless nationalisms and the central states that hold them captive; by the degree and pattern of regional ethnic intermingling; by the defensibility and legitimacy of the borders of new national states; and by the correspondence of these borders with ethnic boundaries.

The Domestic Balance of Power and of Will. Unattained nationalisms are more troublesome under two conditions: (1) the movement has the strength to reach plausibly for statehood; and (2) the central state has the will to resist this attempt.

Stateless nationalisms whose statehood is unattainable will lie dormant, their emergence deterred by the power of the central state. Nationalism becomes manifest and can produce war when the power-balance between the central state and the captive nationalism shifts to allow the possibility of successful secession. Thus two safe conditions exist: where national statehood is already attained; and where it is not attained, but clearly cannot be. The danger zone lies between, in cases where statehood has not been attained yet is attainable or appears to be. In this zone we find wars of nationalist secession.[11] Such conflicts can, in turn, grow into international wars: examples include the 1912–14 Balkan secessionist struggles that triggered World War I, and the 1991–92 Serbo-Croatian conflict.

The Third World nationalisms of the twentieth century erupted partly because the spread of small arms and literacy shifted the balance of power in favor of these nationalisms, against their imperial captors. Nationalism emerged because it could. Likewise, nationalism exploded in the former Soviet Union in the late 1980s partly because Soviet central power had waned.

War is inevitable if central states have the will to resist emerging nationalist/secessionist movements, but these movements can win freedom without violence if that will is missing. Many sub-Saharan African states gained freedom in the 1960s without violence because the European colonial powers lost their imperial will. Likewise, the emergence of non-Russian nationalisms in the former Soviet Union was accompanied by (and encouraged by) the loss of imperial will in Moscow; this loss of will at the center allowed the non-Russians to escape the Soviet empire without waging wars of secession. French decolonization was far more violent, spawning large wars in Vietnam and Algeria, because the French metropole retained its will even after nationalism gained momentum in the French empire.

The will of the central state is largely governed by its domestic politics, but is also determined partly by demographic facts. Specifically, central governments can allow secession more easily if secession would leave a homogeneous rump central state, since permitting secession then sets a less damaging precedent. Thus the Czechs could accept Slovak independence without fear of setting a precedent that would trigger another secession, since there is no potential secessionist group in the rump Czech Republic. Likewise, the United States could grant independence to the Philippines fairly easily in 1946 because the United States had few other colonies, and none of these were large or valuable, hence Philippine independence set no dangerous precedents. Conversely, the Austro-Hungarian empire strongly resisted secessions before 1914 because the empire contained many potential secessionists who might be encouraged if any secession were allowed.

The Demographic Arrangement of National Populations: Are They Intermingled or Homogeneous?
Are nationality populations densely intermingled? If they are, does this create large or small national diasporas? Intermingling raises the risk of communal conflict during the struggle for national freedom, as groups that would be trapped as minorities in a new national state oppose its reach for freedom. Dispersion and intermingling will also trap some co-ethnics outside the boundaries of their nation-states; this raises the danger that new nation-states will pursue diaspora-recovering expansionism after they gain statehood, and the possibility that their abuse of minorities will trigger attack from outside.

These dangers are reduced if national populations are compact and homogenous—diasporas and minorities then occur only if political boundaries fail to follow ethnic boundaries. They are intensified if the nationality is dispersed abroad, and intermingled with others at home. The Czechs, for example, can pursue nationalism with little risk to the peace of their neighborhood, because they have no diaspora abroad, and few minorities at home. They need not limit their goals or learn to accommodate minorities. The 1947 partition of India was a far bloodier process than the 1992 Czech-Slovak divorce partly because Hindus and Moslems were far more intermingled than Czechs and Slovaks. The partition of Yugoslavia has been especially violent partly because nationalities in former Yugoslavia are more densely intermingled than any others in Eastern or Western Europe outside the former Soviet Union.[12]

Overall, nationalism poses greater dangers in Eastern than Western Europe because the peoples of Eastern Europe are more densely intermingled. A survey of Eastern Europe reveals roughly a dozen minority group pockets that may seek independence or be claimed by other countries.[13] The ethnographic structure of the former Soviet Union is even more ominous; an ethnographic map of the former USSR reveals massively intermingled nationalities, scattered in scores of isolated pockets, a mosaic far more tangled and complex than any found elsewhere in Europe except the former Yugoslavia.[14]

Two aspects of intermingling determine the size of the dangers it poses: the scope of intermingling, and the pattern of intermingling. All intermingling causes trouble, but some patterns of intermingling cause more trouble than others.

Groups can be intermingled on a regional scale (regions are heterogeneous, small communities are homogeneous) or local scale (even small communities are heterogeneous, as in Sarajevo). Regional intermingling is more easily managed, because inter-group relations can be negotiated by elites. In contrast, elites can lose control of events when intermingling extends to the local level: conflict can flare against the wishes of elites when unofficial killers seize the agenda by sparking a spiral of private violence. Local intermingling can also produce conflict-dampening personal friendships and inter-ethnic marriages, but the Bosnian conflict shows the limits of this tempering effect. Overall, local intermingling is more dangerous.

The most dangerous pattern of regional intermingling is one that leaves elements of one or both groups insecurely at the mercy of the other, but also allows for the possibility of forcible rescue—either by self-rescue (secession) or external rescue (intervention by an already-free homeland).

If rescue is impossible, then the goal of secession or reunion with a homeland will be abandoned. Israel cannot rescue Soviet Jewry, except by immigration, and Ukraine cannot rescue the Ukrainian diaspora in Russia; hence neither considers forceful rescue. This lowers the risk of war.

If rescue is easy, it may not be attempted, since

the threat of rescue is enough to deter abuse of the diaspora. Russia could fairly easily rescue the Russian minority in the Baltics and perhaps elsewhere on the Russian periphery, because much of the Russian diaspora lies clustered near the Russian border, and Russia holds military superiority over its neighbors. These power realities may deter Russia's neighbors from abusing their Russian minorities, leaving Russia more room to take a relaxed attitude.[15]

It is in-between situations—those where rescue is possible, but only under optimal conditions—that are most dangerous. This situation will tempt potential rescuers to jump through any windows of opportunity that arise. Forceful rescue is then driven by both fear and opportunity—fear that later the abuse of diasporas cannot be deterred by threatening to rescue them (since the difficulty of rescue will rob that threat of credibility), and by the opportunity to rescue the diaspora now by force.[16] Thus Serbia would have probably been unable to rescue the Serb diaspora in normal times: Serbia is too weak, and the Serbian diasporas in Croatia and Bosnia are too distant from Serbia. But rescue was feasible if Serbia made the attempt at a moment of peak Serbian military advantage. Such a moment emerged in 1990, after Serbia consolidated the weaponry of the Yugoslav army under its control, but before the Croatian and Bosnian states could organize strong militaries.[17] In contrast, such a moment may never emerge for Russia, because it can always rescue large parts of its diaspora should the need ever arise, leaving less need to seize an early opportunity.

These in-between situations are most troublesome when the diaspora is separated from the homeland by lands inhabited by others: wars of rescue then cause larger injury. In such cases rescue requires cutting a secure corridor through these lands; this, in turn, requires the forcible expulsion of the resident population, with its attendant horrors and cruelties. In 1991 the Serbian diaspora in Croatia and Bosnia was cut off from the Serb homeland by walls of Moslem-inhabited territory, and the vast Serbian cruelties against the Bosnian Moslems during 1992–93 grew mainly

from Serbia's effort to punch corridors through these walls in order to attach these diasporas to Serbia proper. In contrast, more of Russia's diaspora is contiguous to Russia, hence a Russian war of rescue would do relatively less harm to others innocently in the way (though it would still do plenty of harm.)

Borders: Defensibility, Legitimacy, and Border/Ethnic Correspondence. The risks to peace posed by a nationalism's emergence are governed partly by the defensibility and international legitimacy of the nation's borders, and by the degree of correspondence between these political borders and ethnic boundaries.

The satisfaction of national demands for statehood extends international anarchy by creating more states: hence nationalism's effects are governed partly by the character of the extended anarchy that it creates. Some anarchies are relatively peaceful, others more violent. The acuteness of the security dilemma is a key factor governing the answer. Anarchy is a precondition for international war, hence extending anarchy may expand the risk of war, but this is not always the case: the fragmentation of states can deepen peace if it leaves the world with states that are more difficult to conquer, hence are more secure, than the older states from which they were carved. The character of boundaries helps decide the issue: if the new borders are indefensible, the net impact of the creation of new national states will be warlike; if borders are highly defensible, the net impact may be peaceful.

Defensible boundaries reduce the risk of war because they leave new states less anxious to expand for security reasons, while also deterring others from attacking them. The nations of Western Europe can be more peaceful than those of the East because they are endowed with more defensible borders: the French, Spanish, British, Italian, and Scandinavian nations have natural defenses formed by the Alps and the Pyrenees, and by the waters of the English Channel, the Baltic, and the North Sea. Icelandic nationalism is especially unproblematic because geography makes Iceland unusually secure, and almost incapable of attack. In contrast, the nationalities living on the exposed plains of Eastern Europe and western Asia contend with a harsher geography: with few natural barriers to invasion, they are more vulnerable to attack, hence are more tempted to attack others in pre-emptive defense.[18] They are therefore more likely to disturb the status quo, or to be victims of other disturbers.

The international legitimacy of a new nation's borders helps determine the level of danger raised when it gains independence: if borders lack inter-national legitimacy or are unsettled altogether, de-mands for border changes will arise, providing new occasions for conflict. The successor states of the former Soviet Union find themselves with borders drawn by Stalin or other Bolshevik rulers; these have correspondingly small legitimacy. Israel's post-1948 boundaries at first lacked international legitimacy because they had no historical basis, having arisen simply from truce lines expressing the military outcome of the 1948 war. In contrast, the borders of the recently-freed states of Eastern Europe have greater legitimacy because they have firmer grounding in history, and some were the product of earlier international negotiation and agreement.

Borders may bisect nationalities, or may follow national demographic divides. Nation-bisecting borders are more troublesome, because they have the same effect as demographic inter-mingling: they entrap parts of nationalities within the boundaries of states dominated by other ethnic groups, giving rise to expansionism by the trun-cated nation. Thus Hungary's borders bisect (and truncate) the Hungarian nation, giving rise to a (now dormant but still surviving) Hungarian re-vanchism against Slovakia, Serbia, and Rumania. The Russian/Ukrainian border bisects both nation-alities, creating the potential for movements to ad-just borders in both countries.

The borders of new states can arise in two main ways: from violent military struggle (e.g., Israel) or as a result of cession of sovereignty to existing ad-ministrative units whose boundaries were previ-ously defined by the parent multiethnic state (e.g., former Soviet Union). War-born borders often have the advantage of following ethnic lines, because the cruelties of war often cause ethnic cleansing, and offensives lose strength at ethnic boundaries; inherited administrative borders (e.g., the boundaries of Azerbaijan, which entrap the Ar-menians of Nagorno-Karabakh) more often plant the charge of future conflict by dividing nations and creating diasporas. The peaceful dissolution of the former Soviet Union was thus a mixed blessing: its successor states emerged without violence, but with borders that captured unhappy diasporas be-hind them.

POLITICAL/ENVIRONMENTAL FACTORS: HOW HAVE NEIGHBORS BEHAVED? HOW DO THEY NOW BEHAVE?

The conduct of nationalities and nation-states mir-rors their neighbors' past and present conduct.

Past Conduct: Were Great Crimes Committed? The degree of harmony or conflict between inter-mingled nationalities depends partly on the size of the crimes committed by each against the other in the past; the greater these past crimes, the greater the current conflict. Memories of its neigh-bors' cruelties will magnify an emerging nation's impulse to ingather its diaspora, converting the nation from a diaspora-accepting to a diaspora-annexing attitude. Thus the vast Croatian mass-murders of Serbs during the 1940s were the taproot that fed violent pan-Serbianism after 1990: Serbs vowed "never again," and argued that they must incorporate the Serbian diaspora in Croatia to save it from new pogroms. Past suffering can also spur nations to oppress old tormentors who now live among them as minorities, sparking con-flict with these minorities' home countries. Thus the past horrors inflicted on the Baltic peoples by Stalinism fuels their discrimination against their Russian minorities today, this discrimination, in turn, feeds anti-Baltic feeling in Russia. In contrast, non-victim nations are less aggressive toward both neighbors and minorities. Czech nationalism is be-nign partly because the Czechs have escaped real victimhood; Quebec nationalism is mild for the same reason.

Mass murder, land theft, and population expulsions are the crimes that matter most. Past exterminations foster diaspora-recovering ideologies that are justified by self-protection logic. Past land theft fosters territorial definitions of nationhood (e.g., the Israeli Likud's concept of "the Land of Israel," a place including once-Jewish lands that Likud argues were wrongfully taken by others) and claims to land that excludes the rights of peoples now on that land (the Likud rejects equal rights for the Palestinian inhabitants of these once-Jewish lands; Serbs likewise reject equal rights for Albanian Kosovars who Serbs claim wrongfully took Serb land). Past expulsions and dispersions feed diaspora-intolerance: if others created the diaspora, it is argued, then others should pay the price for restoring the diaspora to the nation by making territorial concessions.

The scope of the dangers posed by past crimes is a function, in part, of whether these crimes are remembered, and whether victims can attach responsibility for crimes to groups that are still present. Crimes that have faded in the victims' memories have a less corrosive effect on intergroup relations; thus mayhem that occurred before written records poses fewer problems than more recent crimes that are better-recorded.

Crimes committed by groups still on the scene pose more problems than crimes committed by vanished groups. This, in turn, is a matter of interpretation: who committed the crime in question? Can inherited blame be attached to any present group? Thus the Ukrainians can assess responsibility for Stalin's vast murders of Ukrainians in several ways. Were they committed by a crazed Georgian? This interpretation is benign: it points the finger at a single man who is long gone from the scene. Were they committed by that now-vanished tribe, the Bolsheviks? This interpretation is also benign: those responsible have miraculously disappeared, leaving no target for violence. Or, more ominously, were these the crimes of the Russian empire and the Russian people? This interpretation would guarantee bitter Russian-Ukrainian conflict, because the crimes in question were so enormous, and many of the "criminals"

live in Ukraine,[19] making ready targets for hatred, and setting the stage for a Russian-Ukrainian conflict-spiral. Such a spiral is more likely because Russians would not accept the blame assigned them: they count themselves among the victims, not the perpetrators, of Bolshevism's crimes, and they would view others' demands that they accept blame as a malicious outrage.

The danger posed by past crimes also depends on the criminal group's later behavior: has it apologized or otherwise shown contrition? Or has it shown contempt for its victims' suffering? Nazi Germany's crimes were among the greatest in human history, but Germany has re-established civil relations with its former victims by acknowledging its crimes and showing contrition, e.g., by postwar German leaders' public apologies and symbolic acts of repentance. Conversely, Turkey has denied the great crimes it committed against the Armenian people during World War I;[20] this display of contempt has sustained an Armenian hatred that is still expressed in occasional acts of violent anti-Turkish retribution.

A final significant factor lies in the degree of coincidence of power and victimhood. Are the groups with the greatest historic grievances also the groups with the greatest power today? Or is past victimhood confined to today's weaker groups? Things are more dangerous when power and aggrievement coincide, since this combination brings together both the motive and the capacity to make trouble; when power and aggrievement are separated, grievances have less effects. On this count the past crimes of the Russian and Bolshevik states leave a less dangerous legacy than the crimes committed in the former Yugoslavia during World War II, because the strongest group in the former Soviet Union (the Russians) is the least aggrieved; in contrast, in former Yugoslavia the strongest group (the Serbs) is the most aggrieved.

Current Conduct: Are Minority Rights Respected?
As noted earlier, nations are less diaspora-accepting if others abuse the rights of that diaspora; such abuse magnifies the impulse to incorporate the territory of the diaspora by force.

Thus Serbia's 1991 attack on Croatia was spurred partly by Croatian threats against the Serbian minority.[21] Likewise, Russia's attitude toward the Russian diaspora will be governed partly by the treatment of the Russian diaspora in their new homelands. Oppressive policies will provoke wider Russian aims.

PERCEPTUAL FACTORS: NATIONALIST SELF-IMAGES
AND IMAGES OF OTHERS

The effects of nationalism depend heavily on the beliefs of nationalist movements, especially their self-images and their images of their neighbors. Nations can co-exist most easily when these beliefs converge—when they share a common image of their mutual history, and of one another's current conduct and character. This can be achieved either by common convergence of images on something close to the "truth," or by convergence on the same distortion of the truth. Relations are worst if images diverge in self-justifying directions. This occurs if nations embrace self-justifying historical myths, or adopt distorted pictures of their own and others' current conduct and character that exaggerate the legitimacy of their own cause. Such myths and distortions can expand a nation's sense of its right and its need to oppress its minorities or conquer its diaspora. If carried to extreme such myths can also transform nationalism from symmetrical to asymmetrical—from a purely self-liberating enterprise into a hegemonistic enterprise.

Chauvinist mythmaking is a hallmark of nationalism, practiced by nearly all nationalist movements to some degree. These myths are purveyed through the schools, especially in history teaching; through literature; or by political elites. They come in three principal varieties: self-glorifying, self-whitewashing, and other-maligning. Self-glorifying myths incorporate claims of special virtue and competence, and false claims of past beneficence toward others. Self-whitewashing myths incorporate false denial of past wrongdoing against others. Both types of myths can lead a nation to claim a right to rule others ("we are especially virtuous, so

our expansion benefits those we conquer"). They also lead a nation to view others' complaints against them as expressions of ungrateful malice: ("we have never harmed them; they slander us by claiming otherwise"). This can produce conflict-spirals, as the nation responds to others' legitimate complaints with hostility, in expectation that the claimant knows its claims are illegitimate and will back down if challenged. The targets of this hostility, in turn, will take it as further evidence of the nation's inherent cruelty and injustice. Self-glorifying myth, if it contains claims of cultural superiority, can also feed false faith in one's capacity to defeat and subdue others, causing expansionist wars of optimistic miscalculation.

Other-maligning myth can incorporate claims of others' cultural inferiority, false blame of others for past crimes and tragedies, and false claims that others now harbor malign intentions against the nation. Such myths support arguments for the rightness and necessity of denying equal rights to minorities living in the national territory, and for subjugating peoples further afield. These minorities and distant peoples will appear to pose a danger if they are left unsuppressed; moreover, their suppression is morally justified by their (imagined) misconduct, past and planned.

Self-whitewashing myths are probably the most common of these three varieties. The dangers they pose are proportional to the gravity of the crimes they whitewash. If small crimes are denied, their denial is disrespect that victims can choose to overlook. The denial may even spring from simple ignorance; if so, it conveys little insult. If great crimes are denied, however, their denial conveys contempt for the victims' very humanity. The denial cannot be ascribed to unintended ignorance; if truly great crimes are forgotten, the forgetting is willful, hence it conveys greater insult. And being willful, the denial implies a dismissal of the crime's wrongness, which in turn suggests an ominous willingness to repeat it. As a result, the denial of great crimes provokes greater hostility from the victims than the denial of minor crimes. Thus Croatian historians and politicians who white-washed the Croatian Ustashi's vast murders of

Serbs during World War II were playing with especially powerful dynamite: the crimes they denied were enormous, hence their denial had serious ramifications, feeding Serb hostility that led to the Serbo-Croatian war of 1991–92. Likewise, the question of historical responsibility for Stalin's crimes in the former Soviet Union is especially explosive because the crimes in question are so vast.

Why are myths purveyed? They emanate largely from nationalist political elites, for whom they serve important political functions. Some of these functions also serve the nation as a whole, while others serve only the narrow interests of the elite. Self-glorifying myths encourage citizens to contribute to the national community—to pay taxes, join the army, and fight for the nation's defense. These purposes are hard to fault, although the myths purveyed to achieve them may nevertheless have pernicious side-effects. Myths also bolster the authority and political power of incumbent elites: self-glorifying and self-whitewashing myths allow elites to shine in the reflected luster of their predecessors' imagined achievements and the imagined glory of the national institutions they control; other-maligning myths bolster the authority of elites by supporting claims that the nation faces external threats, thus deflecting popular hostility away from national elites and toward outsiders. Myths that serve only these purposes injure intercommunal relations without providing countervailing benefits to the general community.

Although mythmaking is ubiquitous among nationalisms, the scope and character of mythmaking varies widely across nations. Myths flourish most when elites need them most, when opposition to myths is weakest, and when publics are most myth-receptive. Four principal factors govern the level of infection by nationalist myth:

The Legitimacy of the Regime (or, if the national movement remains stateless, the legitimacy of the movement's leaders). As just noted, nationalist myths can help politically frail elites to bolster their grip on power. The temptation for elites to engage in mythmaking is therefore inversely proportional to their political legitimacy: the less legitimate their rule, the greater their incentive to make myths.

A regime's legitimacy is in turn a function of its representativeness, its competence and efficiency, and the scope of the tasks that face it. Unrepresentative regimes will face challenge from underrepresented groups, and will sow myths to build the support needed to defeat this challenge. This motive helped fuel the extreme nationalism that swept Europe in the late nineteenth century: oligarchic regimes used chauvinist myths, often spread through the schools, to deflect demands from below for a wider sharing of political and economic power. Corrupt regimes or regimes that lack competence due to underinstitutionalization will likewise deploy chauvinist myths to divert challenges from publics and elites. This is a common motive for mythmaking in the Third World. Finally, regimes that face overwhelming tasks—e.g., economic or social collapse, perhaps caused by exogenous factors—will be tempted to use myths to divert popular impatience with their inability to improve conditions. Thus the Great Depression fueled nationalist mythmaking in some industrial states during the 1930s.

These factors correlate closely with the ebb and flow of nationalist mythmaking through history. Nationalist mythmaking reached high tide in Europe when Europe's regimes had little legitimacy, during 1848–1914. It then fell dramatically as these regimes democratized and their societies became less stratified, which greatly lessened popular challenge to elites.

The Scope of the Demands Posed by the State on its Citizenry. The more the regime asks of its citizens, the harder it must work to persuade its citizens to fulfill these demands; this increases its temptation to deploy nationalist myths for purposes of social mobilization. Regimes at war often use myths to motivate sacrifice by their citizens and to justify their cruelties against others. These myths can live on after the war to poison external relations in later years. Mass revolutionary movements often infuse their movements with mythical propaganda for the same reason; these myths survive after the revolution is won. Regimes that are forced by external threats to sustain large peacetime military efforts are likewise driven to use myths to sustain popular support. This is especially true if they rely on mass armies for their defense. Finally, totalitarian regimes place large demands on their citizens, and use correspondingly large doses of myth to induce their acquiescence.

Domestic Economic Crisis. In societies suffering economic collapse, mythmaking can take scapegoating form—the collapse is falsely blamed on domestic or international malefactors. Here the mythmaking grows from increased receptivity of the audience: publics are more willing to believe that others are responsible when they are actually suffering pain; when that pain is new and surprising, they search for the hand of malevolent human agents. Germany in the 1930s is the standard example.

The Strength and Competence of Independent Evaluative Institutions. Societies that lack free-speech traditions, a strong free press, and free universities are more vulnerable to mythmaking because they lack "truth squads" to counter the nationalist mythmakers. Independent historians can provide an antidote to official historical mythmaking; an independent press is an antidote to official mythmaking about current events. Their absence is a permissive condition for nationalist mythmaking. Wilhelmine Germany illustrates: the German academic community failed to counter the official myths of the era, and often helped purvey them.

Several conclusions follow from this discussion. Democratic regimes are less prone to mythmaking, because such regimes are usually more legitimate and are free-speech tolerant; hence they can develop evaluative institutions to weed out nationalist myth. Absolutist dictatorships that possess a massive military superiority over their citizens are also less prone to mythmaking, because they can survive without it. The most dangerous regimes are those that depend on some measure of popular consent, but are narrowly governed by unrepresentative elites. Things are still worse if these governments are poorly institutionalized, are in-

competent or corrupt for other reasons, or face overwhelming problems that exceed their governing capacities. Regimes that emerged from a violent struggle, or enjoy only precarious security, are also more likely to retain a struggle-born chauvinist belief-system.

Conclusion: Predictions and Prescriptions

What predictions follow? These hypotheses can be used to generate forecasts; applied to Europe, they predict that nationalism will pose little risk to peace in Western Europe, but large risks in Eastern Europe.

Most of the nationalisms of the West are satisfied, having already gained states. Western diasporas are few and small, reflecting the relative homogeneity of Western national demography, and Western minorities are relatively well-treated. The historic grievances of Western nationalities against one another are also small—many of the West's inter-ethnic horrors have faded from memory, and the perpetrators of the greatest recent horror—the Germans—have accepted responsibility for it and reconciled with their victims. The regimes of the West are highly legitimate, militarily secure, and economically stable; hence chauvinist mythmaking by their elites is correspondingly rare. The West European nationalisms that caused the greatest recent troubles, those of Germany and Italy, are now clearly benign, and the conditions for a return to aggressive nationalism are absent in both countries. Outsiders sometimes fear that outbreaks of anti-immigrant extremism in Germany signal the return of German fascism, but the forces of tolerance and decency are overwhelmingly dominant in Germany, and the robust health of German democracy and of German academic and press institutions ensures they will remain dominant. As a result nationalism should cause very little trouble in Western Europe.

In the East the number of stateless nationalisms is larger, raising greater risk that future conflicts will arise from wars of liberation. The collapse of Soviet power shifted the balance of power toward these nationalisms, by replacing the Soviet state with weaker successor states. This shift has produced secessionist wars in Georgia and Moldova, and such wars could multiply. The tangled pattern of ethnic intermingling across the East creates large diasporas. Eastern societies have little tradition of respect for minority rights, raising the likelihood that these diasporas will face abuse; this in turn may spur their homelands to try to incorporate them by force. The borders of many emerging Eastern nations lack natural defensive barriers, leaving the state exposed to attack; some borders also lack legitimacy, and correspond poorly with ethnic boundaries. Some new Eastern regimes, especially those in the former Soviet Union, lack legitimacy and are under-institutionalized, raising the risk that they will resort to chauvinist mythmaking to maintain their political viability. This risk is heightened by the regional economic crisis caused by the transition from command to market economies. Evaluative institutions (free universities and a free press) remain weak in the East, raising the risk that myths will go unchallenged. The Soviet regime committed vast crimes against its subject peoples; this legacy will embitter relations among these peoples if they cannot agree on who deserves the blame.

The Eastern picture is not all bleak. The main preconditions for democracy—high levels of literacy, some degree of industrial development, and the absence of a landed oligarchy—exist across most of the East. As a result the long-term prospects for democracy are bright. Moreover, the East's economic crisis is temporary: the conditions for prosperous industrial economies (a trained workforce and adequate natural resources) do exist, so the crisis should ease once the market transition is completed. These relatively favorable long-term prospects for democracy and prosperity dampen the risk that chauvinist mythmaking will get out of hand. The fact that the new Eastern states managed to gain freedom without violent struggles also left them with fewer malignant beliefs, by allowing them to forgo infusing their societies with chauvinist war propaganda. The power and ethnographic structures of the East, while dan-

gerous, are less explosive than those of Yugoslavia: historic grievances and military power coincide less tightly—there is no other Eastern equivalent of Serbia, having both military superiority and large historical grievances; and ethnographic patterns create less imperative for a diaspora-rescue operation by the state most likely to attempt such a rescue, Russia.

All in all, however, conditions in Eastern Europe are more bad than good; hence nationalism will probably produce a substantial amount of violence in the East over the next several decades.

What policy prescriptions follow? The Western powers should move to dampen the risks that nationalism poses in the East, by moving to channel manipulable aspects of Eastern nationalism in benign directions. Some aspects of Eastern nationalist movements are immutable (e.g., their degree of intermingling, or the history of crimes between them). Others, however, can be decided by the movements themselves (e.g., their attitude toward minorities, their vision of history, and their willingness to reach final border settlements with others); these can be influenced by the West if the movements are susceptible to Western pressure or persuasion. The Western powers should use their substantial economic leverage to bring such pressure to bear.

Specifically, the Western powers should condition their economic relations with the new Eastern states on these states' conformity with a code of peaceful conduct that proscribes policies that make nationalism dangerous. The code should have six elements: (1) renunciation of the threat or use of force; (2) robust guarantees for the rights of national minorities, to include, under some stringent conditions, a legal right to secession; (3) commitment to the honest teaching of history in the schools, and to refrain from the propagation of chauvinist or other hate propaganda; (4) willingness to adopt a democratic form of government, and to accept related institutions—specifically, free speech and a free press; (5) adoption of market economic policies, and disavowal of protectionist or other beggar-thy-neighbor economic policies toward other Eastern states; and (6) acceptance of current national borders, or agreement to settle contested borders promptly through peaceful means. This list rests on the premise that "peaceful conduct" requires that nationalist movements renounce the use of force against others (element 1), and also agree to refrain from policies that the hypotheses presented here warn against (elements 2–6).

Hypothesis I.4 (see Table 1) warns that the risk of war rises when nationalist movements oppress their minorities; hence the code requires respect for minority rights (element 2). Hypothesis II.6 warns that divergent beliefs about mutual history and current conduct and character raise the risk of war; hence the code asks for historical honesty and curbs on official hate propaganda (element 3). Hypothesis II.6.a warns that illegitimate governments have a greater propensity to mythmake, and hypothesis II.6.d warns that chauvinist myths prevail more often if independent evaluative institutions are weak; hence the code asks that movements adopt democracy (to bolster legitimacy) and respect free speech and free press rights (to bolster evaluation) (element 4). Hypothesis II.6.c warns that economic collapse promotes chauvinist mythmaking; hence the code asks movements to adopt market reforms, on grounds that prosperity requires marketization (element 5). Hypothesis II.3.b warns that the risk of war rises if the borders of emerging nation states lack legitimacy; hence the code asks movements to legitimize their borders through formal non-violent settlement (element 6).

The Western powers should enforce this code by pursuing a common economic policy toward the states of the East: observance of the code should be the price for full membership in the Western economy, while non-observance should bring exclusion and economic sanctions. This policy should be married to an economic aid package to assist marketization, also conditioned on code observance.

The Bush and Clinton administrations have adopted elements of this policy, but omitted key aspects. In September 1991, then–Secretary of State James Baker outlined five principles that in-

corporate most of the six elements in the code of conduct outlined above (only element 3—honest treatment of history—was unmentioned), and he indicated that American policy toward the new Eastern states would be conditioned on their acceptance of these principles. During the spring and summer of 1992 the administration also proposed a substantial economic aid package (the Freedom Support Act) and guided it through Congress.

However, Baker's principles later faded from view. Strangely, the Bush administration failed to clearly condition release of its aid package on Eastern compliance with these principles. It also failed to forge a common agreement among the Western powers to condition their economic relations with the Eastern states on these principles. The principles themselves were not elaborated; most importantly, the minority rights that the Eastern states must protect were not detailed, leaving these states free to adopt a watered-down definition. The Bush administration also recognized several new Eastern governments (e.g., Azerbaijan's) that gave Baker's principles only lip service while violating them in practice. The Clinton administration has largely followed in Bush's footsteps: it continued Bush's aid program, but omitted clear political conditions.

There is still time for such a policy, but the clock is running out. A policy resting on economic sticks and carrots will be too weak to end major violence once it begins; hence the West should therefore move to avert trouble while it still lies on the horizon.

NOTES

1. A survey is Anthony D. Smith, *Theories of Nationalism*, 2nd ed. (New York: Harper & Row, 1983). Prominent recent works include: Ernest Gellner, *Nations and Nationalism* (Ithaca: Cornell University Press, 1983); Anthony D. Smith, *The Ethnic Origins of Nations* (Oxford: Basil Blackwell, 1986); E.J. Hobsbawm, *Nations and Nationalism Since 1780* (New York: Cambridge University Press, 1990); Benedict

Anderson, *Imagined Communities: Reflections on the Origin and Spread of Nationalism*, rev. ed. (London: Verso, 1991); Liah Greenfeld, *Nationalism: Five Roads to Modernity* (Cambridge: Harvard University Press, 1992); and Barry R. Posen, "Nationalism, the Mass Army, and Military Power," *International Security*, Vol. 18, No. 2 (Fall 1993), pp. 80–124. * * *

2. * * * [T]he entry under "Nationalism and War" in Louis Snyder's 435-page *Encyclopedia of Nationalism* fills only two pages, and its bibliography lists no works focused on the topic. Louis L. Snyder, *Encyclopedia of Nationalism* (New York: Paragon, 1990), pp. 248–250. * * *

3. My usage of "ethnic community" follows Anthony Smith, who suggests that an ethnic community has six characteristics: a common name, a myth of common ancestry, shared memories, a common culture, a link with a historic territory or homeland (which it may or may not currently occupy), and a measure of common solidarity. See Smith, *Ethnic Origins of Nations*, pp. 22–30. Summarizing Smith nicely is Michael E. Brown, "Causes and Implications of Ethnic Conflict," in Brown, ed., *Ethnic Conflict and International Security*, pp. 3–26 at 4–5.

Smith's second criteria (myth of common ancestry) would exclude immigrant societies of diverse origin that have developed the other five characteristics of ethnic community, such as the immigrant peoples of the United States, Cuba, Argentina, Chile, and Brazil. However, the common usage of "nation" and "nationalism" includes these groups as nations that can have a nationalism, e.g., "American nationalism," "Argentine nationalism," "Chilean nationalism." I define nationalism as a movement of a "national community" as well as an "ethnic community" in order to include these nationalisms. My usage of "national" follows the *Dictionary of the Social Sciences*, which defines "nation" as "the largest society of people united by a common culture and consciousness," and which "occupies a common territory." Julius Gould and William L. Kolb,

eds., *A Dictionary of the Social Sciences* (New York: Free Press of Glencoe, 1964), p. 451.

4. The academic literature defines nationalism in an annoyingly wide range of ways. My definition follows no other exactly, but it amalgamates the more prominent definitions: each of these include at least one element of my definition, that prime loyalty is owed to one's ethnic/culture group, and/or that the group to which prime loyalty is given should have its own state. My usage most closely follows Rupert Emerson and Richard Cottam, who define nationalism (in Cottam's words) as "a belief on the part of a large group of people that they comprise a community, a nation, that is entitled to independent statehood, and a willingness of this group to grant their community a primary and terminal loyalty"; quoted in Shafer, *Faces of Nationalism* [New York: Harcourt Brace Jovanovich, 1972], p. 4. Similar is Hans Kohn, whose nationalists give "supreme loyalty" to their own nationality, and who see "the nation-state as the ideal form of political organization." Ibid. Also similar are E.J. Hobsbawm and Ernest Gellner, who define nationalism as "primarily a principle which holds that the political and national unit should be congruent." Hobsbawm, *Nations and Nationalism since 1780*, p. 9, quoting and adopting Gellner's definition. However, their definition, by describing nationalism as an idea holding that states and nationalities should be coterminous, omits the many nationalisms that would claim their own state while also denying the statehood aspirations of other nationalities, and also omits more modest nationalisms that are content to allow a diaspora beyond their state borders.

5. Wars can result from having too many states, as well as too few. If states are too many, wars of national unification will result, as they did in Germany and Italy in the nineteenth century, and as they might someday in the Arab world. In Europe, however, the problem everywhere is an excess of demand for states over the supply.

6. Alan Thein Durning, *Guardians of the Land: Indigenous Peoples and the Health of the Earth*, Worldwatch Paper No. 112 (Washington, D.C.: Worldwatch Institute, December 1992), p. 9. Durning reports that measured by spoken languages the world has 6000 cultures. Of these some 4000–5000 are indigenous, and comprise some 10 percent of the world's population. * * *

7. These figures are for 1979, and are calculated from John L. Scherer, ed., *USSR Facts and Figures Annual*, Vol. 5 (Gulf Breeze, Fla.: Academic International Press, 1981), pp. 51–52. Of these stateless groups the ten largest are the Tatar (6.3 million), German (1.9 million), Jewish (1.8 million), Chuvash (1.8 million), Dagestan (1.7 million), Bashkir (1.4 million), Mordvin (1.2 million), Polish (1.2 million), Chechen (.8 million), and Udmurt (.7 million).

8. The Chinese state has historically left the overseas Chinese to their own political devices. John E. Wills, "Maritime Asia, 1500–1800: The Interactive Emergence of European Domination," *American Historical Review*, Vol. 98, No. 1 (February 1993), pp. 83–105, at p. 87.

9. Calculated from Scherer, *USSR Facts and Figures Annual*, pp. 49–51.

10. On the greater peacefulness of a defense-dominant world, see Robert Jervis, "Cooperation Under the Security Dilemma," *World Politics*, Vol. 30, No. 2 (January 1978), pp. 167–214.

11. Overall, then, three variables matter: (1) the supply of states; (2) the demand for states; (3) the capacity of submerged nations to acquire states. * * *

12. Moreover, Yugoslavia's one easy secession—that of Slovenia—was easy because the Slovene population was not intermingled with others. * * *

13. These include Hungarians in Romania, Slovakia, and Serbia; Poles in Lithuania, Belarus, Ukraine, and the Czech Republic; Germans in Poland and the Czech Republic; Turks in Bulgaria; Greeks in Albania; Albanians in Serbia and Macedonia; Croats in Bosnia-Herzegovina; and Serbs in Croatia and Bosnia-Herzegovina. Summaries include F. Stephen Larrabee, "Long Memories and Short Fuses: Change and Instability in the Balkans," *International Security*, Vol. 15, No. 3 (Winter 1990/91), pp. 58–91; Istvan Deak, "Uncovering Eastern Europe's Dark History," *Orbis*, Vol. 34, No. 1 (Winter 1989), pp. 51–65. * * *

14. Overall, 16 percent of the titular peoples of the 15 successor states of the former Soviet Union, totalling 39 million people, live outside their home states ("titular peoples": the peoples after whom republics are named, e.g., Armenians, Kazakhs, Russians, etc.). * * *

15. Making this argument is Posen, "The Security Dilemma and Ethnic Conflict," [*Survival*, Vol. 35, No. 1 (Spring 1993),] pp. 32–35.

16. See Posen, "The Security Dilemma and Ethnic Conflict," pp. 32–38.

17. The intensification of fighting between Armenia and Azerbaijan in 1991–92 had similar origins: Armenia moved to free Nagorno-Karabakh at a moment that Armenia's power relative to Azerbaijan's was at its peak.

18. Likewise, Germany has produced the most troublesome Western nationalism partly because German borders are relatively exposed.

19. Ukraine contains 10.5 million Russians, 21 percent of its total population. Calculated from Scherer, *USSR Facts and Figures Annual*, p. 49.

20. On Turkish denial of these murders see Roger W. Smith, "The Armenian Genocide: Memory, Politics, and the Future," in Richard G. Hovannisian, ed. *The Armenian Genocide: History, Politics, Ethics* (New York: St. Martin's, 1992), pp. 1–20. * * *

21. Glenny, "The Massacre of Yugoslavia," [*New York Review of Books*, January 30, 1992,] pp. 30–31; and Glenny, *The Fall of Yugoslavia* [*The Third Balkan War* (London: Penguin, 1992)], pp. 12–14, 123.

BARRY R. POSEN

The Security Dilemma and Ethnic Conflict

The end of the Cold War has been accompanied by the emergence of nationalist, ethnic and religious conflict in Eurasia. However, the risks and intensity of these conflicts have varied from region to region: Ukrainians and Russians are still getting along relatively well; Serbs and Slovenians had a short, sharp clash; Serbs, Croats and Bosnian Muslims have waged open warfare; and Armenians and Azeris seem destined to fight a slow-motion attrition war. The claim that newly released, age-old antipathies account for this violence fails to explain the considerable variance in observable intergroup relations.

The purpose of this article is to apply a basic concept from the realist tradition of international relations theory, "the security dilemma," to the special conditions that arise when proximate groups of people suddenly find themselves newly responsible for their own security. A group suddenly compelled to provide its own protection must ask the following questions about any neighbouring group: is it a threat? How much of a threat? Will the threat grow or diminish over time? Is there anything that must be done immediately? The answers to these questions strongly influence the chances for war.

This article assesses the factors that could produce an intense security dilemma when imperial order breaks down, thus producing an early resort to violence. The security dilemma is then employed to analyse * * * the break-up of Yugoslavia * * * to illustrate its utility. Finally, some actions are suggested to ameliorate the tendency towards violence.

From *Survival* 35, no. 1 (spring 1993): 27–47. Some of the author's notes have been omitted.

The Security Dilemma

The collapse of imperial regimes can be profitably viewed as a problem of "emerging anarchy." The longest standing and most useful school of international relations theory—realism—explicitly addresses the consequences of anarchy—the absence of a sovereign—for political relations among states.[1] In areas such as the former Soviet Union and Yugoslavia, "sovereigns" have disappeared. They leave in their wake a host of groups—ethnic, religious, cultural—of greater or lesser cohesion. These groups must pay attention to the first thing that states have historically addressed—the problem of security—even though many of these groups still lack many of the attributes of statehood.

Realist theory contends that the condition of anarchy makes security the first concern of states. It can be otherwise only if these political organizations do not care about their survival as independent entities. As long as some do care, there will be competition for the key to security—power. The competition will often continue to a point at which the competing entities have amassed more power than needed for security and, thus, consequently begin to threaten others. Those threatened will respond in turn.

Relative power is difficult to measure and is often subjectively appraised; what seems sufficient to one state's defence will seem, and will often be, offensive to its neighbours. Because neighbours wish to remain autonomous and secure, they will react by trying to strengthen their own positions. States can trigger these reactions even if they have no expansionist inclinations. This is the security dilemma: what one does to enhance one's own security causes reactions that, in the end, can make one less secure. Cooperation among states to mute these competitions can be difficult because someone else's "cheating" may leave one in a militarily weakened position. All fear betrayal.

Often statesmen do not recognize that this problem exists: they do not empathize with their neighbours; they are unaware that their own actions can seem threatening. Often it does not matter if they know of this problem. The nature of their situation compels them to take the steps they do.

The security dilemma is particularly intense when two conditions hold. First, when offensive and defensive military forces are more or less identical, states cannot signal their defensive intent—that is, their limited objectives—by the kinds of military forces they choose to deploy. Any forces on hand are suitable for offensive campaigns. For example, many believe that armoured forces are the best means of defence against an attack by armoured forces. However, because armour has a great deal of offensive potential, states so outfitted cannot distinguish one another's intentions. They must assume the worst because the worst is possible.

A second condition arises from the effectiveness of the offence versus the defence. If offensive operations are more effective than defensive operations, states will choose the offensive if they wish to survive. This may encourage pre-emptive war in the event of a political crisis because the perceived superiority of the offensive creates incentives to strike first whenever war appears likely. In addition, in the situation in which offensive capability is strong, a modest superiority in numbers will appear to provide greatly increased prospects for military success. Thus, the offensive advantage can cause preventive war if a state achieves a military advantage, however fleeting.

The barriers to cooperation inherent in international politics provide clues to the problems that arise as central authority collapses in multi-ethnic empires. The security dilemma affects relations among these groups, just as it affects relations among states. Indeed, because these groups have

the added problem of building new state structures from the wreckage of old empires, they are doubly vulnerable.

Here it is argued that the process of imperial collapse produces conditions that make offensive and defensive capabilities indistinguishable and make the offence superior to the defence. In addition, uneven progress in the formation of state structures will create windows of opportunity and vulnerability. These factors have a powerful influence on the prospects for conflict, regardless of the internal politics of the groups emerging from old empires. Analysts inclined to the view that most of the trouble lies elsewhere, either in the specific nature of group identities or in the short-term incentives for new leaders to "play the nationalist card" to secure their power, need to understand the security dilemma and its consequences. Across the board, these strategic problems show that very little nationalist rabble-rousing or nationalistic combativeness is required to generate very dangerous situations.

THE INDISTINGUISHABILITY OF OFFENCE AND DEFENCE

Newly independent groups must first determine whether neighbouring groups are a threat. They will examine one another's military capabilities to do so. Because the weaponry available to these groups will often be quite rudimentary, their offensive military capabilities will be as much a function of the quantity and commitment of the soldiers they can mobilize as the particular characteristics of the weapons they control. Thus, each group will have to assess the other's offensive military potential in terms of its cohesion and its past military record.

The nature of military technology and organization is usually taken to be the main factor affecting the distinguishability of offence and defence. Yet, clear distinctions between offensive and defensive capabilities are historically rare, and they are particularly difficult to make in the realm of land warfare. For example, the force structures of armed neutrals such as Finland, Sweden and Switzerland are often categorized as defensive.

These countries rely more heavily on infantry, which is thought to have weak offensive potential, than on tanks and other mechanized weaponry, which are thought to have strong offensive potential. However, their weak offensive capabilities have also been a function of the massive military power of what used to be their most plausible adversary, the former Soviet Union. Against states of similar size, similarly armed, all three countries would have considerable offensive capabilities—particularly if their infantries were extraordinarily motivated—as German and French infantry were at the outset of World War I, as Chinese and North Vietnamese infantry were against the Americans and as Iran's infantry was against the Iraqis.

Ever since the French Revolution put the first politically motivated mass armies into the field, strong national identity has been understood by both scholars and practitioners to be a key ingredient of the combat power of armies.[2] A group identity helps the individual members cooperate to achieve their purposes. When humans can readily cooperate, the whole exceeds the sum of the parts, creating a unit stronger relative to those groups with a weaker identity. Thus, the "groupness" of the ethnic, religious, cultural and linguistic collectivities that emerge from collapsed empires gives each of them an inherent offensive military power.

The military capabilities available to newly independent groups will often be less sophisticated; infantry-based armies will be easy to organize, augmented by whatever heavier equipment is inherited or seized from the old regime. Their offensive potential will be stronger the more cohesive their sponsoring group appears to be. Particularly in the close quarters in which these groups often find themselves, the combination of infantry-based, or quasi-mechanized, ground forces with strong group solidarity is likely to encourage groups to fear each other. Their capabilities will appear offensive.

The solidarity of the opposing group will strongly influence how each group assesses the magnitude of the military threat of the others. In general, however, it is quite difficult to perform such assessments. One expects these groups to be "exclusive" and, hence, defensive. Frenchmen generally do not want to turn Germans into Frenchmen, or the reverse. Nevertheless, the drive for security in one group can be so great that it produces near-genocidal behaviour towards neighbouring groups. Because so much conflict has been identified with "group" identity throughout history, those who emerge as the leaders of any group and who confront the task of self-defence for the first time will be sceptical that the strong group identity of others is benign.

What methods are available to a newly independent group to assess the offensive implications of another's sense of identity?[3] The main mechanism that they will use is history: how did other groups behave the last time they were unconstrained? Is there a record of offensive military activity by the other? Unfortunately, the conditions under which this assessment occurs suggest that these groups are more likely to assume that their neighbours are dangerous than not.

The reason is that the historical reviews that new groups undertake rarely meet the scholarly standards that modern history and social science hold as norms (or at least as ideals) in the West. First, the recently departed multi-ethnic empires probably suppressed or manipulated the facts of previous rivalries to reinforce their own rule; the previous regimes in the Soviet Union and Yugoslavia lacked any systemic commitment to truth in historical scholarship. Second, the members of these various groups no doubt did not forget the record of their old rivalries; it was preserved in oral history. This history was undoubtedly magnified in the telling and was seldom subjected to critical appraisal. Third, because their history is mostly oral, each group has a difficult time divining another's view of the past. Fourth, as central authority begins to collapse and local politicians begin to struggle for power, they will begin to write down their versions of history in political speeches. Yet, because the purpose of speeches is domestic political mobilization, these stories are likely to be emotionally charged.

The result is a worst-case analysis. Unless proven otherwise, one group is likely to assume that another group's sense of identity, and the cohesion that it produces, is a danger. Proving it to be otherwise is likely to be very difficult. Because the cohesion of one's own group is an essential means of defence against the possible depredations of neighbours, efforts to reinforce cohesion are likely to be undertaken. Propagandists are put to work writing a politicized history of the group, and the mass media are directed to disseminate that history. The media may either willingly, or under compulsion, report unfolding events in terms that magnify the threat to the group. As neighbouring groups observe this, they do the same.

In sum, the military capability of groups will often be dependent on their cohesion, rather than their meagre military assets. This cohesion is a threat in its own right because it can provide the emotional power for infantry armies to take the offensive. An historical record of large-scale armed clashes, much less wholesale mistreatment of unarmed civilians, however subjective, will further the tendency for groups to see other groups as threats. They will all simultaneously "arm"—militarily and ideologically—against each other.

THE SUPERIORITY OF OFFENSIVE OVER
DEFENSIVE ACTION

Two factors have generally been seen as affecting the superiority of offensive over defensive action—technology and geography. Technology is usually treated as a universal variable, which affects the military capabilities of all the states in a given competition. Geography is a situational variable, which makes offence particularly appealing to specific states for specific reasons. This is what matters most when empires collapse.

In the rare historical cases in which technology has clearly determined the offence-defence balance, such as World War I, soldiers and statesmen have often failed to appreciate its impact. Thus, technology need not be examined further, with one exception: nuclear weapons. If a group inherits a nuclear deterrent, and its neighbours do as well, "groupness" is not likely to affect the security dilemma with as much intensity as would be the case in non-nuclear cases. Because group solidarity would not contribute to the ability of either side to mount a counterforce nuclear attack, nationalism is less important from a military standpoint in a nuclear relationship.

Political geography will frequently create an "offence-dominant world" when empires collapse. Some groups will have greater offensive capabilities because they will effectively surround some or all of the other groups. These other groups may be forced to adopt offensive strategies to break the ring of encirclement. Islands of one group's population are often stranded in a sea of another. Where one territorially concentrated group has "islands" of settlement of its members distributed across the nominal territory of another group (irredenta), the protection of these islands in the event of hostile action can seem extremely difficult. These islands may not be able to help one another; they may be subject to blockade and siege, and by virtue of their numbers relative to the surrounding population and because of topography, they may be militarily indefensible. Thus, the brethren of the stranded group may come to believe that only rapid offensive military action can save their irredenta from a horrible fate.[4]

The geographic factor is a variable, not a constant. Islands of population can be quite large, economically autonomous and militarily defensible. Alternatively, they can have large numbers of nearby brethren who form a powerful state, which could rescue them in the event of trouble. Potentially, hostile groups could have islands of another group's people within their states; these islands could serve as hostages. Alternatively, the brethren of the "island" group could deploy nuclear weapons and thus punish the surrounding group if they misbehave. In short, it might be possible to defend irredenta without attacking or to deter would-be aggressors by threatening to retaliate in one way or another.

Isolated ethnic groups—ethnic islands—can produce incentives for preventive war. Theorists argue that perceived offensive advantages make preventive war more attractive: if one side has an advantage that will not be present later and if security can best be achieved by offensive military action in any case, then leaders will be inclined to attack during this "window of opportunity."[5] For example, if a surrounding population will ultimately be able to fend off relief attacks from the home territory of an island group's brethren, but is currently weak, then the brethren will be inclined to attack sooner rather than later.

In disputes among groups interspersed in the same territory, another kind of offensive advantage exists—a tactical offensive advantage. Often the goal of the disputants is to create ever-growing areas of homogeneous population for their brethren. Therefore, the other group's population must be induced to leave. The Serbs have introduced the term "ethnic cleansing" to describe this objective, a term redolent with the horrors of 50 years earlier. The offence has tremendous tactical military advantages in operations such as these. Small military forces directed against unarmed or poorly armed civilians can generate tremendous terror. This has always been true, of course, but even simple modern weapons, such as machine guns and mortars, increase the havoc that small bands of fanatics can wreak against the defenceless: Consequently, small bands of each group have an incentive to attack the towns of the other in the hopes of driving the people away.[6] This is often quite successful, as the vast populations of war refugees in the world today attest.

The vulnerability of civilians makes it possible for small bands of fanatics to initiate conflict. Because they are small and fanatical, these bands are hard to control. (This allows the political leadership of the group to deny responsibility for the actions those bands take.) These activities produce disproportionate political results among the opposing group—magnifying initial fears by confirming them. The presence or absence of small gangs of fanatics is thus itself a key determinant of the ability of groups to avoid war as central political authority erodes. Although almost every society produces small numbers of people willing to engage in violence at any given moment, the rapid emergence of organized bands of particularly violent individuals is a sure sign of trouble.

The characteristic behaviour of international organizations, especially the United Nations (UN), reinforces the incentives for offensive action. Thus far, the UN has proven itself unable to anticipate conflict and provide the credible security guarantees that would mitigate the security dilemma. Once there is politically salient trouble in an area, the UN may try to intervene to "keep the peace." However, the conditions under which peacekeeping is attempted are favourable to the party that has had the most military success. As a general rule, the UN does not make peace: it negotiates cease-fires. Two parties in dispute generally agree to a cease-fire only because one is successful and happy with its gains, while the other has lost, but fears even worse to come. Alternatively, the two sides have fought to a bloody stalemate and would like to rest. The UN thus protects, and to some extent legitimates, the military gains of the winning side, or gives both a respite to recover. This approach by the international community to intervention in ethnic conflict, helps create an incentive for offensive military operations.

WINDOWS OF VULNERABILITY AND OPPORTUNITY

Where central authority has recently collapsed, the groups emerging from an old empire must calculate their power relative to each other at the time of collapse and make a guess about their relative power in the future. Such calculations must account for a variety of factors. Objectively, only one side can be better off. However, the complexity of these situations makes it possible for many competing groups to believe that their prospects in a war would be better earlier, rather than later. In addition, if the geographic situation creates incentives of the kind discussed earlier, the temptation to capitalize on these windows of opportunity may be great. These windows may also prove tempting to those who wish to expand for other reasons.

The relative rate of state formation strongly influences the incentives for preventive war. When central authority has collapsed or is collapsing, the groups emerging from the political rubble will try to form their own states. These groups must choose leaders, set up bureaucracies to collect taxes and provide services, organize police forces for internal security and organize military forces for external security. The material remnants of the old state (especially weaponry, foreign currency reserves, raw material stocks and industrial capabilities) will be unevenly distributed across the territories of the old empire. Some groups may have had a privileged position in the old system. Others will be less well placed.

The states formed by these groups will thus vary greatly in their strength. This will provide immediate military advantages to those who are farther along in the process of state formation. If those with greater advantages expect to remain in that position by virtue of their superior numbers, then they may see no window of opportunity. However, if they expect their advantage to wane or disappear, then they will have an incentive to solve outstanding issues while they are much stronger than the opposition.

This power differential may create incentives for preventive expropriation, which can generate a spiral of action and reaction. With military resources unevenly distributed and perhaps artificially scarce for some due to arms embargoes, cash shortages or constrained access to the outside world, small caches of armaments assume large importance. Any military depot will be a tempting target, especially for the poorly armed. Better armed groups also have a strong incentive to seize these weapons because this would increase their margin of superiority.

In addition, it matters whether or not the old regime imposed military conscription on all groups in society. Conscription makes arms theft quite easy because hijackers know what to look for and how to move it. Gains are highly cumulative because each side can quickly integrate whatever it steals into its existing forces. High cumulativity of conquered resources has often motivated states in the past to initiate preventive military actions.

Expectations about outside intervention will also affect preventive war calculations. Historically, this usually meant expectations about the intervention of allies on one side or the other, and the value of such allies. Allies may be explicit or tacit. A group may expect itself or another to find friends abroad. It may calculate that the other group's natural allies are temporarily preoccupied, or a group may calculate that it or its adversary has many other adversaries who will attack in the event of conflict. The greater the number of potential allies for all groups, the more complex this calculation will be and the greater the chance for error. Thus, two opposing groups could both think that the expected behaviour of others makes them stronger in the short term.

A broader window-of-opportunity problem has been created by the large number of crises and conflicts that have been precipitated by the end of the Cold War. The electronic media provide free global strategic intelligence about these problems to anyone for the price of a shortwave radio, much less a satellite dish. Middle and great powers, and international organizations, are able to deal with only a small number of crises simultaneously. States that wish to initiate offensive military actions, but fear outside opposition, may move quickly if they learn that international organizations and great powers are preoccupied momentarily with other problems.

Croats and Serbs

Viewed through the lens of the security dilemma, the early stages of Yugoslavia's disintegration were strongly influenced by the following factors. First, the parties identified the re-emerging identities of the others as offensive threats. The last time these groups were free of constraint, during World War II, they slaughtered one another with abandon. In addition, the Yugoslav military system trained most men for war and distributed infantry armament widely across the country. Second, the offensive appeared to have the advantage, particularly against Serbs "marooned" in Croatian and Muslim territory. Third, the new republics were not equally powerful. Their power assets varied in terms of people and economic resources; access to the wealth and military assets of the previous regime; access to external allies; and possible outside enemies. Preventive war incentives were consequently high. Fourth, small bands of fanatics soon appeared on the scene. Indeed, the political and military history of the region stressed the role of small, violent, committed groups; the resistance to the Turks; the Ustashe in the 1930s; and the Ustashe state and Serbian Chetniks during World War II.

Serbs and Croats both have a terrifying oral history of each other's behaviour. This history goes back hundreds of years, although the intense Croat-Serb conflict is only about 125 years old. The history of the region is quite warlike: the area was the frontier of the Hapsburg and Turkish empires, and Croatia had been an integral part of the military apparatus of the Hapsburg empire. The imposition of harsh Hungarian rule in Croatia in 1868; the Hungarian divide-and-conquer strategy that pitted Croats and Serbs in Croatia against each other; the rise of the independent Serbian nation-state out of the Ottoman empire, formally recognized in Europe in 1878; and Serbian pretensions to speak for all south Slavs were the main origins of the Croat-Serb conflict. When Yugoslavia was formed after World War I, the Croats had a very different vision of the new state than the Serbs. They hoped for a confederal system, while the Serbs planned to develop a centralized nation-state.[7] The Croats did not perceive themselves to be treated fairly under this arrangement, and this helped stimulate the development of a violent resistance movement, the Ustashe, which collaborated with the Fascist powers during the 1930s.

The Serbs had some reasons for assuming the worst about the existence of an independent Croatian state, given Croatian behaviour during World War II. Ustashe leadership was established in Croatia by Nazi Germany. The Serbs, both communist and non-communist, fought the Axis forces, including the Croats, and each other. (Some Croats also fought in Josef Tito's communist partisan movement against the Nazis.) Roughly a million people died in the fighting—some 5.9% of Yugoslavia's pre-war population.[8] The Croats behaved with extraordinary brutality towards the Serbs, who suffered nearly 500,000 dead, more than twice as many dead as the Croats.[9] (Obviously, the Germans were responsible for many Serbian deaths as well.) Most of these were not killed in battle; they were civilians murdered in large-scale terrorist raids.

The Croats themselves suffered some 200,000 dead in World War II, which suggests that depredations were inflicted on many sides. (The noncommunist, "nationalist" Chetniks were among the most aggressive killers of Croats, which helps explain why the new Croatian republic is worried by the nationalist rhetoric of the new Serbian republic.) Having lived in a pre- and post-war Yugoslavia largely dominated by Serbs, the Croats had reason to suspect that the demise of the Yugoslavian Communist Party would be followed by a Serbian bid for hegemony. In 1971, the Croatian Communist Party had been purged of leaders who had favoured greater autonomy. In addition, the historical record of the Serbs during the past 200 years is one of regular efforts to establish an ever larger centralized Serbian national state on the Balkan Peninsula. Thus, Croats had sufficient reason to fear the Serbs.

Serbs in Croatia were scattered in a number of vulnerable islands; they could only be "rescued" by offensive action from Serbia. Such a rescue, of course, would have been enormously complicated by an independent Bosnia, which in part explains the Serbian war there. In addition, Serbia could not count on maintaining absolute military superiority over the Croats forever: almost twice as many Serbs as Croats inhabit the territory of what was once Yugoslavia, but Croatia is slightly wealthier than Serbia.[10] Croatia also has some natural allies within former Yugoslavia, especially Bosnian Muslims, and seemed somewhat more adept at winning allies abroad. As Croatia adopted the trappings of statehood and achieved international recognition, its military power was expected to grow. From the Serbian point of view, Serbs in Croatia were insecure and expected to become more so as time went by.

From a military point of view, the Croats probably would have been better off postponing their secession until after they had made additional military preparations. However, their experience in 1971, more recent political developments and the military preparations of the Yugoslav army probably convinced them that the Serbs were about to strike and that the Croatian leadership would be rounded up and imprisoned or killed if they did not act quickly.

Each side not only had to assess the other's capabilities, but also its intentions, and there were plenty of signals of malign intent. Between 1987 and 1990, Slobodan Milosevic ended the administrative autonomy within Serbia that had been granted to Kosovo and Vojvodina in the 1974 constitution.[11] In August 1990, Serbs in the Dalmatia region of Croatia held a cultural autonomy referendum, which they defended with armed roadblocks against expected Croatian interference.[12] By October, the Yugoslav army began to impound all of the heavy weapons stored in Croatia for the use of the territorial defence forces, thus securing a vast military advantage over the nascent armed forces of the republic.[13] The Serbian window of opportunity, already large, grew larger. The Croats accelerated their own military preparations.

It is difficult to tell just how much interference the Croats planned, if any, in the referendum in Dalmatia. However, Croatia had stoked the fires of Serbian secessionism with a series of ominous rulings. In the spring of 1990, Serbs in Croatia were redefined as a minority, rather than a constituent nation, and were asked to take a loyalty oath. Serbian police were to be replaced with Croats, as were some local Serbian officials. No offer of cultural autonomy was made at the time. These Croatian policies undoubtedly intensified Serbian fears about the future and further tempted them to exploit their military superiority.

It appears that the Croats overestimated the reliability and influence of the Federal Republic of Germany as an ally due to some combination of World War II history, the widespread misperception created by the European media and by Western political leaders of Germany's near-superpower status, the presumed influence of the large Croatian émigré community in Germany and

Germany's own diplomacy, which was quite favourable to Croatia even before its June 1991 declaration of independence.[14] These considerations may have encouraged Croatia to secede. Conversely, Serbian propaganda was quick to stress the German-Croatian connection and to speculate on future German ambitions in the Balkans.[15] Fair or not, this prospect would have had an impact on Serbia's preventive war calculus.

*   *   *

Conclusion

Three main conclusions follow from the preceding analysis. First, the security dilemma and realist international relations theory more generally have considerable ability to explain and predict the probability and intensity of military conflict among groups emerging from the wreckage of empires.

Second, the security dilemma suggests that the risks associated with these conflicts are quite high. Several of the causes of conflict and war highlighted by the security dilemma operate with considerable intensity among the groups emerging from empires. The kind of military power that these groups can initially develop and their competing versions of history will often produce mutual fear and competition. Settlement patterns, in conjunction with unequal and shifting power, will often produce incentives for preventive war. The cumulative effect of conquered resources will encourage preventive grabs of military equipment and other assets.

Finally, if outsiders wish to understand and perhaps reduce the odds of conflict, they must assess the local groups' strategic view of their situation. Which groups fear for their physical security and why? What military options are open to them? By making these groups feel less threatened and by reducing the salience of windows of opportunity, the odds of conflict may be reduced.

Because the international political system as a whole remains a self-help system, it will be difficult to act on such calculations. Outsiders rarely have major material or security interests at stake in regional disputes. It is difficult for international institutions to threaten credibly in advance to intervene, on humanitarian grounds, to protect groups that fear for the future. Vague humanitarian commitments will not make vulnerable groups feel safe and will probably not deter those who wish to repress them. In some cases, however, such commitments may be credible because the conflict has real security implications for powerful outside actors.

Groups drifting into conflict should be encouraged to discuss their individual histories of mutual relations. Competing versions of history should be reconciled if possible. Domestic policies that raise bitter memories of perceived past injustices or depredations should be examined. This exercise need not be managed by an international political institution; non-governmental organizations could play a role. Discussions about regional history would be an intelligent use of the resources of many foundations. A few conferences will not, of course, easily undo generations of hateful, politicized history, bolstered by reams of more recent propaganda. The exercise would cost little and, therefore, should be tried.

In some cases, outside powers could threaten not to act; this would discourage some kinds of aggressive behaviour. For example, outside powers could make clear that if a new state abuses a minority and then gets itself into a war with that minority and its allies, the abuser will find little sympathy abroad if it begins to lose. To accomplish this, however, outside powers must have a way of detecting mistreatment of minorities.

In other cases, it may be reasonable for outside powers to provide material resources, including armaments, to help groups protect themselves. However, this kind of hard-bitten policy is politically difficult for liberal democratic governments now dominating world politics to pursue, even on humanitarian grounds. In addition, it is an admittedly complicated game in its own right because it is difficult to determine the amount and type of military assistance needed to produce effective defensive forces, but not offensive capabilities. Nev-

ertheless, considerable diplomatic leverage may be attained by the threat to supply armaments to one side or the other.

*   *   *

It will frequently prove impossible, however, to arrange military assets, external political commitments and political expectations so that all neighbouring groups are relatively secure and perceive themselves as such. War is then likely. These wars will confirm and intensify all the fears that led to their initiation. Their brutality will tempt outsiders to intervene, but peace efforts originating from the outside will be unsuccessful if they do not realistically address the fears that triggered the conflicts initially. In most cases, this will require a willingness to commit large numbers of troops and substantial amounts of military equipment to troubled areas for a very long time.

NOTES

1. The following realist literature is essential for those interested in the analysis of ethnic conflict: Kenneth Waltz, *Theory of International Politics* (Reading, MA: Addison Wesley, 1979), Chapters 6 and 8; Robert Jervis, "Cooperation under the security dilemma," *World Politics*, no. 2, January 1978, pp. 167–213; Robert Jervis, *Perception and Misperception in International Politics* (Princeton, NJ: Princeton University Press, 1976), Chapter 3; Thomas C. Schelling, *Arms and Influence* (New Haven, CT: Yale University Press, 1966, 1976), Chapters 1 and 6.

2. See Carl Von Clausewitz, *On War* (Princeton, NJ: Princeton University Press, 1984), pp. 591–92; Robert Gilpin, "The Richness of the Tradition of Political Realism," in Robert E. Keohane, *Neorealism and its Critics* (New York: Columbia University Press, 1986), pp. 300–21, especially pp. 304–308.

3. This problem shades into an assessment of "intentions," another very difficult problem for states in international politics. This issue is

treated as a capabilities problem because the emergence of anarchy forces leaders to focus on military potential, rather than on intentions. Under these conditions, every group will ask whether neighbouring groups have the cohesion, morale and martial spirit to take the offensive if their leaders call on them to do so.

4. It is plausible that the surrounding population will view irredenta in their midst as an offensive threat by the outside group. They may be perceived as a "fifth column," that must be controlled, repressed or even expelled.

5. See Stephen Van Evera, "The cult of the offensive and the origins of the First World War," *International Security*, vol. 9, no. 1, Summer 1984, pp. 58–107.

6. Why do they not go to the defence of their own, rather than attack the other? Here, it is hypothesized that such groups are scarce relative to the number of target towns and villages, so they cannot "defend" their own with any great confidence.

7. James Gow, "Deconstructing Yugoslavia," *Survival*, vol. 33, no. 4, July/August 1991, p. 292; J.B. Hoptner, *Yugoslavia in Crisis 1934–1941* (New York: Columbia University Press, 1962), pp. 1–9.

8. Ivo Banac, "Political change and national diversity," *Daedalus*, vol. 119, no. 1, Winter 1990, pp. 145–150, estimates that 487,000 Serbs, 207,000 Croats, 86,000 Bosnian Muslims and 60,000 Jews died in Yugoslavia during the war.

9. Aleksa Djilas, *The Contested Country* (Cambridge, MA: Harvard University Press, 1991), pp. 103–28. See especially, Chapter 4, "The National State and Genocide: The Ustasha Movement, 1929–1945," especially pp. 120–27, which vividly describes large-scale Croatian murders of Serbs, as well as Jews and Gypsies; however, Djilas does not explain how 200,000 Croats also died.

10. See Sabrina Ramet, *Nationalism and Federalism in Yugoslavia 1962–1991* (Bloomington, IN: Indiana University Press, 2nd ed., 1992), Appendix 2, p. 286.

11. Gow, *op. cit.* in note 7, p. 294. Vojvodina contains the only petroleum and gas in Yugoslavia proximate to Serbia, so this act probably had a strategic motive; see Central Intelligence Agency, *Atlas of Eastern Europe* (Washington, DC: US Government Printing Office, August 1990), p. 10.

12. International Institute for Strategic Studies, *Strategic Survey 1990–1991* (London: Brassey's for the IISS, 1991), p. 167.

13. Gow, *op. cit.* in note 7, p. 299.

14. See John Newhouse, "The diplomatic round," *The New Yorker*, 24 August 1992, especially p. 63. See also John Zametica, *The Yugoslav Conflict*, Adelphi Paper 270 (London: Brassey's for the IISS, 1992), pp. 63–65.

15. Ramet, *op. cit.* in note 10, p. 265.

11 ✧ THE DEMOCRATIC PEACE DEBATE

The democratic peace debate has generated an abundance of theoretical and empirical research. Karen Mingst, in Essentials of International Relations, *uses this debate in chapter 1 to illustrate how the behavioral revolution has influenced contemporary research and in chapter 3 to illustrate liberal institutionalism. The readings in this chapter provide the intellectual and empirical underpinnings to this key debate.*

Two centuries ago, the philosopher Immanuel Kant posited that a group of republican states with representative forms of government that were accountable to their citizens would be able to form an effective league of peace. Michael Doyle (see chapter 2) drew on Kant's insights in explaining why no two democracies have ever fought a war against each other. Among Kant's and Doyle's explanations are the accountability of the governments to the voters, who would have to pay the price of a war; the ethical unacceptability of attacking a justly elected regime whose legitimacy rests on the same principles as one's own; and the ties of interests created by free trade among commercially liberal states.

Realist scholar Christopher Layne, however, argued in 1994 that a closer look at some historical confrontations fails to support the reasoning behind Kant's and Doyle's claims. He points out that in numerous crises during which democracies almost went to war with each other, public opinion was often belligerent. A better explanation for the peaceful outcomes in these cases, he says, is the realist prudence of the militarily weaker side. Moreover, other critics of the democratic peace hypothesis, such as John Mearsheimer in his Norton series book, point out that democracies were scarce until the post-1945 period. Realism, Mearsheimer argues, can easily explain why democracies never fought each other between 1945 and the 1980s: they were too busy containing the geopolitical threat from the rising power of the Soviet Union.

John Oneal and Bruce Russett's book in the Norton series uses state-of-the-art statistical analyses to rebut such objections. They argue that the pattern of behavior among democracies is too distinctive on too many dimensions—such as trade, alliances, and dispute resolution—to be coincidental. The democratic peace is real, they say, and if managed properly, here to stay. Jack Snyder's book in the Norton series, however, offers the reminder that the turbulent early stages of the transition to democracy can increase the risk of war and nationalist conflict, since a nascent civil society and weak democratic institutions can be easily manipulated by powerful elites who play the nationalist card.

IMMANUEL KANT

To Perpetual Peace: A Philosophical Sketch

*   *   *

The state of peace among men living in close proximity is not the natural state * * * ; instead, the natural state is a one of war, which does not just consist in open hostilities, but also in the constant and enduring threat of them. The state of peace must therefore be *established*, for the suspension of hostilities does not provide the security of peace, and unless this security is pledged by one neighbor to another (which can happen only in a state of *lawfulness*), the latter, from whom such security has been requested, can treat the former as an enemy.

First Definitive Article of Perpetual Peace: The Civil Constitution of Every Nation Should Be Republican

The sole established constitution that follows from the idea of an original contract, the one on which all of a nation's just legislation must be based, is re-

From Immanuel Kant, *Perpetual Peace, and Other Essays on Politics, History, and Morals*, trans. Ted Humphrey (Indianapolis: Hackett Publishing, 1983), 110–18. Both the author's and the translator's notes have been omitted. Bracketed editorial insertions are the translator's.

publican. For, first, it accords with the principles of the *freedom* of the members of a society (as men), second, it accords with the principles of the *dependence* of everyone on a single, common [source of] legislation (as subjects), and third, it accords with the law of the equality of them all (as citizens). Thus, so far as [the matter of] right is concerned, republicanism is the original foundation of all forms of civil constitution. Thus, the only question remaining is this, does it also provide the only foundation for perpetual peace?

Now in addition to the purity of its origin, a purity whose source is the pure concept of right, the republican constitution also provides for this desirable result, namely, perpetual peace, and the reason for this is as follows: If (as must inevitably be the case, given this form of constitution) the consent of the citizenry is required in order to determine whether or not there will be war, it is natural that they consider all its calamities before committing themselves to so risky a game. (Among these are doing the fighting themselves, paying the costs of war from their own resources, having to repair at great sacrifice the war's devastation, and, finally, the ultimate evil that would make peace itself better, never being able—because of new and constant wars—to expunge the burden of debt.)

By contrast, under a nonrepublican constitution, where subjects are not citizens, the easiest thing in the world to do is to declare war. Here the ruler is not a fellow citizen, but the nation's owner, and war does not affect his table, his hunt, his places of pleasure, his court festivals, and so on. Thus, he can decide to go to war for the most meaningless of reasons, as if it were a kind of pleasure party, and he can blithely leave its justification (which decency requires) to his diplomatic corps, who are always prepared for such exercises.

The following comments are necessary to prevent confusing (as so often happens) the republican form of constitution with the democratic one: The forms of a nation (*civitas*) can be analyzed either on the basis of the persons who possess the highest political authority or on the basis of the way the people are *governed* by their ruler, whoever he may be. The first is called the form of sovereignty * * *, of which only three kinds are possible, specifically, where either *one*, or *several* in association, or *all* those together who make up civil society possess the sovereign power (Autocracy, Aristocracy and Democracy, the power of a monarch, the power of a nobility, the power of a people). The second is the form of government (*forma regiminis*) and concerns the way in which a nation, based on its constitution (the act of the general will whereby a group becomes a people), exercises its authority. In this regard, government is either *republican* or *despotic*. *Republicanism* is that political principle whereby executive power (the government) is separated from legislative power. In a despotism the ruler independently executes laws that it has itself made; here rulers have taken hold of the public will and treated it as their own private will. Among the three forms of government, *democracy*, in the proper sense of the term, is necessarily a *despotism*, because it sets up an executive power in which all citizens make decisions about and, if need be, against one (who therefore does not agree); consequently, all, who are not quite all, decide, so that the general will contradicts both itself and freedom.

Every form of government that is not *represen-*

tative is properly speaking *without form*, because one and the same person can no more be at one and the same time the legislator and executor of his will (than the universal proposition can serve as the major premise in a syllogism and at the same time be the subsumption of the particular under it in the minor premise). And although the other two forms of political constitution are defective inasmuch as they always leave room for a democratic form of government, it is nonetheless possible that they assume a form of government that accords with the *spirit* of a representative system: As Friederick II at least *said*, "I am merely the nation's highest servant." The democratic system makes this impossible, for everyone wants to rule. One can therefore say, the smaller the number of persons who exercise the power of the nation (the number of rulers), the more they represent and the closer the political constitution approximates the possibility of republicanism, and thus, the constitution can hope through gradual reforms finally to become republican. For this reason, attaining this state that embodies a completely just constitution is more difficult in an aristocracy than in a monarchy, and, except by violent revolution, there is no possibility of attaining it in a democracy. Nonetheless, the people are incomparably more concerned with the form of government than with the form of constitution (although a great deal depends on the degree to which the latter is suited to the goals of the former). But if the form of government is to cohere with the concept of right, it must include the representative system, which is possible only in a republican form of government and without which (no matter what the constitution may be) government is despotic and brutish. None of the ancient so-called republics were aware of this, and consequently they inevitably degenerated into despotism; still, this is more bearable under a single person's rulership than other forms of government are.

Second Definitive Article for a Perpetual Peace: The Right of Nations Shall Be Based on a Federation of Free States

As nations, peoples can be regarded as single individuals who injure one another through their close proximity while living in the state of nature (i.e., independently of external laws). For the sake of its own security, each nation can and should demand that the others enter into a contract resembling the civil one and guaranteeing the rights of each. This would be a federation *of nations*, but it must not be a nation consisting of nations. The latter would be contradictory, for in every nation there exists the relation of *ruler* (legislator) to *subject* (those who obey, the people); however, many nations in a single nation would constitute only a single nation, which contradicts our assumption (since we are here weighing the rights of *nations* in relation to one another, rather than fusing them into a single nation).

Just as we view with deep disdain the attachment of savages to their lawless freedom—preferring to scuffle without end rather than to place themselves under lawful restraints that they themselves constitute, consequently preferring a mad freedom to a rational one—and consider it barbarous, rude, and brutishly degrading of humanity, so also should we think that civilized peoples (each one united into a nation) would hasten as quickly as possible to escape so similar a state of abandonment. Instead, however, each *nation* sees its majesty (for it is absurd to speak of the majesty of a people) to consist in not being subject to any external legal constraint, and the glory of its ruler consists in being able, without endangering himself, to command many thousands to sacrifice themselves for a matter that does not concern them. The primary difference between European and American savages is this, that while many of the latter tribes have been completely eaten by their enemies, the former know how to make better use of those they have conquered than to consume them: they increase the number of their subjects and thus also the quantity of instruments they have to wage even more extensive wars.

Given the depravity of human nature, which is revealed and can be glimpsed in the free relations among nations (though deeply concealed by governmental restraints in law governed civil-society), one must wonder why the word *right* has not been completely discarded from the politics of war as pedantic, or why no nation has openly ventured to declare that it should be. For while Hugo Grotius, Pufendorf, Vattel, and others whose philosophically and diplomatically formulated codes do not and cannot have the slightest legal force (since nations do not stand under any common external constraints), are always piously cited in justification of a war of aggression (and who therefore provide only cold comfort), no example can be given of a nation having foregone its intention [of going to war] based on the arguments provided by such important men. The homage that every nation pays (at least in words) to the concept of right proves, nonetheless, that there is in man a still greater, though presently dormant, moral aptitude to master the evil principle in himself (a principle he cannot deny) and to hope that others will also overcome it. For otherwise the word *right* would never leave the mouths of those nations that want to make war on one another, unless it were used mockingly, as when that Gallic prince declared, "Nature has given the strong the prerogative of making the weak obey them."

Nations can press for their rights only by waging war and never in a trial before an independent tribunal, but war and its favorable consequence, victory, cannot determine the right. And although a *treaty of peace* can put an end to some particular war, it cannot end the state of war (the tendency always to find a new pretext for war). (And this situation cannot straightforwardly be declared unjust, since in this circumstance each nation is judge of its own case.) Nor can one say of nations as regards their rights what one can say concerning the natural rights of men in a state of lawlessness, to wit, that "they should abandon this state." (For as nations they already have an internal, legal constitution and therefore have outgrown the compulsion to subject themselves to another legal constitution that is subject to someone else's concept of right.) Nonetheless, from the throne of its moral legislative power, reason absolutely condemns war as a means of determining the right and makes seeking the state of peace a matter of unmitigated duty. But without a contract among nations peace can be neither inaugurated nor guaranteed. A league of a special sort must therefore be established, one that we can call a *league of peace* (*foedus pacificum*), which will be distinguished from a *treaty of peace* (*pactum pacis*) because the latter seeks merely to stop *one* war, while the former seeks to end *all* wars forever. This league does not seek any power of the sort possessed by nations, but only the maintenance and security of each nation's own freedom, as well as that of the other nations leagued with it, without their having thereby to subject themselves to civil laws and their constraints (as men in the state of nature must do). It can be shown that this *idea of federalism* should eventually include all nations and thus lead to perpetual peace. For if good fortune should so dispose matters that a powerful and enlightened people should form a republic (which by its nature must be inclined to seek perpetual peace), it will provide a focal point for a federal association among other nations that will join it in order to guarantee a state of peace among nations that is in accord with the idea of the right of nations, and through several associations of this sort such a federation can extend further and further.

That a people might say, "There should be no war among us, for we want to form ourselves into a nation, i.e., place ourselves under a supreme legislative, executive, and judicial power to resolve our conflicts peacefully," is understandable. But when a nation says, "There should be no war between me and other nations, though I recognize no

supreme legislative power to guarantee me my rights and him his," then if there does not exist a surrogate of the union in a civil society, which is a free federation, it is impossible to understand what the basis for so entrusting my rights is. Such a federation is necessarily tied rationally to the concept of the right of nations, at least if this latter notion has any meaning.

The concept of the right of nations as a right to go to war is meaningless (for it would then be the right to determine the right not by independent, universally valid laws that restrict the freedom of everyone, but by one-sided maxims backed by force). Consequently, the concept of the right of nations must be understood as follows: that it serves justly those men who are disposed to seek one another's destruction and thus to find perpetual peace in the grave that covers all the horrors of violence and its perpetrators. Reason can provide related nations with no other means for emerging from the state of lawlessness, which consists solely of war, than that they give up their savage (lawless) freedom, just as individual persons do, and, by accommodating themselves to the constraints of common law, establish a *nation of peoples* (*civitas gentium*) that (continually growing) will finally include all the people of the earth. But they do not will to do this because it does not conform to their idea of the right of nations, and consequently they discard in *hypothesis* what is true in *thesis*. So (if everything is not to be lost) in place of the positive idea of *a world republic* they put only the *negative* surrogate of an enduring, ever expanding *federation* that prevents war and curbs the tendency of that hostile inclination to defy the law, though there will always be constant danger of their breaking loose. * * *

*   *   *

CHRISTOPHER LAYNE

Kant or Cant: The Myth of the Democratic Peace

The theory of the "Democratic Peace" raises important theoretical issues: the contention that democratic states behave differently toward each other than toward non-democracies cuts to the heart of the international relations theory debate about the relative salience of * * * domestic politics * * * and of * * * systemic structure * * * explanations of international political outcomes. Democratic peace theory has also come to have a real-world importance as well: Policymakers who have embraced democratic peace theory see a crucial link between America's security and the spread of democracy, which is viewed as the antidote that will prevent future wars. Indeed some democratic peace theorists, notably Bruce Russett, believe that in an international system comprising a critical mass of democratic states, "It may be possible in part to supersede the 'realist' principles (anarchy, the security dilemma of states) that have dominated practice to the exclusion of 'liberal' or 'idealist' ones since at least the seventeenth century."[1] Because of its theoretical claims and policy implications, the democratic peace theory merits careful examination.[2] In this article, I focus primarily on a critique of the persuasiveness of democratic peace theory's causal logic and ask whether democratic peace theory or realism is a better predictor of international outcomes. I then briefly assess the robustness of democratic peace theory's empirical evidence in light of my conclusions about the strength of its explanatory power.

I begin by reviewing the explanations of the Democratic Peace advanced by democratic peace theorists. There are two strands to the theory's causal logic. One attributes the absence of war between democracies to institutional constraints: the restraining effects of public opinion, or of the checks and balances embedded in a democratic state's domestic political structure. The other posits that it is democratic norms and culture—a shared commitment to the peaceful adjudication of political disputes—that accounts for the absence of war between democratic states. As I demonstrate, the institutional-constraints argument fails to provide a compelling explanation for the absence of war between democracies. Thus, democratic peace theory's explanatory power rests on the persuasiveness of the contention that democratic norms and culture explain why, although democratic states fight with non-democracies, they do not go to war with each other.

This article's centerpiece is a test of the competing explanations of international outcomes offered by democratic peace theory and by realism. This test is based on case studies of four "near misses"—crises where two democratic states almost went to war with each other. These four cases are well-documented instances of democratic great powers going to the brink of war without going over it. As such, they present an opportunity to determine which of the competing hypotheses advanced respectively by democratic peace theory and realism best account for international political outcomes.[3] Moreover, they present an easy case for democratic peace theory and a hard case for realism. The selected cases favor democratic peace theory because, in each, the pacifying effect of democratic norms and culture was bolstered by complementary factors (e.g., economic interdependence, or special ties linking the disputants). I

From *International Security* 19, no. 2 (fall 1994): 5–49. Some of the author's notes have been omitted.

deduce, from both the democratic norms and culture argument and from realism, sets of indicators—testable propositions—that should be present if a crisis's outcome is explained by either of the two theories. Using a process-tracing approach, I examine each crisis in detail.

I conclude that realism is superior to democratic peace theory as a predictor of international outcomes. Indeed, democratic peace theory appears to have extremely little explanatory power in the cases studied. Doubts about the validity of its causal logic suggest that the empirical evidence purporting to support democratic peace theory should also be revisited. Democratic peace theorists contend that the theory is validated by a large number of cases. However, a powerful argument can be made that the universe of cases from which it can be tested is actually quite small. This is a crucial issue, because if the theory's empirical support is based on a small-N universe, this magnifies the importance of possible exceptions to the rule that democracies do not fight each other (for example, World War I, the War between the States, the War of 1812). I conclude by discussing democratic peace theory's troublesome implications for post–Cold War American foreign policy.

The Case for a Democratic Peace: Its Claims and its Logic

Democratic peace theory does not contend that democratic states are less war-prone than non-democracies; they are not. The theory does, however, make two important claims, first, that democracies never (or rarely; there is a good deal of variation about this) go to war with other democracies.[4] As Jack S. Levy observes, the "absence of war between democracies comes as close as anything we have to an empirical law in international relations."[5] Second, when democracies come into conflict with one another, they only rarely threaten to use force, because it is "illegitimate" to do so.[6] Democratic peace theory explicitly holds that it is the very nature of democratic political systems that accounts for the fact that democracies do not fight or threaten other democracies.

THE CAUSAL LOGIC

Democratic peace theory must explain an anomaly: democracies are no less war-prone than non-democratic states. Yet, while they will readily threaten and fight non-democracies, they do not threaten or fight other democracies. The key challenge for the theory, then, is to identify the special characteristics of democratic states that restrain them from using coercive threats against, or actually going to war with, other democracies. The theory advances two alternative explanations: (1) institutional constraints; and (2) democratic norms and cultures.[7]

There are two major variants of the institutional constraints argument. Michael Doyle, building on Immanuel Kant, explains that democratic governments are reluctant to go to war because they must answer to their citizens.[8] Citizens pay the price for war in blood and treasure; if the price of conflict is high, democratic governments may fall victim to electoral retribution. Moreover, in democratic states, foreign policy decisions carrying the risk of war are debated openly and not made behind closed doors, which means that both the public and policymakers are sensitized to costs of fighting. A second version of the institutional constraints argument focuses on "checks and balances"; it looks at three specific features of a state's domestic political structure: executive selection, political competition, and the pluralism of the foreign policy decisionmaking process.[9] States with executives answerable to a selection body, with institutionalized political competition, and with decisionmaking responsibility spread among multiple institutions or individuals, should be more highly constrained and hence less likely to go to war.

The democratic norms explanation holds that "the *culture, perceptions, and practices* that permit compromise and the peaceful resolution of conflicts without the threat of violence *within countries* come to apply across national boundaries toward other democratic countries."[10] Democratic states assume both that other democracies also subscribe to pacific methods of regulating political competition and resolving disputes, and that others will apply these norms in their external relations with fellow democracies. In other words, democratic states develop positive perceptions of other democracies. Consequently, Doyle says, democracies, "which rest on consent, presume foreign republics to be also consensual, just and therefore deserving of accommodation."[11] Relations between democratic states are based on mutual respect rooted in the fact that democracies perceive each other as dovish (that is, negotiation or the status quo are the only possible outcomes in a dispute). This perception, it is argued, is based on a form of learning. Democratic states benefit from cooperative relations with one another and they want to expand their positive interactions. In turn, this desire predisposes them to be responsive to the needs of other democratic states, and ultimately leads to creation of a community of interests. As democracies move towards community, they renounce the option to use (or even to threaten to use) force in their mutual interactions.[12]

The democratic ethos—based on "peaceful competition, persuasion and compromise"— explains the absence of war and war-like threats in relations between democratic states. Conversely, the absence of these norms in relations between democracies and non-democracies, it is said, explains the paradox that democracies do not fight each other even though in general they are as war-prone as non-democracies: "When a democracy comes into conflict with a nondemocracy, it will not expect the nondemocratic state to be restrained by those norms [of mutual respect based on democratic culture]. It may feel obliged to adapt to the harsher norms of international conduct of the latter, lest it be exploited or eliminated by the nondemocratic state that takes advantage of the inherent moderation of democracies."[13] Thus it is a fundamental postulate of democratic peace theory that democracies behave in a qualitatively different manner in their relations with each other than they do in their relations with non-democracies.

The Realist Case: The Same Things Over and Over Again

If history is "just one damn thing after another," then for realists international politics is the same damn things over and over again: war, great power security and economic competitions, the rise and fall of great powers, and the formation and dissolution of alliances. International political behavior is characterized by continuity, regularity, and repetition because states are constrained by the international system's unchanging (and probably unchangeable) structure.

The realist paradigm explains why this is so.[14] International politics is an anarchic, self-help realm. "Anarchy," rather than denoting chaos or rampant disorder, refers in international politics to the fact that there is no central authority capable of making and enforcing rules of behavior on the international system's units (states). The absence of a rule-making and enforcing authority means that each unit in the system is responsible for ensuring its own survival and also that each is free to define its own interests and to employ means of its own choice in pursuing them. In this sense, international politics is fundamentally competitive. And it is competitive in a manner that differs crucially from domestic politics in liberal societies, where the losers can accept an adverse outcome because they live to fight another day and can, therefore, ultimately hope to prevail. In international politics, states that come out on the short end of political competition face potentially more extreme outcomes, ranging from constraints on autonomy to occupation to extinction.

It is anarchy that gives international politics its distinctive flavor. In an anarchic system, a state's first goal is to survive. To attain security, states engage in both internal and external balancing for the purpose of deterring aggressors, and of defeating them should deterrence fail. In a realist world, cooperation is possible but is hard to sustain in the face of the competitive pressures that are built into the international political system's structure. The imperative of survival in a threatening environment forces states to focus on strategies that maximize their power relative to their rivals. States have powerful incentives both to seek the upper hand over their rivals militarily and to use their edge not only for self-defense but also to take advantage of others. Because military power is inherently offensive rather than defensive in nature, states cannot escape the security dilemma: measures taken by a state as self-defense may have the unintended consequence of threatening others. This is because a state can never be certain that others' intentions are benign; consequently its policies must be shaped in response to others' capabilities. In the international system, fear and distrust of other states is the normal state of affairs.

Here democratic peace and realism part company on a crucial point. The former holds that changes within states can transform the nature of international politics. Realism takes the view that even if states change internally, the structure of the international political system remains the same. As systemic structure is the primary determinant of international political outcomes, structural constraints mean that similarly placed states will act similarly, regardless of their domestic political systems. As Kenneth Waltz says: "In self-help systems, the pressures of competition weigh more heavily than ideological preferences or internal political pressures."[15] Changes at the unit level do not change the constraints and incentives imbedded at the systemic level. States respond to the logic of the situation in which they find themselves even though this may result in undesirable outcomes, from the breakdown of cooperation to outright war. States that ignore the imperatives of a realist world run the risk of perishing. In a realist world, survival and security are always at risk, and democratic states will respond no differently to democratic rivals than to non-democratic ones.

Testing Democratic Peace Theory

Institutional constraints do not explain the democratic peace. If democratic public opinion really had the effect ascribed to it, democracies would be peaceful in their relations with all states, whether democratic or not. If citizens and policymakers of a democracy were especially sensitive to the human and material costs of war, that sensitivity should be evident whenever their state is on the verge of war, regardless of whether the adversary is democratic: the lives lost and money spent will be the same. Nor is democratic public opinion, *per se*, an inhibitor of war. For example, in 1898 it was public opinion that impelled the reluctant McKinley administration into war with Spain; in 1914 war was enthusiastically embraced by public opinion in Britain and France. Domestic political structure—"checks and balances"—does not explain the democratic peace either. "This argument," as Morgan and Schwebach state, "does not say anything directly about the war-proneness of democracies," because it focuses on an independent variable—decisional constraints embedded in a state's domestic political structure—that is associated with, but not exclusive to, democracies.

Because these explanations fall short, the democratic norms and culture explanation must bear the weight of the democratic peace theory's causal logic. It is there we must look to find that "something in the internal makeup of democratic states" that explains the democratic peace.[16]

Democratic peace theory not only predicts a specific outcome—no war between democracies—but also purports to explain why that outcome will occur. It is thus suited to being tested by the case study method, a detailed look at a small number of examples to determine if events unfold and actors act as the theory predicts. The case study method also affords the opportunity to test the competing explanations of international political outcomes offered by democratic peace theory and by realism. To test the robustness of democratic peace theory's causal logic, the focus here is on "near misses," specific cases in which democratic states had both opportunity and reason to fight each other, but did not.

The case studies in this article use the process-tracing method (opening up the "black box") to identify the factors to which decisionmakers respond, how those factors influence decisions, the actual course of events, and the possible effect of other variables on the outcome. As Stephen

Van Evera says, if a theory has strong explanatory power, process-tracing case studies provide a robust test because decisionmakers "should speak, write, and otherwise behave in a manner consistent with the theory's predictions."[17]

Democratic peace theory, if valid, should account powerfully for the fact that serious crises between democratic states ended in near misses rather than in war. If democratic norms and culture explain the democratic peace, in a near-war crisis, certain indicators of the democratic peace theory should be in evidence: First, public opinion should be strongly pacific. Public opinion is important not because it is an institutional constraint, but because it is an indirect measure of the mutual respect that democracies are said to have for each other. Second, policymaking elites should refrain from making military threats against other democracies and should refrain from making preparations to carry out threats. Democratic peace theorists waffle on this point by suggesting that the absence of war between democracies is more important than the absence of threats. But this sets the threshold of proof too low. Because the crux of the theory is that democracies externalize their internal norms of peaceful dispute resolution, then especially in a crisis, one should not see democracies threatening other democracies. And if threats are made, they should be a last-resort option rather than an early one. Third, democracies should bend over backwards to accommodate each other in a crisis. Ultimata, unbending hard lines, and big-stick diplomacy are the stuff of *Realpolitik*, not the democratic peace.

A realist explanation of near misses would look at a very different set of indicators. First, realism postulates a ratio of national interest to democratic respect: in a crisis, the more important the interests a democracy perceives to be at stake, the more likely that its policy will be shaped by realist imperatives rather than by democratic norms and culture. When vital interests are on the line, democracies should not be inhibited from using threats, ultimata, and big-stick diplomacy against another democracy. Second, even in a crisis involving democracies, states should be very attentive to

strategic concerns, and the relative distribution of military capabilities between them should crucially—perhaps decisively—affect their diplomacy. Third, broader geopolitical considerations pertaining to a state's position in international politics should, if implicated, account significantly for the crisis's outcome. Key here is what Geoffrey Blainey calls the "fighting waterbirds' dilemma," involving concerns that others watching from the sidelines will take advantage of a state's involvement in war; that war will leave a state weakened and in an inferior relative power position *vis-à-vis* possible future rivals; and that failure to propitiate the opposing state in a crisis will cause it to ally with one's other adversaries or rivals.[18]

I have chosen to study four modern historical instances in which democratic great powers almost came to blows: (1) the United States and Great Britain in 1861 ("the *Trent* affair"); (2) the United States and Great Britain in 1895–96 (the Venezuela crisis); France and Great Britain in 1898 (the Fashoda crisis); and France and Germany in 1923 (the Ruhr crisis).[19] I focus on great powers for several reasons. First, international relations theory is defined by great powers: they are the principal components of the international system, and their actions—especially their wars—have a greater impact on the international system than do those of small powers.[20] Moreover, while democratic peace theory should apply to both great and small powers, realist predictions about great power behavior are not always applicable to small powers, because the range of options available to the latter is more constrained.[21] Crises between democratic great powers are a good head-to-head test because democratic peace theory and realism should both be applicable.[22]

The cases selected should favor democratic peace theory for more than the obvious reason that none of them led to war. In each crisis, background factors were present that should have reinforced democratic peace theory's predictions. In the two Anglo-American crises, a common history, culture and language, and economic interdependence were important considerations.[23] In the Fashoda crisis, the factors that led to the 1904 Anglo-French entente were already present and both countries benefited significantly from their economic relations.[24] The Franco-German Ruhr crisis tested both the Wilsonian prescription for achieving security in post–World War I Europe and the belief (increasingly widespread among French and German business elites, and to a lesser extent the political elites) that the prosperity of both states hinged on their economic collaboration.

ANGLO-AMERICAN CRISIS I: THE *TRENT* AFFAIR, 1861

In 1861, tensions arising from the War Between the States brought the Union and Britain to the brink of war. The most important causes of Anglo-American friction stemmed from the Northern blockade of Confederate ports and the consequent loss to Britain of the cotton upon which its textile industry depended. The immediate precipitating cause of the Anglo-American crisis, however, was action of the *USS San Jacinto* which, acting without express orders from Washington, intercepted the British mail ship *Trent* on November 8, 1861. The *Trent* was transporting James M. Mason and John Slidell, the Confederacy's commissioners-designate to Great Britain and France; they had boarded the *Trent*, a neutral vessel, in Havana, Cuba, a neutral port. A boarding party from the *San Jacinto*, after searching the *Trent*, placed Mason and Slidell under arrest. The *Trent* was allowed to complete its voyage while the *San Jacinto* transported Mason and Slidell to Fort Warren in Boston harbor, where they were incarcerated.

When word was received in Britain, the public was overcome with war fever. "The first explosion of the Press, on receipt of the news of the *Trent*, had been a terrific one."[25] An American citizen residing in England reported to Secretary of State William H. Seward, "The people are frantic with rage, and were the country polled I fear 999 men out of 1000 would declare for war."[26] From Edinburgh, another American wrote, "I have never seen so intense a feeling of indignation in my life."[27]

The British government was hardly less bellicose than the public and the press. Fortified by legal opinions holding that Mason and Slidell had been removed from the *Trent* in contravention of international law, the Cabinet adopted a hard-line policy that mirrored the public mood. Prime Minister Lord Palmerston's first reaction to the news of the *Trent* incident was to write to the Secretary of State for War that, because of Britain's "precarious" relations with the United States, the government reconsider cuts in military expenditures planned to take effect in 1862.[28] At the November 29 Cabinet meeting, Palmerston reportedly began by flinging his hat on the table and declaring to his colleagues, "I don't know whether you are going to stand this, but I'll be damned if I do!"[29]

The Cabinet adopted a dual-track approach towards Washington: London used military threats to coerce the United States into surrendering diplomatically, while on the diplomatic side, Foreign Secretary Lord John Russell drafted a note to the Union government in which, while holding firm to the demand that Mason and Slidell be released, he offered Washington an avenue of graceful retreat by indicating that London would accept, as tantamount to an apology, a declaration that the *San Jacinto* had acted without official sanction. Nevertheless, the note that was actually transmitted to Washington was an ultimatum. * * *

Although some, notably including Russell, hoped that the crisis could be resolved peacefully, the entire Cabinet recognized that its decision to present an ultimatum to Washington could lead to war. The British believed that there was one hope for peace: that Washington, overawed by Britain's military power and its readiness to go to war, would bow to London's demands rather than resisting them.[30] As the Undersecretary of State for Foreign Affairs stated, "Our only chance of peace is to be found in working on the fears of the Government and people of the United States."[31]

*   *   *

* * * [A]lthough some papers (notably the *New York Times* and the *New York Daily Tribune*) urged that Washington should placate the British, public opinion strongly favored a policy of standing up to London and refusing to release Mason and Slidell.[32] In response to Britain's hard line, "a rag-

ing war cry reverberated across the Northern states in America."[33] Charles Francis Adams, Jr., whose father was U.S. minister in London at the time, wrote later of the affair: "I do not remember in the whole course of the half-century's retrospect . . . any occurence in which the American people were so completely swept off their feet, for the moment losing possession of their senses, as during the weeks which immediately followed the seizure of Mason and Slidell."[34]

The Lincoln administration was aware of the strength of anti-British sentiment among the public and in Congress (indeed, in early December, Congress passed a resolution commending the *San Jacinto*'s captain for his action). There is some evidence that in order to placate public opinion, President Lincoln was inclined toward holding on to Mason and Slidell, notwithstanding the obvious risks of doing so.[35] Nevertheless, after first toying with the idea of offering London arbitration in an attempt to avoid the extremes of war or a humiliating climb-down, the United States elected to submit to Britain's demands. Given that Washington "could not back down easily," it is important to understand why it chose to do so.

The United States bowed to London because, already fully occupied militarily trying to subdue the Confederacy, the North could not also afford a simultaneous war with England, which effectively would have brought Britain into the War Between the States on the South's side.[36] This was clearly recognized by the Lincoln administration when the cabinet met for two days at Christmas to decide on the American response to the British note. The cabinet had before it two critical pieces of information. First, Washington had just been informed that France supported London's demands (ending American hopes that Britain would be restrained by its own "waterbird" worries that France would take advantage of an Anglo-American war).[37] Second, Washington had abundant information about the depth of the pro-war sentiment of the British public. The American minister in London, Charles Francis Adams, wrote that the English "were now all lashed up into hostility" and that: "The leading newspapers roll out as much fiery lava as Vesuvius

is doing, daily. The Clubs and the army and the navy and the people in the streets generally are raving for war."[38] Senator Charles Sumner passed on to the Lincoln administration letters from the noted Radical members of parliament, Richard Cobden and John Bright. While deploring their government's policy and the tenor of British public opinion, both Cobden and Bright stressed that war would result unless the United States gave in to London. Cobden observed:

> Formerly England feared a war with the United States as much from the dependence on your cotton as from a dread of your power. *Now* the popular opinion (however erroneous) is that a war would give us cotton. And we, of course, consider your power weakened by your Civil War.[39]

Facing the choice of defying London or surrendering to its demands, Washington was compelled to recognize both that Britain was serious about going to war and that such a war almost certainly would result in the Union's permanent dissolution. * * *

The *Trent* affair's outcome is explained by realism, not democratic peace theory. Contrary to democratic peace theory's expectations, the mutual respect between democracies rooted in democratic norms and culture had no influence on British policy. Believing that vital reputational interests affecting its global strategic posture were at stake, London played diplomatic hardball, employed military threats, and was prepared to go to war if necessary. Both the public and the elites in Britain preferred war to conciliation. Across the Atlantic, public and governmental opinion in the North was equally bellicose. An Anglo-American conflict was avoided only because the Lincoln administration came to understand that diplomatic humiliation was preferable to a war that would have arrayed Britain with the Confederacy and thus probably have secured the South's independence.

ANGLO-AMERICAN CRISIS II: VENEZUELA, 1895–96

In 1895–96, the United States and Great Britain found themselves embroiled in a serious diplomatic confrontation arising out of an obscure long-standing dispute between London and Caracas over the Venezuela–British Guiana boundary. By 1895, Caracas was desperately beseeching Washington to pressure London to agree to arbitrate the dispute. The Cleveland administration decided to inject the United States diplomatically into the Anglo-Venezuelan disagreement, but not out of American solicitude for Venezuela's interests or concern for the issue's merits.[40] For the United States, the Anglo-Venezuelan affair was part of a larger picture. By 1895, American policymakers, conscious of the United States's status as an emerging great power, were increasingly concerned about European political and commercial intrusion into the Western Hemisphere.[41] For Washington, the controversy between London and Caracas was a welcome pretext for asserting America's claim to geopolitical primacy in the Western hemisphere. It was for this reason that the United States provoked a showdown on the Anglo-Venezuelan border dispute.[42]

* * *

The outcome of the Venezuelan crisis is better explained by realism than by democratic peace theory. Consistent with realist expectations, both Britain and the United States began planning for war. Although, as democratic peace theory would predict, there was no war fever in either Britain or the United States, there is no evidence that public opinion played any role in London's decision-making process. It was London's decision to reverse its initially uncompromising stance and instead seek an amicable diplomatic solution with Washington that allowed Britain and the United States to avoid war. All available evidence supports the realist explanation that London made this decision solely for strategic reasons.

THE ANGLO-FRENCH STRUGGLE FOR CONTROL
OF THE NILE: FASHODA, 1898

The Fashoda crisis marked the culmination of the Anglo-French struggle for supremacy over Egypt and the headwaters of the Nile.[43] Until 1882 Egypt, although nominally part of the Ottoman Empire,

had been administered by an Anglo-French condominium. In 1882, Britain intervened unilaterally to suppress a nationalist revolt. Because the Suez canal was the vital artery linking Britain with India and its other far eastern imperial interests, strategic considerations overrode London's initial inclination to withdraw quickly from Egypt after the 1882 intervention. By the early 1890s, Lord Salisbury and other British policymakers had determined that in order to safeguard Egypt, Britain had to exert control over the Nile's source and its entire valley.

For France, Britain's post-1882 Egyptian primacy was an affront and, spurred by France's colonial party, Paris periodically looked for ways in which it could compel London to honor its pledge to withdraw from Egypt. The immediate impetus for the French expedition to Fashoda appears to have come from a January 1893 talk given by the hydraulic engineer Victor Prompt at the Egyptian Institute in Paris, which suggested that the flow of water to Egypt could be restricted by damming the Upper Nile. After reviewing Prompt's speech, President of the French Republic Sadi Carnot exclaimed, "we must occupy Fashoda!"[44]

The plan to advance on Fashoda was eagerly embraced by Theophile Delcassé during his 1893–95 tenure first as undersecretary and then as minister for colonies. As a journalist and as a politician, he had been obsessed by the Egyptian question. For Delcassé and other French colonialists, France's prestige and its Mediterranean interests required an end to Britain's occupation of Egypt.[45] In 1896, a plan by marine captain Jean-Baptiste Marchand for an overland expedition to establish French control at Fashoda was approved by Foreign Minister Gabriel Hanotaux and Colonial Minister Emile Chautemps. They did not seek to precipitate an armed confrontation with Britain; they favored an eventual Anglo-French rapprochement and entente. However, they were convinced that French opinion would not accept an entente unless the two powers could reach settlement on the points of dispute between them, including Egypt. Thus, for Hanotaux and Delcassé, the Fashoda expedition was conceived as a lever to force the British to negotiate the Egyptian question and thus to increase France's great-power prestige.

In September 1898, Delcassé was foreign minister. As the conflict loomed, he hoped that it might be averted by Marchand's failure to reach his objective or, if the French expedition did run into British forces, by an agreement that the crisis would be settled diplomatically by London and Paris, not militarily by the opposing forces at Fashoda. Apparently relying on Salisbury's reputation for making "graceful concessions," Delcassé hoped to defuse the crisis by exchanging Marchand's withdrawal for Britain's agreement to reopen the Egyptian question and to discuss giving France an outlet on the Nile.[46] The British, however, had no intention of negotiating. London's position was simple: "Marchand should go, without quibbles or face saving."[47]

French policymakers "deluded themselves" into thinking that by taking Fashoda they could force London to negotiate the Egyptian issue.[48] As early as March 1895, when London had its first intimations about French designs on the upper Nile, Sir Edward Grey, then parliamentary undersecretary for foreign affairs, had stated bluntly that such a move "would be an unfriendly act and would be so viewed in England."[49] In spring 1898, responding to reports that France was driving on the upper Nile, London decided on an all-out reconquest of Sudan.

After victory at Khartoum, Field Marshal Lord Kitchener was ordered to advance to Fashoda and instructed, in the event he encountered French forces, to do nothing that "would in any way imply a recognition on behalf of Her Majesty's Government of a title on behalf of France . . . to any portion of the Nile Valley."[50] On September 19, 1898, Kitchener's forces reached Fashoda, where they were greeted by Marchand's band. Although the opposing forces treated each other with elaborate military courtesy, their meeting plunged London and Paris into a deep diplomatic crisis. The Anglo-French "quarrel was not about Fashoda, or about the fate of the Sudan, or even about the security of the Nile waters and of Egypt; it was about the relative status of France and Britain as Powers."[51]

Once the crisis began, Delcassé quickly recognized that France was in an untenable position. The British ambassador in Paris reported that Delcassé was "prepared to retreat . . . if we can build him a golden bridge."[52] Delcassé believed his maneuvering room was seriously circumscribed by the potentially volatile domestic political situation in France stemming from the Dreyfus affair. To accept a humiliating diplomatic defeat would probably mean the Brisson cabinet's fall and, it was widely feared, even a military coup.[53] Delcassé reportedly begged London, "Do not drive me into a corner."[54] On October 11, he told the British ambassador that if London made it easy for him "in form he would be conciliatory in substance."[55] On October 27 the French ambassador to London, telling Salisbury that Marchand would soon leave Fashoda, pleaded for Britain to make some concession in return.[56]

Meanwhile, notwithstanding both the pleading tone of French diplomacy and the possible repercussions of Britain's stance on French internal politics, London adamantly refused to give Paris an alternative to the bleak choice of ordering Marchand's humiliating withdrawal or going to war. * * * Salisbury was determined "to compel, rather than persuade, the French to withdraw."[57]

London's hard-line diplomacy was overwhelmingly supported by bellicose public opinion. Even before Fashoda, because of the tensions engendered by the Anglo-French colonial rivalry, "war with France was not exactly desired in England, but it would be accepted without hesitation if the occasion arose."[58] Once the crisis began, the press overwhelmingly supported the government's decision to refuse negotiations with France, and during the crisis "the British popular press indulged in an orgy of scurrility."[59] "There was plenty of warlike spirit in the country," and British public opinion was "aggressively jingoistic" over Fashoda.[60] "The unequivocal expression of British opinion" was solidly behind the Cabinet's hard-line policy.[61] This no doubt was true because the British public believed England's prestige was at stake and consequently was "in a mood to respond vigorously" to the French challenge.[62]

The public mood was matched by that of Britain's political elite. As Chancellor of the Exchequer Michael Hicks Beach said on October 19, "The country has put its foot down."[63] The government's uncompromising stance was supported strongly by the opposition Liberal Imperialists, notably Lord Rosebery, H.H. Asquith, and Sir Edward Grey.[64] Rosebery, a former prime minister and foreign secretary, recalled that his Cabinet had warned the French away from the Upper Nile in 1895 and declared that any Cabinet that showed signs of conciliating Paris over Fashoda would be replaced within a week. Indeed when, in the crucial October 27 Cabinet meeting, Salisbury left the impression in some minds that he was leaning towards compromise with Paris, the majority of ministers quickly poured cold water on that idea and the Admiralty was ordered to put the navy on a war footing.

The British knew that if Paris did not capitulate, armed conflict would ensue. London regarded that prospect with equanimity and, indeed, confidence. * * *

In October 1898 the British navy enjoyed a decisive superiority over the French fleet in both numbers and quality, and the outcome of an Anglo-French war was a foregone conclusion.[65] London manifested no reluctance in pressing its strategic advantage. During October, the Royal Navy made preparations for a war with France.[66] * * *

There is no question that France was finally compelled to accept a crushing diplomatic defeat because of its military inferiority *vis-à-vis* Britain. * * * In the end, "Delcassé had no real alternative but to yield; except as an irrational gesture of defiance, war with England was not a possible choice."[67] The Fashoda crisis's outcome was, as Grenville says, "a demonstration of British power and French weakness."[68]

The outcome of the Fashoda crisis is explained by realism, not by democratic peace theory. Believing that vital strategic and reputational interests were at stake, the British ruled out diplomatic accommodation with Paris notwithstanding Delcassé's pleas to be given a face-saving way to extricate France from the crisis. Britain's in-

transigence runs directly counter to democratic peace theory's expectation that relations between democratic states are governed by mutual respect based on democratic norms and culture. Backed strongly by public and elite opinion, London adopted a policy that left Paris with two stark choices: diplomatic humiliation or military defeat in a war. Counter to democratic peace theory's expectations, but consistent with those of realism, Britain made, and was prepared to carry out, military threats against France. Paris caved in to British demands rather than fight a war it could not win.

FRANCO-GERMAN CRISIS: THE RUHR, 1923

The Ruhr occupation, culmination of the post-1918 cold peace, "practically amounted to the renewal of war."[69] The occupation arose from the collision of France's policy of security and Germany's policy of seeking revision of the Versailles Treaty system. The reparations issue was the immediate cause of the Ruhr occupation, but although it had economic significance in itself, its true importance was that Paris and Berlin regarded it as symbolic of the geopolitical competition between them.[70]

For Paris, compelling Germany to adhere strictly to its reparations obligations was seen as crucial to maintaining the Versailles system. Moreover reparations were, as the Ruhr occupation demonstrated, a lever for France to revise Versailles in its favor by imposing political and territorial sanctions on Germany when Berlin defaulted on its payments. For Germany, obtaining modification of reparations was a wedge to open the issue of revising the entire Versailles framework. The "fulfillment" policies adopted by Berlin were designed to force revision by demonstrating that strict compliance with reparations obligations was beyond Germany's capacity and would lead inevitably to Germany's financial and economic collapse.[71]

Although Germany had been defeated and its short-term power constrained by the Versailles settlement, the underlying sources of its geopolitical strength—its industrial base and population—remained intact. French policymakers were obsessed about the resurgence of a German security threat and determined to prevent it by imposing military, territorial and economic restrictions on Germany.

France's postwar German policy was rooted in the aims that Paris had pursued during the war. As early as 1915, Foreign Minister Delcassé had envisioned breaking up the German Reich into a number of small states, coupled with annexation by France, Holland, and Belgium of the Rhine's left bank.[72] By late 1917, Paris had decided to leave a truncated Reich intact while annexing Alsace-Lorraine and the Saar, and creating an independent French satellite state in the Rhineland.[73] France's military and economic security would be enhanced by imposing reparations on Germany and by giving France control of the iron and coal that were crucial to West European industrial supremacy.

After the war, France's objectives did not change. Paris sought military security, reparations, and the establishment of France as Europe's leading steel producer. At Versailles, to avoid alienating Britain and the United States, France abandoned its annexationist aspirations in the Rhineland; however, throughout the period from the Armistice to the Ruhr occupation, Paris covertly supported Rhenish separatism while continuing to harbor hopes of controlling the left bank.[74] Even while appearing to abandon France's territorial claims in the Rhineland, French Premier Clemenceau had achieved much of their essence by coupling the reparations and security issues: under the Versailles Treaty's provisions, as long as Germany remained in default on reparations, French troops could remain in the Rhineland.

The government's German policy was strongly supported by the French public. French public opinion had demanded a peace settlement that would "impose the greatest possible restrictions on Germany's influence and power," and the French public's Germanophobia carried over into the postwar period.[75] Public and policymakers alike believed that Germany should be forced to pay all

of the costs France had sustained in connection with the war (including reconstruction of German-occupied French territory), and official and public opinion were mutually reinforcing. Indeed, French public opinion, which French Prime Minister Poincaré had done much to shape, was so anti-German in late 1922 that it is doubtful that he would have survived politically had he not moved to occupy the Ruhr.[76]

The French military invasion of the Ruhr was prompted by Paris's mounting frustration with Germany's campaign to obtain a significant reduction of its reparations obligations. * * *

In the Ruhr crisis, France did not hesitate to use military force against democratic Weimar Germany in pursuit of French security interests. Indeed, what leaps out from histories of the period between 1915 (when French policymakers began to think seriously about their war aims) and 1923 is the repeated French rejection of * * * arguments that France's postwar security position would be enhanced if Germany were transformed into a democracy. Unlike the British, who soon after the war came to believe a democratic Germany was the key to maintaining the peace in Europe, France preferred to put German democracy at risk rather than abandon its strategy of protecting its security with tangible guarantees. As Walter McDougall observes:

> The Quai d'Orsay perceived little connection between forms of government and foreign policies. The Wilsonian idea that democracies choose peaceful foreign policies, while authoritarian regimes are aggressive, found few disciples in the French government and military. . . . A strong united Germany, whether monarchist or republican, would pose a threat to France and surely come to dominate the economies of the Danubian and Balkan regions.[77]

*   *   *

The Ruhr crisis strongly disconfirms democratic peace theory. In World War I's aftermath, both the public and the elites in France perceived Germany as a dangerous threat to France's security and its great-power status, even though Weimar Germany was a democracy. What mattered to the French was Germany's latent power, not its domestic political structure. Contrary to democratic peace theory's predictions, French policy toward democratic Germany reflected none of the mutual respect based on democratic norms and culture that democracies are supposed to display in their relations with each other. On the contrary, driven by strategic concerns, the French used military power coercively to defend the Versailles system upon which they believed their safety depended, rather than entrust their national security to the hope that Germany's postwar democratic institutions would mitigate the geopolitical consequences flowing from the underlying disparity between German and French power.

Theoretical Conclusions

Proponents have made sweeping theoretical claims for, and have drawn important policy conclusions from, democratic peace theory. These claims rest on a shaky foundation, however. The case studies presented above subject both democratic peace theory and realism to a robust test. It is striking that in each of these four cases realism, not democratic peace theory, provides the more compelling explanation of why war was avoided. Indeed, the democratic peace theory indicators appear not to have played *any* discernible role in the outcome of these crises.

In each of these crises, at least one of the democratic states involved was prepared to go to war (or, in the case of France in 1923, to use military force coercively) because it believed it had vital strategic or reputational interests at stake. In each of these crises, war was avoided only because one side elected to pull back from the brink. In each of the four crises, war was avoided not because of the "live and let live" spirit of peaceful dispute resolution at democratic peace theory's core, but because of realist factors. Adverse distributions of military capabilities explain why France did not fight over Fashoda, and why Germany resisted the French occupation of the Ruhr passively rather than forcibly. Concerns that others would take advantage of the fight (the "waterbirds dilemma") explain why

Britain backed down in the Venezuela crisis, and the Union submitted to Britain's ultimatum in the *Trent* affair. When one actually looks beyond the *result* of these four crises ("democracies do not fight democracies") and attempts to understand *why* these crises turned out as they did, it becomes clear that democratic peace theory's causal logic has only minimal explanatory power.

Although democratic peace theory identifies a correlation between domestic structure and the absence of war between democracies, it fails to establish a causal link. Because democratic peace theory's deductive logic lacks explanatory power, a second look at the theory's empirical support is warranted to see if the evidence is as strong as is commonly believed. The statistical evidence that democracies do not fight each other seems impressive but in fact, it is inconclusive, because the universe of cases providing empirical support for democratic peace theory is small, and because several important cases of wars between democratic states are not counted for reasons that are not persuasive.

QUANTITATIVE SUPPORT FOR THE THEORY:
HOW BIG AN N?

Democratic peace theory purports to be validated by a large number ("N") of cases. A large N is achieved by aggregating the number of possible democratic dyads. Thus Switzerland and Sweden, or Austria and Israel, count as democratic dyads validating democratic peace theory. The result is the appearance of a large number of interactions with little or no conflict between democracies. Notwithstanding the theory's claim, however, the universe of supporting cases is small. There are three reasons why this is so. First, between 1815 and 1945 there were very few democracies (and the N would shrink further if only dyads involving democratic great powers are considered). Second, the possibility of *any* dyad (whether democratic, mixed, or non-democratic) becoming involved in a war is small, because wars are a relatively rare occurrence. States, even great powers, do not spend most of their time at war.[78] As David Spiro points out, if all nations are unlikely to fight wars, the claim that democracies do not fight each other loses much of its power. He states that if nations are rarely at war, and liberal dyads are a small proportion of all possible pairings of nation-states, then perhaps we should be surprised if democracies ever do go to war, but not at the absence of wars among democracies.[79]

Third, not all dyads are created equal. For the purposes of testing democratic peace theory, a dyad is significant only if it represents a case where there is a real possibility of two states going to war. To fight, states need both the *opportunity* (that is, the ability to actually project their power to reach an opponent) and a *reason* to do so. Only dyads meeting these preconditions are part of the appropriate universe of cases from which democratic peace theory can be tested.

Wars between Democracies: Big Exceptions in a Small-N World.   The size of the N is an important question. If the effective universe of cases from which democratic peace theory can be tested is a small N, the importance of exceptions to the rule that democracies do not fight each other is heightened. Here, by their own admissions, democratic peace theorists are on thin ice. For example, referring specifically to the classification of the War of 1812 as one not involving two democracies, Bruce Russett acknowledges that this decision "may seem like a cheap and arbitrary escape" but asserts it is not.[80] It is only intellectual suppleness—the continual tinkering with definitions and categories—that allows democratic peace theorists to deny that democratic states have fought each other.[81]

An important example of this is the War Between the States, which the democratic peace theorists generally rule out on the grounds that it was an internal conflict within a state rather than an international conflict between sovereign states.[82] Yet the events of 1861–65 seem especially relevant because the theory is based explicitly on the premise that the norms and culture that operate within democracies are externalized by them in their relations with other democratic states.[83] Democratic peace theory itself makes relevant the issue of whether democratic norms and culture do, in fact, result in the peaceful resolution of disputes within democracies. The War Between the States cuts to the heart of the democratic peace theory's causal logic: if democratic norms and culture fail to prevent the outbreak of civil war within democracies, what reason is there to believe that they will prevent the outbreak of interstate wars between democracies?

In the case of the Union and the Confederacy, the characteristics at the heart of democratic peace theory—the democratic ethos of respect for other democracies, a political culture that emphasizes the non-violent dispute resolution, the shared benefits of cooperation, the restraining effect of open debate and public opinion—failed conspicuously to assure a peaceful result. Indeed, if a democracy as tightly knit—politically, economically, culturally—as the United States was in 1861 could split into two warring successor states, we should have little confidence that democracy will prevent great power conflicts in an anarchic, competitive, self-help realm like international politics.

An even more important example is the issue of whether Wilhelmine Germany was a democracy. Even if World War I were the only example of democracies fighting each other, it would be so glaring an exception to democratic peace theory as to render it invalid. As even Michael Doyle concedes, the question of whether Wilhelmine Germany was a democracy presents a "difficult case."[84] Indeed, it is such a difficult case that, in a footnote, Doyle creates a new category in which to classify Wilhelmine Germany—that of a bifurcated democracy: pre-1914 Germany was, he says, democratic with respect to domestic politics but not in the realm of foreign policy.[85] Doyle does not consider Imperial Germany to have been a democracy for foreign policy purposes because the executive was not responsible to the Reichstag and, consequently, the foreign policy making process remained, he argues, autocratic.

In fact, however, with respect to foreign policy, Wilhelmine Germany was as democratic as France and Britain. In all three countries, aristocratic or upper-middle-class birth and independent wealth were prerequisites for service in the diplomatic corps and the key political staffs of the foreign office.[86] In all three countries, foreign policy was insulated from parliamentary control and criticism because of the prevailing view that external affairs were above politics.

In democratic France, the Foreign Minister enjoyed virtual autonomy from the legislature, and even from other members of the cabinet.[87] As Christopher Andrew notes, "On the rare occasions when a minister sought to raise a question of foreign policy during a cabinet meeting, he was accustomed to the remark: 'Don't let us concern ourselves with that, gentlemen, it is the business of the foreign minister and the President of the Republic.' "[88] Treaties and similar arrangements were ratified by the president of the Republic (that is, by the cabinet) and the legislature played no role in the treaty making process (although the Senate did have the right to ask to be informed of treaty terms insofar as national security permitted).[89] Notwithstanding the formal principle of ministerial responsibility, the French legislature possessed no mechanisms for effectively supervising or reviewing the government's conduct of foreign policy.[90] Even in democratic France, the executive enjoyed unfettered power in the realm of foreign policy. This concentration of foreign policy making power in the executive had a profound effect on the chain of events leading to World War I. The terms of the Franco-Russian alliance and military convention—the "fateful alliance" that ensured that an Austro-Russian war in the Balkans could not remain localized—were kept secret from the French legislature, public, and press.[91]

In democratic Britain, too, as in France and Germany, crucial foreign policy decisions were taken without consulting Parliament. Notwithstanding the profound implications of the Anglo-French staff talks, which began in January 1906, Foreign Secretary Sir Edward Grey and Prime Minister H.H. Asquith did not inform the Cabinet of their existence.[92] Grey and Asquith feared (and rightly so) that a Cabinet majority would oppose the staff talks and indeed the very idea of more intimate Anglo-French strategic relations. When

questioned in Parliament in 1910, 1911, and 1913 about the Anglo-French military discussions, Grey and Asquith consistently gave false or evasive answers that kept hidden both the nature and the implications of the strategic agreements between London and Paris.[93] Even when Grey and Asquith had to account to the Cabinet, after it learned in November 1911 of the existence of staff talks, they left their colleagues with the incorrect impression that London had undertaken no binding obligations to France.[94] Notwithstanding Grey's and Asquith's constant reiteration (to the French, to Cabinet, and to Parliament) that London retained unimpaired freedom of maneuver, they had, in fact, undertaken a portentous commitment through a constitutionally doubtful process. In the Cabinet's debates about whether Britain should go to war in August 1914, Grey's argument that the Entente, and the concomitant military and naval agreements, had morally obligated Britain to support France proved decisive.[95]

It is apparent that before World War I, the most important and consequential grand strategic decisions made by both Paris (on the Russian alliance) and London (on the entente and military arrangements with France) were made without any legislative control or oversight, notwithstanding both countries' democratic credentials. Form should not be confused with substance. In the realm of foreign policy, France and Britain were no more and no less democratic than the Second Reich.[96]

The case of Wilhelmine Germany suggests that democratic great powers indeed have gone to war against one another (and could do so again in the future). Yet the prevailing view that the Second Reich was not a democracy has powerfully influenced the international relations–theory debate both on the broad question of how domestic political structure affects international outcomes and the specific issue of whether there is a "democratic peace." However, the received wisdom about pre–World War I Germany has been badly distorted by a combination of factors: the liberal bias of most Anglo-American accounts of German history between 1860–1914; the ideologically tinged nature of post-1960 German studies of the Wilhelmine era; and the residual effects of Allied propaganda in World War I, which demonized Germany.[97] The question of whether Wilhelmine Germany should be classified as a democracy is an important one and it deserves to be studied afresh.

AN ALTERNATIVE HYPHOTHESIS * * *

From a realist perspective, democratic peace theory has mistakenly reversed the linkage between international systemic constraints and domestic political institutions. Otto Hintze made the realist argument that a state's internal political structure is highly influenced by external factors.[98] This creates a selection process that explains why some states become democracies while others do not. States that enjoy a high degree of security, like Britain and the United States at the beginning of the twentieth century, can afford the more minimalist state political structures of classical Anglo-American liberalism, because there is no imminent external threat that necessitates a powerful governmental apparatus to mobilize resources for national security purposes. States that live in a highly threatening external environment are more likely to choose either more statist forms of democracy or even authoritarian structures, precisely because national security concerns require that the state have available to it the instruments for mobilizing national power resources.[99] The greater the external threat a state faces (or believes it does), the more "autocratic" its foreign policy making process will be, and the more centralized its political structures will be.

If this hypothesis is true, it suggests that democratic peace theory is looking through the wrong end of the telescope. States that are, or that believe they are, in high-threat environments are less likely to be democracies because such states are more likely to be involved in wars, and states that are likely to be involved in wars tend to adopt autocratic governmental structures that enhance their strategic posture. Thus, as realist theory would predict, international systemic structure is not only the primary determinant of a state's external behavior but may also be a crucial element in shaping its domestic political system. This hypothesis may provide a more useful approach than democratic peace theory to investigating the links between domestic structure and foreign policy.

Policy Conclusions: Why It Matters

The validity of democratic peace theory is not a mere academic concern. Democratic peace theory has been widely embraced by policymakers and foreign policy analysts alike and it has become a lodestar that guides America's post–Cold War foreign policy. Michael Doyle's 1983 conception of a democratic "zone of peace" is now routinely used in both official and unofficial U.S. foreign policy pronouncements. Following the Cold War, a host of commentators have suggested that the export or promotion of democracy abroad should become the central focus of American's post–Cold War foreign policy.[100] From Haiti to Russia, America's interests and its security have been identified with democracy's success or failure. National Security Adviser Anthony Lake said that America's post–Cold War goal must be to expand the zone of democratic peace and prosperity because, "to the extent democracy and market economics hold sway in other nations, our own nation will be more secure, prosperous and influential."[101]

Those who want to base American foreign policy on the extension of democracy abroad invariably disclaim any intention to embark on a "crusade," and profess to recognize the dangers of allowing policy to be based on excessive ideological zeal.[102] These reassurances are the foreign-policy version of "trust me." Because it links American security to the nature of other states' internal political systems, democratic peace theory's logic inevitably pushes the United States to adopt an interventionist strategic posture. If democracies are peaceful but non-democratic states are "troublemakers" the conclusion is inescapable: the former will be truly secure only when the latter have been transformed into democracies, too.

Indeed, American statesmen have frequently expressed this view. During World War I, Elihu

Root said that, "To be safe democracy must kill its enemy when it can and where it can. The world cannot be half democratic and half autocratic."[103] During the Vietnam War, Secretary of State Dean Rusk claimed that the "United States cannot be secure until the total international environment is ideologically safe." These are not isolated comments; these views reflect the historic American propensity to seek absolute security and to define security primarily in ideological (and economic) terms. The political culture of American foreign policy has long regarded the United States, because of its domestic political system, as a singular nation. As a consequence, American policymakers have been affected by a "deep sense of being alone" and they have regarded the United States as "perpetually beleaguered."[104] Consequently, America's foreign and defense policies have been shaped by the belief that the United States must create a favorable ideological climate abroad if its domestic institutions are to survive and flourish.[105]

Democratic peace theory panders to impulses which, however noble in the abstract, have led to disastrous military interventions abroad, strategic overextension, and the relative decline of American power. The latest example of the dangers of Wilsonianism is the Clinton administration's Partnership for Peace. Under this plan, the asserted American interest in projecting democracy into East Central Europe is advanced in support of NATO security guarantees and eventual membership for Poland, Hungary, and the Czech Republic (and some form of U.S. security guarantee for Ukraine). The underlying argument is simple: democratic governments in these countries will guarantee regional peace in the post–Cold War era, but democracy cannot take root unless these countries are provided with the "reassurance" of U.S. or NATO security guarantees.

In fact, however, East Central Europe is bound to be a highly volatile region regardless of whether NATO "moves east." The extension of NATO guarantees eastward carries with it the obvious risk that the United States will become embroiled in a future regional conflict, which could involve major powers such as Germany, Ukraine, or Russia. There is

little wisdom in assuming such potentially risky undertakings on the basis of dubious assumptions about the pacifying effects of democracy.[106]

Democratic peace theory is dangerous in another respect, as well: it is an integral component of a new (or more correctly, recycled) outlook on international politics. It is now widely believed that the spread of democracy and economic interdependence have effected a "qualitative change" in international politics, and that war and serious security competitions between or among democratic great powers are now impossible.[107] There is therefore, it is said, no need to worry about future great power challenges from states like Japan and Germany, or to worry about the relative distribution of power between the United States and those states, unless Japan or Germany were to slide back into authoritarianism.[108] The reason the United States need not be concerned with the great-power emergence of Japan and Germany is said to be simple: they are democracies and democracies do not fight democracies.

Modern-day proponents of a liberal theory of international politics have constructed an appealing vision of perpetual peace within a zone of democracy and prosperity. But this "zone of peace" is a peace of illusions. There is no evidence that democracy at the unit level negates the structural effects of anarchy at the level of the international political system. Similarly, there is no evidence that supports the sister theory: that economic interdependence leads to peace. Both ideas have been around for a long time. The fact that they are so widely accepted as a basis for international relations theory shows that for some scholars, "theories" are confirmed by the number of real-world tests that they fail. Proponents of liberal international relations theory may contend, as Russett does, that liberal approaches to international politics have not failed, but rather that they have not been tried.[109] But this is what disappointed adherents of ideological worldviews always say when belief is overcome by reality.

If American policymakers allow themselves to be mesmerized by democratic peace theory's seductive—but false—vision of the future, the

United States will be ill prepared to formulate a grand strategy that will advance its interests in the emerging world of multipolar great-power competition. Indeed, as long as the Wilsonian worldview underpins American foreign policy, policymakers will be blind to the need to have such a grand strategy, because the liberal theory of international politics defines out of existence (except with respect to non-democracies) the very phenomena that are at the core of strategy: war, the formation of power balances, and concerns about the relative distribution of power among the great powers. But in the end, as its most articulate proponents admit, liberal international relations theory is based on hope, not on fact.[110] In the final analysis, the world remains what it always has been: international politics continues to occur in an anarchic, competitive, self-help realm. This reality must be confronted, because it cannot be transcended. Given the stakes, the United States in coming years cannot afford to have either its foreign policy, or the intellectual discourse that underpins that policy, shaped by theoretical approaches that are based on wishful thinking.

NOTES

1. Bruce Russett, *Grasping the Democratic Peace: Principles for a Post–Cold War World* (Princeton: Princeton University Press, 1993), chap. 7 * * *.
2. In this article, I build upon and expand the criticisms of democratic peace theory found in John J. Mearsheimer, "Back to the Future: Instability in Europe After the Cold War," *International Security*, Vol. 15, No. 1 (Summer 1990), pp. 5–56; and Kenneth N. Waltz, "America as Model for the World? A Foreign Policy Perspective," *PS* (December 1991), pp. 667–670.
3. Other cases of crises between democratic great powers that might be studied include Anglo-French relations during the Liberal *entente cordiale* of 1832–48, Franco-Italian relations during the late 1880s and early 1890s

and, if Wilhelmine Germany is classified as a democracy, the Moroccan crises of 1905–06 and 1911 and the Samoan crises of 1889 and 1899. * * *
4. Melvin Small and J. David Singer first observed the pattern of democracies not fighting democracies in a 1976 article: Small and Singer, "The War-proneness of Democratic Regimes, 1816–1865," *Jerusalem Journal of International Relations*, Vol. 1, No. 4 (Summer 1976), pp. 50–69. * * *
5. Jack S. Levy, "Domestic Politics and War," in Robert I. Rotberg and Theodore K. Rabb, eds., *The Origin and Prevention of Major Wars* (Cambridge: Cambridge University Press, 1989), p. 88.
6. Russett, *Grasping the Democratic Peace*, p. 33; Michael W. Doyle, "Kant, Liberal Legacies, and Foreign Affairs," Part I, *Philosophy and Public Affairs*, Vol. 12, No. 3 (Summer 1983), p. 213.
7. This is the terminology employed by Russett, *Grasping the Democratic Peace*; also see Bruce Russett and Zeev Maoz, "Normative and Structural Causes of Democratic Peace," *American Political Science Review*, Vol. 87, No. 3 (September 1993), pp. 624–638. Russett points out (pp. 40–42) that, although analytically distinct, these two explanations are intertwined.
8. Doyle, "Kant, Liberal Legacies, and Foreign Affairs," pp. 205–235. See also Doyle, "Liberalism and World Politics," *American Political Science Review*, Vol. 80, No. 4 (December 1986), pp. 1151–1169; Russett, *Grasping the Democratic Peace*, pp. 38–40.
9. T. Clifton Morgan and Sally H. Campbell, "Domestic Structure, Decisional Constraints and War: So Why Kant Democracies Fight?" *Journal of Conflict Resolution*, Vol. 35, No. 2 (June 1991), pp. 187–211; and T. Clifton Morgan and Valerie L. Schwebach, "Take Two Democracies and Call Me in the Morning: A Prescription for Peace?" *International Interactions*, Vol. 17, No. 4 (Summer 1992), pp. 305–420.

10. Russett, *Grasping the Democratic Peace*, p. 31 (second emphasis added).

11. Doyle, "Kant, Liberal Legacies, and Foreign Affairs," p. 230. It is also argued that the predisposition of democratic states to regard other democracies favorably is reinforced by the fact that liberal democratic states are linked by mutually beneficial ties of economic interdependence. Democracies thus have strong incentives to act towards each other in a manner that enhances cooperation and to refrain from acting in a manner that threatens their stake in mutually beneficial cooperation. Ibid., pp. 230–232; Rummel, "Libertarianism and International Violence," [*Journal of Conflict Resolution*, Vol. 27, No. 1 (March 1983),] pp. 27–28. For the "interdependence promotes peace" argument see Richard Rosecrance, *The Rise of the Trading State* (New York: Basic Books, 1986). In fact, however, for great powers economic interdependence, rather than promoting peace, creates seemingly important interests that must be defended by overseas military commitments (commitments that carry with them the risk of war). See Christopher Layne and Benjamin C. Schwarz, "American Hegemony—Without an Enemy," *Foreign Policy*, No. 92 (Fall 1993), pp. 5–23.

12. Doyle, "Kant, Liberal Legacies, and Foreign Affairs"; and Harvey Starr, "Democracy and War: Choice, Learning and Security Communities," *Journal of Peace Research*, Vol. 29, No. 2 (1992), pp. 207–213.

13. Russett, *Grasping the Democratic Peace*, p. 33.

14. Classic explications of realism are Kenneth N. Waltz, *Theory of International Politics* (Reading, Mass.: Addison-Wesley, 1979) and Hans J. Morgenthau, rev. by Kenneth W. Thompson, *Politics Among Nations: The Struggle for Power and Peace*, 6th ed. (New York: Knopf, 1985).

15. Kenneth N. Waltz, "A Reply to My Critics," in Robert O. Keohane, ed., *Neorealism and Its Critics* (New York: Columbia University Press, 1986), p. 329.

16. Maoz and Russett, "Normative and Structural Causes," p. 624.

17. Stephen Van Evera, "What Are Case Studies? How Should They Be Performed?" unpub. memo, September 1993, Department of Political Science, MIT, p. 2.

18. Geoffrey, Blainey, *The Causes of War*, 3rd ed. (South Melbourne: Macmillan Co. of Australia, 1988), pp. 57–67. As the parable goes, while the waterbirds fight over the catch, the fisherman spreads his net.

19. * * * Democratic peace theorists have classified all eight states as having been democracies at the time of their involvement in the crises under discussion. See Doyle, "Kant, Liberal Legacies, and Foreign Affairs," Part I, pp. 214–215. Russett, *Grasping the Democratic Peace*, pp. 5–9, briefly discusses the Venezuela and Fashoda crises, but his bibliography has few historical references to these two crises (and related issues), and omits most standard sources.

20. Waltz, *Theory of International Politics*, pp. 72–73.

21. See Robert L. Rothstein, *Alliances and Small Powers* (New York: Columbia University Press, 1968), especially chap. 1.

22. As noted above, other such crises also support my argument.

23. For a brief discussion of the cultural, social, and economic bonds between Britain and the United States during the mid-nineteenth century, see Martin Crawford, *The Anglo-American Crisis of the Mid-Nineteenth Century: The Times and America, 1850–1862* (Athens: University of Georgia Press, 1987), pp. 39–55.

24. Stephen R. Rock, *Why Peace Breaks Out: Great Power Rapprochement in Historical Perspective* (Chapel Hill: University of North Carolina Press, 1989), pp. 91–119.

25. Adams, [*Great*] *Britain and the* [*American*] *Civil War* [New York: Russell and Russell, 1924], Vol. I, p. 216.

26. Quoted in Gordon H. Warren, *Fountain of Discontent: The Trent Affair and Freedom of*

the Seas (Boston: Northeastern University Press, 1981), p. 105.

27. Quoted in Adams, *Britain and the Civil War*, Vol. I, p. 217.

28. Quoted in Norman B. Ferris, *The Trent Affair: A Diplomatic Crisis* (Knoxville: University of Tennessee Press, 1977), p. 44.

29. Ibid., p. 109; Howard Jones, *Union in Peril: The Crisis Over British Intervention in the Civil War* (Chapel Hill: University of North Carolina Press, 1992), pp. 84–85.

30. Jenkins, *[Britain and the] War for the Union*, [2 vols. (Montreal: McGill-Queen's University Press, 1974–80),] p. 214.

31. Quoted in Kenneth Bourne, *Britain and the Balance of Power in North America, 1815–1908* (Berkeley: University of California Press, 1967), p. 219.

32. Ferris, *Trent Affair*, pp. 111–113.

33. Norman B. Ferris, *Desperate Diplomacy: William H. Seward's Foreign Policy, 1861* (Knoxville: University of Tennessee, 1976), p. 194.

34. Quoted in Adams, *Britain and the Civil War*, Vol. I, p. 218.

35. Warren, *Fountain of Discontent*, pp. 184–185; Adams, *Britain and the Civil War*, p. 231. Howard Jones, however, suggests that Lincoln probably intended to give up Mason and Slidell and that he may have been posturing in order to shift to other members of his cabinet the onus of advancing the argument for surrendering them. Jones, *Union in Peril*, pp. 91–92.

36. Ferris, *Trent Affair*, pp. 177–182; Jenkins, *War for the Union*, pp. 223–226; Warren, *Fountain of Discontent*, pp. 181–182.

37. See Jenkins, *War for the Union*, pp. 225–226.

38. Quoted in Ferris, *Trent Affair*, pp. 154, 147 and see also pp. 66–67, 139–141; Jones, *Union in Peril*, p. 89.

39. Quoted in ibid., p. 172 (emphasis in original). Bright's letter warned: "If you are resolved to succeed against the South, *have no war with England.*" Quoted in Adams, *Britain and the Civil War*, p. 232 (emphasis in original).

40. Walter LaFeber demonstrates that the United States injected itself into the crisis to protect its own interests, not Venezuela's. LaFeber, *The New Empire: An Interpretation of American Expansion, 1860–1898* (Ithaca: Cornell University Press, 1963), chap. 6.

41. The relationship between security concerns and American foreign and strategic policy is discussed in Richard D. Challener, *Admirals, General and Foreign Policy, 1898–1914* (Princeton: Princeton University Press, 1973) and J.A.S. Grenville and George B. Young, *Politics, Strategy, and American Diplomacy: Studies in American Foreign Policy, 1873–1917* (New Haven: Yale University Press, 1966).

42. Walter LaFeber, "The Background of Cleveland's Venezuelan Policy: A Reinterpretation," *American Historical Review*, Vol. 66, No. 4 (July 1961), p. 947; Ernest R. May, *Imperial Democracy: The Emergence of America as a Great Power* (New York: Harcourt, Brace and World, 1961), p. 34.

43. For accounts of the Fashoda crisis and its background, the following are excellent sources: William L. Langer, *The Diplomacy of Imperialism, 1890–1902*, 2d ed. (New York: Knopf, 1965), pp. 101–144, 259–302; Ronald Robinson and John Gallagher with Alice Denny, *Africa and the Victorians: The Official Mind of Imperialism* (London: Macmillan, 1981, rev. ed.), pp. 76–159, 290–306; G.N. Sanderson, *England, Europe, and the Upper Nile, 1882–1899* (Edinburgh: Edinburgh University Press, 1965), chaps. 12–15; and Sanderson, "The Origins and Significance of the Anglo-French Confrontation at Fashoda," in Prosser Gifford and William Roger Louis, eds., *France and Britain in Africa: Imperial Rivalry and Colonial Rule* (New Haven: Yale University Press, 1971), pp. 285–332.

44. Quoted in A.J.P. Taylor, "Prelude to Fashoda: The Question of the Upper Nile, 1894–5," *English Historical Review*, Vol. 65, No. 254 (January 1950), p. 54.

45. Christopher Andrew, *Theophile Delcassé and the Making of the Entente Cordiale: A Reap-*

praisal of French Foreign Policy, 1898–1905 (New York: Macmillan, 1968), pp. 21–25.

46. Ibid., p. 100; Roger Glenn Brown, *Fashoda Reconsidered: The Impact of Domestic Politics on French Policy in Africa* (Baltimore: Johns Hopkins University Press, 1970), pp. 92–93.

47. Robinson and Gallagher, *Africa and the Victorians*, p. 371.

48. Langer, *Diplomacy of Imperialism*, pp. 550–551.

49. Quoted in James Goode, *The Fashoda Crisis: A Survey of Anglo-French Imperial Policy on the Upper Nile Question, 1882–1899* (Ph.D. diss., North Texas State University, 1971), p. 150; and Darrell Bates, *The Fashoda Incident of 1898: Encounter on the Nile* (New York: Oxford University Press, 1984), p. 24.

50. Lord Salisbury's instructions quoted in Robinson and Gallagher, *Africa and the Victorians*, p. 368.

51. Sanderson, "Origins and Significance of Fashoda," p. 289.

52. Quoted in Sanderson, *The Upper Nile*, p. 346.

53. Brown, *Fashoda Reconsidered*, pp. 99–100, 127.

54. Quoted in T.W. Riker, "A Survey of British Policy in the Fashoda Crisis," *Political Science Quarterly*, Vol. 44, No. 1 (March 1929), p. 63.

55. Quoted in Keith Eubank, "The Fashoda Crisis Re-examined," *The Historian*, Vol. 22, No. 2 (February 1960), p. 152.

56. Quoted in ibid., p. 154.

57. Sanderson, *The Upper Nile*, p. 334.

58. Ibid., p. 372.

59. Ibid.; Riker, "British Policy in the Fashoda Crisis," pp. 65–67; Sanderson, *The Upper Nile*, p. 348.

60. Robinson and Gallagher, *Africa and the Victorians*, p. 376; Sanderson, *The Upper Nile*, p. 354.

61. Riker, "British Policy in the Fashoda Crisis," pp. 66–67.

62. Sanderson, "Origins and Significance of Fashoda," pp. 295, 300.

63. Quoted in Langer, *Diplomacy of Imperialism*, p. 553.

64. Langer, *Diplomacy of Imperialism*, pp. 552–553; Robinson and Gallagher, *Africa and the Victorians*, pp. 376–378; Riker, "British Policy in the Fashoda Crisis," p. 67; Sanderson, *The Upper Nile*, p. 347.

65. On the Royal Navy's advantages and London's confidence in British sea power, see Marder, *Anatomy of British See Power* [*A History of British Naval Policy in the Pre-Dreadnought Era, 1880–1905* (New York: Knopf, 1940)], pp. 320–331; Langer, *Diplomacy of Imperialism*, pp. 559–560.

66. Marder, *Anatomy of British Sea Power*, pp. 321–328.

67. Sanderson, *The Upper Nile*, p. 362.

68. Grenville, *Lord Salisbury* [*and Foreign Policy at the Close of the Nineteenth Century* (London: Athlone Press, 1964)], p. 218.

69. Royal J. Schmidt, *Versailles and the Ruhr: Seedbed of World War II* (The Hague: Martinus Nijhoff, 1968), p. 17; Marshall M. Lee and Wolfgang Michalka, *German Foreign Policy, 1917–1933: Continuity or Break?* (Leamington Spa, U.K.: Berg, 1987), p. 47; Detlev J.K. Peukert, *The Weimar Republic: The Crisis of Classical Modernity*, trans. Richard Deveson (New York: Hill and Wang, 1992), p. 61; Hermann J. Rupieper, *The Cuno Government and Reparations, 1922–1923: Politics and Economics* (The Hague: Martinus Nijhoff, 1979) p. 96.

70. Peukert, *Weimar Republic*, p. 55; Marc Trachtenberg, *Reparation in World Politics: France and European Economic Diplomacy, 1916–1923* (New York: Columbia University Press, 1980), p. 122; Stephen A. Schuker, *The End of French Predominance in Europe: The Financial Crisis of 1924 and the Adoption of the Dawes Plan* (Chapel Hill: University of North Carolina Press, 1976), p. 6.

71. On Berlin's strategy of seeking revision through fulfillment, see David Felix, *Walther Rathenau and the Weimar Republic: The Politics of Reparations* (Baltimore: Johns Hopkins University Press); and Rupieper, *The Cuno Government*.

72. D. Stevenson, *French War Aims Against Germany, 1914–1919* (Oxford: Clarendon Press, 1982), pp. 26–27.

73. On French war aims see Walter A. McDougall, *France's Rhineland Diplomacy, 1914–1924: The Last Bid for a Balance of Power in Europe* (Princeton: Princeton University Press, 1978), p. 25; Schmidt, *Versailles and the Ruhr*, pp. 22–23; Stevenson, *French War Aims*, pp. 38–39.

74. Stevenson, *French War Aims*, pp. 195–196. The definitive account of France's Rhenish policy is McDougall, *Rhineland Diplomacy*.

75. Stevenson, *French War Aims*, pp. 135–136. Leaders such as Poincaré actively promoted anti-German attitudes, not a particularly difficult task. See Schmidt, *Versailles and the Ruhr*, p. 231.

76. Rupieper, *The Cuno Government*, pp. 88, 96; Schmidt, *Versailles and the Ruhr*, p. 52.

77. McDougall, *Rhineland Diplomacy*, p. 114.

78. On the striking decline in the frequency of great-power war during the past two centuries see Jack S. Levy, *War and the Modern Great Power System, 1495–1975* (Lexington: University Press of Kentucky, 1983), chap. 6.

79. David E. Spiro, "The Insignificance of the Liberal Peace," *International Security*, Vol. 19, No. 2 (Fall 1994), pp. 50–86. Spiro concludes that the statistical evidence for the liberal peace is weak: either the data are ambiguous, or random chance would predict the absence of wars between democracies. Spiro is sympathetic to the democratic peace theory. He suggests that the tendency of liberal states to ally with, instead of opposing, each other is important and probably is rooted in liberal norms.

80. Russett, *Grasping the Democratic Peace*, p. 16. However, sometimes things *are* exactly as they seem. Russett excludes the War of 1812 on the grounds that, prior to the Reform Bill of 1832, Britain was not a democracy. Yet, until the "revolution" that followed Andrew Jackson's 1828 election to the presidency, the United States was not appreciably more democratic than Britain. *The Federalist* and the Constitution itself, in its provision for an Electoral College and indirect election of senators, reflect the desire of the framers to circumscribe egalitarian democratic impulses. In early nineteenth-century America, suffrage was significantly restricted by property and other qualifications imposed at the state level. See Clinton Williamson, *American Suffrage: From Property to Democracy, 1750 to 1860* (Princeton: Princeton University Press, 1960); Paul Kleppner, et al., *The Evolution of American Electoral Systems* (Westport, Conn.: Greenwood Press, 1981).

81. A good example is James L. Ray, "Wars Between Democracies: Rare, or Nonexistent?" *International Interactions*, Vol. 18, No. 3 (1993), pp. 251–276. After readjusting the definition of democracy, Ray takes a brief look at five of the nineteen alleged exceptions to the rule that democratic states do not fight each other and concludes that over the last 200 to 250 years there are no exceptions to the rule.

82. Russett's comments (*Grasping the Democratic Peace*, p. 17) notwithstanding, after secession the War Between the States did take on the cast of an international conflict between two sovereign democratic entities. It certainly was so regarded by contemporaneous observers (and had the Confederacy prevailed, it certainly would be so regarded today). For example, no less a figure than Prime Minister William Gladstone, the arch-apostle of British Liberalism, observed that: "Jefferson Davis and other leaders of the South have made an army; they are making, it appears, a navy; and they have made what is more than either: they have made a nation." Quoted in James M. McPherson, *Battle Cry of Freedom: The Civil War Era* (New York: Oxford University Press, 1988), p. 552.

83. Democratic peace theory "*extends to the international arena* the cultural norms of live-and-let-live and peaceful conflict resolution that operate *within* democracies." Ibid., p. 19 (emphasis added).

84. Doyle, "Kant, Liberal Legacies, and Foreign Affairs," Part I, p. 216, fn 8.

85. Ibid. I do not address the issue of whether any state can in fact have such a tightly compartmentalized political system that it can be democratic in domestic politics but not in foreign policy. I know of no other example of a bifurcated democracy. If this concept of bifurcated democracy were accepted, proponents of democratic peace theory could defend their argument by asserting that, while democratic in the realm of domestic policy, in 1914 Britain and France, like Wilhelmine Germany, also were non-democratic in terms of foreign policy.

86. See Lamar Cecil, *The German Diplomatic Service, 1871–1914* (Princeton: Princeton University Press, 1976); Paul Gordon Lauren, *Diplomats and Bureaucrats: The First Institutional Responses to Twentieth Century Diplomacy in France and Germany* (Stanford: Hoover Institution Press, 1976), pp. 27–29; Frederick L. Schuman, *War and Diplomacy in the French Republic: An Inquiry into Political Motivations and the Control of Foreign Policy* (New York: Whittlesy House, 1931); Zara S. Steiner, *The Foreign Office and Foreign Policy, 1898–1914* (Cambridge: Cambridge University Press, 1969); and Steiner, "The Foreign Office under Sir Edward Grey," in F.H. Hinsley, ed., *British Foreign Policy Under Sir Edward Grey* (Cambridge: Cambridge University Press, 1977), pp. 22–69.

87. Schuman, *War and Diplomacy*, pp. 21, 28–32.

88. Andrew, *Theophile Delcassé*, p. 64.

89. Ibid., p. 22; Lauren, *Diplomats and Bureaucrats*, p. 29.

90. Lauren, *Diplomats and Bureaucrats*, p. 29.

91. Schuman, *War and Diplomacy*, p. 143.

92. See Samuel R. Williamson, *The Politics of Grand Strategy: Britain and France Prepare for War, 1904–1914* (Cambridge: Harvard University Press, 1969).

93. Ibid., pp. 134, 137–138, 202–204, 330–331.

94. Ibid., pp. 198–200.

95. Grey threatened to resign from the Cabinet unless it agreed to take Britain into the war on France's side. Grey's resignation threat was determinative because the non-interventionist Cabinet Radicals realized that their refusal to declare war would lead to the Cabinet's replacement either by a Conservative-Unionist government or by a coalition between the Conservatives and the Liberal Imperialists. See K.M. Wilson, "The British Cabinet's Decision for War, 2 August 1914," *British Journal of International Studies*, Vol. 1, No. 2 (July 1975), pp. 148–159.

96. The classification of Wilhelmine Germany as a democracy is also supported by an analysis of the foreign policy making process of its successor, the Weimar Republic. Although the Weimar Republic invariably is classified as a democracy, in crucial respects, it closely resembled the Second Reich. During the Weimar Republic, the Foreign Office and the Army collaborated to ensure that the processes of formulating foreign policy and grand strategy were insulated from the Reichstag's oversight and control. The leading study is Gaines Post, Jr., *The Civil-Military Fabric of Weimar Foreign Policy* (Princeton: Princeton University Press, 1973). Post observes (p. 358) that the Weimar Republic stands as a "model for the virtual exclusion of the parliamentary or legislative level from politico-military activity in a representative system of government." If Weimar Germany is considered to be a democracy, then how can Wilhelmine Germany be classified as a non-democracy?

97. For a discussion of the leftist ideological biases that color the writings of Fritz Fischer's disciples and a critique of Fischer, Berghahn, Kehr, and Wehler, see Wolfgang J. Mommsen, "Domestic Factors in German Foreign Policy before 1914," *Central European History*, Vol. 6, No. 1 (March 1973), pp. 4–18. An insightful critique of the "failure of liberalism" school is Klaus P. Fischer, "The Liberal Image of German History," *Modern Age*, Vol. 22, No. 4 (Fall 1978), pp. 371–383.

98. This thesis is developed in Otto Hintze, "The Formation of States and Constitutional Development: A Study in History and Politics"; Hintze, "Military Organization and the Organization of the State"; and Hintze, "The Origins of the Modern Ministerial System: A Comparative Study," in Felix Gilbert, ed., *The Historical Essays of Otto Hintze* (New York: Oxford University Press, 1975).

99. This argument is developed in Brian M. Downing. *The Military Revolution and Political Change: Origins of Democracy and Political Change* (Princeton: Princeton University Press, 1992).

100. See for example Joshua Muravchik, *Exporting Democracy: Fulfilling America's Destiny* (Washington, D.C.: AEI Press, 1991); and Larry Diamond, "Promoting Democracy," *Foreign Policy*, No. 87 (Summer 1992), pp. 25–46.

101. "Remarks of Anthony Lake," Johns Hopkins School of Advanced International Studies, Washington, D.C., September 21, 1993 (Washington, D.C.: National Security Council Press Office).

102. Lake stated that the Clinton administration does not propose to embark on a "democratic crusade." Both Doyle and Russett acknowledge that democratic peace theory could encourage democratic states to pursue aggressive policies toward non-democracies, and both express worry at this. Doyle, "Kant, Liberal Legacies, and Foreign Affairs," Part II; Russett, *Grasping the Democratic Peace*, p. 136.

103. Quoted in Russett, *Grasping the Democratic Peace*, p. 33.

104. William Appleman Williams, *Empire As A Way of Life: An Essay on the Causes and Character of America's Present Predicament Along With a Few Thoughts About An Alternative* (New York: Oxford University Press, 1980), p. 53.

105. Lloyd C. Gardner, *A Covenant With Power: America and World Order from Wilson to Reagan* (New York: Oxford University Press,

1984), p. 27. For an excellent critique of the notion that America's domestic ideology must be validated by its foreign policy, see Michael H. Hunt, *Ideology and U.S. Foreign Policy* (New Haven: Yale University Press, 1987).

106. It could be argued that if Hintze's argument is correct (that secure states are more likely to become, or remain, democratic), then extending security guarantees to states like Ukraine, or preserving extant alliances with states like Germany, Japan, and South Korea, is precisely what the United States should do. Indeed, the Bush and Clinton administrations have both subscribed to a worldview that holds that the United States, as the sole remaining superpower, must take responsibility for maintaining regional power balances in Europe and East Asia. By preventing the "renationalization" of other states' security policies and by foreclosing the possibility of regional power vacuums, the United States, it is argued, can preserve the kind of international environment that is conducive to the spread of democracy and economic interdependence. For critiques of this policy see Christopher Layne, "The Unipolar Illusion: Why New Great Powers Will Rise," *International Security*, Vol. 17, No. 4 (Spring 1993), pp. 5–51; Layne, "American Grand Strategy After the Cold War: Primacy or Blue Water?" in Charles F. Hermann, ed., *American Defense Annual* (New York: Lexington Books, 1994); and Layne and Schwarz, "American Hegemony."

107. Robert Jervis, "The Future of World Politics: Will It Resemble the Past?" *International Security*, Vol. 16, No. 3 (Winter 1991/92), pp. 39–73.

108. For an example of this argument see James M. Goldgeier and Michael McFaul, "A Tale of Two Worlds: Core and Periphery in the Post–Cold War Era," *International Organization*, Vol. 46, No. 3 (Spring 1992), pp. 467–491.

109. Russett, *Grasping the Democratic Peace*, p. 9,

says that Kantian and Wilsonian principles have not been given a real chance to operate in international politics.

110. Russett, *Grasping the Democratic Peace*, p. 136, argues that, "understanding the sources of democratic peace can have the effect of a self-fulfilling prophecy. Social scientists sometimes create reality as well as analyze it. Insofar as norms do guide behavior, repeating those norms helps to make them effective. *Repeating the norms as descriptive principles can help to make them true.*" (Emphasis added.)

12   GLOBALIZATION AND GLOBALIZING ISSUES

Globalization is an overarching process discussed at several different junctures in Essentials of International Relations. *Of the recent changes in international relations, none has been as complex as this multifaceted phenomenon, involving economic, political, social, and cultural ramifications.* Human Development Report 1999, *a product of the U.N. Development Programme, argues that globalization represents more than economic and financial growth; it needs to have a "human face." David Held and his collaborators in Great Britain, drawing on their book,* Global Transformations: Politics, Economics, and Culture *(1999), investigate the analytic dimensions of globalization for their piece in the new scholarly journal* Global Governance. *Thomas Friedman, in an excerpt from his national bestseller,* The Lexus and the Olive Tree *(1999), examines the backlash against globalization.*

Arising out of the interconnectedness of globalization, new issues have become part of the global agenda—issues of population, disease, the environment, and human rights. Together these represent the new security concerns for the twenty-first century. Lester R. Brown and Brian Halweil, writing in World Watch, *introduce a number of these issues, including the population explosion, the reversal in the human death rate caused by the AIDS epidemic in Africa and its social consequences, declining agricultural production, and environmental problems.*

In many of these issues of globalization, the rights of the individual are pitted against the rights of the global community. Does a couple have the right of unlimited procreation? What are the rights of the community to protect itself against the scourge of AIDS? Do the rights of the individual take precedence over the rights of the community in the use of land and natural resources? In trying to resolve some of these dilemmas, some people have argued in favor of the enforcement of universal human rights. These are human rights applicable across all peoples and all cultures. Other writers think that the notion of a universality of human rights is but an illusion. Amartya Sen, in the last selection of this chapter, suggests that there is a great diversity of human rights experience among both Western and non-

Western cultures. The application of Western human rights standards across cultures may therefore be problematic. These questions of the entitlements of the individual versus the entitlements of the community address core problems of culture, legality, and morality. In this reader, we have presented different perspectives about the salience of these and other issues, and we challenge students to continue to ponder them.

U.N. DEVELOPMENT PROGRAMME

Globalization with a Human Face

The real wealth of a nation is its people. And the purpose of development is to create an enabling environment for people to enjoy long, healthy and creative lives. This simple but powerful truth is too often forgotten in the pursuit of material and financial wealth." Those are the opening lines of the first *Human Development Report*, published in 1990. This tenth *Human Development Report*—like the first and all the others—is about people. It is about the growing interdependence of people in today's globalizing world.

Globalization Is Not New, but the Present Era Has Distinctive Features. Shrinking Space, Shrinking Time and Disappearing Borders Are Linking People's Lives More Deeply, More Intensely, More Immediately than Ever Before.

More than $1.5 trillion is now exchanged in the world's currency markets each day, and nearly a fifth of the goods and services produced each year are traded. But globalization is more than the flow

From U.N. Development Programme, *Human Development Report 1999* (New York: Oxford University Press, 1999), 1–8.

of money and commodities—it is the growing interdependence of the world's people. And globalization is a process integrating not just the economy but culture, technology and governance. People everywhere are becoming connected—affected by events in far corners of the world. The collapse of the Thai baht not only threw millions into unemployment in South-East Asia—the ensuing decline in global demand meant slowdowns in social investment in Latin America and a sudden rise in the cost of imported medicines in Africa.

Globalization is not new. Recall the early sixteenth century and the late nineteenth. But this era is different:

- *New markets*—foreign exchange and capital markets linked globally, operating 24 hours a day, with dealings at a distance in real time.
- *New tools*—Internet links, cellular phones, media networks.
- *New actors*—the World Trade Organization (WTO) with authority over national governments, the multinational corporations with more economic power than many states, the global networks of non-governmental organizations (NGOs) and other groups that transcend national boundaries.
- *New rules*—multilateral agreements on trade, services and intellectual property,

backed by strong enforcement mechanisms and more binding for national governments, reducing the scope for national policy.

Globalization Offers Great Opportunities for Human Advance— but Only with Stronger Governance

This era of globalization is opening many opportunities for millions of people around the world. Increased trade, new technologies, foreign investments, expanding media and Internet connections are fuelling economic growth and human advance. All this offers enormous potential to eradicate poverty in the 21st century—to continue the unprecedented progress in the 20th century. We have more wealth and technology—and more commitment to a global community—than ever before.

Global markets, global technology, global ideas and global solidarity can enrich the lives of people everywhere, greatly expanding their choices. The growing interdependence of people's lives calls for shared values and a shared commitment to the human development of all people.

The post–cold war world of the 1990s has sped progress in defining such values—in adopting human rights and in setting development goals in the United Nations conferences on environment, population, social development, women and human settlements.

But today's globalization is being driven by market expansion—opening national borders to trade, capital, information—outpacing governance of these markets and their repercussions for people. More progress has been made in norms, standards, policies and institutions for open global markets than for people and their rights. And a new commitment is needed to the ethics of universalism set out in the Universal Declaration of Human Rights.

Competitive markets may be the best guarantee of efficiency, but not necessarily of equity. Liberalization and privatization can be a step to competitive markets—but not a guarantee of them. And markets are neither the first nor the last word in human development. Many activities and goods that are critical to human development are provided outside the market—but these are being squeezed by the pressures of global competition. There is a fiscal squeeze on public goods, a time squeeze on care activities and an incentive squeeze on the environment.

When the market goes too far in dominating social and political outcomes, the opportunities and rewards of globalization spread unequally and inequitably—concentrating power and wealth in a select group of people, nations and corporations, marginalizing the others. When the market gets out of hand, the instabilities show up in boom and bust economies, as in the financial crisis in East Asia and its worldwide repercussions, cutting global output by an estimated $2 trillion in 1998–2000. When the profit motives of market players get out of hand, they challenge people's ethics—and sacrifice respect for justice and human rights.

The challenge of globalization in the new century is not to stop the expansion of global markets. The challenge is to find the rules and institutions for stronger governance—local, national, regional and global—to preserve the advantages of global markets and competition, but also to provide enough space for human, community and environmental resources to ensure that globalization works for people—not just for profits. Globalization with:

- *Ethics*—less violation of human rights, not more.
- *Equity*—less disparity within and between nations, not more.
- *Inclusion*—less marginalization of people and countries, not more.
- *Human security*—less instability of societies and less vulnerability of people, not more.
- *Sustainability*—less environmental destruction, not more.
- *Development*—less poverty and deprivation, not more.

The Opportunities and Benefits of Globalization Need to Be Shared Much More Widely

Since the 1980s many countries have seized the opportunities of economic and technological globalization. Beyond the industrial countries, the newly industrializing East Asian tigers are joined by Chile, the Dominican Republic, India, Mauritius, Poland, Turkey and many others linking into global markets, attracting foreign investment and taking advantage of technological advance. Their export growth has averaged more than 5% a year, diversifying into manufactures.

At the other extreme are the many countries benefiting little from expanding markets and advancing technology—Madagascar, Niger, the Russian Federation, Tajikistan and Venezuela among them.

These countries are becoming even more marginal—ironic, since many of them are highly "integrated," with exports nearly 30% of GDP for Sub-Saharan Africa and only 19% for the OECD. But these countries hang on the vagaries of global markets, with the prices of primary commodities having fallen to their lowest in a century and a half. They have shown little growth in exports and attracted virtually no foreign investment. In sum, today, global opportunities are unevenly distributed—between countries and people (see figure).

If global opportunities are not shared better, the failed growth of the last decades will continue. More than 80 countries still have per capita incomes lower than they were a decade or more ago. While 40 countries have sustained average per capita income growth of more than 3% a year since 1990, 55 countries, mostly in Sub-Saharan Africa and Eastern Europe and the Commonwealth of Independent States (CIS), have had declining per capita incomes.

Many people are also missing out on employment opportunities. The global labour market is increasingly integrated for the highly skilled—corporate executives, scientists, entertainers and the many others who form the global professional elite—with high mobility and wages. But the market for unskilled labour is highly restricted by national barriers.

Inequality has been rising in many countries since the early 1980s. In China disparities are widening between the export-oriented regions of the coast and the interior: the human poverty index is just under 20% in coastal provinces, but more than 50% in inland Guizhou. The countries of Eastern Europe and the CIS have registered some of the largest increases ever in the Gini coefficient, a measure of income inequality. OECD countries also registered big increases in inequality after the 1980s—especially Sweden, the United Kingdom and the United States.

Inequality between countries has also increased. The income gap between the fifth of the world's people living in the richest countries and the fifth in the poorest was 74 to 1 in 1997, up from 60 to 1 in 1990 and 30 to 1 in 1960. In the nineteenth century, too, inequality grew rapidly during the last three decades, in an era of rapid global integration: the income gap between the top and bottom countries increased from 3 to 1 in 1820 to 7 to 1 in 1870 and 11 to 1 in 1913.

By the late 1990s the fifth of the world's people living in the highest-income countries had:

- 86% of world GDP—the bottom fifth just 1%.
- 82% of world export markets—the bottom fifth just 1%.
- 68% of foreign direct investment—the bottom fifth just 1%.
- 74% of world telephone lines, today's basic means of communication—the bottom fifth just 1.5%.

Some have predicted convergence. Yet the past decade has shown increasing concentration of income, resources and wealth among people, corporations and countries:

- OECD countries, with 19% of the global population, have 71% of global trade in goods and services, 58% of foreign direct investment and 91% of all Internet users.

Stark Disparities between Rich and Poor in Global Opportunity
(1997 shares)

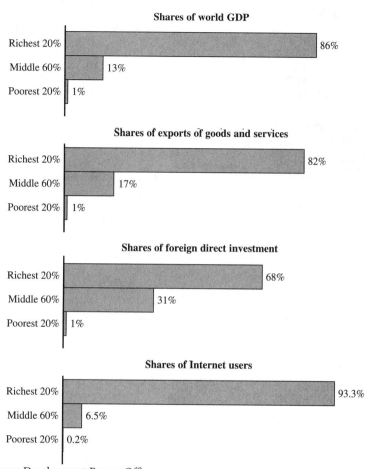

Shares of world GDP

Richest 20% — 86%
Middle 60% — 13%
Poorest 20% — 1%

Shares of exports of goods and services

Richest 20% — 82%
Middle 60% — 17%
Poorest 20% — 1%

Shares of foreign direct investment

Richest 20% — 68%
Middle 60% — 31%
Poorest 20% — 1%

Shares of Internet users

Richest 20% — 93.3%
Middle 60% — 6.5%
Poorest 20% — 0.2%

Source: Human Development Report Office

- The world's 200 richest people more than doubled their net worth in the four years to 1998, to more than $1 trillion. The assets of the top three billionaires are more than the combined GNP of all least developed countries and their 600 million people.
- The recent wave of mergers and acquisitions is concentrating industrial power in megacorporations—at the risk of eroding competition. By 1998 the top 10 companies in pesticides controlled 85% of a $31 billion global market—and the top 10 in telecommunications, 86% of a $262 billion market.

- In 1993 just 10 countries accounted for 84% of global research and development expenditures and controlled 95% of the US patents of the past two decades. Moreover, more than 80% of patents granted in developing countries belong to residents of industrial countries.

All these trends are not the inevitable consequences of global economic integration—but they have run ahead of global governance to share the benefits.

Globalization Is Creating New Threats to Human Security—in Rich Countries and Poor

One achievement of recent decades has been greater security for people in many countries—more political freedom and stability in Chile, peace in Central America, safer streets in the United States. But in the globalizing world of shrinking time, shrinking space and disappearing borders, people are confronting new threats to human security—sudden and hurtful disruptions in the pattern of daily life.

FINANCIAL VOLATILITY AND ECONOMIC INSECURITY

The financial turmoil in East Asia in 1997–99 demonstrates the risks of global financial markets. Net capital flows to Indonesia, the Republic of Korea, Malaysia, the Philippines and Thailand rocketed in the 1990s, reaching $93 billion in 1996. As turmoil hit market after market, these flows reversed overnight—with an outflow of $12 billion in 1997. The swing amounted to 11% of the precrisis GDPs of these countries. Two important lessons come out of this experience.

First, the human impacts are severe and are likely to persist long after economic recovery.

Bankruptcies spread. Education and health budgets came under pressure. More than 13 million people lost their jobs. As prices of essentials rose sharply, real wages fell sharply, down some 40–60% in Indonesia. The consequences go deeper—all countries report erosion of their social fabric, with social unrest, more crime, more violence in the home.

Recovery seems to be on the way, most evidently in Korea and least in Indonesia. But while output growth, payment balances, interest rates and inflation may be returning to normal, human lives take longer to recover. A review of financial crises in 80 countries over the past few decades shows that real wages take an average of three years to pick up again, and that employment growth does not regain precrisis levels for several years after that.

Second, far from being isolated incidents, financial crises have become increasingly common with the spread and growth of global capital flows. They result from rapid buildups and reversals of short-term capital flows and are likely to recur. More likely when national institutions regulating financial markets are not well developed, they are now recognized as systemic features of global capital markets. No single country can withstand their whims, and global action is needed to prevent and manage them.

JOB AND INCOME INSECURITY

In both poor and rich countries dislocations from economic and corporate restructuring, and from dismantling the institutions of social protection, have meant greater insecurity in jobs and incomes. The pressures of global competition have led countries and employers to adopt more flexible labour policies with more precarious work arrangements. Workers without contracts or with new, less secure contracts make up 30% of the total in Chile, 39% in Colombia.

France, Germany, the United Kingdom and other countries have weakened worker dismissal laws. Mergers and acquisitions have come with corporate restructuring and massive layoffs. Sustained economic growth has not reduced unemployment in Europe—leaving it at 11% for a decade, affecting 35 million. In Latin America growth has created jobs, but 85% of them are in the informal sector.

HEALTH INSECURITY

Growing travel and migration have helped spread HIV/AIDS. More than 33 million people were living with HIV/AIDS in 1998, with almost 6 million new infections in that year. And the epidemic is now spreading rapidly to new locations, such as rural India and Eastern Europe and the CIS. With 95% of the 16,000 infected each day living in developing countries, AIDS has become a poor person's disease, taking a heavy toll on life expectancy, reversing the gains of recent decades. For nine countries in Africa, a loss of 17 years in life expectancy is projected by 2010, back to the levels of the 1960s.

CULTURAL INSECURITY

Globalization opens people's lives to culture and all its creativity—and to the flow of ideas and knowledge. But the new culture carried by expanding global markets is disquieting. As Mahatma Gandhi expressed so eloquently earlier in the century, "I do not want my house to be walled in on all sides and my windows to be stuffed. I want the cultures of all the lands to be blown about my house as freely as possible. But I refuse to be blown off my feet by any." Today's flow of culture is unbalanced, heavily weighted in one direction, from rich countries to poor.

Weightless goods—with high knowledge content rather than material content—now make for some of the most dynamic sectors in today's most advanced economies. The single largest export industry for the United States is not aircraft or automobiles, it is entertainment—Hollywood films grossed more than $30 billion worldwide in 1997.

The expansion of global media networks and satellite communications technologies gives rise to a powerful new medium with a global reach. These networks bring Hollywood to remote villages—the number of television sets per 1,000 people almost doubled between 1980 and 1995, from 121 to 235. And the spread of global brands—Nike, Sony—is setting new social standards from Delhi to Warsaw to Rio de Janeiro. Such onslaughts of foreign culture can put cultural diversity at risk, and make people fear losing their cultural identity. What is needed is support to indigenous and national cultures—to let them flourish alongside foreign cultures.

PERSONAL INSECURITY

Criminals are reaping the benefits of globalization. Deregulated capital markets, advances in information and communications technology and cheaper transport make flows easier, faster and less restricted not just for medical knowledge but for heroin—not just for books and seeds but for dirty money and weapons.

Illicit trade—in drugs, women, weapons and laundered money—is contributing to the violence and crime that threaten neighbourhoods around the world. Drug-related crimes increased from 4 per 100,000 people in Belarus in 1990 to 28 in 1997, and from 1 per 100,000 to 8 in Estonia. The weapons trade feeds street crime as well as civil strife. In South Africa machine guns are pouring in from Angola and Mozambique. The traffic in women and girls for sexual exploitation—500,000 a year to Western Europe alone—is one of the most heinous violations of human rights, estimated to be a $7 billion business.

The Internet is an easy vehicle for trafficking in drugs, arms and women through nearly untraceable networks. In 1995 the illegal drug trade was estimated at 8% of world trade, more than the trade in motor vehicles or in iron and steel. Money laundering—which the International Monetary Fund (IMF) estimates at equivalent to 2–5% of global GDP—hides the traces of crime in split seconds, with the click of a mouse.

At the root of all this is the growing influence of organized crime, estimated to gross $1.5 trillion a year, rivalling multinational corporations as an economic power. Global crime groups have the power to criminalize politics, business and the police, developing efficient networks, extending their reach deep and wide.

ENVIRONMENTAL INSECURITY

Chronic environmental degradation—today's silent emergency—threatens people worldwide and undercuts the livelihoods of at least half a billion people. Poor people themselves, having little choice, put pressure on the environment, but so does the consumption of the rich. The growing export markets for fish, shrimp, paper and many other products mean depleted stocks, less biodiversity and fewer forests. Most of the costs are borne by the poor—though it is the world's rich who benefit most. The fifth of the world's people living in the richest countries consume 84% of the world's paper.

Closely related to many other forms of insecurity is the rise of social tensions that threaten political stability and community cohesion. Of the 61 major armed conflicts fought between 1989 and 1998, only three were between states—the rest were civil.

Globalization has given new characteristics to conflicts. Feeding these conflicts is the global traffic in weapons, involving new actors and blurring political and business interests. In the power vacuum of the post–old war era, military companies and mercenary armies began offering training to governments—and corporations. Accountable only to those who pay them, these hired military services pose a severe threat to human security.

New Information and Communications Technologies Are Driving Globalization—but Polarizing the World into the Connected and the Isolated

With the costs of communications plummeting and innovative tools easier to use, people around the world have burst into conversation using the Internet, mobile phones and fax machines. The fastest-growing communications tool ever, the Internet had more than 140 million users in mid-1998, a number expected to pass 700 million by 2001.

Communications networks can foster great advances in health and education. They can also empower small players. The previously unheard voices of NGOs helped halt the secretive OECD negotiations for the Multilateral Agreement on Investment, called for corporate accountability and created support for marginal communities. Barriers of size, time and distance are coming down for small businesses, for governments of poor countries, for remote academics and specialists.

Information and communications technology can also open a fast track to knowledge-based growth—a track followed by India's software exports, Ireland's computing services and the Eastern Caribbean's data processing.

Despite the potential for development, the Internet poses severe problems of access and exclusion. Who was in the loop in 1998?

- *Geography divides.* Thailand has more cellular phones than Africa. South Asia, home to 23% of the world's people, has less than 1% of Internet users.
- *Education is a ticket to the network high society.* Globally, 30% of users had at least one university degree.
- *Income buys access.* To purchase a computer would cost the average Bangladeshi more than eight years' income, the average American, just one month's wage.
- *Men and youth dominate.* Women make up just 17% of the Internet users in Japan, only 7% in China. Most users in China and the United Kingdom are under 30.
- *English talks.* English prevails in almost 80% of all Websites, yet less than one in 10 people worldwide speaks it.

This exclusivity is creating parallel worlds. Those with income, education and—literally—connections have cheap and instantaneous access to information. The rest are left with uncertain, slow and costly access. When people in these two worlds live and compete side by side, the advantage of being connected will overpower the marginal and impoverished, cutting off their voices and concerns from the global conversation.

This risk of marginalization does not have to be a reason for despair. It should be a call to action for:

- *More connectivity:* setting up telecommunications and computer hardware.
- *More community:* focusing on group access, not just individual ownership.
- *More capacity:* building human skills for the knowledge society.

- *More content:* putting local views, news, culture and commerce on the Web.
- *More creativity:* adapting technology to local needs and opportunities.
- *More collaboration:* developing Internet governance to accommodate diverse national needs.
- *More cash:* finding innovative ways to fund the knowledge society everywhere.

Global Technological Breakthroughs Offer Great Potential for Human Advance and for Eradicating Poverty—but Not with Today's Agendas

Liberalization, privatization and tighter intellectual property rights are shaping the path for the new technologies, determining how they are used. But the privatization and concentration of technology are going too far. Corporations define research agendas and tightly control their findings with patents, racing to lay claim to intellectual property under the rules set out in the agreement on Trade-Related Aspects of Intellectual Property Rights (TRIPS).

Poor people and poor countries risk being pushed to the margin in this proprietary regime controlling the world's knowledge:

- In defining research agendas, money talks, not need—cosmetic drugs and slow-ripening tomatoes come higher on the priority list than drought-resistant crops or a vaccine against malaria.
- From new drugs to better seeds, the best of the new technologies are priced for those who can pay. For poor people, they remain far out of reach.
- Tighter property rights raise the price of technology transfer, blocking developing countries from the dynamic knowledge sectors. The TRIPS agreement will enable multinationals to dominate the global market even more easily.

- New patent laws pay scant attention to the knowledge of indigenous people. These laws ignore cultural diversity in the way innovations are created and shared—and diversity in views on what can and should be owned, from plant varieties to human life. The result: a silent theft of centuries of knowledge from some of the poorest communities in developing countries.
- Despite the risks of genetic engineering, the rush and push of commercial interests are putting profits before people.

A broader perspective is needed. Intellectual property rights were first raised as a multilateral trade issue in 1986 to crack down on counterfeit goods. The reach of those rights now goes far beyond that—into the ownership of life. As trade, patents and copyright determine the paths of technology—and of nations—questioning today's arrangements is not just about economic flows. It is about preserving biodiversity. Addressing the ethics of patents on life. Ensuring access to health care. Respecting other cultures' forms of ownership. Preventing a growing technological gap between the knowledge-driven global economy and the rest trapped in its shadows.

The Relentless Pressures of Global Competition Are Squeezing Out Care, the Invisible Heart of Human Development

Caring labour—providing for children, the sick and the elderly, as well as all the rest of us, exhausted from the demands of daily life—is an important input for the development of human capabilities. It is also a capability in itself. And it is special—nurturing human relationships with love, altruism, reciprocity and trust. Without enough care, individuals do not flourish. Without attention and stimulus, babies languish, failing to reach their full potential. And without nurturing from their families, children underperform in school.

Human support to others is essential for social

cohesion and a strong community. It is also essential for economic growth. But the market gives few incentives and few rewards for it. Societies everywhere have allocated women much of the responsibility and the burden for care—women spend two-thirds of their work time in unpaid activities, men only a quarter. Women predominate in caring professions and domestic service. Families, nations and corporations have been free-riding on caring labour provided mostly by women, unpaid or underpaid.

But today's competitive global market is putting pressures on the time, resources and incentives for the supply of caring labour. Women's participation in the formal labour market is rising, yet they continue to carry the burden of care—women's hours spent in unpaid work remain high. In Bangladesh women in the garment industry spend 56 hours a week in paid employment on top of 31 hours in unpaid work—a total of 87 hours, compared with 67 by men. Men's share of unpaid care work is increasing slowly in Europe and other OECD countries but not in most developing countries and in Eastern Europe.

Meanwhile, fiscal pressures are cutting back on the supply of state-provided care services. Tax revenue declined in poor countries from 18% of GDP in the early 1980s to 16% in the 1990s. Public services deteriorated markedly—the result of economic stagnation, structural adjustment programmes or the dismantling of state services, especially in the transition economies of Eastern Europe and the CIS.

And global economic competition has put pressure on the wages for caring labour, as the wage gap increases between tradable and nontradable sectors, and between the skilled and unskilled.

How can societies design new arrangements for care in the global economy? The traditional model of a patriarchal household is no solution—a new approach must build gender equity into sharing the burdens and responsibility for care. New institutional mechanisms, better public policy and a social consensus are needed to provide incentives for rewarding care and increasing its supply and quality:

- Public support for care services—such as care for the elderly, day care for children and protection of social services during crises.
- Labour market policies and employer action to support the care needs of employees.
- More gender balance and equity in carrying the burden of household care services.

Each society needs to find its own arrangements based on its history and conditions. But all societies need to devise a better solution. And all need to make a strong commitment to preserving time and resources for care—and the human bonds that nourish human development.

National and Global Governance Have to Be Reinvented—with Human Development and Equity at Their Core

None of these pernicious trends—growing marginalization, growing human insecurity, growing inequality—is inevitable. With political will and commitment in the global community, they can all be reversed. With stronger governance—local, national, regional and global—the benefits of competitive markets can be preserved with clear rules and boundaries, and stronger action can be taken to meet the needs of human development.

Governance does not mean mere government. It means the framework of rules, institutions and established practices that set limits and give incentives for the behaviour of individuals, organizations and firms. Without strong governance, the dangers of global conflicts could be a reality of the 21st century—trade wars promoting national and corporate interests, uncontrolled financial volatility setting off civil conflicts, untamed global crime infecting safe neighbourhoods and criminalizing politics, business and the police.

With the market collapse in East Asia, with the contagion to Brazil, Russia and elsewhere and with the threat of a global recession still looming, global governance is being re-examined. But the current debate is:

- Too narrow, limited to the concerns of economic growth and financial stability and neglecting broader human concerns such as persistent global poverty, growing inequality between and within countries, exclusion of poor people and countries and persisting human rights abuses.
- Too geographically unbalanced, dominated by the largest economies—usually the G-7, sometimes just the G-1, and only occasionally bringing in the large newly industrializing countries. Most small and poor developing countries are excluded, as are people's organizations.

  Nor does the debate address the current weaknesses, imbalances and inequities in global governance—which, having developed in an ad hoc way, leaves many gaps.
- Multilateral agreements have helped establish global markets without considering their impacts on human development and poverty.

- The structures and processes for global policy-making are not representative. The key economic structures—the IMF, World Bank, G-7, G-10, G-22, OECD, WTO—are dominated by the large and rich countries, leaving poor countries and poor people with little influence and little voice, either for lack of membership or for lack of capacity for effective representation and participation. There is little transparency in decisions, and there is no structured forum for civil society institutions to express their views.
- There are no mechanisms for making ethical standards and human rights binding for corporations and individuals, not just governments.

In short, stronger national and global governance are needed for human well-being, not for the market.

*   *   *

DAVID HELD AND ANTHONY MCGREW, WITH DAVID GOLDBLATT AND JONATHAN PERRATON

Globalization

Globalization: n. a process (or set of processes) that embodies a transformation in the spatial organization of social relations and transactions, generating transcontinental or interregional flows and networks of activity, interaction, and power.

Although everybody talks about globalization, few people have a clear understanding of it. The "big idea" of the late twentieth century is in danger of

From *Global Governance* 5, no. 4 (October/December 1999): 483–96.

turning into the cliché of our times. Can we give it precise meaning and content, or should globalization be consigned to the dustbin of history?

The reason there is so much talk about globalization is that everyone knows that something extraordinary is happening to our world. We can send e-mail across the planet in seconds; we hear that our jobs depend on economic decisions in far-off places; we enjoy films, food, and fashion from all over the world; we worry about an influx of drugs and how we can save the ozone layer. These growing global connections affect all aspects of our lives—but it is still not clear what globalization really means.

There has been a heated debate about whether globalization is occurring at all. The debate rages between those who claim that globalization marks the end of the nation-state and the death of politics and those who dismiss the globalization hype and say that we have seen it all before. This debate has continued for a decade, leading to ever more confusion. It is not that these positions are wholly mistaken. In fact, both capture elements of a complex reality. But it is the wrong debate to have when there is no common ground about what globalization is. Until we know what globalization actually means, we will not be able to understand how it affects our lives, our identities, and our politics.

In this essay, we try to go beyond the rhetoric of entrenched positions and produce a richer account of what globalization is, how the world is changing, and what we can do about it. So what does globalization mean? We show that globalization is made up of the accumulation of links across the world's major regions and across many domains of activity. It is not a single process but involves four distinct types of change:

- It stretches social, political, and economic activities across political frontiers, regions, and continents.
- It intensifies our dependence on each other, as flows of trade, investment, finance, migration, and culture increase.
- It speeds up the world. New systems of transport and communication mean that ideas, goods, information, capital, and people move more quickly.
- It means that distant events have a deeper impact on our lives. Even the most local developments may come to have enormous global consequences. The boundaries between domestic matters and global affairs can become increasingly blurred.

In short, globalization is about the connections between different regions of the world—from the cultural to the criminal, the financial to the environmental—and the ways in which they change and increase over time.

We show that globalization, in this sense, has been going on for centuries. But we also show that globalization today is genuinely different both in scale and in nature. It does not signal the end of the nation-state or the death of politics. But it does mean that politics is no longer, and can no longer be, based simply on nation-states. We cannot predict the future or know what the final outcome of globalization will be. But we can now define the central challenge of the global age—rethinking our values, institutions, and identities so that politics can remain an effective vehicle for human aspirations and needs.

First, we need to understand what is distinctive about globalization today. We can do this only by studying the forms it has taken throughout history in all areas of activity—the environment, the economy, politics, and culture. The thread that ties these things together is people, and so it is with the movements of people that we must start.

People on the Move

Globalization began with people traveling. For millennia, human beings have migrated—settling new lands, building empires, or searching for work. Most migrations in history have not been global. But from the sixteenth century onward, Europeans traveled the world, conquering the Americas and Oceania before making colonial incursions into Africa and Asia. The first great wave of modern migration was the transatlantic slave trade. Nine to twelve million people were shipped as slaves from Africa to the Americas by the mid-nineteenth century. But this was dwarfed by the extraordinary outpouring of Europe's poor to the New World from the mid-nineteenth century onward. More than thirty million people moved in this way between 1880 and World War I.

Levels of global migration have fluctuated dramatically with political and economic conditions. During World War I, international migration plummeted. European migration stopped, beyond a few forced migrations like that of Armenians and

Greeks from Turkey. North America closed its borders and created the first systematic immigration legislation in the modern era. But the bitter struggles and ethnic violence of World War II led to unprecedented levels of forced migrations, refugees, and asylum movements. Ethnic Germans fled the Soviet Union and Eastern Europe. Jews headed for Israel. Pakistan and India exchanged millions of people. And Koreans flooded south.

In the 1950s and 1960s, millions of people poured into Europe, attracted by the rebirth of Western European economies. After the oil shocks of the 1970s, politicians closed many of these migration programs. But they couldn't stop the foreign population and ethnic mix continuing to grow. A combination of family reunions, unpoliceable borders, and sheer demand for labor have continued to drive migration from the European peripheries of Turkey and North Africa and from the distant outposts of old European empires in Asia and Africa. There has also been a takeoff in legal and illegal migration to the United States and Australasia, enormous flows to the oil-rich and labor-scarce Middle East, and new patterns of regional migration throughout the world.

Today, we are living with the consequences of centuries of migration and conquest. There is more ethnic diversity than ever before in states of the Organization for Economic and Community Development (OECD), especially in Europe. The process can never be reversed, particularly when in countries like Sweden more than 10 percent of the population are foreign born. Moreover, the United States is experiencing levels of migration that are comparable to the great transatlantic push of the late nineteenth century. In the mid-1990s, this involved more than a million immigrants per year, mainly from Asia, Latin America, and Central America. And it is not just economic migration. There has also been an astronomical rise in asylum seeking, displaced persons, and refugees from wars as states are created and collapse in the developing world. More than half a million applicants for asylum were received per annum by OECD countries in the 1990s.

International attempts to regulate the flow of people have not succeeded. Some states are highly dependent on migrant labor; others find it difficult to win support for tracking illegal migrants. All states have to reassess what national citizenship is and what it means as an era of diversity transforms identities and cultures. The long history of migration is coming home to roost.

The Fate of National Cultures

When people move, they take their cultures with them. So, the globalization of culture has a long history. The great world religions showed how ideas and beliefs can cross the continents and transform societies. No less important were the great premodern empires that, in the absence of direct military and political control, held their domains together through a common culture of the ruling classes. For long periods of human history, there have been only these global cultures and a vast array of fragmented local cultures. Little stood between the court and the village until the invention of nation-states in the eighteenth century created a powerful new cultural identity that lay between these two extremes.

This rise of nation-states and nationalist projects truncated the process of cultural globalization. Nation-states sought to control education, language, and systems of communication, like the post and the telephone. But as European empires became entrenched in the nineteenth century, new forms of cultural globalization emerged with innovations in transport and communications, notably regularized mechanical transport, and the telegraph. These technological advances helped the West to expand and enabled the new ideas that emerged—especially science, liberalism, and socialism—to travel and transform the ruling cultures of almost every society on the planet.

Contemporary popular cultures have certainly not yet had a social impact to match this, but the sheer scale, intensity, speed, and volume of global cultural communications today is unsurpassed. The accelerating diffusion of radio, television, the Internet, and satellite and digital technologies has made instant communication possible. Many national controls over information have become ineffective. Through radio, film, television, and the Internet, people everywhere are exposed to the values of other cultures as never before. Nothing, not even the fact that we all speak different languages, can stop the flow of ideas and cultures. The English language is becoming so dominant that it provides a linguistic infrastructure as powerful as any technological system for transmitting ideas and cultures.

Beyond its scale, what is striking about today's cultural globalization is that it is driven by companies, not countries. Corporations have replaced states and theocracies as the central producers and distributors of cultural globalization. Private international institutions are not new, but their mass impact is. News agencies and publishing houses in previous eras had a much more limited impact on local and national cultures than the consumer goods and cultural products of global corporations today.

Although the vast majority of these cultural products come from the United States, this is not a simple case of "cultural imperialism." One of the surprising features of our global age is how robust national and local cultures have proved to be. National institutions remain central to public life, and national audiences constantly reinterpret foreign products in novel ways.

These new communication technologies threaten states that pursue rigid closed-door policies on information and culture. For example, China sought to restrict access to the Internet but found this extremely difficult to achieve. In addition, it is likely that the conduct of economic life everywhere will be transformed by the new technologies. The central question is the future impact of cultural flows on our sense of personal identity and national identity. Two competing forces are in evidence: the growth of multicultural politics almost everywhere and, in part as a reaction to this, the assertion of fundamentalist identities (religious, nationalist, and ethnic). Although the balance between these two forces remains highly uncertain, it is clear that only a more open, cosmopolitan outlook can ultimately accommodate itself to a more global era.

The Territorial State and Global Politics

One thousand years ago, a modern political map of the world would have been incomprehensible. It is not just that much of the world was still to be "discovered." People simply did not think of political power as something divided by clear-cut boundaries and unambiguous color patches. But our contemporary maps do not just misrepresent the past. By suggesting that territorial areas contain indivisible, illimitable, and exclusive sovereign states, they may also prove a poor metaphor for the shape of the politics of the future.

Modern politics emerged with and was shaped by the development of political communities tied to a piece of land, the nation-state. This saw the centralization of political power within Europe, the creation of state structures, and the emergence of a sense of order between states. Forms of democracy were developed within certain states, while at the same time the creation of empires saw this accountability denied to others.

Today, we are living through another political transformation, which could be as important as the creation of the nation-state; the exclusive link between geography and political power has now been broken.

Our new era has seen layers of governance spread within and across political boundaries. New institutions have both linked sovereign states together and pooled sovereignty beyond the nation-state. We have developed a body of regional and international law that underpins an emerging system of global governance, both formal and informal, with many layers.

Our policymakers experience a seemingly endless merry-go-round of international summits. Two or three congresses a year convened 150 years ago. Today more than four thousand convene each year. They include summits of the UN, the Group of Seven, the International Monetary Fund, the World Trade Organization, the European Union (EU), the Asia-Pacific Economic Cooperation bloc, the regional forum of the Association of Southeast Asian Nations, and Mercado Común del Sur (Mercosur). These summits and many other official and unofficial meetings lock governments into global, regional, and multilayered systems of governance that they can barely monitor, let alone control.

Attention has tended to focus on the failure of global institutions to live up to the vast hopes that their birth created. But they have significant achievements to their credit. Although the UN remains a creature of the interstate system with well-documented shortcomings, it does deliver significant international public goods. These range from air traffic control and the management of telecommunications to the control of contagious diseases, humanitarian relief for refugees, and measures to protect our oceans and atmosphere.

However, it is regional institutions that have done most to transform the global political landscape. The EU has transformed Europe from postwar disarray to a situation where member states can pool sovereignty to tackle common problems. Despite the fact that many people still debate its very right to exist, the view from 1945 would be of astonishment at how far the EU has come so quickly. Although regionalism elsewhere is very different from the European model, its acceleration in the Americas, in the Asian Pacific, and (somewhat less) in Africa has had significant consequences for political power. Despite fears of Fortress Europe and protectionist blocs, regionalism has been a midwife to political globalization rather than a barrier to it. In fact, many global standards have resulted from negotiations involving regional groupings.

Another feature of the new era is the strengthening and broadening of international law. States no longer have the right to treat their citizens as they think fit. An emerging framework of "cosmopolitan law"—governing war, crimes against humanity, environmental issues, and human rights—has made major inroads into state sovereignty. Even the many states that violate these standards in practice accept general duties to protect their citizens, to provide a basic standard of living, and to respect human rights.

These international standards are monitored and vociferously lobbied for by a growing number of international agencies. In 1996, there were nearly 260 intergovernmental organizations and nearly 5,500 international nongovernmental organizations. In 1909, the former numbered just 37 and the latter a mere 176. There has also been a vast increase in the number of international treaties and regimes, such as the nuclear nonproliferation regime.

The momentum for international cooperation shows no sign of slowing, despite the many vociferous complaints often heard about it. The stuff of global politics already goes far beyond traditional geopolitical concerns and will increase whenever effective action requires international cooperation. Drug smugglers, capital flows, acid rain, and the activities of pedophiles, terrorists, and illegal immigrants do not recognize borders; neither can the policies for their effective resolution.

This transformation of international politics does not mean that the nation-state is dead. The multilateral revolution, rather than replacing the familiar world of nation-states, overlays and complicates it. Many familiar political distinctions and assumptions have been called into question. The context of national politics has been transformed by the diffusion of political authority and the growth of multilayered governance (which we discuss further in the section on governing globalization). But it is not entirely clear which factors will determine how far old institutions can adapt and whether new institutions can be invested with legitimacy.

The Globalization of Organized Violence

Ironically, war and imperial conquest have been great globalizing forces in history. Countries and peoples have met often on the battlefield. Although we live in an era distinguished by the absence of empires, great-power conflict, and interstate war, military globalization is not a thing of the past. It works very differently now but in many ways is more significant than ever. New threats to our security and our responses to these threats have made countries much more interdependent.

One major change comes from weapons themselves. Military competition has always been about developing more powerful weapons. But the last half-century has not just created the most powerful weapons the world has ever seen—including weapons of mass destruction that can travel across entire continents. It has also seen some of these tools of war fall into the hands of an unprecedented number of countries and regimes. This has "shrunk" the world and made it more dangerous. Although the end of the Cold War has undermined the political logic of the global arms dynamic, the Cold War itself accelerated the diffusion of military-technological innovation across the world. Whereas it took two centuries for the gunpowder revolution to reach Europe from China in the Middle Ages, it took less than five decades for India to acquire its existing nuclear capability.

Meanwhile, the same infrastructures that have facilitated global flows of goods, people, and capital have generated new societal security threats. Cyberwar, international and ecological terrorism, and transnational organized crime cannot be satisfactorily dealt with either by traditional military means or solely within a national framework.

These changes have transformed power relationships in the world military order, creating new global and regional risks that demand multilateral action. Global and regional security institutions have become more important. Most states today have chosen to sign up to a host of multilateral arrangements and institutions in order to enhance their security. Few states now see unilateralism or neutrality as a credible defense strategy.

But it is not just the institutions of defense that have become multinational. The way that we make military hardware has also changed. The age of "national champions" has been superseded by a sharp increase in licensing, coproduction agreements, joint ventures, corporate alliances, and subcontracting. This means that few countries today—not even the United States—can claim to have an autonomous military production capacity. This is especially so because key civil technologies such as electronics, which are vital to advanced weapons systems, are themselves the products of highly globalized industries.

Arms producers have also become increasingly reliant on export markets. This is why, despite the end of the Cold War, global arms sales (in real terms) have remained above the level of the 1960s. In fact, since the mid-1990s, their volume has increased. The number of countries manufacturing arms (forty) or purchasing arms (a hundred) is greater than at any time since the crisis-ridden 1930s.

The paradox and novelty of the globalization of violence today is that national security has become a multilateral affair. For the first time in history, the one thing that did most to give nation-states a focus and a purpose, the thing that has always been at the very heart of what sovereignty is, can now be protected only if nation-states come together and pool resources, technology, intelligence, and sovereignty.

The Global Economy

When people are not fighting, they have always made things and sold them to each other. And indeed when most people think about globalization, they think of economics. So what is happening to trade, production, and finance? How do they relate to each other—and how are they changing our world?

TRADE

The world has never been more open to trade than it is today. The dismantling of trade barriers has allowed global markets to emerge for many goods and services. The major trading blocs created in Europe, North America, and the Asian Pacific are not regional fortresses but remain open to competition from the rest of the world. Developing and transition economies have also opened up and seen their shares of world trade rise as a result. The consequence of these trading networks is not just that trade today is greater than ever before. Trade has changed in a way that links national economies together at a deeper level than in the past.

Competitive pressures have blurred the division between trade and domestic economic activity. Countries not only increasingly consume goods from abroad but depend on components from overseas for their own production processes. The massive growth of intraindustry trade, which now forms the majority of trade in manufactures among developed economies, further intensifies competition across national boundaries. The production process can now easily be sliced up and located in different countries—creating a new global division of labor and new patterns of wealth and inequality.

No economic activity can easily be insulated from global competition. A greater proportion of domestic output is traded than in the past. This does not mean that countries' fortunes are simply determined by their national "competitiveness." The basic rules of economics still apply. Countries still specialize according to comparative advantage; they cannot be competitive in everything or nothing. National economies can still gain, overall, from increased trade.

What has changed is the distribution of these gains from trade. These are highly uneven—and in new ways. There are clear winners and losers, both between and within countries. More trade with developing countries hurts low-skilled workers while simultaneously increasing the incomes of more highly skilled workers. National governments may protect and compensate those who lose out from structural change, but employers in tradable industries vulnerable to global competition will increasingly resist the costs of welfare provision. The welfare state is under pressure from both within and without.

Despite the creation of global markets, regulation remains largely national. The banana dispute waged between the EU and the United States illustrates the international friction that trade can generate. The weakness of international regulation also means that we cannot easily correct for market failures and externalities in global markets. The World Trade Organization, a powerful advocate of deregulation and trade liberalization, is in its infancy in harmonizing national regulatory regimes.

It confronts a legitimation deficit—as the banana dispute shows—that can be effectively removed only by greater transparency and by wider participation (of those significantly affected by disputes) in its rule making.

PRODUCTION

Global exports may be more important than ever, but transnational production is now worth even more. To sell to another country, increasingly you have to move there; this is the main way to sell goods and services abroad. The multinational corporation has taken economic interdependence to new levels. Today, 53,000 multinational corporations and 450,000 foreign subsidiaries sell $9.5 trillion of goods and services across the globe every year. Multinational corporations account for at least 20 percent of world production and 70 percent of world trade. A quarter to a third of world trade is intrafirm trade between branches of multinationals.

Such impressive figures nevertheless underestimate the importance of multinational corporations to global economic prosperity: multinationals also form relationships that link smaller national firms into transnational production chains. Although multinationals typically account for a minority of national production, they are concentrated in the most technologically advanced economic sectors and in export industries. They also often control the global distribution networks on which independent exporters depend, especially in developing countries, and are of fundamental importance in the generation and international transfer of technology.

Multinationals are concentrated in developed countries and a small number of developing ones, but their impact is felt across the world. Almost all countries have some inward foreign direct investment and compete intensely for more. Investment is spreading out, with an increasing share to developing countries and rapid increases in Central and Eastern Europe and in China.

How powerful are multinational corporations today? They have developed transnational networks that allow them to take advantage of differences in national cost conditions and regulations. Domestic economies are also suffering because multinational companies are becoming genuinely more multinational as they find it increasingly difficult to win competitive advantage from their home base alone. In the past, even large multinational corporations like Sony retained many national characteristics. Technological advantages were largely realized in their country of origin and were shared among various national stakeholders. This is less and less possible due to the significant growth of transnational corporate alliances, mergers, and acquisitions (such as Chrysler-Daimler) and the tendency of multinationals to invest in foreign innovation clusters.

Nevertheless, multinationals are not "footloose." Production has to take place somewhere, and the costs of shifting can be high—especially where an area of industrial specialization gives strong reasons to stay. But their exit power, as recent events in Sweden and Germany show, has increased over time. And governments increasingly see multinationals as determining the balance of economic power in the world economy, with the power to play different governments off against each other to win extra subsidies for inward investment or changes to regulatory requirements.

In the short term, governments will continue to respond to this pressure by trimming their national regimes to balance domestic priorities and conditions with the demands of global capital. But we can expect increasing pressure for the transnational harmonization of corporate practices, taxes, and business regimes as an escape route from this Dutch auction.

FINANCE

Alongside multinationals the power of global finance has been most central to economic globalization. World financial flows are so large that the numbers are overwhelming. Every day, $1.5 trillion is traded on the foreign exchange markets—as a few thousand traders seem to determine the economic fate of nations. Most countries today are in-

corporated into global financial markets, but the nature of their access to these markets is highly uneven. When foreign exchange markets turn over sixty times the value of world trade, this is not just a staggering increase; it is a different type of activity altogether. The instantaneous transactions of the twenty-four-hour global markets are largely speculative, where once most market activity financed trade and long-term investment.

The fact that these global markets determine countries' long-term interest rates and exchange rates does not mean that the financial markets simply determine national economic policy. But they do radically alter both the costs of particular policy options and, crucially, policymakers' perceptions of costs and risk. Speculative activity on this scale brings both unprecedented uncertainty and volatility—and can rapidly undermine financial institutions, currencies, and national economic strategies. It is not surprising that policymakers take a distinctly risk-averse approach and therefore adopt a more conservative macroeconomic strategy as a result. Even if there is often more room for maneuver with hindsight, future policy will change only marginally when the risks of getting it wrong appear to be, and are, potentially so catastrophic.

The 1997 East Asian crisis forcibly demonstrated the impact of global financial markets and the shifting balance between public and private power. The global financial disruption triggered by the collapse of the Thai baht demonstrated new levels of economic interconnectedness. The "Asian tiger" economies had benefited from the rapid increase of financial flows to developing countries in the 1990s and were held up as examples to the rest of the world. But these heavy flows of short-term capital, often channeled into speculative activity, could be quickly reversed, causing currencies to fall very heavily and far in excess of any real economic imbalances. The inability of the existing international financial regime to prevent global economic turmoil has created a wide-ranging debate on its future institutional architecture—and the opportunity to promote issues of legitimacy, accountability, and effectiveness.

Another important change on the policymaking menu arises from the exchange rate crises of the 1990s. Fixed exchange rates are ceasing to be a viable policy option in the face of global capital flows of this scale and intensity. The choice that countries face is increasingly between floating rates and monetary union—shown by the launch of the euro and discussion of dollarization in Latin America.

Globalization and the Environment

Environmental change has always been with us. What is new today is that some of the greatest threats are global—and any effective response will have to be global too. For most of human history, the main way in which environmental impacts circulated around the earth was through the unintentional transport of flora, fauna, and microbes. The great plagues showed how devastating the effects could be. The European colonization of the New World within a generation wiped out a substantial proportion of the indigenous populations of the Caribbean, Mexico, and parts of Latin America. Over the following centuries, these societies saw their ecosystems, landscapes, and agricultural systems transformed. Early colonialism also damaged the environment in new ways. The Sumatran and Indian forests were destroyed to meet consumer demand in Europe and America. Seals were overhunted to dangerously low levels. And some species of whale were hunted to extinction.

But most forms of environmental degradation were largely local until the middle of this century. Since then, the globalization of environmental degradation has accelerated. Fifty years of resource-intensive and high-pollution growth in the OECD countries and the even dirtier industrialization of Russia, Eastern Europe, and the ex-Soviet states have taken their toll on the environment. The South is now industrializing at breakneck speed, driven by exponential growth of global population. We also know much more about the dangers and the damage that we have caused.

Humankind is increasingly aware that it faces an unprecedented array of truly global and regional environmental problems, which no national community or single generation can tackle alone. We have reacted to global warming; to ozone depletion; to destruction of global rainforests and loss of biodiversity; to toxic waste; to the pollution of oceans and rivers; and to nuclear risks with a flurry of global and regional initiatives, institutions, regimes, networks, and treaties. Transnational environmental movements are also more politically visible than ever. But there has simply not been the political power, domestic support, or international authority so far on a scale that can do any more than limit the very worst excesses of these global environmental threats.

Governing Globalization

Contemporary globalization represents the beginning of a new epoch in human affairs. In transforming societies and world order, it is having as profound an impact as the Industrial Revolution and the global empires of the nineteenth century. We have seen that globalization is transforming our world, but in complex, multifaceted, and uneven ways. Although globalization has a long history, it is today genuinely different both in scale and in form from what has gone before. Every new epoch creates new winners and losers. This one will be no different. Globalization to date has already both widened the gap between the richest and poorest countries and further increased divisions within and across societies. It has inevitably become increasingly contested and politicized.

National governments—sandwiched between global forces and local demands—must now reconsider their roles and functions. But to say simply that states have lost power distorts what is happening, as does any suggestion that nothing much has changed. The real picture is much more complex. States today are at least as powerful, if not more so, than their predecessors on many fundamental measures of power—from the capacity to raise taxes to the ability to hurl force at enemies. But the demands on states have grown very rapidly as well. They must often work together to pursue the public good—to prevent recession or to protect the environment. And transnational agreements, for example dealing with acid rain, will often force national governments to adopt major changes in domestic policy.

So state power and political authority are shifting. States now deploy their sovereignty and autonomy as bargaining chips in multilateral and transnational negotiations, as they collaborate and coordinate actions in shifting regional and global networks. The right of most states to rule within circumscribed territories—their sovereignty—is not on the edge of collapse, although the practical nature of this entitlement—the actual capacity of states to rule—is changing its shape. The emerging shape of governance means that we need to stop thinking of state power as something that is indivisible and territorially exclusive. It makes more sense to speak about the transformation of state power than the end of the state; the range of government strategies stimulated by globalization are, in many fundamental respects, producing the potential for a more activist state.

But the exercise of political and economic power now frequently escapes effective mechanisms of democratic control. And it will continue to do so while democracy remains rooted in a fixed and bounded territorial conception of political community. Globalization has disrupted the neat correspondence between national territory, sovereignty, political space, and the democratic political community. It allows power to flow across, around, and over territorial boundaries. And so the challenge of globalization today is ultimately political. Just as the Industrial Revolution created new types of class politics, globalization demands that we re-form our existing territorially defined democratic institutions and practices so that politics can continue to address human aspirations and needs.

This means rethinking politics. We need to take our established ideas about political equality, social justice, and liberty and refashion these into a coherent political project robust enough for a world where power is exercised on a transnational scale and where risks are shared by peoples across the world. And we need to think about what institutions will allow us to tackle these global problems while responding to the aspirations of the people they are meant to serve.

This is not a time for pessimism. We are caught between nostalgia for causes defeated and ideas lost, and excitement at the new possibilities that we face. We need to think in new ways. Globalization is not bringing about the death of politics. It is reilluminating and reinvigorating the contemporary political terrain.

THOMAS FRIEDMAN

The Backlash

Analysts have been wondering for a while now whether the turtles who are left behind by globalization, or most brutalized or offended by it, will develop an alternative ideology to

From Thomas Friedman, *The Lexus and the Olive Tree: Understanding Globalization* (New York; Farrar, Straus, Giroux, 1999; reprint, New York: Anchor Books, 2000), chap. 15 (page citations are to the reprint edition).

liberal, free-market capitalism. * * * [I]n the first era of globalization, when the world first experienced the creative destruction of global capitalism, the backlash eventually produced a whole new set of ideologies—communism, socialism, fascism—that promised to take the sting out of capitalism, particularly for the average working person. Now that these ideologies have been discredited, I doubt we will see a new coherent, universal ideological re-action to globalization—because I don't believe there is an ideology or program that can remove all of the brutality and destructiveness of capitalism and still produce steadily rising standards of living.

Another reason the backlash against globaliza-tion is unlikely to develop a coherent alternative ideology is because the backlash itself involves so many disparate groups—as evidenced by the coali-tion of protectionist labor unions, environmental-ists, anti-sweatshop protestors, save-the-turtles activists, save-the-dolphins activists, anti–geneti-cally altered food activists and even a group called "Alien Hand Signals," who came together in De-cember 1999 to protest globalization at the Seattle WTO summit. These disparate groups are bound by a common sense that a world so dominated by global corporations, and their concerns, can't help but be a profoundly unfair world, and one that is as hostile to the real interests of human beings as it is to turtles. But when it comes to actually identify-ing what the real interests of human beings are and how they should be protected, these groups are as different as their costumes. The auto work-ers, steelworkers and longshoremen, who were in Seattle to demand more protectionism, doubtlessly couldn't care much whether America allows im-ports of tuna caught in nets that also snare turtles. Indeed, I wouldn't want to be the turtle that gets in the way of one of those longshoremen offloading a boat in Seattle harbor. This makes the power of the backlash hard to predict, because while all the groups can agree that globalization is hurtful to them, they have no shared agenda, ideology or strategy for making it less so for all.

That's why I suspect that the human turtles, and many of those who simply hate the changes that globalization visits on cultures, environment or communities, are not going to bother with an alternative ideology. Their backlash will take a va-riety of different spasmodic forms. The steelwork-ers will lobby Washington to put up walls against foreign steel. Others, such as the radical environ-mentalists who want to save the rain forest, will simply lash out at globalization and all its manifes-

tations, without offering a sustainable economic alternative. Their only message will be: STOP.

As for the poorest human turtles in the devel-oping world, those really left behind by globaliza-tion, they will express their backlash by simply eating the rain forest—each in their own way—without trying to explain it or justify it or wrap it in an ideological bow. In Indonesia, they will eat the Chinese merchants by ransacking their stores. In Russia, they will sell weapons to Iran or turn to crime. In Brazil, they will log the rest of the rain forest or join the peasant movement in the Brazil-ian countryside called "Sem Teto" (Without Roofs), who simply steal what they need. There are an estimated 3.5 million of them in Brazil—agricultural people without land, living in some 250 encampments around the country. Sometimes they live by the roads and just close the roads until they are paid or evicted, sometimes they invade su-permarkets, rob banks or steal trucks. They have no flag, no manifesto. They have only their own unmet needs and aspirations. That's why what we have been seeing in many countries, instead of popular mass opposition to globalization, is wave after wave of crime—people just grabbing what they need, weaving their own social safety nets and not worrying about the theory or ideology.

But while this backlash may be a bit incoherent and only loosely connected, it is very real. It comes from the depth of people's souls and pocketbooks and therefore, if it achieves a critical mass, can in-fluence politics in any country. Societies ignore it at their own peril.

In almost every country that has put on the Golden Straitjacket you have at least one populist party or major candidate who is campaigning all the time now against globalization. They offer var-ious protectionist, populist solutions that they claim will produce the same standards of living, without having to either run so fast, trade so far or open the borders so wide. They all claim that by just putting up a few new walls here and there everything will be fine. They appeal to all the peo-ple who prefer their pasts to their future. In Rus-sia, for instance, the communist members of the Duma continue to lead a backlash against globalization by telling the working classes and pensioners that in the days of the Soviet Union they may have had lousy jobs and been forced to wait in breadlines, but they always knew there would be a job and always knew there would be some bread they could afford at the head of the line. The strength of these populist, antiglobalization candidates depends to a large degree on the weakness of the economy in the country that they are in. Usually, the weaker the economy, the wider the following these simplistic solutions will attract.

But these antiglobalization populists don't only thrive in bad times. In 1998, a majority of the U.S. Congress refused to give the President authority to expand NAFTA to Chile—little Chile—on the argument that this would lead to a loss of American jobs. This wrongheaded view carried the day at a time when the American stock market was at a record high, American unemployment was at a record low and virtually every study showed that NAFTA had been a win-win-win arrangement for the United States, Canada and Mexico. Think of how stupid this was: The U.S. Congress appropriated $18 billion to replenish the International Monetary Fund, so that it could do more bailouts of countries struggling with globalization, but the Congress would not accept expansion of the NAFTA free trade zone to Chile. What is the logic of that? It could only be: "We support aid, not trade."

It makes no sense, but the reason these arguments can resonate in good times as well as bad is that moments of rapid change like this breed enormous insecurity as well as enormous prosperity. They can breed in people a powerful sense that their lives are now controlled by forces they cannot see or touch. The globalization system is still too new for too many people, and involves too much change for too many people, for them to have confidence that even the good job they have will always be there. And this creates a lot of room for backlash demagogues with simplistic solutions. It also creates a powerful feeling in some people that we need to slow this world down, put back some walls or some sand in the gears—not so I can get off, but so I can stay on.

And don't kid yourself, the backlash is not just an outburst from the most downtrodden. Like all revolutions, globalization involves a shift in power from one group to another. In most countries it involves a power shift from the state and its bureaucrats to the private sector and entrepreneurs. As this happens, all those who derived their status from positions in the bureaucracy, or from their ties to it, or from their place in a highly regulated and protected economic system, can become losers—if they can't make the transition to the Fast World. This includes industrialists and cronies who were anointed with import or export monopolies by their government, business owners who were protected by the government through high import tariffs on the products they made, big labor unions who got used to each year winning fewer work hours with more pay in constantly protected markets, workers in state-owned factories who got paid whether the factory made a profit or not, the unemployed in welfare states who enjoyed relatively generous benefits and health care no matter what, and all those who depended on the largesse of the state to protect them from the global market and free them from its most demanding aspects.

This explains why, in some countries, the strongest backlash against globalization comes not just from the poorest segments of the population and the turtles, but rather from the "used-to-bes" in the middle and lower-middle classes, who found a great deal of security in the protected communist, socialist and welfare systems. As they have seen the walls of protection around them coming down, as they have seen the rigged games in which they flourished folded up and the safety nets under them shrink, many have become mighty unhappy. And unlike the turtles, these downwardly mobile groups have the political clout to organize against globalization. The AFL-CIO labor union federation has become probably the most powerful political force against globalization in the United States. Labor unions covertly funded a lot of the advertising on behalf of the demonstrations in Seattle to encourage grass-roots opposition to free trade.

One of my first tastes of this middle-class backlash against globalization came by accident when I was in Beijing talking to Wang Jisi, who heads the North America desk at the Chinese Academy of Social Sciences. We drifted from talking about America to talking about his own life in a China that was rapidly moving toward the free market, which many Chinese both welcome and fear. "The market mechanism is coming to China, but the question is how to impose it," said Wang. "I depend on my work unit for my housing. If all the housing goes to a free-market system, I might lose my housing. I am not a conservative, but when it comes to practical issues like this, people can become conservatives if they are just thrown onto the market after being accustomed to being taken care of. * * * *"

You don't have to have been a communist worker bee to feel this way. Peter Schwartz, chairman of the Global Business Network, a consulting firm, once told me about a conversation he had before being interviewed in London for an economics program on the BBC: "The British reporter for the show, while escorting me to the interview, was asking me about some of my core ideas. I alluded to the idea that Britain was a good example of the takeoff of the entrepreneurial economy—particularly compared to the rest of Europe—and that the best indicator of the difference was the difference in unemployment in the U.K. and continental Europe. At that point he said to me: 'Isn't that terrible? Unemployment benefits are now so low in Britain it isn't worth staying on the dole anymore and people have to go to work.' "

Schwartz then added: "There are people who see this transformation [to globalization] as a big loss, not a gain. They are losing not just a benefit but something they perceived as a right—the notion that modern industrial societies are so wealthy that it is the right of people to receive generous unemployment insurance."

If you want to see this war between the protected and the globalizers at its sharpest today, go to the Arab world. In 1996, Egypt was scheduled to host the Middle East Economic Summit, which was to bring together Western, Asian, Arab and Israeli business executives. The Egyptian bureaucracy fought bitterly against holding the summit.

In part, this was politically inspired by those in Egypt who did not feel Israel had done enough vis-à-vis the Palestinians to really merit normalization. But in part it was because the Egyptian bureaucrats, who had dominated the Egyptian economy ever since Nasser nationalized all the big commercial institutions in the 1960s, intuitively understood that this summit could be the first step in their losing power to the private sector, which was already being given the chance to purchase various state-owned enterprises and could eventually get its hands on the state-controlled media. The Islamic opposition newspaper *al-Shaab* denounced the economic summit as "the Conference of Shame." For the first time, though, the Egyptian private sector got itself organized into power lobbies—the American-Egypt Chamber of Commerce, the President's Council of Egyptian business leaders and the Egypt Businessmen's Association—and tugged President Mubarak the other way, saying that hosting a summit with hundreds of investors from around the world was essential to produce jobs for an Egyptian workforce growing by 400,000 new entrants each year. President Mubarak went back and forth, finally siding with the private sector and agreeing to host the summit, and bluntly declaring in his opening speech: "This year Egypt joined the global economy. It will live by its rules." But the Egyptian bureaucracy, which does not want to cede any power to the private sector, is still fighting that move, and every time there is a downturn in the global economy, such as the Asian collapse in 1998, the Egyptian bureaucrats go to Mubarak and say, "See, we told you so. We need to slow down, put up some new walls, otherwise what happened to Brazil will happen to us."

For a long time, I thought that this Egyptian reluctance to really plug into the globalization system was rooted simply in the ignorance of bureaucrats, and a total lack of vision from the top. But then I had an eye-opening experience. I did an author's tour of Egypt in early 2000, meeting with students at Cairo University, journalists at Egyptian newspapers and business leaders in Cairo and Alexandria to talk about the Arabic edition of this book.

Two images stood out from this trip. The first was riding the train from Cairo to Alexandria in a car full of middle- and upper-class Egyptians. So many of them had cell phones that kept ringing with different piercing melodies during the two-hour trip that at one point I felt like getting up, taking out a baton and conducting a cell-phone symphony. I was so rattled from ringing phones, I couldn't wait to get off the train. Yet, while all these phones were chirping inside the train, outside we were passing along the Nile, where bare-foot Egyptian villagers were tilling their fields with the same tools and water buffalo that their ancestors used in Pharaoh's day. I couldn't imagine a wider technology gap within one country. Inside the train it was A.D. 2000, outside it was 2000 B.C.

The other image was visiting Yousef Boutrous-Ghali, Egypt's M.I.T.-trained minister of economy. When I arrived at his building the elevator operator, an Egyptian peasant, was waiting for me at the elevator, which he operated with a key. Before he turned it on, though, to take me up to the minister's office, he whispered the Koranic verse "In the name of God, the Merciful, the Compassionate." To a Westerner, it is unnerving to hear your elevator operator utter a prayer before he closes the door, but for him this was a cultural habit, rooted deep in his tradition. Again, the contrast: Mr. Boutrous-Ghali is the most creative, high-tech driver of globalization in Egypt, but his elevator man says a prayer before taking you up to his office.

These scenes captured for me the real tension at the heart of Egypt: while its small, cell-phone-armed, globalizing elites were definitely pushing to get online and onto the global economic train, most others feared they would be left behind or lose their identity trying to catch it. Indeed I was struck, after a week of discussing both the costs and benefits of globalization, how most Egyptians, including many intellectuals, could see only the costs. The more I explained globalization, the more they expressed unease about it. It eventually struck me that I was encountering what anthropologists call "systematic misunderstanding." Systematic misunderstanding arises when your framework and the other person's framework are so fundamentally different that it cannot be corrected by providing more information.

The Egyptians' unease about globalization is rooted partly in a justifiable fear that they still lack the technological base to compete. But it's also rooted in something cultural—and not just the professor at Cairo University asked me: "Does globalization mean we all have to become Americans?" The unease goes deeper, and you won't understand the backlash against globalization in traditional societies unless you understand it. Many Americans can easily identify with modernization, technology and the Internet because one of the most important things these do is increase individual choices. At their best, they empower and emancipate the individual. But for traditional societies, such as Egypt's, the collective, the group, is much more important than the individual, and empowering the individual is equated with dividing the society. So "globalizing" for them not only means being forced to eat more Big Macs, it means changing the relationship of the individual to his state and community in a way that they feel is socially disintegrating.

"Does globalization mean we just leave the poor to fend for themselves?" one educated Egyptian woman asked me. "How do we privatize when we have no safety nets?" asked a professor. When the government here says it is "privatizing" an industry, the instinctive reaction of Egyptians is that something is being "stolen" from the state, said a senior Egyptian official.

After enough such conversations I realized that most Egyptians—understandably—were approaching globalization out of a combination of despair and necessity, not out of any sense of opportunity. Globalization meant adapting to a threat coming from the outside, not increasing their own freedoms. I also realized that their previous ideologies—Arab nationalism, socialism, fascism or communism—while they may have made no economic sense, had a certain inspirational power. But globalism totally lacks this. When you tell a traditional society it has to streamline, downsize and get with the Internet, it is a challenge that is devoid of any redemptive or inspirational force. And that is why, for all of globalization's obvious power to elevate living standards, it is going to be a tough, tough sell to all those millions who still say a prayer before they ride the elevator.

This tug-of-war is now going on all over the Arab world today, from Morocco to Kuwait. As one senior Arab finance official described this globalization struggle in his country: "Sometimes I feel like I am part of the Freemasons or some secret society, because I am looking at the world so differently from many of the people around me. There is a huge chasm between the language and vocabulary I have and them. It is not that I have failed to convince them. I often can't even communicate with them, they are so far away from this global outlook. So for me, when I am pushing a policy issue related to globalization, the question always becomes how many people can I rally to this new concept and can I create a critical mass to effect a transition? If you can get enough of your people in the right places, you can push the system along. But it's hard. On so many days I feel like I have people coming to me and saying, 'We really need to repaint the room.' And I'm saying, 'No, we really need to rebuild the whole building on a new foundation.' So their whole dialogue with you is about what color paint to use, and all you can see in your head is the whole new architecture that needs to be done and the new foundations that need to be laid. We can worry about the color of paint later! Brazil, Mexico, Argentina, they now have that critical mass of people and officials who can see this world. But most developing countries are not there yet, which is why their transition is still so uncertain."

In Morocco, the government is privatizing simply by selling many state-owned enterprises to the same small economic clique tied to the royal palace that once dominated the state monopolies. This is why 3 percent of Morocco's population controls 85 percent of the country's wealth. Morocco's universities, which uniquely combine the worst of the socialist and French education systems, each year turn out so many graduates who cannot find jobs, and have no entrepreneurial or technical skills suited for today's information

economy, that Morocco now has a "Union of Unemployed University Graduates."

As more countries have plugged into the globalization system and the Fast World, still another new backlash group has started to form—the wounded gazelles. This group comprises people who feel they have tried globalization, who have gotten hammered by the system, and who, instead of getting up, dusting themselves off and doing whatever it takes to get back into the Fast World are now trying artificially to shut it out or get the rules of the whole system changed. The poster boy for this group is Malaysia's Prime Minister Mahathir. Hell hath no wrath like a globalizer burned. On October 25, 1997, in the midst of the Asian economic meltdown, Mahathir told the Edinburgh Commonwealth Summit that the global economy—which had poured billions of dollars of investments into Malaysia, without which its spectacular growth would never have been possible—had become "anarchic."

"This is an unfair world," Mahathir fumed. "Many of us have struggled hard and even shed blood in order to be independent. When borders are down and the world becomes a single entity, independence can become meaningless."

Not surprisingly, in 1998 Mahathir was the first Asian globalizer to impose capital controls in an effort to halt the wild speculative swings in his own currency and stock market. When Singapore's Minister for Information, George Yeo, described Mahathir's move at the time, he said, "Malaysia has retreated to a lagoon and is trying to anchor its boats, but the strategy is not without risk."

Indeed it is not. If you think you can retreat permanently into an artificially constructed third space, and enjoy all the rising living standards of the Fast World without any of the pressures, you are really fooling yourself and your people. Nevertheless, Mahathir's retreat, which proved to be only temporary, was received with a certain amount of sympathy in the developing world—although it was not copied by anyone. As we enter this second decade of globalization, there is an increasing awareness among those countries that have resisted the Golden Straitjacket and the Fast World that they cannot go on resisting. And they know that a strategy of retreat will not produce growth over the long run. For several years I would meet Emad El-Din Adeeb, editor of the Egyptian journal *Al Alam Al Youm*, at different World Bank meetings and other settings, and for several years he would express to me strong reservations about Egypt joining this globalization system. When I saw him in 1999, at the Davos Forum, he said to me, "O.K., I understand we need to get prepared for this globalization and that is partly our responsibility. There is a train that is leaving and we should have known this and done our homework. But now you should slow the train down a bit and give us a chance to jump on."

I didn't have the heart to tell him that I had just come from a press lunch with Bill Gates. All the re-porters there kept asking him, "Mr. Gates, these Internet stocks, they're a bubble, right? Surely, they're a bubble. They must be a bubble?" Finally, an exasperated Gates said to the reporters: Look, of course they're a bubble, but you're all missing the point. This bubble is going to attract so much new capital to this Internet industry that it is going to drive innovation "faster and faster." So there I was: in the morning listening to Bill Gates telling me that the Fast World was about to get even faster and in the afternoon listening to Adeeb tell me he wanted to hop on but could someone just slow it down a bit.

I wish we could slow this globalization train down, I told Adeeb, but there's no one at the controls.

*   *   *

LESTER R. BROWN AND BRIAN HALWEIL

Breaking *Out* or Breaking *Down*

In Some Parts of the World, the Historic Trend toward Longer Life Has Been Abruptly Reversed

On October 12 of this year, the world's human population is projected to pass 6 billion. The day will be soberly observed by population and development experts, but media attention will do nothing to immediately slow the expansion. During that day, the global total will swell by another 214,000—enough people to fill two of the world's largest sports stadiums.

Even as world population continues to climb, it is becoming clear that the several billion additional people projected for the next half century are not likely to materialize. What is not clear is how the growth will be curtailed. Unfortunately, in some countries, a slowing of the growth is taking place only partly because of success in bringing birth rates down—and increasingly because of newly emergent conditions that are raising death rates.

Evidence of this shift became apparent in late October, 1998, when U.N. demographers released their biennial update of world population projections, revising the projected global population for 2050. Instead of rising in the next 50 years by more than half, to 9.4 billion (as computed in 1996), the 1998 projection rose only to 8.9 billion. The good news was that two-thirds of this anticipated slowdown was expected to be the result of falling fertility—of the decisions of more couples to have fewer children. But the other third was due to rising death rates, largely as a result of rising mortality from AIDS.

From *World Watch* (September/October 1999): 20–29.

This rather sudden reversal in the human death rate trend marks a tragic new development in world demography, which is dividing the developing countries into two groups. When these countries embarked on the development journey a half century or so ago, they followed one of two paths. In the first, illustrated by the East Asian nations of South Korea, Taiwan, and Thailand, early efforts to shift to smaller families set in motion a positive cycle of rising living standards and falling fertility. Those countries are now moving toward population stability.

In the second category, which prevails in sub-Saharan Africa (770 million people) and the Indian subcontinent (1.3 billion), fertility has remained high or fallen very little, setting the stage for a vicious downward spiral in which rapid population growth reinforces poverty, and in which some segments of society eventually are deprived of the resources needed even to survive. In Ethiopia, Nigeria, and Pakistan, for example, demographers estimate that the next half-century will bring a doubling or near-tripling of populations. Even now, people in these regions each day awaken to a range of daunting conditions that threatens to drop their living standards below the level at which humans can survive.

We now see three clearly identifiable trends that either are already raising death rates or are likely to do so in these regions: the spread of the HIV virus that causes AIDS, the depletion of aquifers, and the shrinking amount of cropland available to support each person. The HIV epidemic is spiraling out of control in sub-Saharan Africa. The depletion of aquifers has become a major threat to India, where water tables are falling almost everywhere. The shrinkage in cropland per person threatens to force reductions in food consumed per person, increasing malnutrition—and threatening lives—in many parts of these regions.

Containing one-third of the world's people, these two regions now face a potentially dramatic shortening of life expectancy. In sub-Saharan Africa, mortality rates are already rising, and in the Indian subcontinent they could begin rising soon. Without clearly defined national strategies for quickly lowering birth rates in these countries, and without a commitment by the international community to support them in their efforts, one-third of humanity could slide into a demographic black hole.

Birth and Death

Since 1950, we have witnessed more growth in world population than during the preceding 4 million years since our human ancestors first stood upright. This post-1950 explosion can be attributed, in part, to several developments that reduced death rates throughout the developing world. The wider availability of safe drinking water, childhood immunization programs, antibiotics, and expanding food production sharply reduced the number of people dying of hunger and from infectious diseases. Together these trends dramatically lowered mortality levels.

But while death rates fell, birth rates remained high. As a result, in many countries, population growth rose to 3 percent or more per year—rates for which there was no historical precedent. A 3 percent annual increase in population leads to a twenty-fold increase within a century. Ecologists have long known that such rates of population growth—which have now been sustained for close to half a century in many countries—could not be sustained indefinitely. At some point, if birth rates did not come down, disease, hunger, or conflict would force death rates up.

Although most of the world has succeeded in reducing birth rates to some degree, only some 32 countries—containing a mere 12 percent of the world's people—have achieved population stability. In these countries, growth rates range between 0.4 percent per year and minus 0.6 percent per year. With the exception of Japan, all of the 32 countries are in Europe, and all are industrial. Although other industrial countries, such as the United States, are still experiencing some population growth as a result of a persistent excess of births over deaths, the population of the industrial world as a whole is not projected to grow at all in the next century—unless, perhaps, through the arrival of migrants from more crowded regions.

Within the developing world, the most impressive progress in reducing fertility has come in East Asia. South Korea, Taiwan, and Thailand have all reduced their population growth rates to roughly one percent per year and are approaching stability. (See table, this page.) The biggest country in Latin America—Brazil—has reduced its population growth to 1.4 percent per year. Most other countries in Latin America are also making progress on this front. In contrast, the countries of sub-Saharan Africa and the Indian subcontinent have lagged in lowering growth rates, and populations are still rising ominously—at rates of 2 to 3 percent or more per year.

Graphically illustrating this contrast are Thailand and Ethiopia, each with 61 million people. Thailand is projected to add 13 million people over the next half century for a gain of 21 percent. Ethiopia, meanwhile, is projected to add 108 million for a gain of 177 percent. (The U.N.'s projections are based on such factors as the number of children per woman, infant mortality, and average life span in each country—factors that could change in time, but meanwhile differ sharply in the two countries.) The deep poverty among those living in sub-Saharan Africa and the Indian subcontinent has been a principal factor in their rapid population growth, as couples lack access to the kinds of basic social services and education that allow control over reproductive choices. Yet, the population growth, in turn, has only worsened their poverty—perpetuating a vicious cycle in which hopes of breaking out become dimmer with each passing year.

After several decades of rapid population growth, governments of many developing countries are simply being overwhelmed by their crowding—and are suffering from what we term "demographic fatigue." The simultaneous challenges of educating growing numbers of children, creating jobs for the swelling numbers of young people coming into the job market, and confronting such environmental consequences of rapid population growth as deforestation, soil erosion, and falling water tables, are undermining the capacity of governments to cope. When a major new threat arises, as has happened with the HIV virus, governments often cannot muster the leadership energy and fiscal resources to mobilize effectively. Social problems that are easily contained in industrial societies can become humanitarian disasters in many developing ones. As a result, some of the latter may soon see their population growth curves abruptly flattened, or even thrown into decline, not because of falling birth rates but because of fast-rising death rates. In some countries, that process has already begun.

Projected Population Growth in Selected Developing Countries, 1999 to 2050

	1999 (millions)	2050 (millions)	Growth from 1999 to 2050 (millions)	Growth from 1999 to 2050 (percent)
Developing Countries That Have Slowed Population Growth:				
South Korea	46	51	5	+11
Taiwan	22	25	3	+14
Thailand	61	74	13	+21
Developing Countries Where Rapid Population Growth Continues:				
Ethiopia	61	169	108	+177
Nigeria	109	244	135	+124
Pakistan	152	345	193	+127

Source: United Nations, Global Population Projections, 1998.

Shades of the Black Death

Industrial countries have held HIV infection rates under 1 percent of the adult population, but in many sub-Saharan African countries, they are spiraling upward, out of control. In Zimbabwe, 26 percent of the adult population is infected; in Botswana, the rate is 25 percent. In South Africa, a country of 43 million people, 22 percent are infected. In Namibia, Swaziland, and Zambia, 18 to 20 percent are. (See table, this page.) In these countries, there is little to suggest that these rates will not continue to climb.

In other African nations, including some with large populations, the rates are lower but climbing fast. In both Tanzania, with 32 million people, and Ethiopia, with its 61 million, the race is now 9 percent. In Nigeria, the continent's largest country with 111 million people, the latest estimate now puts the infection rate also at 9 percent and rising.

What makes this picture even more disturbing is that most Africans carrying the virus do not yet know they are infected, which means the disease can gain enormous momentum in areas where it is still largely invisible. This, combined with the social taboo that surrounds HIV/AIDS in Africa, has made it extremely difficult to mount an effective control effort.

Barring a medical miracle, countries such as Zimbabwe, Botswana, and South Africa will lose at least 20 percent of their adult populations to AIDS within the next decade, simply because few of those now infected with the virus can afford treatment with the costly antiviral drugs now used in industrial countries. To find a precedent for such a devastating region-wide loss of life from an infectious disease, we have to go back to the decimation of Native American communities by the introduction of small pox in the sixteenth century from Europe or to the bubonic plague that claimed roughly a third of Europe's population in the fourteenth century (see table, next page).

Reversing Progress

The burden of HIV is not limited to those infected, or even to their generation. Like a powerful storm or war that lays waste to a nation's physical infrastructure, a growing HIV epidemic damages a nation's social infrastructure, with lingering demographic and economic effects. A viral epidemic that grows out of control is likely to reinforce many of the very conditions—poverty,

Countries Where HIV Infection Rate Among Adults Is Greater Than Ten Percent

Country	Population (millions)	Share of Adult Population Infected (percent)
Zimbabwe	11.7	26
Botswana	1.5	25
South Africa	43.3	22
Namibia	1.6	20
Zambia	8.5	19
Swaziland	0.9	18
Malawi	10.1	15
Mozambique	18.3	14
Rwanda	5.9	13
Kenya	28.4	12
Central African Republic	3.4	11
Cote d'Ivoire	14.3	10

Source: UNAIDS

Profiles of Major Epidemics Throughout Human History

Epidemic and Date	Mode of Introduction and Spread	Description of Plague and Its Effects on Population
Black Death in Europe, 14th century	Originating in Asia, the plague bacteria moved westward via trade routes, entering Europe in 1347; transmitted via rats as well as coughing and sneezing.	One fourth of the population of Europe was wiped out (an estimated 25 million deaths); old, young, and poor hit hardest.
Smallpox in the New World, 16th century	Spanish conquistadors and European colonists introduced virus into the Americas, where it spread through respiratory channels and physical contact.	Decimated Aztec, Incan, and native American civilizations, killing 10 to 20 million.
HIV/AIDS, worldwide, 1980 to present	Thought to have originated in Africa; a primate virus that mutated and spread to infect humans; transmitted by the exchange of bodily fluids, including blood, semen, and breast milk.	More than 14 million deaths worldwide thus far; an additional 33 million infected; one-fifth of adult population infected in several African nations; strikes economically active populations hardest.

Source: Jared Diamond, *Guns, Germs, and Steel: The Fates of Human Societies*, 1997; UNAIDS.

illiteracy, malnutrition—that gave it an opening in the first place.

Using life expectancy—the sentinel indicator of development—as a measure, we can see that the HIV virus is reversing the gains of the last several decades. For example, in Botswana life expectancy has fallen from 61 years in 1990 to 44 years in 1999. By 2010, it is projected to drop to 39 years—a life expectancy more characteristic of medieval times than of what we had hoped for in the twenty-first century.

Beyond its impact on mortality, HIV also reduced fertility. For women, who live on average scarcely 10 years after becoming infected, many will die long before they have reached the end of their reproductive years. As the symptoms of AIDS begin to develop, women are less likely to conceive. For those who do conceive, the likelihood of spontaneous abortion rises. And among the reduced number who do give birth, an estimated 30 percent of the infants born are infected and an additional 20 percent are likely to be infected before they are weaned. For babies born with the virus, life expectancy is less than 2 years. The rate of population growth falls, but not in the way any family-planning group wants to see.

One of the most disturbing social consequences of the HIV epidemic is the number of orphans that it produces. Conjugal sex is one of the surest ways to spread AIDS, so if one parent dies, there is a good chance the other will as well. By the end of 1997, there were already 7.8 million AIDS orphans in Africa—a new and rapidly growing social subset. The burden of raising these AIDS orphans falls first on the extended family, and then on society at large. Mortality rates for these orphans are likely to be much higher than the rates for children whose parents are still with them.

As the epidemic progresses and the symptoms become visible, health care systems in developing countries are being overwhelmed. The estimated cost of providing antiviral treatment (the standard regimen used to reduce symptoms, improve life quality, and postpone death) to all infected individuals in Malawi, Mozambique, Uganda, and Tanzania would be larger than the GNPs of those countries. In some hospitals in South Africa, 70 percent of the beds are occupied by AIDS patients. In Zimbabwe, half the health care budget now goes to deal with AIDS. As AIDS patients increasingly monopolize nurses' and doctors' schedules, and drain funds from health care budgets, the capacity to provide basic health care to the general population—including the immunizations and treatments for routine illnesses that have underpinned the decline in mortality and the rise in life expectancy in developing countries—begins to falter.

Worldwide, more than half of all new HIV infections occur in people between the ages of 15 and 24—an atypical pattern for an infectious disease. Human scourges have historically spread through respiratory exposure to coughing or sneezing, or through physical contact via shaking hands, food handling, and so on. Since nearly everyone is vulnerable to such exposure, the victims of most infectious diseases are simply those among society at large who have the weakest immune systems—generally the very young and the elderly. But with HIV, because the primary means of transmission is unprotected sexual activity, the ones who are most vulnerable to infection are those who are most sexually active—young, healthy adults in the prime of their lives. According to a UNAIDS report, "the bulk of the increase in adult death is in the younger adult ages—a pattern that is common in wartime and has become a signature of the AIDS epidemic, but that is otherwise rarely seen."

One consequence of this adult die-off is an increase in the number of children and elderly who are dependent on each economically productive adult. This makes it more difficult for societies to save and, therefore, to make the investments needed to improve living conditions. To make matters worse, in Africa it is often the better educated, more socially mobile populations who have the highest infection rate. Africa is losing the agronomists, the engineers, and the teachers it needs to sustain its economic development. In South Africa, for example, at the University of Durban-Westville, where many of the country's future leaders are trained, 25 percent of the students are HIV positive.

Countries where labor forces have such high infection levels will find it increasingly difficult to attract foreign investment. Companies operating in countries with high infection rates face a doubling, tripling, or even quadrupling of their health insurance costs. Firms once operating in the black suddenly find themselves in the red. What has begun as an unprecedented social tragedy is beginning to translate into an economic disaster. Municipalities throughout South Africa have been hesitant to publicize the extent of their local epidemics or scale up control efforts for fear of deterring outside investment and tourism.

The feedback loops launched by AIDS may be quite predictable in some cases, but could also destabilize societies in unanticipated ways. For example, where levels of unemployment are already high—the present situation in most African nations—a growing population of orphans and displaced youths could exacerbate crime. Moreover, a country in which a substantial share of the population suffers from impaired immune systems as a result of AIDS is much more vulnerable to the spread of other infectious diseases, such as tuberculosis, and waterborne illness.

In Zimbabwe, the last few years have brought a rapid rise in deaths due to tuberculosis, malaria, and even the bubonic plague—even among those who are not HIV positive. Even without such synergies, in the early years of the next century, the HIV epidemic is poised to claim more lives than did World War II.

Sinking Water Tables

While AIDS is already raising death rates in sub-Saharan Africa, the emergence of acute water shortages could have the same effect in India. As population grows, so does the need for water. Home to only 358 million people in 1950, India will pass the one-billion mark later this year. It is projected to overtake China as the most populous nation around the year 2037, and to reach 1.5 billion by 2050.

As India's population has soared, its demand for water for irrigation, industry, and domestic use has climbed far beyond the sustainable yield of the country's aquifers. According to the International Water Management Institute (IWMI), water is being pumped from India's aquifers at twice the rate the aquifers are recharged by rainfall. As a result, water tables are falling by one to three meters per year almost everywhere in the country. In thousands of villages, wells are running dry.

In some cases, wells are simply drilled deeper—if there is a deeper aquifer within reach. But many villages now depend on trucks to bring in water for household use. Other villages cannot afford such deliveries, and have entered a purgatory of declining options—lacking enough water even for basic hygiene. In India's western state of Gujarat, water tables are falling by as much as five meters per year, and farmers now have to drill their wells down to between 700 and 1200 feet to reach the receding supply. Only the more affluent can afford to drill to such depths.

Although irrigation goes back some 6,000 years, aquifer depletion is a rather recent phenomenon. It is only within the last half century or so that the availability of powerful diesel and electric pumps has made it possible to extract water at rates that exceed recharge rates. Little is known about the total capacity of India's underground supply, but the unsustainability of the current consumption is clear. If the country is currently pumping water at double the rate at which its aquifers recharge, for example, we know that when the aquifers are eventually depleted, the rate of pumping will necessarily have to be reduced to the recharge rate—which would mean that the amount of water pumped would be cut in half. With at least 55 percent of India's grain production now coming from irrigated lands, IWMI speculates that aquifer depletion could reduce India's harvest by one-fourth. Such a massive cutback could prove catastrophic for a nation where 53 percent of the children are already undernourished and underweight.

Impending aquifer depletion is not unique to India. It is also evident in China, North Africa and the Middle East, as well as in large tracts of the United States. However, in wealthy Kuwait or Saudi Arabia, precariously low water availability per person is not life-threatening because these countries can easily afford to import the food that they cannot produce domestically. Since it takes 1,000 tons of water to produce a ton of grain, the ability to import food is in effect an ability to import water. But in poor nations, like India, where people are immediately dependent on the natural-resource base for subsistence and often lack money to buy food, they are limited to the water they can obtain from their immediate surroundings—and are much more endangered if it disappears.

In India—as in other nations—poorer farmers are thus disproportionately affected by water scarcity, since they often cannot get the capital or credit to obtain bigger pumps necessary to extract water from ever-greater depths. Those farmers who can no longer deepen their wells often shift their cropping patterns to include more water-efficient—but lower-yielding—crops, such as mustard, sorghum, or millet. Some have abandoned irrigated farming altogether, resigning themselves to the diminished productivity that comes with depending only on rainfall.

When production drops, of course, poverty deepens. When that happens, experience shows that most people, before succumbing to hunger or starvation, will migrate. On Gujarat's western coast, for example, the overpumping of underground water has led to rapid salt-water intrusion as seawater seeps in to fill the vacuum left by the freshwater. The groundwater has become so saline that farming with it is impossible, and this has driven a massive migration of farmers inland in search of work.

Village communities in India tend to be rather insular, so that these migrants—uprooted from their homes—cannot take advantage of the social safety net that comes with community and family bonds. Local housing restrictions force them to camp in the fields, and their access to village clinics, schools, and other social services is restricted. But while attempting to flee, the migrants also bring some of their troubles along with them.

Navroz Dubash, a researcher at the World Resources Institute who examined some of the effects of the water scarcity in Gujarat, notes that the flood of migrants depresses the local labor markets, driving down wages and diminishing the bargaining power of all landless laborers in the region.

In the web of feedback loops linking health and water supply, another entanglement is that when the *quantity* of available water declines, the *quality* of the water, too, may decline, because shrinking bodies of water lose their efficacy in diluting salts or pollutants. In Gujarat, water pumped from more than 700 feet down tends to have an unhealthy concentration of some inorganic elements, such as fluoride. As villagers drink and irrigate with this contaminated water, the degeneration of teeth and bones known as fluorosis has emerged as a major health threat. Similarly, in both West Bengal, India and Bangladesh, receding water tables have exposed arsenic-laden sediments to oxygen, converting them to a water-soluble form. According to UNDP estimates, at least 30 million people are exposed to health-impairing levels of arsenic in their drinking water.

As poverty deepens in the rural regions of India—and is driven deeper by mutually exacerbating health threats and water scarcities—migration from rural to urban areas is likely to increase. But for those who leave the farms, conditions in the cities may be no better. If water is scarce in the countryside, it is also likely to be scarce in the squatter settlements or other urban areas accessible to the poor. And where water is scarce, access to adequate sanitation and health services is poor. In most developing nations, the incidence of infectious diseases, including waterborne microbes, tuberculosis, and HIV/AIDS, is considerably higher in urban slums—where poverty and compromised health define the way of life—than in the rest of the city.

In India, with so many of the children undernourished, even a modest decline in the country's ability to produce or purchase food is likely to increase child mortality. With India's population expected to increase by 100 million people per decade over the next half century, the potential losses of irrigation water pose an ominous specter not only to the Indian people now living but to the hundreds of millions more yet to come.

Shrinking Cropland Per Person

The third threat that hangs over the future of nearly all the countries where rapid population growth continues is the steady decline in the amount of cropland remaining per person—a threat both of rising population and of the conversion of cropland to other uses. In this analysis, we use grainland per person as a surrogate for cropland, because in most developing countries the bulk of land is used to produce grain, and the data are much more reliable. Among the more populous countries where this trend threatens future food security are Nigeria, Ethiopia, and Pakistan—all countries with weak family-planning programs.

As a limited amount of arable land continues to be divided among larger numbers of people, the average amount of cropland available for each person inexorably shrinks. Eventually, it drops below the point where people can feed themselves. Below 600 square meters of grainland per person (about the area of a basketball court), nations typically begin to depend heavily on imported grain. Cropland scarcity, like water scarcity, can easily be translated into increased food imports in countries that can afford to import grain. But in the poorer nations of sub-Saharan Africa and the Indian subcontinent, subsistence farmers may not have access to imports. For them, land scarcity readily translates into malnutrition, hunger, rising mortality, and migration—and sometimes conflict. While most experts agree that resource scarcity alone is rarely the cause of violent conflict, resource scarcity has often compounded socioeconomic and political disruptions enough to drive unstable situations over the edge.

Thomas Homer-Dixon, director of the Project on Environment, Population, and Security at the University of Toronto, notes that "environmental scarcity is, without doubt, a significant cause of today's unprecedented levels of internal and international migration around the world." He has examined two cases in South Asia—a region plagued by land and water scarcity—in which resource constraints were underlying factors in mass migration and resulting conflict.

In the first case, Homer-Dixon finds that over the last few decades, land scarcity has caused millions of Bangladeshis to migrate to the Indian states of Assam, Tripura, and West Bengal. These movements expanded in the late 1970s after several years of flooding in Bangladesh, when population growth had reduced the grainland per person in Bangladesh to less than 0.08 hectares. As the average person's share of cropland began to shrink below the survival level, the lure of somewhat less densely populated land across the border in the Indian state of Assam became irresistible. By 1990, more than 7 million Bangladeshis had crossed the border, pushing Assam's population from 15 million to 22 million. The new immigrants in turn exacerbated land shortages in the Indian states, setting off a string of ethnic conflicts that have so far killed more than 5,000 people.

In the second case, Homer-Dixon and a colleague, Peter Gizewski, studied the massive rural-to-urban migration that has taken place in recent years in Pakistan. This migration, combined with population growth within the cities, has resulted in staggering urban growth rates of roughly 15 percent a year. Karachi, Pakistan's coastal capital, has seen its population balloon to 11 million. Urban services have been unable to keep pace with growth, especially for low-income dwellers. Shortages of water, sanitation, health services and jobs have become especially acute, leading to deteriorating public health and growing impoverishment.

"This migration . . . aggravates tensions and violence among diverse ethnic groups," according to Homer-Dixon and Gizewski. "This violence, in turn, threatens the general stability of Pakistani society." The cities of Karachi, Hyderabad, Islamabad, and Rawalpindi, in particular, have become highly volatile, so that "an isolated, seemingly chance incident—such as a traffic accident or short-term breakdown in services—ignites explosive violence." In 1994, water shortages in Islamabad provoked widespread protest and violent confrontation with police in hard-hit poorer districts.

Without efforts to step up family planning in Pakistan, these patterns are likely to be magnified. Population is projected to grow from 146 million today to 345 million in 2050, shrinking the grainland area per person in Pakistan to a miniscule 0.036 hectares by 2050—less than half of what it is today. A family of six will then have to produce its food on roughly one-fifth of a hectare, or half an acre—the equivalent of a small suburban building lot in the United States.

Similar prospects are in the offing for Nigeria, where population is projected to double to 244 million over the next half century, and in Ethiopia, where population is projected to nearly triple. In both, of course, the area of grainland per person will shrink dramatically. In Ethiopia, if the projected population growth materializes, it will cut the amount of cropland per person to one-third of its current 0.12 hectares per person—a level at which already more than half of the country's children are undernourished. And even as its per capita land shrinks, its long-term water supply is jeopardized by the demands of nine other rapidly growing, water-scarce nations throughout the Nile River basin. But even these projections may underestimate the problem, because they assume an equitable distribution of land among all people. In reality, the inequalities in land distribution that exist in many African and South Asian nations mean that as the competition for declining resources becomes more intense, the poorer and more marginal groups face even harsher deprivations than the averages imply.

Moreover, in these projections we have assumed that the total grainland area over the next half-century will not change. In reality this may be overly optimistic simply because of the ongoing conversion of cropland to nonfarm uses and the loss of cropland from degradation. A steadily growing population generates a need for more homes, schools, and factories, many of which will be built on once-productive farmland. Degradation, which may take the form of soil erosion or of the waterlogging and salinization of irrigated land, is also claiming cropland.

Epidemics, resource scarcity, and other societal stresses thus do not operate in isolation. Several disruptive trends will often intersect synergistically, compounding their effects on public health, the environment, the economy, and the society. Such combinations can happen anywhere, but the effects are likely to be especially pernicious—and sometimes dangerously unpredictable—in such places as Bombay and Lagos, where HIV prevalence is on the rise, and where fresh water and good land are increasingly beyond the reach of the poor.

Regaining Control of Our Destiny

The threats from HIV, aquifer depletion, and shrinking cropland are not new or unexpected. We have known for at least 15 years that the HIV virus could decimate human populations if it is not controlled. In each of the last 18 years, the annual number of new HIV infections has risen, climbing from an estimated 200,000 new infections in 1981 to nearly 6 million in 1998. Of the 47 million people infected thus far, 14 million have died. In the absence of a low-cost cure, most of the remaining 33 million will be dead by 2005.

It may seem hard to believe, given the advanced medical knowledge of the late twentieth century, that a controllable disease is decimating human populations in so many countries. Similarly, it is hard to understand how falling water tables, which may prove an even greater threat to future economic progress, could be so widely ignored.

The arithmetic of emerging resource shortages is not difficult. The mystery is not in the numbers, but in our failure to do what is needed to prevent such threats from spiraling out of control.

Today's political leaders show few signs of comprehending the long-term consequences of persistent environmental and social trends, or of the interconnectedness of these trends. Despite advances in our understanding of the complex— often chaotic—nature of biological, ecological, and climatological systems, political thought continues to be dominated by reductionist thinking that fails to target the root causes of problems. As a result, political action focuses on responses to crises rather than prevention.

Leaders who are prepared to meet the challenges of the next century will need to understand that universal access to family planning not only is essential to coping with resource scarcity and the spread of HIV/AIDS, but is likely to improve the quality of life for the citizens they serve. Family planning comprises wide availability of contraception and reproductive healthcare, as well as improved access to educational opportunities for young women and men. Lower birth rates generally allow greater investment in each child, as has occurred in East Asia.

Leaders all over the world—not just in Africa and Asia—now need to realize that the adverse effects of global population growth will affect those living in nations such as the United States or Germany, that seem at first glance to be relatively protected from the ravages now looming in Zimbabwe or Ethiopia. Economist Herman Daly observes that whereas in the past surplus labor in one nation had the effect of driving down wages only in that nation, "global economic integration will be the means by which the consequences of overpopulation in the Third World are generalized to the globe as a whole." Large infusions of job-seekers into Brazil's or India's work force that may lower wages there may now also mean large infusions into the global workforce, with potentially similar consequences.

As the recent Asian economic downturn further demonstrates, "localized instability" is becoming an anachronistic concept. The consequences of social unrest in one nation, whether resulting from a currency crisis or an environmental crisis, can quickly cross national boundaries. Several nations, including the United States, now recognize world population growth as a national security issue. As the U.S. Department of State Strategic Plan, issued in September 1997, explains, "Stabilizing population growth is vital to U.S. interests. . . . Not only will early stabilization of the world's population promote environmentally sustainable economic development in other countries, but it will benefit the United States by improving trade opportunities and mitigating future global crises."

One of the keys to helping countries quickly slow population growth, before it becomes unmanageable, is expanded international assistance for reproductive health and family planning. At the United Nations Conference on Population and Development held in Cairo in 1994, it was estimated that the annual cost of providing quality reproductive health services to all those in need in developing countries would amount to $17 billion in the year 2000. By 2015, the cost would climb to $22 billion.

Industrial countries agreed to provide one-third of the funds, with the developing countries providing the remaining two-thirds. While developing countries have largely honored their commitments, the industrial countries—and most conspicuously, the United States—have reneged on theirs. And in late 1998, the U.S. Congress—mired in the quicksand of anti-abortion politics—

withdrew all funding for the U.N. Population Fund, the principal source of international family planning assistance. Thus was thrown aside the kind of assistance that helps both to slow population growth and to check the spread of the HIV virus.

In most nations, stabilizing population will require mobilization of domestic resources that may now be tied up in defense expenditures, crony capitalism or government corruption. But without outside assistance, many nations may still struggle to provide universal family planning. For this reason, delegates at Cairo agreed that the immense resources and power found in the First World are indispensable in this effort. And as wealth further consolidates in the North and the number living in absolute poverty increases in the South, the argument for assistance grows more and more compelling. Given the social consequences of one-third of the world heading into a demographic nightmare, failure to provide such assistance is unconscionable.

AMARTYA SEN

Universal Truths: Human Rights and the Westernizing Illusion

My students seem to be very concerned and also very divided on how to approach the difficult subject of human rights in non-Western societies. Is it right, the

From *Harvard International Review* 20, no. 3 (summer 1998): 40–43. This article is a revised version of the Commencement Address given at Bard College on May 24, 1997. Related arguments were presented in Professor Sen's Morgenthau Memorial Lecture ("Human Rights and Asian Values") at the Carnegie Council on Ethics and International Affairs on May 1, 1997, and published by the Carnegie Council.

question is often asked, that non-Western societies should be encouraged and pressed to conform to "Western values of liberty and freedom"? Is this not cultural imperialism? The notion of human rights builds on the idea of a shared humanity. These rights are not derived from citizenship of any country, or membership of any nation, but taken as entitlements of every human being. The concept of universal human rights is, in this sense, a uniting idea. Yet the subject of human rights has ended up being a veritable battleground of political debates and ethical disputes, particularly in their application to non-Western societies. Why so?

A Clash of Cultures?

The explanation for this is sometimes sought in the cultural differences that allegedly divide the world, a theory referred to as the "clash of civilizations" or a "battle between cultures." It is often asserted that Western countries recognize many human rights, related for example to political liberty, that have no great appeal in Asian countries. Many people see a big divide here. The temptation to think in these regional and cultural terms is extremely strong in the contemporary world.

Are there really such firm differences on this subject in terms of traditions and cultures across the world? It is certainly true that governmental spokesmen in several Asian countries have not only disputed the relevance and cogency of universal human rights, they have frequently done this disputing in the name of "Asian values," as a contrast with Western values. The claim is that in the system of so-called Asian values, for example in the Confucian system, there is greater emphasis on order and discipline, and less on rights and freedoms.

Many Asian spokesmen have gone on to argue that the call for universal acceptance of human rights reflects the imposition of Western values on other cultures. For example, the censorship of the press may be more acceptable, it is argued, in Asian society because of its greater emphasis on discipline and order. This position was powerfully articulated by a number of governmental spokesmen from Asia at the Vienna Conference on Human Rights in 1993. Some positive things happened at that conference, including the general acceptance of the importance of eliminating economic deprivation and some recognition of social responsibility in this area. But on the subject of political and civil rights the conference split through the middle, largely on regional lines, with several Asian governments rejecting the recognition of basic political and civil rights. In this argument, the rhetoric of "Asian values" and their differences from Western priorities played an important part.

If one influence in separating out human rights as specifically "Western" comes from the pleading of governmental spokesmen from Asia, another influence relates to the way this issue is perceived in the West itself. There is a tendency in Europe and the United States to assume, if only implicitly, that it is in the West—and only in the West—that human rights have been valued from ancient times. This allegedly unique feature of Western civilization has been, it is assumed, an alien concept elsewhere. By stressing regional and cultural specificities, these Western theories of the origin of human rights tend to reinforce, rather inadvertently, the disputation of universal human rights in non-Western societies. By arguing that the valuing of toleration, of personal liberty, and of civil rights is a particular contribution of Western civilization, Western advocates of these rights often give ammunition to the non-Western critics of human rights. The advocacy of an allegedly "alien" idea in non-Western societies can indeed look like cultural imperialism sponsored by the West.

Modernity as Tradition

How much truth is there in this grand cultural dichotomy between Western and non-Western civilizations on the subject of liberty and rights? I believe there is rather little sense in such a grand dichotomy. Neither the claims in favor of the specialness of "Asian values" by governmental spokesmen from Asia, nor the particular claims for the uniqueness of "Western values" by spokesmen from Europe and America can survive much historical examination and critical scrutiny.

In seeing Western civilization as the natural habitat of individual freedom and political democracy, there is a tendency to extrapolate backwards from the present. Values that the European Enlightenment and other recent developments since the eighteenth century have made common and widespread are often seen, quite arbitrarily, as part of the long-run Western heritage, experienced in the West over millennia. The concept of universal human rights in the broad general sense of entitlements of every human being is really a relatively new idea, not to be much found either in the ancient West or in ancient civilizations elsewhere.

There are, however, other ideas, such as the value of toleration, or the importance of individual freedom, which have been advocated and defended for a long time, often for the selected few. For example, Aristotle's writings on freedom and human flourishing provide good background material for the contemporary ideas of human rights. But there are other Western philosophers (Plato and St. Augustine, for example) whose preference for order and discipline over freedom was no less pronounced than Confucius' priorities. Also, even those in the West who did emphasize the value of freedom did not, typically, see this as a fight of all human beings. Aristotle's exclusion of women and slaves is a good illustration of this non-universality. The defenses of individual freedom in Western tradition did exist but took a limited and contingent form.

Confucius and Co.

Do we find similar pronouncements in favor of individual freedom in non-Western traditions, particularly in Asia? The answer is emphatically yes. Confucius is not the only philosopher in Asia, not even in China. There is much variety in Asian intellectual traditions, and many writers did emphasize the importance of freedom and tolerance, and some even saw this as the entitlement of every human being. The language of freedom is very important, for example, in Buddhism, which originated and first flourished in South Asia and then spread to Southeast Asia and East Asia, including China, Japan, Korea, and Thailand. In this context it is important to recognize that Buddhist philosophy not only emphasized freedom as a form of life but also gave it a political content. To give just one example, the Indian emperor Ashoka in the third century BCE presented many political inscriptions in favor of tolerance and individual freedom, both as a part of state policy and in the relation of different people to each other. The domain of toleration,

Ashoka argued, must include everybody without exception.

Even the portrayal of Confucius as an unmitigated authoritarian is far from convincing. Confucius did believe in order, but he did not recommend blind allegiance to the state. When Zilu asks him how to serve a prince, Confucius replies, "Tell him the truth even if it offends him"—a policy recommendation that may encounter some difficulty in contemporary Singapore or Beijing. Of course, Confucius was a practical man, and he did not recommend that we foolhardily oppose established power. He did emphasize practical caution and tact, but also insisted on the importance of opposition. "When the [good] Way prevails in the state, speak boldly and act boldly. When the state has lost the Way, act boldly and speak softly," he said.

The main point to note is that both Western and non-Western traditions have much variety within themselves. Both in Asia and in the West, some have emphasized order and discipline, even as others have focused on freedom and tolerance. The idea of human rights as an entitlement of every human being, with an unqualified universal scope and highly articulated structure, is really a recent development; in this demanding form it is not an ancient idea either in the West or elsewhere. But there are limited and qualified defenses of freedom and tolerance, and general arguments against censorship, that can be found both in ancient traditions in the West and in cultures of non-Western societies.

Islam and Tolerance

Special questions are often raised about the Islamic tradition. Because of the experience of contemporary political battles, especially in the Middle East, the Islamic civilization is often portrayed as being fundamentally intolerant and hostile to individual freedom. But the presence of diversity and variety within a tradition applies very much to Islam as well. The Turkish emperors were often more tolerant than their European contemporaries. The Mughal emperors in India, with one exception, were not only extremely tolerant, but some even theorized about the need for tolerating diversity. The pronouncements of Akbar, the great Mughal emperor in sixteenth century India, on tolerance can count among the classics of political pronouncements, and would have received more attention in the West had Western political historians taken as much interest in Eastern thought as they do in their own intellectual background. For comparison, I should mention that the Inquisitions were still in full bloom in Europe as Akbar was making it a state policy to tolerate and protect all religious groups.

A Jewish scholar like Maimonides in the twelfth century had to run away from an intolerant Europe and from its persecution of Jews for the security offered by a tolerant Cairo and the patronage of Sultan Saladin. Alberuni, the Iranian mathematician, who wrote the first general book on India in the early eleventh century, aside from translating Indian mathematical treatises into Arabic, was among the earliest of anthropological theorists in the world. He noted and protested against the fact that "depreciation of foreigners . . . is common to all nations towards each other." He devoted much of his life to fostering mutual understanding and tolerance in his eleventh-century world.

Authority and Dissidence

The recognition of diversity within different cultures is extremely important in the contemporary world, since we are constantly bombarded by oversimplified generalizations about "Western civilization, . . . Asian values," "African cultures," and so on. These unfounded readings of history and civilization are not only intellectually shallow, they also add to the divisiveness of the world in which we live. Boorishness begets violence.

The fact is that in any culture people like to argue with each other, and often do. I recollect being amused in my childhood by a well-known poem in Bengali from nineteenth century Calcutta. The poet is describing the horror of death, the sting of mortality. "Just think," the poem runs, "how terri-

ble it would be on the day you die / Others will go on speaking, and you will not be able to respond." The worst sting of death would appear to be, in this view, the inability to argue, and this illustrates how seriously we take our differences and our debates.

Dissidents exist in every society, often at great risk to their own security. Western discussion of non-Western societies is often too respectful of authority—the governor, the Minister, the military leader, the religious leader. This "authoritarian bias" receives support from the fact that Western countries themselves are often represented, in international gatherings, by governmental officials and spokesmen, and they in turn seek the views of their "opposite numbers" from other countries.

The view that Asian values are quintessentially authoritarian has tended to come almost exclusively from spokesmen of those in power and their advocates. But foreign ministers, or government officials, or religious leaders do not have a monopoly in interpreting local culture and values. It is important to listen to the voices of dissent in each society.

National and Cultural Diversity

To conclude, the so-called "Western values of freedom and liberty," sometimes seen as an ancient Western inheritance, are not particularly ancient, nor exclusively Western in their antecedence. Many of these values have taken their full form only over the last few centuries. While we do find some anticipatory components in parts of the ancient Western traditions, there are other such anticipatory components in parts of non-Western ancient traditions as well. On the particular subject of toleration, Plato and Confucius may be on a somewhat similar side, just as Aristotle and Ashoka may be on another side.

The need to acknowledge diversity applies not only between nations and cultures, but also within each nation and culture. In the anxiety to take adequate note of international diversity and cultural divergences, and the so-called differences between "Western civilization," "Asian values," "African culture," and so on, there is often a dramatic neglect of heterogeneity within each country and culture. "Nations" and "cultures" are not particularly good units to understand and analyze intellectual and political differences. Lines of division in commitments and skepticism do not run along national boundaries—they criss-cross at many different levels. The rhetoric of cultures, with each "culture" seen in largely homogenized terms, can confound us politically as well as intellectually.

CREDITS

Chapter 1: Approaches and History

2: From Thucydides, *Complete Writings: The Peloponnesian War*, trans. Richard Crawley (New York: Modern Library, 1951), adapted by Suresht Bald, Williamette University.

6: Reprinted by permission of *Foreign Affairs*. © 1987 by the Council on Foreign Relations, Inc.

11: © 1986 by John Gaddis. Reprinted by permission of the author.

Chapter 2: Contending Perspectives

27: Reprinted with permission from *Foreign Policy*. © 1998 by the Carnegie Endowment for International Peace.

35: © 1967 by Alfred A. Knopf, Inc. Reprinted by permission of Alfred A. Knopf, a division of Random House, Inc.

39: © 1986 by the American Political Science Association and Michael Doyle. Reprinted with the permission of the publisher and the author.

52: © 1966 by The Monthly Review. Reprinted with permission.

60: © 1992 by Columbia University Press. Reprinted by permission of the publisher.

Chapter 3: New Frontiers in International Political Theory

70: © 1979 by McGraw-Hill. Reprinted with the permission of The McGraw-Hill Companies.

91: Reprinted with the permission of John Ruggie and Taylor & Francis Books Ltd.

120: © 1997 by the International Studies Association.

Chapter 4: The International System

139: © 1977 by Hedley Bull. Reprinted by permission of the publisher.

143: © 1967 by Hans Morgenthau. Reprinted by permission of Alfred A. Knopf, a division of Random House, Inc.

149: © 1974 by Cambridge University Press. Reprinted with the permission of Cambridge University Press.

157: © 1999 by the President and Fellows of Harvard College and the Massachusetts Institute of Technology.

174: Reprinted by permission of *Foreign Affairs*. © 1993 by the Council on Foreign Relations, Inc.

180: © 1996 by The Economist Newspaper Group, Inc. Reprinted with permission. Further reproduction prohibited.